OECD

ECONOMIC

OUTLOOK

73

JUNE 2003

OECD

ORGANISATION FOR ECONOMIC CO-OPERATION AND DEVELOPMENT

The Organisation for Economic Co-operation and Development (OECD)

was set up under a Convention, signed in Paris on 14 December 1960, which provides that the OECD shall promote policies designed:

− *To achieve the highest sustainable economic growth and employment and a rising standard of living in member countries while maintaining financial stability, and thus to contribute to the development of the world economy.*

− *To contribute to sound economic expansion in member as well as non-member countries in the process of economic development.*

− *To contribute to the expansion of world trade on a multilateral, non-discriminatory basis in accordance with international obligations.*

The original member countries of the OECD are: Austria, Belgium, Canada, Denmark, France, Germany, Greece, Iceland, Ireland, Italy, Luxembourg, the Netherlands, Norway, Portugal, Spain, Sweden, Switzerland, Turkey, the United Kingdom and the United States. The following countries became members subsequently through accession at the dates indicated hereafter: Japan (28 April 1964), Finland (28 January 1969), Australia (7 June 1971), New Zealand (29 May 1973), Mexico (18 May 1994), the Czech Republic (21 December 1995), Hungary (7 May 1996), Poland (22 November 1996), Korea (12 December 1996) and Slovak Republic (14th December 2000). The Commission of the European Communities takes part in the work of the OECD (Article 13 of the OECD Convention).

The French version of the *OECD Economic Outlook* is entitled *Perspectives économiques de l'OCDE.*

The *OECD Economic Outlook* is published on the responsibility of the Secretary-General of the OECD. The assessments given of countries' prospects do not necessarily correspond to those of the national authorities concerned. The OECD is the source of statistical material contained in tables and figures, except where other sources are explicitly cited.

TABLE OF CONTENTS

Conventional signs

$	US dollar	.	Decimal point
¥	Japanese yen	I, II	Calendar half-years
£	Pound sterling	Q1, Q4	Calendar quarters
€	Euro	Billion	Thousand million
mbd	Million barrels per day	Trillion	Thousand billion
..	Data not available	s.a.a.r.	Seasonally adjusted at annual rates
0	Nil or negligible	n.s.a.	Not seasonally adjusted
–	Irrelevant		

Summary of projections[a]

	2002	2003	2004	2002		2003		2004	
				I	II	I	II	I	II
				Percentage changes from previous period					
Real GDP									
United States	2.4	2.5	4.0	3.5	2.7	1.7	3.8	4.1	3.8
Japan	0.3	1.0	1.1	1.0	3.5	0.0	0.6	1.2	1.4
Euro area	0.9	1.0	2.4	1.1	1.1	0.9	1.4	2.6	2.9
European Union	1.0	1.2	2.4	1.2	1.4	1.0	1.5	2.6	2.8
Total OECD	1.8	1.9	3.0	2.5	2.4	1.4	2.4	3.2	3.2
Real total domestic demand									
United States	3.0	2.8	4.0	4.2	3.3	2.1	3.8	4.2	3.8
Japan	-0.3	0.5	0.4	-0.4	3.2	-0.6	-0.2	0.5	0.7
Euro area	0.3	1.1	2.4	0.4	1.0	1.0	1.5	2.6	2.9
European Union	0.7	1.3	2.5	0.7	1.5	1.1	1.6	2.8	3.0
Total OECD	1.9	2.0	2.9	2.4	2.8	1.4	2.4	3.1	3.1
				Per cent					
Inflation[b]									
United States	1.1	1.6	1.3	0.9	1.3	2.0	1.2	1.5	1.3
Japan	-1.7	-2.2	-1.8	-1.7	-2.6	-2.1	-1.8	-1.8	-1.8
Euro area	2.4	1.9	1.7	2.5	2.1	1.9	1.8	1.6	1.6
European Union	2.5	1.9	1.8	2.8	2.1	1.9	1.9	1.8	1.8
OECD *less* Turkey	1.4	1.3	1.2	1.5	1.2	1.5	1.2	1.2	1.2
Total OECD	2.1	1.7	1.4	2.0	1.7	1.9	1.5	1.4	1.3
				Per cent of labour force					
Unemployment									
United States	5.8	6.0	5.8	5.7	5.8	6.0	6.1	5.9	5.7
Japan	5.4	5.7	5.7	5.3	5.4	5.6	5.8	5.7	5.7
Euro area	8.2	8.8	8.7	8.1	8.3	8.7	8.8	8.8	8.6
European Union	7.6	8.0	7.9	7.5	7.7	8.0	8.1	8.0	7.9
Total OECD	6.9	7.2	7.0	6.8	7.0	7.1	7.2	7.1	6.9
				Per cent of GDP					
Current account balance									
United States	-4.8	-5.4	-5.5	-4.6	-5.0	-5.4	-5.4	-5.5	-5.5
Japan	2.8	3.1	3.9	3.0	2.6	2.9	3.4	3.8	4.1
Euro area	1.1	1.4	1.4	0.9	1.3	1.3	1.4	1.4	1.4
European Union	0.9	1.0	1.0	0.7	1.0	1.0	1.0	1.0	0.9
Total OECD	-1.1	-1.2	-1.2	-1.0	-1.1	-1.2	-1.1	-1.1	-1.1
				Per cent					
Short-term interest rate[c]									
United States	1.8	1.4	3.0	1.9	1.6	1.3	1.4	2.6	3.5
Japan	0.1	0.0	0.0	0.1	0.0	0.0	0.0	0.0	0.0
Euro area	3.3	2.3	2.3	3.4	3.3	2.5	2.1	2.1	2.5
				Percentage changes from previous period					
World trade[d]	3.6	5.9	8.8	5.9	7.9	4.1	7.5	9.3	9.4

Note: Apart from unemployment rates and interest rates, half-yearly data are seasonally adjusted, annual rates.

a) Assumptions underlying the projections include:
 - no change in actual and announced fiscal policies;
 - unchanged exchange rates as from 26 March 2003; in particular 1$ = 120.10 yen and 0.936 euros;
 - the cut-off date for other information used in the compilation of the projections is 4 April 2003

b) GDP deflator.

c) United States: 3-month eurodollars; Japan: 3-month CDs; euro area: 3-month interbank rates. See box on policy and other assumptions underlying the projections.

d) Growth rate of the arithmetic average of world merchandise import and export volumes.

Source: OECD.

EDITORIAL: A PROGRESSIVE BUT UNSPECTACULAR RECOVERY

Since we published our previous *OECD Economic Outlook*, six months ago, growth in the OECD has proved disappointing. The US recovery is still fragile and somewhat weaker than expected, while economies in the euro area have undershot an already modest forecast by a wide margin. In Japan, volatile movements in exports and investment have not broadened into a genuine recovery.

There are many reasons for this new bout of economic weakness and evaluating their respective importance is no easy task.

Worries about oil prices, anxiety in the face of war, fear of terrorism and epidemics, loss of confidence in international governance... The list of the so-called geopolitical and psychological factors is long. And their role in the recent waning of business and consumer confidence is indeed quite palpable.

Nonetheless, despite their overwhelming presence in the public debate, these elements of turbulence should not overshadow some important economic issues that will shape the world recovery. The brisk reconstruction of Iraq and good progress towards a more secure world would obviously help, but they will not translate into a robust recovery unless enough underlying economic momentum has been regained. This momentum depends, in turn, on how far OECD economies have purged past imbalances (over-investment, inflated share prices, balance sheet exposure...), and how much support is being provided by economic policies.

Despite the prevailing uncertainties and the current weakness in activity, this Outlook still sees a progressive if unspectacular world recovery as the most likely scenario. While a relapse into recession cannot be totally ruled out, it remains a low-probability outcome.

This sluggish but by no means catastrophic scenario is based on a careful assessment of the current balance of risks. Looking at recent geopolitical developments, it appears that the most acute source of risk has now receded. With the ending of war and securing of Iraqi oil fields, the threat of an oil crisis sending the world economy into outright recession has subsided. However, the more diffuse perception of a still insecure economic environment may prevail for some time, prolonging wait-and-see attitudes in the areas of investment and spending on major consumer durables.

On the economic front, some of the obstacles that previously stood in the way of a recovery have been progressively lifted. This is particularly true of business spending. In the United States, the initial capital overhang has been largely eliminated and investment has stabilised, thereby removing a hugely negative contribution to growth. Business spending is now better placed to take over the baton from consumers. In Europe, inventories are generally seen as light and may play a useful role in restarting the economy. More generally, fiscal and monetary conditions across the OECD remain accommodating enough to support an incipient recovery.

On a less positive note, household demand will probably take some time to accelerate in a context where wage earners are still worried about adverse labour-market developments and home owners, in the United Kingdom and the United States in particular, may face downward corrections in housing markets.

Restructuring of the weak balance sheets inherited from earlier over-investment may also damp the recovery. This might not only be true for US and UK households, but applies as well to businesses in Europe, where profits are lagging and indebtedness has reached high levels. A striking example of excessive leverage can be found in the telecommunications sector, which is analysed in some detail in Chapter IV of this *Outlook*. Current financial difficulties, however substantial, should not be an excuse for delaying the course of economic reforms and a further opening of telecom markets.

Beyond the example of the telecoms sector, one of the challenges facing policymakers is, indeed, that they should resolutely push ahead with economic reforms without waiting for a fully-fledged recovery to materialise. A "double-handed" strategy is called for, where the authorities show a readiness to intervene in the short run to support the economy should it flag again, while at the same time providing economic agents with a sense of long-term direction and governance to re-establish confidence.

Looking first at macroeconomic policies, there seems to be little room for manoeuvre left for fiscal policies beyond the use of automatic stabilisers. Public deficits OECD-wide will reach 3½ per cent of GDP in 2003. This marked deterioration stems from a cyclical weakness in tax receipts, but also reflects a serious worsening in the underlying position of public finances which will take time and effort to redress. This plunge into deep deficit is all the more worrying since in many countries prospective deficits associated with ageing are large, due to the slow pace of reform of pension and health care systems. Indeed, a number of countries have little alternative but to begin the process of consolidating their fiscal position without delay. Running prudent fiscal policies is also essential to the conduct of stabilisation policies because they will help avoid premature hikes in long-term interest rates.

In this context, monetary policy is best placed to steer the recovery. While, at present, monetary conditions appear well-adapted to the conjunctural situation in the United States, there is a case for a significant easing in the euro area, where growth may remain below potential during the next few quarters, while core inflation is decelerating. In Japan, more aggressive liquidity provision combined with a decisive restructuring of the financial sector is advisable.

To regain economic momentum, a renewed commitment to economic reform will be key in many OECD countries. The case for economic reform remains very strong in the larger European countries and Japan, which ceased to converge to the United States in terms of GDP per capita in the 1980s and lost ground for the first time since World War II during the 1990s. The areas where emphasis should be placed are summarised in Chapter V of this *Outlook*.

The same reforms that boost potential growth in the medium term could also, in the short run, increase the resilience of economies in the face of conjunctural shocks. It may not be a pure coincidence if, as noted in this report, those countries which have grown most rapidly over the past decade are also those which have withstood shocks the most easily, while those which have performed worst in the long run also experienced the most abrupt departure from trend over the past three years.

Providing a sense of long-term direction means, in many countries, setting and implementing an ambitious agenda for growth. Its aims would range from improved corporate governance in the United States to raising employment and productivity in Europe and Japan. In Germany, where structural weaknesses are standing in the way of a robust recovery, an ambitious reform plan centred on labour markets and social security institutions is now being discussed which, if fully implemented, would help unlock the growth potential of the economy.

In a period of diplomatic friction and loss of confidence in collective governance, progress in trade talks will also be important. More generally, efforts to maintain and strengthen international economic integration remain essential to world prosperity. Recent OECD empirical research, summarised in Chapters VI to VIII of this *Outlook*, shows how foreign direct investment could be fostered by improving regulatory frameworks. Preserving the world economic system through improved security is certainly central but proactive measures to facilitate the flow of capital and the associated knowledge and expertise are vital too.

16 April 2003

Jean-Philippe Cotis
Chief Economist

I. GENERAL ASSESSMENT
OF THE MACROECONOMIC SITUATION

Overview: a slow recovery

The upturn is hesitant and drawn-out, with confidence fragile. The short-term weakness foreseen in the previous *OECD Economic Outlook* is proving to be unexpectedly protracted, against the background of sharp swings in the oil price, sizeable exchange rate shifts and continuing equity price erosion. Forward-looking indicators suggest a deferral of the area-wide upturn until later in 2003. This year, OECD GDP growth is thus likely to only marginally exceed the 1¾ per cent recorded in 2002 (Table I.1). At the same time, regional growth disparities are rising, with the output gap set to widen less markedly in the United States than in the euro area.

Economic activity is hesitant...

Sluggish growth in the near term is partly related to the geopolitical uncertainties created by the Iraq crisis. The rapid resolution to the conflict, and the more settled geopolitical climate that is assumed to follow, should allow investor and consumer confidence to strengthen gradually, with positive effects on demand. The headwinds which were holding back the recovery at the time of the previous *Outlook* have abated somewhat, as interest rates have declined and the capital overhang has been reduced. Monetary policies and fiscal easing in several countries, notably the United States, continue to support demand, in a context of declining core inflation. If, as assumed, oil prices remain around $25 per barrel, OECD growth should revert to around 3 per cent – exceeding its potential rate – in 2004. There remains, however, a degree of uncertainty regarding the underlying cyclical momentum of the OECD-area economy, relating to persistent imbalances and, in some economies, insufficient structural reform. But while the risks are mainly negative they are not exclusively on the downside.

... but should revive later in 2003, subject to negative risks

Table I.1. **Output growth**

Percentage changes in GDP

	2001	2002	2003	2004
United States	0.3	2.4	2.5	4.0
Japan	0.4	0.3	1.0	1.1
Euro area	1.5	0.9	1.0	2.4
European Union	1.6	1.0	1.2	2.4
Total OECD	0.8	1.8	1.9	3.0

Source: OECD.

Nature of the cycle and geopolitical risks

Major forces acting

The business cycle has some unusual features...

Two unusual sets of short-term influences are at play in the current conjuncture. The first relates to the nature of the cyclical downturn, which started in all the major OECD regions during 2001. The slowdown was not, as on many occasions in the past, generated by monetary tightening in response to increasing inflationary pressure and/or growing international imbalances. Rather, it was characterised by a classical over-investment cycle. Corporate balance sheet and excess capacity problems have been more severe than in earlier recessions and have taken longer to be worked off. However, because inflation pressures were generally subdued, central banks have been able to respond vigorously. The second set of influences arises from the pervasive geopolitical uncertainty deriving from the Iraq crisis, together with ongoing security risks in other regions and those related to global terrorism. Besides the effect on energy prices, this has hurt already fragile corporate and consumer confidence. Both sets of influences were combined with an unusually severe bear market in equities, following the bursting of the stock market bubble.

... which impair conjunctural visibility

Viewed in this double perspective, the strength of the upturn is determined by: *i)* how geopolitical tensions and oil prices will evolve; *ii)* responses to the policies in place; and *iii)* most importantly, the extent to which the imbalances built up during the boom have unwound and corporate sector headwinds abated.

Impact of geopolitical tensions

Oil prices have gyrated...

Perhaps the most direct global economic manifestation of the geopolitical tensions has been the volatility of oil prices. Higher oil prices played a key role in ending the already mature expansion in 1990-91, but came this time early in the recovery stage and whilst inflation trends were generally benign, so the parallels are limited. Over the year to mid-March, spot oil prices rose from $20 to $35 per barrel for Brent crude.[1] Apart from a substantial and rising war-premium, this increase also reflected the supply shortfalls caused by strikes in Venezuela and Nigeria, the demand boost from unusually cold weather in North America and Japan, and unusually low OECD crude oil stocks. In the early stages of the war, oil prices plummeted, and by early April 2003 they were hovering around $25 per barrel, with futures quotes showing market expectations they would stay at this level – the mid-point of the range targeted by OPEC – over the coming year.

... and geopolitical risks have weighed on consumer and business confidence

The crisis over Iraq has affected the global economy in other, more diffuse ways than fluctuations in oil prices (Figure I.1). In particular, equity markets have remained turbulent, as the pricing of risk has become very difficult. Investors have been searching for safe havens, causing shifts in relative prices between equities on the one hand and gold and government bonds on the other.[2] Household confidence has fallen to levels approaching those observed during the Gulf crisis in the early 1990s; and while business confidence has held more steady, it has more recently tended to follow suit. The link between swings in confidence (especially

---

1. In real terms, this increase is only half as large as the surge that followed Iraq's invasion of Kuwait in 1990.
2. For an analysis of behaviour across markets, see Leigh, A., J. Wolfers and E. Zitzewitz, "What do financial markets think of war in Iraq?", *NBER Working Papers*, No. 9587, 2003; and Rigobon, R. and B. Sack, "The effects of war risk on US financial markets", *NBER Working Papers*, No. 9609, 2003.

Figure I.1. **Tensions and uncertainties in the global economy, spring 2003**

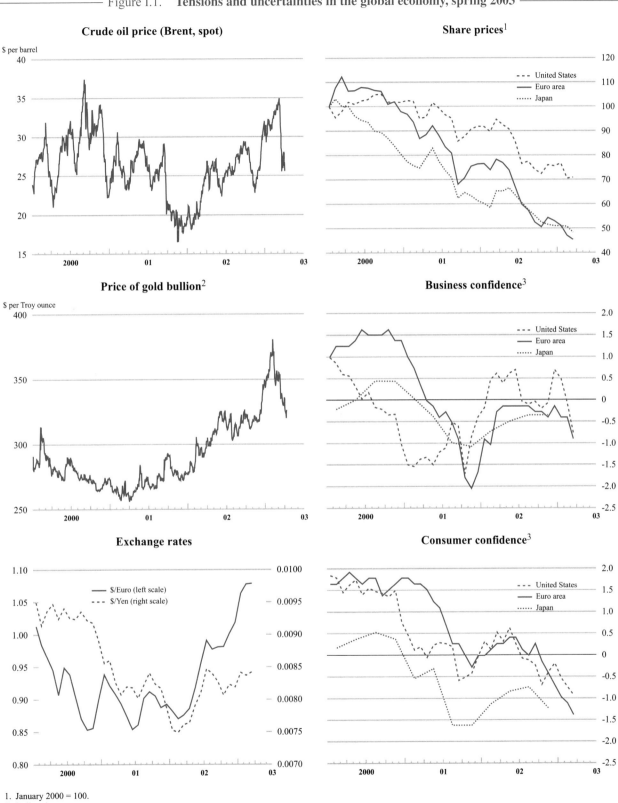

1. January 2000 = 100.
2. Daily prices.
3. All series have been normalised at the average for the period for which data are available and are presented in units of standard deviation.
Source: OECD, *Main Economic Indicators*, Datastream and the US Energy Information Administration.

business sentiment) and fluctuations in activity becomes less predictable when changes in confidence are driven by political rather than economic factors, as has recently been the case. Estimates of the direct costs of war, as incorporated in the OECD projections, are spelled out in Box I.2 below.

Consumption responses to the policies in place

Consumption has held up in a number of countries...

The downturn has prompted substantial demand-supportive policy responses (described below), the most powerful effects of which can be seen in relatively strong personal consumption in a number of countries. Tax cuts and/or low interest rates have boosted household spending in the United States, the United Kingdom, Australia and Spain, partly via buoyant residential property markets (both directly in housing construction and indirectly through property-wealth effects). Interest rate effects have also been conspicuous in the US motor vehicle sector. These positive influences have been vying with the negative effect of volatile and fragile household confidence and financial wealth losses.[3] In the euro area at large – but especially reflecting developments in Germany and Italy – policy measures have not sufficed to sustain household spending growth. In Japan, consumption, though by no means strong, has been a steadying factor in aggregate demand growth.

... financed by rising household debt

These rather disparate outcomes are reflections of differences in the balance sheet behaviour of households. Household spending has been sustained, in some countries, by taking on debt, which now exceeds 100 per cent of disposable income in the United States and 120 per cent in the United Kingdom. Mortgage equity with-drawal, in particular, has played a substantial role. Debt increases have had a coun-terpart in rising house prices and household net wealth has been cushioned, to some extent, from equity price falls. Moreover, debt service flows have been contained by lower interest rates and households have used refinancing opportunities to pay down expensive consumer credit.[4] In continental Europe, steep equity price falls have to be seen in the context of much narrower household share ownership, while refinancing of mortgages is more difficult and property markets have been less buoyant. As a consequence, house prices and low interest rates have a smaller impact on consump-tion, even though housing forms a relatively large part of household wealth. In Japan, the protracted weakness in equity and property prices is cushioned, at least in a statistical sense, by rising real household wealth held as government debt, despite concerns about future pensions and taxes.

Financial headwinds and the investment cycle

Financial stress has eased

Financial headwinds have abated, though equities remain volatile

The financial headwinds noted in the previous *Outlook* have abated, albeit not completely. Long-term interest rates have remained low and spreads on corporate bonds have narrowed substantially, although this is due in part to the drying up of high-risk credit demand and/or lenders becoming more selective. The number of profit downgrades has fallen to more normal levels. Stock markets are still unsettled, however, even though price-earnings ratios have come closer to their historical

---

3. In the United States, the residual drag on household consumption from past equity falls was recently estimated by Federal Reserve staff to amount to 1 percentage point in 2003 and ½ percentage point in 2004, under the benign assumption that equity prices would move in line with income this year and next.
4. See Aizcorbe, A., A. Kennickell and K. Moore, "Recent changes in US family finances: evidence from the 1998 and 2001 Survey of Consumer Finances", *Federal Reserve Bulletin*, January 2003.

Figure I.2. **Variability of output and investment growth**

Percentage change from previous period, annual rate

——— Private non-residential fixed investment   - - - GDP

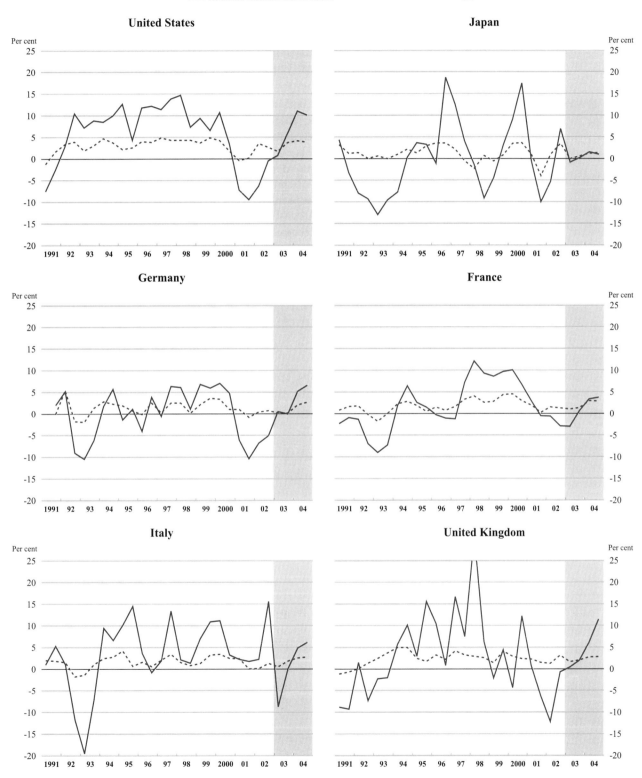

Source: OECD.

averages. Equity price declines have been particularly pronounced in Europe and Japan. In Europe, this may reflect the fact that profit margins have been squeezed by rising unit labour costs, while in Japan corporate and financial restructuring still has a long way to go. Moreover, some sectors of the financial markets (life insurers in the United Kingdom, banks in Germany) are still suffering balance sheet strains, with repercussions on their own equity market value and on share prices generally via a lower institutional demand for shares. These explanations apart, shares still look more richly valued in the United States than elsewhere.

Credit conditions remain supportive

On the positive side, banks in the major countries, outside Japan and to a lesser extent Germany, entered the recent downturn in a healthy condition, with favourable capital and liquidity positions and low risk exposures. Most of the capital losses from the investment boom of the late 1990s ended up outside the banking system, both in the United States and Europe. More recently, some signs of stress have emerged due to the increased incidence of corporate defaults. However, there is no evidence of any generalised credit squeeze in OECD economies.[5] In Germany, bank lending is contracting in real terms, but this may be partly explained by the fact that real interest rates are relatively high compared with other euro area countries.

What is left of the capital overhang?

The slump in investment is deeper than in past downturns...

The economic boom of the late 1990s saw a substantial increase in business investment, mostly reflecting strong growth in machinery and equipment, notably in the information and communications technology sector (ICT). Fuelled by the stock market and the rapid decline in computer prices, investment attained unsustainable levels, in particular in the United States. The slowdown has, to a large extent, reflected a need to reduce the ensuing capital overhang. For the past two years, capital spending has fallen well short of long-term trend, especially, but by no means uniquely, in the United States, where business investment dropped sharply in 2001 and 2002. The cumulative decline for the OECD area was almost 6 per cent over these two years.

Figure I.3. **Private investment spending in the United States and the euro area**

Percentage change from previous period at annual rate

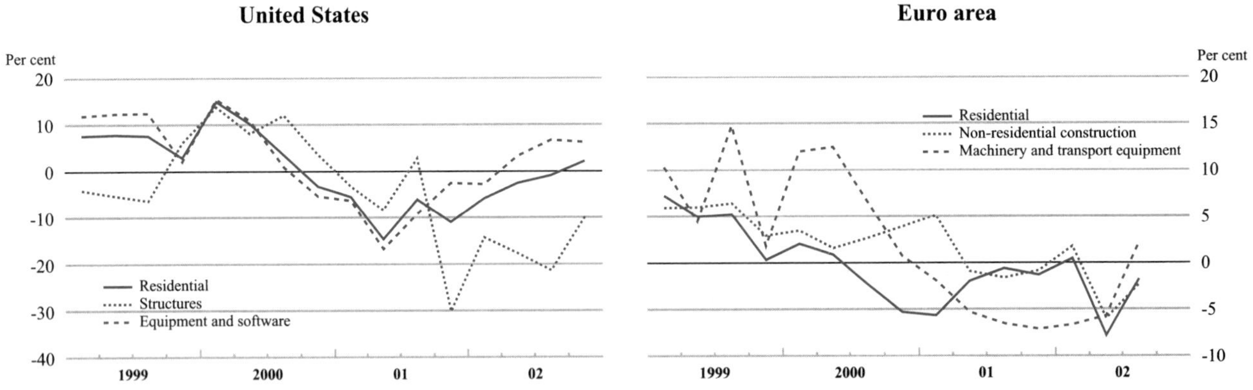

Source: OECD.

---

5. For supporting evidence in the US case, see Stiroh, K. and C. Metli, "Now and then: the evolution of loan quality for US banks", Federal Reserve Bank of New York, *Current Issues in Economics and Finance*, Vol. 9, No. 4, 2003.

Business investment amounts to no more than a third of private consumption spending, but is normally the most volatile component of final demand, and has accounted for as much of recent variations in output as has household demand (Figure I.2).

Following two years of retrenchment, the bulk of the excess capital stock has in all likelihood been worked off (Box I.1). Business fixed investment appears to have bottomed out in the United States, albeit with certain sectoral weaknesses (Figure I.3). Spending on high-tech investment (equipment and software) began to recover from the spring of 2002, though moderately so. However, investment in machinery and equipment continued to contract in 2002 in the euro area. In Japan, where corporate restructuring is proceeding, capital spending picked up during the second half of 2002, but this rebound is not expected to be sustained. Moreover, capacity utilisation rates in manufacturing remain below historical averages in all three major regions (though most significantly in the United States), suggesting that some excess capital still exists in sectors relying on more durable assets, such as structures (Figure I.4). Also holding back a decisive investment recovery are the relatively high levels of debt built up during the boom years, most conspicuously perhaps in the telecommunications sector.[6]

... and the global capital overhang has been largely eliminated...

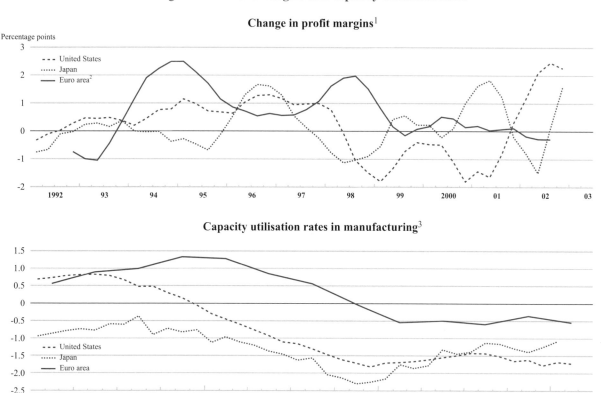

Figure I.4. **Profit margins and capacity utilisation rates**

Change in profit margins[1]

Capacity utilisation rates in manufacturing[3]

1. Approximated by GDP deflator divided by unit labour costs in the business sector, year-on-year percentage changes, moving average on 4 quarters.
2. Whole economy.
3. All series have been normalised at the average for the period for which data are available and are presented in units of standard deviation.
Source: OECD, *Main Economic Indicators*; European Central Bank, Monthly Bulletin.

6. See Chapter IV, "After the telecommunications bubble".

Box I.1. What is left of the capital overhang?

Non-residential fixed capital formation accelerated in the second half of the 1990s in a number of OECD countries – particularly the United States, the United Kingdom, Italy, Canada, Australia, Denmark, the Netherlands, Spain, and Sweden – durably outpacing GDP. Despite the trend decline in the relative price of investment, its share in nominal GDP also rose during that period. The subsequent global slowdown in activity saw investment spending drop sharply, especially in the United States.[1] At the same time, equity prices collapsed. This fuelled concerns that a "capital overhang" had been built up during the boom years, foreshadowing a spell of subdued investment growth long enough for the excess capital to be worked off.[2]

Several pieces of evidence seem to corroborate the view that by the turn of the millennium too much capital had been put in place too soon. A recent cross-country study based on a system of panel cointegration equations for gross business investment found that in a number of OECD countries investment rose more than could be explained by output growth, the cost of capital and financial market development.[3] Specifically, only one-third to one-half of the increase in business investment between 1995 and 1999 in the United States, the United Kingdom, Canada, Austria and Denmark could be attributed to these fundamentals. A significant portion of the increase also failed to be captured in these equations in the cases of Australia, the Netherlands and Sweden. Although Japan did not witness any investment surge during the 1990s, the study also showed over-investment in this case.[4] At a slightly more disaggregated level, unsustainably rapid investment growth in some sectors supported the notion of an overhang. Globally, this has been a widespread perception as regards ICT, in part but not solely related to the frontloading of Y2K-related outlays. In the United States, such over-accumulation has been documented, albeit on a limited scale, concerning computer and communications equipment but also trucks.[5] Further evidence of an over-hang includes very low capacity utilisation rates in US manufacturing, which remain far below their levels of the early 1990s recession.[6]

However, it is unlikely that at the economy-wide level there now remains significant excess capital in North America or in Europe. Indeed, the overhang symptoms listed above are subject to some caveats. *First*, in several countries, rapid investment growth represented a catch-up following a period of investment decline or stagnation. *Second*, the cited cross-country regressions did not allow for the possibility that economies were in the process of adjusting to a regime of higher trend output growth. Nor did they take into account the likely shift to higher depreciation rates (not least in connection with the growing share in the capital stock of fast-depreciating computer, equipment and software), which *ceteris paribus* raises gross investment requirements.[7] *Third*, the overall, net US capital-output ratio (measured as the net capital stock divided by net domestic product) is not out of line with its long-run historical average.[8] *Fourth*, any such overhang as did emerge in computer and software equipment was bound to erode rapidly, given that depreciation rates are so much higher in that sector. In fact, US nominal and *a fortiori* real high tech spending started to turn around in 2002.

Some local or sectoral pockets of capital overhang may nonetheless persist, notably for some more durable types of capital. Commercial real estate vacancy rates in particular have shot up in the United States, as well as in a number of other OECD countries. This is partly related to the longer lags inherent in this type of investment project, which takes several years to be completed. In the telecommunications sector, as well, some overcapacity may remain, although it does not necessarily signal excessive past investment and probably coexists with capacity shortages, *e.g.* as regards the "last mile".[9]

1. US non-residential fixed investment declined cumulatively by close to 11 per cent in 2001-02, against a briefer and shallower contraction of barely 5 per cent in the recession of the early 1990s. Elsewhere, however, the recent drop has been smaller so far than that witnessed in the early 1990s (although it is almost as large in the United Kingdom).
2. It has also led some to describe the current cycle as an "Austrian" one. See Oppers, S., "The Austrian theory of business cycles: old lessons for modern economic policy?", *IMF Working Papers*, No. 02/2, 2002.
3. See Pelgrin, F., S. Schich and A. de Serres, "Increases in business investment rates in OECD countries in the 1990s: how much can be explained by fundamentals?", *OECD Economics Department Working Papers*, No. 327, 2002.
4. Comparing the market and the replacement value of physical assets, another recent study reaches the same conclusion. See Ando, A., D. Christelis and T. Miyagawa, "Inefficiency of corporate investment and distortion of savings behavior in Japan", *NBER Working Papers*, No. 9444, 2003.
5. See "Evaluating the evidence of a capital overhang in the US economy", in *United States: Selected Issues*, IMF Country Report, No. 02/165, 2002.
6. Again, this contrasts with developments in Europe, where capacity utilisation rates remain close to historical averages.
7. See Pelgrin *et al.*, *op. cit.*, and Tevlin, S. and K. Whelan, "Explaining the investment boom of the 1990s", *Journal of Money, Credit and Banking*, Vol. 35, No. 1. Depreciation rates may well fall back somewhat, however, in the context of a protracted slowdown.
8. This is so in nominal terms. In real terms, the net US capital-output ratio probably exceeds its long-run average.
9. For example, it is rational to install more optical fibre than can be used in the short run, since this material is long-lasting and the bulk of the investment costs stem from digging the trenches and installing the fibre.

Falling capital investment has been associated with a reassessment of future profitability in many sectors. Many corporations have seen their capital base come under pressure, and cutbacks in capital spending, tight inventory management, and labour shedding/productivity increases have become the main vehicles for improving their balance sheets. Profit margins have been helped by sustained productivity gains in the United States, but have been held back by the typically slower labour market adjustment in continental Europe and – where defined-benefit occupational pensions are the norm (United States, United Kingdom, Netherlands) – by the need to top up corporate pension funds. In this context, even in the absence of geopolitical events and uncertainty, the upturn would in all likelihood be moderate, dependent for some time on expansionary macroeconomic policies.

… with improved profits in the United States, but less so elsewhere

Strength and general dynamics of the upturn

Lower oil prices and supportive policies…

The projections have been built on the assumptions that the acute risk attaching to the oil price has subsided, and that the more diffuse uncertainties attaching to the aftermath of the Iraq war will dissipate more gradually. The oil price is taken as averaging $25 from the second quarter of 2003 onwards (Table I.2). Hence, the projected impact of recent price spikes on output and inflation is limited. The negative effect of uncertainty on confidence would, at the same time, give way to conditions where, in particular for business investment, the option value of waiting falls rather quickly to more normal levels.

Oil prices are assumed to stay around $25 per barrel

Macroeconomic policies remain expansionary, although to differing degrees, on both sides of the Atlantic (see Box I.2). Monetary indicators suggest that the monetary policy impulse is greatest in the United States. However, policy rates across the OECD area are at or near historical lows and the OECD projections embody a further 50 basis point decline in short-term interest rates in the euro area. Money market rates are assumed to remain low for some time, before rising as the recovery

Monetary policies remain supportive…

Table I.2. **Oil and non-oil commodity prices**

	2000	2001	2002	2003	2004
	Percentage changes				
OECD import oil price (cif)	62.1	-15.8	2.4	7.8	-3.8
Non-oil commodity prices[a]	3.1	-8.6	-0.3	9.5	5.1
	$ per barrel				
Memorandum item:					
OECD import oil price (cif)[b]	28.0	23.6	24.1	26.0	25.0

a) Total Hambourg commodity price index, excluding energy. OECD estimates and projections for 2003-04.
b) The historical data for the OECD crude oil import prices are average cif unit prices as calculated by the International Energy Agency; that is, they include cost, insurance and freight but exclude import duties. OECD estimates and projections for 2003-04.
Source: Hamburg Institute for Economic Research (HWWA), International Energy Agency and OECD.

Box I.2. Policy and other assumptions underlying the central projections[1]

Fiscal policy assumptions are based as closely as possible on legislated tax and spending provisions (current policies or "current services"). Where policy changes have been announced but not legislated, the procedure is to incorporate them if the assessment is that they will be implemented in a shape close to that announced. For the present projections the implications are as follows:

- The US projection embodies the main thrust of the Administration's tax proposals, which bring forward tax cuts that were built into the 2001 Tax Act and change the personal income tax treatment of dividends. It also incorporates the $75 billion supplemental appropriations request submitted by the President to Congress on 25 March 2003.

- The projection for Japan incorporates the supplementary budget for fiscal year (FY) 2002, passed by the Diet in early 2003, as well as the FY 2003 Budget, passed by the Diet in March 2003.

- Measures to meet budget deficit objectives under the Stability and Growth Pact are incorporated provided they are enshrined in law or about to be legislated.

Policy-controlled interest rates are set in line with the stated objectives of the relevant monetary authorities with respect to inflation and activity. In the United States, the federal funds target rate, which was last lowered to 1¼ per cent in November 2002, is assumed to rise gradually from late 2003 to 3½ per cent a year later, as some withdrawal of policy stimulus becomes appropriate in order to maintain price stability. In the euro area, the main refinancing rate, lowered by ¼ percentage point in early March to 2½ per cent, is assumed to be cut by ½ percentage point over the coming months, and to start gradually moving up from around mid-2004. In Japan, short-term interest rates are assumed to remain close to zero throughout the projection period.

The projections assume unchanged exchange rates from those prevailing on 26 March 2003, at one US dollar equals ¥ 120.1 and € 0.936. For Turkey, the exchange rate is assumed to depreciate in line with projected inflation.

The baseline assumption is that, following the fairly swift resolution of the Iraq crisis, with limited collateral damage, geopolitical uncertainty more generally will dissipate, leading to a return to "normality" in the second half of this year.

Since early 2002, oil prices have responded to production cutbacks and political tensions in the Middle East, falling sharply in March 2003, and the working hypothesis is that OECD oil import prices average $25 per barrel from the second quarter of 2003 onwards.

The cut-off date for information used in the projections was 4 April 2003.

---

1. Details of assumptions for individual countries are provided in the corresponding country notes.

---

firms and it becomes necessary to adjust the stance of policy. Despite increasing budget deficits, long yields have remained low. Steeper yield curves are expected only late in the projection period.

... though financial conditions are affected by exchange rate shifts

Relative financial conditions have, however, been affected by substantial exchange rate movements (Figure I.5). The dollar has weakened notably since last autumn and even more so from its peak in early 2002. A large part of the adjustment has fallen on the euro, against which the dollar has lost almost a quarter of its value in the year to early April 2003. The dollar has also fallen by 11 per cent against the yen.[7] The British pound as well has weakened substantially since last autumn.

Fiscal policy is expansionary in many countries

Fiscal positions have deteriorated sharply in the course of the downturn, both for cyclical and for structural reasons, and part of the associated impulse (amounting to a swing in the cyclically-adjusted deficit of over 1½ per cent of GDP for the OECD area as a whole in the course of 2001-02) has still to come through. Looking

---

7. Over the same period, non-Japan Asia continued to rapidly build up foreign exchange reserves, as many countries in the region resisted currency appreciation, thereby pushing an additional burden on the euro area and Japan.

Figure I.5. **Real effective exchange rates**

Average since 1980 = 100[1]

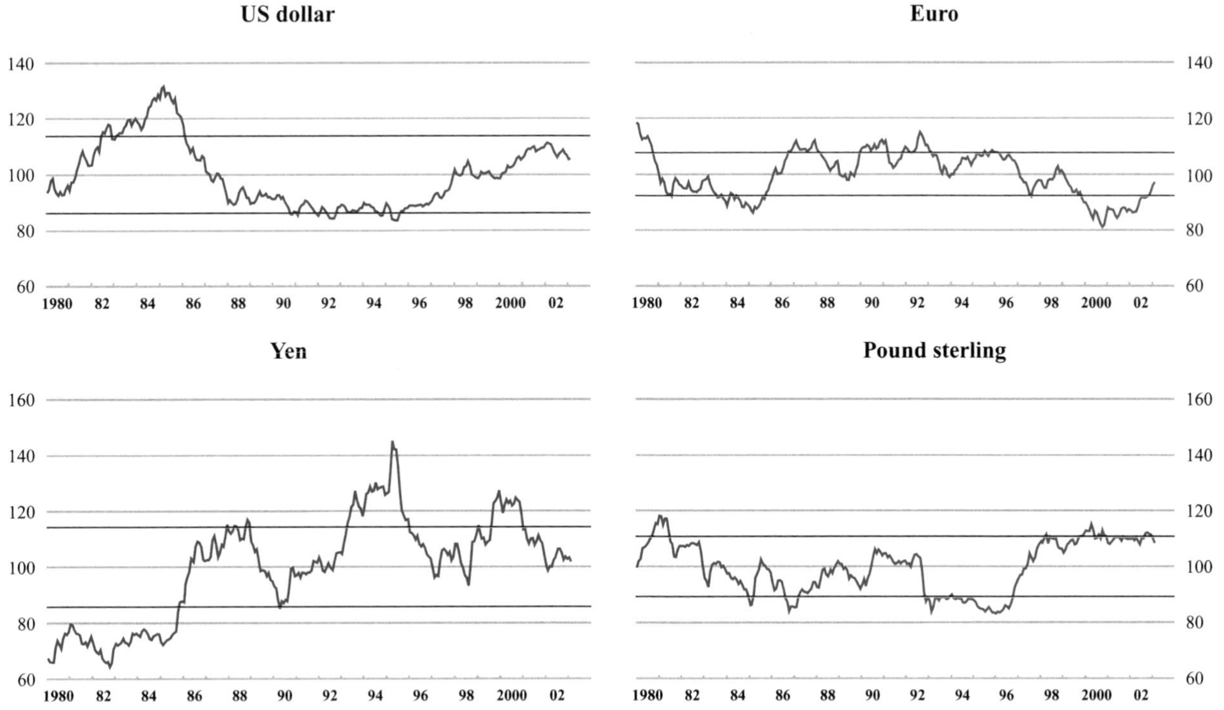

US dollar

Euro

Yen

Pound sterling

1. Horizontal lines delineate +/- one standard deviation from the average since 1980.
Source: OECD, *Main Economic Indicators*.

forward, the OECD overall fiscal deficit is expected to widen further in 2003, partly because of built-in stabilisers. As well, an additional *ex ante* stimulus is likely to accrue from a further increase in the cyclically-adjusted deficit amounting to a little under ½ per cent of GDP. The fiscal stance is set to loosen in particular in the United States, the United Kingdom, Austria and Finland. In the euro area as a whole, the stance becomes a bit more restrictive in 2003, mainly reflecting significant tightening programmed for Germany. In Japan, the stance is expansionary this year, reflecting the increase in expenditures in the fiscal year (FY) 2002 supplementary budget and the planned tax cuts in the FY 2003 budget. Budget deficits in several OECD transition economies should shrink, while remaining uncomfortably large (5 to 6½ per cent of GDP). Australia, Canada and Korea would continue to record budget surpluses.

... should underpin stronger but uneven growth from late 2003

Following a weak end-year quarter, the latest information on consumer spending, durable goods orders and purchasing manager intentions points to some modest growth pick-up in the first quarter of this year in the United States and less so in Europe. Empirical work at the OECD using high frequency data to forecast growth in the very short term points to continued modest growth in the second quarter in the euro area and possibly some slowing in the United States (Table I.3). In Japan,

Growth is uneven across OECD regions in early 2003

———————— Table I.3. **Very short-term output growth projections** ————————

Per cent, quarter-on-quarter, seasonally-adjusted [a]

	Outcome 2002 Q4	Estimates 2003 Q1	Projections 2003 Q2
United States	0.4	0.7 (0.2 – 1.2)	0.4 (-0.1 – 0.9)
Euro area	0.2	0.3 (0.1 – 0.5)	0.3 (0.0 – 0.6)
Germany	0.0	0.3 (-0.1 – 0.7)	0.3 (-0.3 – 0.9)
France	0.2	0.3 (0.0 – 0.6)	0.1 (-0.3 – 0.5)
Italy	0.4	0.3 (0.0 – 0.7)	0.4 (0.0 – 0.8)
United Kingdom	0.4	0.2 (-0.1 – 0.5)	0.5 (0.1 – 0.9)

a) Based on available conjunctural indicators published until 1 April 2003. In parentheses is the associated ± 1 standard error range.
Source: OECD.

surveys and leading indicators suggest that following an apparent spurt in late 2002, growth may have stalled in early 2003.

Inventories may be normalising   The inventory cycle is playing a neutral – perhaps even positive – role at this stage. Inventory adjustment has come to an end in the United States, and a build-up of stocks may add to demand at least in the early part of this year. In the euro area, business surveys also point to a modest improvement: the balance of firms finding stocks excessive has diminished, although not in Germany. The stock-output ratio in Japan continued to decline throughout 2002 and is edging below its long-term trend.

———————— Table I.4. **Contributions to changes in real GDP** ————————

Per cent of GDP in previous period

	2001	2002	2003	2004
United States				
Final domestic demand	1.7	2.5	2.7	3.9
of which: Business investment	-0.8	-0.8	0.2	1.2
Stockbuilding	-1.4	0.7	0.3	0.3
Net exports	-0.2	-0.8	-0.6	-0.3
GDP	0.3	2.4	2.5	4.0
Japan				
Final domestic demand	1.0	0.1	0.4	0.3
of which: Business investment	0.2	-0.6	0.2	0.2
Stockbuilding	0.0	-0.4	0.1	0.0
Net exports	-0.7	0.7	0.6	0.8
GDP	0.4	0.3	1.0	1.1
Euro area				
Final domestic demand	1.4	0.4	1.1	2.0
of which: Business investment	0.1	-0.3	-0.1	0.5
Stockbuilding	-0.4	-0.1	0.0	0.3
Net exports	0.5	0.5	0.0	0.1
GDP	1.5	0.9	1.0	2.4
OECD				
Final domestic demand	1.3	1.6	1.9	2.8
of which: Business investment	-0.3	-0.5	0.2	0.8
Stockbuilding	-0.7	0.3	0.2	0.2
Net exports	0.3	-0.1	-0.1	0.0
GDP	0.8	1.8	1.9	3.0

Source: OECD.

Against this background, the US recovery is expected to be driven by a very gradual strengthening of business fixed investment and modest re-stocking. Household consumption growth is, meanwhile, projected to slow as the mortgage-refinancing effects abate and a weak labour market negatively affects consumer spending propensities, at least in 2003. Moreover, a significant part of the Administration's proposed tax cut is assumed to be saved. Federal government spending may rise strongly, but this may to some extent be offset by restraint at the state and local level. Despite the weaker dollar, the drag from net exports is projected to diminish only slowly, with exports being held back by less than robust growth of export markets. Overall, and in year-average terms, growth will remain relatively subdued in 2003 at around 2½ per cent, but accelerate to 4 per cent in 2004 (Table I.4).

The United States will lead the cyclical upturn...

Activity in the euro area is expected to grow only modestly this year and next, while intra-regional growth trends are becoming increasingly divergent, with among the larger economies Germany and the Netherlands lagging France and Spain. In the near term, private consumption is likely to remain weak in the face of deteriorating employment prospects (Table I.5). With exports recovering only moderately (in part due to the stronger euro), significant unused capacity and pressures on profit margins, business investment may only gather momentum in 2004. As unemployment stops rising in 2004, consumption should regain some of its normal strength. All this sums up to a very gradual recovery in 2003, before growth picks up, but only to around potential rates, in 2004.

... with the euro area trailing...

The Japanese economy is not expected to sustain the growth performance recorded in 2002, when it grew by 2½ per cent during the year (but by 0.3 per cent

... and Japan slowing down

Table I.5. **Euro area: summary of projections**

	1999 current prices		2000	2001	2002	2003	2004
	Billion euros	Per cent of GDP	Percentage changes, volume				
Private consumption	3 587 .4	57.3	2.6	1.8	0.7	1.2	2.1
Government consumption	1 247 .4	19.9	2.2	2.1	2.7	1.6	1.2
Gross fixed capital formation	1 316 .1	21.0	5.1	-0.2	-2.3	0.2	2.7
Residential	364 .4	5.8	1.3	-3.1	-1.5	0.8	1.0
Business	794 .3	12.7	7.4	0.4	-2.2	-0.6	3.8
Government	157 .4	2.5	2.7	3.2	-4.5	3.1	0.9
Final domestic demand	6 150 .8	98.2	3.1	1.4	0.4	1.1	2.0
Stockbuilding[a]	19 .1	0.3	0.0	-0.4	-0.1	0.0	0.3
Total domestic demand	6 169 .9	98.5	3.0	1.0	0.3	1.1	2.4
Net exports[a]	92 .4	1.5	0.6	0.5	0.5	0.0	0.1
GDP at constant prices			3.6	1.5	0.9	1.0	2.4
GDP at current prices	6 262 .3	100.0	5.0	3.9	3.2	3.0	4.1
Memorandum items							
Harmonised consumer price index			2.4	2.5	2.4	2.0	1.6
Private consumption deflator			2.1	2.4	2.2	1.7	1.4
Total employment			2.3	1.5	0.4	-0.1	0.7
Unemployment rate			8.4	8.0	8.2	8.8	8.7
General government financial balance [b]			0.1	-1.6	-2.3	-2.5	-2.4
Current account balance [b]			-0.4	0.2	1.1	1.4	1.4
Output gap [c]			1.1	0.3	-0.9	-1.8	-1.5

a) Contributions to changes in real GDP (percentage of real GDP in previous year), actual amount in the first column.
b) As a percentage of GDP.
c) As a percentage of potential GDP.
Source: OECD.

year-on-year).[8] Going forward, growth is expected to average 1 per cent in 2003-04 and to be driven largely by exports, as subdued wage growth and deteriorating employment prospects will restrain household spending. Despite some improvement in profit expectations, continuing corporate restructuring will weigh on business investment.

Labour markets are worsening and disinflation continues

The recovery has been jobless in the United States...

In the United States, aggressive labour shedding against the background of strong productivity growth (Table I.6) has allowed relatively strong *per capita* income growth to be maintained while reducing unit labour costs and partially rebuilding profits. While output has increased by 3 per cent since the onset of the recession in March 2001, employment has shrunk. Even more so than in the early 1990s, the upturn has been a "jobless" one. Nevertheless, the US labour market having entered this recession tighter than it had been in 30 years, the unemployment rate remains lower than in the aftermath of most recent recessions, at just under 6 per cent.

... and unemployment is rising in the euro area and Japan

In the euro area, unemployment remained fairly stable in the early phases of the downturn. This may be partly thanks to the ongoing impact of labour market reforms, which have been pricing low-productivity workers into jobs, as well as to the fact that the initial slowdown was milder than across the Atlantic. Comparatively stronger employment protection rules may also have delayed layoffs, despite the rising share of flexible work contracts. Unemployment has, however, started to rise more rapidly since, and now stands at 8¾ per cent of the labour force. In Japan, unemployment currently stands near a historical peak, at 5¼ per cent of the labour force, despite a falling participation rate.

Disinflation is likely to continue

Inflation is generally low or trending down in core terms, but with exceptions (Canada and some smaller euro area countries). In the United States, although inflation has tended to pick up, reflecting rising energy prices and stronger import prices resulting from a weaker dollar, it will remain moderate. As higher energy prices unwind, inflation should slow, consistent with the negative output gap prevailing over the entire projection period. In the euro area, where the output gap is widening sharply and rising oil prices were largely offset by euro appreciation, inflation is projected to decline from 2½ per cent in 2002 to 1½ per cent in 2004, as measured by the harmonised index of consumer prices. Inflation in Germany and Switzerland would approach zero. In Japan, deflation is not expected to abate, and the consumption deflator should continue to decline by about 1½ per cent per year.

World trade should regain momentum

World trade will rebound, but external imbalances worsen

World trade growth slowed late in 2002 as global economic activity lost some of its strength and world ICT markets relapsed. It is projected to pick up gradually in the course of 2003, as OECD activity firms (Table I.7). Reflecting the uneven recovery, current account imbalances are projected to increase. The US current account deficit is set to rise by ¾ per cent of GDP between 2002 and 2004, to 5½ per cent of GDP, while the Japanese and euro area surpluses would increase by 1 per cent and ¼ per cent of GDP respectively over the same period.

---

8. This was, however, partly due to the adoption of a new definition of the national accounts deflators that showed a stronger deflation than had previously been expected. Nominal GDP declined 1½ per cent in 2002.

——— Table I.6. **Productivity, unemployment, output gaps and inflation** ———

	2001	2002	2003	2004
	Per cent			
Labour productivity growth				
United States	0.2	3.9	2.0	2.3
Japan	0.8	1.7	1.6	1.3
Euro area	-0.1	0.5	1.3	1.8
European Union	0.3	0.7	1.5	2.0
Total OECD	0.3	2.2	1.8	2.0
Employment growth				
United States	0.0	-0.3	0.9	1.4
Japan	-0.5	-1.3	-0.6	-0.2
Euro area	1.5	0.4	-0.1	0.7
European Union	1.4	0.5	0.0	0.7
Total OECD	0.5	0.1	0.4	1.0
	Percentage of labour force			
Unemployment rate				
United States	4.8	5.8	6.0	5.8
Japan	5.0	5.4	5.7	5.7
Euro area	8.0	8.2	8.8	8.7
European Union	7.3	7.6	8.0	7.9
Total OECD	6.4	6.9	7.2	7.0
	Per cent			
Output gaps[a]				
United States	-1.1	-1.5	-2.1	-1.2
Japan	-0.6	-1.5	-1.8	-2.0
Euro area	0.3	-0.9	-1.8	-1.5
European Union	0.2	-0.9	-1.7	-1.4
Total OECD	-0.4	-1.2	-1.8	-1.4
Inflation[b]	GDP deflator			
United States	2.4	1.1	1.6	1.3
Japan	-1.6	-1.7	-2.2	-1.8
Euro area	2.4	2.4	1.9	1.7
European Union	2.4	2.5	1.9	1.8
Total OECD *less* Turkey	2.0	1.4	1.3	1.2
Total OECD	2.9	2.1	1.7	1.4
	Consumer price index			
United States	2.8	1.6	2.4	1.7
Japan	-0.7	-0.9	-0.9	-1.0
Euro area[c]	2.5	2.4	2.0	1.6

a) Per cent of potential GDP.
b) Percentage change from previous period.
c) Harmonised index of consumer prices.
Source: OECD.

Beyond the near-term, the relative dynamism of the non-OECD Asian economies as a whole, and in particular China and Dynamic Asia,[9] is likely to continue to be a positive contributor to growth in global trade. Non-OECD Asia accounted for close to 45 per cent of global trade volume growth in 2002 and is projected to account for over 30 per cent this year – approximately double the share of these economies in total world trade. China's strong real GDP growth performance in 2002 has been driven

Domestic demand remains relatively strong in Asia...

---

9. Dynamic Asia economies include Hong Kong, China; Chinese Taipei; Indonesia; Malaysia; the Philippines; Singapore and Thailand.

————— Table I.7. **World trade and current account summary** —————

	2001	2002	2003	2004
Merchandise trade volume		Percentage changes		
World trade[a]	-0.2	3.6	5.9	8.8
of which: Manufactures	-1.1	3.8	6.1	9.4
OECD exports	-0.5	2.7	4.6	7.9
OECD imports	-0.7	2.5	4.9	7.5
Non-OECD exports	-0.6	7.6	9.8	11.3
Non-OECD imports	2.8	5.2	8.3	12.6
Intra-OECD trade[b]	-1.0	1.5	3.4	6.6
OECD exports to non-OECD	2.1	5.6	9.1	12.4
OECD imports from non-OECD	-0.2	8.0	9.8	10.6
Trade prices				
OECD exports[c]	-2.6	1.1	7.8	1.3
OECD imports[c]	-3.3	0.7	8.2	1.3
OECD terms-of-trade with rest of the world[d]	2.0	0.4	-0.7	0.2
Current account balances		Per cent of GDP		
United States	-3.9	-4.8	-5.4	-5.5
Japan	2.1	2.8	3.1	3.9
Euro area	0.2	1.1	1.4	1.4
European Union	0.1	0.9	1.0	1.0
OECD	-1.0	-1.1	-1.2	-1.2
		$ billion		
United States	-393	-503	-587	-629
Japan	88	114	129	160
Euro area	15	73	105	115
European Union	10	75	98	99
OECD	-255	-289	-338	-345
Non-OECD	100	129	184	181
World	-155	-159	-154	-164

Note: Regional aggregates include intra-regional trade.
a) Growth rates of the arithmetic average of world import volumes and world export volumes.
b) Arithmetic average of the intra-OECD import and export volumes implied by the total OECD trade volumes and the estimated trade flows between the OECD and non-OECD areas based on the 1995 structure of trade values.
c) Average unit values in US$.
d) The OECD terms of trade are calculated as the ratio of OECD export to OECD import prices, excluding intra-OECD trade.
Source: OECD.

largely by domestic demand, which was boosted by exceptionally strong growth in government investment spending and by booms in real estate investment and consumer durables, all of which are likely to ease over the coming two years. As a result, growth is likely to depend increasingly on progress on structural reforms.

… and Russia…

The global slowdown has had a limited negative impact on activity in Russia, where GDP growth is expected to remain robust in 2003-04. The main contributing factors are rising investment in oil and utilities and strong private consumption. Despite high oil-driven capital inflows, inflation should continue to decline gradually, supported by the ongoing real appreciation of the rouble.

… but weak in Latin America

Import demand from Latin America will remain weak, following unexpectedly large adjustments of current account deficits in the region. In Brazil in particular, the current account deficit shrank from 4.6 per cent of GDP in 2001 to 1.8 per cent in

2002, due to depressed demand and intense import substitution. The deficit is projected to decline further this year, reflecting *inter alia* continued adherence to prudent macroeconomic policies. Argentina now displays a sizeable current account surplus and is only slowly recovering from the 2002 recession, as political uncertainties and financial blockages hinder the resumption of growth.

Risks remain mainly on the downside

Significant uncertainties attach to the strength of the cyclical recovery, independently of those created by geopolitical tensions. Possible aggravating factors include balance-sheet stress in the household sector, a failure of investment to pick up, a disorderly unwinding of international imbalances or some combination thereof. At the same time, oil prices and business and consumer confidence are subject to a wide range of possible outcomes. The majority of these risks would seem to be on the downside. Even so, activity could well stage a stronger than foreseen comeback in response to an ending of war and successful stabilisation in Iraq, and to the recent macroeconomic policy impulses that have yet to fully work their way through.

Downside risks continue to dominate

As noted, the more acute risks attaching to a surge in oil prices faded as the risk of serious damage to oil production and distribution infrastructure receded. But significant and lasting changes in oil prices – in either direction – cannot be ruled out. Simulations with the OECD's INTERLINK model suggest that a $10 increase (decrease) in the average OECD import price of oil would, if sustained for a year, lead to a ¼ per cent decline (rise) in OECD area-wide growth and ½ percentage point increase (fall) in headline inflation.[10] The actual impact of an unexpected shift in oil prices, however, would depend on the context and might differ from what past experience seems to imply, not least because inflation is now benign and well-anchored.

Oil price risks are no longer only on the upside

An underlying cyclical risk is that the consumption impulse could wane before investment recovers. This might translate into a more rapid increase in the household saving ratio towards long-run historical averages than embodied in the projection (Figure I.6). There are several dimensions to this risk:

Consumption could be weaker

- Housing prices could fall, either in response to an interest rate shock (possibly in connection with worsening fiscal concerns) or for other reasons, causing household balance sheet strains to emerge.[11, 12]

---

10. The impact on Japanese and euro area growth would be stronger than that in the United States, reflecting their respective dependence on net oil imports. The underlying assumptions are specified in Dalsgaard, T., C. André and P. Richardson, "Standard shocks in the OECD Interlink model", *OECD Economics Department Working Papers*, No. 306, 2001.

11. In this connection, it should also be noted that US housing market risk is concentrated in the portfolios of two large and modestly capitalised government-sponsored agencies, which may be a problem if it were to materialise. See Poole, W., "Housing in the economy", Speech delivered at the Office of Federal Housing Enterprise Oversight Symposium, Washington DC, 10 March 2003.

12. In the United Kingdom, debt-to-income ratios have risen most rapidly for the lowest-income mortgage-holding households, and ratios of unsecured debt to income more than doubled for the lowest-income households. These are the ones most vulnerable to shocks increasing financial stress, such as unexpected interest rate hikes or spells of unemployment. See Cox, P., J. Whitley and P. Brierley, "Financial pressures in the UK household sector: evidence from the British Household Panel Survey", *Bank of England Quarterly Bulletin*, Winter, 2002. Housing market bubble symptoms have arguably also been observed in other OECD countries, including Spain and Australia.

Figure I.6. **Saving and investment in the United States**

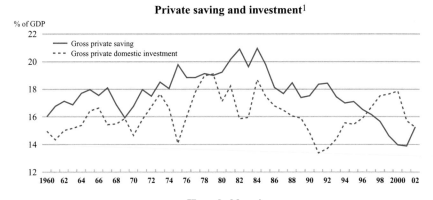

1. There is a statistical discrepancy in the national accounts, reflecting conflicting information from source data regarding product and income, with gross saving exceeding gross investment (by 1.1 per cent of GDP in 2002).
Source: US Bureau of Economic Analysis and OECD.

– Further equity price declines are still a source of potential instability. Price-earnings ratios remain relatively high in North America compared with long-run averages and with those in Europe,[13] while expected equity price volatility remains elevated. Even if equity prices do not drop any further, household consumption could be affected by an increase in saving as pension plan holders gradually realise the extent of the losses they effectively incurred.

– While lower interest rates have allowed corporations to consolidate their accounts by rolling over or refinancing loans, profit margins remain generally quite low and pricing power weak.[14] This implies not only a risk of further deferred investment but also of accelerated labour-market adjustment, especially in the euro area, where unit labour costs have been under pressure. The ensuing increase in uncertainty would push up precautionary saving.

---

13. However, following recent corporate governance scandals and the ensuing tightening of regulation (see Box I.3 in the previous *Outlook*), reported and forecast earnings may have become more conservative, implying that price-earnings ratios may look higher than they otherwise would have.
14. Even in the United States, non-financial corporate profits are still relatively low, at 7.5 per cent of GDP in 2002 (as against an average of 8.7 per cent over the last four decades).

Box I.3.   Economic consequences of the spread of severe acute respiratory syndrome

An atypical form of pneumonia, called severe respiratory syndrome (SARS), emerged in China in late 2002. It has been spreading considerably since, leading to an emergency travel advisory issued by the World Health Organisation and to precautions being taken by healthcare professionals around the world. The early manifestations of the disease are non-specific, resembling symptoms of the common cold or influenza, making it difficult to detect in timely fashion. By mid-April 2003, over 3 200 cases had been reported in 24 countries, with 154 deaths, mostly in mainland China and in Hong Kong, but also *inter alia* in Singapore, Vietnam and Canada.[1]

The economic impact of this epidemic depends largely on how promptly and effectively the virus can be brought under control. Preventive measures have been taken in the coun-tries most directly affected, but they have disrupted traffic and business. A cheaper method of prevention or a cure have yet to be discovered. More specifically, the SARS has pushed stock prices down and taken a toll on airlines, tour-ism and retailing in several non-OECD Asian countries and has affected travel to or from New Zealand and Canada. In several countries, some workplaces have temporarily closed or employees are being invited or obliged to stay at home. A number of Japanese firms are restricting travel by employees to Singapore and other Asian cities. The ultimate macroeco-nomic repercussions of the epidemic are difficult to ascertain at this early stage, but past experience with other disease outbreaks[2] suggests that local or sectoral impacts in the most seriously affected countries could be significant if the emer-gency were to worsen and persist.

---

1. For a clinical perspective, see "A major outbreak of severe acute respiratory syndrome in Hong Kong", *New England Journal of Medicine*, 7 April 2003, and for an up-to-date count, *www.who.int/csr/sarscountry/en/*.
2. For example the meat-related diseases in the late 1990s (Box I.4 in *OECD Economic Outlook*, No. 69, June 2001).

On top of the above geopolitical and economic tensions, a new risk has recently emerged, with the spreading of an atypical form of pneumonia (Box I.3). It has caused significant disruptions in several countries, particularly China and Hong Kong. Its effect on the global outlook is as yet very uncertain. It will depend *inter alia* on how effective containment measures are, on how rapidly its propagation is understood and on whether a vaccine or cure is discovered.

A new epidemiological risk has surfaced

The external counterpart of low private and declining public saving in the United States is a large and rising current account deficit, which is set to widen to 5½ per cent of GDP by 2004, despite the recent dollar depreciation. The experience of the late 1980s suggests that the narrowing of the external gap need not be disrup-tive, but it may also point to the possibility of further exchange rate adjustment, not least if central banks in Asia were to significantly reduce the pace at which they build up dollar reserves.

External imbalances remain of concern

Macroeconomic policy challenges

The severity of the downswing has been limited by the relaxation of macroeco-nomic policy, especially in the United States. Even so, persistent cyclical weaknesses and downside risks raise the issue of whether additional policy stimulus is in order. Where there remains scope for further monetary policy action, this may indeed have to be used. On the fiscal side, however, any new discretionary fiscal measures need to be set against longer-run sustainability considerations and control over spending

Some rebalancing of the policy mix may be needed

has to improve. In some cases, consolidation ought to start even before the recovery is well established.

Monetary policy: how much more can it help?

Monetary policy has cushioned the downturn

Against the background of low inflation and widening output gaps (Figure I.7), central banks have brought down policy-controlled interest rates near or to historical lows.[15] This has helped contain the amplitude of the downturn and, given the lags associated with monetary policy, will continue to support demand in the course of 2003. At the same time, falling bond yields and buoyant house prices have, in a number of cases, limited the extent of adverse wealth effects of collapsing equity prices. Going forward, loosening monetary policy for cyclical reasons may, in some countries, aggravate domestic or external imbalances. In others, there is more clearly scope for further interest rate cuts, although monetary policy alone cannot put economies back on a balanced and sustainable growth path.

Figure I.7. **Resource utilisation, inflation and interest rates**

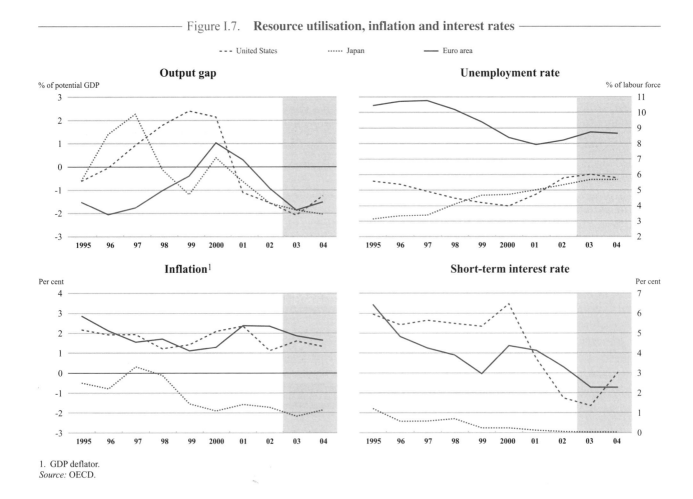

1. GDP deflator.
Source: OECD.

15. Australia, Canada, Korea, Mexico and New Zealand are the only exceptions among OECD countries (excluding Turkey), and even there, interest rates are low in historical perspective.

In the United States, nominal short-term interest rates are at their lowest levels in over four decades, following a cumulative 475 basis point cut in the Federal Reserve's target rate in the course of 2001 and an additional 50 basis point cut in November 2002. In real terms, short-term interest rates are essentially nil or negative, depending on which price index is used. This loose stance has generously supported credit and demand, notably in the consumer durables and housing sectors. The room for lowering the federal funds rate is now limited, but on current OECD projections, there is no need to cut the policy rate further. Indeed, as the recovery strengthens in 2004, it will be desirable to start moving the policy rate back towards neutrality.

There is little room or need to cut interest rates in the United States

In Europe, with the exception of Switzerland, nominal short-term interest rates have remained well above their US counterparts. The Eurosystem cut its minimum refinance rate by 25 basis points in early March 2003, bringing the policy rate back to the level of its 1999 trough, which, however, is still 125 basis points above the corresponding US rate. Based on expected inflation, real short-term interest rates in the euro area are still, on average, close to 1 per cent. There is scope to bring the policy rate down further, given that core inflation is trending down against the background of a significant near-term widening in the output gap. Moreover, the effective exchange rate has appreciated substantially in recent months.

There is more scope to ease interest rates in the euro area...

In the United Kingdom, the Bank of England cut its repo rate by 25 basis points in February 2003, after a prolonged wait-and-see period, and despite the persistent vigour of house price inflation. But with growth more resilient and fiscal policy more stimulative than in the euro area, there seems to be much less of a need for further cuts.

... but less so in the United Kingdom

In Japan, short-term interest rates have been zero almost uninterruptedly since 1999. Liquidity injections have been stepped up several times, so that banks' current account balances at the Bank of Japan have quadrupled over the last two years. The range of assets purchased by the central bank has been broadened.[16] Even so, year on year, broad money has recently been expanding at a rate of only about 2 per cent, while private bank lending has continued to contract by 2 to 3 per cent. While liquidity creation may have helped contain the acceleration of deflation,[17] it has clearly not been sufficient to pull the general price level back up. Exchange rate appreciation since early 2002 (which several bouts of effectively sterilised official intervention on the foreign exchange market failed to prevent) has also contributed to depressing the domestic price level.

In Japan, monetary action has not ended deflation...

Continued liquidity expansion is necessary to prevent worsening deflation, including via the purchase of foreign currency denominated assets. But as long as the monetary policy transmission mechanism is defective, "quantitative easing" in the form of liquidity injections against domestic collateral will not suffice. Bank balance sheets are saddled with very large amounts of non-performing loans (NPLs). As

... and further easing is needed, with structural reforms

---

16. The Bank of Japan also purchases shares held by commercial banks (and is authorised to accumulate up to ¥ 3 trillion of such shares itself), but the purpose is to reduce bank balance sheet instability rather than to boost liquidity.
17. The intensity of deflation may be understated, however, by the official consumer price index series (see Ariga, K. and K. Matsui, "Mismeasurement of the CPI", *NBER Working Papers*, No. 9436, 2003). Also, a new version of the Bank of Japan's wholesale price index, aiming at better accounting for changes in the quality of goods, shows the annual rate of deflation to be around one percentage point stronger than suggested by the old index.

described in more detail in the previous *Outlook*, new measures were introduced in late 2002 to address the NPL problem more aggressively and to work off the existing stock of bad loans. The supervisory agency has launched a second round of special inspections and there are signs that banks are indeed acting more expeditiously to recognise and work off bad loans as well as to close unprofitable branches. The expertise of foreign banks in bad loan restructuring is also starting to be called upon more. However, consistent and more far-reaching efforts are necessary to resolve this problem while implementing broad structural reform to reinvigorate credit demand.

Fiscal policy: room for manoeuvre has essentially been exhausted

Further fiscal loosening is inadvisable

In most OECD countries, the fiscal outlook (see Table I.8) is now far more sombre than in the late 1990s, owing to cyclical setbacks, higher spending and a series of deficit-financed tax cuts, but also to the often belated action to address longer-run fiscal pressures. In some cases, traditional methods of assessing the fiscal stance have failed to correct for a number of transitory factors masking underlying weaknesses, which has contributed to delaying remedial measures or prompted fiscal expansion that may be unsustainable in the long term. In particular, the tax receipts associated with the asset price booms of the late 1990s tended to be treated, implicitly,

Table I.8.   **General government financial balances**

Per cent of GDP / Potential GDP

	2001	2002	2003	2004
United States				
Actual balance	-0.5	-3.4	-4.6	-4.2
Cyclically-adjusted balance	-0.2	-2.9	-4.0	-3.9
Cyclically-adjusted primary balance	2.1	-1.0	-2.1	-2.0
Japan[a]				
Actual balance	-6.1	-7.1	-7.7	-7.8
Cyclically-adjusted balance	-5.9	-6.7	-7.2	-7.2
Cyclically-adjusted primary balance	-4.6	-5.6	-5.8	-5.8
Euro area				
Actual balance	-1.6	-2.3	-2.5	-2.4
Cyclically-adjusted balance	-1.8	-1.9	-1.6	-1.6
Cyclically-adjusted primary balance	1.7	1.4	1.6	1.5
European Union				
Actual balance	-1.1	-2.0	-2.3	-2.2
Cyclically-adjusted balance	-1.2	-1.6	-1.4	-1.5
Cyclically-adjusted primary balance	2.0	1.5	1.5	1.3
OECD[b]				
Actual balance	-1.3	-2.9	-3.6	-3.5
Cyclically-adjusted balance	-1.4	-2.8	-3.2	-3.2
Cyclically-adjusted primary balance	1.1	-0.6	-1.0	-1.1

Note: Actual balances are as a per cent of nominal GDP. Cyclically-adjusted balances are as a per cent of potential GDP. The cyclically-adjusted balance excludes one-off revenues from the sale of mobile telephone licences. The primary cyclically-adjusted balance is the cyclically-adjusted balance less net debt interest payments.

a) Includes deferred tax payments on postal saving accounts amounting to 0.6 and 0.2 per cent of GDP in 2001 and 2002, respectively.

b) Total OECD figures for the actual balance exclude Mexico, Switzerland and Turkey and those for the cyclically-adjusted balance further exclude the Czech Republic, Hungary, Korea, Luxembourg, Poland and the Slovak Republic.

Source: OECD.

as a permanent improvement on the revenue side. Underlying trends have also been masked by a number of one-off operations, *e.g.* securitisation of public assets or receivables, debt swaps, privatisations and tax amnesties.[18] Identifying underlying "structural" fiscal trends is therefore difficult (Box I.4). But against the backdrop of mounting ageing-related pressures,[19] it is clear that there is, in general, little if any scope for new fiscal stimulus over and above the cushion provided by the automatic stabilisers. In some cases, consolidation cannot be delayed even if it is pro-cyclical. Rapidly rising deficits and debts would risk pushing up real long-term interest rates and crowding out private activity, as in the early 1980s and early 1990s.

The turnaround in the fiscal position has been particularly marked in the United States. Adjusting for the cycle in activity (but not for any additional impact of the cycle in asset prices nor for any other special factors), the swing from 2000 to 2002 amounted to 3.8 percentage points of GDP. This constitutes the largest two-year fiscal expansion in decades and has brought longer-run fiscal sustainability concerns to the fore. The President's budget proposals for FY 2004, which are built into the OECD projection, involve significant additional loosening, both in the form of tax cuts and via higher spending, particularly on security and health care, and may add close to 1 per cent of GDP to what the deficit would otherwise have been (Figure I.8). Some of the measures, such as the acceleration of the personal income tax relief foreseen in the 2001 Economic Growth and Tax Relief Reconciliation Act, should help support household consumption later this year and next, even if part of the extra disposable income is likely to be saved. The war-related outlays should also end up boosting domestic demand. In contrast, the intensity and timing of the stimulus to be expected from some of the other proposals, notably the exclusion of dividends from individual taxable income, remains difficult to assess.[20]

Large budget deficits are likely to persist in the United States...

The newly proposed tax cuts are seen by the US Administration as structural reform initiatives more than as attempts at fiscal fine-tuning. But coupled with some costly new spending initiatives and with the $75 billion supplemental appropriations request submitted to Congress in March 2003,[21] they imply that fiscal deficits will continue to pre-empt large amounts of national saving well beyond the point where the current cyclical slack has been absorbed. Apart from uncertainty about the eventual budgetary costs of the war in Iraq, the risk of significantly higher deficits is compounded, over the longer term, by the absence of a medium-run anchor that would tie down spending growth, as the now expired Budget Enforcement Act helped do during the 1990s. In addition, some foreseeable future tax changes, for example as regards the alternative minimum tax,[22] will also contribute to widening the fiscal gap. Based on past experience (Figure I.9), higher

... with possible adverse consequences over the longer run

---

18. Fiscal deficits may also be understated by "below-the-line" treatment of capital injections into state-owned enterprises where they really represent subsidies.
19. For a detailed discussion, see "Fiscal sustainability: the contribution of fiscal rules", *OECD Economic Outlook*, No. 72, December 2002.
20. Moreover, with state governments facing a severe fiscal crisis, spending cutbacks and tax increases at sub-national level are partly offsetting federal stimulus.
21. This request is built on the assumption of a rapid and decisive US military action in Iraq and does not extend beyond the end of the current fiscal year (30 September 2003). The amount approaches the total fiscal cost of the first Gulf War (which is estimated at around $80 billion at today's prices), and represents 0.7 percentage point of GDP.
22. The alternative minimum tax – originally established to ensure that high-income earners could not abuse tax shelters – is not indexed for inflation and the 2001 tax reform did not cut it alongside the ordinary income tax. If it were to remain as is, it would encroach on a rapidly rising fraction of middle-income earners.

Box I.4. Re-assessing cyclically-adjusted balances

Traditional methods of correcting budget deficits for the cycle in economic activity do not adjust for asset price cycles or one-off operations (tax amnesties, securitisations).[1] Regarding the former, movements in asset prices generate capital gains and losses, which impact on tax revenues with various lags. These movements are not necessarily correlated with cycles in economic activity, and can be seen as structural where the fundamentals determining asset prices (such as profit and productivity growth and risk premia) have undergone change. Where they have not, however, the cyclically-adjusted balance may give too favourable a "structural" picture by not recognising the temporary nature of tax buoyancy due to asset price fluctuations. This appears to have occurred during the recent asset price boom.

Measuring non-discretionary fluctuations in tax revenue. In several OECD countries, total government receipts as a percentage of GDP surged in the latter part of the 1990s and subsequently contracted sharply, mostly reflecting changes in household direct taxes. For example, in the United States, these grew from 10.1 per cent of GDP in 1992 to a historical peak of 13.1 per cent in 2000 but had fallen back to 10.7 per cent by 2002. In the United Kingdom, they rose from 11.8 per cent of GDP in 1993 to 13.4 per cent in 2001 and then dropped back to 12.5 per cent in 2002. Other OECD countries including Canada and Sweden have experienced similar tax revenue swings. Corporate income taxes have followed the same pattern, but to a much lesser extent.

A simple *ex post* measure of the "unexpected" deviation in the effective tax rate is what cannot be explained by cyclical variations in output and identifiable discretionary fiscal policy measures. In the United States, this difference cumulatively amounted to 3.3 per cent of GDP between 1997 and 2001 for direct household taxes. In 2002, revenues then undershot by 0.6 per cent of GDP. Thus, the sensitivity of tax revenues to GDP may differ substantially from that used to derive cyclically-adjusted revenues.

Asset price cycles and tax revenues. Direct taxes do not vary linearly with GDP. Factors altering the receipts-to-GDP ratio include the progressivity of the household income tax, the volatility of corporate profits, the non-symmetrical tax treatment of profits and losses, deferred taxation and the fact that taxable income does not include all components of GDP. Another factor leading to variations in the receipts-to-GDP ratio is the rise and fall of asset prices. As equity prices rise, capital gains accrue. When they are realised, gains show up as taxable income for households and/or corporations depending on national legislation. In the United States, taxes on households capital gains grew from $27 billion in FY 1992 to $120 billion in FY 2000 (close to 12 per cent of total direct taxes paid by households) before dropping to an estimated $55 billion in FY 2002. Similarly, in Finland taxes on capital gains paid by households (accruals basis) rose from € 0.5 billion in 1998 to € 1.2 billion in 2000 (6 per cent of total direct taxes paid by households) before collapsing to € 0.4 billion in 2002. It is capital gains realisations that are taxed rather than capital gains accruals, and they tend to lag movements

in asset prices. Indeed, after a bull market such as that of the 1990s, a sizeable amount of accrued gains remains to be realised, and equity sales in a falling market can still result in taxable gains, albeit reduced.

Financial market swings may also affect tax receipts through their effect on stock options. Estimates for the United States show that income from stock options rose from negligible amounts in the early 1990s to about $50 billion in 1997, and to over $100 billion in 2000 (*i.e.* about 2 per cent of wages and salaries). This may have yielded individual income tax receipts of around $40 billion in 2000, with most of that income probably concentrated among the highest earnings taxpayers and thus taxed at the highest rates. Preliminary data suggest that income from stock options may have halved in 2001 and fallen even further in 2002. Similarly, in Finland direct taxes on stock options have risen from € 0.1 billion in 1998, to € 0.6 billion in 2000 (also representing about 2 per cent of total wages and salaries) before falling to € 0.3 billion in 2002. However, as income earned is reported as part of wage and salary income when the options are exercised, it is at the same time deductible from the corporate income tax. Given these offsetting effects on corporate profits, changes in equity prices and income tend to generate much smaller changes in total taxable income and total tax receipts.

Rising asset values may also affect receipts through other routes:

– In the United Kingdom, receipts from the stamp duty – a tax on land and property transactions and on equity transfers – increased from 0.3 per cent of GDP in 1996 to 0.8 per cent in 2000, owing to buoyant property and equity markets and, to a lesser extent, to past increases in tax rates. Receipts have flattened since, reflecting the offsetting impact of house and equity price changes.

– In Denmark, the return on pension funds' investments is taxable. The fall in equity prices and the recent change in tax rates resulted in a significant drop in revenue, which fell from a peak of 1.2 per cent of GDP in 1999 to virtually zero in 2001 and 2002.

– In Greece, financial and capital transactions taxes have more than doubled between 1995 and 2000, reaching 1.6 per cent of GDP in 2000.

Accounting for asset price changes. The figure below shows the effect of excluding direct tax revenues that are particularly sensitive to asset prices on cyclically-adjusted balances in two countries (but it does not attempt to incorporate a "normal" element of such revenues in the adjusted balance). In the United States, direct taxes from capital gains realised by households rose from an average of 0.5 per cent of GDP in the first half of the 1990s to 1.1 per cent between 1998 and 2000, before falling abruptly in 2002. In Finland, the massive swing in equity prices in 2001 and 2002 caused a loss of revenue equivalent to nearly 1 per cent of GDP, accounting for a significant part of the "discretionary" easing in the fiscal stance since 2000.

Box I.4.   **Re-assessing cyclically-adjusted balances** *(cont.)*

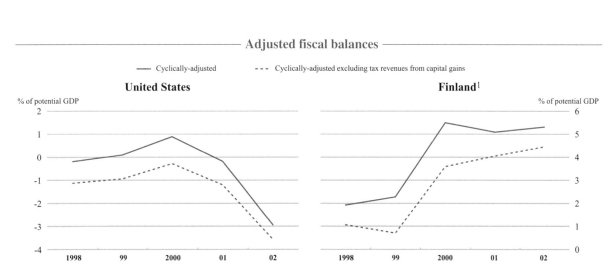

—————————————————————————— Adjusted fiscal balances ——————————————————————————

—— Cyclically-adjusted   - - - Cyclically-adjusted excluding tax revenues from capital gains

United States

Finland[1]

1. Excludes also tax revenues from stock options.
Source: OECD.

Other non-structural changes. One-off budgetary operations further complicate the interpretation of cyclically-adjusted balances. The OECD has consistently deducted the budgetary proceeds from the sales of UMTS licences. However, other possible budgetary operations should be taken into account as well:

–   In some EU countries (Austria, Finland, Greece, Ireland and Italy), governments have securitised financial or non-financial assets and revenue flows.[2] The impact of these operations on the general government fiscal balance and debt depends on how the special purpose vehicle's payment to the general government is recorded. To secure consistency across EU countries, Eurostat released guidelines in 2002 on the recording in national accounts of securitisation operations. The implementation of the new guidelines has been reflected in an upward adjustment of the deficit for Italy by about ¾ per cent of GDP in 2001 and of the debt position for Austria and Greece (by about 3½ per cent of GDP in 2000-01 for Greece).

–   In a number of countries, government asset sales have, at times, contributed to the improvement in cyclically-adjusted balances, amounting to ¼ per cent of GDP in 2001-02 in Belgium and to ¼ per cent of GDP in FY 2000-01 in Australia.

–   Tax amnesties have been used in many countries. In Italy, for example, a partial tax amnesty providing temporary incentives for the repatriation of financial assets illegally held abroad was passed in 2001. The legalisation of such assets was made conditional on the payment of a penalty of 2.5 per cent of the value of the assets declared. This measure could generate revenues of 0.1 per cent of GDP in 2002.

Policy implications. In sum, careful calculation and interpretation of "structural" budget balances is warranted in light of the large non-cyclical, but temporary, shifts in government revenues observed recently in OECD countries. Overstating structural budget positions can lead governments to raise spending or reduce taxes to an extent which compromises future budget management during subsequent downturns.

———————————

1. The OECD, the IMF and the European Commission use a broadly similar approach to compute cyclically-adjusted balances. See OECD, *Sources and methods of the OECD Economic Outlook*; Hagemann, R., "The structural budget balance: the IMF's methodology", *IMF Working Papers*, No. 99/95, 1999; and European Commission, *Public Finances in EMU 2002*, Brussels, 2002.

2. Securitisation is defined here as an arrangement where the owner of an asset (or sometimes revenue flows not attached to an asset) transfers the ownership to another unit, often called a special purpose vehicle, which borrows to pay the seller, generally in the form of securities issued on its own account.

Figure I.8. **US Federal budget prospects two years apart**

Fiscal years[1]

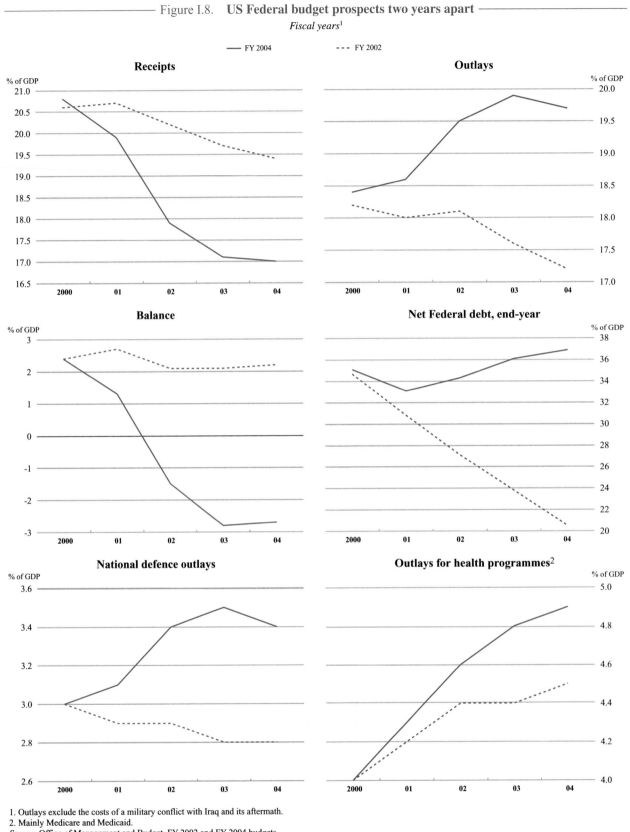

1. Outlays exclude the costs of a military conflict with Iraq and its aftermath.
2. Mainly Medicare and Medicaid.
Source: Office of Management and Budget, FY 2002 and FY 2004 budgets.

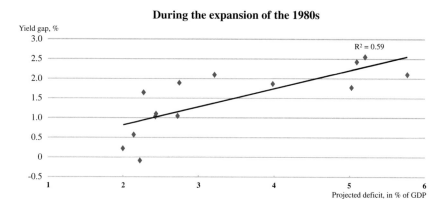

——— Figure I.9. **Projected US deficit and yield gap** ———
Semi-annual observations[1]

During the expansion of the 1980s

During the expansion of the 1990s

1. Expansion periods are those defined by the NBER Business Cycle Dating Committee. Observations dates correspond to the winter and summer CBO reports on the fiscal outlook. The yield gap is defined as the 5-year government bond minus the 3-month T-bill rate. The projected deficit is the CBO projection of the cumulative deficit over the next five fiscal years, in per cent of GDP.
Source: Congressional Budget Office, Federal Reserve.

deficits may translate into higher real long-term interest rates once the recovery gathers steam.[23]

The stability and convergence programmes presented by European Union (EU) member states on the eve of the 2001 downturn foresaw that for the euro area as a whole, the general government deficit would have fallen to 0.3 per cent of GDP by 2002 and would have disappeared altogether by 2003. The outcome was, instead, a deficit of 2.3 per cent of GDP in 2002, mostly reflecting much weaker-than-projected growth but also, in some cases, tax cuts and persistent overruns on health spending (notably in France and Germany). The deterioration in the fiscal balance was of a similar magnitude in the United Kingdom, although there a discretionary acceleration in spending accounts for a larger portion of the shift.[24] In

In several EU countries, sizeable deficits have re-emerged...

23. A picture similar to Figure I.9 would be obtained with real long-term interest rates instead of the difference between long and short rates, and with a ten-year rather than a five-year horizon (but the number of observations would be smaller, as the Congressional Budget Office did not project ten years ahead during the 1980s). Even so, such correlations have only a suggestive value, as interest rates are influenced by other factors, including the business cycle.
24. In 2003, budgetary outlays related to the war in Iraq may amount to 0.3 per cent of GDP.

general, the automatic stabilisers have functioned unimpeded in euro area countries and, having a larger impact than across the Atlantic, they played a more important role in cushioning the downturn.

... triggering policy reactions...   With deficits exceeding or approaching the 3 per cent of GDP threshold embodied in the Stability and Growth Pact, the excessive deficit procedure has been activated for Germany, Portugal, and, more recently, France. The European Commission has also expressed concern regarding underlying fiscal weakness in Italy, temporarily masked by several one-off operations. While France and Italy have not announced any permanent fiscal adjustment measures since, the German and Portuguese governments have introduced tax hikes and spending cuts to bring their deficits down. However, in both cases, as in a number of other countries, the official national growth assumptions underpinning the budget projections seem to err on the optimistic side, implying that deficits are set to remain above or near the 3 per cent of GDP mark longer than programmed. This is all the more likely where programmes lack specific adjustment measures beyond 2003. In fact, on current policies, the deficit is projected to distinctly exceed 3 per cent of GDP in France and Germany in each of the three years to 2004.[25]

... but further measures are called for   Even over the medium run, when the near-term cyclical slack is absorbed, deficits in the three largest euro area countries would not decline much, if at all, unless significant new measures are taken (see Appendix). This would clearly breach the commitment to bring fiscal positions into balance or surplus and put upward pressure on long-term real interest rates. While an overly rapid fiscal correction could prove counter-productive against the backdrop of widening output gaps, sticking to a gradual medium-term adjustment path for structural balances of at least ½ percentage point of GDP *per annum* is necessary, not simply to preserve the credibility of the policy framework, but because of the age-related spending pressures that are about to intensify over the next few years. In the short run, fiscal consolidation should facilitate an accommodative monetary stance and be facilitated by it. Over the longer run, the best way to cope with fiscal pressures, however, is to push ahead where needed with labour market, pension and health care reform.

Japan's fiscal imbalances remain most worrying   Japan remains a fiscal outlier among OECD countries, with a deficit again exceeding 7 per cent of GDP in 2002 and a rapidly rising gross public debt ratio, which exceeded 140 per cent of GDP at the end of 2002. With yields on long-term government bonds below one per cent, their price can barely rise any further, and holders of public debt – notably the banks – are exposed to a major downside risk. In 2003, the deficit is to widen a bit further, reflecting the spending increases enshrined in the FY 2002 supplementary budget (for public works and unemployment benefits) as well as the tax cuts built into the FY 2003 budget, which are only partly offset by consolidation measures on the spending side. As a result, the stance of fiscal policy is loosening slightly in 2003.[26] The stimulative impact of the new tax cuts is open to doubt insofar as tax credits to spur business investment may be ineffective in a context where many firms face over-capacity. Tax reform is indeed needed in Japan but

---

25. Fiscal deficits are much larger in many EU accession countries, notably in the Czech Republic, Hungary, Poland and the Slovak Republic. See for example Coricelli, F. and V. Ercolani, "Cyclical and structural deficits on the road to accession: fiscal rules for an enlarged European Union", *CEPR Discussion Papers*, No. 3672, 2002.

26. Estimates of the output gap are particularly fragile in the case of Japan, so that cyclical adjustment can only be done on an indicative basis. It should also be noted that owing to low tax elasticities, a large output gap does not translate into that big a cyclical deficit in Japan.

should rather involve streamlining tax relief and allowances so as to broaden the tax base, while improving the incentive structure of the tax system.[27] On the spending side, introducing more formal rules capping outlays could make it easier to bring about the needed degree of fiscal discipline.

Stepping up structural reform to boost growth and resilience to shocks

Macroeconomic performance obviously depends not just on the quality of the monetary and fiscal policy mix, but also on the timing, nature and intensity of exogenous shocks and on the resilience of growth to them. This resilience is influenced by institutions and structural policies, since sound structural fundamentals allow adverse shocks to be overcome at a lower cost. Indeed, the disparities in economic performance during the current cycle are partly related to differences in the flexibility of response to shocks among OECD economies.

Structural policies influence current macroeconomic performance

Among the larger OECD economies,[28] the resilience during the recent slowdown has to some extent mirrored growth performance since the mid-1990s, which has varied considerably (Table I.9). At one end of the spectrum, Canada, Australia, France and Spain stand out with a relatively limited deceleration in activity. At the other end, the output gap is widening very considerably in Japan and Germany. Despite massive macroeconomic policy stimulus, the US output gap opens up more than in the euro area.[29] To some extent, these divergent fortunes reflect differences in shocks: Germany for example is still digesting the massive unification shock, while Australia's specialisation meant that it was less exposed to the ICT boom-and-bust.

The momentum and resilience of growth varies...

However, the impact of any given shock depends on an economy's institutional features, as shaped over time by structural policy. For example, where the labour market institutions are such that unemployment spells tend to be protracted, adverse shocks are more likely to lead to the marginalisation of the longer-term unemployed. Thus downward pressure on wages is weaker and hence the return to lower unemployment takes longer.[30] Not coincidentally, Canada, Australia and Spain are among the OECD countries where structural reforms have made significant progress during the 1990s, while Germany and Japan are among those where they have made least headway.[31] In the case of Germany, structural bottlenecks undermine domestic flexibility: when long-lasting shocks hit, calling for labour reallocation from the tradeables to the non-tradeables sector, very strict employment protection legislation, wage rigidities and other regulations hinder

... as does vulnerability to shocks

27. See the *OECD Economic Survey of Japan*, Paris, 2002.
28. The sample includes the 12 largest OECD economies based on nominal GDP at market exchange rates.
29. As noted above, while discretionary fiscal policy and monetary loosening were less aggressive in the euro area, the automatic stabilisers are about twice as powerful there, thus helping more effectively to contain the amplitude of the slowdown. In addition, compared with pre-1999 shocks, some euro area countries at least have been partly shielded by membership in a common currency area, which *inter alia* served to limit interest rate tensions.
30. See Blanchard, O. and J. Wolfers, "The role of shocks and institutions in the rise of European unemployment: the aggregate evidence", *Economic Journal*, Vol. 110, Issue 462, 2000.
31. See the corresponding recent *OECD Economic Surveys*.

─────── Table I.9. **Growth momentum and resilience in the larger OECD countries** ───────

Fastest growing 1995-2002				Output gap			
Real GDP		**Labour productivity**			2002		**Cumulative 2001-2004**
Per cent				*Per cent of potential GDP*			
Korea	5.3	Korea	4.4	Canada	0.2	Canada	0.2
Australia	3.8	United States	2.0	France	-0.2	France	-1.3
Canada	3.4	Australia	1.9	Australia	-0.3	Australia	-2.9
Spain	3.3	**Total OECD**	1.7	Spain	-0.8	Spain	-3.5
United States	3.2	Canada	1.5	*Euro area*	-0.9	United Kingdom	-3.8
Netherlands	2.9	Japan	1.4	Netherlands	-1.0	*Euro area*	-3.9
Total OECD	2.7	United Kingdom	1.4	United Kingdom	-1.0	Netherlands	-4.6
United Kingdom	2.7	France	1.0	**Total OECD**	-1.2	**Total OECD**	-4.8
Mexico	2.6	Italy	1.0	Germany	-1.3	Italy	-5.4
France	2.3	*Euro area*	1.0	United States	-1.5	Germany	-5.6
Euro area	2.2	Germany	1.0	Japan	-1.5	United States	-5.9
Italy	1.8	Spain	0.8	Italy	-1.6	Japan	-6.0
Germany	1.4	Netherlands	0.8				
Japan	1.2	Mexico	0.5				

Note: Comparable output gap estimates are not available for Korea and Mexico.
Source: OECD.

adjustment, aggravating the deterioration of the labour market and the depth of the slow-down. Given Germany's relative size, its lack of resilience has significant spillover effects to neighbouring EU countries, dragging down the performance of the euro area at large. In contrast, Korea sailed through the recent downturn at impressive speed, in large part thanks to the drastic structural reforms undertaken in the wake of the 1997 crisis.

To raise or uphold trend growth, structural reform is needed...

Thus, structural reform is important to improve resilience to shocks. It is also needed to bolster or maintain potential growth.[32] On current policies, growth can be expected to slow significantly over time in a number of OECD countries (see Appendix). This will exacerbate the fiscal pressures associated with ageing populations.[33] Stepping up structural reform, especially in the euro area and in Japan, will unlock latent potential, raise living standards and facilitate the absorption of these pressures.

... in labour markets...

Labour market reform progressed during the 1990s. However, unemployment rates continue to differ considerably across OECD countries, and employment rates vary even more, especially for older age groups, signaling that human resources are not fully used.[34] In the case of Japan, a recent study estimates that removing the impediments restricting labour mobility between firms and discouraging female labour force participation could push up total labour supply by 13 to 18 per cent and thereby raise annual GDP growth by nearly 1 percentage point for a decade.[35] In the

───────────────

32. See Chapter V, "Structural policies and growth".
33. See Dang, T.T., P. Antolin and H. Oxley, "Fiscal implications of ageing: projections of age-related spending", *OECD Economics Department Working Papers,* No. 305, 2001.
34. See "Increasing employment: the role of later retirement", *OECD Economic Outlook,* No. 72, December 2002.
35. See Hiroshi, O. and M. Rebick, "Constraints on the level and efficient use of labor in Japan", in M. Blomström, J. Corbett, F. Hayashi and A. Kashyap (eds), *Structural Impediments to Growth in Japan,* University of Chicago Press, forthcoming. This would, however, imply a participation rate of 83 to 86 per cent, higher even than those currently observed in Nordic European countries.

case of Germany, a government-sponsored commission put forward a set of reform proposals focused on active labour market measures, which it is hoped could halve the unemployment rate within three years.[36] This may be an overstatement of their impact, given the limited scope of the proposals, but the government has since stated its intention to introduce more fundamental and wide-ranging reforms.

There is also ample scope in most OECD countries for product market improvements conducive to faster growth and higher standards of living. Recent OECD work shows how lowering entry barriers and improving the regulatory framework can enhance competition and raise multi-factor productivity (MFP). In the larger euro area countries and in Greece, where heavy regulation has widened the technology gap *vis-à-vis* best practice abroad, the removal of trade and administrative barriers might increase MFP growth in manufacturing by 0.1 to 0.2 percentage point over a considerable period. In addition, progressively bringing down barriers to entry in service sectors to the OECD-wide average could add 0.1 to 0.2 percentage point to overall business sector MFP growth in Greece, Italy or Portugal.[37] Recognising these potential gains, the European Commission is preparing a new action plan to speed up the completion of the single market for services. Tangible progress in the context of the Doha Round of trade liberalisation would work in the same direction.

... product markets...

Addressing capital market shortcomings is also necessary to boost economy-wide growth and employment. In the United States, the focus has lately been on corporate governance reform and financial market regulations.[38] In Europe, the emphasis is on the implementation of the EU financial services and risk capital action plans, which are somewhat behind schedule. The benefits to be expected from further EU integration are significant: estimates of the macroeconomic impact of the associated reduction in the cost of equity, bond and bank finance point to a permanent EU-wide gain on the order of one percentage point for GDP and ½ percentage point for employment.[39] In Japan, financial system rehabilitation and reform is of course an indispensable element of a broader set of measures needed for the economy to pull out of stagnation and deflation, as stressed in many earlier editions of the *Outlook*.

... and capital markets

---

36. See Hartz Kommission, *Moderne Dienstleistungen am Arbeitsmarkt*, Berlin, 16 August 2002, which is analysed further in the *OECD Economic Survey of Germany*, Paris, 2003.
37. The estimates quoted here come from Nicoletti, G. and S. Scarpetta, "Regulation, productivity and growth: OECD evidence", *OECD Economics Department Working Papers*, No. 347, 2003 and are subject to the usual caveats associated with econometric analyses.
38. See Box I.3 in *OECD Economic Outlook*, No. 72, December 2002.
39. See London Economics, *Quantification of the Macro-Economic Impact of Integration of EU Financial Markets*, Final report to the European Commission, November 2002. Another study finding substantial gains is Giannetti, M., L. Guiso, T. Jappelli, M. Padula and M. Pagano, "Financial market integration, corporate financing and economic growth", *European Economy*, Economic Papers, No. 179, 2002. For more details and references, see the *OECD Economic Survey of the Euro Area*, Paris, 2002.

Appendix: The medium-term reference scenario

The medium-term reference scenario shows area-wide growth of around 3 per cent

The medium-term reference scenario extends the current short-term projections to the end of 2008 (see Tables I.10 to I.12).[40] It is essentially driven by the supply side of economies. Growth in output for any country beyond 2004 is assumed to be a combination of growth in potential output and a contribution from the closing of the output

Table I.10. **Medium-term reference scenario summary**

Per cent

	Real GDP growth 2005-2008	Inflation rate[a] 2004	Inflation rate[a] 2008	Unemployment rate[b] 2004	Unemployment rate[b] 2008	Current balance[c] 2004	Current balance[c] 2008	Long-term interest rate 2004	Long-term interest rate 2008
Australia	3.8	2.6	2.3	5.8	5.5	-3.7	-3.1	6.3	6.5
Austria	2.6	1.1	1.0	5.9	4.7	0.3	0.4	4.4	5.7
Belgium	2.7	1.2	1.1	7.7	6.9	5.3	5.1	4.4	5.7
Canada	3.1	2.1	2.1	7.0	7.1	2.2	2.2	5.7	6.0
Czech Republic	2.8	2.3	2.0	7.2	6.8	-5.1	-4.5	2.8[d]	6.0[d]
Denmark	2.2	2.3	2.0	4.4	4.7	3.6	3.6	4.5	5.6
Finland	2.3	1.5	1.4	9.0	8.0	7.2	5.3	4.5	5.7
France	2.1	1.4	1.3	9.2	8.8	2.2	2.3	4.4	5.6
Germany	2.0	0.4	0.8	8.3	7.0	3.2	3.4	4.3	5.5
Greece	3.1	3.4	2.8	9.1	9.0	-5.8	-5.7	4.4	5.7
Hungary	4.3	4.5	3.0	6.4	6.1	-3.8	-4.0	7.3[d]	7.5[d]
Iceland	2.8	2.6	2.5	3.0	3.0	-0.9	-0.9	8.0	6.0
Ireland	4.0	3.2	2.8	5.2	5.1	0.8	0.8	5.3	5.5
Italy	2.3	1.9	1.5	8.9	8.6	0.0	0.0	4.5	5.7
Japan	1.7	-1.6	-1.6	5.7	3.9	3.9	4.1	1.1	1.7
Korea	5.2	3.3	3.1	3.0	3.0	0.2	0.3	6.7	6.7
Mexico	4.3	3.5	3.0	2.4	2.3	-2.8	-3.0	8.8	8.6
Netherlands	2.4	1.3	1.2	5.0	3.5	2.5	2.1	4.4	5.6
New Zealand	3.0	2.0	2.0	5.3	5.4	-4.6	-4.3	6.2	6.5
Norway	1.6	1.6	2.0	4.6	3.6	13.2	12.0	5.7	7.0
Poland	4.1	2.3	2.2	19.9	16.5	-4.5	-4.3	6.0[d]	6.0[d]
Portugal	2.9	2.2	2.0	6.3	3.8	-5.5	-4.6	4.5	5.7
Slovak Republic	4.2	6.1	5.1	16.8	14.8	-6.1	-5.8	7.7	6.5
Spain	3.1	2.4	1.9	11.7	9.4	-3.2	-3.3	4.2	5.5
Sweden	2.3	1.7	2.0	4.3	4.5	4.4	4.4	4.8	5.5
Switzerland	1.5	0.3	0.4	3.4	1.8	12.2	11.8	2.4	3.1
Turkey	4.7	17.1	10.9	10.6	9.5	-2.6	-2.0	19.0	14.4
United Kingdom	2.6	1.0	2.0	5.2	5.1	-2.0	-1.9	5.1	5.5
United States	3.5	1.2	1.0	5.8	5.0	-5.5	-5.6	5.0	5.8
Euro area	2.4	1.4	1.3	8.7	7.6	1.4	1.4	4.4	5.6
European Union	2.4	1.4	1.4	7.9	7.1	0.9	0.9	4.5	5.6
Total of above OECD countries	2.9	1.1[e]	1.0[e]	7.0	6.0	-1.2	-1.3	4.4[e]	5.2[e]

Note: For further details see *OECD Economic Outlook* Sources and Methods (*http://www.oecd.org/eco/sources-and-methods*).
a) Percentage change from the previous period in the private consumption deflator.
b) Per cent of labour force.
c) Per cent of nominal GDP.
d) Short-term interest rate.
e) Excluding Turkey.
Source: OECD.

---

40. Assumptions underlying the medium-term reference scenario are outlined in Box I.5.

Table I.11. **Fiscal trends in the medium-term reference scenario**

As a percentage of nominal GDP

	Financial balances[a]		Net financial liabilities[b]		Gross financial liabilities[c]		Gross public debt (Maastricht definition)[d]	
	2004	2008	2004	2008	2004	2008	2004	2008
Australia	0.5	0.1	4	2	20	18	..	..
Austria	-1.1	-0.4	49	44	66	61	66	61
Belgium	0.2	0.8	90	74	99	83	99	83
Canada	1.0	1.0	34	24	75	65	..	..
Czech Republic	-6.2	-4.5	..	..	..	..	..	..
Denmark	1.9	2.2	2	-6	48	39	42	34
Finland	2.9	2.6	-47	-49	45	42	40	38
France	-3.3	-3.3	44	50	71	75	64	67
Germany	-3.3	-2.7	52	58	67	72	65	71
Greece	-0.7	-1.0	..	..	99	88	99	88
Hungary	-5.0	-3.3	..	..	..	..	..	..
Iceland	0.1	0.6	23	19	43	39	..	..
Ireland	-1.2	-1.0	..	..	31	29	31	28
Italy	-2.8	-2.8	94	90	118	115	105	103
Japan	-7.8	-7.6	89	119	164	194	..	..
Korea	3.9	3.7	-39	-42	19	29	..	..
Netherlands	-2.0	-0.3	42	39	53	50	53	50
New Zealand	0.5	0.9	17	11	38	39	..	..
Norway	10.7	9.6	-100	-122	20	22	..	..
Poland	-5.9	-3.8	..	..	..	..	..	..
Portugal	-2.7	-1.1	..	..	59	54	59	54
Slovak Republic	-5.1	-3.5	..	..	..	..	..	..
Spain	-0.2	0.3	36	28	63	55	52	47
Sweden	1.2	1.2	-6	-9	58	55	52	49
United Kingdom	-2.2	-1.6	30	32	52	54	41	45
United States	-4.2	-2.4	49	51	66	68	..	..
Euro area	-2.4	-1.9	56	56	76	76	70	70
European Union	-2.2	-1.8	50	50	73	72	66	67
Total of above OECD countries	-3.5	-2.6	51	56	81	86		

Note: For further details see *OECD Economic Outlook* Sources and Methods (*http://www.oecd.org/eco/sources-and-methods*).

a) General government fiscal surplus (+) or deficit (-) as a percentage of GDP.

b) Includes all financial liabilities minus financial assets, as defined by the System of National Accounts (where data availability permits) and covers the general government sector, which is a consolidation of central government, state and local government and the social security sector.

c) Includes all financial liabilities, as defined by the System of National Accounts (where data availability permits) and covers the general government sector, which is a consolidation of central government, state and local government and the social security sector.

d) Debt ratios are based on debt figures for 2002, provided by Eurostat, and GDP figures from national authorities, projected forward in line with the OECD projections for GDP and general government financial liabilities.

Source: OECD.

gap. Growth in potential for the OECD as a whole is expected to slow to below 2½ per cent *per annum* over the period, falling more substantially for some countries in the later years. This slowing reflects the combined effects of a decrease in trend growth of the labour force, partly offset by small increases in trend labour productivity growth.

Since most OECD economies are forecast to be operating well below output potential in 2004, the closing of output gaps implies that growth in subsequent years exceeds estimated potential. OECD-wide real GDP is projected to expand at close to 3 per cent *per annum* over the period. The area-wide rate of unemployment drops to

Unemployment falls, inflation remains low, but fiscal deficits persist

Table I.12. **Growth in potential GDP and its components**

Annual averages, percentage points

| | Output gap | Potential GDP growth | | Potential labour productivity growth (output per employee) | | Potential employment growth | | Components of potential employment[a] | | | | | |
| | | | | | | | | Potential labour force participation rate | | Working age population | | Structural unemployment[b] | |
	2004	1996-2004	2005-2008	1996-2004	2005-2008	1996-2004	2005-2008	1996-2004	2005-2008	1996-2004	2005-2008	1996-2004	2005-2008
Australia	-1.4	3.8	3.5	2.0	2.4	1.7	1.1	0.1	0.0	1.4	1.0	0.2	0.0
Austria	-2.5	2.3	2.0	1.9	1.9	0.4	0.1	0.1	0.1	0.3	-0.1	0.0	0.1
Belgium	-2.4	2.1	2.1	1.2	1.5	0.9	0.5	0.5	0.2	0.2	0.3	0.2	0.0
Canada	0.2	3.3	3.2	1.6	2.0	1.7	1.2	0.3	0.1	1.2	1.0	0.2	0.0
Denmark	-0.3	2.3	2.1	2.0	2.0	0.3	0.1	-0.1	0.0	0.2	0.1	0.2	0.0
Finland	-0.4	2.8	2.2	2.1	1.9	0.6	0.3	0.1	0.0	0.3	0.2	0.3	0.1
France	-0.8	2.2	1.9	1.3	1.5	0.8	0.4	0.3	0.0	0.3	0.4	0.2	0.1
Germany	-2.0	1.5	1.5	1.2	1.3	0.2	0.2	0.4	0.3	-0.1	-0.2	-0.1	0.1
Greece	1.1	3.1	3.4	2.5	3.0	0.6	0.4	0.5	0.2	0.2	0.0	0.0	0.1
Iceland	0.7	2.9	3.1	1.6	2.0	1.2	1.0	0.0	0.0	1.3	0.9	-0.1	0.1
Ireland	2.1	7.1	4.5	3.6	3.1	3.3	1.3	0.7	0.2	1.8	0.9	0.8	0.1
Italy	-1.5	1.8	1.9	1.3	1.5	0.4	0.4	0.4	0.5	-0.1	-0.1	0.2	0.1
Japan	-2.0	1.3	1.1	1.2	1.2	0.1	-0.1	0.4	0.3	-0.2	-0.4	-0.1	0.0
Netherlands	-2.4	2.8	1.8	1.2	1.1	1.5	0.6	0.8	0.2	0.4	0.4	0.3	0.0
New Zealand	0.3	3.1	3.1	1.4	1.9	1.6	1.2	0.2	0.1	1.2	1.0	0.2	0.0
Norway	-0.3	2.6	2.0	1.7	1.5	0.9	0.5	0.1	0.0	0.6	0.5	0.2	0.0
Spain	-1.2	2.9	2.7	1.0	1.1	1.8	1.7	1.0	1.0	0.6	0.3	0.3	0.4
Sweden	0.0	2.3	2.3	2.1	1.8	0.3	0.4	-0.3	-0.1	0.5	0.6	0.1	0.0
Switzerland	-1.4	1.3	1.2	0.7	0.8	0.6	0.3	0.0	0.0	0.5	0.3	0.1	0.0
United Kingdom	-1.2	2.5	2.3	1.9	2.0	0.6	0.4	0.1	0.1	0.4	0.3	0.2	0.0
United States	-1.2	3.3	3.1	1.9	2.1	1.4	1.0	0.0	-0.1	1.3	1.0	0.0	0.0
Euro area	-1.5	2.1	2.0	1.3	1.4	0.7	0.5	0.4	0.3	0.2	0.1	0.1	0.1
Total OECD	-1.3	2.5	2.4	1.6	1.8	0.9	0.6	0.2	0.1	0.7	0.4	0.1	0.0

a) Percentage point contributions to potential employment growth.
b) Estimates of the structural rate of unemployment are based on the concepts and methods described in "Revised OECD measures of structural unemployment", *Economic Outlook,* No. 68, 2000.
Source: OECD.

around 6 per cent, while inflation remains broadly unchanged at 2004 levels. Despite fairly robust recovery, fiscal balances remain in significant deficit for the area as a whole. This reflects continuing large deficits for the major European economies and Japan, partially offset by gradual improvement for the United States.

Growth is robust in the United States beyond 2004... Potential output for the United States is projected to grow at a little over 3 per cent over the medium term, with increasing growth in labour productivity being offset by declining growth in the working-age population and the labour force. With output below potential for much of the period, inflation continues at a low rate. The fiscal balance remains in substantial deficit, albeit improving over the period, reflecting both the cyclical improvement and the expiry of temporary tax breaks on business investment in late 2004. Overall, the deficit falls to around 2½ per cent of GDP by 2008.

> ### Box I.5. **Assumptions underlying the medium-term reference scenario**
>
> The medium-term reference scenario is conditional on the following assumptions for the period beyond the short-term projection horizon:
>
> - Gaps between actual and potential output are eliminated by 2008 in all OECD countries.
> - Unemployment returns to its structural rate (the NAIRU) in all OECD countries by 2008.[1]
> - Commodity prices and most exchange rates remain broadly unchanged in real terms.
> - Monetary policies are directed at keeping inflation low, or bringing it down in line with medium-term objectives.
>
> - Fiscal policies are assumed to remain broadly unchanged (*i.e.* the cyclically-adjusted primary budget balance is held approximately unchanged from one year to the next),[2] or to follow medium-term programmes where these are well-defined parts of the institutional framework for fiscal policy.
>
> The main purpose of the medium-term reference scenario is to provide a basis for comparisons with other scenarios based on alternative assumptions and to provide insights on the possible build-up or unwinding of specific imbalances and tensions in the world economy over the medium term. The reference scenario does not embody a specific view about the timing of future cyclical events.
>
> ---
>
> 1. The concept and measurement of structural unemployment rates are discussed in more detail in Chapter V, "Revised OECD measures of structural unemployment", *OECD Economic Outlook* 68, December 2000.
> 2. This implicitly assumes that the authorities take measures to offset underlying changes in primary structural balances.

Within the euro area, potential output growth, averaging 2 per cent *per annum* beyond 2004, is much lower than in the United States, reflecting lower growth in both the working age population and trend labour productivity. At the same time, the cyclical position in 2004 is similar to what is observed in the United States with a negative output gap of 1½ per cent of GDP. Overall, there is a significant contribution from the closure of the gap, leading to GDP growth of around 2½ per cent *per annum* over the period. Unemployment falls by almost one percentage point to around 7½ per cent, but inflation remains subdued. Despite the recovery, the fiscal deficit for the euro area as a whole remains at almost 2 per cent of GDP in 2008. The general government deficit is, at present policy settings, projected to remain slightly above 3 per cent of GDP for France, with rising public debt interest payments broadly offsetting the cyclical contribution from the closing of the gap.[41] Significant deficits also persist in Germany and Italy and, to a lesser extent, Greece and Ireland. With the exception of the United Kingdom, which also remains in significant deficit, the fiscal positions of other European Union member countries move steadily towards balance or remain in significant surplus.

... but more modest in Europe, where fiscal deficits persist

Potential output growth in Japan is projected to slow, given declines in the working-age population and relatively slow growth in the capital stock and trend labour productivity. To close the output gap from 2004 levels, GDP growth accelerates to above 1½ per cent *per annum* and the unemployment rate falls by almost 2 percentage points to around 4 per cent. Deflation nonetheless persists over the period and interest rates remain low.[42] As a result, the public debt interest burden remains proportionally much lower than in other countries experiencing high levels

In Japan, growth remains weak and the fiscal position unsustainable

---

41. See Box I.5 and the main text for specific details of the underlying fiscal assumptions.
42. Assessing the relationship between the output gap and inflation is particularly difficult in the current Japanese deflationary environment. The judgement taken over the medium-term horizon is that the change in the output gap also has some effect on inflation, *i.e.* that the higher growth required to close the output gap balances the deflationary pressures arising from the output gap itself.

of public debt. Nonetheless, with continuing large structural fiscal deficits of up to 8 per cent of GDP, in part reflecting the ongoing fiscal costs associated with population ageing, public debt continues to accumulate at an unsustainable rate.

World trade grows robustly but current account imbalances persist

Given fairly robust GDP growth in the OECD area, growth in world trade, at around 8 per cent per annum, remains at around the historical average of the 1990s.[43] For the area as a whole, the current account balance remains in small deficit over the medium term although, in the absence of major changes in potential growth rates or trade openness and at broadly unchanged real exchange rates, there is little overall adjustment in the current external imbalances between regions. For the euro area, the current account remains in surplus at around 1½ per cent of GDP; the US deficit stabilises at around 5½ per cent of GDP, with an increasing outflow of investment income as net foreign debt continues to accumulate, while Japan remains in a position of large surplus, at around 4 per cent of GDP.

---

43. In part, this reflects robust underlying growth for China and the dynamic Asian economies.

II. DEVELOPMENTS IN INDIVIDUAL OECD COUNTRIES

United States

The economy has been soft recently. Household spending has advanced more modestly as higher energy prices have pinched real incomes. Yet business investment has stabilised and appears set to recover following the end of the war in Iraq, while rising military expenditures are providing a boost to demand. Growth is expected to rebound sharply by the autumn assuming the conflict is resolved by early summer. Household, business and foreign demand – the latter buoyed by the drop in the dollar – are all projected to strengthen markedly in 2004. Inflation should fall back as energy prices reverse and slack persists following several years of growth below potential.

Monetary policy has remained supportive, but interest rates will need to be raised once growth picks up. The proposed tax cuts and further increases in expenditure, not least the jump in defence purchases, will widen the federal government deficit sharply. This will have to be reversed in coming years. While the planned tax rate reductions and reforms to dividend taxation are attractive from an efficiency perspective, these proposed changes should be part of a more revenue-neutral reform package.

After advancing solidly in the first half of 2002, the pace of activity slowed in the latter part of the year. Both consumption and residential investment posted more modest gains. This reflected the stagnant labour market, a waning impetus from attractive terms available on mortgage and consumer durable financing and the passing of the boost to income from earlier tax cuts. Moreover, the technical stimulus to growth from a resumption in stockbuilding moderated and net exports continued to exert a significant drag as growth in the rest of the OECD was also sub-par. Government spending, particularly at the state and local level, also grew more slowly in the second half of last year. In contrast, business fixed investment stabilised after dropping for two years, with gains in equipment and software outlays largely offsetting lower spending on non-residential structures.

Growth slowed in the second half of 2002…

United States

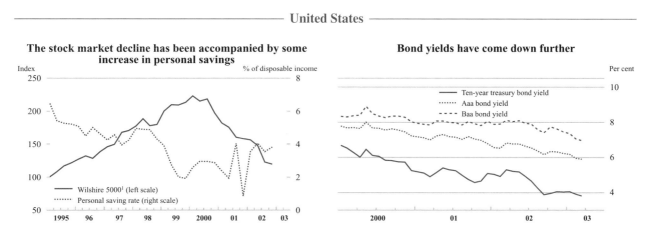

The stock market decline has been accompanied by some increase in personal savings

Index

Wilshire 5000[1] (left scale)
Personal saving rate (right scale)

% of disposable income

Bond yields have come down further

Ten-year treasury bond yield
Aaa bond yield
Baa bond yield

Per cent

1. Wilshire 5000 divided by disposable income, set equal to 100 in the first quarter of 1995.
Source: Board of Governors of the Federal Reserve System, Bureau of Economic Analysis and Thomson Financial.

United States: **Employment, income and inflation**

Percentage changes from previous period

	2000	2001	2002	2003	2004
Employment[a]	1.5	0.0	-0.9	0.6	1.7
Unemployment rate[b]	4.0	4.8	5.8	6.0	5.8
Employment cost index	4.6	4.1	3.7	2.8	2.7
Compensation per employee[c]	6.5	2.3	2.3	3.4	3.3
Labour productivity[c]	2.6	0.2	3.9	2.0	2.3
Unit labour cost[c]	3.8	2.1	-1.5	1.4	1.0
GDP deflator	2.1	2.4	1.1	1.6	1.3
Consumer price index	3.4	2.8	1.6	2.4	1.7
Private consumption deflator	2.5	2.0	1.4	2.0	1.2
Real household disposable income	4.8	1.8	4.3	3.0	3.8

a) Whole economy, for further details see *OECD Economic Outlook* Sources and Methods,
   (http://www.oecd.org/eco/sources-and-methods).
b) As a percentage of labour force.
c) In the business sector.
Source: OECD.

... and may remain subdued
through mid-year

Recent indicators suggest continued weakness in the first half of this year. Equity markets have been volatile, while consumer confidence has dropped. An important part of this uncertainty stemmed from heightened tensions related to Iraq, although the share market fluctuations may also reflect the lingering impact on risk appetites of the burst stock-market bubble and corporate governance concerns. In any case, personal savings can be expected to rise over this year. The recovery in the manufacturing sector also appears to have stalled, with the weak data on orders pointing to another slowing this spring.

Higher oil and other energy
prices are restraining demand

The conflict in the Middle East and the earlier strikes in Venezuela resulted in a sharp run-up in petroleum prices. The cold winter and lean stock levels have also led to sharp increases in natural gas and electricity prices. With energy accounting for about 5 per cent of consumption expenditures, higher prices have eroded household

---
United States

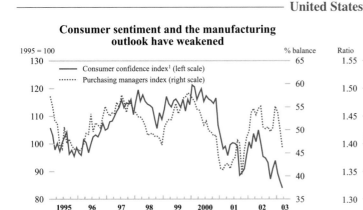

Consumer sentiment and the manufacturing outlook have weakened

Past declines have brought business demand to low levels

1. University of Michigan.
Source: Institute for Supply Management, US Census Bureau and OECD.

─────────────── United States: **Financial indicators** ───────────────

	2000	2001	2002	2003	2004
Household saving ratio[a]	2.8	2.3	3.7	4.6	4.8
General government financial balance[b]	1.4	-0.5	-3.4	-4.6	-4.2
Current account balance[b]	-4.2	-3.9	-4.8	-5.4	-5.5
Short-term interest rate[c]	6.5	3.7	1.8	1.4	3.0
Long-term interest rate[d]	6.0	5.0	4.6	4.1	5.0

a) As a percentage of disposable income.
b) As a percentage of GDP.
c) 3-month euro-dollar.
d) 10-year government bonds.
Source: OECD.

purchasing power thus far this year. The drag on demand should prove modest and temporary, if oil and natural gas prices drop through the spring and summer as expected. Moreover, the energy price shock will contribute to a further widening in the current account deficit, which has weighed increasingly on the exchange rate.

The Federal Reserve has provided a substantial impetus to demand since beginning to cut the federal funds rate more than two years ago, with the federal funds rate holding at 1¼ per cent since last November. However, the effects of the stimulus have begun to wane: while the level of house and consumer durable purchases remains strong, their contribution to growth has slowed. Even so, with demand projected to advance modestly over the first half of this year, no further cuts in the funds rate are projected in the near term. If demand has advanced, as expected, by the autumn, a gradual move toward a more neutral monetary stance should begin at that point.

Interest rates are projected to rise once growth accelerates…

─────────────── United States: **Demand and output** ───────────────

	1999	2000	2001	2002	2003	2004
	Current prices billion $	Percentage changes, volume				
Private consumption	6 246.5	4.3	2.5	3.1	2.3	3.6
Government consumption	1 336.3	2.8	3.7	4.4	5.3	2.0
Gross fixed investment	1 881.9	5.5	-2.6	-1.8	1.4	5.9
Public	304.7	2.4	3.3	4.4	1.4	0.6
Residential	403.7	1.1	0.3	3.9	0.7	1.3
Non-residential	1 173.5	7.8	-5.2	-5.7	1.7	9.5
Final domestic demand	9 464.7	4.3	1.6	2.4	2.6	3.8
Stockbuilding[a]	59.5	0.0	-1.4	0.7	0.3	0.3
Total domestic demand	9 524.3	4.4	0.4	3.0	2.8	4.0
Exports of goods and services	989.4	9.7	-5.4	-1.6	4.0	9.0
Imports of goods and services	1 239.2	13.2	-2.9	3.7	6.4	7.8
Net exports[a]	- 249.9	-0.9	-0.2	-0.8	-0.6	-0.3
GDP at market prices	9 274.4	3.8	0.3	2.4	2.5	4.0

Note: National accounts are based on official chain-linked data. This introduces a discrepancy in the identity between
   real demand components and GDP. For further details see *OECD Economic Outlook* Sources and Methods,
   (http://www.oecd.org/eco/sources-and-methods).
a) Contributions to changes in real GDP (percentage of real GDP in previous year), actual amount in the first column.
Source: OECD.

——————————————— United States: **External indicators** ———————————————

	2000	2001	2002	2003	2004
			$ billion		
Merchandise exports	772.0	718.8	682.6	723	806
Merchandise imports	1 224.4	1 145.9	1 166.9	1 285	1 399
Trade balance	- 452.4	- 427.2	- 484.4	- 562	- 594
Invisibles, net	42.1	33.8	- 19.1	- 25	- 36
Current account balance	- 410.3	- 393.4	- 503.4	- 587	- 629
			Percentage changes		
Merchandise export volumes [a]	11.3	- 5.9	- 3.6	3.6	9.9
Merchandise import volumes [a]	13.5	- 3.3	3.9	6.6	7.7
Export performance [b]	- 1.0	- 4.9	- 6.1	- 1.8	0.9
Terms of trade	- 3.5	2.3	1.2	- 1.4	0.4

a) Customs basis.
b) Ratio between export volume and export market of total goods.
Source: OECD.

... and fiscal policy must move to reduce the deficit over the medium run

The projection incorporates the Administration's 2004 budget proposal and additional expenditures totalling $75 billion over 2003 and 2004 related to the war with Iraq. In 2002, federal government purchases of goods and services expanded by more than 10 per cent, and the jump in defence purchases will contribute to another double-digit increase in expenditures this year. Federal revenues dropped more than 6 per cent in 2002. Moreover, the Administration's proposed tax cuts, which consist largely of expanded child tax credits, accelerated reductions in marginal tax rates and the elimination of the double taxation of dividends, would lower revenues in 2003 and 2004 by ¼ per cent and more than ¾ per cent of GDP, respectively. While higher spending and tax cuts have contributed to growth over the past two years and should do so again, at least modestly, they have generated a projected federal deficit of just under $400 billion, or about 3½ per cent of GDP, in both 2003 and 2004. The growing deficit is one factor contributing to a projected rise in long-term interest rates of over 100 basis points by the end of 2004. A renewed focus on spending priorities and tax law changes will be necessary to generate a reduction in federal deficits over the next few years. State and local governments have also seen weak revenues and are projected to run a deficit of about 1¼ per cent of GDP this year. However, a slowing in expenditures and some tax increases should result in a smaller deficit in 2004. Overall, the general government deficit is projected to exceed 4½ per cent of GDP in 2003 before edging down in 2004.

Growth should accelerate as uncertainty with Iraq is resolved

The slow pace of growth in the first half of this year should be followed by stronger gains, as energy prices subside and confidence returns after the end of the war in Iraq. Consumption expenditures are expected to rise only modestly until the second half of this year. But thereafter a recovery in the labour market and improved balance sheets should lead to more robust spending by households. While business fixed investment is being held back by the same concerns as are weighing on consumer confidence and equity markets, the sharp reduction in capital stock growth brought about by the correction in investment over the past two years, along with the continued rise in demand, point to the prospect of a notable acceleration in purchases later in the year. In addition, an improvement in worldwide demand and the depreciation of the dollar are expected to contribute to an acceleration in exports in 2004. Risks to the outlook remain substantial but are not only on the downside. Bad news regarding the geopolitical situation or continued household pessimism following the war may lower growth. On the other hand, the impetus from fiscal loosening and a pickup in business and foreign demand could generate a more pronounced acceleration.

Japan

The economic expansion stalled in the second half of 2002 as a result of a slowdown in export growth. Although the outlook for domestic demand remains weak, a rebound in world trade growth in the second half of 2003 may prompt a mild recovery, with output growth of around 1 per cent in both 2003 and 2004. Such an upturn would be unlikely to reduce unemployment or the rate of deflation. Indeed, a possible strengthening of deflationary pressures poses a downside risk to the projection, as do continued financial sector fragility and the strains associated with a further rise in public debt.

Monetary policy should focus on ending deflation through further increases in liquidity. The accelerated resolution of non-performing loans, in line with the government's objective, should be a priority, accompanied if necessary by the direct injection of public funds. If the bad debt problem were addressed more aggressively, fiscal policy should allow the automatic stabilisers to respond to any negative effects on output and employment. But it is also essential to set out a medium-term fiscal consolidation framework incorporating targets for spending. The economy needs to be revitalised through an acceleration of corporate restructuring and the implementation of structural reforms on a broad front.

The economic upturn that started in early 2002 lost momentum in the second half of the year as export growth slowed, in part due to the appreciation of the yen. The export slowdown triggered a decline in industrial production in the final quarter of 2002 and a rise in the unemployment rate to a record high. However, the resilience of private domestic demand prevented the economy from falling into another recession. The household sector has reduced its saving rate in the face of falling real wages to sustain private consumption. Deflation in the private consumption deflator has persisted at a 1½ per cent annual rate in the context of falling nominal wages and a significant negative output gap. An expected 10 per cent rise in corporate profits in fiscal year (FY) 2002 supported a modest rise in business investment in the second half of 2002 in an otherwise fragile financial environment.

Economic activity is flat following a slowdown in export growth

The government has launched a number of initiatives to address problems in the financial and corporate sectors, including the Industrial Revitalisation Corporation, which will purchase loans beginning in FY 2003 from banks in cases where the borrowers are judged to be viable. The success of such measures to ensure the survival of firms under restructuring will depend on the extent to which the authorities can avoid

The non-performing loan problem is being addressed

— Japan —

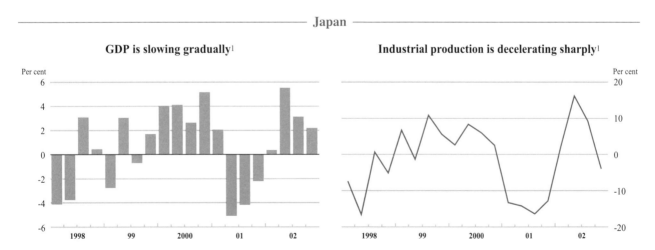

GDP is slowing gradually[1]

Per cent

Industrial production is decelerating sharply[1]

Per cent

1. Series adjusted for seasonal variations, volumes, annualised percentage change over preceding quarter.
Source: Economic and Social Research Institut and Ministry of Economy, Trade and Industry.

—————— Japan: **Employment, income and inflation** ——————

Percentage changes from previous period

	2000	2001	2002	2003	2004
Employment	-0.2	-0.5	-1.3	-0.6	-0.2
Unemployment rate[a]	4.7	5.0	5.4	5.7	5.7
Compensation of employees	0.7	-0.4	-2.3	-1.3	-0.7
Unit labour cost	-2.1	-0.8	-2.6	-2.3	-1.8
Household disposable income	-1.5	-2.9	-1.4	-1.0	-0.9
GDP deflator	-1.9	-1.6	-1.7	-2.2	-1.8
Consumer price index	-0.7	-0.7	-0.9	-0.9	-1.0
Private consumption deflator	-1.2	-1.5	-1.5	-1.6	-1.6

a) As a percentage of labour force.
Source: OECD.

moral hazard problems. In the October 2002 programme, the authorities set an objective of halving the ratio of non-performing loans (NPLs) to total loans in the major banks by March 2005. The programme also introduced stricter assessment and provisioning for loans based on a discounted cash flow method. In addition, the Financial Services Agency is conducting a second round of special inspections focusing on large borrowers. Given that these measures will tend to increase the required level of provisioning, major banks are trying to strengthen their capital base by issuing shares and pursuing mergers. However, the outlook for increasing capital adequacy ratios is uncertain, in part because the treatment of deferred tax assets, which currently account for 40 per cent of Tier I capital, is under review. Moreover, the low level of equity prices, which have fallen by another 25 per cent since mid-2002, has a negative effect on bank balance sheets, given the high level of shareholding. In sum, the capital base of the banks is likely to remain weak, making them risk averse.

Credit and money supply trends are weak

Bank lending fell by 2½ per cent in the final quarter of 2002, despite further monetary easing by the Bank of Japan. In October, the Bank raised the quantitative target on the current accounts held with it by banks by ¥ 5 trillion to a range of ¥ 15 to 20 trillion. The target was raised by another ¥ 2 trillion when the new postal

—————— **Japan** ——————

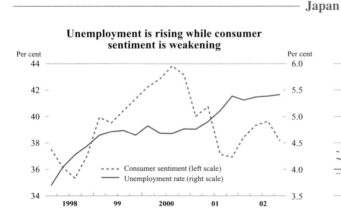

Unemployment is rising while consumer sentiment is weakening

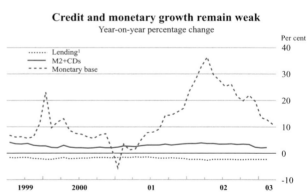

Credit and monetary growth remain weak
Year-on-year percentage change

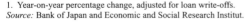

1. Year-on-year percentage change, adjusted for loan write-offs.
Source: Bank of Japan and Economic and Social Research Institut.

———————— Japan: **Financial indicators** ————————

	2000	2001	2002	2003	2004
Household saving ratio[a]	9.8	6.9	5.8	5.8	5.8
General government financial balance[b]	-7.4	-6.1	-7.1	-7.7	-7.8
Current account balance[b]	2.5	2.1	2.8	3.1	3.9
Short-term interest rate[c]	0.2	0.1	0.1	0.0	0.0
Long-term interest rate[d]	1.7	1.3	1.3	0.9	1.1

a) As a percentage of disposable income.
b) As a percentage of GDP.
c) 3 month CDs.
d) 10-year government bonds.
Source: OECD.

---

corporation opened an account at the central bank in April 2003. To achieve this target, the Bank also increased outright purchases of long-term government bonds to ¥ 1.2 trillion per month in October. Despite this additional easing, the year-on-year growth rate of the broad money supply (M2 plus certificates of deposit) continued to decelerate from 3½ per cent in mid-2002 to 2 per cent in early 2003. The central bank started purchasing shares held by major banks in November, in order to help them reduce their exposure to the equities market.

With the economy losing momentum and deflation persisting, fiscal policy has focused more on concerns about short-term weakness. The fiscal stance is expected to be slightly expansionary in 2003, with cyclically-adjusted net lending by the general government projected to rise to 7.2 per cent of GDP from 6.7 per cent in 2002, despite planned cuts in current expenditure and an increase in social security contributions. The larger deficit reflects the rise in expenditures in the FY 2002 supplementary budget and the planned tax cuts in the FY 2003 budget. The FY 2002 supplementary budget boosted spending by 2.5 trillion yen in net terms (0.5 per cent

The fiscal policy stance has shifted from neutral to slightly expansionary

---

———————— Japan: **Demand and output** ————————

	1999	2000	2001	2002	2003	2004
	Current prices trillion ¥	Percentage changes, volume (1995 prices)				
Private consumption	286.6	1.0	1.7	1.4	0.6	0.7
Government consumption	82.9	4.7	2.5	2.3	2.0	1.9
Gross fixed investment	133.5	2.9	-1.2	-4.0	-1.3	-1.5
Public[a]	39.4	-9.2	-4.2	-4.7	-5.6	-6.9
Residential	20.2	0.7	-5.4	-4.8	-5.2	-3.9
Non-residential	73.9	9.6	1.1	-3.6	1.3	1.1
Final domestic demand	502.9	2.1	1.1	0.1	0.4	0.3
Stockbuilding[b]	- 1.7	0.3	0.0	-0.4	0.1	0.0
Total domestic demand	501.2	2.4	1.1	-0.3	0.5	0.4
Exports of goods and services	51.1	12.3	-6.1	8.1	7.7	9.4
Imports of goods and services	43.3	9.4	0.1	2.0	3.6	4.2
Net exports[b]	7.9	0.5	-0.7	0.7	0.6	0.8
GDP at market prices	509.1	2.8	0.4	0.3	1.0	1.1

a) Including public corporations.
b) Contributions to changes in real GDP (percentage of real GDP in previous year), actual amount in the first column.
Source: OECD.

─────────────── Japan: **External indicators** ───────────────

	2000	2001	2002	2003	2004
	\$ billion				
Merchandise exports	459.3	383.8	395.8	442	488
Merchandise imports	342.6	313.5	302.1	336	356
Trade balance	116.6	70.3	93.8	106	131
Invisibles, net	2.9	17.4	19.8	23	29
Current account balance	119.5	87.7	113.6	129	160
	Percentage changes				
Merchandise export volumes[a]	9.0	- 10.9	9.6	8.2	9.6
Merchandise import volumes[a]	11.1	- 1.9	1.6	4.7	4.3
Export performance[b]	- 6.7	- 8.0	4.0	0.2	- 1.7
Terms of trade	- 5.1	0.5	- 1.0	- 3.0	- 1.0

a) Customs basis.
b) Ratio between export volume and export market of total goods.
Source: OECD.

of GDP), primarily for unemployment benefits and public works. The FY 2003 budget includes a net 1.8 trillion yen tax cut, including the introduction of new tax credits for business investment and a reduction in tax rates on inheritance.

An upturn in world trade may generate a mild recovery

Most recent indicators suggest some weakening in domestic demand in the first half of 2003. Consumer confidence has declined, reflecting the higher unemployment rate, which is projected to continue rising despite further falls in nominal wages that are intended to preserve jobs. Moreover, the scope for further declines in the saving rate to sustain private consumption appears limited, given that Japan's once high household saving rate has fallen below the OECD average. Business investment is also likely to remain weak, at least until the second half of 2003, when a rebound in world market growth should boost exports. Such a recovery could lift output growth to around 1 per cent in both 2003 and 2004. A modest upturn of this scale would not suffice to narrow the output gap and slow deflation from its 1½ per cent pace.

There are a number of domestic risks to an export-led upturn

While continued weakness in external demand could delay the recovery, there are a number of domestic risks as well. Perhaps most important is financial fragility, notably the possibility of a correction in the government bond market, given the continued large increases in public debt. Further declines in share prices would also weaken sentiment and bank balance sheets. Finally, the plan to accelerate the resolution of non-performing loans may have a significant impact on the outlook. While progress in this regard is essential to achieving a sustained and robust recovery, it may have negative impacts on the labour market and household confidence in the short run.

Germany

Output came close to stagnating in 2002. While fixed investment fell further and private consumption contracted, this was counterbalanced by continuing, albeit weak, export growth. With domestic demand having firmed somewhat at the turn of the year, the trough of the downswing might have been reached. But the economy seems likely to grow very slowly through 2003, as consumption and investment remain subdued and a significant pickup in exports is unlikely before 2004. Unemployment is set to remain high. As the upswing broadens in 2004, GDP growth is projected to pick up to around 1¾ per cent, slightly above potential.

The general government deficit totalled 3.6 per cent of GDP in 2002 and – based on current legislation – will remain above three per cent in 2003. Coherent expenditure reforms are required to reduce the structural deficit and raise the growth path of the economy. Furthermore, the slowing of the economic expansion reinforces the need for fundamental reform to make labour markets more flexible and improve incentives for work. The government has announced important measures designed to tackle these issues, and these should be implemented as soon as possible.

The German economy barely grew in 2002, reflecting the weakness in domestic demand. Private consumption contracted and investment in machinery and equipment and construction remained deeply in recession for the year as a whole. Exports grew only moderately but, with imports falling, the rise in net exports roughly offset the fall in domestic demand. Domestic demand firmed somewhat towards the end of the year, and destocking appears to have slowed, suggesting that the trough of the downswing might have been reached.

Economic activity is very weak...

Forward-looking indicators also suggest that the business cycle might have reached its bottom, but activity is likely to remain weak over the months to come. Business confidence remains at low levels reflecting a high degree of uncertainty over economic developments. Unsettled expectations about fiscal consolidation measures are adding to uncertainty. Domestic orders have stabilised but export orders are still volatile. Consumer sentiment remains depressed at levels last seen more than five years ago, reflecting rising unemployment and the adverse income effects associated with hikes in indirect taxes and a sizeable increase in fuel prices.

... but the cycle appears to have bottomed out

Employment continues to decline and unemployment to rise despite slowing labour force participation. Nonetheless, recent wage settlements in the public sector confirm the

Employment continues to fall

Germany

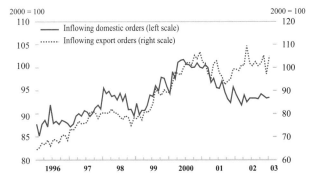

Business expectations are still weak[1]

1991 = 100
— Current situation
— Six month expectation

Domestic orders have stabilised[2]

2000 = 100
— Inflowing domestic orders (left scale)
······ Inflowing export orders (right scale)

1. Industry, western Germany.
2. Industry, volume.
Source: Ifo Institut für Wirtschaftsforschung; Deutsche Bundesbank.

──────── Germany: **Employment, income and inflation** ────────

Percentage changes from previous period

	2000	2001	2002	2003	2004
Employment	1.8	0.4	-0.6	-1.0	0.0
Unemployment rate[a]	7.3	7.3	7.8	8.3	8.3
Compensation of employees	3.9	1.9	0.9	1.5	2.0
Unit labour cost	1.0	1.3	0.7	1.2	0.2
Household disposable income	2.9	3.8	1.0	1.3	2.1
GDP deflator	-0.3	1.4	1.6	0.8	0.6
Consumer price index	1.5	2.1	1.3	0.8	0.4
Private consumption deflator	1.5	1.9	1.4	0.8	0.4

a) As a percentage of labour force.
Source: OECD.

pick-up in wage growth emanating from last year's wage round in major parts of the economy, notably the metal and engineering and the chemical industries. The government is beginning to take actions to address Germany's labour market problems. At the turn of the year new legislation came into force, designed to improve the efficiency of job placement of the unemployed and to increase the flexibility of employment in small jobs. Then in March the government announced important measures to increase the flexibility of the labour market and raise incentives to take up work and hire labour. Commissions have also been established to prepare reforms designed to increase the efficiency and viability of the health care and pension systems.

Monetary conditions could damp economic activity

Headline inflation (the Harmonised Index of Consumer Prices) has stabilised at around 1¼ per cent on a year-on-year basis since summer 2002, despite rising oil prices and increases in indirect taxes at the turn of the year. Core inflation – net of energy and food items – has decelerated over the same period, reflecting the appreciation of the euro and the weakness of demand. Continued disinflation is likely to imply a rise in real short-term interest rates that could damp economic activity. Bank lending has been stagnating in nominal terms. Apart from subdued economic

──────── **Germany** ────────

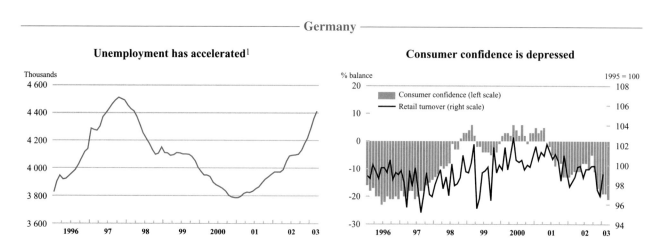

Unemployment has accelerated[1]

Consumer confidence is depressed

1. Seasonally adjusted, registered unemployment.
Source: Deutsche Bundesbank; OECD.

—————————————————— Germany: **Financial indicators** ——————————————

	2000	2001	2002	2003	2004
Household saving ratio[a]	9.8	10.1	10.4	10.5	10.8
General government financial balance[b]	1.1[c]	-2.8	-3.6	-3.7	-3.3
Current account balance[b]	-1.1	0.2	2.5	2.9	3.2
Short-term interest rate[d]	4.4	4.2	3.3	2.3	2.3
Long-term interest rate[e]	5.3	4.8	4.8	4.2	4.3

a) As a percentage of disposable income.
b) As a percentage of GDP.
c) Including proceeds of sales of mobile telephone licences (around 2.5 per cent of GDP).
d) 3-month interbank rate.
e) 10-year government bonds.
Source: OECD.

activity, this development might also reflect some tightening of credit supply as a result of deteriorating bank profits and balance sheets, notably on account of accelerating bankruptcies among industrial firms.

The general government budget deficit deteriorated by ¾ percentage point in 2002 to 3.6 per cent of GDP, overshooting the government's consolidation target by a wide margin and giving rise to an excessive deficit procedure. On top of an already high structural deficit, a substantial widening of the output gap, continuing significant tax shortfalls, and a sizeable deficit in the health funds were the main factors behind this development.

The general government deficit overshot 3 per cent of GDP in 2002...

The government has presented a consolidation package designed to reduce the general government deficit to below 3 per cent of GDP in 2003, though the largest part of the package has not yet been approved by the second chamber of parliament.

... and will remain high in the absence of further measures

—————————————————— Germany: **Demand and output** ——————————————

	1999	2000	2001	2002	2003	2004
	Current prices billion euros	Percentage changes, volume (1995 prices)				
Private consumption	1 156.5	1.4	1.5	-0.6	0.5	1.4
Government consumption	378.8	1.2	0.8	1.5	0.8	0.4
Gross fixed investment	426.1	2.5	-5.3	-6.7	-0.5	1.8
Public	37.8	-2.9	-3.4	-5.7	1.8	-3.5
Residential	143.5	-2.6	-7.1	-5.9	-0.1	-1.4
Non-residential	244.9	6.2	-4.5	-7.3	-1.1	4.2
Final domestic demand	1 961.4	1.6	-0.2	-1.5	0.4	1.3
Stockbuilding[a]	0.9	0.2	-0.6	0.1	0.2	0.3
Total domestic demand	1 962.3	1.8	-0.8	-1.5	0.6	1.6
Exports of goods and services	587.0	13.7	5.0	2.6	3.2	6.0
Imports of goods and services	570.7	10.5	1.0	-2.1	4.3	6.1
Net exports[a]	16.3	1.0	1.4	1.6	-0.2	0.2
GDP at market prices	1 978.6	2.9	0.6	0.2	0.3	1.7
Memorandum items						
Investment in machinery and equipment	181.0	9.3	-4.4	-7.7	0.7	5.4
Construction investment	245.2	-2.6	-6.0	-5.9	-1.5	-1.3

a) Contributions to changes in real GDP (percentage of real GDP in previous year), actual amount in the first column.
Source: OECD.

Germany: **External indicators**

	2000	2001	2002	2003	2004
	\$ billion				
Merchandise exports	550.2	571.3	614.5	718	773
Merchandise imports	491.8	480.6	491.2	578	623
Trade balance	58.4	90.7	123.3	140	150
Invisibles, net	- 78.9	- 87.1	- 73.0	- 73	- 75
Current account balance	- 20.5	3.5	50.3	67	75
	Percentage changes				
Merchandise export volumes[a]	12.8	4.7	4.4	4.4	6.0
Merchandise import volumes[a]	9.9	2.4	- 0.3	4.8	6.3
Export performance[b]	- 0.2	3.6	1.7	- 0.1	- 2.3
Terms of trade	- 5.7	2.0	2.4	0.2	0.2

a) Customs basis.
b) Ratio between export volume and export market of total goods.
Source: OECD.

This concerns various measures generating higher revenues from income, business and indirect taxes, including an amnesty to induce repatriation of savings transferred abroad for the purpose of tax evasion. Based on current legislation and observed recent consolidation trends – notably reductions in government employment and subsidies and in investment (net of flood relief spending) – the OECD projects the structural deficit to improve by about ½ percentage point in 2003. However, with the output gap widening further and growth likely to undershoot the official projection, no reduction in the general government deficit is projected for this year in the absence of further consolidation measures. In 2004 the deficit is likely to fall to some 3¼ per cent.

Activity is likely to remain subdued in 2003

With activity likely to remain weak through much of 2003, average growth for the year as a whole is projected to be below ½ per cent. Inflation is likely to slow further, despite higher wage growth. While both higher wage growth and lower inflation support real disposable incomes, *ceteris paribus*, private consumption is likely to be subdued for some quarters to come, as unemployment continues to rise and consumer sentiment is depressed. Construction investment is being temporarily boosted in the first half of 2003 on account of ongoing flood relief measures, but is projected to fall back again thereafter. World trade is expected to recover in the second half of the year, and accelerating exports will be the main driving force for the economy in both 2003 and 2004. Consumption will strengthen gradually as labour shedding bottoms out, and the recovery will be supported by income tax reductions in 2004. With foreign and domestic demand rising, investment in machinery and equipment will also pick up. As the recovery broadens in 2004, growth is projected to increase to some 1¾ per cent, slightly above potential.

Risks to these projections are significant

External risks relate to the pace at which international tensions dissipate. However, if far-reaching labour market reforms were carried through and public sector reform were forthcoming, business confidence might strengthen and investment rates could be higher than projected. On the other hand, if the share of non-performing loans turns out to be larger than perceived, credit supply might tighten, with adverse effects on activity.

France

GDP grew by 1.2 per cent in 2002, with robust personal and government consumption offsetting a decline in investment and a sharp fall in inventories. Inflation pressures have reversed although unemployment is up only marginally. Output is projected to rise by only around 1¼ per cent overall in 2003, the product of weak conditions in the first half and an acceleration in the second half that should see the economy expand by more than 2½ per cent in 2004. Meanwhile, consumer price inflation should decelerate to around 1½ per cent in 2003, before stabilising.

Fiscal policy relaxed substantially in 2002 and the authorities expect the deficit to reach 3½ per cent of GDP this year. As a result, government debt is likely to rise to more than 60 per cent of GDP. Although measures in place should permit the deficit to fall in 2004, significant additional efforts will need to be made to restrain the pace at which expenditures rise if the authorities are to achieve their goal of reducing the deficit below 3 per cent of GDP.

Growth was weak in 2002

The economy grew by only 1.2 per cent in 2002, with strong private and government consumption the principal sources of growth. Investment activity, which had been weak in the first half of the year, declined in the second half and firms continued to meet demand by reducing inventories. On the external side, both exports and imports of intermediate goods decelerated sharply in the fourth quarter, reflecting a reduction in world trade. Overall, the net contribution of trade to growth was slightly positive. Meanwhile, the appreciation of the euro allowed the trade surplus to improve further, notwithstanding higher oil prices. High frequency data concerning the first quarter of 2003 suggest that growth remains weak.

Employment is stable and inflation is now declining

Overall, the labour market has resisted the slowdown. While the unemployment rate has risen somewhat, at 9.2 per cent in February 2003, it remains close to its structural rate and employment is still increasing. At the same time, continued moderate increases in wages and unit labour costs have contributed to disinflationary pressures. Partly as a result, both headline and core inflation, expressed in year-over-year terms, began declining towards the end of 2002. Notwithstanding an uptick in February, further declines in inflation appear to be in store given low monthly rates of core inflation and the recent decline in energy prices.

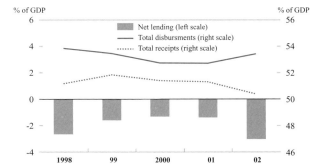

France

Private and public consumption drive growth[1]

Fiscal imbalances are growing

1. From previous quarter at annual rates.
2. Including change in stock.
Source: National Institute for Statistics and Economic Studies (INSEE) and OECD.

France: **Employment, income and inflation**

Percentage changes from previous period

	2000	2001	2002	2003	2004
Employment	2.5	1.6	0.4	-0.1	0.7
Unemployment rate[a]	9.4	8.6	8.9	9.3	9.2
Compensation of employees	4.9	5.0	3.7	2.6	3.5
Unit labour cost	0.7	3.1	2.5	1.4	0.9
Household disposable income	4.5	5.0	4.1	2.8	3.7
GDP deflator	0.5	1.5	1.7	1.5	1.6
Consumer price index	1.8	1.8	1.9	1.6	1.4
Private consumption deflator	1.2	1.4	1.5	1.4	1.4

a) As a percentage of labour force.
Source: OECD.

Financial conditions remain easy...

In this overall context and despite the appreciation of the euro and falling inflation expectations, monetary conditions remain broadly accommodative. Moreover, while there are some signs of rising levels of indebtedness, the debt financing costs of firms remain low, and credit remains readily available. At the household level balance sheets continue to look healthy.

... and fiscal policy has relaxed significantly

Fiscal policy relaxed sharply in 2002, as the general government deficit more than doubled to 3.1 per cent of GDP. While cyclical factors were at play, about two thirds of the deterioration was due to discretionary measures. Furthermore, notwithstanding an announced cut in spending of € 1.5 billion and the putting aside of a precautionary reserve of € 2.5 billion, the authorities project that the deficit will reach 3.4 per cent of GDP in 2003 and that the debt to GDP ratio will rise to more than 60 per cent.

Short-term indicators suggest continued slow growth

The slowdown has now entered its fourth quarter and the output gap has turned negative. As a result, firms report far fewer production bottlenecks and recruitment difficulties, while capacity utilisation rates are falling and are currently below their

---

France

Core inflation has moderated[1]

Per cent
.... Headline inflation
—— Core inflation

Firm's debt servicing costs are low[2]

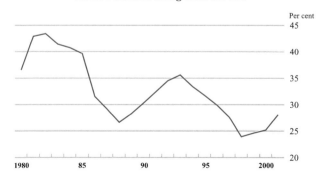

Per cent

1. Year-on-year percentage changes.
2. Interest payments on debt divided by net operating surplus.
Source: National Institute for Statistics and Economic Studies (INSEE) and OECD.

——————————————— France: **Financial indicators** ———————————————

	2000	2001	2002	2003	2004
Household saving ratio[a]	10.8	11.5	12.2	12.0	12.1
General government financial balance [b]	-1.4	-1.5	-3.2	-3.6	-3.3
Current account balance [b]	1.3	1.6	2.1	2.4	2.2
Short-term interest rate[c]	4.4	4.2	3.3	2.3	2.3
Long-term interest rate[d]	5.4	4.9	4.9	4.3	4.4

a) As a percentage of disposable income.
b) As a percentage of GDP.
c) 3-month interbank rate.
d) 10-year benchmark government bonds.
Source: OECD.

long-term averages. Business indicators suggest continued weak growth over the near term, while consumer confidence has weakened markedly in recent months.

Taking these factors into account, GDP is projected to increase by only 1¼ per cent this year, reflecting slow growth in the first half followed by a gradual pick-up. Stagnant employment and weaker wage growth will slow the pace of consumer demand, notwithstanding planned hikes to the minimum wage and last year's tax cuts. From the middle of the year, investment activity should begin to pick up as uncertainty dissipates. This, coupled with a slowing of the destocking process, should see GDP beginning to accelerate in the second half and into 2004, when it is projected to increase by 2½ per cent. Although the labour market is forecast to continue deteriorating during the first half of this year, the rise in unemployment should be moderate. By the same token, however, employment is not expected to respond quickly to the recovery in activity as firms make more intensive use of their existing labour force. Overall, weak labour-market and demand conditions are projected to cause headline and core inflation to decline substantially during 2003, before stabilising the following year as the output gap closes.

The recovery should begin during the second half of 2003...

——————————————— France: **Demand and output** ———————————————

	1999	2000	2001	2002	2003	2004
	Current prices billion euros	Percentage changes, volume (1995 prices)				
Private consumption	742.8	2.8	2.8	1.8	1.6	2.2
Government consumption	315.7	2.9	2.4	3.5	2.7	1.6
Gross fixed investment	259.9	8.3	2.6	-0.6	-1.4	2.3
General government	40.4	11.1	6.0	0.2	-1.1	0.8
Household	64.4	4.1	-0.9	0.2	-0.1	1.8
Other	155.1	9.2	3.0	-1.1	-2.0	2.8
Final domestic demand	1 318.4	3.9	2.6	1.7	1.2	2.1
Stockbuilding[a]	5.6	0.4	-1.0	-0.6	-0.1	0.8
Total domestic demand	1 324.0	4.3	1.6	1.1	1.1	2.9
Exports of goods and services	350.3	13.6	1.5	1.5	2.6	5.2
Imports of goods and services	320.0	15.0	0.9	1.2	2.5	6.5
Net exports[a]	30.2	-0.1	0.2	0.1	0.1	-0.2
GDP at market prices	1 354.3	4.2	1.8	1.2	1.2	2.6

a) Contributions to changes in real GDP (percentage of real GDP in previous year), actual amount in the first column.
Source: OECD.

————— France: **External indicators** —————

	2000	2001	2002	2003	2004
	\$ billion				
Merchandise exports	298.9	292.1	306.6	351	377
Merchandise imports	302.1	288.9	295.7	338	368
Trade balance	- 3.2	3.2	10.9	13	9
Invisibles, net	20.4	17.9	18.5	26	29
Current account balance	17.2	21.2	29.4	39	38
	Percentage changes				
Merchandise export volumes[a]	13.3	1.6	2.2	2.7	5.4
Merchandise import volumes[a]	15.5	0.4	1.6	2.5	6.9
Export performance[b]	1.0	- 0.6	0.8	- 1.7	- 2.1
Terms of trade	- 3.4	0.8	1.0	0.8	0.1

a) Customs basis.
b) Ratio between export volume and export market of total goods.
Source: OECD.

... but its strength and timing remains uncertain

The timing and strength of the projected recovery will depend importantly on the reactions of enterprises and consumers to international events in the near term. If business confidence or developments elsewhere in the OECD worsen, the pace of layoffs may pick up. This could affect consumer demand both directly and indirectly, further weakening business conditions and provoking a period of negative growth. In contrast, if the uncertainty concerning demand conditions lifts and investment activity picks up more quickly than projected, then the pace of recovery would be stronger, possibly even pushing the economy back into a position of excess demand in 2004.

Italy

Growth continued to be sluggish in 2002 because of flagging domestic confidence and weak export performance. A recovery is expected to begin only in the second half of 2003 and to gather strength in 2004, driven by low real interest rates, reviving confidence, and accelerating world demand. Inflation, as measured by the Harmonised Index of Consumer Prices, is expected to decelerate, stabilising at 1¾ per cent by the end of 2004.

Labour market liberalisation and wage moderation underpin an ongoing structural shift towards more labour-intensive production, but greater wage differentiation is desirable to encourage further the demand for low-skill labour. More public expenditure restraint will be needed in both the short and medium term to reduce the high tax wedge, while also allowing for a satisfactory pace of debt reduction. Total factor productivity growth is low and strengthening it will require policies to promote product market competition and innovation.

GDP grew by only 0.4 per cent in 2002, though private investment accelerated towards the end of the year, responding strongly to the anticipated ending of government incentives. Government expenditure and stockbuilding provided some further support to growth. On the whole, however, both domestic and foreign demand were held back by a marked deterioration of confidence in response to global geopolitical and financial market tensions. With investment growth falling back and consumer confidence sagging, domestic demand weakness is likely to continue through the first half of this year. Export performance will probably deteriorate further following the sharp appreciation of the euro.

The economy was weak in 2002 and early 2003

Solid employment creation has been registered despite sluggish GDP growth, thanks to the continuing impact of the liberalisation of labour contracts. Fiscal interventions for 2003 are likely to have mixed labour market effects, as tax incentives to hiring have been tightened but marginal tax rates are being reduced for low income workers. Early in 2003, the Parliament approved a further batch of structural measures that – if implemented quickly – could help to maintain the momentum of reform. Wage moderation has continued, as contractual wages are geared to the rate of inflation. However, unit labour costs have accelerated as productivity growth has fallen, for both cyclical and structural reasons. A Bank of Italy survey suggests that labour costs are becoming the

Employment growth is relatively robust

— Italy —

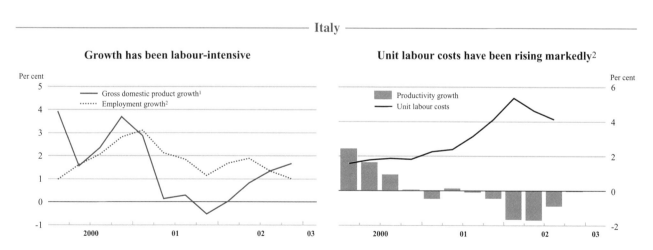

Growth has been labour-intensive

Per cent
— Gross domestic product growth[1]
······ Employment growth[2]

Unit labour costs have been rising markedly[2]

Per cent
▨ Productivity growth
— Unit labour costs

1. Seasonnally adjusted data, at annual rate.
2. Year-on-year percentage changes.
Source: OECD.

—————— Italy: **Employment, income and inflation** ——————

Percentage changes from previous period

	2000	2001	2002	2003	2004
Employment	1.9	2.0	1.5	0.5	1.2
Unemployment rate[a]	10.7	9.6	9.1	9.2	8.9
Compensation of employees	5.0	4.8	4.3	3.9	4.9
Unit labour cost	1.8	3.0	3.9	2.9	2.4
Household disposable income	4.6	4.8	4.2	3.6	4.1
GDP deflator	2.1	2.7	2.7	2.7	2.6
Consumer price index	2.6	2.3	2.6	2.3	1.9
Private consumption deflator	2.9	2.7	3.0	2.4	1.9

a) As a percentage of labour force.
Source: OECD.

main reason for concern by many companies. A slowing of employment growth is expected in 2003, with a delayed reaction of labour shedding to the economic downturn partly offsetting the employment-creating impacts of further labour market reforms.

Inflation has risen but should eventually fall back

Prices accelerated in the second half of 2002 despite demand weakness, with core inflation rising to over 3 per cent. Besides the push from rising unit labour costs, temporary factors continued to play a role, as the effects of the euro changeover, which seem to have been stronger than elsewhere in the euro area, continued to operate throughout the year. Moreover, the utilities price freeze was lifted in December 2002. Inflation may ease during 2003, thanks to the moderating influence of euro appreciation and the imposition of administrative controls on pharmaceutical prices. However, the pass-through of temporarily higher world oil prices will keep inflation from falling much below 2½ per cent in the first half of 2003. Thereafter, moderating influences should take over, with core inflation falling to below 2 per cent by the end of 2004.

The fiscal deficit has stabilised...

The general government deficit improved slightly in 2002 from 2001 in spite of the growth slowdown. This reflected a number of measures taken in order to limit slippage from Stability Programme targets and to maintain the public debt-to-GDP

—————— **Italy** ——————

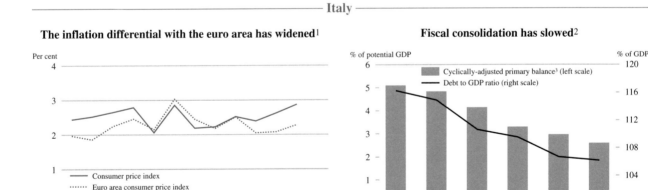

The inflation differential with the euro area has widened[1]

Per cent

— Consumer price index
······· Euro area consumer price index

Fiscal consolidation has slowed[2]

% of potential GDP   % of GDP

▓ Cyclically-adjusted primary balance[3] (left scale)
— Debt to GDP ratio (right scale)

1. Year-on-year percentage changes.
2. Data for 2003 are estimates.
3. Less securitisation operations.
Source: OECD.

———————————————— Italy: **Financial indicators** ————————————————

	2000	2001	2002	2003	2004
Household saving ratio[a]	14.5	15.4	16.0	16.1	15.9
General government financial balance [b,c]	-0.7	-2.7	-2.5	-2.4	-2.8
Current account balance[b]	-0.5	0.0	-0.5	-0.1	0.0
Short-term interest rate[d]	4.4	4.2	3.3	2.3	2.3
Long-term interest rate[e]	5.6	5.2	5.0	4.6	4.5

a) As a percentage of disposable income.
b) As a percentage of GDP.
c) Excludes the impact of swaps and forward rate transactions on interest payments. These operations are however included in the financial balance reported to the European Commission for purposes of the excessive deficit procedure.
d) 3-month interbank rate.
e) 10-year government bonds.
Source: OECD.

ratio on its downward trajectory. These included tighter controls on central government spending, a strengthened health spending agreement with the regions, and an enlargement of the business tax base. Special operations also played a role, namely securitisation of real estate assets and a tax amnesty on the repatriation of capital from abroad. The debt ratio fell thanks to a swap of government bonds held by the Central Bank which reduced their total face value. In 2003, the deficit is expected to remain at just under 2½ per cent of GDP, reflecting offsetting tendencies. The full impact of savings measures taken in 2002 will be felt and a new series of one-off securitisation operations and tax amnesties will be introduced. Furthermore, low average interest rates on public debt will reduce the debt service burden. On the other hand, measures to advance the government's structural reform agenda have been introduced, notably tax cuts to businesses and lower-income households.

———————————————— Italy: **Demand and output** ————————————————

	1999	2000	2001	2002	2003	2004
	Current prices billion euros	Percentage changes, volume (1995 prices)				
Private consumption[a]	667.9	2.7	1.0	0.4	1.0	2.4
Government consumption	199.5	1.6	3.6	1.7	1.2	1.1
Gross fixed investment	210.6	7.1	2.6	0.5	1.1	3.5
Machinery and equipment	123.7	8.0	2.2	0.6	0.0	3.7
Construction	87.0	5.9	3.2	0.3	2.7	3.3
Residential	47.9	5.3	1.7	0.9	2.2	2.6
Non-residential	39.1	6.7	5.1	-0.3	3.4	4.1
Final domestic demand	1 078.1	3.4	1.8	0.7	1.1	2.4
Stockbuilding[b]	7.1	-1.1	0.0	0.4	-0.3	-0.1
Total domestic demand	1 085.2	2.3	1.8	1.1	0.8	2.3
Exports of goods and services	283.0	11.7	1.1	-1.0	4.4	5.5
Imports of goods and services	260.3	8.9	1.0	1.5	3.8	5.4
Net exports[b]	22.7	0.9	0.1	-0.7	0.2	0.1
GDP at market prices	1 108.0	3.1	1.8	0.4	1.0	2.4

a) Final consumption in the domestic market by households.
b) Contributions to changes in real GDP (percentage of real GDP in previous year), actual amount in the first column.
Source: OECD.

——————————————— Italy: **External indicators** ———————————————

	2000	2001	2002	2003	2004
	\$ billion				
Merchandise exports	240.6	245.1	253.8	298	320
Merchandise imports	231.0	229.5	236.7	276	296
Trade balance	9.6	15.6	17.1	22	24
Invisibles, net	- 15.3	- 15.9	- 22.8	- 23	- 23
Current account balance	- 5.8	- 0.3	- 5.7	- 1	0
	Percentage changes				
Merchandise export volumes[a]	10.2	0.3	1.6	4.4	5.7
Merchandise import volumes[a]	8.3	- 0.7	1.7	3.8	5.8
Export performance[b]	- 2.6	- 0.8	- 0.6	- 0.5	- 2.2
Terms of trade	- 7.4	2.0	0.5	0.2	0.0

a) Customs basis.
b) Ratio between export volume and export market of total goods.
Source: OECD.

... but may widen sharply in 2004

For 2004, the Italian Stability Programme envisages a target deficit ratio of 0.6 per cent of GDP. The objective is ambitious given: *i)* that growth is quite likely to be slower than assumed by the government, and *ii)* the lack, thus far, of savings measures to offset the substantial permanent budgetary costs of recently announced reforms. Unless such measures are soon forthcoming, the deficit ratio would be close to the 3 per cent Maastricht limit in 2004 despite the ongoing favourable impacts of low real interest rates and an already-announced continuation of the securitisation operation programme. On present policies, including one-off measures, the cyclically-adjusted primary surplus is projected to decline from 3.5 per cent in 2002 to around 2 per cent of GDP in 2004.

Recovery is expected by the latter half of 2003

A mild recovery is expected to start in the third quarter of 2003, gathering strength towards end-year and through 2004. Overall, growth is projected to reach only 1 per cent in 2003 and to rise to just under 2½ per cent in 2004. Improving export growth, in response to a recovery in world trade, should lead to an improvement in business prospects and so encourage higher capital spending by firms. Historically low real interest rates and a declining corporate tax burden will provide further stimulus to investment. The rebound in consumption may be less marked especially in 2003 as unemployment rises temporarily and precautionary savings respond, partly offsetting the impacts of low interest rates and tax cuts.

Major risks stem from fiscal, labour market and global tensions

A major risk to the projections attaches to the severe fiscal constraint facing Italy. The phasing out of one-off measures will have negative impacts on the deficit and debt if permanent expenditure cuts cannot be found to replace them. The fiscal situation moreover remains vulnerable to any unexpected jump in interest rates, given the still high level of the debt. Also, heightened tensions between the social partners over labour market and other reforms might result in unexpected wage and price pressures. Finally, there are clear global risks threatening the recovery of both foreign and domestic demand during 2003.

United Kingdom

The UK economy has so far shown greater resilience in weathering the downturn than any other major European economy. An expansionary fiscal stance and a reduced drag from net exports should ensure a slight pick-up in growth this year, despite a slowdown in consumption. As business investment and exports revive, the output gap should begin to close in 2004 with inflation falling back to the official target.

The recent and prospective deterioration in the government financial balance is not an immediate cause for concern given the relatively low level of debt. The "golden rule" is likely to be met over the current cycle, but with a worse starting position there will be a greater challenge in meeting it over the next cycle. The recent easing of monetary policy, while justified by signs of weakening domestic and international demand, may fuel the housing market and does nothing to reduce the risk of a sudden fall in house price inflation or even possibly an abrupt fall in the level of house prices.

GDP growth slowed to 1.8 per cent in 2002, which was still more than double the euro area's growth rate. The expenditure composition of growth has, however, remained polarised. In each of the past seven years consumption has grown significantly faster than output and net exports have acted as a drag on activity. In addition, public consumption also increased strongly in 2002, while both business investment and exports fell.

Growth has slowed

Private consumption remained buoyant in 2002 despite substantial falls in equity wealth because house price inflation, recently running at annual rates of 20 to 25 per cent, has led to partially compensating increases in housing wealth. It has also led to a sharp rise in the secured debt-to-income ratio so that an increasing share of consumers' expenditure is being financed by mortgage equity withdrawal. However, a fall in retail sales in January and February, suggests a sharp weakening in consumption in early 2003. Although there are signs that the housing market is slowing, the pronounced decline in consumer confidence is probably linked to the war in Iraq, and may be a more important factor behind this weakness.

Consumption has recently weakened

Real business investment has declined by over 12 per cent between the end of 2000 and the beginning of 2002, and has since shown no sign of recovery despite continued output growth. This weakness reflects a fall in profitability, bleak

Business investment and exports are weak

United Kingdom

Consumption is driving growth

Per cent

Legend:
- Consumption[1]
- Investment[2]
- Net exports
- GDP growth

Household wealth is supported by housing[3]

Per cent

Legend:
- Housing wealth
- Net financial assets

1. Public and private.
2. Including stockbuilding.
3. In per cent of disposable income.
Source: National Statistics and OECD.

United Kingdom: **Employment, income and inflation**

Percentage changes from previous period

	2000	2001	2002	2003	2004
Employment	1.1	0.8	0.7	0.2	0.5
Unemployment rate[a]	5.5	5.1	5.2	5.4	5.2
Compensation of employees	6.5	5.9	4.8	4.5	4.5
Unit labour cost	3.3	3.8	3.0	2.4	1.9
Household disposable income	5.4	7.4	3.5	3.5	3.6
GDP deflator	2.2	2.3	3.2	1.8	2.3
Consumer price index[b]	2.1	2.1	2.2	3.1	2.8
Private consumption deflator	0.7	0.9	0.8	0.9	1.0

a) As a percentage of labour force.
b) Retail price index excluding mortgage payments RPIX.
Source: OECD.

---

prospects for demand in the manufacturing sector and, more recently, geopolitical uncertainties. Another recent factor, which may also delay an investment recovery, is that companies may be diverting funds into shoring up company pension schemes that have been adversely affected by the fall in equity prices. While overall export volumes have broadly maintained their market share since 1999, manufacturing export volumes fell by more than 6 per cent in the fourth quarter of 2002, but this could reflect the effect of erratic factors that may well be reversed in early 2003.

Interest rates have been cut recently

The Monetary Policy Committee of the Bank of England cut the official repo rate by ¼ percentage point in February 2003, on the basis of prospective weakness in both external and domestic demand conditions. This was despite inflation, measured by the retail price index, excluding mortgage interest payment (RPIX) having risen to an annual rate of 2.7 per cent, above the 2½ per cent target, partly as a consequence of a rising contribution from housing depreciation costs following the escalation of house prices. Other measures of inflation remain low and stable. For example, the inflation rate according to the harmonised measure of consumer prices has been

---

United Kingdom

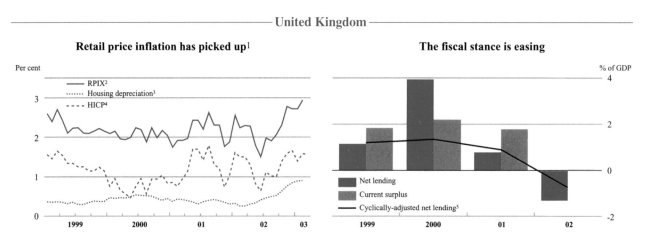

Retail price inflation has picked up[1]

The fiscal stance is easing

1. Year-on-year percentage changes.
2. Retail price index, all items excluding mortgage interest payments, seasonally-adjusted data.
3. Contribution to RPIX inflation.
4. Harmonised consumer price index.
5. In per cent of potential GDP.
Source: National Statistics and OECD.

———————————————— United Kingdom: **Financial indicators** ————————————

	2000	2001	2002	2003	2004
Household saving ratio[a]	4.3	5.5	5.2	5.5	5.8
General government financial balance [b]	3.9	0.8	-1.3	-1.9	-2.2
Current account balance [b]	-2.0	-1.3	-0.8	-1.4	-2.0
Short-term interest rate[c]	6.1	5.0	4.0	3.8	4.3
Long-term interest rate[d]	5.3	4.9	4.9	4.5	5.1

a) As a percentage of disposable income.
b) As a percentage of GDP.
c) 3-month interbank rate.
d) 10-year government bonds.
Source: OECD.

among the lowest in the European Union. Wage inflation has remained relatively stable, consistent with an unemployment rate close to the structural rate of unemployment at just over 5 per cent.

The general government financial balance declined from a surplus of ¾ per cent of GDP in 2001 to a deficit of 1¼ per cent of GDP in 2002, and on a cyclically-adjusted basis the fiscal stance eased by 1¾ per cent of GDP. About half of this can be explained by the increase in spending on goods and services, primarily aimed at improving long-standing weaknesses in the health service and education. The remainder is due to greater-than-expected weakness in the "tax take", particularly corporate tax revenues, which have been adversely affected by the decline in asset prices. The projections were finalised before the Budget on 9 April, which confirmed plans for strong growth in public spending while no major changes in taxation were announced. Continued growth in public spending implies that the fiscal stance will ease by around ½ per cent of GDP this year. In the absence of any recovery in the corporate tax take, and despite the previously announced increase in national

The fiscal stance has eased

——————————————— United Kingdom: **Demand and output** ————————————

	1999	2000	2001	2002	2003	2004
	Current prices billion £	Percentage changes, volume (1995 prices)				
Private consumption	591.6	5.2	4.1	3.8	2.2	2.3
Government consumption	166.6	2.1	2.5	3.8	2.1	2.8
Gross fixed investment	153.5	1.9	1.0	-3.2	1.9	6.7
Public[a]	11.5	5.3	4.2	10.3	9.6	17.0
Private residential	33.8	0.8	-3.5	12.2	3.2	2.1
Private non-residential	108.2	1.8	1.6	-8.0	0.5	6.4
Final domestic demand	911.7	4.0	3.3	2.6	2.2	3.1
Stockbuilding [b]	6.3	-0.1	-0.6	-0.1	0.3	0.4
Total domestic demand	918.0	3.9	2.6	2.5	2.4	3.4
Exports of goods and services	236.6	10.1	0.9	-1.0	2.1	8.4
Imports of goods and services	252.2	11.7	2.3	1.5	2.9	9.6
Net exports [b]	- 15.6	-1.1	-0.6	-0.9	-0.5	-1.1
GDP at market prices	902.5	3.1	2.1	1.8	2.1	2.6

a) Including nationalised industries and public corporations.
b) Contributions to changes in real GDP (percentage of real GDP in previous year), actual amount in the first column.
Source: OECD.

——————— United Kingdom: **External indicators** ———————

	2000	2001	2002	2003	2004
	\$ billion				
Merchandise exports	284.5	273.8	279.1	301	329
Merchandise imports	330.4	322.0	331.0	367	403
Trade balance	- 45.9	- 48.2	- 52.0	- 66	- 74
Invisibles, net	17.1	30.3	38.9	42	37
Current account balance	- 28.7	- 17.9	- 13.1	- 24	- 37
	Percentage changes				
Merchandise export volumes[a]	11.4	0.8	- 1.8	0.5	9.0
Merchandise import volumes[a]	11.8	2.9	1.4	2.2	9.6
Export performance[b]	- 0.6	0.8	- 4.1	- 3.9	1.2
Terms of trade	0.9	0.5	2.2	- 1.1	0.0

a) Customs basis.
b) Ratio between export volume and export market of total goods.
Source: OECD.

insurance contributions that will come into force this April, the general government deficit is projected to widen further to 2¼ per cent of GDP by 2004.

Growth will pick up as exports and then investment recover

Various indicators, in particular a fall in the purchasing managers' index and weak retail sales, suggest a slowdown in growth in early 2003. Even once effects on consumer confidence associated with the war in Iraq have dissipated, several factors may contribute to a slowdown in private consumption. These include a gradual fall in house price inflation, a decline in the terms of trade, and the effect of increases in national insurance contributions and slower employment growth on disposable income. Nevertheless, consumption may still grow at about 2 per cent in 2003 and 2004, although this would be the slowest rate of growth since the mid-1990s. Exports are likely to recover gradually with export market growth, and should make some modest gains in market share over the next two years following the fall in the effective exchange rate by nearly 5 per cent during the first quarter of 2003. It is only next year, once business fixed investment recovers and world trade strengthens, that output growth of over 2½ per cent will exceed that of potential.

Inflation will return to target

In the near term, RPIX inflation is likely to rise above 3 per cent as a consequence of continued pressure from housing depreciation costs, prospective increases in council taxes as well as an increase in imported inflation following the depreciation of sterling. Nevertheless, with output remaining below potential, the housing component of inflation declining and oil prices assumed to remain at current levels, inflation should fall back towards the target in 2004. As the output gap begins to close in 2004, short-term interest rates will need to rise to contain future inflationary pressure.

Downside risks predominate

Downside risks to both domestic and external demand predominate. A fall in the level of house prices, which in relation to average earnings are close to the peak reached in the late 1980s, could lead to a sharp retrenchment of consumers' expenditure. Exports could suffer if the recovery of world trade is delayed, which would dampen the projected recovery in business investment. Conversely, inflation might return more slowly to the target if recent price increases were to feed through into higher wage settlements, which could in turn lead to a somewhat tighter stance of monetary policy.

Canada

After a very strong performance during most of last year, output slowed down markedly in the autumn, mainly because of faltering export demand. Output growth is likely to have remained weak through the winter, but the pause is expected to be fairly short-lived. Economic fundamentals are sound, and activity should pick up in the second half of this year if the US recovery accelerates as expected and the present uncertainties diminish. Even though the recent rise in inflation was partly due to one-off factors, price pressures are beginning to build.

The Bank of Canada will need to raise interest rates further this year and next in order to avoid overheating. The planned shift in the fiscal stance, due to a substantial increase in spending, increases these overheating risks. Even though the medium-term fiscal situation is still solid, the government will eventually need to control the underlying sources of spending pressures, particularly in the health care system.

Economic activity was buoyant in the first three quarters of 2002, driven by interest-sensitive housing and consumer durable spending, but slowed thereafter. Nevertheless, Canadian GDP growth continued to exceed US outcomes, as it has since 1999. Weaker external conditions contributed to the slowdown. Exports, particularly those of manufactures, contracted in the fourth quarter, reflecting faltering US demand. Moreover, the recovery of business investment stalled in the second half of the year, probably influenced by global uncertainties and weak stock market prices, and the rebuilding of inventories contributed much less to output growth than it had earlier in the year. By contrast, private consumption expenditure, supported by expanding employment and incomes, continued to bolster economic activity.

Output growth slowed in the latter part of 2002

Job creation was the key factor supporting consumer confidence and personal expenditure throughout 2002. Despite more moderate output growth in the latter part of the year, employment continued to grow at a remarkably rapid pace. However, the unemployment rate declined by only ½ percentage point, since a substantial rise in participation continued to add to the labour force. Employment gains are expected to continue in 2003 and 2004, albeit at a more moderate pace.

... but employment gains remained vigorous

GDP growth is likely to remain below its potential rate in the first half of this year, but is expected to accelerate again in the second half and in 2004, led by export demand and business investment. At present, the underlying factors that slowed

The current cyclical slowdown should be short-lived

Canada

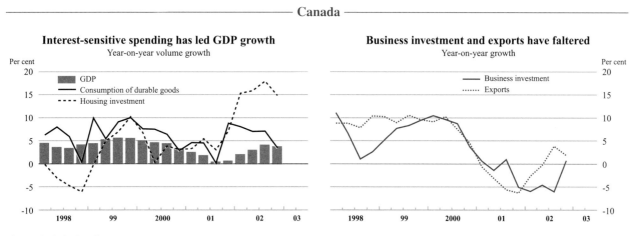

Source: Statistics Canada.

—————————— Canada: **Employment, income and inflation** ——————————

Percentage changes from previous period

	2000	2001	2002	2003	2004
Employment	2.6	1.1	2.2	2.1	1.7
Unemployment rate[a]	6.8	7.2	7.7	7.3	7.0
Compensation of employees	8.4	4.4	4.6	5.2	5.3
Unit labour cost	3.7	2.8	1.2	2.4	1.9
Household disposable income	6.9	4.4	4.5	4.9	5.9
GDP deflator	3.9	1.0	1.2	3.5	2.1
Consumer price index	2.7	2.5	2.2	3.7	2.1
Private consumption deflator	2.1	1.9	1.9	2.8	2.1

a) As a percentage of labour force.
Source: OECD.

economic activity in the latter part of last year are still at work. In addition, the impact of higher energy prices could damp consumer expenditure temporarily. However, export market growth can be expected to pick up later in the year as the US recovery quickens. Moreover, the fundamentals are in place for a vigorous investment rebound once uncertainty subsides, since capacity utilisation is rather high, profits are continuing to rise and business confidence, although lower than one year ago, is still well above historical averages. At the same time, households continue to benefit from recent employment gains and remain relatively optimistic.

The recent rise in inflation is not entirely due to temporary factors

Headline inflation was above 4 per cent in the early part of this year. Although this was partly due to a combination of base effects and one-off factors (including higher energy and car insurance prices), there is evidence that price pressures are becoming more broadly based. Expectations of higher inflation could become more entrenched given that output is already slightly above its potential level. So far, signs of labour market tightness have not yet appeared and wage behaviour has remained moderate. But the unemployment rate, at around 7½ per cent, is probably not far from its structural level. And to the extent that last year's large participation gains were due to cyclical effects, they are unlikely to be repeated in the near future.

—————————— **Canada** ——————————

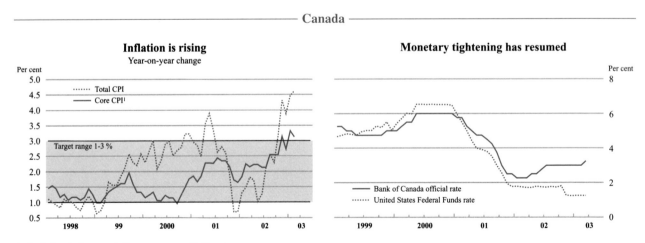

1. Excluding the 8 most volatile components and indirect taxes.
Source: Statistics Canada.

——————— Canada: **Financial indicators** ———————

	2000	2001	2002	2003	2004
Household saving ratio[a]	4.8	4.6	4.4	3.8	4.5
General government financial balance[b]	3.1	1.8	1.3	1.1	1.0
Current account balance[b]	2.6	2.8	1.5	2.0	2.2
Short-term interest rate[c]	5.8	4.0	2.6	3.6	4.6
Long-term interest rate[d]	5.9	5.5	5.3	5.3	5.7

a) As a percentage of disposable income.
b) As a percentage of GDP.
c) 3-month deposit rate.
d) 10-year government bonds.
Source: OECD.

To counteract these risks, the Bank of Canada raised official interest rates by a quarter of a percentage point in early March, resuming the process of gradually withdrawing monetary stimulus that started in the spring of last year. Nevertheless, the monetary stance is still largely supportive of economic activity. Further tightening over the remainder of this year and next will be required to curb domestic expenditure, particularly if export demand picks up as expected.

... and monetary policy is being tightened

Fiscal policy is expected to become significantly more expansionary this year and in 2004. In the recent budget the federal government introduced substantial new spending for the next three years and eliminated some business taxes. More than half of the additional spending will be used to fund provincial health expenditures. All in all, the new measures are expected to reduce the federal surplus by about ½ percentage point of GDP this year and next. As it has been its policy in recent

The fiscal stance is becoming more expansionary

——————— Canada: **Demand and output** ———————

	1999	2000	2001	2002	2003	2004
	Current prices billion CAD	Percentage changes, volume				
Private consumption	561.0	3.7	2.6	2.9	2.8	2.9
Government consumption	185.3	2.3	3.3	2.0	3.7	3.2
Gross fixed investment	195.3	6.5	1.7	2.5	3.4	5.2
Public[a]	22.6	3.0	11.5	8.7	5.4	5.2
Residential	45.9	3.5	4.7	16.0	0.8	-1.7
Non-residential	126.8	8.2	-1.1	-3.9	4.2	8.4
Final domestic demand	941.6	4.0	2.5	2.6	3.1	3.5
Stockbuilding[b]	5.3	0.4	-1.3	0.8	0.2	0.1
Total domestic demand	946.9	4.5	1.0	3.5	3.3	3.5
Exports of goods and services	421.8	8.0	-3.8	0.8	4.4	7.3
Imports of goods and services	388.2	8.2	-5.8	0.8	6.1	8.0
Net exports[b]	33.6	0.3	0.6	0.0	-0.4	0.1
Error of estimate[b]	0.0	0.0	-0.1	0.1	0.0	0.0
GDP at market prices	980.5	4.5	1.5	3.4	2.7	3.4

Note: National accounts are based on official chain-linked data. This introduces a discrepancy in the identity between real demand components and GDP. For further details see *OECD Economic Outlook* Sources and Methods, *(http://www.oecd.org/eco/sources-and-methods).*
a) Excluding nationalized industries and public corporations.
b) Contributions to changes in real GDP (percentage of real GDP in previous year), actual amount in the first column.
Source: OECD.

———————————————————— Canada: **External indicators** ————————————————————

	2000	2001	2002	2003	2004
			$ billion		
Merchandise exports	286.5	268.0	261.4	293	322
Merchandise imports	244.7	226.5	226.9	252	278
Trade balance	41.8	41.4	34.5	41	45
Invisibles, net	- 23.1	- 21.9	- 23.5	- 25	- 26
Current account balance	18.6	19.5	11.0	16	19
			Percentage changes		
Merchandise export volumes[a]	9.0	- 4.3	0.6	4.1	7.4
Merchandise import volumes[a]	9.5	- 5.9	1.1	6.1	8.0
Export performance[b]	- 4.2	- 0.7	- 2.8	- 2.4	- 0.4
Terms of trade	4.8	- 0.7	- 1.9	3.0	0.3

a) Customs basis.
b) Ratio between export volume and export market of total goods.
Source: OECD.

years, the government has made use of all the fiscal room projected to be available. As a result, excluding the contingency buffers built into the projections, the government is now expecting a balanced budget both in 2003 and 2004, in spite of improving cyclical conditions. The general government financial balance looks more favourable, in part because it includes the rising financial surplus of the public pension systems (those of the federal government and Quebec), although it is also expected to deteriorate when adjusted for cyclical effects. Indeed, the government's overall financial situation is fundamentally sound, and public debt is projected to continue declining as a share of GDP.

Risks are mostly to the downside in the short term

Downside risks to the projection are related, in the short term, mainly to a more protracted global uncertainty and a shallower pick-up in world trade. But further into the projection period there are risks of overheating in the event of a simultaneous vigorous acceleration of exports, investment and public expenditure superimposed on persistently strong household demand.

Australia

Robust economic growth continued through the second half of 2002, despite sluggish exports that reflected the severe drought and the weak global economy. With the residential construction boom likely to peter out, GDP growth may slow somewhat in 2003, but then accelerate in 2004 along with the projected global recovery and higher farm output. Unemployment should fall further, with inflation remaining under control, given sizeable productivity gains and wage moderation.

To maintain price stability, monetary policy will need to become less accommodating once the drought effects have faded and signs of a global pick-up become clearer. The government should maintain its fiscal objective of keeping the budget balanced over the economic cycle. Longer-run growth prospects would be improved by further reforms in the areas of welfare, private pensions, education, competition and labour markets, to encourage more people to participate in the workforce, remain in employment, and further raise their productivity.

GDP grew by 3½ per cent in 2002, led by surging residential construction, robust household consumption and a recovery in business investment. Buoyant domestic demand was underpinned by high levels of business and consumer confidence, historically low interest rates, rising terms of trade, strong productivity growth, and a generous subsidy to first-time home buyers. It entailed a widening of the current external deficit in the second half of 2002 to around 5 per cent of GDP.

Domestic demand was barely affected by the global downturn

Employment gathered strength in 2002, and the unemployment rate continued to fall, to just over 6 per cent in early 2003, although still exceeding estimates of the structural rate of unemployment. As in previous years, part-time employment was more dynamic than full-time employment. Notwithstanding robust growth and the earlier exchange rate depreciation, consumer price inflation has been kept in line with the Reserve Bank's 2 to 3 per cent inflation target over the cycle, with underlying inflation measures being somewhat lower. Good inflation performance has been underpinned by wage moderation and strong labour productivity growth.

Employment recovered and inflation remained under control

Following the interest rate hikes in May and June 2002 by altogether 50 basis points to 4.75 per cent, the Reserve Bank has refrained from further tightening, in view of the loss of momentum in the global economy and the severe drought. A return to more neutral monetary conditions is incorporated in the projections for 2003-04.

Monetary policy has become less expansionary…

Australia

Household debt service remains manageable

% of disposable income (left scale)
% of disposable income (right scale)

— Household debt (left scale)
······· Debt interest payments (right scale)

The corporate debt burden is low

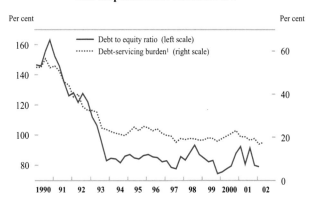

Per cent (left scale)
Per cent (right scale)

— Debt to equity ratio (left scale)
······· Debt-servicing burden[1] (right scale)

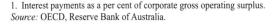

1. Interest payments as a per cent of corporate gross operating surplus.
Source: OECD, Reserve Bank of Australia.

———————————— Australia: **Demand, output and prices** ————————————

	1999	2000	2001	2002	2003	2004
	Current prices billion AUD	\multicolumn{5}{c}{Percentage changes, volume}				
Private consumption	365.0	3.2	3.1	4.1	3.5	3.2
Government consumption	108.2	5.8	1.5	4.3	2.5	3.5
Gross fixed capital formation	144.8	-0.4	-1.3	14.1	6.2	5.5
Final domestic demand	618.1	2.8	1.8	6.3	4.0	3.8
Stockbuilding *a*	5.1	-0.9	-0.1	-0.2	0.1	0.1
Total domestic demand	623.2	1.9	1.7	6.2	4.1	3.9
Exports of goods and services	113.8	10.8	1.4	-0.1	3.4	8.4
Imports of goods and services	130.3	7.1	-4.1	11.9	6.9	8.2
Net exports *a*	- 16.5	0.6	1.3	-2.6	-0.9	-0.2
Statistical discrepancy *a*	0.0	0.4	-0.2	0.0	-0.1	0.0
GDP at market prices	606.7	3.0	2.8	3.5	3.2	3.8
GDP deflator	_	4.3	3.0	2.7	1.8	2.6
Memorandum items						
Consumer price index	_	4.5	4.4	3.0	2.5	2.5
Private consumption deflator	_	3.3	3.5	2.1	2.5	2.6
Unemployment rate	_	6.3	6.8	6.3	6.1	5.8
Household saving ratio *b*	_	3.4	3.0	0.3	0.5	0.8
General government financial balance *c*	_	0.3	-0.6	-0.1	0.2	0.5
Current account balance *c*	_	-3.4	-2.0	-4.1	-3.9	-3.7

Note: National accounts are based on official chain-linked data. This introduces a discrepancy in the identity between real demand components and GDP. For further details see *OECD Economic Outlook* Sources and Methods, *(http:// www.oecd.org/eco/sources-and-methods).*
a) Contributions to changes in real GDP (percentage of real GDP in previous year), actual amount in the first column.
b) As a percentage of disposable income.
c) As a percentage of GDP.
Source: OECD.

... while fiscal policy is firming

Higher subsidies to first-time home-owners and increased security-related expenditures lent moderate support to domestic demand in 2002. Reflecting expected strengthening activity, the Commonwealth Budget for 2002-03 aims for a return of the underlying cash balance to small surplus, and larger budget surpluses are projected over the medium-term.

Growth should remain strong with inflation low

Though the drought will impact on growth in 2003, the expected improvement in the global environment should help the economy to expand at around 3¼ per cent in 2003 and 3¾ per cent in 2004. The demand for labour should continue to rise, but strong productivity gains are expected to help to keep labour costs and inflation under control. Rising incomes and real-estate wealth, as well as comparatively low debt-servicing costs for households, should support consumer confidence and private consumption. The residential construction boom could be nearing its end, but surveys suggest that business investment will pick up further, underpinned by low financing costs, healthy company profitability and low corporate debt. Exports are expected to recover in line with overseas markets, which will help to bring the current external deficit back below 4 per cent of GDP.

The risks to the outlook are on the downside

The major risk attached to the projection is that the slowdown of the world economy could be longer-lasting than expected, with adverse effects on exports and in particular on business confidence. Moreover, it is not yet clear if the house price boom is a bubble that will eventually burst, with a negative impact on household financial positions and spending, or an adaptation to an era of strong real income growth and low interest rates. On the upside, a faster-than-projected recovery in major trading partners could generate stronger demand for Australian exports, while the domestic economy could also display more momentum than anticipated.

Austria

GDP growth weakened at the turn of the year, due to shrinking domestic demand. A gradual, export driven recovery is expected later in 2003. Meanwhile, rising unemployment will continue to depress household confidence while investment plans are held back by international uncertainty. Growth can be expected to pick up later this year and into 2004 as high growth in neighbouring accession countries impacts positively on growth in Austria and fiscal policy offers some support.

By allowing the structural deficit to deteriorate by ½ per cent of GDP in 2003 the new Austrian government is giving less priority than its predecessor to maintaining a balanced budget. The scheduled tax reductions for 2004 and 2005 will be partly debt financed and may act pro-cyclically. Returning to a balanced budget in later years, as intended, requires coherent measures on the expenditure side, linking fiscal consolidation with structural reform.

Real GDP growth weakened in the second half of 2002 on account of subdued domestic demand while exports supported growth. Business investment fell sharply, in line with deteriorating expectations. Employment declined and the registered unemployment rate increased to some 7 per cent at the beginning of 2003 (seasonally adjusted), almost ½ percentage point higher than a year earlier, a substantial increase in foreign labour adding to this process. With the negative output gap having risen, core inflation has declined. However, headline inflation (the Harmonised Index of Consumer Prices) has not fallen, largely on account of higher energy prices.

Activity slowed in the second half of 2002

The balancing of the general government budget in 2001 – achieved largely through revenue-raising measures and some one-off effects – could not be repeated in 2002. The failure to maintain a lasting budget balance is likely to have contributed to the fragility of the business climate. The government's new fiscal programme foresees gross tax reductions in two steps (the smaller part in 2004 and the larger part in 2005), totalling € 3½ billion (1.6 per cent of GDP). This package is to be partially financed by ongoing and intended reforms of the public administration, as well as the pension and healthcare systems. The remainder is to come from energy tax increases and debt financing. This may turn out to be pro-cyclical given the projected shape of the recovery, according to which GDP growth approaches its potential rate in 2004.

The budget deficit is increasing again

Austria

Confidence remains fragile

Orders have ceased to improve

% balance

— Business climate[1, 2]
...... Production plans[2]
- - - Consumer confidence[2]

— Total order stocks[2]
...... Foreign order stocks[2]

1. Anticipated business conditions.
2. Seasonally adjusted. Balance of positive-negative replies.
Source: WIFO Institut für Wirtschaftsforschung and OECD.

———————————— Austria: **Demand, output and prices** ————————————

	1999	2000	2001	2002	2003	2004
	Current prices billion euros	Percentage changes, volume (1995 prices)				
Private consumption	112.0	3.3	1.5	0.9	1.3	1.9
Government consumption	39.0	0.0	-0.5	1.3	0.5	0.7
Gross fixed capital formation	46.2	5.9	-2.2	-4.8	0.8	2.9
Final domestic demand	197.3	3.3	0.2	-0.3	1.0	1.9
Stockbuilding *a*	2.1	-0.7	-0.4	0.0	0.0	0.0
Total domestic demand	199.4	2.6	-0.2	-0.3	1.0	1.9
Exports of goods and services	89.6	13.4	7.4	2.6	3.0	6.4
Imports of goods and services	91.3	11.6	5.9	0.0	3.0	6.4
Net exports *a*	- 1.7	0.8	0.8	1.4	0.1	0.2
GDP at market prices	197.2	3.5	0.7	1.0	1.1	2.0
GDP deflator	_	1.4	1.6	1.3	1.7	1.1
Memorandum items						
Consumer price index	_	2.0	2.3	1.7	1.4	1.0
Private consumption deflator	_	1.5	2.0	1.8	1.4	1.1
Unemployment rate *b*	_	4.7	4.8	5.3	5.9	5.9
Household saving ratio *c*	_	8.3	7.4	7.5	7.6	7.8
General government financial balance *d*	_	-1.5	0.2	-0.6	-1.3	-1.1
Current account balance *d*	_	-2.6	-2.2	0.3	0.2	0.3

a) Contributions to changes in real GDP (percentage of real GDP in previous year), actual amount in the first column.
b) See data annex for details.
c) As a percentage of disposable income.
d) As a percentage of GDP.
Source: OECD.

The recovery will not gain momentum until late 2003

Two location-specific factors provide positive impulses for economic recovery. First, Austria is benefiting from the high growth rates of its neighbouring accession countries. Second, the Austrian tourist industry is located near to its customers and therefore benefits from increasing risk aversion among travellers. Nevertheless, current business cycle indicators do not suggest an upturn of economic activity over the next months. Private consumption will remain subdued in 2003 as unemployment continues to rise. Fixed investment will, however, temporarily benefit from the government's stimulation package and reconstruction spending relating to the floods in autumn last year. Real GDP growth is expected to gather momentum later in the year, when the recovery in world trade compensates for the weakness in domestic demand. All in all, GDP growth is projected to amount to 1.1 per cent in 2003, but to pick up to 2 per cent – around its potential rate – in 2004 as the international recovery broadens. Core inflation will continue to decelerate given the negative output gap. The labour market will not improve before 2004, as companies are engaged in significant labour shedding and job creation is facing widespread regulatory and regional bottlenecks.

Budget developments could affect business sentiment

Downward risks mainly stem from the possibility of a delayed recovery of domestic demand, especially if the government has to resort to revenue increases to consolidate public finances. On the upside, renewed reform efforts in Germany could have a positive effect on business activities and foreign direct investment in the region, with direct and indirect benefits for Austria.

Belgium

Economic growth is likely to remain weak in the first half of 2003, but to rise thereafter, reaching 3 per cent in 2004 as the international economy recovers and business investment picks up. Inflation is likely to fall to 1¼ per cent in 2004, reflecting significantly lower increases in unit labour costs and favourable import price developments.

Wage increases should be limited to levels provided for in the accord for 2003-04 so as to maintain international price competitiveness. The government should not allow the budget to fall into deficit so as not to erode the credibility of its debt-reduction strategy; this strategy entails running budget surpluses until 2030 so as to pre-fund the budget costs of population ageing, which will begin to build as from 2010.

As in other euro area countries, the economic recovery slowed markedly in the second half of 2002; real GDP growth fell to just 0.2 per cent in the fourth quarter. The improvement in export markets during the first half of the year fizzled out, obliging firms further to reduce productive capacity. Business investment continued to fall, resulting in the severest annual downturn since 1993. So also did employment, pushing up the unemployment rate to 7¾ per cent in early 2003, which is above the OECD estimate of the structural rate. In response to deteriorating labour market prospects, falling stock markets and an uncertain international environment, consumer confidence has also been falling since last summer. Similarly, business confidence has been deteriorating over this period and is now pointing to continued weak growth in the first half of 2003. Both underlying and consumer price inflation fell sharply through 2002 to around 1½ per cent in recent months, partly owing to the abolition of television licence fees in Flanders and Brussels, which reduced inflation by 0.3 percentage point (and will have the same effect in 2003). Despite weak economic conditions, hourly wage increases accelerated to 4 per cent in 2002, reflecting delays both in implementing the 2001-02 wage accord and in granting indexed increases. A lower wage accord (5.4 per cent per hour) has been agreed for 2003-04, with most of the increase to be delayed until 2004.

The economic recovery has stalled

The market services sector excluding services to households, which represents about 43 per cent of GDP, has unusually displayed counter-cyclical behaviour during this business cycle, reaching a peak in late 2001 when the rest of the economy reached a

The service sector has flattened the recovery profile

Belgium

Weak services have slowed the recovery

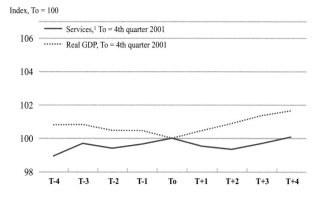

Employment is still weak

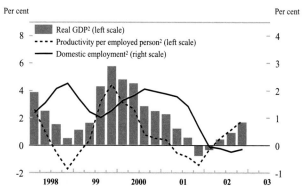

1. Market sector excluding services to households (NACE codes N, O and P).
2. Percentage changes from corresponding quarter of the previous year.
Source: National Bank of Belgium; National Accounts Institute and OECD.

————————————— Belgium: **Demand, output and prices** —————————————

	1999	2000	2001	2002	2003	2004
	Current prices billion euros	Percentage changes, volume (1995 prices)				
Private consumption	126.6	3.3	1.0	0.6	1.0	2.0
Government consumption	50.0	2.4	2.1	1.5	1.5	1.8
Gross fixed capital formation	49.6	3.2	0.5	-2.6	0.5	2.5
Final domestic demand	226.2	3.1	1.1	0.1	1.0	2.1
Stockbuilding ^{a}	- 0.5	0.2	-0.5	0.2	0.3	0.1
Total domestic demand	225.7	3.3	0.5	0.4	1.4	2.2
Exports of goods and services	178.4	8.5	1.2	-1.0	2.6	6.6
Imports of goods and services	168.3	8.3	0.8	-1.5	2.8	6.8
Net exports ^{a}	10.1	0.5	0.3	0.3	0.0	0.3
GDP at market prices	235.8	3.7	0.8	0.7	1.3	2.3
GDP deflator	_	1.3	1.9	2.2	2.0	1.5
Memorandum items						
Consumer price index	_	2.7	2.4	1.6	1.4	1.2
Private consumption deflator	_	2.3	2.5	1.9	1.7	1.2
Unemployment rate	_	6.9	6.7	7.3	7.8	7.7
Household saving ratio ^{b}	_	13.4	13.0	13.7	13.8	14.1
General government financial balance ^{c}	_	0.1	0.4	0.0	0.0	0.2
Current account balance ^{c}	_	4.1	4.0	4.7	5.0	5.3

Note: Corrected for calendar effects.
a) Contributions to changes in real GDP (percentage of real GDP in previous year), actual amount in the first column.
b) As a percentage of disposable income.
c) As a percentage of GDP.
Source: OECD.

trough. This attenuated the downturn but subsequent weakness has slowed the recovery. Business services held up particularly well in 2001 but have since been very weak as they adjusted to more normal levels. With this adjustment now largely complete, the market services sector should once again grow at rates more in line with the rest of the economy.

The cyclical deterioration in the budget balance is being offset

The government recently announced measures, mainly on the expenditure side, to ensure that the budget remains in balance in 2003 despite a reduction in the projected growth rate in order to maintain credibility in the government's long-term commitment to drive down the high level of public debt. This will contribute to the continued fall in debt interest payments and allow further fiscal consolidation (necessary to finance population ageing costs) while pursuing personal income tax cuts. These are expected to reduce tax revenue by 0.4 per cent of GDP in 2003 and by a further 0.1 per cent of GDP in 2004. Further reductions in employers' social security contributions are also scheduled (reducing labour costs per employee by 0.1 percentage point in 2003 and in 2004). Corporate income tax reform, which came into effect at the beginning of this year, is intended to be revenue neutral.

The recovery should gather strength in the second half of 2003

Economic growth is projected to remain weak during the first half of 2003 but subsequently to strengthen as the international economy recovers and business investment picks up, rising to around trend in 2004 and leaving a substantial negative output gap. As employment growth is only likely to recover with a lag, unemployment may rise to 7¾ per cent in 2003 and remain at that rate in 2004. Inflation is projected to fall to around 1¼ per cent in 2004, reflecting the easing of domestic inflation pressures and the strengthening of the euro. The main risk to this outlook is that businesses and households may delay expenditures in view of the highly uncertain international environment. A more rapid international recovery, on the other hand, would particularly benefit the internationally highly integrated Belgian economy.

Czech Republic

Output growth is projected to strengthen progressively from 2 per cent in 2002 to 3½ per cent by 2004, driven by strong consumption and exports, especially those of foreign-investment firms. Massive currency appreciation has engendered a very sharp disinflation and price increases are expected to remain subdued.

Fiscal policy has become increasingly expansionary and needs to be tightened from the expenditure side in order to balance the macroeconomic policy mix. A determined pursuit of corporate governance and labour market reforms is needed to facilitate the re-employment of workers whose jobs are being made redundant by industrial restructuring.

Strong currency appreciation up to mid-2002 has resulted in a marked disinflation, driven by falling prices of tradables, cheap energy imports and small increases in regulated prices. The resulting positive surprise in real disposable income growth, which was also raised by large public-sector wage hikes and increased social transfers, underpinned buoyant private consumption. At the same time, the adverse impact of the strong koruna on cost competitiveness has hit the domestic business sector hard and has led to an acceleration of industrial restructuring. Business investment has decelerated and the pace of layoffs has picked up, resulting in the rapid growth of registered unemployment to record levels. Taking advantage of the still generous disability and early-retirement benefits, more elderly unemployed have become inactive while involuntary unemployment measured by labour force surveys has declined. The current account deficit declined to 5⅓ per cent of GDP in 2002, despite flood-related falls in tourism receipts as exports decelerated less than imports. Exports have accelerated recently in spite of the continued weakness of external demand in the European Union (EU), while a similar pick-up in imports suggests a revival of investment demand.

Currency appreciation has led to disinflation and the current account has improved

Fiscal policy continues on an excessively expansionary path, mainly reflecting the rapid growth of government wages, pensions and other social transfers. This is bound to increase further the public debt, the level of which is already considerable when off-budget liabilities are included. Given the time period necessary to implement a major fiscal consolidation package, including the relevant legislative changes related to cuts in mandatory programme spending, no significant budget savings have been projected to take place next year. Monetary conditions remain tight with

Fiscal policy is easy while monetary policy is tight

Czech Republic

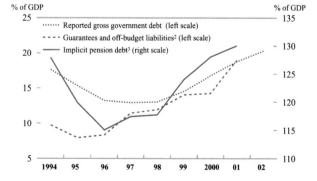

Currency appreciation has helped to subdue inflation

Public debt has increased significantly

1. Year-on-year percentage change of monthly data.
2. Liabilities of the Consolidation Bank group and risk-adjusted state guarantees.
3. Assets which would have to be built up to cover the pension system deficits over the next 50 years.
Source: National authorities; OECD estimates.

——————— Czech Republic: **Demand, output and prices** ———————

	1999	2000	2001	2002	2003	2004
	Current prices billion CZK	Percentage changes, volume (1995 prices)				
Private consumption	1 019.2	2.5	3.6	4.0	4.1	4.5
Government consumption	373.3	-1.0	5.3	5.7	1.8	1.4
Gross fixed capital formation	528.3	5.3	5.5	0.6	3.2	3.5
Final domestic demand	1 920.8	2.7	4.5	3.2	3.4	3.6
Stockbuilding [a]	5.8	1.3	0.7	0.3	0.0	0.0
Total domestic demand	1 926.6	4.0	5.1	3.4	3.3	3.6
Exports of goods and services	1 152.6	17.0	11.9	2.8	6.3	9.8
Imports of goods and services	1 176.9	17.0	13.6	4.3	6.3	9.2
Net exports [a]	- 24.3	-1.0	-2.3	-1.7	-0.7	-0.5
GDP at market prices	1 902.3	3.3	3.1	2.0	3.0	3.5
GDP deflator	_	1.1	6.3	2.6	2.5	3.6
Memorandum items						
Consumer price index	_	3.9	4.8	1.8	2.0	3.1
Private consumption deflator	_	2.8	3.8	-0.1	2.0	2.3
Unemployment rate	_	8.9	8.2	7.3	7.2	7.2
Household saving ratio [b]	_	13.0	13.0	11.3	11.1	10.8
General government financial balance [c]	_	-4.0	-2.8	-4.5	-6.3	-6.2
Current account balance [c]	_	-5.3	-5.7	-5.3	-5.3	-5.1

a) Contributions to changes in real GDP (percentage of real GDP in previous year), actual amount in the first column.
b) As a percentage of disposable income.
c) As a percentage of GDP.
Source: OECD.

inflation undershooting its target corridor. Buoyant foreign direct investment and expectations of EU accession in May 2004 have kept the Czech koruna under pressure. But since mid-2002 the Czech National Bank has succeeded in stabilising the rate at a high level, by sterilising privatisation-related inflows, cutting policy interest rates to all-time lows and intervening in the foreign exchange market. Continued fiscal expansion may, however, require a tightening in policy rates.

Exports should pick up again, and inflation will return to target

Recovery in western Europe and improved production potential, resulting from ongoing industrial restructuring driven by foreign-investment firms, should result in an export-driven expansion despite the strong koruna. GDP growth is expected to pick up from 2 per cent in 2002 to 3 per cent in 2003 and 3½ per cent in 2004. The large fiscal impulses of 2002-03 will diminish in 2004 but by then household income growth should pick up to sustain private consumption growth and investment should also pick up, bringing output close to its potential level. Assuming exchange-rate stability, inflation is likely to increase to within the corridor targeted by the Central Bank within a year and remain within that range, despite a likely uptick in prices connected with indirect tax harmonisation prior to EU accession. Dependent employment is projected to decline again this year, reflecting punitive payroll tax rates, but the continued strong growth of self-employment may result in a small increase in total employment. This pattern of unbalanced and subdued employment growth is likely to persist over the projection period and is consistent with a slow decline of the unemployment rate, as measured in the labour force survey. Aside from the possibility of another delay in the recovery in western Europe, the most serious downward risk to the economic expansion would be posed by the adoption of a weak fiscal consolidation programme which fails to control the growth of social transfers. That would undermine policy credibility, erode confidence and lead to additional monetary tightening, while having negative impacts on competitiveness.

Denmark

The pace of activity has slowed in the face of weak exports, although domestic demand remains firm. Growth prospects are expected to brighten as the international situation improves and firms regain sufficient confidence to increase investment and hiring. Unemployment has drifted upwards but is still lower than its structural rate. Labour shortages could re-emerge as the expansion quickens, accompanied by accelerating wages.

With accommodating monetary conditions, the tax cuts planned for 2004 need to be accompanied by concrete measures to trim expenditure growth to avoid adding unhelpful stimulus to an economy already operating close to capacity. Further initiatives to get more people into work and reduce reliance on public benefits would help to ease these pressures.

The Danish economy was treading water in the second half of last year as the weakness in foreign markets finally impacted and exports fell marginally. Private consumption continued to rise at an annualised rate of around 2¼ per cent in the second half of last year, but a fall in consumer confidence and car sales around the beginning of the year portends some hesitation about spending in the first half of 2003. Business indicators suggest that production may remain sluggish in the first half of this year, as new orders have softened again and confidence remains weak: this may lead to a postponement of some business investment plans until prospects brighten. Nevertheless, additions to capacity along with shrinking private sector employment over the course of 2002 have boosted labour productivity. Job creation has continued in the public sector, albeit at a reduced annual pace of around ½ per cent. This has attenuated the impact of cyclical weakness on unemployment, with the standardised rate standing at 4¾ per cent in the first quarter of this year. This is lower than the OECD estimate of its structural level. Compensation per employee has decelerated a little, but overall the labour market remains relatively tight, while output remains only slightly below estimated potential.

Domestic activity remains solid, but exports have faltered

Monetary policy continues to mirror developments in the euro area, as the National Bank keeps the krone within narrow bands around its central parity *vis-à-vis* the euro. Monetary conditions may remain relatively easy over the projection period, given that Denmark's cyclical position is stronger than that of the euro area.

Monetary conditions will support growth

— Denmark —

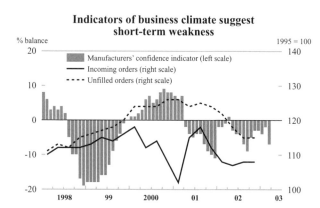

Consumption growth remains solid

Indicators of business climate suggest short-term weakness

1. 4-quarter moving average.
Source: Statistics Denmark; OECD.

————————— Denmark: **Demand, output and prices** —————————

	1999	2000	2001	2002	2003	2004
	Current prices billion DKK	Percentage changes, volume (1995 prices)				
Private consumption	599.5	-1.9	0.4	2.1	1.9	2.2
Government consumption	312.1	1.1	2.1	0.9	1.0	0.9
Gross fixed capital formation	240.9	9.1	1.3	1.3	1.1	3.2
Final domestic demand	1 152.6	1.3	1.0	1.6	1.5	2.1
Stockbuilding [a]	- 2.6	0.6	-0.3	-0.4	0.2	0.0
Total domestic demand	1 149.9	2.0	0.8	1.2	1.7	2.1
Exports of goods and services	459.6	13.1	3.2	3.4	3.1	7.5
Imports of goods and services	401.8	11.9	1.8	2.5	3.5	7.1
Net exports [a]	57.8	0.9	0.7	0.5	0.0	0.6
GDP at market prices	1 207.7	2.8	1.4	1.6	1.6	2.6
GDP deflator	_	3.1	2.0	1.1	2.4	2.6
Memorandum items						
Consumer price index	_	2.9	2.4	2.4	2.4	2.3
Private consumption deflator	_	3.5	2.6	2.3	2.3	2.3
Unemployment rate	_	4.4	4.3	4.5	4.7	4.4
Household saving ratio [b]	_	4.8	6.0	6.2	6.0	6.1
General government financial balance [c]	_	2.5	2.8	1.8	1.6	1.9
Current account balance [c]	_	1.5	3.1	2.9	2.9	3.6

a) Contributions to changes in real GDP (percentage of real GDP in previous year), actual amount in the first column.
b) As a percentage of disposable income.
c) As a percentage of GDP.
Source: OECD.

Tax cuts could add further stimulus

Fiscal policy is expected to add some stimulus to activity next year, as it remains unclear whether the government will succeed in constraining public expenditure growth sufficiently to offset the announced tax cuts. The general government surplus looks set to strengthen to almost 2 per cent of GDP in 2004, but further spending restraint will be needed to finance the planned tax cuts to 2007.

The pick up in activity could lead to supply pressures

The rate of expansion is expected to be modest in the first half of this year, as consumers and businesses postpone some spending, but then to quicken from the second half to reach around 2½ per cent in 2004. Export growth is projected to rebound as global demand accelerates, while the stimulus from easy monetary conditions and tax cuts should underpin private domestic demand. Employment is likely to expand again next year by around ½ per cent, with a corresponding fall in the unemployment rate. With real GDP increasing faster than its potential rate next year, the output gap is likely to close, and labour shortages could start to re-emerge. This is likely to lead to some acceleration in wages and prices. The main source of risk is the evolution of foreign demand.

Finland

A recent deterioration in the international outlook suggests that last years' recovery may be stalled until the second half of 2003. Once world trade picks up, the rise in exports should lead both to a revival in investment and a closing of the output gap, although unemployment will remain above the euro area average.

The surge in government consumption, if sustained, is likely to endanger the previous government's fiscal targets, which are appropriate in the light of imminent budget pressures from an ageing population. It will also severely constrain any scope for much-needed cuts in the tax burden on labour, which are needed to address high structural unemployment.

GDP in the fourth quarter of 2002 was 2¾ per cent higher than a year earlier, compared to a rise of only 1¼ per cent for the euro area as a whole. Much of this recovery was driven by exports, which were up 7 per cent over the same period, with the output of the main exporting industries, electronics and forestry, up 20 and 10 per cent, respectively. Most of these gains were made in the middle of the year, but the outlook appears to have deteriorated rapidly since the start of 2003, with a fall in survey measures of business confidence which are usually a reliable leading indicator. These developments are related to the deteriorating outlook for international demand, particularly from the rest of the euro area. The continued appreciation of the euro may also mean that many export industries will struggle to maintain market share, although this is probably less true for mobile telephone exports, where there may be scope to cut profit margins.

The outlook has deteriorated sharply

The deterioration in export prospects, combined with weak business investment, which had already fallen sharply at the end of 2002, suggests growth in the first half of 2003 may be meagre and dependent on the buoyancy of consumption and an expansionary fiscal stance. Thereafter, as world trade recovers, higher exports should lead to a revival in business investment and stockbuilding, generating growth of about 3½ per cent in 2004. Unemployment, which has remained stubbornly high at just over 9 per cent, is unlikely to fall much below that level by 2004.

Growth will not exceed potential until 2004

Inflation as measured by the Harmonised Index of Consumer Prices fell to 1½ per cent at the beginning of 2003, below the euro area average. With the output gap opening up and the euro appreciating, inflation is likely to decline further. Nevertheless, the

Inflation will fall

Finland

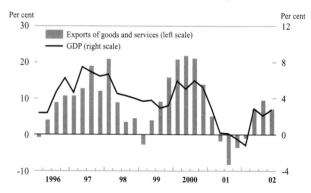

Industrial output and confidence are weak

Exports are the key to recovery[1]

1. Seasonally-adjusted volume data, growth over same period of previous year.
Source: Statistics Finland, Eurostat and OECD.

─────────────────── Finland: **Demand, output and prices** ───────────────────

	1999	2000	2001	2002	2003	2004
	Current prices billion euros	Percentage changes, volume (2000 prices)				
Private consumption	60.2	3.3	1.7	2.1	2.3	2.1
Government consumption	25.9	0.4	1.2	4.0	2.0	2.0
Gross fixed capital formation	23.6	4.0	3.8	-1.0	-1.3	2.6
Final domestic demand	109.7	2.8	2.0	1.8	1.4	2.2
Stockbuilding *a*	0.0	0.9	-0.2	-1.2	0.3	0.5
Total domestic demand	109.7	3.7	1.8	0.6	1.8	2.8
Exports of goods and services	45.3	19.3	-2.3	5.6	3.1	6.9
Imports of goods and services	35.1	16.9	-0.2	1.7	3.5	6.3
Net exports *a*	10.2	2.2	-0.9	1.8	0.1	0.9
GDP at market prices	120.0	5.5	0.6	1.6	2.2	3.4
GDP deflator	_	2.9	3.6	1.3	1.5	1.3
Memorandum items						
Consumer price index	_	3.0	2.7	2.0	1.4	1.2
Private consumption deflator	_	3.7	3.4	1.7	2.3	1.5
Unemployment rate	_	9.8	9.2	9.1	9.2	9.0
General government financial balance *b*	_	6.9	5.1	4.7	3.1	2.9
Current account balance *b*	_	7.7	7.1	7.6	6.7	7.2

a) Contributions to changes in real GDP (percentage of real GDP in previous year), actual amount in the first column.
b) As a percentage of GDP.
Source: OECD.

extent of any fall will be limited by wage agreements already in place that imply average wages will increase by around 4 per cent in 2003 and 3 per cent in 2004.

The fiscal stance may be easing

The fiscal projections, particularly for 2004, are somewhat speculative given continuing discussions on the nature of a new coalition government following the March general election. Tax revenues are likely to be weak as the one-off factors that boosted corporate tax revenues and brought forward the payment of capital gains tax into 2002 expire, and as indirect tax revenues on alcohol and tobacco are reduced in 2004 due to European Union harmonisation measures. On the expenditure side there was a sharp increase in real general government consumption of 4 per cent in 2002, although one percentage point of this increase is of a technical nature relating to a sectoral re-classification of activities. Nevertheless, the underlying increase conflicts with the previous government's stated objective of holding central government expenditure (albeit more broadly defined) at its 1999 level in real terms. Given budget commitments, real expenditure is likely to increase further in 2003. If this momentum carries forward, the general government surplus could fall by almost two per cent of GDP by 2004. Whilst this would still imply a surplus of nearly 3 per cent of GDP in 2004, it would mean that the surplus objectives of the previous government, set at 3½ per cent of GDP for general government and 1½ to 2 per cent of GDP for central government, would be missed.

Major risks relate to the upswing in world trade

The major risk concerns the timing of the upswing in world trade, which if delayed might lead to labour shedding and falls in consumer confidence and demand. On the other hand, there is also scope for upside surprises if there is a positive reaction to the third generation of mobile phones. A boom in the electronics industry on the scale experienced in the second half of the 1990s would lift trend potential growth for the whole economy by as much as ½ per cent *per annum*, though such a scenario is no doubt an optimistic one.

Greece

Real GDP continued to grow strongly year-on-year in 2002, but slowed in the second half when both domestic and external demand weakened. Output growth is set to pick up again during 2003, driven by a recovery in foreign demand and strong investment growth. Inflation, though easing, is expected to remain above the euro area average, partly reflecting differences in cyclical positions. The current account deficit, which edged up to 6½ per cent of GDP in 2002, is projected to narrow gradually.

The necessary rapid reduction of the high debt-to-GDP ratio requires tighter control of primary government expenditure and greater efficiency in public sector administration. Recent steps to reform the social security and tax systems are welcome. Further structural reforms in the labour and product markets, including a more determined opening of network industries to competition, are essential for sustained non-inflationary growth.

The economy expanded briskly in 2002, despite the global slowdown. Real output is estimated to have grown by 4 per cent year-on-year, continuing to outpace the euro area average. Growth was boosted by strong government consumption and solid investment, driven by low real interest rates, rapidly expanding housing loans, the inflows from the Third Community Support Framework and preparations for the 2004 Olympic Games. Private consumption also remained robust, underpinned by buoyant consumer credit, generous wage awards and tax cuts. However, the growing uncertainty surrounding global economic prospects and the continuing slump of the stock market have sapped confidence, and output growth slowed in the second half. Average unemployment in 2002 remained high, at around 10 per cent. The current account deficit increased somewhat in 2002, to 6½ per cent of GDP.

Output growth has slowed and the current account deficit has widened

Harmonised consumer price inflation, although falling from its early 2002 spike, averaged 3.9 per cent in 2002, with the differential *vis-à-vis* the euro area rising to 1.7 percentage points. Bad weather conditions and the rise in energy prices added further to headline inflation in early 2003. Core inflation also remained high, averaging 3.6 per cent in 2002, with service prices rising particularly fast.

The inflation differential with the euro area remained high

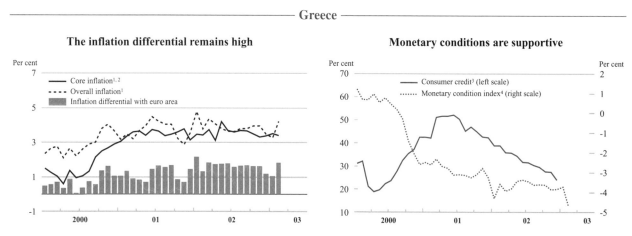

Greece

The inflation differential remains high

Per cent

— Core inflation[1,2]
- - - Overall inflation[1]
▓ Inflation differential with euro area

Monetary conditions are supportive

Per cent / Per cent

— Consumer credit[3] (left scale)
······ Monetary condition index[4] (right scale)

1. Harmonised index of consumer price, year-on-year percentage changes.
2. Excluding energy, food, alcohol and tobacco.
3. Year-on-year percentage changes. Provisional data for December 2002.
4. Weighted sum of the relative change in the real effective exchange rate and the absolute change in the short-term real interest rate compared with their 1995-2002 average.
Source: OECD; Bank of Greece.

———————————— Greece: **Demand, output and prices** ————————————

	1999	2000	2001	2002	2003	2004
	Current prices billion euros	Percentage changes, volume (1995 prices)				
Private consumption	79.8	2.6	2.9	2.5	2.7	2.9
Government consumption	17.4	2.0	-0.9	6.2	0.0	0.2
Gross fixed capital formation [a]	24.5	8.0	5.9	6.7	8.6	6.8
Final domestic demand	121.6	3.7	3.0	3.9	3.7	3.5
Stockbuilding [b,c]	- 0.4	0.3	0.1	0.0	0.0	0.0
Total domestic demand	121.3	3.9	3.1	3.9	3.7	3.5
Exports of goods and services	23.1	19.7	-1.6	-4.5	2.9	7.3
Imports of goods and services	31.5	14.5	-3.4	-2.7	3.3	5.2
Net exports [b]	- 8.4	-0.1	0.7	-0.2	-0.3	0.1
GDP at market prices	112.9	4.2	4.1	4.0	3.6	3.9
GDP deflator	_	3.4	3.4	3.7	3.5	3.6
Memorandum items	_					
Consumer price index	_	2.9	3.7	3.9	3.4	3.5
Private consumption deflator	_	3.2	3.1	3.5	3.3	3.4
Unemployment rate	_	11.1	10.4	10.0	9.5	9.1
General government financial balance [d]	_	-1.9	-1.4[e]	-1.2	-1.0	-0.7
Current account balance [d,f]	_	-6.9	-6.2	-6.5	-6.2	-5.8

a) Excluding ships operating overseas.
b) Contributions to changes in real GDP (percentage of real GDP in previous year), actual amount in the first column.
c) Including statistical discrepancy.
d) As a percentage of GDP.
e) Including proceeds of sales of mobile telephone licences (around 0.5 per cent of GDP).
f) On settlement data basis.
Source: OECD.

Monetary conditions are supportive...

Despite the sharp appreciation of the euro, monetary conditions remained easy in 2002, with real short-term interest rates averaging around zero. Although consumer credit expansion has slowed, it was still growing by around 24 per cent in December 2002 (year-on-year), while housing loans expanded by 36 per cent.

... while the fiscal balance is in modest deficit

The general government deficit is now estimated at 1.2 per cent of GDP in 2002, broadly unchanged from the previous year. The 2003 budget targets a deficit of 0.9 per cent of GDP. It includes a new tax package as part of the ongoing comprehensive reform of the tax system, with an estimated fiscal cost of between 0.8 and 1 per cent of GDP, spread over the period 2003-04. The budget balance is projected by the OECD to improve gradually to a deficit of 0.7 per cent of GDP by 2004.

Output growth is expected to pick up in the course of 2003

Economic activity is expected to rebound in the course of 2003, in line with the international recovery. Because of the weak carry-over, year-on-year growth may ease to 3½ per cent in 2003, before edging up to around 4 per cent in 2004. Activity should continue to benefit from the preparations for the 2004 Olympic Games, low interest rates and the inflows of European structural funds. Moreover, the implementation of the new tax package included in the 2003 Budget, along with further employment gains, should stimulate consumption expenditure. Imports are expected to pick up but the recovery in world demand should also boost exports, eliminating the drag from the external sector in 2004. Inflation is projected to decline, but is likely to remain around 3½ per cent over the next two years because of strong domestic activity. A downward risk to the outlook is that the international slowdown may become more protracted than envisaged.

Hungary

Activity remained strong through 2002 in spite of the international slowdown, because of an exceptional electoral fiscal stimulus. A transition from fiscal to export-led growth will begin in 2003 but, because of important competitiveness losses and the delayed international recovery, GDP growth will ease somewhat before picking up in 2004.

The policy mix needs to be rebalanced. A credible medium-term public expenditure framework should be introduced to help consolidation. Monetary easing is welcome but should depend on the ability of the social partners to moderate wage growth consistent with inflation targets.

The economy bottomed out in the second half of 2001 and strengthened through the election year 2002 on the back of very strong household income and consumption growth stimulated by government policies, in particular increases in the minimum wage and strong public sector wage rises. The fiscal impulse also entailed growing government consumption and investment. In spite of an absolute fall in private business investment, final domestic demand grew by over 7 per cent.

Exceptional fiscal stimulus fueled domestic demand...

GDP growth remained moderate, however, because of a negative swing in the contribution of stockbuilding and net exports amounting to over 4 per cent of GDP. Competitiveness losses resulting from rapid wage growth and currency appreciation – a combination leading to the largest relative unit labour cost increases in the OECD area in 2002 – hit the service balance particularly hard. Manufacturing exports initially resisted well, but strains became apparent at the end of the year. In spite of decelerating imports of capital goods and export-related inputs, the current account deficit rose from 3.4 per cent of GDP in 2001 to 4 per cent in 2002 (in spite of a favourable effect from the change in measurement methodology). Supported by temporary factors, including the slowdown of international prices, continuing restraint on regulated prices and currency appreciation, inflation ended the year at 4.8 per cent, close to the central value of the inflation target ($4\frac{1}{2} \pm 1$).

... but competitiveness losses moderated the impact on growth

The general government deficit of 8.4 per cent of GDP[1] would need to come down substantially in 2003, if the government is to meet its domestic and international commitments. The authorities declared an ESA95 deficit target of less than $4\frac{1}{2}$ per cent of GDP for 2003 and their strategy of achieving euro area eligibility by 2007-08 implies bringing the deficit below 3 per cent by 2005. Several factors make this difficult to achieve,

Fiscal consolidation is needed, as monetary policy is constrained

Hungary

The policy mix is unbalanced

Competitiveness has deteriorated

1. The index measures the change in the real interest rate and the real exchange rate, an increase represents a tightening. See Sources and Methods.
2. In 1998 prices.
3. Unit labour costs in manufacturing in US dollars relative to a weighted average of those of trade partners. An increase in the index indicates a deterioration of the competitive position.
Source: OECD.

1. OECD estimate for 2002 based on GFS data and aiming at approximating the main ESA adjustments while excluding all government liabilities incurred in previous years.

——————————— Hungary: **Demand, output and prices** ———————————

	1999	2000	2001	2002	2003	2004
	Current prices billion HUF	Percentage changes, volume (1998 prices)				
Private consumption	5 974.0	4.4	4.9	9.8	5.5	3.8
Government consumption	2 454.8	1.9	0.1	2.6	1.4	0.0
Gross fixed capital formation	2 724.5	7.7	3.1	5.9	2.6	2.1
Final domestic demand	11 153.4	4.7	3.4	7.3	4.0	2.6
Stockbuilding [a]	523.4	0.7	-1.2	-1.7	0.2	0.6
Total domestic demand	11 676.8	5.1	2.1	5.3	4.0	3.1
Exports of goods and services	6 038.3	21.8	9.1	5.9	4.6	8.0
Imports of goods and services	6 321.6	21.1	6.3	8.9	5.8	7.0
Net exports [a]	- 283.3	0.0	1.7	-2.0	-1.0	0.5
GDP at market prices	11 393.5	5.2	3.8	3.3	3.1	3.7
GDP deflator	–	9.7	9.0	8.8	7.1	4.3
Memorandum items						
Consumer price index	–	9.8	9.2	5.3	5.2	4.6
Private consumption deflator	–	9.9	8.6	4.5	5.1	4.5
Unemployment rate	–	6.5	5.8	5.9	6.0	6.4
General government financial balance[b,c]	–	-2.9	-5.2	-8.4	-5.6	-5.0
Current account balance [b]	–	-6.3	-3.4	-4.0	-4.5	-3.8

a) Contributions to changes in real GDP (percentage of real GDP in previous year), actual amount in the first column.
b) As a percentage of GDP.
c) OECD estimate which adjusts official GSF data, see *Economic Survey of Hungary,* 2002.
Source: OECD.

including the fiscal carry-over from the autumn 2002 wage increases, political promises to maintain the level of social transfers and official growth projections of 4 per cent for 2003 that appear optimistic in view of the deterioration of competitiveness. The OECD projects that the withdrawal of fiscal stimulus will begin in 2003 but at a slower rate than planned by the government. The Central Bank expects headline inflation to reach 5.2 per cent at the end of 2003, well above the initial target of 2½ to 4½ per cent. This reflects the phasing out of temporary disinflation factors and the lagged effect of wage increases. At the same time, strong currency appreciation – reflecting the confirmation of European Union accession prospects and the expectation of monetary tightening – pushed the Central Bank to cut policy rates by 300 basis points. This is not sustainable in a domestically driven excess demand environment without undermining the credibility of the inflation targets. To soften the monetary policy dilemma between inflation and competitiveness objectives fiscal consolidation is needed; but since such consolidation is expected to be slow, monetary tightening is assumed through the projection period.

Growth depends on the international recovery and restored competitiveness

GDP growth is projected to decelerate to just above 3 per cent in 2003, but to pick up again with the international recovery. However, growth acceleration depends on the restoration of Hungary's international competitiveness through wage moderation and strong productivity growth, which entails some increase in unemployment. The resulting slowdown in household incomes and consumption should be offset by the recovery of business investment, including foreign direct investment. The projection would be put at risk if wage and public spending were not to moderate to the extent assumed, with consequences on competitiveness and fiscal balances. The further tightening of monetary conditions that would be required in this case could well abort the fragile expansion.

Iceland

With major imbalances having been corrected, recovery is likely to gather pace around the middle of the year when large-scale investments in power-intensive industries will begin to boost demand and push growth above potential rates.

Tighter monetary conditions will be required once growth picks up and a positive output gap re-emerges in order to prevent overheating in the middle of the decade. Fiscal policy will need to support this effort by moving toward a restrictive stance. In particular, it will be important to avoid an overlap of public infrastructure investments with the gearing-up of the power-intensive projects.

The economy shrank by ½ per cent in 2002. The upturn in the latter part of the year was modest and activity seems to have strengthened little since then. While there has been a revival in private consumption and residential construction appears to have kept growing, business investment has remained depressed. At the same time, the growth contribution of net exports has decreased. The current account has nevertheless remained in broad balance. Sluggish growth has meant that the unemployment rate has kept rising, exceeding 3 per cent in seasonally-adjusted terms. This has contributed to a marked fall in wage drift. Helped by a renewed strengthening in the exchange rate, consumer price inflation has eased to around 2 per cent, which is a remarkable turnaround given that it was almost 10 per cent at the beginning of 2002. Underlying inflation has also been below or at the central bank's 2½ per cent target.

Recovery has been hesitant...

Against this backdrop and the weaker-than-expected momentum of the economy, the central bank reduced its policy interest rate further, to 5.3 per cent in mid-February, the lowest level since 1994. The projections assume a gradual rise in the policy interest rate beginning in the second half of this year. Indeed, inflation expectations have already drifted upward somewhat, probably reflecting the impact of the forthcoming major investment projects. The timing and magnitude of interest-rate increases will depend on the momentum of the economy and further currency developments, but it would seem that much of the adjustment of the equilibrium exchange rate to the expected effects of the investment projects has already occurred. In keeping with their stated policy principles, the authorities intended to maintain a modest

... prompting monetary and fiscal easing...

Iceland

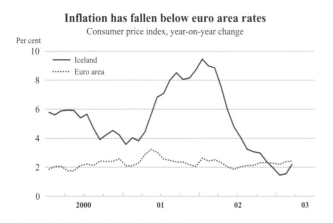

Inflation has fallen below euro area rates
Consumer price index, year-on-year change

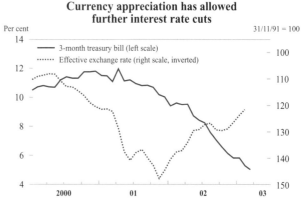

Currency appreciation has allowed further interest rate cuts

Source: Central Bank, Statistics Iceland and OECD.

—————————————— Iceland: **Demand, output and prices** ——————————————

	1999	2000	2001	2002	2003	2004
	Current prices billion ISK	Percentage changes, volume (1990 prices)				
Private consumption	358.7	4.0	-3.0	-1.2	0.5	2.0
Government consumption	142.1	3.8	2.9	3.1	2.0	2.5
Gross fixed capital formation	135.0	14.8	-6.3	-13.0	10.6	11.2
Final domestic demand	635.8	6.3	-2.7	-3.0	2.8	4.1
Stockbuilding *a*	0.1	0.5	-0.9	0.4	0.0	0.2
Total domestic demand	635.9	6.7	-3.4	-2.6	2.8	4.3
Exports of goods and services	212.2	5.0	7.9	2.9	4.0	4.5
Imports of goods and services	241.5	8.0	-9.0	-2.4	6.0	6.5
Net exports *a*	- 29.3	-1.6	6.8	2.0	-0.7	-0.8
GDP at market prices	606.6	5.5	3.1	-0.6	2.1	3.5
GDP deflator	_	2.9	9.1	5.2	2.8	3.2
Memorandum items						
Consumer price index	_	5.1	6.4	5.2	2.5	2.6
Private consumption deflator	_	4.5	8.1	3.9	2.5	2.6
Unemployment rate	_	2.3	2.3	3.1	3.3	3.0
General government financial balance *b*	_	2.5	0.5	0.2	0.0	0.1
Current account balance *b*	_	-10.3	-4.3	0.3	-0.2	-0.9

a) Contributions to changes in real GDP (percentage of real GDP in previous year), actual amount in the first column.
b) As a percentage of GDP.
Source: OECD.

budget surplus in 2003, similar to that achieved in the past two years, implying a slightly restrictive fiscal stance. But in February the government announced a substantial bringing forward of public investments planned for 2005-06 (mainly road building) that is now to be carried out over the rest of 2003 and 2004. This has been followed by similar announcements at the municipal level. Overall, however, the general government budget position seems likely to remain in broad balance.

... which should contribute to activity gathering momentum

Following modest economic expansion in the first half of this year, the construction of a hydropower facility in eastern Iceland and subsequent work on a new aluminium smelter that it would serve, along with public infrastructure investment, will lift growth above its estimated potential rate of just below 3 per cent. This should have spill-over effects on domestic demand, which has been held back by the need for repairing balance sheets after the spending spree in the late 1990s. Export demand is likely to be less supportive to growth than during the downturn, given the adverse effect on competitiveness of the higher exchange rate. However, higher fishing quotas and firming market growth should underpin exports going forward. With import demand picking up because of the increased construction, the current balance is expected to move into deficit. The unemployment rate is projected to peak at around 3½ per cent before receding gradually. Given the current slack in the economy, inflation is expected to remain near the target over the projection period. Nonetheless, inflationary pressures are likely to build as work on the aluminium-related investment projects accelerates in the middle of the decade, requiring a prompt and ideally pre-emptive policy response.

Ireland

After unexpected resilience in 2002, real GDP growth is forecast to slow to 3¼ per cent in 2003, before rebounding to 4¼ per cent in 2004 with the strengthening of export market growth. Wage pressure is expected to weaken throughout the forecast period. While inflation is also forecast to fall, it is likely to remain above the European Union average, reflecting persistent price pressures in the service sector.

Now that private sector wages have begun to adjust to slower growth, the planned increase in public sector pay should be strictly conditional upon demonstrated higher efficiency in that sector. The projected public finance position looks healthy, but its realisation will require significant efforts to tighten control over expenditures.

Real GDP growth in 2002 of around 6 per cent, itself a significant decline from the Celtic Tiger era, was largely accounted for by the strong performance of the bio-medical and pharmaceutical sectors. On the demand side, an absolute decline in machinery and equipment investment was more than offset by continued solid growth in housing construction, public investment and government consumption, associated with a sharp rise in public employment.

Output growth in 2002 was narrowly based...

The economy has lost momentum since late 2002, with a further slowdown in exports and a substantial weakening in business confidence. The purchasing manager index for manufacturers fell in March for the sixth successive month, while that for the service sector has remained almost flat. The demand for labour slackened throughout 2002, leading to a rise in the unemployment rate from its historical lows of 3.7 per cent in the first half of 2001 to 4.5 per cent in March 2003. Yet, inflation remains high due to rapid price increases in service-producing industries.

... and has lost momentum more recently

The adjustment in income expectations to a slower growth environment has begun to take hold. With acute shortages of labour having eased, the recent wage agreement of 7 per cent over the next eighteen months will help moderate wage growth and inflation. Public sector wages, however, are expected to rise sharply in 2003 and 2004 as the benchmarking exercise allows a phased level adjustment *vis-à-vis* equivalent jobs in the private sector.

Wages are set to moderate but not in the public sector

Ireland

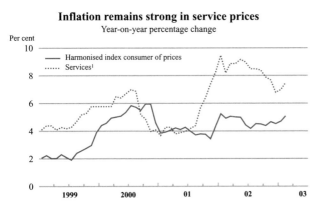

Inflation remains strong in service prices
Year-on-year percentage change

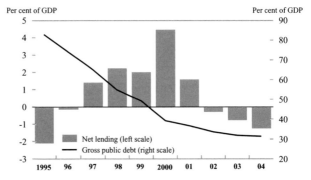

The budget balance continues to worsen[2]

1. The decline in inflation in Q4 2000 was associated with a change in the survey on the cost of child services from a yearly to quarterly frequency.
2. OECD estimates for 2002-2004.
Source: Central Statistics Office and OECD.

———————————— Ireland: **Demand, output and prices** ————————————

	1999	2000	2001	2002	2003	2004
	Current prices billion euros	Percentage changes, volume (1995 prices)				
Private consumption	43.2	9.0	5.0	2.5	3.0	3.5
Government consumption	12.5	7.6	10.5	8.7	1.5	0.7
Gross fixed capital formation	21.3	7.0	1.0	-0.7	-0.2	2.1
Final domestic demand	77.0	8.2	4.9	2.8	2.0	2.7
Stockbuilding [a]	0.4	0.3	-0.4	-0.2	0.2	0.1
Total domestic demand	77.4	8.5	4.4	2.5	2.2	2.7
Exports of goods and services	79.0	20.6	6.7	4.9	3.5	7.1
Imports of goods and services	66.6	21.2	6.1	1.8	3.0	6.5
Net exports [a]	12.4	2.4	1.6	3.6	1.1	1.8
GDP at market prices	89.8	10.0	6.0	6.0	3.2	4.2
GDP deflator	_	4.3	5.3	4.9	4.0	3.6
Memorandum items						
Consumer price index	_	5.3	4.0	4.7	4.1	3.2
Private consumption deflator	_	4.0	4.2	4.8	4.2	3.2
Unemployment rate	_	4.3	3.9	4.2	5.0	5.2
General government financial balance [b]	_	4.5	1.6	-0.3	-0.8	-1.2
Current account balance [b]	_	0.1	-0.3	-0.2	-1.1	0.8

a) Contributions to changes in real GDP (percentage of real GDP in previous year), actual amount in the first column.
b) As a percentage of GDP.
Source: OECD.

The 2003 budget accords better with the slower growth environment

The budget balance deteriorated, from a surplus of 4½ per cent of GDP in 2000 to an estimated deficit of 0.3 per cent in 2002. This reflected tax revenue shortfalls due to slower economic growth and tax measures, as well as continued strong spending pressures. The 2003 budget marks a departure from the two previous budgets, in that it relies on increased taxation and allows a smaller increase in spending. Tax revenue estimates are more cautious, while the rapid increase in government consumption is to be contained by limiting new recruitment. Even so, general government net borrowing is expected to increase to 0.8 per cent of GDP this year and further to 1.2 per cent in 2004. Spending pressure is likely to remain strong in such areas as infrastructure development, public sector pay and health care.

Growth will slacken in 2003 before rebounding

The current weak trend in activity is expected to prevail during 2003, but is forecast to give way to a modest acceleration in 2004 with the assumed recovery of export markets and the fading impact of euro appreciation. Private consumption is projected to increase at only a moderate rate, reflecting lower income growth, while government consumption is expected to slow sharply and business investment to continue to fall in 2003 before rebounding during 2004. On the other hand, both public and housing investment, the latter supported by favourable tax treatment and low interest rates, are projected to remain buoyant through the forecast period. Reflecting wage moderation and the impact of the past euro appreciation, consumer price inflation, as measured by the harmonised index, is expected to come down from 4¾ per cent in 2002 to 3¼ per cent in 2004. The extent of the decline in 2003 will be limited by the planned increase in public charges and indirect taxes.

Failure to control the public sector wage bill is a major risk

An open economy like Ireland will remain vulnerable to a further appreciation of the euro and geopolitical risks. Domestically, a major risk would be a failure actually to stop the rapid increase in public employment and to control public sector pay, which would adversely affect the fiscal position and/or inflation prospects.

Korea

Domestic demand decelerated at the end of 2002 in a context of geopolitical uncertainty that may continue well into 2003. Nevertheless, with a recovery in world demand expected in the second half of 2003, output growth may return to around 6 per cent in 2004. The unemployment rate is likely to remain near 3 per cent, while core inflation may rise to the top of the 2.5 to 3.5 per cent target range.

A gradual increase in interest rates may be necessary to keep inflation within its target zone, as the pace of growth picks up. Moving ahead with the privatisation of state-owned banks is important to cover part of the cost of financial-sector restructuring, while helping to promote corporate restructuring. Given this cost, as well as future spending pressures, the emphasis on fiscal consolidation has been appropriate.

Growth was more than 6 per cent in 2002 as a rebound in exports in the second half of the year took over from strong domestic demand, which weakened at the end of 2002. The buoyant Chinese economy was the key factor, with Korean exports to China rising nearly 50 per cent (year-on-year in dollar value) in the second half of 2002. With output accelerating, the unemployment rate fell to around 3 per cent, resulting in double-digit wage hikes. Despite a substantial increase in unit labour costs, core consumer price inflation has remained stable at around 3 per cent.

Output growth accelerated in 2002...

Domestic demand slowed in a context of geopolitical uncertainty that has led to a deterioration in household and business confidence and a 17 per cent fall in the stock market since October. In addition, policies to restrain bank lending to households – which soared more than 50 per cent during the first nine months of 2002 – have dampened private consumption. Such steps reflected concern about the increased exposure of banks to households, which have raised their financial liabilities from 86 per cent of their disposable income in 1998 to an estimated 120 per cent at the end of 2002. The government has also introduced a series of tax and regulatory measures to calm the overheated real estate market. Subsequently, apartment prices stabilised in the final quarter of 2002, following a 40 per cent rise since the beginning of 2001. This was accompanied by a decline in investment in housing, despite the continued relaxed stance of monetary policy. The overnight call rate has

... despite weakened confidence and policy measures to slow demand

Korea

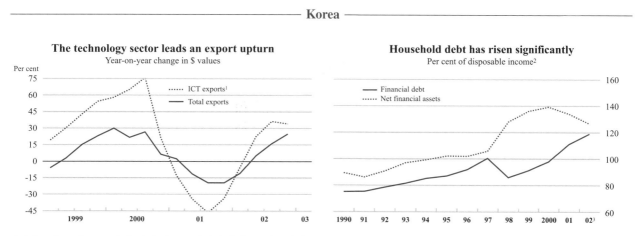

The technology sector leads an export upturn
Year-on-year change in $ values

······ ICT exports[1]
—— Total exports

Household debt has risen significantly
Per cent of disposable income[2]

—— Financial debt
······ Net financial assets

1. Information and communication technology products, including semi-conductors.
2. Financial assets and liabilities of the individual sector. OECD estimates of disposable income for 2001 and 2002.
3. End of June 2002.
Source: Bank of Korea and Korea Statistical Office.

––––––––––––––––––––––––– Korea: **Demand, output and prices** –––––––––––––––––––––––––

	1999	2000	2001	2002	2003	2004
	Current prices trillion KRW	Percentage changes, volume (1995 prices)				
Private consumption	271.1	7.9	4.7	6.8	3.2	4.3
Government consumption	50.1	0.1	1.3	2.9	2.0	2.0
Gross fixed capital formation	134.2	11.4	-1.8	4.8	2.4	5.0
Final domestic demand	455.4	8.2	2.3	5.8	2.8	4.3
Stockbuilding *a*	- 5.4	-0.2	-0.1	-0.2	0.0	0.0
Total domestic demand	450.0	8.1	2.2	5.7	2.9	4.4
Exports of goods and services	204.4	20.5	0.7	14.9	12.8	11.9
Imports of goods and services	171.3	20.0	-3.0	16.4	11.4	11.5
Net exports *a*	33.1	3.1	1.4	2.0	2.7	2.4
Statistical discrepancy *a*	- 0.4	-0.7	-0.2	-0.4	0.0	0.0
GDP at market prices	482.7	9.3	3.1	6.3	5.2	6.0
GDP deflator	_	-1.1	2.5	1.7	0.5	1.4
Memorandum items						
Consumer price index	_	2.3	4.1	2.8	3.8	3.3
Private consumption deflator	_	2.2	4.1	3.0	3.8	3.3
Unemployment rate	_	4.1	3.7	3.0	3.2	3.0
Household saving ratio *b*	_	11.5	9.4	9.6	10.0	10.8
Consolidated central government balance *c*	_	1.1	1.3	3.8	1.0	1.4
Current account balance *c*	_	2.7	1.9	1.3	0.3	0.2

a) Contributions to changes in real GDP (percentage of real GDP in previous year), actual amount in the first column.
b) As a percentage of disposable income.
c) As a percentage of GDP.
Source: OECD.

remained at 4¼ per cent since May 2002, 25 basis points above its record low point set during the 2001 downturn.

Fiscal policy has been restrictive

The stance of fiscal policy in 2002 was somewhat restrictive, with the consolidated central government budget surplus rising from 1¼ per cent of GDP in 2001 to 3¾ per cent in 2002. Such an improvement should help cope with the costs incurred for financial-sector restructuring, amounting to a total of KRW 157 trillion (27 per cent of GDP). About half of this may be recovered through privatising state-owned banks and resolving non-performing loans. However, KRW 49 trillion of the remainder will be paid by the government budget between 2003 and 2006. Excluding such costs, the fiscal stance in 2003 appears slightly contractionary.

Sustaining the expansion depends on overseas demand

Economic growth is likely to decelerate to around 5¼ per cent in 2003 as a result of the weakness of domestic demand and a slowing in external demand in the first half of the year. Core inflation may pick up to around 3½ per cent in 2003, while the lagged effects of high oil prices are likely to push headline inflation to nearly 4 per cent, before moderating in 2004. Given the rise in household debt during the past few years and weak confidence, sustaining the expansion through 2004 is likely to depend on overseas demand. The projected pick-up in world trade beginning in the second half of 2003 may return output growth to 6 per cent in 2004. While the external environment is the major risk to a continued expansion, restructuring the large number of firms with weak balance sheets could pose a temporary drag on the economy. However, a rebound in the information and communications technology sector could lead to faster-than-expected growth.

Luxembourg

With the lead sector of the economy, financial services, still in difficulty, GDP is expected to stagnate in 2003, under-performing the European Union for the third year in a row. More recently, conditions in domestically oriented sectors have also deteriorated. As a consequence, overall activity will not turn around before mid-2003, when the economy should benefit from a recovery of international financial services markets.

Government expenditures should be brought in line with lower trend GDP growth (3 to 4 per cent) as soon as possible to avoid a sustained deterioration in the budget balance, which would disrupt confidence.

The economy lost further steam during 2002 and might currently be in recession. The financial sector contracted for the second consecutive year. Falling stock valuations depressed prices and volumes of financial transactions, leading to a significant decline in services exports (representing about 100 per cent of GDP) and terms of trade. The difficulties in international activities spread to domestic demand in the second half of 2002. Retail data and consumer confidence indicate weakening private consumption, while construction orders point to falling residential investment and delayed implementation of public investment projects.

Economic growth is slow

Growth in domestic employment has slowed sharply but has remained positive, pointing to poor productivity outcomes. Many firms kept hiring for fear of not finding enough staff during the next upswing in sectors that had experienced bottlenecks in the recent past. This may explain why growth in employment of cross-border workers has not fallen further but rather levelled off at about 4.5 per cent year-on-year since mid-2002. National employment, however, is currently expanding by less than the resident labour force, leading to an increase in the unemployment rate, which edged up by 1 percentage point during the last six months to 3.8 per cent in January. Softening labour markets and earlier declines in inflation contributed to wage pressures easing considerably in 2002 (wages are indexed). Headline inflation was broadly stable, as underlying inflation decreased and energy prices increased.

Unemployment is rising

From 2000 to 2002 the budget surplus fell from over 6 to 2½ per cent of GDP, reflecting weak GDP growth and a structural deterioration. Tax cuts (amounting to 1.2 per cent of GDP in 2001 and 2.5 per cent in 2002) were accompanied by real

The budgetary situation has deteriorated significantly

Luxembourg

The financial sector has under-performed other sectors[1]

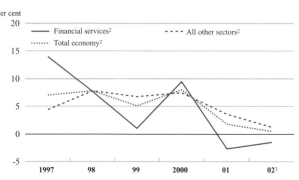

Confidence indicators point to weak activity[4]

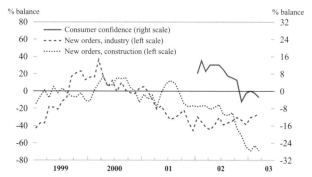

1. Real value added.
2. Year-on-year percentage changes.
3. Estimate.
4. Balance of positive and negative replies.
Source: Central Service of Statistics and Economic Studies (STATEC); Central Bank of Luxembourg and OECD.

———————————— Luxembourg: **Demand, output and prices** ————————————

	1999	2000	2001	2002	2003	2004
	Current prices billion euros	Percentage changes, volume (1995 prices)				
Private consumption	8.1	3.3	3.6	1.6	0.2	1.5
Government consumption	3.1	4.3	7.5	6.3	6.5	3.2
Gross fixed capital formation	4.5	-6.3	5.9	-4.3	-3.1	3.4
Final domestic demand	15.7	0.7	5.0	1.0	0.7	2.3
Stockbuilding [a]	0.1	-0.9	1.0	0.0	0.0	0.2
Total domestic demand	15.7	-0.3	6.3	1.0	0.7	2.5
Exports of goods and services	25.3	19.1	1.2	-1.7	0.1	4.8
Imports of goods and services	22.5	14.0	4.5	-2.2	0.4	5.0
Net exports [a]	2.8	8.3	-4.0	0.5	-0.4	0.5
GDP at market prices	18.6	8.9	1.0	0.5	0.3	2.7
GDP deflator	_	2.8	2.3	0.2	0.6	2.2
Memorandum items						
Consumer price index	_	3.8	2.4	2.1	2.3	1.2
Private consumption deflator	_	2.6	2.8	2.2	2.2	1.4
Unemployment rate	_	2.6	2.6	3.0	4.0	3.9
General government financial balance [b]	_	6.1	6.4	2.6	0.2	-1.0

a) Contributions to changes in real GDP (percentage of real GDP in previous year), actual amount in the first column.
b) As a percentage of GDP.
Source: OECD.

government consumption and investment expenditures growing by 6½ per cent per year on average. Exceptionally strong corporate income tax revenues, due to particular efforts to reduce tax arrears, prevented the balance from deteriorating even more. This effect will also boost revenues in 2003 but not in 2004. The government plans to restrict growth in nominal expenditure to 5 per cent in 2004, a rate that is judged to be compatible with a stable share of expenditure in trend GDP. Nevertheless, there is projected to be a further deterioration in the budget balance, which will swing into deficit.

The recovery is contingent on financial markets turning around

As business conditions are weak, firms are likely to cut investment and gradually revise labour hoarding policies, leading to a slight decline in private sector employment during the summer. Nevertheless, with equity prices stabilising and financial market volatility returning towards more normal levels, a gradual recovery in the financial sector could begin later this year. Moreover, the revival of growth in the euro area will boost goods exports. The recovery will spill over to the domestic economy in 2004. Inflation is likely to come down broadly in line with that in the euro area in the course of 2003 and even below in 2004, because of the larger weight of energy products. Indexation arrangements could turn out to be a risk for competitiveness if oil prices were to be higher than assumed. Another risk to the outlook would be further falls in asset prices.

Mexico

The economy is experiencing a weak recovery, based on higher exports of manufactures to the United States. GDP growth is expected to gather pace as confidence improves and firms increase investment. The passthrough from currency depreciation will be moderated by tight policies and inflation is expected to fall. The current account deficit, which narrowed to a record low in 2002, is expected to widen gradually as activity gains momentum.

Economic policies were tightened in 2002 and early 2003 in the context of a weaker peso and stalling disinflation. This stance needs to be maintained to keep disinflation and fiscal consolidation on target and retain market confidence. Implementation of the reform of the electricity industry and the tax system would boost investor confidence and growth prospects.

Growth remained sluggish in the second half of 2002, despite a recovery in exports to the United States. Reflecting higher oil prices and still weak import demand, the current account deficit narrowed in 2002, to $14 billion (2¼ per cent of GDP). Net foreign direct investment totalled close to that amount. The peso has depreciated significantly since its April 2002 peak, reflecting uncertainties related to the US economy – with which the Mexican cycle is highly synchronised – and the lack of progress in structural reform. Disinflation stalled after mid-year, reflecting hikes in administered prices (gas and electricity) and farm prices. Consumer price inflation was 5.7 per cent in December, exceeding the central bank target by more than 1 percentage point. However, core inflation was much below this, as weak activity damped the passthrough from import prices and the monetary stance was tightened. At the beginning of 2003, the strength of the economic upturn remained uncertain: investment was still strongly negative while employment picked up slightly in the formal sector.

Exports underpin the still weak recovery

The public sector financial deficit would have come in at 0.7 per cent of GDP, just below target in 2002, but the cost of liquidating a small development bank and creating a new institution for the rural sector pushed it up to 1¼ per cent of GDP. Meanwhile, the broader public sector borrowing requirement (PSBR) was below 3 per cent of GDP. Higher oil revenue in the second half of 2002 helped to offset lower-than-budgeted tax receipts, so that spending did not have to be cut again. The

Fiscal and monetary policies remain tight

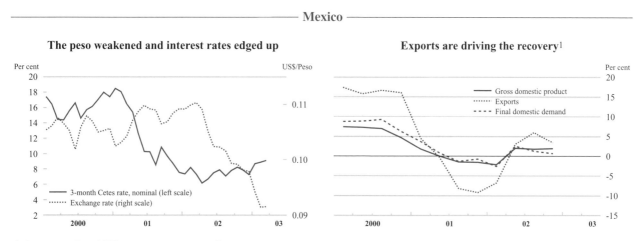

Mexico

The peso weakened and interest rates edged up   **Exports are driving the recovery**[1]

1. At constant prices of 1993, year-on-year percentage change.
Source: OECD, Bank of Mexico.

—————————————— Mexico: **Demand, output and prices** ——————————————

	1999	2000	2001	2002	2003	2004
	Current prices billion MXN	Percentage changes, volume (1993 prices)				
Private consumption	3 084.1	8.2	2.7	1.2	2.4	4.2
Government consumption	506.5	2.0	-1.2	-1.3	2.8	3.0
Gross fixed capital formation	973.8	11.4	-5.8	-1.3	3.0	5.5
Final domestic demand	4 564.4	8.2	0.6	0.5	2.6	4.3
Stockbuilding *a*	109.3	0.3	-0.2	0.5	0.0	0.3
Total domestic demand	4 673.7	8.3	0.4	1.0	2.5	4.4
Exports of goods and services	1 414.3	16.4	-3.6	1.4	5.2	8.2
Imports of goods and services	1 488.6	21.5	-1.5	1.6	4.8	9.3
Net exports *a*	- 74.2	-1.8	-0.7	-0.1	0.0	-0.7
GDP at market prices	4 599.4	6.6	-0.3	0.9	2.5	3.9
GDP deflator	–	12.2	6.4	4.6	4.1	3.6
Memorandum items						
Consumer price index	–	9.5	6.4	5.0	4.4	3.5
Private consumption deflator	–	10.3	7.2	4.8	4.4	3.5
Unemployment rate *b*	–	2.2	2.4	2.7	2.7	2.4
Current account balance *c*	–	-3.1	-2.9	-2.2	-2.5	-2.8

a) Contributions to changes in real GDP (percentage of real GDP in previous year), actual amount in the first column.
b) Based on the National Survey of Urban Employment.
c) As a percentage of GDP.
Source: OECD.

2003 public sector budget deficit is targeted at 0.5 per cent of GDP, with the objective of achieving balance by 2005, in line with the government medium-term programme. By then, the PSBR is to be brought down to around 2 per cent of GDP. The Central Bank tightened its policy stance three times in the first quarter of 2003, to bring inflation expectations down in line with the inflation target range of 3 per cent plus or minus 1 per cent at end year. The three-month *Cetes* rate, which was around 7 per cent in August, has moved back up to just below 9 per cent at the end of March. Real interest rates are assumed to remain close to their recent levels of about 5 per cent in 2003, edging down only slightly in 2004.

The recovery should gain momentum from mid-2003...   Improving labour market prospects should help restore consumer confidence from mid-2003 and exports are expected to quicken in line with foreign markets. But with no stimulus expected from macroeconomic policies and given the standstill on the reform agenda, the recovery in investment is likely to be slow and GDP growth could be more subdued than in the late 1990s. The current account deficit is expected to edge up to a little less than 3 per cent of GDP by 2004, mostly financed by foreign direct investment. Barring shocks to inflation from administered prices or farm prices, headline and core inflation should converge to within the Central Bank target range of 3 (±1) per cent by December 2003.

... depending on US growth and structural reforms   The main risks to the outlook concern external developments, including world oil prices, financial markets and, above all, the speed of the projected recovery in the United States. The main domestic uncertainty relates to Mexico's structural agenda. Approval of the tax and electricity reforms in particular would help to create an environment more supportive of private investment, including foreign direct investment, and GDP growth could be much stronger from early 2004.

Netherlands

Economic activity has weakened, but should begin to strengthen from the second half of 2003 as the international economy recovers, de-stocking slows and business investment begins to pick up. Real GDP growth may reach 2 per cent in 2004, which would nonetheless leave a substantial negative output gap. Given the sub-par growth outlook, employment growth is set to remain weak, increasing the unemployment rate to 5 per cent in 2004. With lower domestic cost pressures, inflation is projected to fall to 1½ per cent in 2004.

Improving competitiveness and enhancing employment prospects will depend on the resumption of wage moderation. It is important to remove the incentives to leave the labour force prematurely via benefit programmes. The government should take measures to adjust public spending to lower trend growth and return the budget to balance. The objective of paying-off debt by 2030, thereby pre-funding the additional budget costs associated with population ageing, should be restored.

The nascent economic recovery by mid-2002 faltered markedly in the rest of the year, as in other euro area countries, with output growth falling close to zero in the fourth quarter. With the strengthening in export markets not proving to be lasting, firms reduced business investment and employment. Unemployment has increased to 3 per cent in recent months, but remains below the OECD estimate of the structural rate (around 3½ per cent). Faced with deteriorating labour market prospects, an uncertain international environment, falling stock markets and the associated increases in pension contribution rates, consumer confidence has plunged to its lowest level since 1983. At the same time, business confidence has deteriorated, although less markedly, and is now pointing towards continued stagnation in investment in the first half of 2003.

The pace of recovery has faltered

Underlying and consumer price inflation fell sharply in 2002 to around 2¾ per cent in recent months, reflecting the elimination of the effect of indirect tax increases in 2001 and the appreciation of the euro. Although wage increases edged down in 2002, they remained high at around 4¼ per cent. This, together with rising employer pension contribution rates, weak productivity growth and euro appreciation has resulted in a further loss of competitiveness. The social partners have agreed a ceiling

Inflation has fallen, but competitiveness has worsened

Netherlands

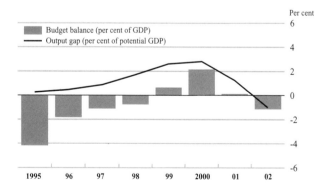

Weak confidence is likely to weigh on growth

The budget balance is under cyclical pressure

1. Percentage changes from corresponding quarter of the previous year.
Source: OECD.

——————————————— Netherlands: **Demand, output and prices** ———————————————

	1999	2000	2001	2002	2003	2004
	Current prices billion euros	Percentage changes, volume				
Private consumption	187.6	3.6	1.2	1.0	1.2	2.3
Government consumption	85.5	1.9	3.1	3.8	0.2	0.8
Gross fixed capital formation	84.2	3.5	-0.8	-3.1	-0.7	1.2
Final domestic demand	357.3	3.2	1.2	0.7	0.6	1.7
Stockbuilding [a]	0.5	-0.3	0.2	-0.7	0.1	0.9
Total domestic demand	357.8	2.8	1.4	-0.1	0.6	2.7
Exports of goods and services	225.4	10.9	1.7	-1.4	1.4	7.0
Imports of goods and services	209.1	10.6	1.9	-2.2	1.4	8.7
Net exports [a]	16.2	0.8	0.0	0.4	0.1	-0.6
GDP at market prices	374.1	3.3	1.3	0.3	0.7	1.9
GDP deflator	_	4.2	5.3	3.4	2.6	1.9
Memorandum items						
Consumer price index	_	2.3	5.1	3.9	2.4	1.5
Private consumption deflator	_	3.5	4.6	3.5	2.3	1.3
Unemployment rate	_	2.6	2.0	2.5	4.1	5.0
Household saving ratio [b]	_	6.7	9.6	10.7	10.9	10.8
General government financial balance [c]	_	2.2	0.1	-1.1	-1.6	-2.0
Current account balance [c]	_	2.1	2.1	2.1	3.1	2.5

Note: National accounts are based on official chain-linked data. This introduces a discrepancy in the identity between real demand components and GDP. For further details see *OECD Economic Outlook* Sources and Methods, *(http:// www.oecd.org/eco/sources-and-methods).*
a) Contributions to changes in real GDP (percentage of real GDP in previous year), actual amount in the first column.
b) As a percentage of disposable income, including savings in life insurance and pension schemes.
c) As a percentage of GDP.
Source: OECD.

of 2¼ to 2½ per cent for contractual wage increases in 2003, which reflects lower inflation and productivity growth and which should help to restore profitability.

The cyclical deterioration in the budget balance is being partly offset

The cyclical deterioration in the budget balance is being partly offset by structural expenditure and tax measures. These should limit the budget deficit to 1.6 per cent of GDP in 2003. The coalition government in the process of being formed is likely to introduce additional measures of around 3 per cent of GDP over the period 2004-07, part of which has been taken into account in the projections (for the budget balance in 2004, a small net effect of around 0.3 per cent of GDP has been included). The measures should be aimed at restoring budget surpluses and moving towards paying off all government debt by 2003.

Recovery should resume in the second half of 2003

The economy is projected to continue to stagnate in the first half of 2003 but subsequently to strengthen as the international economy recovers, lifting growth to around trend in 2004 but leaving a substantial negative output gap. With improving prospects for demand and profitability, firms are likely to reduce de-stocking and increase investment. Employment growth, however, is likely to remain weak, pushing up unemployment to 5 per cent in 2004, well above the OECD estimate of the structural rate. Inflation is projected to fall to around 1½ per cent in 2004, reflecting a sharp fall in domestic cost pressures and the strengthening of the euro. A main risk to this outlook is that pension fund contributions may need to rise further in the future, weighing on consumer sentiment and raising labour costs.

New Zealand

Activity is expected to slow in 2003 after four years of healthy growth. Continued strength in domestic demand will not suffice to offset the damping effects of weaker terms of trade and a sharply higher currency. However, the slowdown is likely to be short-lived, with growth returning to its medium-term potential rate of 3 per cent in 2004.

The currency appreciation has taken the pressure off monetary policy, as it should drive inflation down to the middle of the 1 to 3 per cent target range. Hence, interest rates can be left unchanged for the time being. The budget remains in surplus, and the government is prudently not raising expenditure in response to higher-than-expected revenues until it is confident that the fiscal surprise will prove permanent.

Activity was buoyant last year, with GDP growing by 4½ per cent. The export sector was robust in the first half of last year, but weakened considerably thereafter. However, domestic demand picked up to ensure a vigorous finish to the year. The labour market is very tight, with unemployment below 5 per cent and participation rates close to historical peaks. Consequently, inflation has picked up, with most measures of core inflation near 3 per cent.

Economic activity has been strong...

The main drivers of growth last year were the lagged impact of high terms of trade and a weak currency, both of which lifted farm incomes, with flow-through effects to the rest of the economy. A high rate of immigration also contributed to a residential construction boom. These forces have begun to wane. The terms of trade have fallen by around 10 per cent from their peak, and the (trade-weighted) exchange rate has increased by 30 per cent from a deeply depressed level. Immigration, which has slowed only slightly, is likely to have a much smaller impact on residential construction growth over the next year, as the building industry is running at full capacity. Instead, demand pressures will drive up house prices.

... but some of the driving forces have eased

Persistent strength in domestic demand is likely to carry the economy forward for the first six to nine months of this year. Rising employment, a pick-up in wage growth, and the wealth effect of higher house prices are all expected to contribute to solid consumer spending, at least in the cities. Spending in rural areas, however, will probably weaken. Export growth is projected to remain weak for most of 2003, due to sluggish global demand and the currency appreciation. The stronger New Zealand

Domestic demand momentum should partly offset weaker exports

New Zealand

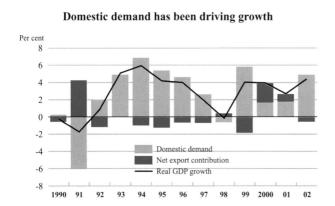

Source: Reserve Bank of New Zealand and OECD.

———————————— New Zealand: **Demand, output and prices** ————————————

	1999	2000	2001	2002	2003	2004
	Current prices billion NZD	Percentage changes, volume				
Private consumption	65.1	2.0	2.2	3.8	3.4	2.6
Government consumption	20.1	-1.9	3.5	4.6	2.9	2.5
Gross fixed capital formation	20.3	7.4	-1.7	8.0	4.9	2.7
Final domestic demand	105.4	2.3	1.6	4.8	3.6	2.6
Stockbuilding *a*	1.4	-0.5	0.2	0.2	-0.2	0.0
Total domestic demand	106.8	1.7	1.8	4.9	3.4	2.6
Exports of goods and services	32.2	6.8	2.0	7.6	4.6	6.4
Imports of goods and services	33.2	0.2	1.4	8.8	6.3	5.6
Net exports *a*	- 1.0	2.1	0.2	-0.2	-0.5	0.3
GDP (expenditure) at market prices	105.8	3.9	2.0	4.6	2.9	2.9
GDP deflator	_	2.4	4.8	0.3	1.1	2.5
Memorandum items						
GDP (production)	_	4.0	2.7	4.4	3.1	2.9
Consumer price index	_	2.6	2.6	2.7	2.0	2.0
Private consumption deflator	_	2.1	2.1	1.5	1.6	2.0
Unemployment rate	_	6.0	5.3	5.2	5.1	5.3
General government financial balance *b*	_	0.9	1.8	1.3	0.8	0.5
Current account balance *b*	_	-5.2	-2.8	-3.1	-4.6	-4.6

Note: National accounts are based on official chain-linked data. This introduces a discrepancy in the identity between real demand components and GDP. For further details see *OECD Economic Outlook* Sources and Methods, *(http:// www.oecd.org/eco/sources-and-methods).*
a) Contributions to changes in real GDP (percentage of real GDP in previous year), actual amount in the first column.
b) As a percentage of GDP.
Source: OECD.

dollar will also hurt the price-sensitive tourism industry next summer. In 2004, however, export growth should recover in step with the world economy. Business investment should pick up as well, since capacity utilisation rates have been high for some time, but this is unlikely to occur until global uncertainties – both geopolitical and economic – begin to fade.

Monetary and fiscal settings remain prudent

The appreciating exchange rate has taken much of the pressure off monetary policy. While domestically-generated inflation (the prices of non-tradables) was around 4 per cent last year and is rising, it is being offset by decelerating import prices, resulting in consumer price inflation being driven below 2 per cent this year. But it is likely to edge up again when the impact of the currency appreciation subsides. Consequently, official interest rates, which are currently around "neutral" levels, do not need to change for the time being. On the fiscal side, the government's accounts remain in healthy surplus, and tax revenues are substantially higher than forecast, even after adjusting for the unexpectedly buoyant economy. The government is prudently not spending these windfall revenues until it is confident that they are here to stay.

There are several risks to the outlook

Apart from uncertainty about the strength and timing of the global recovery, risks include the impact of the summer drought, the highly uncertain outlook for residential construction and the possibility that the effects of the tight labour market feed into wages and prices. The current account deficit, which is forecast to rise to its long-run average of 5 per cent of GDP, combined with the high net foreign debt position, may increase the country's vulnerability to swings in investor sentiment.

Norway

Growth, which was already subdued since 1998, slowed further in 2002 as wages and the exchange rate soared, squeezing mainland industry. Activity will remain subdued this year, but should pick up in 2004 as monetary policy easing feeds through and the global economy recovers. The unemployment rate is expected to peak at 4½ per cent, with inflation remaining low.

The authorities should not ease fiscal policy beyond the room for manoeuvre provided by the fiscal guidelines since easing would lead to further crowding-out of exposed industries. Wage moderation is needed to contain cost pressures, and work disincentives stemming from the disability and early retirement schemes should be reduced to stimulate labour supply.

Growth of mainland GDP has continued to ease from the 1998 cyclical peak, to only 1¼ per cent in 2002, and the first signs of slack have appeared. Overall GDP (including oil and gas production) grew by 1 per cent. Consumption and government spending stayed buoyant, but business investment fell sharply, taking a further hit in 2002 as businesses anticipated the removal of the investment surtax at the end of the year. Residential investment peaked in 2002 as high interest rates restrained demand and house prices levelled off. Gains in export market share by the traditional (non-oil and gas) sector reported for 2002 are unlikely to be sustained as profit margins have been squeezed. With layoffs accelerating, the unemployment rate edged up to 4.1 per cent by the end of 2002 – a percentage point above its 1998 low. Core inflation (excluding indirect taxes and energy) dropped below the official 2½ per cent target but headline inflation soared due to a weather-related surge in electricity prices during the winter.

The mainland economy is cooling off

Mainland industry has been severely squeezed since the economy peaked in 1998. The large interest rate spread against major currencies and the oil price hike propelled the external value of the krone to record highs. Meanwhile wage increases have averaged 5½ per cent *per annum*. The external economic environment has also been weakening since the autumn of 2002, prompting the Bank of Norway to cut its official sight deposit rate in three equal steps from 7 to 5½ per cent between December 2002 and March 2003. With the exchange rate falling back considerably as a result, monetary conditions have eased substantially. While further monetary easing cannot be ruled out, the projections assume policy rates to stay on hold as wages may not come down sufficiently to warrant further easing.

Monetary policy eased after profits were squeezed

Norway

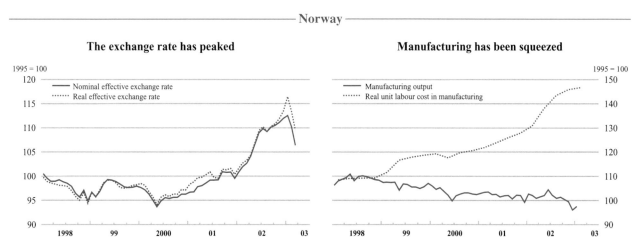

The exchange rate has peaked

Manufacturing has been squeezed

Source: OECD.

―――――――――― Norway: **Demand, output and prices** ――――――――――

	1999	2000	2001	2002	2003	2004
	Current prices billion NOK	Percentage changes, volume (1999 prices)				
Private consumption	584.3	3.9	2.6	3.3	2.5	2.5
Government consumption	263.7	1.3	2.7	4.5	0.5	1.1
Gross fixed capital formation	271.8	-3.6	-4.2	-3.3	2.1	0.6
Final domestic demand	1 119.8	1.5	1.0	2.2	1.9	1.8
Stockbuilding *a*	20.7	0.8	-0.5	0.0	0.0	0.0
Total domestic demand	1 140.6	2.4	0.4	2.1	1.9	1.7
Exports of goods and services	486.2	4.0	4.1	-0.5	0.4	3.8
Imports of goods and services	393.8	2.7	0.9	1.7	2.3	3.2
Net exports *a*	92.5	1.0	1.6	-0.7	-0.5	0.8
GDP at market prices	1 233.0	2.8	1.9	1.0	1.1	2.1
GDP deflator	–	15.9	1.9	-0.7	2.6	2.6
Memorandum items						
Mainland GDP at market prices *b*	–	2.5	1.7	1.3	0.9	1.9
Consumer price index	–	3.1	3.0	1.3	3.2	1.6
Private consumption deflator	–	3.0	2.4	0.7	3.2	1.6
Unemployment rate	–	3.4	3.5	4.0	4.5	4.6
Household saving ratio *c*	–	4.5	3.7	7.0	5.5	5.9
General government financial balance *d*	–	15.0	14.8	12.8	11.3	10.7
Current account balance *d*	–	14.9	15.3	13.7	12.2	13.2

a) Contributions to changes in real GDP (percentage of real GDP in previous year), actual amount in the first column.
b) GDP excluding oil and shipping.
c) As a percentage of disposable income.
d) As a percentage of GDP.
Source: OECD.

Fiscal policy is set to be moderately supportive

On current plans the fiscal stimulus should be modest. The fiscal policy guidelines introduced in 2001 allow the government to channel receipts equivalent to an *ex ante* 4 per cent real rate of return on the Government Petroleum Fund (which exceeds 40 per cent of GDP) into the budget. The resulting demand impulse is officially estimated to have been around ½ per cent of potential mainland GDP in 2002, but this will not be sustained in 2003. A drop in the market value of the capital in the Petroleum Fund – due to the slump in stock markets and currency appreciation – has reduced the government's leeway to tap resources from the Fund. Accordingly, fiscal easing stemming from the 2003 budget is only roughly half of that in 2002 and, barring a reversal of the capital losses on the Fund, should not pick up again in 2004.

Activity should pick up

Growth in mainland GDP is projected to recover from ¾ per cent in 2003 to 1¾ per cent in 2004. Business and residential investment are set to remain weak but buoyant investment in the oil and gas sector, which is included in mainland demand, could provide an offset. Consumption growth should pick up as employment prospects improve and electricity prices come down. Mainland exports are projected to stay weak initially, but the global recovery should underpin a pick up in 2004. With new gas fields coming on stream, overall GDP should recover from 1 per cent in 2003 to 2 per cent in 2004. Wage growth is projected to come down a little and, with productivity accelerating, underlying inflation should stay on target.

Fiscal slippage could undermine the recovery

If calls for fiscal stimulus are met, monetary conditions may again need to tighten, unless stronger wage moderation provides an offset. Exposed industries would then be squeezed further.

Poland

Output growth has averaged just over 1 per cent during the last two years, with the unemployment rate rising to over 20 per cent. Helped by strong export competitiveness, gradually increasing business profits and growing confidence as Poland moves closer to European Union membership, growth is projected to strengthen, reaching 3½ per cent in 2004. Headline inflation is also expected to pick up somewhat in the short-term, reflecting the effective depreciation of the currency.

Substantial cuts in nominal interest rates and a depreciation of the zloty have eased monetary conditions. Further monetary easing is desirable given the slow pace of the recovery relative to potential and still high real interest rates. But this needs to be supported by a strong effort to bring government spending under control. To maintain a favourable business climate and the attractiveness of Poland to foreign investors, structural reforms in labour and product market should be pursued in earnest.

Real GDP grew by 1½ per cent in the second half of 2002, confirming the mild acceleration that had begun earlier in the year. Private and government consumption were the main sources of domestic demand expansion, while the decline in investment activity moderated. Although the zloty strengthened against the dollar, a much stronger euro appreciation led to a marked depreciation in effective terms. As a result, exports picked up strongly and the current account deficit declined. Although recent industrial production data have been mixed, there are signs that profitability and demand conditions are improving, particularly within sectors that serve foreign markets.

Economic activity has accelerated mildly

Even with the incipient recovery, the output gap remains large, which, along with moderate food prices, has helped inflation to fall. As a result, headline inflation was well below the mid-point of the official target range of 3 per cent at the end of 2002. The contraction of the labour market continued, but because labour force withdrawals have moderated, unemployment increased markedly, reaching a historical high of 20 per cent of the labour force in the fourth quarter of last year.

Inflation and employment have declined

The underlying domestic forces acting on the economy are a mix of loose fiscal policy and tight monetary policy. The budget for 2003 rests upon revenue estimates that are based on optimistic macroeconomic assumptions, and no major steps have been taken to rein in government spending, particularly in the extensive extra-budgetary sector. As a

Fiscal policy remains loose, while real interest rates are high

— Poland —

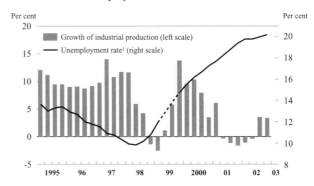

Real interest rates remain high

Unemployment is at record levels

1. The LFS Survey was not carried out in Q2 and Q3 1999.
Source: OECD.

——————————————— Poland: **Demand, output and prices** ———————————————

	1999	2000	2001	2002	2003	2004
	Current prices billion PLZ	Percentage changes, volume				
Private consumption	396.4	2.8	2.0	3.3	1.8	2.0
Government consumption	95.6	1.1	0.4	1.3	1.7	1.8
Gross fixed capital formation	156.7	2.7	-8.8	-7.2	3.5	7.0
Final domestic demand	648.6	2.5	-0.6	0.8	2.1	2.9
Stockbuilding *a*	5.6	0.4	-1.2	0.0	0.0	0.0
Total domestic demand	654.2	2.8	-1.6	0.8	2.1	2.9
Exports of goods and services	160.8	23.2	3.1	5.7	8.5	13.6
Imports of goods and services	199.9	15.6	-5.4	2.5	7.4	10.9
Net exports *a*	- 39.1	1.3	3.1	1.1	0.4	1.1
Statistical discrepancy *a*	0.0	-0.1	-0.6	-0.7	-0.2	-0.5
GDP at market prices	615.1	4.0	1.0	1.3	2.3	3.5
GDP deflator	_	11.3	4.2	1.4	1.0	1.9
Memorandum items						
Consumer price index	_	10.1	5.5	1.9	1.4	2.3
Private consumption deflator	_	11.5	5.0	1.6	1.4	2.3
Unemployment rate	_	16.1	18.2	19.9	20.4	19.9
General government financial balance *b*	_	-3.0	-5.1	-5.7	-6.2	-5.9
Current account balance *b*	_	-6.1	-2.9	-3.5	-4.5	-4.5

Note: National accounts are based on official chain-linked data. This introduces a discrepancy in the identity between real demand components and GDP. For further details see *OECD Economic Outlook* Sources and Methods, *(http:// www.oecd.org/eco/sources-and-methods)*.
a) Contributions to changes in real GDP (percentage of real GDP in previous year), actual amount in the first column.
b) As a percentage of GDP.
Source: OECD.

result, the general government deficit is projected to increase to more than 6 per cent of GDP. Meanwhile, the Polish National Bank has continued to deliver small cuts in its policy rates and the currency has depreciated. While monetary conditions have become more supportive of demand, they remain tight overall since inflation has fallen almost as quickly as nominal rates, keeping real interest rates high.

A mild, export-driven recovery is expected

Looking forward, real GDP growth is projected to accelerate mildly reaching 3½ per cent in 2004. On the upside, an improving export outlook and the prospect of European Union (EU) accession should make for a gradual recovery of investment, marking an end to the capital stock adjustment process that began in 2001. However, the response of private consumption may well be slower, due to the expectation of declining employment for some time to come. The expansion in investment demand, combined with the large fiscal deficit, is projected to push the current account deficit above 4 per cent of GDP in 2004. Although wage growth is expected to be moderate, headline inflation may pick up somewhat in the second half of 2003, reflecting the pass through of the currency depreciation, while underlying inflation will remain relatively stable.

The recovery of investment depends on political stability

The main risks attaching to the projections relate to the possibility that domestic political uncertainty could perturb the EU accession process. Should this happen, the pick-up in foreign direct investment might stall and a high interest rate premium on government bonds could become more entrenched, adversely affecting fiscal developments. This could strain monetary policy easing with the result that the overall recovery of the Polish economy would be delayed.

Portugal

Activity contracted in the second half of 2002, reflecting falling domestic demand and exports. Although lagging that of the euro area, a gradual recovery is projected in 2003 mainly driven by external demand. While narrowing slightly, the output gap is projected to remain large in 2004. Against this background, the inflation differential vis-à-vis the euro area is expected to narrow significantly.

Despite recent progress, the need for fiscal consolidation remains the main priority facing the authorities. Forceful implementation of recent structural measures will be required to rein in public spending.

Economic activity has stalled

After a vigorous expansionary phase, the Portuguese economy was among the weakest in the euro area in 2002, with a real GDP growth of ½ per cent. In particular, activity contracted in the second half of the year, reflecting negative contributions from both domestic and external demand. Employment started to decline in the fourth quarter 2002 and the unemployment rate rose to 6.2 per cent at year-end, its highest level since end-1997. The core inflation differential *vis-à-vis* the euro area widened in 2002, reflecting persistently higher wage increases than in the rest of the euro area and the impact of the standard value added tax (VAT) rate rise in June 2002. Reflecting sluggish domestic demand and a slight improvement in the terms of trade, the current account deficit continued to narrow in 2002 to 7½ per cent of GDP (excluding capital transfers). In early 2003, short-term indicators, including business and household confidence, showed no signs of a pick-up, and unemployment rose further in January and February. Against this background, nominal wage increases implicit in collective agreements for the private sector decelerated somewhat in early 2003.

Fiscal consolidation remains a major challenge

In response to the 2001 fiscal slippage, which triggered the launching of the European Union's excessive deficit procedure, tough corrective actions to reduce the deficit were taken in 2002. They included both emergency measures, mainly spending freezes and a VAT rate increase, and deep reforms to control and allocate public spending better. The emergency measures combined with a tax amnesty and last minute one-off operations (bringing in additional revenues of about 1½ per cent of GDP) helped to cut the deficit to 2.7 per cent of GDP in 2002. The 2002 emergency measures are scheduled to be

Portugal

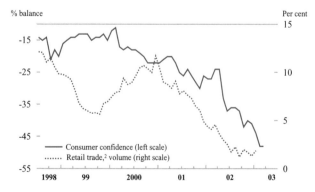

The labour market has deteriorated markedly

Growth of employment,[1] n.s.a. (left scale)
Standardised unemployment rate, s.a. (right scale)

While consumer confidence has worsened

Consumer confidence (left scale)
Retail trade,[2] volume (right scale)

1. Year-on-year percentage changes. Break in 2002 due to changes in methodology and recording practices.
2. Year-on-year percentage changes. 6-month moving average.
Source: OECD, Ministry of Finance; National Institute of Statistics (INE).

——————————— Portugal: **Demand, output and prices** ———————————

	1999	2000	2001	2002	2003	2004
	Current prices billion euros	Percentage changes, volume (1995 prices)				
Private consumption	67.4	2.6	1.2	0.7	0.5	1.6
Government consumption	21.3	4.0	3.4	3.2	-0.3	-0.3
Gross fixed capital formation	29.5	4.4	0.1	-5.2	-2.4	4.2
Final domestic demand	118.1	3.3	1.3	-0.4	-0.3	1.8
Stockbuilding[a]	1.1	-0.3	0.0	0.0	-0.1	0.0
Total domestic demand	119.2	3.1	1.3	-0.4	-0.4	1.8
Exports of goods and services	32.1	8.0	1.9	2.0	3.2	7.7
Imports of goods and services	43.3	5.4	0.9	-0.4	0.8	5.4
Net exports[a]	- 11.2	0.3	0.2	0.9	0.8	0.4
GDP at market prices	108.0	3.7	1.6	0.5	0.3	2.3
GDP deflator	_	3.2	4.8	4.6	3.6	2.3
Memorandum items						
Consumer price index	_	2.8	4.4	3.7	3.2	2.2
Private consumption deflator	_	2.8	4.2	3.6	3.1	2.2
Unemployment rate	_	4.0	4.1	5.1	6.4	6.3
Household saving ratio[b]	_	9.5	10.7	11.9	12.2	12.1
General government financial balance[c]	_	-2.9[d]	-4.3	-2.7	-3.2	-2.7
Current account balance[c]	_	-10.5	-9.6	-7.6	-6.0	-5.5

a) Contributions to changes in real GDP (percentage of real GDP in previous year), actual amount in the first column.
b) As a percentage of disposable income.
c) As a percentage of GDP.
d) Including proceeds of sales of mobile telephone licences (around 0.3 per cent of GDP).
Source: OECD.

phased out progressively by 2004, while the effect of structural reforms will become increasingly important. Given weak activity and the need to compensate for the one-off measures adopted in 2002, the 2.4 per cent budget target for 2003 seems unlikely to be achieved. Even reducing the structural deficit by ½ per cent of GDP, recently stated as the official objective, would require further consolidation efforts. Hence the OECD projection incorporates some slippage. The cyclically-adjusted budget deficit is assumed to decline gradually by around ¼ per cent of GDP in 2003 and close to ½ per cent of GDP in 2004. This projection includes the corporate tax cut scheduled for 2004, though this cut may be postponed if the effects of structural fiscal reforms are smaller than expected.

Exports will drive the pick-up from the second half of 2003

The adjustment of private domestic demand components is likely to continue in 2003. Against this background, and with government consumption declining, the recovery will have to be driven by external demand. Private demand components would strengthen only in 2004 as confidence returns and the labour market starts to improve. The current labour slack and a persistently large output gap, together with the fact that the VAT hike will pass out of the statistics after the middle of this year, should help inflation to decelerate significantly, reducing the differential *vis-à-vis* the euro area to ½ percentage point by end-2004.

Major risks concern consumer behaviour and external demand

On the domestic front, the main risk comes from consumer behaviour in the short term. With unemployment rising, there is a risk that household expenditure could be even weaker than projected in the first half of 2003. It is also important that private wage increases moderate significantly to reflect the economic weakness, otherwise international competitiveness would deteriorate further, putting at risk the export-led recovery. The main external uncertainty still concerns the timing and speed of the projected recovery in Europe.

Slovak Republic

Output growth seems likely to decelerate somewhat this year from the 4½ per cent growth of 2002 as the fiscal impulse is withdrawn while effects of price liberalisation and structural reforms initially damp demand. Inflation had decelerated to 3 per cent due to transitory factors and is picking up again temporarily as a consequence of energy prices increasing toward cost-recovery levels. The high current account deficit is expected to narrow as exports from foreign-controlled firms come on stream.

The scheduled tightening of fiscal policy is welcome, as an excessive loosening occurred last year. This should allow the central bank to soften the exchange-rate impact of strong capital inflows, helping domestic industry to maintain cost competitiveness. The determined pursuit of the ambitious structural reform programme is commendable and should lift productive potential towards levels already achieved by other accession countries in the region.

Output growth accelerated last year, underpinned by booming private and government consumption as a result of strong real wage growth, triggered by an unexpectedly rapid disinflation and spectacular wage increases in the government sector. 2002 was an election year. In contrast, real investment spending declined. Lower imports of investment goods were reflected in the improving merchandise trade balance. But the diminishing services surplus resulting from lower net tourism receipts meant that the current account deficit remained above 8 per cent of GDP. Foreign direct investment (FDI) inflows were twice as high, entailing mainly privatisation receipts but also a rapid expansion of greenfield projects.

GDP growth has been driven by robust consumption…

Headline inflation fell in 2002, as prices of food and imported energy declined and the increase of regulated prices to cost-recovery levels was postponed to this year and next. Unemployment fell despite stagnant employment in response to a shrinking labour market. Increased inactivity is partly explained by rising numbers of partial disability and welfare benefit recipients. Due to the punitive indirect wage costs, dependent employment declined while self-employment increased as small firms continued to hire former employees as contractors.

… while disinflation benefited from temporary factors

The macroeconomic policy mix continued to be characterised by loose fiscal policy and tight monetary conditions. Rapid currency appreciation occurred in the wake of strong capital inflows following the September elections, which resulted in

The macroeconomic policy mix is out of balance

Slovak Republic

FDI inflows and trend productivity growth increased

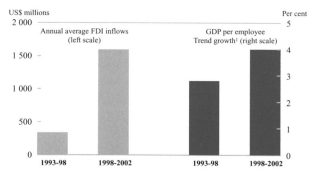

Inflation and unemployment have declined

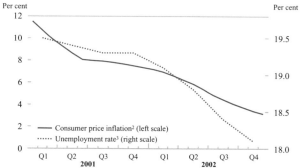

1. Trend estimated using Hodrick Prescott filter with lambda 400 on semiannual data.
2. Inflation is expressed by the 12-month moving average.
3. Standardised seasonnally adjusted unemployment rate.
Source: National Bank of Slovakia; Slovak Statistical Office and OECD.

──────────── Slovak Republic: **Demand, output and prices** ────────────

	1999	2000	2001	2002	2003	2004
	Current prices billion SKK	Percentage changes, volume (1995 prices)				
Private consumption	470.6	-1.8	3.9	5.3	3.0	3.2
Government consumption	165.6	1.3	5.1	4.0	2.5	2.0
Gross fixed capital formation	252.9	1.2	9.6	-0.9	3.7	5.2
Final domestic demand	889.0	-0.4	5.7	3.2	3.1	3.6
Stockbuilding [a]	- 17.1	0.4	1.4	0.8	0.0	0.0
Total domestic demand	871.9	0.0	7.2	4.0	3.1	3.5
Exports of goods and services	510.0	13.8	6.5	5.9	5.9	8.2
Imports of goods and services	546.2	10.2	11.7	5.3	5.2	7.1
Net exports [a]	- 36.2	2.2	-4.0	0.3	0.4	0.7
GDP at market prices	835.7	2.2	3.3	4.4	3.6	4.3
GDP deflator	_	6.4	5.4	4.0	7.4	5.2
Memorandum items						
Consumer price index	_	12.0	7.3	3.1	8.7	7.4
Private consumption deflator	_	10.5	5.6	2.4	7.1	6.1
Unemployment rate	_	18.8	19.3	18.6	17.7	16.8
General government financial balance [b]	_	-10.7	-7.3	-7.2	-6.2	-5.1
Current account balance [b]	_	-3.8	-8.6	-8.1	-6.9	-6.1

a) Contributions to changes in real GDP (percentage of real GDP in previous year), actual amount in the first column.
b) As a percentage of GDP.
Source: OECD.

the formation of a reform-oriented government. The central bank has since cut policy interest rates by 175 basis points and intervened in the foreign exchange market, broadly stabilising the exchange rate *vis-à-vis* the euro.

Budget consolidation plans may be realised only with a lag

The 2003 budget aims to reduce the fiscal deficit from 7 per cent of GDP in 2002 to 5 per cent this year. This ambitious target is unlikely to be met, given the expected delay in the implementation of the fundamental healthcare, pension, tax and labour market reforms outlined in the government programme. On the basis of currently legislated measures, the fiscal deficit is projected to decline gradually to 5 per cent of GDP in 2004. The budgeted decline of public investment expenditure appears to be counterproductive and ought to be substituted by deep cuts in public employment, which remains at one of the highest levels, relative to business employment, in the OECD. However, the employment of lower-skilled workers is currently hampered by high replacement rates and excessive payroll taxes needed to finance them.

Structural reforms and price liberalisation will temporarily damp growth

Despite the continued weakness of external demand, exports to the European Union (EU) area accelerated rapidly in recent months, reflecting the ongoing restructuring by FDI firms. However, steep adjustments in regulated prices, cuts in social transfers and rising indirect taxes are likely to lead to subdued private consumption growth. Thus GDP growth is likely to decelerate temporarily, before picking up again in 2004 with a strengthening recovery in western Europe. This, and further improvements to the supply-side responsiveness resulting from continued FDI inflows, should result in export-driven GDP growth of over 4 per cent in 2004.

Premature appreciation could risk a loss of competitiveness

The principal downward risk is posed by market expectations of massive FDI inflows linked to the 2004 EU accession, which may strengthen the koruna to an extent that damages the competitiveness of domestic industry.

Spain

Growth slowed to 2 per cent in 2002, due to weaker private consumption and investment and sluggish foreign demand, but growth has remained higher than the euro area average. Inflation has declined rather little and the differential with the euro area persists. Activity should strengthen from the second half of this year, halting the rise in unemployment, with GDP likely to grow above potential in 2004.

In early 2003 a personal income tax cut was implemented, while the new Fiscal Stability Law entered into force, which obliges all levels of administration to aim at a balanced budget. The fiscal stance is, nevertheless, broadly neutral, which seems appropriate in view of the relatively small negative output gap. The inflation differential should be tackled by structural reforms rather than by tightening fiscal policy, most importantly by changes to the wage bargaining system to reduce nominal wage rigidities and by further enhancing competition in certain sectors.

Despite the acceleration of public consumption, domestic demand slowed to 2 per cent in the second half of 2002 due to weakening private consumption. The construction sector was resilient, however, while equipment investment, which had fallen for three consecutive semesters, started to recover. Despite the sharp acceleration of exports in the third quarter, the net contribution of foreign demand to growth was only moderately positive since imports were much more dynamic than exports at the end of the year. For 2002 as a whole, GDP growth slowed moderately to 2 per cent. Employment growth also lost momentum, and the unemployment rate rose to 11.5 per cent in the last quarter of 2002. Activity indicators provide a mixed picture for the months to come, and do not point to an immediate upturn. Business orders have improved and employment has picked up somewhat, but car sales have continued falling while consumer confidence has dropped to a seven-year low. Inflation rose to 4 per cent in December but declined in early 2003 due to the freeze of indirect taxes and the waning of the euro changeover effect. However, the differential with the euro area, which is partly the consequence of exceptional factors, has remained high at over 1 per cent. Wage inflation has remained stable, with agreed wages growing at around 3 per cent, implying a decline in real wages, although catch-up clauses for higher-than-expected inflation now cover a large number of wage agreements and could push up wages at the end of 2003.

Growth slowed moderately in 2002, but the inflation differential persisted

In 2002, the general government budget was close to balance, despite lower than projected growth, largely owing to stronger than expected income tax receipts. For 2003, the new Budget Stability Law implies that all levels of administration will have

The fiscal stance will be neutral over the projection period

Spain

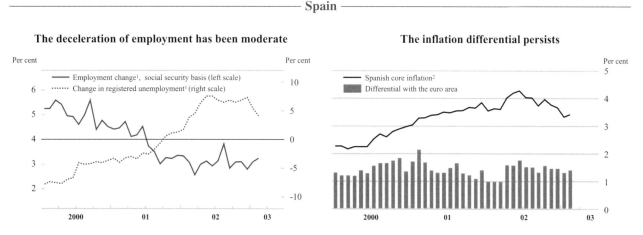

The deceleration of employment has been moderate

Per cent — Employment change[1], social security basis (left scale)
······· Change in registered unemployment[1] (right scale)

The inflation differential persists

Per cent — Spanish core inflation[2]
▓ Differential with the euro area

1. Year-on-year percentage changes.
2. The break in 2001 of the Spanish harmonised consumer price index has been corrected using the national CPI data.
Source : Ministry of Labour and Social Affairs, INE, EUROSTAT and OECD, *Main Economic Indicators.*

——————————————— Spain: **Demand, output and prices** ———————————————

	1999	2000	2001	2002	2003	2004
	Current prices billion euros	Percentage changes, volume (1995 prices)				
Private consumption	335.2	3.9	2.5	1.9	2.3	3.2
Government consumption	98.6	5.0	3.1	3.8	3.5	3.0
Gross fixed capital formation	136.1	5.7	3.2	1.4	2.6	4.1
Final domestic demand	570.0	4.5	2.8	2.1	2.6	3.4
Stockbuilding [a]	2.6	-0.1	0.0	0.1	0.0	0.0
Total domestic demand	572.6	4.4	2.7	2.2	2.6	3.4
Exports of goods and services	155.5	10.1	3.4	1.4	3.3	6.1
Imports of goods and services	162.8	10.6	3.5	2.2	4.7	6.8
Net exports [a]	- 7.4	-0.3	-0.1	-0.3	-0.5	-0.4
GDP at market prices	565.2	4.2	2.7	2.0	2.1	3.1
GDP deflator	_	3.5	4.2	4.4	3.0	2.4
Memorandum items						
Consumer price index	_	3.5	2.8	3.6	2.9	2.4
Private consumption deflator	_	3.2	3.3	3.6	2.9	2.4
Unemployment rate [b]	_	11.0	10.5	11.4	12.0	11.7
Household saving ratio [c]	_	10.6	10.2	10.1	10.4	10.2
General government financial balance [d]	_	-0.6	-0.1	-0.1	-0.4	-0.2
Current account balance [d]	_	-3.5	-2.6	-2.6	-3.0	-3.2

a) Contributions to changes in real GDP (percentage of real GDP in previous year), actual amount in the first column.
b) Spanish data on labour force, employment and unemployment are revised since 1976 using the methodology applied by the Labour Force Survey as from 2002. Revisions are made by the OECD based on information from the official Statistical Office in Spain. They imply a downward revision of the unemployment rate by 2.5 points in 2001.
c) As a percentage of disposable income.
d) As a percentage of GDP.
Source: OECD.

to balance their budget, including the autonomous communities, which will benefit from a new financing system that accompanies their greater spending and tax-raising powers. The budget, which is based on a 3 per cent growth projection for 2003, includes a cut in the personal income tax, with an estimated revenue loss of ½ per cent of GDP. A deficit of close to ½ per cent of GDP is likely to be recorded in 2003, implying a neutral fiscal stance. A small cyclical deficit does not violate the spirit of the Budget Stability Law, which allows for some flexibility in its implementation.

An export-led rebound is expected for the second half of 2003

Activity should recover in the second half of the year, mainly reflecting a better international environment, although the appreciation of the euro will result in a negative contribution of net exports to growth of about ½ percentage point. Equipment investment should rise as prospects improve, while construction is likely to remain strong. Private consumption will be bolstered by the personal income tax cut and stronger employment growth. Overall, GDP is expected to grow by slightly above 2 per cent in 2003, and by more than 3 per cent in 2004, which is above potential. With the labour force growing rapidly, the unemployment rate is expected to rise further in 2003, but to decline again during 2004. Inflation is likely to moderate as the output gap remains negative, and should fall to 2½ per cent by the end of the projection period. Weaker than projected international demand could delay the recovery, and without improvement of the international climate, consumer and business confidence could deteriorate, dragging down equipment investment and consumption. Over the medium term, a persistent inflation differential with the euro area is worrying as it progressively erodes competitiveness.

Sweden

The economy lost steam in the second half of 2002 due to weak export performance and falling business investment. A recovery in exports should make for stronger growth over the course of 2003, and prospects look bright for next year as the international situation improves and investment picks up. Developments in the telecommunications sector remain a source of downside risk, whereas rising wage pressures may imply an upside risk to inflation.

The fiscal position is still sound, with structural surpluses of around 1¼ per cent of GDP. However, following the large tax cuts in 2002, further fiscal stimulus would not be helpful. The proposed measures to curb the number of sickness beneficiaries should be implemented without delay. Monetary policy should be tightened gradually from the second half of 2003 as activity quickens.

Output growth slowed in the second half of 2002 after a notable rebound in the second quarter of the year, with lower exports and business investment accounting for most of the setback. A rising unemployment rate indicates a slight easing of labour market pressures and has also affected consumer confidence, which has steadily declined.

Activity has slowed and unemployment has risen...

Although manufacturers generally expect further reductions in employment, business confidence has improved markedly in recent months, primarily due to rising export orders. Along with brisk retail sales, this indicates a more positive outlook for 2003. Year-on-year consumer price inflation jumped by more than 1 percentage point in the first two months of 2003 as electricity prices surged following cold weather conditions, while measures of inflation excluding energy have been stable.

... but business indicators point to renewed growth

The significant fiscal stimulus coming from the large income tax cuts and other expansionary fiscal measures in 2002 is expected to fuel private consumption throughout the projection period, although local government tax increases in 2003 reduce the gains to households and spending behaviour may remain prudent. The overall fiscal stance is projected to be broadly neutral over the projection period, although the automatic stabilisers will pare back the actual budget surplus by nearly ½ percentage point in 2003 before being reversed again in 2004.

Previous fiscal stimulus will support private consumption...

Monetary policy was eased further in March of this year as the *Riksbank* lowered short-term interest rates by 25 basis points, following cuts amounting to 50 basis points in the last quarter of 2002. However, inflation expectations remain firmly above the

... and monetary policy has eased

Sweden

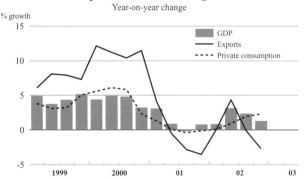

Exports have weakened again
Year-on-year change

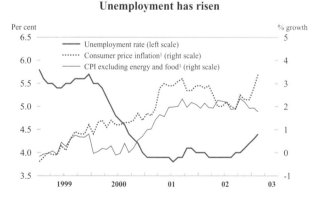

Unemployment has risen

1. Year-on-year.
Source: Statistics Sweden; OECD.

——————————— Sweden: **Demand, output and prices** ———————————

	1999	2000	2001	2002	2003	2004
	Current prices billion SEK	Percentage changes, volume				
Private consumption	1 015.7	5.0	0.2	1.3	2.2	2.6
Government consumption	571.4	-1.1	0.9	2.1	0.8	0.8
Gross fixed capital formation	358.3	6.6	0.8	-2.5	0.2	4.4
Final domestic demand	1 945.5	3.6	0.5	0.8	1.4	2.4
Stockbuilding [a]	5.3	0.5	-0.4	-0.1	0.1	0.0
Total domestic demand	1 950.8	4.1	0.0	0.6	1.5	2.4
Exports of goods and services	885.3	11.3	-0.8	0.4	2.2	7.5
Imports of goods and services	757.6	11.5	-3.5	-2.7	2.0	7.0
Net exports [a]	127.7	0.9	1.1	1.3	0.3	1.0
GDP at market prices	2 078.5	4.4	1.1	1.9	1.5	2.8
GDP deflator	_	1.3	2.0	1.3	2.3	2.3
Memorandum items						
Consumer price index	_	1.3	2.6	2.4	2.4	1.8
Private consumption deflator	_	1.1	2.1	2.0	2.3	1.7
Unemployment rate [b]	_	4.7	4.0	4.0	4.5	4.3
Household saving ratio [c]	_	2.4	5.2	8.2	7.2	6.8
General government financial balance [d,e]	_	3.4	4.6	1.1	0.7	1.2
Current account balance [d]	_	3.9	3.9	4.1	3.9	4.4

Note: National accounts are based on official chain-linked data. This introduces a discrepancy in the identity between real demand components and GDP. For further details see *OECD Economic Outlook* Sources and Methods, *(http://www.oecd.org/eco/sources-and-methods)*.
a) Contributions to changes in real GDP (percentage of real GDP in previous year), actual amount in the first column.
b) Based on monthly Labour Force Surveys.
c) As a percentage of disposable income.
d) As a percentage of GDP.
e) Maastricht definition.
Source: OECD.

2 per cent target and output is close to the OECD's estimate of potential, cautioning against further easing. Gradual hikes in interest rates are likely to be needed from the second half of 2003 as both domestic and external demand pick up.

Economic prospects are still bright for 2004...

As the previous policy stimulus feeds through and foreign demand gains momentum, output growth is projected to recover gradually to reach 2¾ per cent in 2004. Accelerating private consumption may drive up domestic demand and additional impetus is projected from renewed growth in business investment in 2004. A rise in unemployment is foreseen this year, as more private sector jobs are cut, but business employment is projected to recover partially in 2004. Overall, the labour market remains fairly tight, providing little scope for wage increases to moderate. Average annual consumer price inflation should fall back to around 1¾ per cent in 2004 as the effects of recent energy price rises are reversed, thus pulling down inflation rates in the early months of next year.

... but sensitive to the difficulties in the telecommunications sector

Prospects for the telecommunications sector are particularly uncertain, as significant signs of improvement have yet to emerge, and the risks there are probably still on the downside. Wage pressures remain a general concern, especially as the effective labour supply could be eroded by further increases in sickness absenteeism. In particular, high wage demands by municipal workers might spread to the rest of the labour market and feed through to inflation.

Switzerland

The weakness of the external environment, especially in Europe, and the strength of the Swiss franc have continued to put a hold on activity, which stagnated in 2002. The pick-up in production linked to the international recovery should be close to ½ per cent in 2003, before accelerating to nearly 2 per cent in 2004, putting an end to the rise in unemployment. Lower inflation could result in virtual price stability.

The Swiss National Bank should maintain its expansionary monetary policy until the upturn is firmly established. A further cyclical deterioration in the federal budget in 2003 would be acceptable, but adopting an expansionary programme that erodes the structural deficit of the Confederation would not be desirable. More determined efforts to encourage competition would help increase growth potential.

Despite a slight upturn in the second half of 2002, activity stagnated last year. Domestic demand was very weak owing to the sharp fall in investment, while exports barely increased due to the depressed external environment, particularly in Germany, and to the appreciation of the franc. The international weakening of the financial and tourism sectors, both of which are particularly important for the Swiss economy, put a hold on activity. Despite the continued increase in the unemployment rate to 3.9 per cent in February 2003, the highest level in four years, consumption was resilient and household confidence has shown a slight improvement since the Autumn 2002. However, recent cyclical indicators do not point to an improvement in coming months and further job losses are expected. Due to higher energy prices, headline inflation reached 1¼ per cent in March 2003 (year-on-year), but core inflation remained subdued, at ½ per cent over the same period.

The weakness of activity persists

In March 2003, the National Bank lowered again the three-month LIBOR fluctuation band by ½ percentage point to 0-¾ per cent. The Bank envisages keeping the LIBOR in the lower end of this band, *i.e.* at around ¼ per cent. This easing of conditions aims at offsetting the appreciation of the franc against the dollar. The exchange rate against the euro has remained stable since the events of 11 September 2001 until the beginning of 2003. The effective nominal appreciation of the Swiss franc with

Monetary policy has been eased again

Switzerland

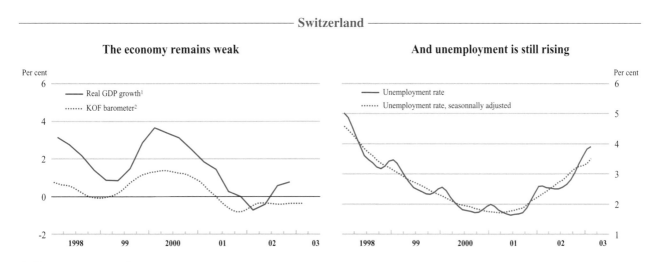

The economy remains weak

And unemployment is still rising

1. Year-on-year percentage changes.
2. The KOF barometer is a leading indicator of future GDP growth, with an average lead of 6 to 9 months.
Source: National Swiss Bank; KOF; OECD, *Quarterly National Accounts.*

——————— Switzerland: **Demand, output and prices** ———————

	1999	2000	2001	2002	2003	2004
	Current prices billion CHF	Percentage changes, volume (1990 prices)				
Private consumption	234.7	2.0	1.8	0.9	0.8	1.8
Government consumption	57.3	1.5	2.6	1.9	0.1	0.4
Gross fixed capital formation	78.1	5.8	-5.2	-6.5	-0.6	3.1
Final domestic demand	370.1	2.9	0.1	-0.8	0.4	1.8
Stockbuilding [a]	- 2.3	-0.3	0.7	-0.5	0.0	0.0
Total domestic demand	367.8	2.5	0.8	-1.3	0.4	1.8
Exports of goods and services	157.7	10.0	-0.1	0.4	3.0	4.9
Imports of goods and services	136.9	8.5	-0.3	-2.6	2.5	4.7
Net exports [a]	20.8	0.6	0.1	1.4	0.2	0.1
GDP at market prices	388.5	3.2	0.9	0.1	0.6	1.9
GDP deflator	_	1.2	1.4	0.4	0.8	0.4
Memorandum items						
Consumer price index	_	1.6	1.0	0.6	0.7	0.3
Private consumption deflator	_	1.1	1.2	0.8	0.7	0.3
Unemployment rate	_	2.0	1.9	2.8	3.7	3.4
Current account balance [b]	_	13.2	9.1	11.9	11.9	12.2

a) Contributions to changes in real GDP (percentage of real GDP in previous year), actual amount in the first column.
b) As a percentage of GDP.
Source: OECD.

respect to the 2001 average is at present 7 per cent, and 5 per cent in real terms. In the projections, monetary policy is assumed to remain expansionary as long as the upturn is not firmly established.

The federal budget is in structural deficit

Exceptional receipts of nearly 1 per cent of GDP limited the general government budget deficit to 0.4 per cent of GDP in 2002. At the federal level, the budget shortfall of CHF 3.3 billion (¾ per cent of GDP excluding exceptional receipts), instead of the CHF 300 million forecast, not only reflects a cyclical drop in revenues but also a larger than expected structural deficit. For 2003, the Confederation budget, which is based on a growth assumption of 1.3 per cent, aims at structural balance, which corresponds to a deficit of CHF 250 million. As recognised by the authorities, this objective seems to be out of reach, as are the targets included in the financial plan until 2006. A programme of medium-term budgetary cuts could be adopted before the summer, but this will not prevent an overshoot of the federal budget this year, nor a structural deficit, which will have to be offset in subsequent years in accordance with the debt containment rule.

The recovery depends on the external environment

The recovery of activity depends on how the international environment evolves, though it will not come before the second half of the year. Growth is thus likely to be modest in 2003 before picking up and exceeding potential in 2004, supported by monetary policy. The usual lag between employment and activity is likely to prevent any rapid decrease in unemployment, which could be around 3½ per cent in 2004. Given a negative output gap and the fall in import prices, inflation could decline further leading to price stability during the projection period. The main risk surrounding this scenario concerns the evolution of the external environment and the exchange rate, whose possible appreciation could penalise Switzerland even in the event of an international recovery.

Turkey

Following the deep recession in 2001, the economy expanded by almost 8 per cent in 2002, with the end-year inflation rate falling to just under 30 per cent, well below the target of 35 per cent. Slower growth is projected in 2003, mainly because of the continuing reluctance of domestic banks to lend, higher real interest rates, and the war in Iraq. Inflation is projected to pick up in the first half of 2003, reflecting recent currency depreciation, the lagged effects of high oil prices and a seasonal hike in agricultural prices, before falling towards, though probably not reaching, the 20 per cent target by end-year.

The establishment of a single party government with a sizeable majority after the November 2002 general elections was initially welcomed by the financial markets. Nonetheless, a significant fiscal slippage has raised concerns. Adherence to expenditure targets and steady implementation of the structural reforms in the banking sector and elsewhere remain the key to maintaining the declining trend in inflation and creating the conditions for a durable recovery.

Growth performance in 2002 was much better than expected, bringing the annual growth rate to 7.8 per cent. A prolonged inventory build-up was the main driver. Nonetheless, final domestic demand remained weak because of still high unemployment and the continued cautiousness by banks in their lending activities during the bank restructuring.

Economic recovery has been better than expected in 2002...

Mainly owing to weak domestic demand and cumulative real appreciation of the exchange rate up to end-2002, both underpinned by tight monetary policy, inflation slowed significantly in 2002. In early 2003, however, the pace of disinflation fell back in response to rising oil prices, the recent renewed depreciation of the exchange rate, and especially high increases in public and agricultural prices. The inflation rate is thus projected to decline only modestly for the year as a whole, from around 30 per cent at end-2002 to 27 per cent by end-2003.

... with a slowing inflation rate

After a long period of unstable coalition governments, the establishment of a single party government following the general elections in November 2002 led to a number of favourable developments in financial markets. Real long-term interest rates fell below 20 per cent and the exchange rate declined below 1.6 million lira per

The real interest rate is still high

— Turkey —

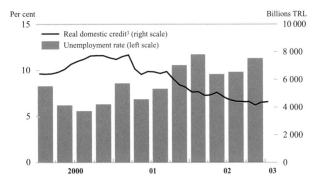

Real interest rates remain high

Per cent / Per cent

- - - Nominal interest rate (right scale)
— Consumer price index[1] (right scale)
▮ Real interest rate[2] (left scale)

Credit conditions and employment are unfavorable

Per cent / Billions TRL

— Real domestic credit[3] (right scale)
▮ Unemployment rate (left scale)

1. Year-on-year growth.
2. Calculated using 12-month ahead inflation or expected inflation.
3. Using consumer price index as deflator.
Source: OECD, State Institute of Statistics.

——————————— Turkey: **Demand, output and prices** ———————————

	1999	2000	2001	2002	2003	2004
	Current prices trillion TRL	Percentage changes, volume (1987 prices)				
Private consumption	55 928	6.2	-9.2	2.0	2.9	3.2
Government consumption	11 748	7.1	-8.5	5.4	2.8	3.1
Gross fixed capital formation	16 931	16.9	-31.5	-0.8	7.9	11.0
Final domestic demand	84 606	8.9	-15.1	1.7	3.9	4.9
Stockbuilding *a*	1 149	1.1	-4.0	7.0	-0.3	-1.6
Total domestic demand	85 755	9.8	-18.5	9.2	3.4	3.0
Exports of goods and services	17 972	19.2	7.4	11.0	8.7	12.1
Imports of goods and services	20 801	25.4	-24.8	15.7	12.9	13.9
Net exports *a*	-2 829	-3.0	12.4	-0.9	-1.1	-0.3
Statistical discrepancy *a*	-5 510	0.1	0.0	0.0	0.3	0.0
GDP at market prices	77 415	7.4	-7.5	7.8	2.5	2.6
GDP deflator	–	49.9	54.8	43.7	26.2	14.3
Memorandum items						
Consumer price index	–	54.9	54.4	45.0	30.3	17.5
Private consumption deflator	–	50.0	58.8	40.5	32.0	17.1
Unemployment rate	–	6.6	8.5	10.6	10.5	10.6
Current account balance *b*	–	-4.9	2.4	-1.0	-1.9	-2.6

a) Contributions to changes in real GDP (percentage of real GDP in previous year), actual amount in the first column.
b) As a percentage of GDP.
Source: OECD.

dollar in December. The revelation of higher-than-expected public spending in 2002 and the outbreak of the war in Iraq then sapped financial market confidence, and nominal interest rates surged by more than 10 percentage points in March relative to end-2002, entailing a renewed rise in the long term real interest rate to over 30 per cent.

Fiscal balances deteriorated...

Performance on the budget front was disappointing in 2002. Primary budget spending rose rapidly, especially in the months surrounding the end-year elections, mainly stemming from personnel outlays, direct income support for farmers, transfers to social security institutions and tax rebates for exporters. At the same time, budget revenues were weaker than expected due to declining tax compliance. The consolidated public sector primary surplus is estimated to have fallen to around 4 per cent of GNP, from around 6 per cent in the previous year against a 2002 target of 6½ per cent. With interest payments also higher than expected, at 19 per cent of GNP, the overall fiscal deficit overshot its 2002 target of 9.6 per cent by some 4½ percentage points of GNP. The government has pledged, however, that the primary budget surplus target of 6½ per cent agreed with the International Monetary Fund will be met in 2003. This would necessitate the implementation of the fiscal measures that have already been specified in the 2003 Budget Law.

... leading to further increases in the debt stock

By February 2003, the total domestic debt stock had risen significantly relative to end-2002, because of increasing nominal interest rates and a declining maturity. This unfavourable development in the debt dynamics was due both to fiscal slippages and to worsening market confidence as a result of the slowing progress in structural reforms since May 2002. The high shares of foreign currency denominated/linked securities and floating rate papers in the total domestic debt stock, currently amounting to 31 and 42 per cent, respectively, render the debt burden especially susceptible to exchange rate and interest rate fluctuations.

Growth is projected to weaken in 2003 and 2004 relative to 2002, mainly because of higher real interest rates and adverse economic impacts stemming from the Iraq war. Real GDP is, nevertheless, expected to grow at around 2½ to 3 per cent in both years thanks to a continuing strong export performance, though the downside risks emanating from Iraq may be particularly important for Turkey. Repeated budget slippages would impact on the financial and exchange-rate markets, threatening the viability of the recovery as well as the disinflation process. Further delays in structural reforms would not only risk the efforts to ease the debt burden but also seriously jeopardise the attainability of the objectives set forth in the stabilisation programme.

Growth prospects are clouded by downside risks

III. DEVELOPMENTS IN SELECTED NON-MEMBER ECONOMIES

Economic activity continued to recover in the non-member Asian region throughout most of 2002, led by double-digit growth in exports. The expansion gained further momentum during the second half in China, but decelerated in Dynamic Asia in response to the renewed weakness in the United States and other OECD countries. Growth in Dynamic Asia should rebound in 2003 if OECD markets recover, but is subject to significant risks from geopolitical tensions, along with structural problems and the potential fallout from the outbreak of disease in several economies. China is less exposed to external risks, but further progress on structural reforms to achieve more balanced growth in the domestic economy are likely to be needed to sustain rapid growth in real GDP beyond the near-term.

Economic growth in Russia and other Newly Independent and South-East European States slowed to below 5 per cent in 2002. In a weak global environment, growth was mainly driven by strongly expanding internal demand, boosted in many countries by sizeable increases in wages and social benefits. Growth is expected to remain robust in 2003 at around 4 to 5 per cent, both for Russia and the region, but may slow further in 2004. In some countries, including Russia, higher growth in commodities and basic manufactures, compared to more complex manufactured goods, may increase the future vulnerability of these economies to external shocks.

South-America is slowly recovering from the regional recession of 2002. The new administration in Brazil has reassured markets in pursuing prudent macroeconomic policies and starting to undertake further structural reforms. In Argentina, the real economy is showing signs of recovery, despite the political uncertainty. Other countries in the region display mixed performances, with growth picking up in Chile whereas Venezuela is facing a severe recession. In addition to the restoration of confidence in the region, a demand push from abroad, notably from OECD countries, would be important to strengthen the incipient economic recovery.

Real GDP, domestic demand, and exports in the Asian region recovered strongly during 2002, but performances diverged during the second half as demand from OECD countries faltered and world Information and Communications Technology (ICT) markets turned down. In contrast to China, export and import growth in the Dynamic Asian Economies (DAE) came to a virtual halt by end of the second half and economic activity decelerated. Economies most dependent on ICT production were hardest hit, notably Singapore, where real GDP was virtually flat in the second half compared to the first half, as well as the Philippines and Chinese Taipei. Nevertheless, real GDP growth of the DAE averaged 3 per cent for 2002 as a whole, compared to nearly zero growth in 2001, and the regional current account surplus continued to increase.

Economic activity in the Asian region recovered in 2002

Provided OECD, and particularly ICT, markets recover, real GDP growth in DAE should pick up further in 2003. With core inflation low except in Indonesia, monetary policy is likely to remain supportive of real growth. However geopolitical tensions surrounding Iraq, whose adverse effects on regional tourism, stock prices, foreign direct investment (FDI), and confidence could persist beyond the near-term, along with the outbreak of severe acute respiratory syndrome (SARS) pose greater than normal downside risks to the DAE outlook. In addition to its direct impact, a prolonged slump in external demand could aggravate internal structural problems and thereby further depress economic performance in some economies, notably in Thailand and Indonesia, where private sector debt strains remain serious, and in Chinese Taipei and Hong Kong, China, which have been experiencing deflation.

Growth should pick up further in the Dynamic Asian Economies in 2003

Activity slowed in the Newly Independent States and in South-East Europe

Russia and other Newly Independent States and South-East Europe experienced a slowdown of economic activity from almost 6 per cent in 2001 to somewhat below 5 per cent in 2002. The slowdown was partly due to weak external demand, and partly to continued structural problems. Growth performances converged, as most countries expanded between 4 and 6 per cent. Notable exceptions were Kazakhstan and Azerbaijan, where expansion in the oil sector fuelled economic growth rates of roughly twice the average for the zone. In most countries gradual disinflation continued, generally helped by the relative strengthening of the local currency with respect to the dollar.

Activity in South America is slowly picking up from the 2002 downturn

After a sharp economic downturn in the first half of 2002, South America experienced a trend reversal in the second half of the year, with the exception of Venezuela. This incipient recovery was mainly driven by strong improvements in the trade account, linked to the strong and persistent depreciation of exchange rates in various countries. Nevertheless, the GDP of the region still contracted by about 1 per cent in 2002, due in part to a 40 per cent drop of foreign direct investment (FDI) inflows to the region. For 2003, growth could increase somewhat, but there are major downside risks. In Argentina, while the severe recession is bottoming out, the recovery has not been supported by major policy actions awaiting the new government. Venezuela's economy may contract sharply in 2003 due to the temporary interruption of oil production and other economic activity and the associated drop in consumption. In Brazil, the smooth government transition in January and the orthodox policies put in place by the new administration have somewhat lessened the pressure on the exchange rate. Despite this development, inflationary pressures have persisted, requiring several increases in the base interest rate, and this in turn is limiting domestic demand growth. The outlook for Chile seems more favourable as exports are expected to grow, under the influence of the free trade agreements with the European Union and the United States, while consumer demand is recovering. Overall, depressed domestic demand and little room for manoeuvre for expansionary policies imply that an increase in foreign demand, mostly from OECD countries, as well as a recovery in foreign investment, will be decisive for the pick-up of growth in South America.

China

Real GDP growth accelerated further in the second half of 2002

China's real GDP growth accelerated further in the second half of 2002 to reach 8 per cent for the year as a whole, compared with the 7.3 per cent increase in 2001. GDP growth accelerated further in the first quarter of 2003, to its fastest pace since 1997. The unexpectedly strong growth performance has been driven by domestic demand, while the contribution of net exports was smaller than in 2001.

Domestic demand growth has been driven by government investment

Government fixed investment spending continues to be the largest contributor to growth. Real estate investment surged by 22 per cent year-on-year in 2002, but with vacancy rates over 10 per cent in major cities, concerns are rising that a new bubble may be in the making. Despite a rise in enterprise profits as a result of accelerating sales, business capital spending has remained relatively weak, due to limited access to credit by non-state enterprises and to continued excess capacity.

Private consumption growth has picked up

The slowdown of household spending in the first half of 2002 was followed by a sharp rebound in the second half. Personal consumption spending has been concentrated on durables, led by passenger cars, and has been especially strong in coastal cities. Growth in rural incomes and consumption continue to be weak, however. The

Table III.1. **Projections for China**[a]

	2001	2002	2003	2004
Real GDP growth	7.3	8.0	7.7	7.1
Inflation	0.7	-0.8	-0.2	0.0
Fiscal balance (% of GDP)	-2.6	-3.0	-3.0	-3.2
Current account balance ($ billion)	17.4	18.5	17.6	15.1
Current account balance (% of GDP)	1.5	1.5	1.3	1.1

a) The figures given for GDP and inflation are percentage changes from the previous year. Inflation refers to the consumer price index.
Source: Figures for 2001 and most of 2002 are from national sources. Figures for 2003-04 are OECD estimates and projections.

spending on consumer durables in part reflects a stock adjustment to the rise in individual home ownership sparked by housing reforms and to the fall in automobile prices in 2002 in the wake of tariff cuts.

China's exports registered exceptionally strong growth in 2002, reaching 22 per cent, year-on-year. Export growth has been concentrated on Asia and Europe (21 and 20 per cent, respectively) reflecting a strong rebound of imports in the former and increasing market share in both regions. Imports also surged in 2002, reaching a growth rate of 21 per cent (year-on-year), driven by strong exports and domestic infrastructure spending, and further boosted by recovering domestic consumption and by tariff and quota reductions related to entry into the World Trade Organisation (WTO). FDI inflows rose by 13 per cent in 2002 compared to 2001, reaching $53 billion.

Exports have been spurred by further market share gains

Deflation has eased somewhat as a result of strong consumption spending, higher oil prices and a rise in food prices due to severe weather conditions. However, there has been little change in the underlying conditions behind the deflation, notably excess supplies in much of industry.

Deflation has eased but the underlying sources remain

Despite the rapid growth in 2002, domestic demand growth is likely to slow during 2003-04 as the real estate investment boom cools and as the stock adjustment in autos and other consumer durables now underway eases. The outbreak of severe acute respiratory syndrome could further depress growth, particularly if it is not quickly contained. The external contribution to GDP may also decline somewhat as gains in export market shares slow. The incoming government thus faces the challenge of achieving more balanced growth while boosting job creation to contain rising unemployment. The scope for macroeconomic stimulus is limited by the already low level of interest rates, the rising budget deficit and the prospectively large future increases in government debt likely to be needed to recapitalise the banking system and carry out other reforms.

Domestic demand growth is likely to slow in 2003-04

Accordingly, sustaining real GDP growth is likely to depend increasingly on structural reforms. Key in this regard are financial sector reforms to end the present virtual credit crunch in lending to non-state and other small and medium sized enterprises (including rural enterprises). Equally important are measures to transform state-owned enterprises into profit-oriented commercial firms with the technology and other capabilities to enable them to be competitive. Public finances also need to be extensively reformed to provide better support to rural areas and a social safety net for those displaced by reforms. Reforms already taken represent important steps toward these goals but are unlikely to be sufficient. There has been much discussion over the past year of new major policy initiatives, particularly in the financial sector, but as yet no official decisions have been taken.

Further structural reforms are needed

The Russian Federation

Russian GDP continues to expand, but growth is increasingly uneven

Russia's GDP growth slowed to 4.3 per cent in 2002. While the service sector boomed, fuelled by real wage increases of above 15 per cent, growth in investment and industrial production continued to slow. Industrial growth was concentrated in the oil, metal and food processing sectors, with the rest of industry by and large stagnating. Exports rose in value terms, driven by higher export volumes. With import growth moderating, the current account surplus remained above 9 per cent of GDP, though decreasing somewhat.

Macroeconomic policies remain sound...

Inflation continued to decline gradually, supported by the continuing real appreciation of the rouble against the dollar. The central bank's recent move to inflation targeting also points to enhanced determination to stem inflation. Overall, external competitiveness was little affected in 2002, as the effective real exchange rate remained almost unchanged due to the rouble's depreciation against the euro. The recent introduction of more efficient monetary policy instruments – as repo and reverse repo operations – will facilitate liquidity management and sterilisation. In turn, this should reduce to some extent the trade-off between accepting higher inflation or allowing faster appreciation of the real exchange rate that characterised the previous monetary regime. Given underlying inflationary pressures and high oil-driven capital inflows, achieving the 2003 inflation target of 10 to 12 per cent without damaging the competitiveness of the Russian economy will be challenging. On the fiscal side a substantial part of increased revenues from higher oil prices in 2002 were channeled into a reserve fund (set up originally to provide for high debt repayments in 2003), as have been recent privatisation revenues. The transformation of this reserve fund into a stabilisation fund against government revenue shortfalls during periods of low oil prices is currently under discussion. The 2003 budget, while expansionary, plans for a small surplus, and in addition has a substantial built-in buffer as it is based on oil prices of around $20 per barrel.

... and there has been some progress on structural reform

Electricity reform made substantial progress as the Duma approved the plan to split up the monopoly electricity company along functional lines and to introduce competition in the sector. While the situation for small and medium sized enterprises remains difficult, deregulation policies recently approved have led to some improvement in the business climate. The current revision of the bankruptcy law should help

—————— Table III.2. **Projections for the Russian Federation**^{a} ——————

	2001	2002	2003	2004
Real GDP growth	5.0	4.3	5.0	3.5
Inflation	18.6	15.1	14.0	11.0
Fiscal balance (% of GDP)^b	2.9	1.0	0.1	1.0
Primary fiscal balance (% of GDP)^c	5.6	3.4	2.7	3.0
Current account balance ($ billion)	35.0	32.2	34.0	25.0
Current account balance (% of GDP)	11.3	9.3	8.5	5.5

a) The figures given for GDP are percentage changes from previous year. Inflation refers to the end-of-year consumer price index.
b) Consolidated budget (including federal, regional and municipal budgets, excluding off-budget funds).
c) Federal Budget.
Source: Figures for 2001 and most of 2002 are figures from national sources. Figures for 2003-04 are OECD projections.

to make property rights more secure. There has also been some recent progress on railway and pension reform and the government has started to tackle regulatory, administrative, and military reforms. While the reform process is taking time, the recent large investment of British Petroleum (BP) in the Russian oil sector suggests improving confidence among the international business community in the capacity of the current government to deliver on reforms.

Continuing strong domestic demand will sustain robust real GDP growth in 2003. Investment, mainly in oil and utilities, has recently picked up, and private consumption will continue to be strong due to a further rise in disposable income. The latter is, however, likely to abate after parliamentary elections take place in late 2003.

Growth is likely to continue in 2003…

Further expansion in oil production and planned investments in utilities are likely to sustain moderate growth beyond 2003. Growth in the oil sector, and a further shift away from more complex and less competitive manufactured goods into commodities and basic manufactures should contribute to increase overall productivity levels. These developments may, however, increase the vulnerability of the Russian economy to external shocks, while rising wages and real exchange rate appreciation risk undermining growth in other industrial sectors. To stem these developments, further structural reforms, particularly in the area of taxation and banking, will be needed to facilitate the reallocation of resources to potentially more dynamic sectors.

… but its unbalanced nature may pose threats in the medium-long term

Brazil

The Brazilian economy performed somewhat better in the second half of 2002 compared to the first half. Several factors explain this trend. The adjustment of the trade imbalance accelerated due to the major exchange rate depreciation. After the elections, confidence improved, leading to a modest recovery in investment. Finally, the economic spurt in the second half (year-on-year) partly reflects a depressed base of comparison in the second half of 2001, when economic activity was low due to the energy crisis. Noteworthy, in parallel to these developments, Brazil faced a large shortfall of private capital inflows, including commercial credit lines and FDI. In this context, the financial package of the International Monetary Fund was critical in lessening the pressures on the balance of payments.

The Brazilian economy is recovering from the confidence shock…

Responding to the inflationary effects of the exchange rate depreciation, the monetary authorities raised the base interest rate during the second half of 2002. Nevertheless, inflation came in above the end-2002 target and inflationary pressures persisted in the first months of 2003. This led the central bank to tighten monetary policy further. The exchange rate shock and increases in the base interest rate raised the public debt, which is largely indexed to these two variables. The public finances remained on track but, to provide for the increased cost of servicing the debt, the government has had to increase the primary surplus to almost 4 per cent of GDP in 2002.

… but the large exchange rate depreciation generated inflationary pressures

The remarkably smooth government transition in January and the commitment of the new administration to pursue a prudent monetary stance and fiscal austerity have re-established confidence. Accordingly, exchange rate pressures diminished and the public debt to GDP ratio has improved since the elections. However, slow

Presently there is no room for expansionary macroeconomic policies…

Table III.3.   **Projections for Brazil**[a]

	2001	2002	2003	2004
Real GDP growth	1.4	1.5	2.0	3.0
Inflation	7.7	12.5	14.0	9.0
Fiscal balance (% of GDP)[b]	-3.6	-4.6	-4.5	-3.0
Primary fiscal balance (% of GDP)	3.8	3.9	4.3	4.0
Current account balance ($ billion)	-23.2	-8.6	-5.0	-6.0
Current account balance (% of GDP)	-4.6	-1.8	-1.1	-1.1

a) The figures given for GDP and inflation are average percentage changes from the previous period. Inflation refers to the end-year consumer price index (IPCA).
b) Harmonised concept excluding revaluations of public debt due to changes in the exchange rate.
Source: Figures for 2001 and 2002 are from national sources. Figures for 2003-04 are OECD estimates and projections

economic growth is putting the finances of the states and municipalities under pressure. Fiscal policy is due to be further tightened during 2003, with a foreseen increase in the primary surplus achieved in large part by severe public expenditure cuts. These restrictive macroeconomic policies will continue to restrain domestic demand. An increase in net exports will not be easy, given the already high degree of capacity utilisation and weak demand of Brazil's trading partners. Moreover, increasing productive capacity by investment is constrained by high real domestic interest rates and limited international credit.

... but the outlook may improve with increased confidence

In this context, implementation of structural reforms is a key element in the confidence-building process. The government has submitted proposals in the areas of tax and pension reform to the congress. Sticking to the reform agenda is a necessary condition to strengthen confidence, which would allow the exchange rate to stabilise, reduce inflationary pressures, and decrease domestic interest rates. In principle, these trends should be accompanied by renewed international credit lines. Under this favourable scenario, the debt burden would be alleviated and investment and consumption boosted. An improved international environment would also increase exports by the end of 2003 and in 2004, fostering economic growth. Under a more pessimistic scenario, government efforts to pursue reforms would either not materialise, or not be rewarded by increased capital inflows and economic growth. The political and social difficulties associated with such a scenario create uncertainties to the outlook.

IV. AFTER THE TELECOMMUNICATIONS BUBBLE

Introduction

The turn of the century saw a "boom and bust" investment cycle in the industries of information and communications technology (ICT) of most OECD countries.[1] The telecommunications sector, in particular, increased its capital spending sharply in the 1990s, after governments opened the market to new entrants. Investment was also spurred by the introduction of marketable new technologies – notably mobile phones and Internet access services. The new regulatory environment, rapid technological innovation and potential for new service development excited the appetite of the investment community. This led to large flows of equity issuance, debt floatation and bank credit. Awash with cash, companies were able to finance large-scale investment projects, notably the construction of vast fibre-optic cable, and pay high prices for the rights to use third generation wireless spectrum networks. When it became clear that the "hype" for the telecommunications sector had gone too far, expectations returned to more realistic levels, investors became much more prudent and financing evaporated. This left companies with severely impaired balance sheets and large non-profitable fixed assets. While demand for telecommunications services continues to grow strongly, the path to recovery is requiring a period of retrenchment and restructuring before investors' and creditors' confidence can be restored.

The burst of the bubble left telecom firms with impaired balance sheets

In most cases, market forces have been allowed to correct past imbalances, without public interference. It is generally considered that competitive markets are the appropriate environment to encourage adjustment through restructuring. Some participants and observers nonetheless suggest that regulators should provide a degree of relief during this difficult phase, to moderate competition and encourage new investment. It has also been argued that a number of European governments sold spectrum licences at excessive prices in 2000 and 2001 – at the peak of the bubble – and that consequently the "rules of the game" should be relaxed in order to make new mobile telephony investments profitable.

Governments have let market forces drive the restructuring

After examining the present economic situation of the telecommunications sector, this chapter discusses these policy issues. Several findings emerge:

- First, the restructuring of the sector is well underway. Companies have entered into negotiations with creditors to reorganise their liabilities and strengthen their balance sheets. This is facilitated in some countries by legal

Confidence is slowly coming back

---

1. This chapter was drafted jointly by the OECD's Economics Department and the Directorate for Science, Technology and Industry. It draws heavily on *OECD Communications Outlook: 2003 Edition*.

provisions for debt renegotiations – such as Chapter 11 of the US Bankruptcy Law – while elsewhere debt restructuring is more gradual. Thanks to this progress, confidence is slowly coming back.

Demand for telecom services remains strong

– Second, empirical evidence suggests that the macroeconomic impact of the sector's restructuring is small, reflecting its relatively limited GDP weight, but with significant upstream effects, notably on equipment suppliers. Judged from the robust demand from consumers and businesses, however, the telecommunications services and equipment sectors should return to steady growth once financial restructuring is completed.

A fundamental shift in regulatory policy is not justified at this stage

– Third, present circumstances do not appear to justify a fundamental shift in regulatory policy. Dynamic competition is still hampered in some market segments, in particular high-speed Internet access, which deprives consumers and businesses from some windfall benefits of ICT innovations. Regulators are adapting their framework to changing circumstances, rolling back regulation where competition has emerged, and strengthening it where incumbents still retain dominant positions. They are also taking steps to make regulation more technology-neutral, which would spur inter-modal competition (cable, wireless, fixed lines, satellite) and help resolve some of the present problems with the unbundling of local loops (access of new entrants to subscribers' lines). More generally, financial help from governments does not seem to be a promising way to support the sector's recovery.

The high prices of UMTS licences in Europe is one of several factors of stress

– Finally, available evidence does not clearly suggest that the European auctions of Universal Mobile Telecommunications System (UMTS) licences were inefficient. It does not show either that auctions were responsible for the current financial stress of European operators, although it was one of the various factors. Nonetheless, a reform of some regulatory aspects of third generation (3G) licences might be considered, in particular transferability, as this would facilitate market entry, spur competition and speed up the launching of this new type of network. Changing this important rule after having solid spectrum rights might however be seen as providing a government subsidy, because it would make the rights more valuable without changing their price.

A reversal of fortunes

Governments have opened telecom markets to new entrants

The regulatory framework of the telecommunications industry changed radically during the past decade in almost all OECD countries, particularly after 1996-97 (Box IV.1). As technological innovation made competition increasingly possible in the long-distance and international telephony markets, policy makers sought to liberalise the access of new entrants. New independent regulatory agencies were established with a mandate to open markets to competition, prevent incumbents from abusing their position and avoid collusion between operators. Following these decisions, telecommunications markets became more competitive (Figure IV.1). Other actions were undertaken to liberalise the industry, including number portability and carrier selection. In addition, progress was made towards the privatisation of state-owned operators.

Box IV.1. **The OECD-wide regulatory reform in telecommunications markets**

All OECD countries are committed to having competitive markets for telecommunications.[1] Regulatory frameworks were adapted during the second half of the 1990s to open telecommunications markets to competition and establish an environment conducive to lower prices. New legislation was adopted in the United States under the Telecommunications Act of 1996 and in the European Union under the Telecommunications Directive of 1997. Sector-specific National Regulatory Agencies (NRAs) were set up to complement the roles of economy-wide competition authorities. Fixed line telecommunications markets were opened for a broad range of services – from international to local calls. Incumbents were required to grant new entrants access to their networks both for voice telephony and high-speed Internet access. Other liberalisation measures included the privatisation or partial privatisation of incumbent public operators; the opening of the sector to foreign ownership; price regulation for services where dominant positions prevail; and other mea-

sures such as number portability that enhance consumer choice. As a result of these regulatory measures, competition has intensified and consumers have benefited from greater choice, lower prices and higher quality services. New entrants have gained sizeable shares in the markets for long-distance national and international calls (OECD, 2003a), although the degree of competition prevailing in the United States – which opened its long distance market in the mid-1980s – is not yet matched in all OECD countries. In the new markets of mobile telephony and Internet access services, the absence of pre-established market positions has facilitated competition. In mobile telephony, nearly all countries have at least three operators, but the subsidiaries of the incumbent fixed operators often have established predominant market share.[2] All countries have a plethora of companies providing Internet dial-up (low-speed) access, but little competition prevails for broadband (high-speed) access as the subsidiaries of fixed line often incumbents dominate the market.

1. Turkey, the last country to open its market, will do so in early-2004 and has already established a regulatory framework for competition.
2. Except in the United Kingdom and the United States where incumbents do not dominate the mobile telephone market.

Fast market growth was projected...

The liberalisation of the sector, together with the emergence of new telecommunications technologies (Box IV.2) resulted in high expectations for future revenues and earnings, boosting share prices and allowing unprecedented levels of borrowing. A bright future was predicted for the industry.[2] For instance, some analysts predicted

Investors expected rapid increases in revenue and earnings

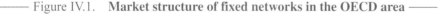

Figure IV.1. **Market structure of fixed networks in the OECD area**

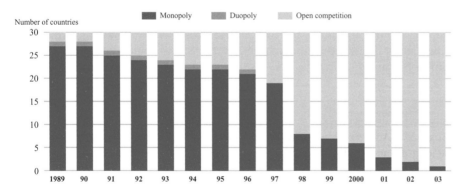

Source: OECD (2003a), *Communications Outlook.*

2. In May 1997, for instance, William Moroney, President of the Multi Media Telecommunications Association predicted that "the road signs all indicate that, basically, the sky is the limit for communication companies".

Box IV.2.   **New telecommunications technologies**

Many technological innovations reached the telecommunications market in the 1990s. New optical technologies made it possible to multiply the transmission capacity of fibre-optic cables. Together with innovation in computers and software this raised the speed at which computers send and receive data and access the Internet. Asymmetric digital subscriber line (ADSL) helped to upgrade traditional copper wires and offer broadband (high-speed) access. Cellular mobile operators constructed second generation networks and, in many OECD

countries, their customer base grew rapidly, in some cases surpassing the number of fixed network subscribers. The third generation of mobile telephones (Universal mobile telecommunications systems) was promised to become a breakthrough in mobile access to Internet. Technological innovation remains dynamic, which is likely to further change the telecommunications landscape in the future. New wireless technologies – such as Wireless-Fidelity (Wi-Fi) and other wireless networks – are likely to influence future trends in the sector.

---

a doubling of Internet traffic every 90 days and double-digit growth in revenues for services and equipment.[3] Research analysts at large investment banks encouraged investors to buy shares and bonds issued by telecommunications companies, which they saw as having promising prospects.[4]

... but expectations of double-digit revenue growth were over-optimistic...

Revenue growth has declined, but traffic keeps on increasing

These high expectations however were not realised. For example, while Internet traffic did grow rapidly (doubling every year), its expansion was significantly slower than earlier predictions.[5] Also, double-digit increases in telecommunications revenue never materialised. During 1996-2001, telecommunications revenue in the OECD area grew by 7.2 per cent annually on average, but slowed to 1.6 per cent in 2001 under the pressure of the economic downturn. According to preliminary indications for the United States and France,[6] revenues may have been roughly flat in 2002, reflecting a combination of price competition and growing traffic.[7]

... and borrowing was excessive

Telecom companies have encountered severe financial difficulties...

With revenues increasing much less rapidly than expected, the business plans of telecommunications operators became highly vulnerable and market sentiment changed rapidly. Creditors and investors revised their expectations of earnings growth towards more realistic levels when they became aware of the degradation of net margins and the increase in debt stocks. It also became clear that the wave of

---

3. Telecommucations Industry Association (TIA) (1997).
4. See for instance the testimony of J.B. Grubman before the US House Committee on Financial Services Hearing regarding Worldcom, 8 July 2002.
5. Coffman and Odlyzko (2001).
6. Fixed line telecommunications revenue in the United States is estimated by Merrill Lynch to have declined by 7 per cent in 2002. In contrast, revenue from wireless telephony increased by 17 per cent in 2002 and revenues from data transfer by 33 per cent. In France, overall telecommunications revenue was stagnating by mid-2002, according to the regulatory agency (*Autorité de régulation des télécommunications*), while traffic increased by 5.6 per cent at constant prices. These numbers should be used with caution, however, because the definition of telecommunications revenue may vary considerably, as well as their consolidation.
7. The overall growth of communication traffic reflects diverging trends across market segments. Fixed line voice telephony traffic tends to stagnate or decline, whereas wireless and Internet access grow strongly.

mergers and acquisitions in the sector, especially in Europe, had taken place at excessively high prices, and that take-over companies might have to significantly write-down the value of acquired assets. Confidence was further undermined in June 2002 when Worldcom, one of the largest US telecommunications long-distance operators, issued a first financial restatement of $3.8 billion and subsequently defaulted on its debt payments. This raised the fear that inappropriate accountancy and governance practices had prevailed in the sector.[8] Stock markets reacted by pushing telecommunications equity prices down, notably in Europe and Japan where they had previously recorded the most spectacular increases (Figure IV.2). The negative sentiment spilled over to the bond market. Rating firms downgraded many operators or put them under review. Several large firms – including Worldcom and Global Crossing – filed for bankruptcy under Chapter 11 in the United States and AT&T Canada undertook a similar proceeding.[9] This led to a wave of defaults on telecommunications corporate bonds and contributed to the largest cycle of defaults on bonds since the 1930s. Defaults on corporate bonds worldwide reached $163 billion in 2002, of

— Figure IV.2.   **Share price indices of selected telecommunications operators** —

United States and Japan

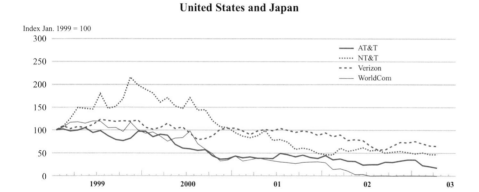

Europe

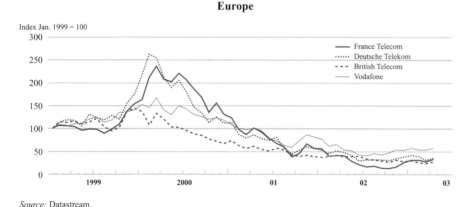

Source: Datastream.

---

8. The role of research analysts at large investment banks was also put into questions, and some banks agreed to pay fines in settlement of cases regarding their dealings.

9. According to Bankruptcy.com, among the largest 15 public companies in the United States that went bankrupt in 2002, eight were communications operators: Worldcom (assets of $104 billion), Global Crossing ($31 billion), Adelphia Communications ($22 billion), NTL ($13 billion), XO Communications ($8 billion), Williams Communications ($6 billion), McLeod USA ($5 billion) and Asia Global Crossing ($4 billion).

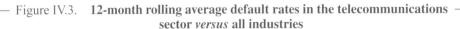

Figure IV.3. **12-month rolling average default rates in the telecommunications sector *versus* all industries**

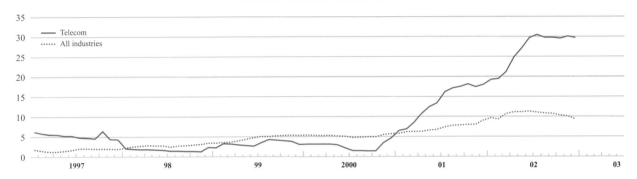

Source: Standard & Poor's CreditPro® 6.2.

which 56.4 per cent in the telecommunications sector,[10] including some investment grade companies[11] (Figure IV.3). The fear of bankruptcy and default resulted into a sharp increase in corporate bond spreads in the middle of 2002. The overall impact on bond markets was, however, limited. Telecom defaults represented 3.2 per cent of the value of bonds outstanding, more than during the previous peak in 1991, but not enough to trigger systemic risk or a credit crunch.[12]

... and some legal challenges

The combination of financial excesses and corporate governance malpractice has triggered a number of legal challenges. In the United States, ongoing grand jury subpoenas into companies' accounting practices and lawsuits filed by various groups (minority shareholders, bondholders and other creditors) brought uncertainty regarding future financial obligations. The quality of information provided to shareholders at the time of mergers and acquisitions has also been challenged before the courts in some European countries. Operators are still attempting to unravel some complex legal issues linked to their international expansion.[13]

The industry is in the middle of a deep financial restructuring

Firms are restructuring their balance sheets

Burdened by high debts, many operators have embarked on restructuring programmes to cut costs, reduce debt, sell assets and strengthen balance sheets. In the United States, firms that filed for bankruptcy under Chapter 11 are negotiating with the various groups of claimants to obtain majority approval[14] for the reorganisation of their liabilities. During the re-negotiation period, firms do not exit the market and

---

10. Moody' Investors Services (2003), *Default and Recovery Rates of Corporate Bond Issuers,* Global Credit Research, February.
11. Investment grade companies that defaulted in North America included AT&T Canada, MCI Wordcom, Inc., and its subsidiary SkyTel Communications, Teleglobe and Qwest Communications International.
12. Bernanke (2003).
13. For instance, France Telecom has been involved in complex legal issues involving its stake in a German wireless company (Mobilcom).
14. Under the provisions of the US Bankruptcy Reform Act of 1978 and supplementary legislation in 1994, the management of firms that file for bankruptcy under Chapter 11 has 120 days to prepare a reorganisation plan (this period can be extended by the courts), and a further two months to gain the approval of the creditors. The reorganisation plan must be approved by the majority of creditors (representing two-thirds of claims) in each class of claimants.

continue to provide their services. Management in some companies was able to gain majority approval for the restructuring of their debts. Reorganisation plans have typically cancelled all existing equity shares, which ceased to be valid, and provided for an exchange of bonds against newly floated shares, at a fraction of the face value. Some firms have also bought back or traded their liabilities (or their subsidiaries' debts) at a significant discount from face value, thus reducing their indebtedness. In Canada, similar steps were taken.[15] In continental Europe, where bankruptcy procedures similar to Chapter 11 do not exist, several incumbents that have accumulated very large debts have embarked on gradual approaches to reduce their obligations. They typically combine sales of non-essential assets, reductions in investment and current spending, debt refinancing and new equity issuance. In countries where companies are still partially state-owned, government funding and loan guarantees are also envisaged.[16]

The direct macroeconomic impact of this restructuring is not substantial, reflecting the telecommunications sector's relatively small weight in national economies (between 2 and 4 per cent of GDP), but it has a significant upstream impact on equipment suppliers and technology firms and contributes to reduced high-tech share prices.

The direct macroeconomic impact is limited...

Investment is being sharply cut back...

The telecommunications industry invested heavily until 2000, when spending on infrastructure reached nearly $230 billion in the OECD (about 4 per cent of total business fixed investment). Starting in 2001, long-distance carriers severely slashed their capital expenditure, having no inventories to run down and little operating costs to cut in the short-term. In 2001, investment fell to $194 billion. Anecdotal evidence regarding telephone equipment manufacturers suggests that capital expenditure was cut even more aggressively in 2002. According to some estimates,[17] capital spending by US telecommunications service providers may have dropped by 47 per cent in 2002, bringing it back to the level recorded in 1997.[18] This retrenchment of capital spending is hurting companies upstream, notably equipment suppliers which had to downsize their activities (Figure IV.4).

... but upstream ripple effects are negative for equipment suppliers

For the time being, investment spending cuts appear to be a sensible response to current conditions, and there are no signs that the quality of services has deteriorated. If sustained for a long period, such low level of capital spending may however eventually weaken the capacity of operators to deliver higher-quality services and deploy new technologies. Mobile phone operators must for instance invest to launch their UMTS network, even though they have postponed and downscaled their plans. Internet service providers need to invest to increase their capacity in offering broadband services.

Investment remains sufficient for high-quality services

---

15. For instance, AT&T Canada obtained approval from its bondholders on a plan to restructure the company's balance sheet and equity. Under the plan, bondholders and other affected creditors receive approximately 17.4 per cent on their claims (part in cash, part in shares of the company).
16. France Telecom for instance announced a three-pronged approach to restructure its debt of € 68 billion. The company is seeking to reduce spending by € 15 billion, raise € 15 billion in new equity (including € 9 billion from the government) and refinance € 15 billion in maturities.
17. TIA (2002).
18. The investment level in 1997 was relatively high historically, but the investment retrenchment is nonetheless severe.

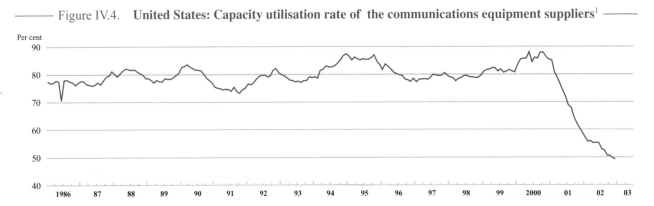

——— Figure IV.4. **United States: Capacity utilisation rate of the communications equipment suppliers**[1] ———

1. Refers to the NAIC industry classification 3342, which includes Telephone Apparatus Manufacturing (NAICS 33421); Radio and Television Broadcasting and Wireless Communications Equipment Manufacturing (NAICS 33422); and Other Communications Equipment Manufacturing (NAICS 33429).
Source: US Federal Reserve.

... but evidence on R&D spending cuts is inconclusive

Some companies are cutting back on R&D, but not all

The telecommunications industry is likely to have cut back its spending on research and development to improve financial results, although available evidence suggests that this was not the case for all operators. Until 2001, leading telecommunications carriers maintained research and development (R&D) expenditure in the order of $6 to $7 billion, in part because some countries regulation require them to allocate a certain amount of their turnover for this activity. In less regulated environments, however, private firms reduced their spending on research and development back to levels of the mid-1990s. Telephone equipment suppliers, which make the bulk of R&D spending on telecommunications technologies, appear to have sharply curtailed their R&D activities in the face of financial challenges.[19]

Confidence seems to be returning slowly

Demand for telecom services is strong

Notwithstanding the financial difficulties, the medium-term prospect for telecommunications services appears promising. Consumer demand for telecommunications services continues to grow, as judged by the increase in the number of subscribers (Figure IV.5). OECD-wide data on this point goes only to 2001 but evidence from large markets suggests that the number of subscribers expanded further in 2002. Forthcoming technologies are likely to stimulate it further. The future of individual market segments is however difficult to predict, not least because of technological uncertainties. Households may also shift away from fixed lines to mobile phones, thus exacerbating the problems of fixed line operators, although the magnitude of this substitution is difficult to predict.

---

19. According to TIA (2002), the following cuts have been announced: Lucent's Bell Labs reduced R&D spending by about a third from fiscal year 2001 ($3.5 billion) to fiscal year 2002 ($2.3 billion); CIENA cut R&D spending by 26 per cent between 31 October 2001 and 31 July 2002; Cisco's R&D spending was down 10 per cent from 31 October 2001 to 31 July 2002; Nortel Networks reduced R&D spending by 28 per cent for the period from 30 September 2001 to 30 June 2002; Tellabs cut its R&D spending by 13 per cent between June 2001 and 31 March 2002; and Ericsson announced plans in 2002 to cut its R&D costs by $773 million and to close half of its 80 R&D offices world-wide.

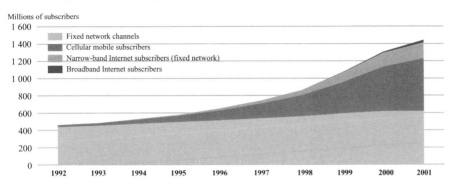

Figure IV.5. Telephone and Internet subscribers in the OECD

Source: OECD (2003a), *Communications Outlook.*

Policy implications

A debate is underway on the appropriate regulatory policy response to telecommunications' companies financial stress

Despite promising medium-term prospects, the present telecom sector retrenchment is painful, some companies are liquidated, spending is cut and jobs are lost. In these circumstances, some observers have argued that regulators should ease their pro-competition stance to help operators restore healthy balance sheets. Available evidence does not demonstrate, however, that the present financial stress stems from regulatory policy decisions made since the mid-1990s. Incumbents have lost market shares to new entrants following liberalisation but, as noted, the overall market size has grown rapidly and incumbents have generally been able to maintain or even increase revenues. Regulatory policy is of course not a goal in itself and measures constraining firm behaviour should eventually be rolled-back, once a competitive environment has been established. Available evidence suggests however that regulatory interventions are still necessary. In some markets, the ongoing consolidation reduces the number of competitors, which alleviates competitive pressure. In addition, incumbents still dominate certain services.

Should regulatory policy be softened to help financial restructuring?

The consolidation underway may reduce competitive pressure

Like in other sectors that saw many entrants fail, the telecommunications sector is presently consolidating as small firms are going out of business or are being acquired by larger firms. This reduces the number of competitors and may have an upward impact on prices. Available evidence suggests for instance that telecommunications services are contributing much less to disinflation in the euro area, after having been an important moderating factor and despite the ongoing price decline of technology equipment (Figure IV.6). In the United States, long-distance prices are

The number of competitors is declining

Figure IV.6. **Telecom services contribution to core inflation in the euro area**[1]

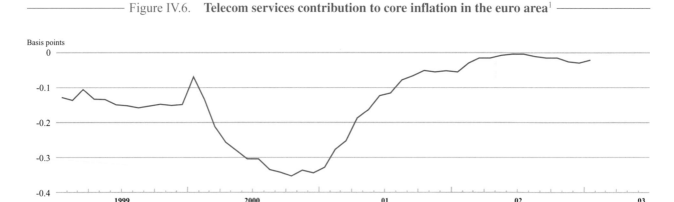

1. Refers to the 12-month percentage change of the HICP index for Telephone and telefax services for the euro-12 area, multiplied by the weight of this index in HICP Core inflation index (overall index excluding energy, food, alcohol and tobacco).
Source: Eurostat.

still on the decline, but there is little sign that the pace of increase in local charges is slowing, despite the opening of this market to competition.[20]

Competition is making slow progress in services requiring access to local loops in the European Union

Unbundling is progressing, after a slow start

Available evidence suggests that competition does not yet prevail in a number of market segments. In some wireless communication markets, the small number of operators requires the intervention of regulators to prevent collusion. The unbundling of the local loop is also exemplary of the difficulties encountered by regulators. Indeed, mixed progress has been made across countries in fostering the penetration of Internet broadband access (Figure IV.7). In the European Union, the opening of local loops was required by a decision of July 2000 and by subsequent national decisions. Implementing legislation is however raising difficult regulatory issues, notably in relation to access prices. Incumbents initially set prices for the use of their infrastructure and lines at levels high enough to discourage access. In addition, they have used delaying tactics related for instance to the need for "collocation" in the operator premises. The pressure of regulators eventually improved conditions for competition, and notably helped reduce the prices charged by incumbent operators.[21] As a result, the number of subscribers has been growing relatively fast and, by October 2002, about 4 per cent of the European Union's 187 million lines had broadband access.[22] The bulk of this is, however, provided by incumbent telecommunications companies. New entrants are pursuing aggressive marketing strategies to gain market shares, with limited results so far.

---

20. While measuring consumer spending on telecommunications services is straightforward, the average price of such services is more difficult to assess. Wireless telephone and Internet access providers offer flat monthly subscription packages, covering different menus of services, which makes it difficult to assess the average price of services really supplied (such as the cost of telephone calls per minute). Hence, some national statistical agencies for the time being exclude mobile phone and Internet services from their consumer price baskets.

21. In the European Union, the monthly rental of fully unbundled loop averages € 12.8 and the connection charges € 103.6, with considerable variance across countries.

22. European Commission (2002).

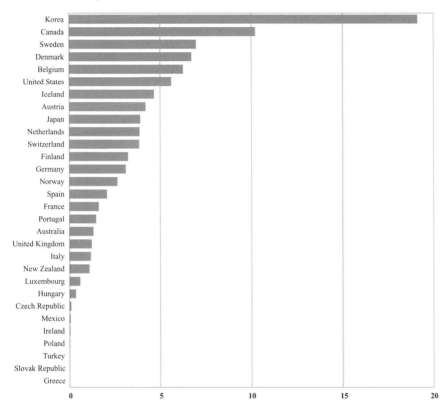

**Figure IV.7. Broadband penetration rates in OECD countries,
June 2002**

Number of DSL,[1] cable modem lines and other broadband[2] per 100 inhabitants

1. Digital subscriber lines.
2. Other broadband technologies include: satellite broadband Internet, fibre-to-the home Internet access, ethernet LANs
   and fixed wireless subscribers (at downstream speeds greater than 256 kbps).
Source: OECD (2003a), *Communications Outlook.*

Recent decisions by the US Federal Communication Commission removed some unbundling obligations

In the United States, the 1996 Telecommunications Act required that Incumbent Local Exchange Carriers unbundle their networks and provide access to new entrants, both for voice telephony and broadband Internet access. The Act allowed long-distance companies to enter the market for local calls, hence introducing competition in a segment of the market where "Baby Bell" companies[23] previously had a monopoly. It also made it possible for new entrants to provide high-speed Internet access services via a connection to copper wire networks. In its Triennial Review proceeding concerning incumbent local exchange carriers' network unbundling obligations in February 2003, the Federal Communication Commission (FCC) decided to soften its direct pressure on Baby Bells by delegating unbundling rulings to individual States, which were deemed better placed to assess inter-modal on local competition conditions. States will therefore be responsible

Some regulatory relief to incumbents in the United States

---

23. "Baby Bells" are the local exchange carriers that were created following the break-up of AT&T. They are specialised in local services (local calls, Internet access).

for deciding whether local loops should be unbundled and for regulating the prices of such services. At the same time, the FCC lifted Baby Bells' obligations to open their fibre-optic cable network to competitors, which may encourage local companies to invest into such networks, but may also weaken competition in related services. In addition, line-sharing obligations, which are seen as an important form of access for broadband access providers, will be eliminated over a three-year period.

Rapid progress was made recently in Japan

In Japan, competition has promoted high-speed Internet access

In Japan, regulators required local loop unbundling in March 2000. The incumbents tried however to retain their dominant positions by setting high access prices. Further pressure was exercised by regulators to ease access.[24] Measures were introduced to set rules for collocation, allow for self-installation of equipment by new entrants and prevent the incumbent companies (Nippon Telegraph and Telephone Corporation, NTT, East and West) from accessing privileged information on subscribers. NTT companies were also obliged to provide the necessary information to support competitors in getting access. The overall effect has been to make Japan a fast growing market for high-speed Internet access. New entrants were providing over 60 per cent of the broadband lines in Japan by end-2002.

The time has not come to roll-back regulatory action

Overall, the example of local loop unbundling shows that the task of opening markets to competition is not yet completed, and that incumbents are still successful in dominating some market segments. While they may eventually relent to regulatory pressure, delaying tactics seem to have been used by incumbents to gain dominant market shares in new markets, which then makes it difficult for new entrants to carve a niche. Hence, there does not seem to be a strong case for providing regulatory relief to distressed incumbents. This would deprive the overall economy from the productivity gains that have been associated with rapid advance in technological innovation.[25]

Towards a technology-neutral regulatory policy?

Although a softer policy stance does not appear to be warranted, there is, however, evidence that regulatory policy should become more technology-neutral in several OECD countries. Technological innovation in recent years has made it possible to provide the same services through different technologies. Voice telephony can be provided via fixed lines, mobile phones, and increasingly via cable television networks, satellite and Internet, with power lines perhaps an additional transmission channel in the future. New networks can compete with old networks. In some cases, however, the same company owns both old and new networks, which may impede competition. While progress has been made in some countries to promote inter-modal competition, many restrictions still prevail in others. The decision by the European Union to introduce a new technology-neutral Regulatory Framework in July 2003 is a step in this direction.

Should the allocation of UMTS licences in Europe be revisited?

The European Union allocation of 3G licences has come under debate

In addition to fixed spending on assets, telecommunications operators spent considerable amounts to purchase spectrum licences, notably in the European Union. The amount committed to buy licences for UMTS services reached close to € 100 billion (Table IV.1). Initially heralded as successful market-based sales of public goods, the allocation of licences in Europe has come under growing scrutiny and debate.

---

24. In December 2000, the charge for unbundled line sharing was reduced from ¥ 800 to ¥ 187 per month (from about $6.15 to only $1.45).
25. OECD (2003b).

Table IV.1.   **Allocation of G3 licences in OECD countries**

	Award Date	Licensing Method	Revenue raised million $US	Remarks
Australia	Mar 2001	Auction	610	48 lots split into 6 licenses
Austria	Nov 2000	Auction	618	6 licenses
Belgium	Mar 2001	Auction	421	3 licenses
Canada	Feb 2001	Auction	931	5 licenses
Czech Republic	Dec 2001	Auction	200	2 licenses
Denmark	Sep 2001	Auction	472	4 licenses
Finland	Mar 1999	Beauty contest	-	licenses awarded to 4 companies, nominal entrance fee
France	Jun 2002	Beauty contest with fee	1 106	2 companies awarded licenses, 2 licenses still available; entrance fee set at $4.5 billion each, reduced to $553 million each plus 1% of revenue
Germany	Aug 2000	Auction	51 000	6 licenses
Greece	Jul 2001	Hybrid auction	414	3 licenses
Ireland	mid-2002	Beauty contest with fee	173	4 licenses, but only 3 bidders
Italy	Oct 2000	Hybrid auction	10 070	5 licenses
Japan	Jun 2000	Beauty contest	-	3 licenses, no fees
Korea	Aug 2001	Beauty contest with fee	2 886	3 licenses
Netherlands	Jul 2000	Auction	2 508	5 licenses
New Zealand	Jan 2001	Auction	60	4 paying licenses, plus one given for free to cover the Maori people
Norway	Nov 2000	Beauty contest with fee	88	4 licenses; each winner paying $11.8 million plus $2.2 million per year over the duration of the license (12 years)
Poland	Dec 2001	Beauty contest with entrance fee	1 839	3 licenses
Portugal	Dec 2000	Beauty contest with fee	360	4 licenses
Spain	Mar 2000	Beauty contest with fee	480	4 licenses
Sweden	Dec 2000	Beauty contest	44	4 licenses, with annual tax of 0.15% of income each year
Switzerland	Dec 2000	Auction	120	4 licenses
United Kingdom	Jun 2000	Auction	35 400	5 licenses
United States	Jan 2001[a]	Auction	16 857	C and F Block Broadband PCS licenses, 35 winning bidders, other earlier broadband PCS auctions not included here

a) Not 3G licenses.
Source: www.*3Gnewsroom.com;* TIA; ITU; FCC.

A debate has emerged on the efficiency of 3G licences in Europe

The European Union required in late 1998 that member states allocate 3G licences before end-2001, preferably through auctions. The United Kingdom and Germany, which were among the early movers, were able to raise considerable revenues. All other member states sold their licences at much lower prices. The diversity of outcomes at the European auctions raises a number of important questions. If the same scarce public good (radio spectrum) was sold in similar countries at very different prices, this might suggest that the auction mechanism was not efficient. Empirical evidence does not indicate that this was the case. licence prices fell in 2001 because market sentiment towards the telecom sector cooled dramatically during the

Available evidence does not demonstrate that auctions were inefficient

period, reducing the amounts that firms and their share-holders were ready to bid. In addition, some auctions appear to have been poorly tailored and failed to attract new entrants. Using the same auction technique as previous governments did prove to be a mistake, as bidders learnt from past experience how to avoid paying excessively high prices. Well-designed auctions appear to have been efficient. While there is therefore no obvious basis for changing the regulatory stance on grounds that the winners paid too much, careful consideration is required for the implementation of auctions, as the final price may be too high or too low under the influence of the auction design.[26]

licences are one of many factors behind current financial difficulties

Irrespective of the analysis on the efficiency of spectrum auctions, the high price paid for UMTS licences is not the main explanatory factor of the financial difficulties experienced by telecommunications operators. In the United States, where these licences have not yet been allocated, financial distress in the telecommunications sector is at least as severe as in Europe. Also, there is no empirical evidence that the share prices of auction winners fared worse than those of auction losers.

A number of regulatory aspects of UMTS services are debated

Nonetheless, a number of decisions regarding UMTS services regulations are under debate in the current, more difficult environment. Regulatory measures have been suggested to facilitate the financial viability of UMTS networks and accelerate the launching of services. A first proposal is to allow the sharing of infrastructure. Some national regulators are allowing operators to share small parts of their networks, mostly for environmental reasons and to reduce negative externalities.[27] Allowing the sharing of larger parts of infrastructure may however reduce competition and encourage the collusion of operators. Another initiative under consideration would allow operators to transfer their licence through secondary market trading. This could be equivalent to a subsidy, however, because it would make a product more valuable after its price has been set. In addition, if spectrum trading is allowed for part of licences, it might lead to a situation where licences are fragmented among several licence holders for the same frequency band. Nonetheless, such a measure would promote competition, because it would put back on the market licences bought by operators now unable to invest in 3G infrastructure. As such, it might be a good measure to avoid a reduction in the number of operators and a decline in competition (Didier and Lorenzi, 2002). A third suggestion is to extend the time period during which the radio spectrum rights can be utilised, in view of the delays in launching services. While suggestions for changing the "rules of the game" are plentiful, it may prove difficult to put them into practice. Changing the rules after having allocated the spectrum may encourage auction losers to challenge regulators in courts and create further legal uncertainties.

---

26. Binmore and Klemperer (2002); Klemperer (2002); and Cable, Henley and Holland (2002).
27. In Germany, for instance, the sharing of sites, masts, antennas, cables and combiners is permitted under certain conditions.

BIBLIOGRAPHY

BERNANKE, B.S. (2003), *Balance Sheets and the Recovery*, Remarks delivered at the 41st Winter Institute, St. Cloud State University, Minnesota, February.

BINMORE, K. and P. KLEMPERER (2002), "The biggest auction ever: the sale of the British 3G Telecom licences", *The Economic Journal*, No. 112, March.

CABLE, J., A. HENLEY and K. HOLLAND (2002), "Pot of Gold or Winner's Curse? An Event Study of the Auctions of 3G Mobile Telephone licences in the UK", *Fiscal Studies*, Vol. 23, No. 4.

COFFMAN, K.G. and A.M. ODLYZKO (2001), *Growth of the Internet*, AT&T Labs, *mimeo*.

DIDIER, M. and J.H. LORENZI (2002), *Enjeux économiques de l'UMTS*, Rapport du Conseil d'analyse économique, La Documentation française, Paris.

EUROPEAN COMMISSION (2002), *Eighth implementation report on the telecommunications regulatory package,* Brussels, December.

KLEMPERER, P. (2002), "Some observations on the Dutch and German 2G Telecom Auctions", *mimeo*, September.

OECD (2003a), *Communications Outlook 2003*, Paris.

OECD (2003b), *The Sources of Economic Growth in OECD Countries*, Paris.

TIA (Telecommunications Industry Association) (1997), "Telecom Market Projected to Achieve Double-Digit Growth through year 2000", Press Release, May 1997, Washington, DC.

TIA (Telecommunications Industry Association) (2002), *Investment, capital spending and service quality in US telecommunications networks: a symbiotic relationship, mimeo*.

V. STRUCTURAL POLICIES AND GROWTH

Introduction

Throughout the 1960s and 1970s, countries with lower GDP *per capita* were generally growing relatively faster than richer ones, leading to a gradual convergence in income levels. This convergence process appears to have reversed during the 1990s, at least among the largest OECD economies, as growth in the United States rose above that observed in Japan and in the major European Union countries. The US growth revival and the related reversal in the convergence process have led to a renewed interest in analysing the relative contribution of institutions, structural policies and other fundamental factors to the growth performance over time and across countries. During the past few years, the OECD has completed a major programme of analysis and empirical research on the sources of economic growth, leading to a broad set of policy recommendations and priority areas for reforms contained in the recent publication, *The Sources of Growth in OECD Countries*.[1] Building on this, as well as on previous in-depth analysis conducted in the context of the *OECD Jobs Strategy*, this Chapter provides an overview of the links between structural polices and labour and product market performance. More specifically, the Chapter reviews the main factors thought to have contributed to differences across countries in the degree of labour resource utilisation, in the intensity of physical and human capital use as well as in the pace of technological progress. In doing so, it provides a number of performance and policy indicators which can be used to assess progress achieved in structural reform.[2]

Recent growth trends have brought structural policies back to the forefront

Diverging growth trends

During the 1960s and 1970s, the pattern of growth across countries was broadly consistent with the conventional view according to which countries lagging in terms of labour productivity and GDP *per capita* gradually close the gap *vis-à-vis* the leading country (the United States). After stalling during the 1980s, the convergence process appears to have reversed during the 1990s, at least among the largest OECD economies, with trend GDP *per capita* growing faster in the United States than in Japan and the large European Union (EU) member countries (Table V.1). Nonetheless, convergence towards US GDP *per capita* has continued for some countries where growth also accelerated after 1995, in particular Canada, Spain, Australia, Sweden, Finland, Ireland and Greece.

Growth rates in GDP per capita have diverged between the largest economies...

---

1. A short summary of the detailed analysis can be found in *The Policy Agenda for Growth* (available on line at: *www.oecd.org/pdf/M00040000/M00040320.pdf*).
2. A version of this chapter including a much wider selection of indicators in tabular or graphical format can be found in de Serres (2003).

Table V.1. **Average trend growth in GDP per capita**
over selected periods

	1980-1995	1995-2002	Change between first and second period
Australia	1.7	2.6	0.8
Austria	2.0	1.9	0.0
Belgium	1.9	2.0	0.2
Canada	1.3	2.5	1.3
Czech Republic	..	2.0	..
Denmark	1.8	2.0	0.2
Finland	1.6	3.5	1.9
France	1.5	1.9	0.4
Germany[a]	1.6	1.4	-0.3
Greece	0.6	3.0	2.4
Hungary	..	3.9	..
Iceland	1.2	2.3	1.1
Ireland	3.8	7.1	3.3
Italy	2.0	1.5	-0.5
Japan	2.9	0.6	-2.3
Korea	6.7	4.3	-2.4
Luxembourg	4.2	3.7	-0.6
Mexico	0.2	2.3	2.1
Netherlands	1.7	2.2	0.5
New Zealand	1.3	2.2	1.0
Norway[b]	1.5	2.0	0.4
Poland	..	4.1	..
Portugal	3.1	2.5	-0.6
Slovak Republic	..	1.7	..
Spain	2.3	2.7	0.4
Sweden	1.3	2.5	1.2
Switzerland	0.9	0.8	-0.1
Turkey	2.1	0.4	-1.8
United Kingdom	2.1	2.2	0.1
United States	2.0	2.3	0.3
Weighted averages			
European Union	1.8	2.0	0.2
Total OECD[c]	2.1	1.9	-0.2

a) West Germany before 1991. For 1980-1995 average excludes 1991.
b) Mainland only.
c) Excluding Czech Republic, Hungary, Poland and Slovak Republic.
Source: OECD *Economic Outlook,* No 72.

... reflecting changes in growth of labour productivity and hours worked

A closer examination of the proximate sources of change in total GDP growth after 1995 shows that while trend labour productivity accelerated in the United States, it slowed in the European Union and Japan, resulting in a convergence of productivity growth rates across the three major economies (Figure V.1). In the case of the European Union, the impact on GDP growth from the slowdown in productivity per hour was partly offset by an increase in employment growth. Despite such improvement in labour market performance, even faster employment growth in the United States accounted for most of the differences in growth in GDP *per capita* between the two economies. Japan is the only country having faced a deceleration in both productivity and labour resource utilisation. Conversely, only a few countries

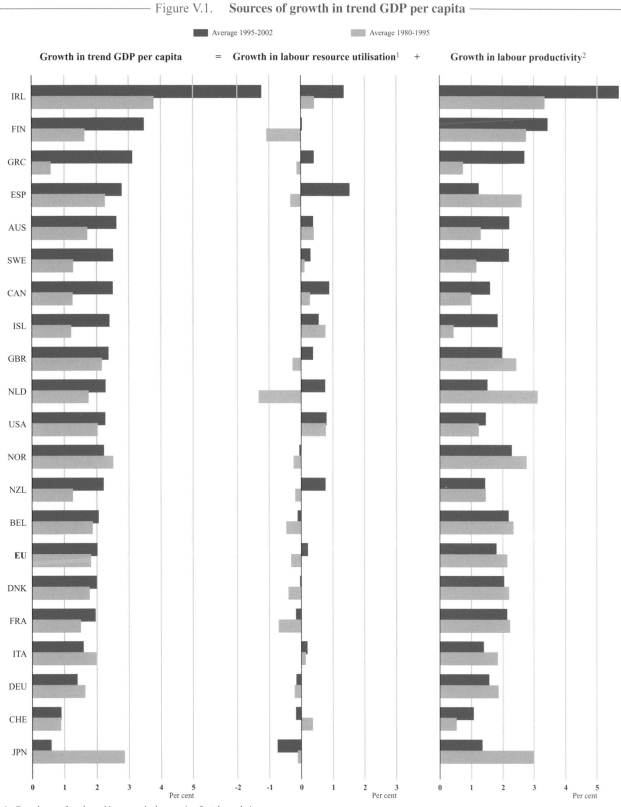

Figure V.1. **Sources of growth in trend GDP per capita**

■ Average 1995-2002   ▨ Average 1980-1995

Growth in trend GDP per capita   =   **Growth in labour resource utilisation**[1]   +   **Growth in labour productivity**[2]

1. Growth rate of total trend hours worked as a ratio of total population.
2. Growth of trend GDP per hour worked.
Source: OECD.

(Canada, Sweden, Finland, Ireland and Greece) enjoyed a clear improvement in both sources of growth in GDP *per capita* after 1995.

Resuming the convergence
process calls for policy changes

Considering that GDP *per capita* in both the European Union and Japan remains around 30 per cent behind that in the United States, the pause – and even reversal – in the convergence process points to the need for changing policies so as to stimulate growth in the two lagging areas. Differences in the sources of the real income gap *vis-à-vis* the United States suggest, however, that the policy priorities faced by the European Union and Japan may be different. In the case of Japan, the gap in GDP *per capita* is due entirely to the lagging performance in productivity. In the EU case, while the process of catch-up in GDP *per capita* had already stalled in the 1980s, convergence in productivity levels continued until the mid-1990s, narrowing the gap to less than 10 per cent of the US level (although this partly reflected the shedding of low-skilled labour). As a result, the relatively low employment rates, combined with the smaller number of hours worked per person employed, account for most of the difference in GDP *per capita* relative to the United States.

Explaining the differences in labour resource utilisation

To the extent that it seems natural for people to demand more leisure as their real income levels go up, an increasing use of labour potential both in terms of employment and hours worked does not necessarily imply a welfare improvement. It is likely, however, that the large discrepancies observed in cross-country employment rates have more to do with the pervasive influence of structural policies on incentives both to hire and to take-up work than with differences in preferences for leisure.

Rising employment rates would
help confront adverse
demographic trends

A look at the sources of growth in labour resource utilisation in EU countries since the mid-1990s shows that the continued decline in average hours worked per person employed was more than offset by the positive impact from rising participation and employment rates (Figure V.2). While such positive trends cannot go on indefinitely, there is still scope in some countries for employment and participation rates to offset the projected negative contribution from demographics. In fact, despite the considerable progress achieved in some of the member countries (the United Kingdom, the Netherlands and Ireland) during the past decade, structural unemployment still remains relatively high in the European Union, leaving significant room for improvement. Related to this, the incidence of long-term unemployment remains quite high in EU countries compared with Japan and the United States and it has not diminished during the 1990s.

Where they occur, weak
employment rates concern
specific groups

Furthermore, the problem of high unemployment in several EU member countries is compounded by low participation rates, resulting in even larger cross-country differences in overall employment rates.[3] Yet, the situation of prime-age males is fairly similar across most OECD countries. The problem of low labour resource

---

3. This is in contrast with the performance of other European countries (Iceland, Switzerland and the Scandinavian countries) which have the highest employment rates among OECD countries.

Figure V.2.   **Sources of growth in trend labour resource utilisation**

Average over 1995-2002

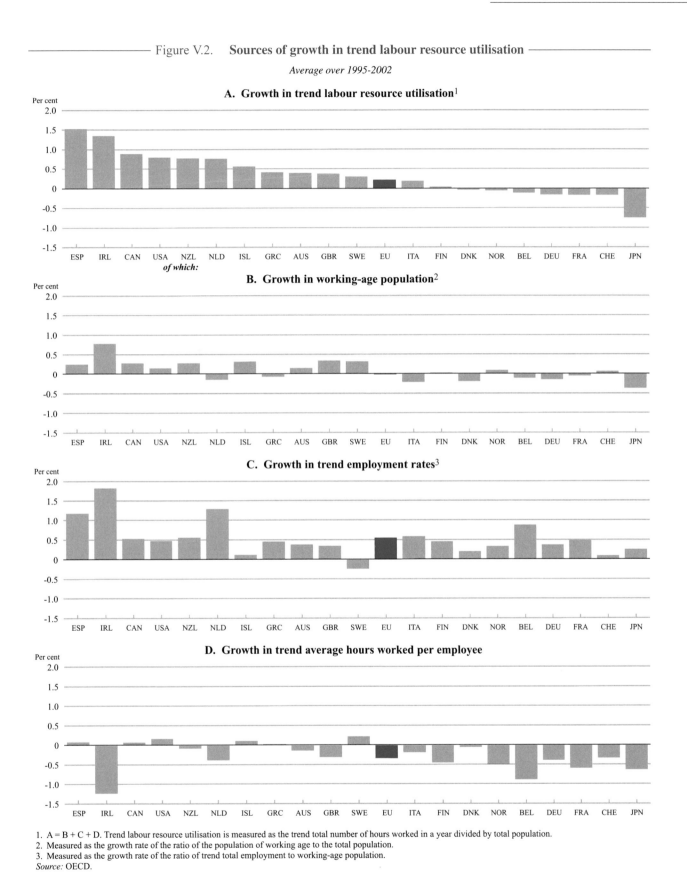

1. A = B + C + D. Trend labour resource utilisation is measured as the trend total number of hours worked in a year divided by total population.
2. Measured as the growth rate of the ratio of the population of working age to the total population.
3. Measured as the growth rate of the ratio of trend total employment to working-age population.
Source: OECD.

utilisation in the European Union is thus concentrated in much lower participation and employment rates of young, old and female workers.

The key policies to raise labour utilisation are well known

The key structural policies responsible for the diverse labour market performance are well known and their influence has been the object of a comprehensive analysis in the context of the *OECD Jobs Strategy* (OECD, 1999a). They can be regrouped into two broad categories: *i)* the tax and benefit system which includes unemployment support and tax wedges and *ii)* labour and product market regulation which covers employment protection legislation, rules regarding minimum wages and other working conditions as well as administrative burdens on the start-up of firms and other barriers to competition. Some of the policy instruments, such as the minimum wage and the level of the out-of-work benefits relative to in-work net income, may have a direct impact on structural unemployment *via* wage floors or by raising workers' reservation wage. For many other policies, however, the main impact is rather indirect, operating *via* their combined effects on the speed and extent of real wage adjustment, the persistence of unemployment and the resilience of labour markets to shocks. In all cases, such policies have been introduced with specific objectives in mind and negative employment effects as an unintended side-effect. Nonetheless, in many cases those objectives may be obtained through other policy instruments with less undesirable side-effects. In other cases, consideration of the negative consequences would justify some compromise in terms of the primary objectives.

Tax and benefit system

Achieving social objectives with minimum impact on incentives is a challenge...

In reforming the system of tax and benefits, policymakers are frequently confronted with a trade-off between meeting social objectives and minimising disincentives to work. For instance, unemployment benefits provide needed support to individuals and households experiencing job losses. However, high replacement rates can raise the structural unemployment rate by lowering the gap between the income from work and the income received on support. This is particularly the case if high replacement rates are accompanied by a lengthy entitlement period. An extended benefit period can contribute to lengthening the average unemployment spell, thus leading to a loss of human capital and a reinforcement of insider-outsider mechanisms,[4] potentially reducing the overall wage sensitivity to labour market conditions.

... as illustrated by the difficulty in lowering high replacement rates...

Indicators combining replacement rates and duration of benefits show that unemployment income support relative to the wage level can be quite high in several countries (Figure V.3, panel A), especially in the case of the long-term unemployed whose earnings' potential in the labour market is often less than that of the average production worker (Figure V.3, panel C). Yet, despite empirical evidence that high replacement rates and long benefit duration can have a sizeable impact on structural unemployment, reform in this area has proved to be difficult.[5] In fact, the gross replacement rate indicator has continued to rise in many countries between 1995 and 1999 (Figure V.3, panel B).

---

4. A labour market characterised by a strong insider-outsider mechanism is one where unemployed workers (outsiders) have little or no influence on the outcome of wage bargaining between employees (insiders) and firms' managers, even when the unemployment rate is relatively high. As a result, the real wage fails to adjust in a way that would facilitate the re-absorption of unemployed workers.
5. For empirical evidence on the effect of replacement rates on unemployment rates in OECD countries, see Elmeskov *et al.* (1998) and Nickell and Layard (1998).

Figure V.3.   Estimates of gross and net replacement rates

A. Gross replacement rates, 1999, overall average[1]

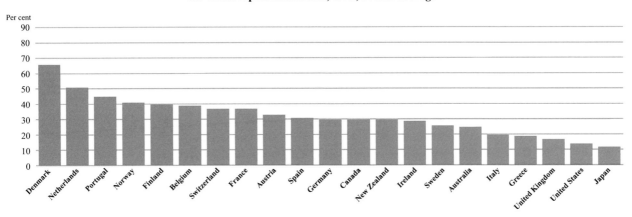

B. Change in gross replacement rates between 1995 and 1999

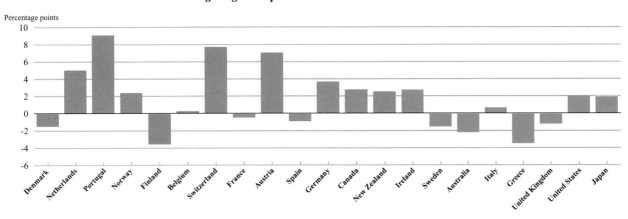

C. Net replacement rates for long-term unemployed, 1999[2]

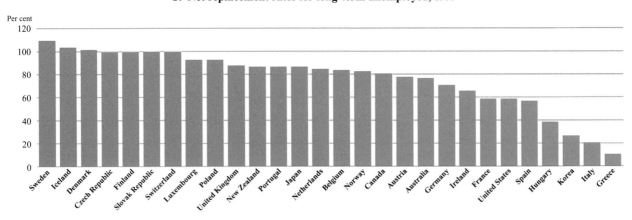

1. Average of gross rates computed for different family situations, earning levels and durations of unemployment.
2. After tax and including family and housing benefits for long-term benefit recipients; situation corresponding to a couple with 2 children and a single earner paid 66.7% of the average production worker's salary.
Source: OECD.

*... but countries have improved
the trade-off by tightening
requirements*

Most countries have nevertheless taken measures to improve the trade-off. While the level and duration of benefits have generally been maintained to avoid adverse social consequences, eligibility and work-availability requirements have been tightened. For instance, the minimum amount of time spent in employment required to satisfy qualifying criteria has been raised and the scope for turning down job offers repeatedly without facing some penalty has been reduced. Furthermore, eligibility to benefits for certain groups has been made conditional on enrolling in various schemes such as schooling, vocational training, voluntary work or a subsidised job. In return, governments are providing more intensive job-search assistance, including personalised job counselling and follow-ups so as to improve matching. Some countries have managed to combine high replacement rates with high employment rates (Denmark, Switzerland and Iceland). The majority of countries have raised active support to the unemployed in order to reduce long-term dependence on benefits, although the amount of resources spent on active labour market policies (ALMPs) varies substantially across countries both in terms of GDP and as a per cent of total expenditures on active and passive measures. Past experience has shown that ALMPs need to be both well designed and well targeted (Martin, 2000).[6] Otherwise, the cost can rise quickly and the higher employment prospects of participants may be more than offset by significant dead-weight losses and the adverse effect of raising taxes to finance such programmes.

*The trade-offs are particularly
difficult for workers with low
earnings potential*

The trade-offs involved in the case of low productivity workers at the margin of the labour market can be particularly painful considering their low earnings potential. First, a significant reduction in out-of-work benefits could push many into poverty. Second, to avoid this, many countries have chosen to provide in-work benefits or payroll tax rebates combined with a minimum wage, in both cases incurring fiscal costs. Third, to limit the fiscal costs, the benefits are typically means-tested, but a rapid withdrawal as earned income increases generates high marginal effective tax rates, lowering incentives to increase work effort beyond a certain threshold (poverty trap). Fourth, raising the threshold for benefit withdrawal and/or lowering its pace pushes the problem of high marginal effective tax rates further up the earnings scale and can rapidly increase the budgetary cost, which may imply higher tax rates.

*Some countries have increased
in-work benefits for low income
workers...*

These concerns notwithstanding, several countries have favoured measures to top-up wages of low-income households with in-work benefits. In addition, even though these benefits remain for the most part means-tested, the phasing-out has been made more gradual. While the Earned Income Tax Credit and the Working Family Tax Credit programmes implemented respectively in the United States and the United Kingdom represent well-known examples of schemes aimed at improving in-work benefits of low-wage earners, similar measures also exist in France, Canada, Australia, Finland, Belgium, Ireland and New Zealand.

*... while others are lowering tax
wedges to stimulate labour
demand*

In order to lower the cost of low-paid jobs and stimulate labour demand, several countries have reduced the wedge between the wage paid by the employers and the take-home pay of employees by cutting labour taxes (in particular employers' and/or employees' contributions to social security). After rising steadily from the mid-1970s to the mid-1990s, tax wedges have been reduced in several countries, includ-

---

6. For instance, a recent study assessing the various programmes available in Sweden for unemployed adults found that employment subsidies are by far the most effective in having a sustained impact on labour market attachment, though the cost-effectiveness of such measures remains highly questionable owing to large negative displacement and dead-weight effects (Sianesi, 2002).

ing in some EU member countries (France, Italy and the Netherlands) where wedges were (and still are) relatively high. In fact, the reduction in tax wedges in the late 1990s may have been a key factor behind the relatively strong EU employment performance, especially in countries where the measures were indeed targeted at the low paid jobs.[7] In these countries, high payroll taxes had had particularly deleterious employment effects on low productivity workers, since they could not be shifted to labour in the form of lower wages, owing to statutory or negotiated wage floors. However, in a context of deteriorating public finances, the scope for further reductions in tax wedges may be limited without tighter control on expenditure.

Considering the particularly high rate of inactivity among workers aged between 55 and 65, one area which could be given particular attention is the incentives for early retirement resulting from existing public pension and other benefit schemes.[8] Indeed, in a large number of countries where the official retirement age remains at 65, the average effective withdrawal age is up to several years lower. The effective retirement age has declined over time even as life expectancy at that age has increased significantly. In many countries, such patterns have been encouraged by public pension policies of high replacement rates combined with a low return on extra years spent in work beyond a certain age or number of years of contributions. More importantly, special early retirement programmes, unemployment-related benefits and disability schemes have provided older workers with an early route out of the labour market. Yet, in countries where participation rates of older workers are high, so are their employment rates suggesting no inherent barriers to employment at an old age. Considering that the burden of early retirement on output and public finances is set to intensify over the next decades, the disincentives to work at older ages should be removed.

Older workers' low activity rates result from various benefit schemes

Labour and product-market regulation

Employment protection legislation (EPL) provides a good example of the possible effect of labour market institutions on structural unemployment *via* their influence on the shock transmission mechanism. By raising the cost of dismissal it reduces the incidence of lay-offs and hence the flow into unemployment. On the other hand, strict firing restrictions make firms more hesitant in their hiring process, making it harder for the unemployed to re-enter employment (Boeri *et al.*, 2000). The direct net effect of EPL on unemployment is thus ambiguous (OECD, 1999b).

While the direct effect of EPL on unemployment is ambiguous...

Even so, EPL may have adverse indirect effects by reducing the speed of real wage adjustment as well as aggregate wage flexibility. The lower job turnover associated with strict EPL often implies an increase in the average duration of unemployment and the proportion of long-term unemployment, raising persistence and potentially reducing the impact of unemployment on wage setting. As noted earlier, it is striking to observe that countries with rising shares of long-term unemployed are also the ones generally facing increases in structural unemployment rates (Figure V.4). While this

... it may have adverse indirect effects on the proportion of long-term unemployed

---

7. While reductions in labour taxes usually have a positive impact on employment, whether or not they also stimulate labour supply depends on the extent to which part of the benefits accrues to employees in the form of higher after-tax wages. Hence, the net effect on unemployment may depend on employers' and employees' respective bargaining power and, at least in the short run, on the labour market situation at the time the cuts are introduced.
8. For a discussion of policies and institutions having an impact on the retirement age, see Chapter V in OECD (2002a).

———————— Figure V.4.   **Changes in long-term unemployment and structural unemployment rates** ————————

Between 1990 and 2001,[1] in percentage points

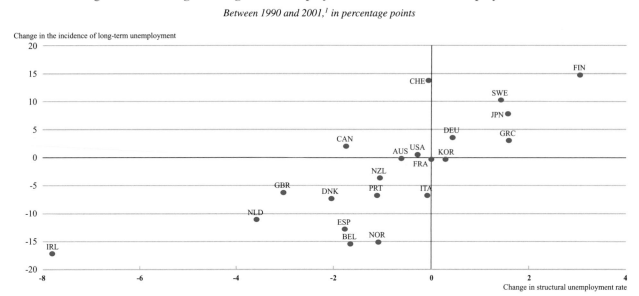

1. 1991-2001 for Finland and Switzerland; 1990-1999 for Ireland, Netherlands; 1990-2000 for Germany.
Source: OECD and *Employment Outlook*, June 2002.

says nothing about the direction of causality, it is at least consistent with the notion that adverse shocks, even temporary ones, are more likely to raise unemployment persistently in countries where policies contribute to strengthen insider-outsider mechanisms.

Reform of EPL has concentrated on temporary contracts

Although reform of EPL has taken place in Europe during the past decade, the general tendency has been towards the easing of regulations affecting temporary contracts, with little change on regular contracts. This has been accompanied since the mid-1990s by a substantial increase in many countries in the share of temporary jobs in total employment (Germany, France, Italy, the Netherlands, Portugal and Spain).[9] While these developments may have contributed to lower labour adjustment costs, the burden of adjustment is heavily concentrated on one category of workers, raising equity concerns. At the same time, the power of "insiders" (who are typically employed on permanent contracts) in wage bargaining may have increased as they could feel even more sheltered from unemployment than before, possibly reducing the responsiveness of wages to shocks.

Uniform minimum wages may affect specific categories of workers

As in the case of EPL, the net direct incidence of a statutory minimum wage on overall employment could arguably be limited, especially when it is set at a moderate level relative to the average wage. However, even though the level beyond which the adverse employment effects dominate is bound to vary across groups and regions, a uniform rate is often applied nation-wide, with the risk of affecting disproportionately specific categories of workers, such as youth in search of a first job experience. While any negative impact of statutory minimum wages is likely to have fallen in the

———————

9. The combination of easier regulation for temporary contracts with strict EPL for permanent ones is only one among several factors behind the rise in the share of temporary employment (see Chapter III in OECD, 2002b). Some evidence of a significant impact has been found in the cases of Spain (Dolado *et al.*, 2001), France, (Blanchard and Landier, 2001) and Italy (Nannincini, 2001).

past decade, owing in many cases to their gradual erosion in relative terms, they remain high in some countries (*e.g.* France, Australia and Ireland), which may prevent relative wages from reflecting productivity differentials

While many countries do not have a statutory minimum wage, binding floors on the wage of less productive workers are sometimes imposed via an extension of collective agreement from unionised to non-unionised segments. In some cases (*e.g.* the Netherlands and Belgium), these floors can exceed the statutory minimum wage. The difference between the proportion of employees covered by collective contracts and the proportion represented by unions provides some indications of the potential extent of economy-wide binding floors arising from this practice. The degree of extended coverage tends to be particularly high in euro area countries (except in Finland and Ireland).

Extension of collective agreements also imposes a wage floor

Empirical evidence has shown that labour market performance can also be influenced by product market regulations having an impact on the degree of competition. Regulatory reforms aimed at lowering trade barriers, the stringency of state control and firms' entry costs can stimulate output and employment by raising the elasticity of product demand, reducing thereby price mark-ups and lessening labour-market segmentation. Progress in reforming such regulation may have boosted employment rates by between ½ and 2½ percentage points across OECD countries over the past two decades (Nicoletti *et al.*, 2001). Clearly, an increase in product market competition puts downward pressures on wages in the short run, especially in highly protected sectors where the scope for rent-seeking behaviour by workers is largest. Indeed, one of the reasons why reforming labour market policies has proved difficult in many countries is the associated rent enjoyed by specific groups that are well positioned to resist (Blanchard and Giavazzi, 2001). In the longer run, however, stronger competition tends to boost real wages *via* its favourable impact on productivity.

Product-market regulatory reforms can boost employment in the longer run

Explaining the differences in the intensity of physical and human capital formation

Physical capital

Business investment (particularly in machinery and equipment) has long been identified as one of the key drivers of output growth (Ahn and Hemmings, 2000; Harris, 1999; De Long and Summers, 1992).[10] First, an increase in the quantity of physical capital has a direct positive, albeit transitory, influence on labour productivity growth through capital deepening. Second, investment in new machinery and equipment can also lead to a sustained increase in productivity growth if capital-embodied technical changes are introduced more quickly. However, this presumes that investment takes place in an environment that is conducive to innovation and where profitable opportunities exist, lest capital formation translates into diminishing returns rather than a strong output performance.

Investment in physical capital boosts output growth

---

10. Empirically, the correlation between physical investment (as a share of GDP) and growth in GDP *per capita* and/or labour productivity stands out as particularly significant and robust (OECD, 2003a).

Investment in ICT-capital has varied across countries...

Furthermore, the impact on growth could also differ according to the composition of investment. Of particular interest is the relative importance of information and communication technologies (ICT) given their alleged contribution to the US growth performance of the late 1990s. Indeed, all countries have since the early 1980s experienced a significant increase in the share of ICT in total investment, albeit to an extent that varies substantially across countries (Figure V.5).[11] The United States appears to maintain a significant lead.

... reflecting in part differences in relative prices of equipment

In several countries, a low rate of ICT investment can be partly explained by a relatively high purchasing price of computer and telecommunication hardware. Even though ICT equipment is an internationally traded good, substantial cross-country price variations have persisted, reflecting in part differences in taxation, but also the presence of significant non-tariff barriers related to technical standards, import licensing and public procurement.

Financial market development is important to spur investment in general...

Cross-country differences in the level and composition of investment continue to be shaped by domestic factors having an influence on the overall cost of capital and access to finance, although foreign direct investment and other capital flows may be growing in significance. Recent empirical work has underscored the importance of domestic financial market development on output growth performance, *via* its impact on risk-diversification and investment (Leahy *et al.*, 2001). As well, financial markets and institutions play an important role in the monitoring of corporate performance and in imposing discipline on corporate governance. One area where access to finance can play a critical role is in the development of new, innovative products or technologies which by nature tend to be high-risk activities. In this regard, the

Figure V.5. **ICT investment in selected OECD countries**

In current price, as a percentage of non-residential gross fixed capital formation, total economy

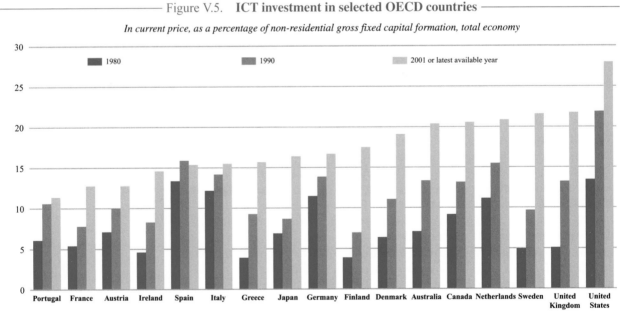

Source: OECD (2003b).

---

11. The differences shown in the shares could partly reflect discrepancies in the measurement and treatment of software investment across countries.

contribution of venture capital to strong entrepreneurial activity in the United States has been recognised as an important ingredient behind the growth performance,[12] although this influence is difficult to assess with precision.

Data on venture capital investment show that substantial cross-country variations prevailed over the period 1998-2001, both in terms of the overall amount invested and the share devoted to activities in the early stage and the expansion phase of developments, with euro area countries generally trailing significantly behind the United States and Canada (Figure V.6). Similar divergences are reflected in less formal indicators such as the funding of activity by business angel networks. Yet, the development of an active venture capital market in the euro area would seem particularly important given the prevalence of a bank-based financial system and the difficulty of new firms with risky projects and little collateral to attract bank loans.[13] Several countries have introduced tax incentives and have more actively supported the business angel network.[14] This notwithstanding, investment in venture capital in several European countries has been limited by the absence of large pension funds and, where such funds exist, by rules preventing these as well as other institutional

... while the presence of venture capital markets is essential for innovative activities...

Figure V.6. **Venture capital[1] investment by stages**

Per cent of GDP, 1998-2001

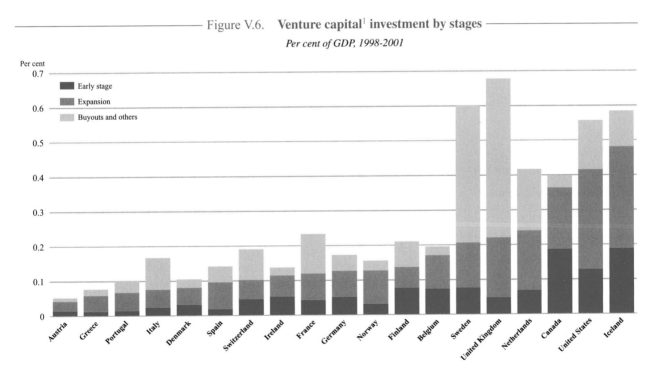

1. The definition of private equity/venture capital varies across countries. Countries are ranked according to the sum of early age and expansion.
Source: OECD; Baygan and Freudenberg (2000).

12. See Kortum and Lerner (2000). Exploiting firm-level data, the authors found that a dollar of venture capital had a bigger impact on patenting in the United States than a dollar of business R&D, although this may reflect the influence of other factors (such as the quality of research infrastructures) not properly controlled for in the empirical analysis.
13. See Audretsch and Lehmann (2002) for evidence that technology-based start-ups are more likely to suffer from financing gaps and lower performance if their access to finance is largely restricted to traditional banks.
14. Tax incentives tend to have a limited impact on venture capital activity owing to the fact that the largest investors are often tax-exempt (see Baygan, 2003).

investors from investing in venture capital. In comparison, pension funds have been an important source of venture capital in the United States, the United Kingdom, Australia, Sweden, Finland and New Zealand (OECD, 2001a).[15]

... requiring the support of well-functioning secondary markets

The development of venture capital also requires the support of well-functioning secondary financial markets for high-tech firms to allow investors to recover their funds via the flotation of start-ups.[16] More generally, the financing of new firms and innovative activity raises the difficulty of assessing prospects based on most accurate information. In this regard, principles of sound management, contract enforcement and transparency are essential features of financial markets.

Human capital

Investment in human capital is also important for growth

As is the case for physical capital, the accumulation of skills and competencies – broadly referred to as human capital – has a direct, though temporary, impact on output growth *via* the improvement in the "quality" of labour input. In fact, recent empirical work suggests that one extra year of average education (roughly equivalent to a 10 per cent rise in human capital) has in the past raised output *per capita* in the long run by around 4 to 7 per cent on average across OECD countries (Bassanini and Scarpetta, 2001).[17] Human capital formation may also have a permanent impact on output growth if a higher level of skills and knowledge facilitates the adoption of new technologies and/or the process of innovation, leading to an acceleration of technical progress. While the empirical literature has so far produced only mixed support for the latter assumption (Temple, 2001) – at least among developed countries – recent evidence based on a more comprehensive data set suggests that the economy-wide returns to investment in primary and secondary education may be larger than those enjoyed by individuals (OECD, 2003a).

Educational achievements have improved in most countries

Given the absence of direct measures, human capital is usually assessed in terms of educational attainment. The latter can in turn be measured on the basis of various indicators, such as the average number of years of education or the percentage of population that has reached a certain level of education.[18] Both indicators suggest that educational achievements have improved significantly in most countries over the past two or three decades and that the cross-country variations have also narrowed. Nevertheless, the percentage of the population having completed at least upper secondary education varies from over 90 per cent in the group of leading countries, to less than 70 per cent in others (Figure V.7). The gap is particularly large in the case of Portugal, Turkey and Mexico.

---

15. The absence of a venture capital industry has been cited as one of the factors behind the slowdown in R&D productivity in Japan during the 1990s. The reason is the greater difficulty for established firms to partner with more entrepreneurial and efficient firms to foster product development in the absence of venture capital (Branstetter and Nakamura, 2003).

16. While the demise of the Neuer Market may, in this respect, be seen as a setback, its failure may also be a consequence of the lack of economies of scale of European secondary markets.

17. These results were obtained over a period during which low-educated cohorts were being replaced by workers with higher levels of education. It is not clear that additional schooling will have as large an impact on average across OECD countries in the future.

18. For purposes of comparison, the levels identified are usually determined on the basis of the International Standard Classification of Education (ISCED), which classifies educational programmes according to various objective criteria. Under this classification, upper secondary education corresponds to level 3 and tertiary education to levels 5A and 6.

──────── Figure V.7. **Percentage of the population that has attained a certain level of education, 2001** ────────

By age group

▲ 25 to 34 year-olds ● 45 to 54 year-olds

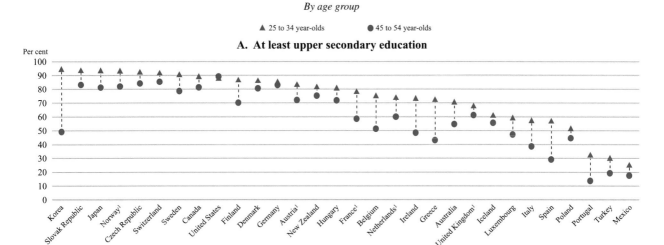

A. At least upper secondary education

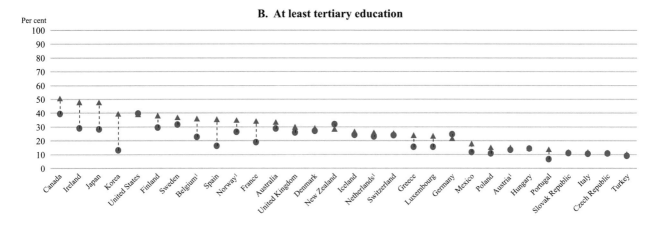

B. At least tertiary education

1. Year of reference: 2000.
Source: OECD.

It is broadly recognised that widespread basic educational services brings benefits to the society and this recognition has led governments in all countries to be involved not only as a source of financing but in most cases as a direct provider. In 1999, OECD countries spent from 2.7 per cent of GDP (Japan) to over 5 per cent (Sweden) of what are essentially public funds on schooling at the primary and secondary levels, which typically corresponds to the years of compulsory education (Table V.2). As is the case for physical capital the appropriateness of the amount invested should, to some extent, be judged against some measures of return on capital. Unfortunately, the latter can be particularly hard to measure in the case of compulsory education. Even so, there seems to be no clear correspondence between the amounts invested and the performance in terms of educational attainment and student abilities across countries which suggest that potential efficiency gains could be reaped by further reform. Indeed, the results from an OECD study on tests of 15 year-old students' abilities in reading, mathematics and sciences show that the

While government investment in compulsory education brings benefit for society…

──────── Table V.2.   **Spending at various levels of education** ────────

1999, Per cent of GDP

	Public spending on education				Total spending on educational institutions
	Primary and secondary[a]	Tertiary	*of which:* Student grants[b]	All levels of education	All levels of education
Australia	3.8	1.2	0.4	5.0	5.8
Austria	4.1	1.7	0.2	6.3	6.3
Belgium	3.5	1.5	0.2	5.5	5.5
Denmark	4.8	2.4	0.8	8.1	6.7
Finland	3.8	2.1	0.3	6.2	5.8
France	4.2	1.1	0.1	6.0	6.2
Germany	3.0	1.1	0.1	4.7	5.6
Greece	2.4	1.1	0.0	3.6	3.9
Ireland	3.1	1.2	0.2	4.3	4.6
Italy	3.2	0.8	0.1	4.5	4.8
Japan	2.7	0.5	0.0	3.5	4.7
Netherlands	3.1	1.3	0.3	4.8	4.7
New Zealand	4.8	1.2	0.3	6.3	..
Norway	4.6	2.0	0.6	7.4	6.6
Portugal	4.2	1.0	0.1	5.7	5.7
Spain	3.3	0.9	0.1	4.5	5.3
Sweden	5.1	2.1	0.6	7.7	6.7
Switzerland	4.0	1.2	0.0	5.5	5.9
United Kingdom	3.3	1.1	0.4	4.7	5.2
United States	3.5	1.4	0.3	5.2	6.5
Country mean	3.7	1.3	0.3	5.5	5.6

a) Includes post-secondary non-tertiary education.
b) Scholarships/other grants to households and student loans.
Source: OECD, *Education at a Glance*, 2002; OECD.

countries doing relatively well are not necessarily the ones spending the most per student (OECD, 2001b).

... the extent of public involvement in tertiary education raises issues

At the tertiary level, an important share of the return on investment in human capital appears to accrue to the individual, raising questions about the extent of government involvement. In addition, given the significant sociological barriers that have historically kept children from poor and less-educated families away from tertiary education, low tuition fees often imply redistribution from poor to middle and upper-middle class families, raising equity concerns. The risk that a significant increase in tuition fees would lower private returns and hence participation in tertiary education could be lessened by an easier access to government-backed unsubsidised student loans.[19]

───────────────

19. Higher tuition fees may also help to reduce the time spent by some students in education over and above the statutory duration required to obtain a diploma, which is a problem in some countries.

Educational attainment represents only one facet of human capital development. Maintaining or improving workers' mobility generally requires providing them with opportunities and incentives to up-grade their skills throughout their professional life *via* vocational training or adult education. The lack of mobility may inhibit the scope for firms to bring about the changes in work practice and organisational structures that are often required to better exploit technologies, limiting thereby their own incentive to invest in the latter (OECD, 2003b). Even though the importance of adult education has grown during the past two decades, the share of adults aged over 35 in total enrolments remains fairly low, except in Australia, the United Kingdom and Sweden. This is partly due to the fact that, under existing institutional arrangements, which in many countries favour earlier retirement, financial incentives to invest in adult education diminish rapidly with age as the amortisation period for the investment shrinks (Blöndal *et al.*, 2002).

Training is an important aspect of labour market flexibility

As regards vocational training, given the various forms that it can take and also considering the problems in measuring on-the-job training, comparable indicators of performance are difficult to develop. Nevertheless, drawing on different sources of survey-based training statistics, an OECD study found significantly different levels of formal training across countries, with relatively low levels observed in southern European countries such as Greece, Italy, Portugal and Spain and relatively high levels in the United Kingdom, France and most Nordic countries (OECD, 1999b).

The amount of training varies across countries...

Perhaps more significantly, the study also confirmed earlier findings that in most countries, less-educated workers and those working on a part-time and/or temporary contract basis are much less likely to receive training, especially when employed by a small firm. Many countries pursue policies to enhance training via subsidies or mandated employer spending on the premise that too little is provided. However, the appropriate amount of training is difficult to assess, suggesting that a focus on giving the right incentives might be more appropriate.

... but in most cases, less-educated workers are less likely to be trained

Explaining the differences in technological progress

Strong investment, in particular in new technologies such as ICT, has a direct impact on output and productivity growth via capital deepening or embodiment effects. However, the positive growth impact from the latter is likely to be transitory and last the time required to complete the transition to a higher level of capital intensity. Hence, for investment to have a durable impact on output and productivity growth, it must generate positive externalities over and above the direct benefits from raising employees' skills or from equipping them with more powerful machines. The significance of externalities, also referred to as *disembodied* technological progress, is often assessed using estimates of multi-factor productivity (MFP). Such estimates show that while MFP growth increased in English speaking and Nordic countries during the 1990s, it fell in Continental Europe and Japan, albeit in several cases from a relatively high level (Figure V.8).

Fostering MFP gains is key to long-term growth

MFP growth usually arises from eliminating the slack in the use of inputs, from the adoption of state-of-the-art technology and related organisational practices (catching-up to technological frontier) and/or from direct innovations in either goods produced or the production process (pushing out the frontier). While numerous fac-

MFP growth requires incentives to innovate and adopt best-practices

—— Figure V.8. **Multi-factor productivity growth over selected periods** ——

Business sector, 1990s and 1980s
(based on cyclically-adjusted series)

Countries where MFP growth accelerated   **Countries where MFP growth decelerated**

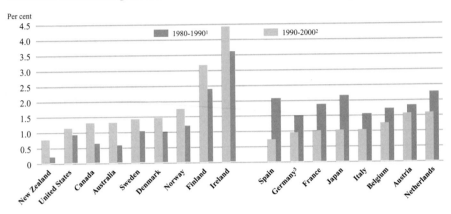

1. 1983-1990 for Belgium, Denmark and Ireland, 1985-1990 for Austria and New Zealand.
2. 1990-1996 for Ireland and Sweden, 1990-1997 for Austria, Belgium and New Zealand, 1990-1998 for Netherlands, 1990-1999 for Australia, Denmark, France, Italy, Japan and 1991-2000 for Germany.
3. West Germany before 1991.
Source: OECD.

tors can affect MFP *via* either channel, recent empirical work based on sectoral data has underscored the important influence of product market competition, R&D intensity as well as labour market regulation and institutions (OECD, 2003a).

Promoting product-market competition helps to raise MFP growth...

There is a broad consensus that the incentives to actively seek efficiency gains via the *catching-up* process can be underpinned by policies and institutional settings strengthening product market competition. In particular, overly stringent product market regulation can have a key influence on the strength of competition in domestic markets either by exerting a direct control on economic activities, by imposing various barriers to entrepreneurial activity (through legal restrictions on market access or administrative burdens on new firm creation), or by maintaining high barriers to trade and foreign direct investment. In this regard, the parallel increase in market size (allowing firms to benefit from economies of scale) and exposure to foreign competition is seen as one of the main benefits from growing international trade and may explain the significant impact of cross-border activities on output growth observed in most empirical studies.

... but progress in reforming product-market regulation has been uneven

While all OECD countries have eased anti-competition regulation (barriers to entry or operational restrictions) during the 1980s and 1990s, some have gone much further than others, not least those that have benefited from an acceleration in MFP during the 1990s (the United States, Australia, Finland and New Zealand). Indeed, a positive link between pro-competition regulation and MFP growth is supported by cross-country evidence at the industry level, even after controlling for R&D investment and industry-specific factors (Nicoletti and Scarpetta, 2003). Regulatory measures having an impact on entry costs are particularly relevant for industries facing rapidly-changing technology, such as ICT-producing or ICT-using industries, given that the contribution of new firms to productivity growth appears to be much stronger in these industries than in the rest of the economy.

The strong and positive impact of R&D intensity on productivity growth has also been shown in various studies, both on the basis of aggregate and sectoral data.[20] Indeed, because of the perceived externalities, most countries provide support to R&D *via* direct expenditure and, in some cases, via tax incentives on private R&D. This notwithstanding, the intensity of both public and private R&D expenditure varies significantly across countries (Figure V.9). In the case of private R&D, the variations reflect also factors such as market size and industrial structure which are not directly amenable to innovation policy. Nevertheless, authorities in a growing number of countries have established explicit R&D targets to narrow the gap *vis-à-vis* leading countries.[21] Yet, although a certain proportion of public R&D funding is considered as necessary to stimulate private R&D, the stimulating effect may diminish beyond a certain threshold.[22]

R&D investment is necessary to foster innovation but public R&D can only go so far

Figure V.9. **Expenditure on R&D in OECD countries**

Total expenditure on R&D as a percentage of GDP, 1980s and 1990s

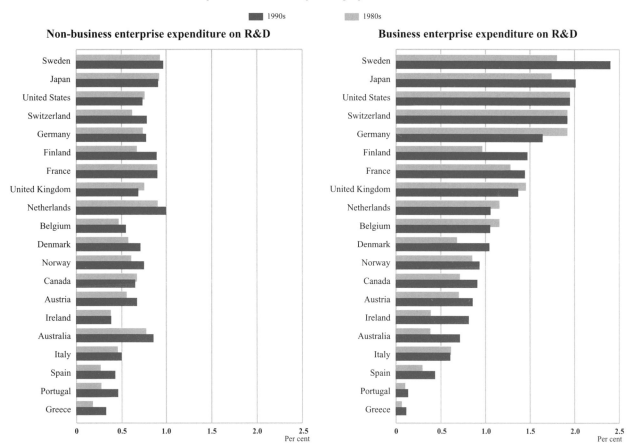

Source: OECD (2003a).

20. See Guellec and van Pottelsberghe (2001) for evidence based on aggregate data and Scarpetta and Tressel (2002) for empirical support based on sectoral data.
21. See Sheehan and Wyckoff (2003) for a review of the economic and policy implications of efforts to meet targets for R&D spending.
22. Such a threshold has been estimated in one study at around 13 per cent of business R&D (Guellec and van Pottelsberghe, 2000).

Product and labour-market regulation may have an impact on private R&D spending

Some of the differences in private R&D spending across countries within comparable industries could reflect the important influence that the policy environment may have on the private incentives to engage in innovative activity. Indeed, it appears a significant part of cross-country variations in R&D intensity within industries can be attributed to differences in product market regulation.[23] The evidence also suggests that labour market regulation plays an important role. This may be especially the case in industries where taking advantage of new opportunities requires significant labour re-allocation. By raising the cost of labour adjustment, stringent employment protection legislation reduces both the return to innovation and the incentive to spend on R&D.[24] In addition to these effects on R&D intensities in individual sectors, structural policy may also affect overall R&D investment through changes in the industry mix. Indeed, analysis indicates that the sectoral composition of the economy matters, as the bulk of R&D activity is concentrated in specific industries.

Stimulating entrepreneurial activity requires allowing firms to enter and exit

Although strong investment in R&D is a key determinant of innovation, other factors are important. For instance, the use and development of new technology requires firms to be able to experiment, and hence to be given the possibility of failure and re-entry. In this regard, having a bankruptcy regime allowing firms to exit with a limited social and financial stigma or burden on firms' owners and managers may boost innovative activity. However, stimulating entrepreneurial activity by facilitating both entry and exit may bring benefits beyond the impact on innovation. For instance, it may lessen the incentives for managers to make business decisions so as to delay as much as possible declaring bankruptcy even when the latter becomes inevitable, improving thereby resource allocation. Furthermore, the threat of exit, combined with competitive pressures from potential entrants, may stimulate productivity growth within firms by raising managerial effort. However, facilitating exit while providing investors with adequate protection in case of business failures may represent a difficult policy challenge.

---

23. See Chapter VII in OECD (2002c).
24. The positive impact on R&D from a reduction in the stringency of EPL is estimated to be particularly strong in the case of high-tech industries (usually requiring higher turnover) in countries where the industrial system is characterised by low or intermediate levels of co-ordination (*e.g.* France, Spain and Portugal). See Chapter VI in OECD (2002a).

BIBLIOGRAPHY

AHN, S. and P. HEMMINGS (2000), "Policy influences on economic growth in OECD countries: An evaluation of the evidence", *OECD Economics Department Working Papers*, No. 246.

AUDRETSCH, D.B. and E. LEHMANN (2002), "Debt or equity? The role of venture capital in financing the new economy in Germany?", *CEPR Discussion Paper Series*, No. 3656.

BASSANINI, A. and S. SCARPETTA (2001), "The driving forces of economic growth: Panel data evidence for the OECD countries", *OECD Economic Studies*, No. 33.

BAYGAN, G. (2003), "Venture capital policy review: United Kingdom", *OECD STI Working Papers*, No. 2003/1.

BAYGAN, G. and M. FREUDENBERG (2000), "The internationalisation of venture capital activity in OECD countries: Implications for measurement and policy", *OECD STI Working Papers,* No. 2000/7.

BLANCHARD, O. and F. GIAVAZZI (2001), "Macroeconomic effects of regulation and deregulation in goods and labor markets", *NBER Working Paper Series*, No. 8120.

BLANCHARD, O. and A. LANDIER (2001), "The perverse effects of partial labour market reform: Fixed duration contracts in France", *NBER Working Paper Series*, No. 8219.

BLÖNDAL, S., S. FIELD and N. GIROUARD (2002), "Investment in human capital through upper-secondary and tertiary education", *OECD Economic Studies*, No. 34.

BOERI, T., G. NICOLETTI and S. SCARPETTA (2000), "Regulation and labour market performance", *CEPR Discussion Paper*, No. 2420.

BRANSTETTER, L. and Y. NAKAMURA (2003), "Is Japan's innovative capacity in decline?", *NBER Working Paper Series*, No. 9438.

DE LONG, J.B. and L.H. SUMMERS (1992), "Equipment investment and economic growth: How strong is the nexus?", *Brookings Papers on Economic Activity,* No. 2.

DE SERRES, A. (2003), "Structural policies and growth: A non-technical overview", *OECD Economics Working Papers* (forthcoming)

DOLADO, J.J., C. GARCIA-SERRANO and J.F. JIMENO (2001), "Drawing lessons from the boom of temporary jobs in Spain", University of Alcala, *mimeo.*

ELMESKOV, J., J. MARTIN and S. SCARPETTA (1998), "Key lessons for labour market reforms: Evidence from OECD countries' experiences", *Swedish Economic Policy Review*, No. 2.

GUELLEC, D. and B. VAN POTTELSBERGHE (2001), "R&D and productivity growth: Panel data analysis of 16 OECD countries", *OECD Economic Studies*, No. 33.

GUELLEC, D. and B. VAN POTTELSBERGHE (2000), "The impact of public R&D expenditure on business R&D", *OECD STI Working Papers*, No. 2000/4.

HARRIS, R. (1999), "Determinants of Canadian productivity growth: issues and prospects", *Industry Canada Discussion Paper*, No. 8.

KORTUM, S. and J. LERNER (2000), "Assessing the contribution of venture capital to innovation", *Rand Journal of Economics*, 31.

LEAHY, M., S. SCHICH. G. WEHINGER. F. PELGRIN and T. THORGEIRSSON (2001), "Contributions of financial systems to growth in OECD countries", *OECD Economics Department Working Papers*, No. 280.

MARTIN, J. (2000), "What works among active labour market policies: evidence from the OECD countries' experiences", *OECD Economic Studies,* No. 30.

NANNINCINI, T. (2001), "The take-off of temporary help in employment in the Italian labor market", European University Institute, Florence, *mimeo.*

NICKELL, S. and R. LAYARD (1998), "Labour market institutions and economic performance ", *Centre for Economic Performance Discussion Paper*, No. 407.

NICOLETTI, G. and S. SCARPETTA (2003), "Regulation, productivity and growth: OECD evidence", *OECD Economics Department Working Papers*, No. 347.

NICOLETTI, G., A. BASSANINI, E. ERNST, S. JEAN, P. SANTIAGO and P. SWAIM (2001), "Product and labour markets interactions in OECD countries", *OECD Economics Department Working Papers*, No. 312.

OECD (1999a), *Implementing the OECD Jobs Strategy: Assessing Policy and Performance*, Paris.

OECD (1999b), *Employment Outlook*, Paris.

OECD (2001a), *The New Economy: Beyond the Hype*, Paris.

OECD (2001b), *Knowledge and Skills for Life; First Results from PISA 2000*, Paris.

OECD (2002a), *OECD Economic Outlook,* No. 72, Paris.

OECD (2002b), *Employment Outlook*, Paris.

OECD (2002c), *OECD Economic Outlook,* No. 71, Paris.

OECD (2003a), *The Sources of Economic Growth in OECD Countries*, Paris.

OECD (2003b), *Seizing the benefits of ICT in a digital economy*, Paris.

SCARPETTA, S. and T. TRESSEL (2002), "Productivity and convergence in a panel of OECD industries: Do regulations and institutions matter?", *OECD Economics Department Working Papers*, No. 342.

SHEEHAN, J. and A. WYCKOFF (2003), "Targeting R&D: Economic and policy implications of increasing R&D spending", *OECD STI Working Papers*, No. 2003/8 (forthcoming).

SIANESI, B. (2002), "Differential effects of Swedish labour market programmes for unemployed adults during the 1990s", *IFAU Working Paper,* No. 2002:5.

TEMPLE, J. (2001), "Growth effects of education and social capital in the OECD countries", *OECD Economic Studies*, No. 33.

VI. TRENDS IN FOREIGN DIRECT INVESTMENT IN OECD COUNTRIES

Introduction

Foreign direct investment (Box VI.1) is considered to be an important driver of economic growth in OECD countries (OECD, 2002a, 2002b). This is because the internationalisation of production helps to better exploit the advantages of enterprises and countries, increase competitive pressures in OECD markets and stimulate technology transfer and innovative activity. In consequence, there is a wide consensus that policy should aim at reducing or eliminating hindrances to foreign direct investment (FDI) as long as this does not conflict with other legitimate policy objectives.

Foreign direct investment has beneficial effects on the economy

This issue of the Economic Outlook explores several important features of FDI in OECD countries. This chapter reviews recent trends and patterns in FDI and the related activity of foreign affiliates. It is followed by chapters on regulations restricting foreign ownership of businesses and on the quantitative impact of various policy- and non-policy-related factors on FDI.

Box VI.1. Foreign direct investment: definition and data sources

FDI is an activity in which an investor resident in one country obtains a lasting interest in, and a significant influence on the management of, an entity resident in another country. This may involve either creating an entirely new enterprise (so-called "greenfield" investment) or, more typically, changing the ownership of existing enterprises (via mergers and acquisitions). Other types of financial transactions between related enterprises, like reinvesting the earnings of the FDI enterprise or other capital transfers, are also defined as foreign direct investment.

FDI activity can be measured in two different ways: financial investment flows and stocks, and "real" activity of foreign affiliates in host countries. Financial FDI data are compiled according to the concepts used for balance of payments (flows) and international investment position (stocks) statistics (OECD, 2001a). Information on the activity of foreign affiliates is collected through national surveys concerning several aspects of business activity, and is compiled by the OECD (OECD, 2001b). The country,

industry and period coverages of these data are still limited. The coverage of the two measures differs because FDI flows and stocks conventionally relate to ownership of 10 per cent or more of the shares or voting power in an enterprise, while the data on the activities of foreign affiliates include only enterprises with foreign ownership of 50 per cent or more.

While the financial data are more widely available, they suffer from various measurement problems. For instance, reported bilateral FDI flows may not always reflect accurately internationalisation patterns, because the proximate destination of these flows (country or industry-wise) may not be the final one, due to the role played by foreign-owned financial intermediaries in host countries (Borga and Mataloni, 2001). Furthermore, despite substantial progress made in harmonising definitions and data collection methods some cross-country inconsistencies remain: while a majority of countries report data on investment positions at book values, some measure the positions in market values.

Patterns of FDI

Foreign direct investment increased sharply in the late 1990s...

FDI flows remained relatively stable for much of the 1990s; picked up significantly towards the end of the decade;[1] and fell back somewhat in 2001 – but to levels some three-times those at the start of the 1990s (Figure VI.1). The internationalisation of production hence increased significantly during the 1990s, approximately doubling the real inward FDI position of the average OECD country (measured in constant 1996 purchasing power parities) from $81 billion to $158 billion over the 1990-2000 period. The marked slowdown of flows at the beginning of the new decade mostly reflected a correction to sustainable levels rather than a reversal of a trend, and the importance of cross-border ownership of assets continues to increase, mirroring the substantial role of multinational enterprises (MNEs) in the global economy.

... consisting mainly of mergers and acquisitions in developed countries

OECD countries accounted for over 80 per cent of global outward FDI in 2000, with most of the activity consisting of mergers and acquisitions (including privatisation deals) of existing businesses (OECD, 2002c) as compared with greenfield investment.[2] The United States and the European Union (EU) countries held more than three-quarters of total OECD inward and outward FDI positions in 1998 (Figure VI.2). Of the EU countries, the United Kingdom, Germany and France were the largest suppliers and receivers of FDI. The Netherlands was also a notably large investor, while Belgium/Luxembourg was a relatively big host to foreign businesses.[3]

Foreign direct investment relative to GDP differs across countries...

FDI positions have grown significantly faster than GDP in virtually all OECD countries over the 1990s (Figure VI.3). Relative to the size of the economy, FDI is particularly large in smaller countries, such as the outward positions of the Netherlands and Switzerland, and the inward positions of Ireland, Belgium/Luxembourg and New Zealand. In new OECD members only inward FDI plays an important role in the economy, while in Japan outward FDI is much higher than inward FDI.

——————— Figure VI.1. **FDI flows within the OECD area**[1] ———————

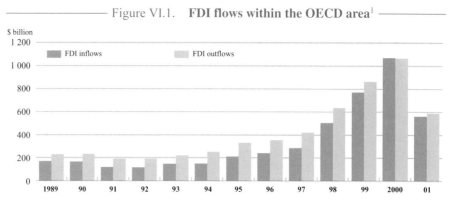

1. Not adjusted for breaks in series.
Source: OECD.

---

1. The peak in FDI coincided with the sharp equity-price increase in the late 1990s and therefore a significant part of it may reflect a pure valuation phenomenon.
2. Greenfield investment has been very important for the new Central European members of the OECD, but the value of such investment is small compared with the bulk of total OECD investment.
3. Data for Belgium and Luxembourg were only collected at the level of Belgo-Luxembourg economic union until 2002.

─────── Figure VI.2. **Distribution of OECD FDI positions in 1998**[1] ───────

Inward positions

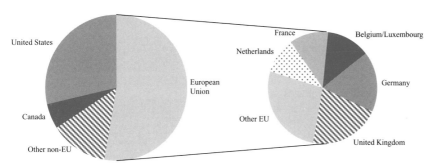

Outward positions

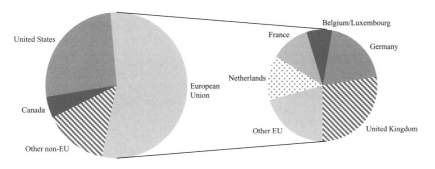

1. The charts are based on bilateral data. As the method used for valuing FDI positions varies across countries, the resulting shares are undervalued for countries that report book values (*e.g.* the United States).
Source: OECD.

The patterns of total FDI invested or hosted by OECD countries mask wide differences in the extent of bilateral FDI relations. In 1998 (the latest year for which bilateral data are reasonably complete) the number of host partners varied across investing countries, ranging from below 10 for Hungary and Turkey to above 20 for many EU countries, the United States and Canada. Moreover, while many countries tended to evenly distribute their FDI across partners, some of them (*e.g.* Canada, Korea, Denmark and the United Kingdom) concentrated FDI on a few host countries. Similarly, FDI in some host countries (Austria, Canada, the United Kingdom and Mexico) mostly comes from just a few investor countries.

... as do the bilateral patterns...

Openness and proximity factors are likely explanations for some of these patterns. A significant share of FDI in the OECD area takes place between countries bound by regional trade agreements and among geographically close countries. Thus, most European countries tend to host relatively more FDI originating from EU countries than from elsewhere,[4] while FDI in Canada and Mexico originates to a

... with geographical and openness factors playing an important role

---

4. Moreover, this "specialisation" pattern has become more accentuated over time with the greater integration of the EU countries spurred by the single market programme and the economic and monetary union.

Figure VI.3. **FDI positions in OECD countries, 1980s and 1990s**[1]

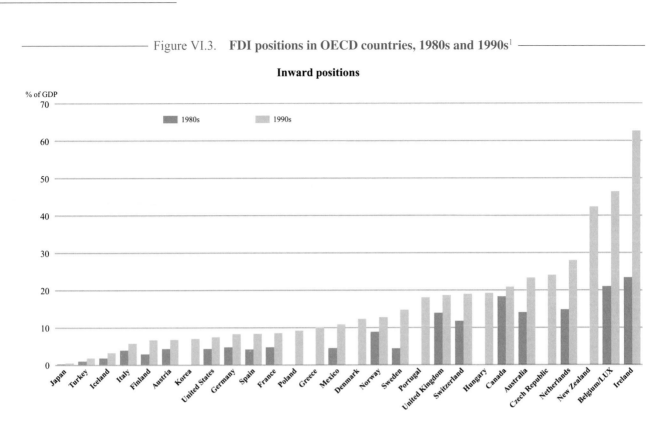

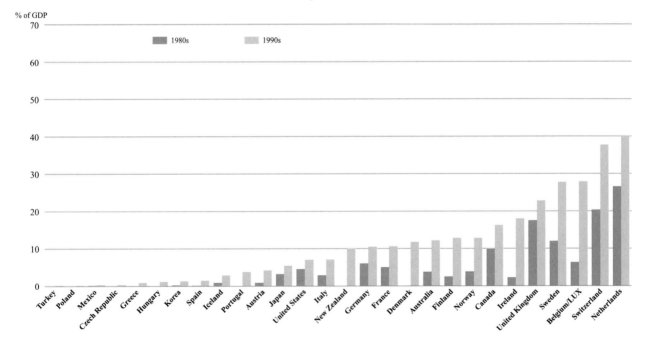

1. Average values over the two periods. For countries where FDI position data are not available, values of bilateral positions reported by their OECD partners were summed up to obtain an approximate measure of multilateral FDI positions.
Source: OECD.

large extent from the United States. Similarly, Pacific shore countries tend to host more FDI from the United States and/or Japan than from other OECD countries.[5]

The share of economic activity accounted for by foreign affiliates in host countries (and in each industry) provides a good indication of the actual degree of internationalisation of production in the OECD area. Data on foreign affiliates is sparse, but available information suggests that the surge in FDI flows observed during the late 1990s was mirrored by a significant increase in the activity of foreign affiliates in the OECD area (OECD, 2002c). In most of the countries for which data are available for the late 1990s, employment of foreign affiliates generally accounted for 1 to 4 per cent of total business employment (Figure VI.4).[6] Exceptions were Hungary and Belgium, which had much higher shares of foreign affiliates in manufacturing and services, respectively, and, at the other extreme, Japan, where their presence was particularly low in both sectors.

Foreign affiliates' activities are concentrated in a few industries

A closer look at the industry distribution of foreign affiliates suggests that their activity tends to be concentrated in a few industries (Figure VI.5).[7] In manufacturing, foreign affiliates' presence (as measured by sectoral employment shares) is particularly

—————— Figure VI.4.   **Activity of foreign affiliates in selected OECD countries, 1990s**[1] ——————

Employment as a per cent of business sector employment

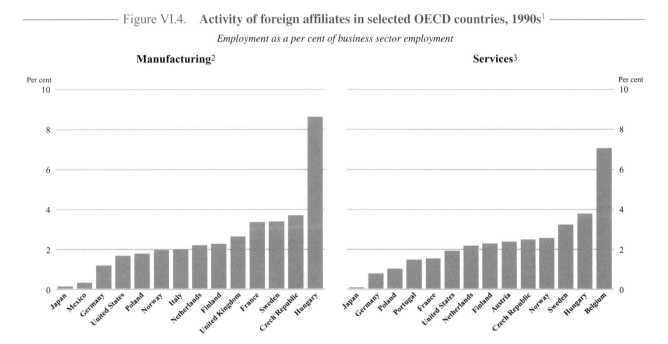

1. Activities of foreign affiliates are classified into industries according to the principal activity of the affiliate. Data are means over available years. The country coverage in manufacturing and services is different.
2. Employment of foreign affiliates in manufacturing is an aggregate corresponding to Total Manufacturing (ISIC rev. 3).
3. Employment of foreign affiliates in services in an aggregate corresponding to Total Services (ISIC rev. 3).
Source: OECD.

---

5. The wide variation in bilateral FDI flows and positions cannot be explained purely by these factors, two counterexamples being Ireland and the United Kingdom whose bilateral FDI positions with the United States are at least as important (as a share in GDP) as those with other EU countries.
6. The shares are computed relative to total business employment to control for possible inconsistencies in the way foreign affiliates and domestic firms are classified across industries (see Box VI.1).
7. The employment shares are higher in Figure VI.5 than in Figure VI.4 because employment is measured relative to sectoral employment and not relative to total business employment.

Figure VI.5. **Percentage share of employment in foreign affiliates in selected industries**

OECD average, 1990s[1]

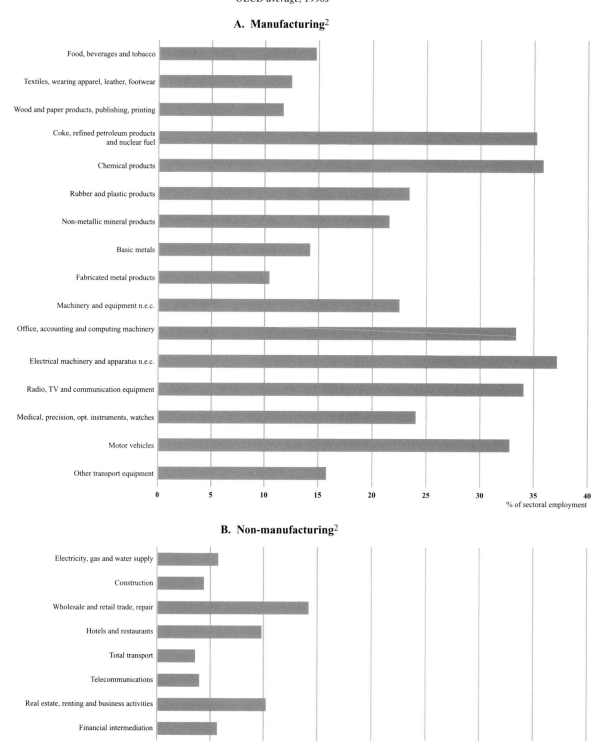

A. Manufacturing[2]

Food, beverages and tobacco
Textiles, wearing apparel, leather, footwear
Wood and paper products, publishing, printing
Coke, refined petroleum products and nuclear fuel
Chemical products
Rubber and plastic products
Non-metallic mineral products
Basic metals
Fabricated metal products
Machinery and equipment n.e.c.
Office, accounting and computing machinery
Electrical machinery and apparatus n.e.c.
Radio, TV and communication equipment
Medical, precision, opt. instruments, watches
Motor vehicles
Other transport equipment

0   5   10   15   20   25   30   35   40
% of sectoral employment

B. Non-manufacturing[2]

Electricity, gas and water supply
Construction
Wholesale and retail trade, repair
Hotels and restaurants
Total transport
Telecommunications
Real estate, renting and business activities
Financial intermediation

0   5   10   15   20   25   30   35   40
% of sectoral employment

1. Simple average. The data cover 19 OECD countries. Available years and sector coverage differ across countries.
2. Activities of foreign affiliates are classified into industries according to the principal activity of the affiliate. Sectoral employment is consistent with this classification.
Source: Directorate for Science, Technology and Industry, OECD.

high in industries producing ICT equipment, petroleum products, chemicals and motor vehicles. These industries seem to be characterised by relatively high economies of scale, the possibility to transfer and exploit locally the specific knowledge of the parent company[8] and, for some of them, the possibility to fragment production into stages. In non-manufacturing, foreign presence is strongest in industries where proximity to local markets is a particularly important condition for supplying the products: distribution, followed at a distance by business services and hotels and restaurants (*i.e.* tourism).[9] In other industries, the relatively low degree of internationalisation may be partly related to the absence of scale economies and opportunities to fragment production, or to the fact that they have been traditionally sheltered from foreign ownership by national governments (see Chapter VII).

Foreign direct investment and trade

The growing interdependency of OECD economies has not only manifested itself in the increase in FDI over the past two decades but also in a parallel increase in foreign trade. These two phenomena appear to be closely linked:[10] both seem to be at least partly affected by factors related to distance, location and size of the economy (for FDI, see Chapter VIII) and, at the same time, they appear to exert a significant reciprocal influence.

Foreign direct investment is positively correlated with trade flows…

The relationships between foreign direct investment and foreign trade at the firm or industry level depend on whether the FDI activity is aimed at "substituting" or "complementing" the export activity (Box VI.2). In services, trade and FDI can be expected to be largely complementary, because establishing commercial presence

… but the underlying relationships are complex

Box VI.2. Trade and different types of FDI

As pointed out by recent research (Markusen, 2002), the interdependence of trade and FDI derives from the fact that the decision to export or invest abroad for producing locally is increasingly taken by the same units, the multinational enterprise. As the main objective of horizontal MNEs is to access foreign markets, exporting or investing abroad are two substitute activities. MNEs will choose one or the other on the basis of their relative returns, which depend among other things on the cost of trade, the cost of FDI and econo-

mies of scale they can enjoy by duplicating production plants in foreign countries. By contrast, the objective of vertical MNEs is to take advantage of cross-country absolute and comparative advantage patterns by locating plants in different countries that specialise in different stages of production. Therefore, trade and vertical FDI are complementary activities: MNEs will typically export components to foreign affiliates and re-export to the home (or other) markets the goods produced abroad.

---

8. Technically, this possibility exploits so-called "firm-level" economies of scale, arising when a common input (knowledge in a specific area) can be used in a non-rival way by both the parent and foreign affiliates.
9. Recorded FDI in the services sectors accounts for an increasing share of total FDI flows, estimated to be around 65 per cent at the end of the 1990s (OECD 2002c). This is likely to be a conservative estimate of the actual share because some firms are still classified as belonging to the manufacturing sector though they are increasingly offering services.
10. The correlation between various measures of foreign trade and foreign direct investment flows and positions is significantly positive (Nicoletti *et al.*, 2003).

abroad generally brings stronger services trade.[11] In manufacturing, both types of FDI are widely practised. Recent evidence suggests that horizontal MNEs, which aim at accessing foreign markets by replicating abroad the production of a final good, may be prevalent in the OECD area, partly reflecting the increasing similarity in factor costs and endowments among Member countries (OECD, 2002d). However, MNEs' strategies have also been shown to vary across OECD countries, with horizontal strategies dominating in some countries and vertical strategies, in which production is fragmented in stages to exploit cross-country comparative advantages, dominating in others. The co-movement of FDI and trade at the aggregate level may reflect both the balance between horizontal and vertical strategies at the firm level and the influence of third factors that are likely to drive both phenomena, such as the generalised growth in income levels. OECD (2002e) further discusses the relationship between trade and FDI.

---

11. Foreign commercial presence tends to increase bilateral trade in transport services (*e.g.* supplying goods to foreign affiliates in the distribution sector), communications (*e.g.* data transactions with foreign affiliates in the financial, telecommunications or tourism sectors), and the like.

BIBLIOGRAPHY

BORGA, M. and R.J. MATALONI (2001), "Direct investment positions for 2000: country and industry detail", *Survey of Current Business,* July.

MARKUSEN, J.R. (2002), Multinational Firms and the Theory of International Trade, Cambridge: MIT Press.

NICOLETTI, G., S. GOLUB, D. HAJKOVA, D. MIRZA and K. YOO (2003), "Policies and international integration: Influences on trade and foreign direct investment", *OECD Economics Department Working Papers*, (forthcoming).

OECD (2001a), International Investment Statistics Yearbook: 1980/2000 – 2001 Edition, Paris.

OECD (2001b), Measuring Globalisation. The Role of Multinationals in OECD Economies. Manufacturing and Services. 2001 Edition, Paris.

OECD (2002a), *Foreign Direct Investment and Development: Where Do We Stand?*, Paris.

OECD (2002b), *Foreign Direct Investment for Development – Maximising Benefits, Minimising Costs*, Paris.

OECD (2002c), "Trends and recent developments in foreign direct investment", *International Investment Perspectives*, Paris.

OECD (2002d), *OECD Economic Outlook* No. 71, Paris.

OECD (2002e), "The relationship between trade and foreign direct investment: A survey", TD/TC/WP(2002)14/FINAL, Paris.

VII. FOREIGN DIRECT INVESTMENT RESTRICTIONS IN OECD COUNTRIES

Introduction

Attitudes and policies towards liberalisation of international capital flows have been subject to considerable controversy.[1] This is because free capital movements raise concerns about loss of national sovereignty and other possible adverse consequences. Foreign direct investment (FDI), even more than other types of capital flows, has historically given rise to such concerns, since it may involve a controlling stake by often large multinational enterprises over which domestic authorities, it is feared, have little power. For these reasons, governments have sometimes imposed restrictions on inward FDI. In recent decades, however, an increasing consensus on the benefits of inward FDI has led to reconsideration of these restrictions and this has been reflected in formal agreements on such capital flows (Box VII.1).

Inward foreign direct investment has often been restricted

Box VII.1. International investment agreements

Formal international agreements on foreign direct investment are far less extensive than on international trade, despite the importance of FDI in the world economy. However, the 1990s have seen a substantial rise in the number of bilateral investment protection treaties, and regional and bilateral trade agreements in which investment disciplines figure prominently. These agreements include North American Free Trade Agreement (NAFTA), the recent agreements concluded by Singapore with European Fair Trade Association (EFTA), Japan and Australia and the Association Agreement between the European Community and Chile. The European Union (EU) had already completely liberalised intra-EU capital movements in the late 1980s.

The OECD has been an important actor in international discussions and agreements on FDI.[1] At present the OECD Code of Liberalisation of Capital Movements forms the only multilateral framework in force on international capital flows, including FDI. Under the Code, countries bind themselves to agreed measures liberalising capital movements. Moreover, under the OECD Declaration on International Investment and Multinational Enterprises, the 30 OECD countries and 7 non-OECD adhering countries are committed to accord national treatment to foreign enterprises operating in their territories and to encourage their multinational enterprises to engage in responsible business conduct in a variety of areas.

There are several investment-related provisions in the agreements related to the World Trade Organisation (WTO). The Uruguay Round led to an agreement on Trade Related Investment Measures (TRIMS) that restricts *inter alia* domestic-content requirements. The General Agreement on Trade in Services (GATS) covers all modes of service delivery, including "commercial presence" which is closely related to FDI. The GATS commitments, however, apply only to industries where countries have explicitly agreed to open their markets to foreign providers. In 1996, the WTO also created the Working Group on the Relationship Between Trade and Investment, a forum for discussion among WTO countries. At the Doha Ministerial Conference in November 2001, the WTO members agreed on the principle of undertaking negotiations on a multilateral framework after the 2003 WTO ministerial meeting at Cancun (see OECD, 2002b).

1. Further discussion of OECD experience with investment rules and multilateral initiatives concerning FDI can be found at *www.oecd.org/daf/investment* and in Graham (2000), Robertson (2002) and Sauvé and Wilkie (2000).

---

1. See OECD (2002*a*) for an overview of policies towards international capital mobility, with a focus on the experience of OECD countries.

This chapter shows that restrictions on FDI are...

This chapter reviews restrictions on FDI inflows in OECD countries. The barriers covered include limitations on foreign ownership, screening or notification procedures, and management and operational restrictions. The main findings are as follows:

... generally low...

– Overall FDI restrictions are generally low in the OECD area at present but important in the case of a few countries.

... concentrated in the service sectors...

– FDI restrictions are concentrated in service sectors with almost no overt constraints in manufacturing.

... and have fallen since 1980

– Barriers to foreign ownership have significantly fallen in virtually all OECD countries over the past two decades.

The different types of FDI barriers

Formal restrictions on FDI include limits on foreign ownership...

Restrictions on foreign ownership are the most obvious barriers to inward FDI. They typically take the form of limiting the share of companies' equity capital that non-residents are allowed to hold in a target sector, *e.g.* to less than 50 per cent, or even prohibit any foreign ownership. Examples of majority domestic ownership requirements include airlines in the European Union and North American countries, telecommunications in Japan, and coastal and freshwater shipping in the United States. Exclusive domestic ownership is also often applied to natural resources sectors with the aim of giving citizens access to the associated rents. For example, foreign ownership is banned in the fishing and energy sectors in Iceland, and in the oil sector in Mexico. Although not specifically aimed at excluding foreign shareholders, statutory state monopolies are tantamount to a ban on foreign investment.

... screening and approval procedures...

Obligatory screening and approval procedures can also be used to limit FDI though their constraining effects depend on the implementation of such practices. Stipulations that foreign investors must show economic benefits can increase the cost of entry and therefore may discourage the inflow of foreign capital. Such provisions apply, for instance, for a few industries in Japan and for the acquisition of more than 49 per cent of any existing enterprise in Mexico. Prior approval of FDI, such as mandated for all FDI projects in a few OECD countries, could also limit foreign capital inflow if it is taken as a sign of an ambivalent attitude towards free FDI, even though it may not be vigorously enforced. Simple pre- or post-notification (as required in *e.g.* Japan) is, however, unlikely to have much impact on capital inflows.

... and constraints on foreign personnel and operational freedom

Other formal restrictions that can discourage FDI inflows include constraints on the ability of foreign nationals either to manage or to work in affiliates of foreign companies and other operational controls on these businesses. Stipulations that nationals or residents must form a majority of the board of directors, as in insurance companies in member countries of the European Union, in financial services industries in Canada and in transport industries in Japan, may undermine foreign owners' control over their holdings and hence make them more hesitant to invest under such circumstances. Similarly, if regulations restrict the employment of foreign nationals (as *e.g.* in Turkey), investors may judge that they cannot make use of the necessary expertise to make their investment worthwhile. Also, operational requirements, such as the restrictions *vis-à-vis* non-members on cabotage in most European Union countries for maritime transport may limit profits of foreign-owned corporations and hence the amount of funds foreign investors are willing to commit.

Apart from the formal barriers discussed above, FDI flows can be held back by opaque informal public or private measures. Indeed, claims abound that such practices are used systematically to limit foreign ownership of domestic businesses. Thus, the US Trade Representative has frequently stated that the system of corporate control in Japan has hampered investment by US companies and that regulatory practices in telecommunications in the European Union work as *de facto* FDI restraining measure. Similarly, the Japanese Ministry of Trade and Economy claims that FDI in financial services in the United States is restricted by the diverse and complex set of regulations at the state level and that barriers relating to interconnections hamper foreign entry into telecommunications in the European Union. Also, the European Union cites the continuing role of administrative guidance to firms in Japan by government officials as a practice that hampers foreign ownership of Japanese enterprises.

Informal barriers may also be important

The openness of OECD countries to inward FDI *circa* 1998-2000

Notwithstanding the numerous barriers in specific activities, an aggregate indicator of FDI restrictions (Box VII.2) suggests that the OECD countries are generally open to foreign direct investment inflows (Figure VII.1).[2] There are, however, significant differences between countries.[3] The most open countries are in the European Union. Since 1992, intra-EU FDI flows are almost completely unrestricted. Furthermore, a number of EU countries have minimal overt restrictions on inflows from non-EU countries. Nonetheless, there are some important differences in restrictions imposed by EU countries on non-EU investors and, therefore, even the European Union is not a completely unified bloc in terms of policies towards inward FDI. The countries with the highest levels of overall restrictions are Iceland, Canada, Turkey, Mexico, Australia, Austria, Korea and Japan. The United States is slightly below the OECD mean.

Overall FDI restrictions are now low in most OECD countries...

Around 2000, equity restrictions were particularly heavy in Mexico, Turkey and Korea, but also remained relatively stringent in Canada and the United States. Management and operational restrictions were notably strong in Japan, Iceland and Canada. In a few countries (Iceland, Australia, New Zealand, Canada and Spain) statutory screening requirements were relatively pervasive.[4]

... and concentrated on ceilings on foreign equity holdings...

---

2. There have been important changes in some countries since 2000 that are not reflected in the results reported here.
3. With an aggregate restrictiveness indicator that excludes screening requirements, the least and most open countries generally remain the same as those in Figure VII.1, the main exceptions being New Zealand (that moves from below to above average openness) and Spain (that moves from average to above average openness). Australia also moves towards a more open stance, though it remains below the OECD average.
4. The indicators are unable to capture differences in the enforcement of restrictions, which might be particularly important for screening requirements. For example, some countries simply perform basic checks such as whether an investor has a criminal record.

| Box VII.2. | **Indicators of FDI restrictions** |

Some indicators of overall FDI barriers are based on a count of the number of restrictions.[1] While this has the advantage of simplicity, some restrictions are more important than others. For example, a ban on foreign ownership is much more restrictive than a screening or a reporting requirement. The OECD FDI restrictiveness indicators therefore weigh different restrictions according to their perceived significance, even though such a procedure entails some arbitrary judgements. They are based on a variant of the methodology applied by the Australian Productivity Commission in a similar study for the APEC countries (Hardin and Holmes, 1997). The OECD indicators cover restrictions in nine sectors (subdivided in 11 subsectors), of which seven are services industries, where the bulk of FDI restrictions is generally found. This information is then aggregated into a single measure for the economy as a whole. Details of the methodology and data sources can be found in Golub (2003).

Some limitations of the measures should be noted. The indicators cover mainly statutory barriers, abstracting from most of the other direct or indirect obstacles impinging on FDI, such as those related to corporate governance mechanisms and/or hidden institutional or behavioural obstacles that discriminate against foreign firms.[2] It is also possible that some countries are more forthcoming than others in self-reporting their restrictions. It could then be that more transparent countries receive higher scores, not because they are in fact more restrictive, but because they are more complete in their reporting. The extent of enforcement of statutory restrictions, especially those concerning screening requirements, may also vary. Finally, standardising and putting into context idiosyncratic restrictions in individual countries often involve an element of judgement.

1. See *e.g.* Hoekman (1995) and Sauvé (2003).
2. Non-statutory barriers to FDI are very difficult to ascertain and quantify. However, some of them were included in the indicators, such as the absolute barrier represented by full state ownership of business enterprises and hidden institutional or behavioural barriers documented in official reports.

Figure VII.1. **FDI restrictions in OECD countries, 1998/2000: breakdown by type of restriction[1]**

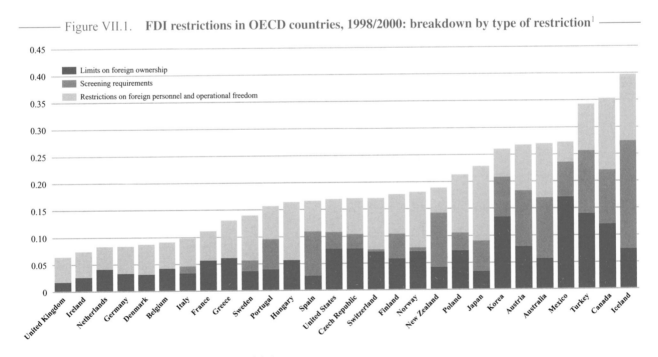

1. The indicator ranges from 0 (least restrictive) to 1 (most restrictive).
Source: OECD.

—— Figure VII.2. **Cross-sectoral patterns of FDI restrictions, 1998/2000**[1] ——

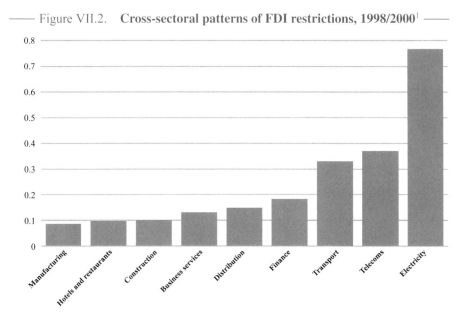

1. The indicator ranges from 0 (least restrictive) to 1 (most restrictive).
Source: OECD.

The overall level of barriers masks wide differences across sectors.[5] Figure VII.2 suggests that, on average, the bulk of restrictions are found in non-manufacturing industries.[6] FDI inflows into manufacturing are almost completely free, aside from economy-wide restrictions such as notification or screening requirements. Within non-manufacturing, electricity, transport and telecommunications are the most constrained industries, followed by finance, while the other services industries are on average relatively unrestricted. Again, these average patterns mask cross-country differences in the extent of restrictions in non-manufacturing industries. In 1998-2000, barriers in the European Union were relatively low in all these industries, while in Canada, Korea, Mexico, Turkey and, to a lesser extent, Australia and New Zealand, they where at or above the OECD average in many of them. They were concentrated in the transport industry in the United States and in telecommunications in Japan.

... in non-manufacturing sectors

The liberalisation of FDI since 1980

Figure VII.3 shows that the liberalisation of FDI flows has been substantial over the past two decades in all OECD countries except the United States and Japan, both of which had what in 1980 were relatively low statutory restrictions.[7] Particularly dramatic changes have occurred in several EU countries, notably Portugal, France and Finland. To a large extent, the generalised decline in barriers reflects full liberalisation of capital flows within the European Union (completed in the early 1990s) and

FDI restrictions have declined steeply since 1980

---

5. For further details about FDI restrictions at the industry level in OECD countries, see Golub (2003).
6. A simple count of restrictions affecting different industries shows that 67 per cent of all restrictions concern the services sector.
7. Due to data limitations, results here are limited to a smaller set of OECD countries.

———————————————— Figure VII.3. **FDI restrictions in OECD countries, 1980-2000**[1] ————————————————

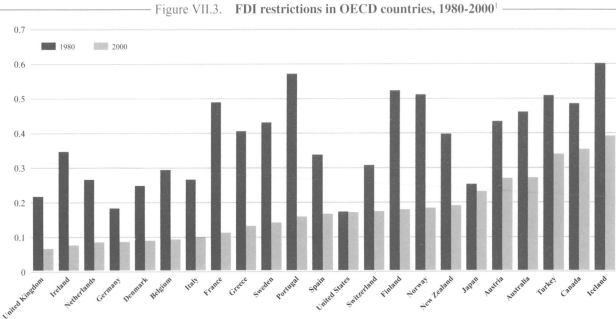

1. The indicator ranges from 0 (least restrictive) to 1 (most restrictive).
Source: OECD.

the concomitant extensive privatisations both in the European Union and elsewhere, which have opened up previously sheltered public firms and monopolies to foreign capital. The fall in FDI barriers throughout the OECD area has been particularly noticeable in the telecommunications and air transport sectors, which were almost completely closed in the early 1980s (Figure VII.4).

———————————————— Figure VII.4. **Evolution of FDI restrictions in selected sectors, 1981-1998**[1] ————————————————

OECD average[2]

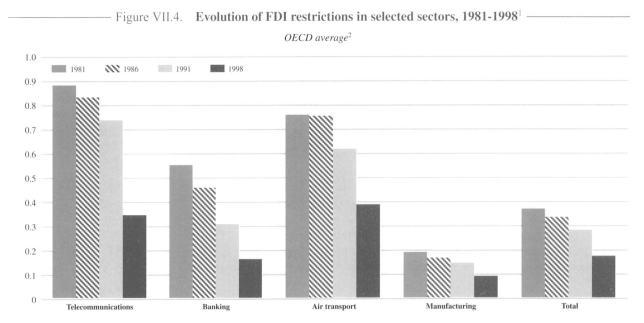

1. The indicator ranges from 0 (least restrictive) to 1 (most restrictive).
2. Average for 23 OECD countries.
Source: OECD.

BIBLIOGRAPHY

GOLUB, S. (2003), "Measures of restrictions on inward foreign direct investment for OECD countries", *OECD Economics Department Working Papers*, forthcoming.

GRAHAM, E.M. (2000), *Fighting the Wrong Enemy*, Institute for International Economics, Washington.

HARDIN, A. and L. HOLMES (1997), *Service Trade and Foreign Direct Investment*, Australian Productivity Commission.

HOEKMAN, B. (1995), "Assessing the general agreement on trade in services", in W. Martin and L.A. Winters (eds.), *The Uruguay Round and the Developing Countries*, World Bank Discussion Paper No. 307.

OECD (2002a), *Foreign Direct Investment for Development – Maximising Benefits, Minimising Costs*, Paris.

OECD (2002b), *Foreign Direct Investment and Development: Where Do We Stand?*, Paris.

ROBERTSON, D. (2002), "Multilateral Investment Rules", in Bora, B. (ed.) *Foreign Direct Investment: Research Issues,* Routledge, London.

SAUVE, P. and C. WILKIE (2000), "Investment liberalisation in GATS", in Sauve, P and R.M. Stern (eds.), *GATS 2000*: *New Direction in Services Trade Liberalisation*, Brookings: Washington.

SAUVE, P. (2003), "Collective Action Issues in Investment Rule-Making", Background Paper for Global Economic Prospects 2003: Investing to Unlock Global Opportunities, World Bank, Washington DC.

VIII. POLICY INFLUENCES ON FOREIGN DIRECT INVESTMENT

Introduction

Structural policies play an important role in determining foreign direct investment (FDI) in the OECD area. The Uruguay trade round, regional trade agreements and bilateral and multilateral investment accords have reduced direct barriers to FDI, and the current trade negotiations under the World Trade Organisation (WTO) auspicies aim at continuing this trend. However, restrictions to FDI are still significant in some countries and industries (see preceding Chapter). At the same time, there is growing recognition that labour market policies and product market regulations may have a significant indirect impact on the activities of multinational enterprises (MNEs).[1]

Structural policies can influence foreign direct investment patterns

This chapter aims at identifying policy influences on bilateral and overall FDI patterns in the OECD area. It considers both explicit trade and FDI restrictions and domestic regulations that affect competition and labour market adaptability. On the basis of the results obtained in this analysis, the effects on FDI of policies aimed at further increasing border openness and easing domestic product and labour market regulations are then explored. The main findings are as follows:

This chapter suggests that…

- FDI restrictions and, to a lesser extent, tariff barriers are estimated to curb significantly FDI stocks in protected countries. Limits to foreign ownership and governance discourage the activity of foreign affiliates, especially in some important non-manufacturing industries such as electricity, transport and telecommunications. Therefore, progress towards reducing remaining border barriers, as has been proposed in the ongoing Doha trade round, would favour closer economic integration among OECD economies.

… foreign direct investment is hampered by trade and FDI restrictions…

- Restrictive product- and labour-market regulations can also act as barriers to FDI. Countries where domestic product-market regulations impose unnecessary costs on businesses and create barriers to entry tend to have lower stocks of foreign capital. Similarly, strict employment protection legislation (EPL) and high labour income taxation also seem to lower inward FDI positions.

… as well as by some product and labour market policies…

- The alignment of FDI restrictions and product market regulations on those of the most liberal country could significantly increase the total OECD-wide inward FDI position, with gains for individual countries proportional to the extent of current restrictions. Substantial gains could also be obtained by further structural reforms in OECD labour markets.

… and that it could be raised significantly by reforms in these areas

---

1. The taxation of foreign affiliates' income is also likely to be an important determinant of FDI. This issue is scheduled to be addressed in a later issue of the Economic Outlook.

Policy and other determinants of foreign direct investment

Non-policy factors only partially explain OECD patterns of FDI...

Recent OECD analysis (Box VIII.1) suggests that differences in bilateral FDI positions across Member countries are explained about equally by policy and non-policy factors (Figure VIII.1). Among the latter, transport and/or communication costs tend to deter FDI between distant countries,[2] while such investment tends to increase with the combined market size of partner countries, because its returns partly depend on the possibility to reap economies of scale. Differences in the supply of physical and human capital also affect bilateral FDI patterns because they influence relative production costs across countries.[3]

... the rest being explained by differences in policies

The most important policy effects on bilateral FDI patterns seem to come from border policies and labour market arrangements. Detailed analysis shows that the contribution of border policies is equally split between the impact of FDI restrictions and other openness factors, such as participation in free-trade areas and tariff and non-tariff barriers. The labour tax wedge is the most influential component of labour market arrangements, with EPL playing a lesser role. Finally, anti-competitive product

Box VIII.1.   Policies and FDI: the OECD empirical analysis

The OECD has analysed the effects of policies on FDI using a large data set that covers bilateral FDI relationships between 28 OECD countries over the past two decades. The focus was on three sets of policies: explicit restrictions to trade and FDI; regulations affecting domestic competition; and policies that affect labour costs and the adaptability of labour markets. OECD countries' policies in labour and product markets were proxied by policy indicators described in OECD (1999; 2001) and Nicoletti and Scarpetta (2003). These were supplemented by indicators of non-tariff barriers (OECD, 1997), new indicators of tariffs (Bouet *et al.*, 2001) and FDI restrictions (see Chaper VII). The analysis relating policies to FDI also accounted for a large number of non-policy-related factors, including geographical distance, market size, transport costs, differences in the availability of physical and human capital, and other country- and period-specific effects, including cross-country differences in cyclical positions.[1]

The results of the empirical analysis can be used to quantify the long-run effects of policies that remove direct and indirect impediments to FDI on OECD-wide FDI integration and individual countries' FDI positions. In practice, this is done using the estimated coefficients of policy variables to project the impact of changes in policies on FDI. The results of these simulations are only suggestive of what could happen under different policy scenarios, notably because the applied coefficients may be imprecise due to the difficulty of disentangling the pure effects of policy and non-policy factors in the empirical analysis. Moreover, the estimated models on which the simulations are based do not account for all possible interactions between policy changes and FDI flows among OECD countries. The quantitative effects highlighted in these simulations also partly depend on the configuration of policies and the distribution of FDI positions in the baseline scenario. Details on sources, methodologies and results can be found in Nicoletti *et al.* (2003).

1. FDI can also be affected by strategic considerations related to expected developments in the behaviour of markets and other investors. These effects could not be accounted for in the analysis.

---

2. Transport costs may affect the returns to FDI to the extent that it is aimed at producing goods that are re-exported back to the home country or other distant markets.
3. The positive influence of dissimilarities in factor proportions on FDI aimed at fragmenting production into different stages is emphasised in Helpman (1984) and Helpman and Krugman (1985). On the other hand, FDI aimed at producing finished goods in local markets generally requires factor proportions to be similar (Markusen, 2002).

—— Figure VIII.1. **Contributions of policies and other factors to explaining** ——
cross-country differences in bilateral outward FDI positions, 1980-2000[1, 2]

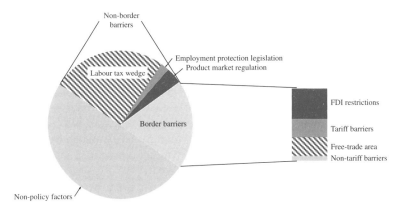

1. The contributions are based on coefficients estimated in panel regressions of bilateral outward FDI positions on non-policy factors (distance, transport costs, market size, similarity in size and factor endowments, and other country and time-specific effects) and policy influences (FDI restrictions, tariff and non-tariff barriers, participation in free-trade areas, and product and labour market arrangements). The regressions cover bilateral FDI positions between 28 OECD countries over the 1980-2000 period.
2. To compute the contributions, the absolute values of the deviations of the bilateral outward FDI positions from the OECD average, explained by each of the policy and non-policy factors, are averaged over the 1980-2000 period and summed over countries. These sums are then expressed as a percentage of the sum (over countries) of the period averages of the overall deviations of bilateral outward FDI positions from the OECD average.
Source: OECD.

market regulations were found to explain a smaller but still significant part of the deviations of inward FDI positions from the OECD average.[4]

The OECD analysis suggests that free-trade areas tend, on balance, to encourage FDI both among signatory countries and, in areas that are closely integrated, also with respect to third-party countries. By enlarging the overall size of the market, these agreements tend to increase the scope for reaping economies of scale through FDI aimed at accessing local markets (so-called "horizontal" FDI) for both signatory and non-signatory countries.[5] Moreover, the reduction in trade costs tends to increase FDI flows that are aimed at re-exporting final or intermediate products into the home country or into other signatory countries (so-called "vertical" FDI).[6] These positive influences on FDI appear to outweigh the tendency of free-trade areas to lower the relative cost of supplying a foreign market via trade compared with local production, which would in principle depress FDI flows.

The European Union (EU) appears to have prompted particularly strong FDI responses among its members, perhaps due to the much closer integration in the EU

Foreign direct investment thrives in free-trade areas...

4. Policies can also affect FDI indirectly, for example by improving the quality of a country's infrastructure capital or the skills of its labour force.
5. This could partly explain the wave of within-EU mergers and acquisitions that followed the European Single Market Programme.
6. More precisely, horizontal FDI flows to foreign affiliates that replicate the production of some of the same goods and services in both the home and host countries, while vertical FDI fragments the production of a good or service into stages located in different countries.

single market than in other free-trade areas [such as the North American Free Trade Agreement (NAFTA)].[7] For countries that will join the European Union in 2004 FDI effects could be sizeable, with outward and inward FDI positions estimated to double relative to their average levels in the 1990s in some of these countries.[8]

... reacting positively to both low tariffs and low investment restrictions...

Outside free-trade areas, OECD estimates suggest that tariff barriers between the host and investor country or between the host and third-party countries discourage foreign investment. This reflects the costs that tariffs impose on re-importing to the home country, or exporting to third-party countries, the final or intermediate goods produced by foreign affiliates.[9] Furthermore, as discussed in Chapter VII, FDI restrictions often set limits on investment by foreign companies, as well as on management and organisational choices of foreign affiliates in the host country.

... which encourage the activity of foreign affiliates

The increase in investment flows resulting from lower FDI restrictions would translate into an expansion of the activities of foreign affiliates in the affected industries. While the industry distribution of FDI in OECD economies can be influenced by a number of policy and non-policy factors, on average, the presence of foreign affiliates (measured by their sectoral employment shares) is currently much larger in industries where FDI restrictions are relatively low, such as manufacturing and some competitive services (*e.g.* distribution, tourism and business services) (Figure VIII.2). Where barriers have been traditionally high and widespread, such as in finance and especially network industries, the activity of foreign affiliates is still weak.

Foreign direct investment can be deterred by labour market policies...

OECD empirical results suggest that labour market arrangements can influence the cross-country patterns of FDI as strongly as direct restrictions to trade and FDI. These arrangements are generally driven by policy objectives that are unrelated to FDI, but they have important side effects on the level and geographical allocation of FDI flows. Strict employment protection legislation and, especially, high labour tax wedges appear to divert FDI to locations where labour market arrangements are perceived as less costly. These results would seem to imply that, on average, the costs of job protection and labour taxation are not fully shifted onto lower (after-tax) wages.[10] The negative effects of strict employment protection legislation on inward FDI may also be due to the fact that this legislation is likely to affect not only the returns expected from foreign investment but also their variability (*e.g.* by influencing the

---

7. The finding that FDI is boosted by EU membership is consistent with related evidence by Pain (1997) and Pain and Lansbury (1997). Positive effects of EU membership on FDI from third-party countries were also found by Dunning (1997) and Barrell and Pain (1998). The lack of these effects in other free-trade areas can partly be explained by higher average tariffs and stricter rules of origin.

8. The gains are due to both increased transactions with other EU countries and (to a lesser extent) increased trade and investment flows from non-EU countries. However, these results are likely to overestimate the actual post-accession gains to the extent that FDI stocks have already been affected by the expectation of EU membership.

9. On the other hand, high bilateral tariffs can generate so-called "tariff-jumping" behaviour by MNEs, aimed at bypassing border barriers by producing locally. The same kind of relationship could *a fortiori* be expected between horizontal FDI and non-tariff barriers, since the latter often raise absolute barriers to market access (*e.g.* quantitative restrictions). Indeed, empirical estimates suggest that, on average, non-tariff barriers have a positive effect on incoming FDI in OECD countries, while tariffs have a negative effect at the aggregate level, suggesting that the "tariff jumping" motive is weak.

10. In principle, higher non-wage labour costs should lead to a compensating reduction in wages in the longer term, because the initial increase in total labour costs should depress labour demand and wages should respond to the induced increase in unemployment. However, if wages are not downward flexible due to institutional rigidities (such as statutory or bargained wage floors or the workings of tax/benefit systems), the shifting of non-wage costs onto wages may be only partial, in which case labour will bear the cost in the form of higher unemployment.

Figure VIII.2.   **Foreign affiliates' activities and FDI restrictions in selected industries**[1]

OECD average

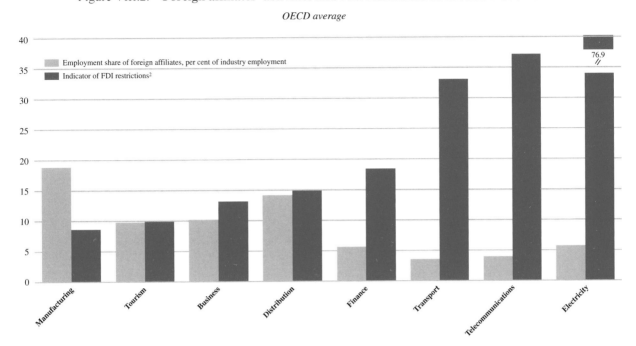

1. For this figure, the indicator ranges from 0 (least restrictive) to 100 (most restrictive).
2. See Chapter VII in this issue.
Source: OECD.

capacity of foreign affiliates to respond to supply or demand shocks), thereby increasing the risk that investors face in the host country.[11] Also, cost shifting in the face of high labour-income taxation may be particularly difficult for MNEs, whose employees have a higher cross-country mobility, especially at the highly-skilled and managerial levels.

Labour market arrangements in the home country can also affect, in conflicting ways, the amount of outward FDI by resident MNEs. On the one hand, MNEs may have incentives to localise production in other countries, where labour market rules and taxation are less stringent. On the other hand, strict provisions may prevent firms from doing so, by hindering their potential for reorganising production or growing in size. OECD estimates suggest that the latter effect dominates, with strict labour market arrangements at home curbing outward FDI as well.

Product market regulations can raise production costs or entry barriers for MNEs both at home and in host country markets. Such regulation generally does not discriminate between local and foreign firms, but it has distorting effects on FDI flows because it affects market access and the relative rates of return expected from investing in different locations. As shown in Figure VIII.3, there appears to be an inverse relationship between the strictness of regulations and inward FDI

... as well as by a lack of competition in product markets

11. Since MNEs can choose *ex ante* where to locate their investment, they may still tend to move where the risk/return ratio is lowest. It is also possible that foreign investors may find the implications of restrictive EPL provisions more difficult to ascertain than domestic investors (due to an asymmetry of information) and hence face higher costs.

Figure VIII.3. **Product market regulation and FDI positions, 1990-1998[1]**

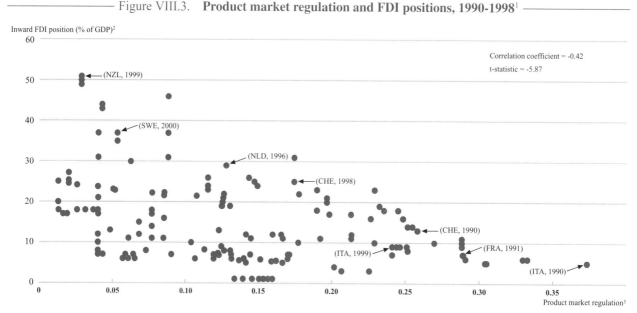

1. Each point shows the combination of regulation and FDI in a given country and period. Some of these country/period combinations are shown for illustrative purposes.
2. The data on the vertical axis are the percentage shares in GDP of inward FDI positions of OECD countries in each year. The data on the horizontal axis are the levels of regulation in OECD countries in each year.
3. Product of the indicator of economy-wide regulation in 1998 and the indicator of barriers to entry in seven non-manufacturing industries over the 1980-1998 period. 0-1 scale from least to most restrictive of competition.
Source: OECD.

positions.[12] Indeed, detailed empirical analysis suggests that regulations that curb competition or impose unnecessary costs on the firms involved in bilateral FDI transactions make the host country less attractive for international investors located in countries where regulations are laxer. Thus, the deterring influence of barriers to entry and cost-increasing regulations appears to outweigh other potential effects, such as the incentives that lack of competition in the host country may create for FDI aimed at acquiring (or merging foreign parents with) local firms endowed with market power.

Foreign direct investment effects of policy reform

Policy reforms have increased inward FDI in several countries

OECD analysis suggests that, relative to the OECD average, policy influences on FDI appear to have played different roles in different countries over the past two decades (Figure VIII.4). For instance, while labour market arrangements seem to have had a relatively positive influence on inward FDI positions in English-speaking countries, Japan and Portugal, they have tended to depress them in other European

---

12. While regulations that bar entry or raise costs may deter FDI, regulations that are aimed at protecting intellectual property rights (IPR) may increase the attractiveness of the host country for international investors because protection of IPR makes it more difficult to imitate their firm-specific knowledge assets (*e.g.* through the movement of managers or employees from the foreign affiliate to local firms). See Smith (2001).

———————— Figure VIII.4. **Policies and inward FDI positions**[1] ————————

Contributions to explaining the deviations from OECD average, 1980-2000[2]

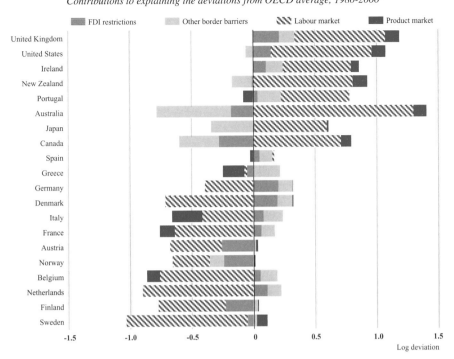

1. "Other border barriers" contains the contribution of tariff and non-tariff barriers and of membership in a free-trade area. "Labour market" contains the contributions of the relative indicator of the tax wedge on labour income and of the relative indicator of employment protection legislation. "Product market" contains the contribution of the relative level of barriers to entry.
2. The contributions are based on coefficients estimated in panel regressions of bilateral outward FDI positions on non-policy factors (distance, transport costs, market size, similarity in size and factor endowments, and other country and time-specific effects) and policy influences (FDI restrictions, tariff and non-tariff barriers, participation in free trade areas, and product and labour market arrangements). The regressions cover bilateral FDI positions between 28 OECD countries over the 1980-2000 period.
Source: OECD.

countries. Similarly, while in most European countries and the United States open-ness factors are estimated to have played a positive role, comparatively restrictive border measures are likely to have depressed inward FDI positions relative to the OECD average in Canada, Australia and, to a lesser extent, Japan, Norway and Finland. On the basis of the analysis discussed above, the contribution of product market regulation was significant for countries having either a relatively liberal approach (the United States, the United Kingdom, Australia, New Zealand, Canada, Sweden and Ireland), where it pushed up relative inward FDI positions, or a rela-tively restrictive approach (some continental European countries), where it pulled down relative inward FDI positions.

While trade and FDI liberalisation have been extensive over the past two decades, further opening up borders would increase FDI integration among OECD countries. For instance, the average effect of lifting such restrictions can be substan-tial, with particularly strong increases in FDI to be obtained from the removal of for-eign equity ceilings (Table VIII.1). Also, based on the estimates discussed above, an OECD-wide alignment of remaining FDI restrictions on those of the least restrictive OECD country (the United Kingdom, according to the indicator presented in Chapter VII) might increase OECD-wide inward FDI positions by almost 20 per cent

Lifting border restrictions would increase FDI...

—————————— Table VIII.1. **FDI positions: the hypothetical effect** ——————————
of removing FDI restrictions[a]

Average across countries

	Per cent change in inward FDI position
Removal of foreign equity ceilings	77.9
Removal of approval and national interest tests	21.2
Easing of nationality requirements on management [b]	10.1

a) The simulations are based on coefficients estimated in panel regressions of bilateral outward FDI positions and flows
on non-policy factors (distance, transport costs, market size, similarity in size and factor endowments, and other country
and time-specific effects) and policy influences (FDI restrictions, tariff and non-tariff barriers, participation in free trade
areas, and product and labour market arrangements). The regressions cover bilateral FDI relationships between 28
OECD countries over the 1980-2000 period.
b) From majority of domestic managers to only one or more domestic managers.
Source: OECD.

(Figure VIII.5, panel A). This scenario implies country-specific reforms that differ in
content and scope depending on the patterns of FDI restrictions in place, but typically they would imply lifting screening requirements and restrictions on foreign
shareholdings, and substantially reducing other restrictions (*e.g.* on the nationality of
management, board composition and movement of people). In the liberalisation scenario, relatively restrictive countries could increase their inward FDI positions by
between 40 and 80 per cent, but even in countries that are estimated to be already relatively open the gains could amount to around 20 per cent of their initial inward
position.[13] While these results illustrate the potential consequences of liberalisation
for FDI, the scenario obviously does not address the issue of whether and how to
deal with the policy objectives currently being pursued by FDI restrictions.

As with the lifting of border restrictions, in many OECD countries policy
reforms that reduce entry barriers and cost-increasing product and labour market
arrangements would significantly boost area-wide FDI integration. For instance,
domestic competition-oriented policies that result in an alignment of product-market
regulations on those of the least restrictive OECD country are estimated to increase
OECD-wide inward FDI positions by over 10 per cent relative to their average level
in the 1990s (Figure VIII.5, panel B). Since bilateral outward positions are estimated
to depend on the relative stringency of regulation in the home and host countries, relatively restrictive host countries – such as Greece, Italy and France – that receive
FDI from relatively liberal countries could increase their FDI instocks by as much as
55 to 80 per cent through regulatory reform. Conversely, countries that are relatively
liberal could see the relative attractiveness of their product markets either broadly
unchanged (such as in the United States, New Zealand and Sweden) or even reduced
(such as in the United Kingdom and Australia).

... and easing product and labour market regulations

Structural reforms in labour markets may also increase FDI integration according to OECD estimates. Such policy scenarios are not easy to construct because the
functioning of labour markets depends on a large number of interrelated factors,

———————————

13. In the simulations, the initial stock is defined as the average inward position over the 1990s.

Figure VIII.5.   **Policies and inward FDI positions: the scope for further integration**[1]

Panel A: Lifting FDI restrictions[2]

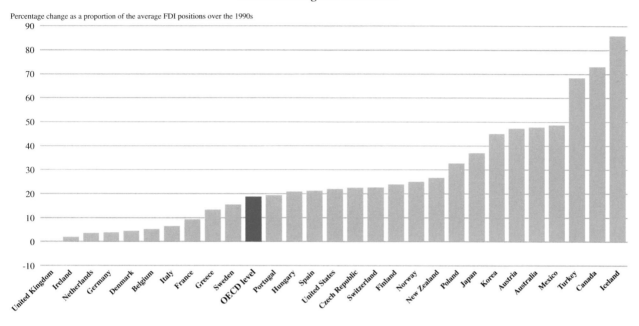

Percentage change as a proportion of the average FDI positions over the 1990s

Panel B: Easing product market regulations[2]

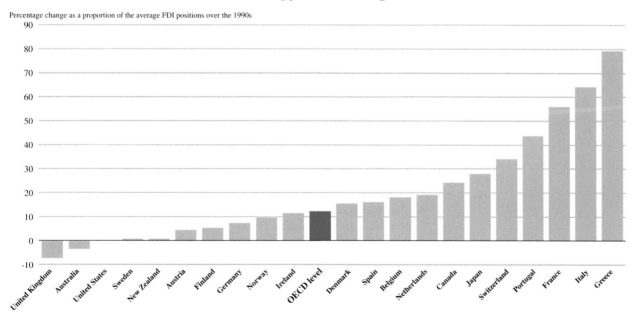

Percentage change as a proportion of the average FDI positions over the 1990s

1. The simulations are based on coefficients estimates in panel regressions of bilateral outward FDI positions on non-policy factors (distance, transport costs, market size, similarity in size and factor endowments, and other country and time-specific effects) and policy influences (FDI restrictions, tariff and non-tariff barriers, participation in free trade areas, and products and labour market arrangements). The regressions cover bilateral FDI positions between 28 OECD countries over the 1980-2000 period.
2. Alignment of restrictions and regulations on those of the most liberal OECD country.
Source: OECD.

sometimes implying trade-offs between several of them (such as between social insurance and employment protection provisions), and no clear benchmarks exist for EPL and labour income taxation. Nonetheless, OECD analysis suggests, for instance, that an alignment of labour tax wedges to the OECD median value (38 per cent) in countries whose wedges are currently above this level could increase the OECD-wide inward FDI position by 5 per cent relative to baseline. This result presupposes that other taxes could be raised or public expenditures cut, so as to preserve sustainable public finances, without any impact on FDI positions.

BIBLIOGRAPHY

BARRELL, R. and N. PAIN (1998), "Real exchange rates, agglomerations and irreversibilities: macroeconomic policy and FDI in EMU", *Oxford Review of Economic Policy*, 14/3.

BOUET, A., L. FONTAGNE, M. MIMOUNI and X. PICHOT (2001), "Market access maps: a bilateral and disaggregated measure of market access", *CEPII documents de travail No. 18*.

DUNNING, J.H. (1997), "The European internal market programme and inbound foreign direct investment", *Journal of Common Market Studies*, 35.

HELPMAN, E. (1984), "A simple theory of trade with multinational corporations", *Journal of Political Economy* 92.

HELPMAN, E. and P. KRUGMAN (1985), *Market Structure and International Trade*, Cambridge, MIT Press.

MARKUSEN, J.R. (2002), *Multinational Firms and the Theory of International Trade*, Cambridge, MIT Press.

NICOLETTI, G. AND S. SCARPETTA (2003), "Regulation, productivity and growth", Economic Policy, No. 36.

NICOLETTI, G., S. GOLUB, D. HAJKOVA, D. MIRZA and K. YOO (2003), "Policy influences and international integration: Influences on trade and foreign direct investment", *OECD Economics Department Working Papers*, forthcoming.

OECD (1997), *Indicators of Tariff & Non-tariff Trade Barrier*, Paris.

OECD (1999), *Implementing the OECD Jobs Strategy: Assessing Performance and Policy*, Paris.

OECD (2001), *OECD Economic Outlook* No. 70, Paris.

PAIN, N. (1997), "Continental drift: European integration and the location of UK foreign direct investment", *The Manchester School*, LXV *Supplement*.

PAIN, N. and M. LANSBURY (1997), "Regional economic integration and foreign direct investment: the case of German investment in Europe", *National Institute Economic Review*, No. 160.

SMITH, P.J. (2001), "How do foreign patent rights affect U.S. exports, affiliate sales, and licences?" *Journal of International Economics* Vol. 55.

Special chapters in recent issues of *OECD Economic Outlook*

No. 72, December 2002

Fiscal sustainability: the contribution of fiscal rules
Increasing employment: the role of later retirement
Product market competition and economic performance
Inflation persistence in the euro area

No. 71, June 2002

Economic consequences of terrorism
Ongoing changes in the business cycle
Intra-industry and intra-firm trade and the internationalisation of production
Productivity and innovation: the impact of product and labour market policies

No. 70, December 2001

Saving and investment: determinants and policy implications
Investment in human capital through post-compulsory education and training
The cross-market effects of product and labour market policies
Agricultural policy reform: the need for further progress

No. 69, June 2001

Fiscal implications of ageing: projections of age-related spending
Challenges for tax policy in OECD countries
Encouraging environmentally sustainable growth: experience in OECD countries
Productivity and firms dynamics: evidence from microdata

No. 68, December 2000

Links between policy and growth: cross-country evidence
Revised OECD measures of structural unemployment
House prices and economic activity
Trends in immigration and economic consequences

No. 67, June 2000

Regulatory reform in network industries: past experience and current issues
Recent growth trends in OECD countries
E-commerce: impacts and policy challenges
Recent labour-market performance and structural reforms
Monetary policy in a changing financial environment

No. 66, December 1999

The size and role of automatic fiscal stabilisers
Making work pay
Public debt management at the cross-roads
Cross-country patterns of product market regulation

No. 65, June 1999

Labour market performance and the OECD jobs strategy
Policy challenges arising from climate change
The recent experience with capital flows to emerging market economies
Causes of the recent widening of OECD current account imbalances
Trends in market openness

This annex contains data on some main economic series which are intended to provide a background to the recent economic developments in the OECD area described in the main body of this report. Data for 2002 to 2004 are OECD estimates and projections. The data on some of the tables have been adjusted to internationally agreed concepts and definitions in order to make them more comparable as between countries, as well as consistent with historical data shown in other OECD publications. Regional totals and sub totals are based on those countries in the table for which data are shown. Aggregate measures contained in the Annex, except the series for the euro area (see below), are computed on the basis of 1995 GDP weights expressed in 1995 purchasing power parities (see following page for weights). Aggregate measures for external trade and payments statistics, on the other hand, are based on current year exchange for values and base year exchange rates for volumes.

The OECD projection methods and underlying statistical concepts and sources are described in detail in documentation that can be downloaded from the OECD Internet site:

- *OECD Economic Outlook* Sources and Methods (*www.oecd.org/eco/sources-and-methods*).
- *OECD Economic Outlook* Database Inventory (*www.oecd.org/eco/data/eoinv.pdf*).
- The construction of macroeconomic series of the euro area (*www.oecd.org/eco/data/euroset.htm*).

NOTE ON STATISTICAL TREATMENT OF GERMANY,
THE CZECH REPUBLIC, HUNGARY, POLAND,
THE SLOVAK REPUBLIC AND THE EURO AREA AGGREGATE

In this publication, the following should be noted:

- Data up to end-1990 are for western Germany only; unless, otherwise indicated, they are for the whole Germany from 1991 onwards. In tables showing percentage changes from previous year, data refer to the whole Germany from 1992 onwards. When data are available for western Germany only, a special mention is made in a footnote to the table.

- For the Czech Republic, Hungary, Poland and Slovak Republic most data are available from 1993 onwards. In tables showing percentage changes from the previous year, the Czech Republic, Hungary, Poland and the Slovak Republic are included from 1994 onwards.

- Greece entered the euro area on 1 January 2001. In order to ensure comparability of the euro area data over time, Greece has been included in the calculation of the euro area throughout.

Country classification

OECD

Seven major OECD countries	Canada, France, Germany, Italy, Japan, United Kingdom and United States.
European Union	Austria, Belgium, Denmark, Finland, France, Germany, Greece, Ireland, Italy, Luxembourg, Netherlands, Portugal, Spain, Sweden and United Kingdom.
Euro area	Austria, Belgium, Finland, France, Germany, Greece, Ireland, Italy, Luxembourg, Netherlands, Portugal and Spain.

Non-OECD

Africa and the Middle East	Africa and the following countries (Middle East): Bahrain, Cyprus, Iran, Iraq, Jordan, Kuwait, Lebanon, Oman, Qatar, Saudi Arabia, Syrian Arab Republic, United Arab Emirates and Yemen.
Dynamic Asian Economies (DAEs)	Chinese Taipei; Hong Kong, China; Indonesia; Malaysia; the Philippines; Singapore and Thailand.
Other Asia	Non-OECD Asia and Oceania, excluding China, the DAEs and the Middle East.
Latin America	Central and South America.
Central and Eastern Europe	Albania, Bulgaria, Romania, the Newly Independent States of the former Soviet Union, and the Baltic States.

Weighting scheme for aggregate measures
Per cent

Australia	1.80	Mexico	2.96
Austria	0.82	Netherlands	1.56
Belgium	1.06	New Zealand	0.30
Canada	3.26	Norway	0.49
Czech Republic	0.61	Poland	1.29
Denmark	0.57	Portugal	0.65
Finland	0.46	Slovak Republic	0.23
France	5.71	Spain	2.84
Germany	8.31	Sweden	0.87
Greece	0.64	Switzerland	0.86
Hungary	0.44	Turkey	1.65
Iceland	0.03	United Kingdom	5.23
Ireland	0.31	United States	35.16
Italy	5.48		
Japan	13.95	Total OECD	100.00
Korea	2.45	*Memorandum items:*	
Luxembourg	0.07	European Union	34.54
		Euro area	27.88

Note: Based on 1995 GDP and purchasing power parities (PPPs).

Irrevocable euro conversion rates
National currency unit per euro

Austria	13.7603	Ireland	0.787564
Belgium	40.3399	Italy	1 936.27
Finland	5.94573	Luxembourg	40.3399
France	6.55957	Netherlands	2.20371
Germany	1.95583	Portugal	200.482
Greece	340.750	Spain	166.386

Source: European Central Bank.

National accounts reporting systems and base-years

Many countries are changing from the SNA68/ESA79 methodology for the national accounts data.
In the present edition of the OECD Economic Outlook, the status of national accounts in the OECD countries is as follows :

	Expenditure accounts	Household accounts	Government accounts	Use of chain weighted price indices	Benchmark/ base year
Australia	SNA93 (1959)	SNA93 (1959)	SNA93 (1959)	YES	2000/2001
Austria	ESA95 (1988)	ESA95 (1995)	ESA95 (1976)	NO	1995
Belgium	ESA95 (1970)	ESA95 (1995)	ESA95 (1970)	NO	1995
Canada	SNA93 (1955)	SNA93 (1955)	SNA93 (1981)	YES	1997
Czech Republic	SNA93 (1994)	SNA93 (1994)	SNA93 (1992)	NO	1995
Denmark	ESA95 (1988)	ESA95 (1988)	ESA95 (1971)	NO	1995
Finland	ESA95 (1995)	ESA95 (1995)	ESA95 (1995)	NO	2000[a]
France	ESA95 (1978)	ESA95 (1978)	ESA95 (1978)	NO	1995
Germany[b]	ESA95 (1960)	ESA95 (1970)	ESA95 (1980)	NO	1995
Greece	ESA95 (1960)	Not available	ESA95 (1960)	NO	1995[a]
Hungary	SNA93 (1995)	Estimated from SNA93	SNA93 (1991)	NO	1998
Iceland	SNA93 (1970)	Not available	SNA93 (1990)	NO	1990
Ireland	ESA95 (1990)	ESA95 (1990)	ESA95 (1990)	NO	1995
Italy	ESA95 (1982)	ESA95 (1980)	ESA95 (1980)	NO	1995
Japan	SNA93 (1980q1)[c]	SNA93 (1990)[c]	SNA93 (1990)[c]	NO	1995
Korea	SNA93 (1970)	SNA93 (1975)	SNA93 (1975)	NO	1995
Luxembourg	ESA95 (1970)	Not available	ESA95(1990)	NO	1995
Mexico	SNA93 (1980)	Not available	Not available	NO	1993
Netherlands	ESA95 (1995)	ESA95 (1995)	ESA95 (1995)	YES	1995
New Zealand	SNA93 (1987)	SNA93 (1986)	SNA93 (1986)	YES	1995/96
Norway	SNA93 (1978)	SNA93 (1978)	SNA93 (1978)	NO	2000[a]
Poland	SNA93 (1991)	SNA93 (1991)	SNA93 (1991)	YES	1995
Portugal	ESA95 (1995)	ESA95(1995)	ESA95 (1977)	NO	1995
Slovak Republic	SNA93 (1993)	SNA93 (1995)	SNA93 (1994)	NO	1995
Spain	ESA95 (1995)	ESA95 (1995)	ESA95 (1995)	NO	1995
Sweden	ESA95 (1980)	ESA95 (1993)	ESA95 (1980)	YES	1995
Switzerland	SNA68	SNA68	Not available	NO	1990
Turkey	SNA68	SNA68	SNA68	NO	1987
United Kingdom	ESA95 (1987)	ESA95 (1987)	ESA95 (1987)	NO	1995
United-States	NIPA (SNA93) (1959q1)	NIPA (SNA93) (1959q1)	NIPA (SNA93) (1960q1)	YES	1996

a) SNA: System of National Accounts. ESA: European Standardised Accounts. NIPA: National Income and Product Accounts. GFS: Government Financial Statistics.
The numbers in brackets indicate the starting year for the time series.
b) Data prior to 1991 refer to the new SNA93/ESA95 accounts for western Germany data..
c) Spliced to SNA68.

Annex Tables

Interest Rates and Exchange Rates

External Trade and Payments

Other Background Data

Annex Table 1. Real GDP

Percentage change from previous period

	Average 1975-85	1986	1987	1988	1989	1990	1991	1992	1993	1994	1995	1996	1997	1998	1999	2000	2001	2002	Projections 2003	Projections 2004
Australia	3.0	1.5	5.0	4.5	4.5	1.4	-0.7	2.4	3.8	4.7	4.0	4.0	3.6	5.5	4.4	3.0	2.8	3.5	3.2	3.8
Austria	2.4	2.1	1.6	3.4	4.2	4.7	3.3	2.3	0.4	2.6	1.6	2.0	1.6	3.9	2.7	3.5	0.7	1.0	1.1	2.0
Belgium	2.1	1.8	2.4	4.6	3.6	3.0	1.8	1.3	-0.7	3.3	2.3	0.8	3.9	2.1	3.2	3.7	0.8	0.7	1.3	2.3
Canada	3.2	2.4	4.3	5.0	2.6	0.2	-2.1	0.9	2.3	4.8	2.8	1.6	4.2	4.1	5.4	4.5	1.5	3.4	2.7	3.4
Czech Republic	..	..	..	..	..	..	..	..	..	2.6	5.9	4.3	-0.8	-1.0	0.5	3.3	3.1	2.0	3.0	3.5
Denmark	2.6	3.6	0.3	1.2	0.2	1.0	1.1	0.6	0.0	5.5	2.8	2.5	3.0	2.5	2.6	2.8	1.4	1.6	1.6	2.6
Finland	2.9	2.5	4.2	4.7	5.1	0.0	-6.3	-3.3	-1.1	4.0	3.8	3.9	6.4	4.9	3.4	5.5	0.6	1.6	2.2	3.4
France	2.3	2.3	2.5	4.2	4.2	2.6	1.0	1.3	-0.9	1.9	1.8	1.1	1.9	3.5	3.2	4.2	1.8	1.2	1.2	2.6
Germany	2.2	2.4	1.5	3.7	3.9	5.7	5.1	2.2	-1.1	2.3	1.7	0.8	1.4	2.0	2.0	2.9	0.6	0.2	0.3	1.7
Greece	2.1	0.5	-2.3	4.3	3.8	0.0	3.1	0.7	-1.6	2.0	2.1	2.4	3.6	3.4	3.6	4.2	4.1	4.0	3.6	3.9
Hungary	..	..	..	..	..	..	..	..	..	2.9	1.5	1.3	4.6	4.9	4.2	5.2	3.8	3.3	3.1	3.7
Iceland	4.3	6.3	8.5	-0.1	0.3	1.2	-0.5	-3.3	0.9	4.1	0.1	5.1	4.6	5.5	4.0	5.5	3.1	-0.6	2.1	3.5
Ireland	3.5	-0.4	4.7	5.2	5.8	8.5	1.9	3.3	2.7	5.8	9.9	8.1	10.9	8.8	11.1	10.0	6.0	6.0	3.2	4.2
Italy	3.0	2.5	3.0	3.9	2.9	2.0	1.4	0.8	-0.9	2.2	2.9	1.1	2.0	1.8	1.7	3.1	1.8	0.4	1.0	2.4
Japan	3.9	2.9	4.4	6.5	5.2	5.2	3.3	1.0	0.3	1.0	1.9	3.4	1.8	-1.1	0.1	2.8	0.4	0.3	1.0	1.1
Korea	7.4	11.0	11.0	10.5	6.1	9.0	9.2	5.4	5.5	8.3	8.9	6.8	5.0	-6.7	10.9	9.3	3.1	6.3	5.2	6.0
Luxembourg	2.4	10.0	4.0	8.5	9.8	5.3	8.6	1.8	4.2	3.8	1.3	3.7	7.7	7.5	6.0	8.9	1.0	0.5	0.3	2.7
Mexico	4.3	-3.6	1.8	1.3	4.2	5.1	4.2	3.6	2.0	4.5	-6.2	5.1	6.8	4.9	3.7	6.6	-0.3	0.9	2.5	3.9
Netherlands	1.9	2.8	1.4	3.0	5.0	4.1	2.5	1.7	0.9	2.6	3.0	3.0	3.8	4.3	4.0	3.3	1.3	0.3	0.7	1.9
New Zealand	1.7	0.6	0.8	2.6	0.6	0.5	-1.9	0.8	4.7	6.2	3.9	3.5	3.1	-0.5	4.8	3.9	2.0	4.6	2.9	2.9
Norway	4.0	3.6	2.0	-0.1	0.9	2.0	3.1	3.3	2.7	5.3	4.4	5.3	5.2	2.6	2.1	2.8	1.9	1.0	1.1	2.1
Poland	..	..	..	..	..	..	..	..	..	5.3	7.0	6.0	6.8	4.8	4.1	4.0	1.0	1.3	2.3	3.5
Portugal	3.0	4.1	6.4	7.5	6.4	4.0	4.4	1.1	-2.0	1.0	4.3	3.5	4.0	4.6	3.8	3.7	1.6	0.5	0.3	2.3
Slovak Republic	..	..	..	..	..	..	..	..	..	5.2	6.5	5.8	5.6	4.0	1.3	2.2	3.3	4.4	3.6	4.3
Spain	1.6	3.3	5.5	5.1	4.8	3.8	2.5	0.9	-1.0	2.4	2.8	2.4	4.0	4.3	4.2	4.2	2.7	2.0	2.1	3.1
Sweden	1.6	2.7	3.3	2.6	2.7	1.1	-1.1	-1.7	-1.8	4.2	4.0	1.3	2.4	3.6	4.6	4.4	1.1	1.9	1.5	2.8
Switzerland	1.6	1.6	0.7	3.1	4.3	3.7	-0.8	-0.1	-0.5	0.5	0.5	0.3	1.7	2.4	1.5	3.2	0.9	0.1	0.6	1.9
Turkey	3.6	7.0	9.5	2.1	0.3	9.3	0.9	6.0	8.0	-5.5	7.2	7.0	7.5	3.1	-4.7	7.4	-7.5	7.8	2.5	2.6
United Kingdom	1.9	4.2	4.2	5.2	2.2	0.8	-1.4	0.2	2.5	4.7	2.9	2.6	3.4	2.9	2.4	3.1	2.1	1.8	2.1	2.6
United States	3.4	3.4	3.4	4.2	3.5	1.8	-0.5	3.1	2.7	4.0	2.7	3.6	4.4	4.3	4.1	3.8	0.3	2.4	2.5	4.0
Euro area	2.3	2.4	2.5	4.1	4.0	3.6	2.5	1.4	-0.8	2.3	2.3	1.4	2.3	2.9	2.8	3.6	1.5	0.9	1.0	2.4
European Union	2.3	2.8	2.8	4.2	3.6	3.1	1.9	1.1	-0.3	2.8	2.5	1.7	2.6	2.9	2.8	3.5	1.6	1.0	1.2	2.4
Total OECD	3.2	3.1	3.6	4.6	3.8	3.1	1.3	2.1	1.4	3.2	2.6	3.0	3.5	2.7	3.1	3.8	0.8	1.8	1.9	3.0

Note: The adoption of new national account systems, SNA93 or ESA95, has been proceeding at an uneven pace among OECD member countries, both with respect to variables and the time period covered. As a consequence there are breaks in many national series. Moreover, some countries are using chain-weighted price indices to calculate real GDP and expenditures components. See Table "National Account Reporting Systems and Base-years" at the beginning of the Statistical Annex and *OECD Economic Outlook Sources and Methods* (*http://www.oecd.org/eco/sources-and-methods*).

Source: OECD.

Annex Table 2. Nominal GDP
Percentage change from previous period

	Average 1975-85	1986	1987	1988	1989	1990	1991	1992	1993	1994	1995	1996	1997	1998	1999	2000	2001	2002	2003 (Proj.)	2004 (Proj.)
Australia	12.5	8.2	13.2	13.5	11.9	6.4	1.6	3.7	5.1	5.6	5.5	6.4	5.3	5.7	5.2	7.4	5.9	6.3	5.1	6.5
Austria	7.4	5.1	3.8	4.7	7.3	8.2	7.2	6.0	3.4	5.4	4.2	3.3	2.5	4.5	3.4	5.0	2.3	2.3	2.8	3.2
Belgium	7.8	4.7	4.1	7.0	8.5	5.9	4.7	4.8	3.3	5.5	3.6	2.1	5.1	3.7	4.6	5.0	2.7	2.9	3.3	3.9
Canada	10.8	5.5	9.1	9.7	7.3	3.4	0.8	2.2	3.8	6.0	5.1	3.3	5.5	3.7	7.2	8.6	2.6	4.6	6.3	5.6
Czech Republic	..	..	..	..	..	..	..	..	..	13.9	16.8	13.5	7.2	9.5	3.4	4.3	9.6	4.6	5.5	7.2
Denmark	11.0	8.4	5.0	4.6	5.4	4.7	3.9	3.5	1.4	7.3	4.6	5.1	5.2	3.5	4.5	5.9	3.5	2.7	4.1	5.3
Finland	12.3	6.9	8.6	13.2	11.6	5.5	-4.5	-2.5	1.2	6.0	8.1	3.6	8.5	8.7	3.1	8.6	4.3	2.9	3.6	4.8
France	12.2	7.6	5.5	7.6	7.6	5.6	4.0	3.3	1.5	3.7	3.5	2.5	3.1	4.4	3.7	4.7	3.3	2.9	2.7	4.2
Germany	5.9	5.7	3.3	5.3	6.4	9.1	8.8	7.4	2.5	4.9	3.8	1.8	2.1	3.1	2.6	2.6	2.0	1.8	1.2	2.4
Greece	21.9	19.5	12.6	21.7	18.8	20.7	23.5	15.6	12.6	13.4	12.1	9.9	10.7	8.8	6.7	7.7	7.6	7.8	7.3	7.6
Hungary	..	..	..	..	..	..	..	..	..	23.0	27.4	22.8	23.9	18.1	12.9	15.4	13.1	12.4	10.5	8.1
Iceland	49.6	33.3	29.7	22.7	20.1	18.2	8.2	-0.1	3.1	6.2	3.0	7.3	8.0	10.7	6.9	8.5	12.5	4.6	4.9	6.8
Ireland	16.7	6.1	7.0	8.6	11.7	7.7	3.8	6.2	8.0	7.5	13.2	10.3	15.5	15.6	15.7	14.6	11.6	11.2	7.3	8.0
Italy	19.3	10.6	9.4	11.0	9.5	10.4	9.1	5.3	3.0	5.8	8.1	6.4	4.5	4.6	3.3	5.3	4.6	3.1	3.8	5.1
Japan	8.1	4.6	4.3	7.3	7.3	7.7	6.3	2.6	0.8	1.1	1.4	2.6	2.2	-1.2	-1.4	0.9	-1.2	-1.4	-1.2	-0.7
Korea	23.0	16.7	17.2	18.8	12.2	20.6	21.1	13.5	12.9	16.5	16.7	10.9	8.3	-2.0	8.6	8.1	5.7	8.1	5.7	7.5
Luxembourg	9.0	9.9	4.0	11.5	14.2	8.0	10.6	5.6	10.4	7.5	3.8	5.4	11.2	9.8	9.3	12.0	3.3	0.7	0.9	5.0
Mexico	45.0	67.0	145.2	103.8	31.8	34.6	28.5	18.6	11.6	13.3	29.3	37.5	25.7	21.0	19.5	19.5	6.1	5.6	6.8	7.6
Netherlands	6.7	2.9	0.7	4.0	6.2	6.4	5.4	4.1	2.7	5.0	5.0	4.2	5.9	6.1	5.6	7.6	6.6	3.7	3.3	3.8
New Zealand	15.7	16.0	14.1	10.3	5.7	3.8	-1.4	2.3	7.8	7.3	6.4	6.0	3.5	1.0	4.7	6.3	6.9	4.9	4.0	5.4
Norway	12.5	2.6	9.1	4.8	6.7	5.9	5.6	2.7	5.1	5.2	7.3	9.5	8.2	1.9	8.9	19.1	3.9	0.3	3.8	4.7
Poland	..	..	..	..	..	..	..	..	..	44.5	36.9	25.9	21.8	17.2	11.1	15.8	5.2	2.7	3.3	5.5
Portugal	25.0	25.4	17.1	19.5	17.6	17.6	14.9	12.7	5.2	8.3	7.9	6.7	7.9	8.5	7.0	7.0	6.5	5.1	3.9	4.7
Slovak Republic	..	..	..	..	..	..	..	..	..	19.6	17.0	10.5	12.7	9.4	7.8	8.7	8.9	8.5	11.2	9.7
Spain	16.6	14.5	11.8	11.3	12.1	11.4	9.7	7.7	3.5	6.4	7.8	6.0	6.4	6.8	7.1	7.8	6.9	6.5	5.2	5.6
Sweden	11.6	9.5	8.3	9.1	10.9	10.0	6.1	-0.8	0.8	6.6	7.6	2.5	4.0	4.4	5.3	5.7	3.2	3.2	3.9	5.2
Switzerland	4.8	4.8	3.5	6.0	7.5	8.2	5.2	2.6	2.2	2.2	1.6	0.7	1.5	2.3	2.2	4.4	2.3	0.5	1.4	2.4
Turkey	48.5	45.5	46.3	72.9	75.9	72.9	60.3	73.5	81.3	95.2	100.7	90.3	95.2	81.1	48.2	60.9	43.2	54.9	29.3	17.3
United Kingdom	12.9	7.5	9.9	11.6	9.8	8.4	5.2	4.2	5.2	6.1	5.6	6.0	6.4	6.0	5.0	5.3	4.5	5.1	4.0	5.0
United States	9.9	5.7	6.5	7.7	7.5	5.7	3.2	5.6	5.1	6.2	4.9	5.6	6.5	5.6	5.6	5.9	2.6	3.6	4.1	5.3
Euro area	11.4	8.1	6.0	8.1	8.4	8.7	7.4	5.8	2.8	5.2	5.2	3.6	4.0	4.7	4.0	5.0	3.9	3.2	3.0	4.1
European Union	12.4	8.5	7.0	8.9	8.9	8.9	7.3	5.5	3.2	5.5	5.6	4.2	4.5	4.9	4.2	5.1	4.0	3.5	3.2	4.2
Total OECD	12.8	9.5	11.8	12.7	10.1	9.4	7.1	6.6	5.4	7.9	7.9	7.4	7.4	6.0	5.5	6.6	3.7	3.9	3.1	4.5
Memorandum item																				
OECD less high inflation countries [a]	11.0	6.9	6.9	8.5	8.2	7.5	5.5	5.1	3.9	5.5	5.0	4.8	5.1	4.0	4.1	5.1	2.8	3.0	2.8	4.1

Note: The adoption of new national account systems, SNA93 or ESA95, has been proceeding at an uneven pace among OECD member countries, both with respect to variables and the time period covered. As a consequence there are breaks in many national series. See Table "National Account Reporting Systems and Base-years" at the beginning of the Statistical Annex and *OECD Economic Outlook* Sources and Methods (http://www.oecd.org/eco/sources-and-methods).

a) High inflation countries are defined as countries which have had 10 per cent or more inflation in terms of the GDP deflator on average during the last 10 years based on historical data. Consequently, Hungary, Mexico, Poland and Turkey are excluded from the aggregate.

Source: OECD.

Annex Table 3. **Real private consumption expenditure**

Percentage change from previous period

	Average 1975-85	1986	1987	1988	1989	1990	1991	1992	1993	1994	1995	1996	1997	1998	1999	2000	2001	2002	Projections 2003	Projections 2004
Australia	2.9	1.8	1.9	3.9	5.6	2.7	0.6	2.5	1.6	3.7	4.7	3.2	4.0	4.5	4.9	3.2	3.1	4.1	3.5	3.2
Austria	2.5	1.9	2.6	3.1	4.3	4.5	2.5	3.0	0.8	2.4	2.6	3.2	1.7	2.7	2.3	3.3	1.5	0.9	1.3	1.9
Belgium	2.4	2.7	1.7	3.3	3.4	3.1	3.0	1.8	-0.3	2.4	1.6	0.9	2.3	3.0	2.2	3.3	1.0	0.6	1.0	2.0
Canada	2.7	3.7	4.2	4.3	3.4	1.2	-1.6	1.5	1.8	3.0	2.1	2.6	4.6	2.8	3.9	3.7	2.6	2.9	2.8	2.9
Czech Republic	..	..	..	..	..	..	..	..	..	5.3	5.9	7.9	2.4	-1.6	1.7	2.5	3.6	4.0	4.1	4.5
Denmark	1.7	5.7	-1.5	-1.0	-0.1	0.1	1.6	1.9	0.5	6.5	1.2	2.5	2.9	2.3	0.7	-1.9	0.4	2.1	1.9	2.2
Finland	2.6	4.0	5.1	5.3	4.6	-0.6	-3.8	-4.4	-3.1	2.6	4.4	3.6	3.5	4.4	3.5	3.3	1.7	2.1	2.3	2.1
France	2.1	3.5	2.6	2.4	3.2	2.7	0.7	0.8	-0.2	0.9	1.3	1.3	0.1	3.6	3.5	2.8	2.8	1.8	1.6	2.2
Germany	2.0	3.9	3.7	2.6	3.2	4.1	4.6	2.7	0.1	1.1	2.1	1.0	0.6	1.8	3.7	1.4	1.5	-0.6	0.5	1.4
Greece	3.4	-1.5	2.7	6.1	6.3	2.6	2.9	2.3	-0.8	1.9	2.5	2.4	2.7	3.5	2.9	2.6	2.9	2.5	2.7	2.9
Hungary	..	..	..	..	..	..	..	..	..	0.2	-7.1	-4.3	1.9	4.8	5.4	4.4	4.9	9.8	5.5	3.8
Iceland	4.6	6.9	16.2	-3.8	-4.2	0.5	0.8	-3.1	-4.7	2.9	2.2	5.4	5.5	10.1	7.3	4.0	-3.0	-1.2	0.5	2.0
Ireland	2.5	2.0	3.3	4.5	6.5	1.4	1.8	2.9	2.9	4.4	3.6	6.5	7.2	7.7	9.3	9.0	5.0	2.5	3.0	3.5
Italy	3.3	4.0	3.8	4.0	3.7	2.1	2.9	1.9	-3.7	1.5	1.7	1.2	3.2	3.2	2.6	2.7	1.0	0.4	1.0	2.4
Japan	3.4	3.2	4.1	5.0	4.7	4.5	2.9	2.6	1.4	2.7	1.8	2.4	0.9	-0.1	0.2	1.0	1.7	1.4	0.6	0.7
Korea	6.3	8.2	7.5	8.5	10.1	9.6	8.0	5.5	5.6	8.2	9.6	7.1	3.5	-11.7	11.0	7.9	4.7	6.8	3.2	4.3
Luxembourg	2.1	3.5	4.6	6.0	4.8	3.8	7.0	-2.3	2.1	4.0	2.1	4.0	4.0	7.8	2.6	3.3	3.6	1.6	0.2	1.5
Mexico	3.6	-2.6	-0.1	1.8	7.3	6.4	4.7	4.7	1.5	4.6	-9.5	2.2	6.5	5.4	4.3	8.2	2.7	1.2	2.4	4.2
Netherlands	1.7	2.6	2.7	0.6	3.3	3.9	2.7	0.8	0.5	0.9	3.0	4.0	3.0	4.8	4.7	3.6	1.2	1.0	1.2	2.3
New Zealand	0.7	4.0	2.4	2.7	1.1	0.1	-1.3	0.1	2.8	5.8	4.0	5.1	2.4	2.0	3.9	2.0	2.2	3.8	3.4	2.6
Norway	3.3	5.0	-0.8	-2.0	-0.6	0.7	1.5	2.2	2.4	3.3	3.7	6.5	3.2	2.7	3.3	3.9	2.6	3.3	2.5	2.0
Poland	..	..	..	..	..	..	..	..	..	..	3.7	8.6	6.9	4.8	5.2	2.8	2.0	3.3	1.8	1.6
Portugal	0.7	5.6	5.3	6.8	2.9	6.4	4.2	4.7	1.1	1.0	0.6	3.0	3.3	5.0	5.1	2.6	1.2	0.7	0.5	1.6
Slovak Republic	..	..	..	..	..	..	..	..	..	..	4.0	8.8	5.7	6.3	3.3	-1.8	3.9	5.3	3.0	3.2
Spain	1.1	3.4	6.0	4.9	5.4	3.5	2.9	2.2	-1.9	1.1	1.7	2.2	3.2	4.4	4.7	3.9	2.5	1.9	2.3	3.2
Sweden	0.7	5.2	5.3	2.6	1.2	-0.4	1.0	-1.3	-3.0	1.9	1.1	1.6	2.7	3.0	3.8	5.0	0.2	1.3	2.2	2.6
Switzerland	1.5	2.3	2.2	1.7	2.3	1.2	1.6	0.1	-0.9	1.0	0.6	0.7	1.4	2.3	2.2	2.0	1.8	0.9	0.8	1.8
Turkey	4.7	5.8	-0.3	1.2	-1.0	13.1	2.7	3.2	8.6	-5.4	4.8	8.5	8.4	0.6	-2.6	6.2	-9.2	2.0	2.9	3.2
United Kingdom	2.1	6.6	5.0	7.5	3.3	1.0	-1.5	0.6	3.2	3.3	1.9	3.8	3.8	3.8	4.5	5.2	4.1	3.8	2.2	2.3
United States	3.5	4.2	3.3	4.0	2.7	1.8	-0.2	2.9	3.4	3.8	3.0	3.2	3.6	4.8	3.9	4.3	2.5	3.1	2.3	3.6
Euro area	2.2	3.5	3.5	3.2	3.7	3.1	2.7	1.9	-0.9	1.3	1.9	1.6	1.6	3.1	3.6	2.6	1.8	0.7	1.2	2.1
European Union	2.2	4.1	3.8	3.8	3.5	2.7	2.1	1.6	-0.3	1.7	1.9	2.0	2.1	3.2	3.7	3.0	2.1	1.2	1.4	2.2
Total OECD	3.1	3.9	3.5	4.1	3.6	3.0	1.4	2.4	1.7	2.8	2.2	2.9	2.9	3.0	3.8	3.5	2.1	2.3	1.8	2.7

Note: The adoption of new national account systems, SNA93 or ESA95, has been proceeding at an uneven pace among OECD member countries, both with respect to variables and the time period covered. As a consequence there are breaks in many national series. Moreover, some countries are using chain-weighted price indices to calculate real GDP and expenditures components. See Table "National Account Reporting Systems and Base-years" at the beginning of the Statistical Annex and *OECD Economic Outlook* Sources and Methods (*http://www.oecd.org/eco/sources-and-methods*).

Source: OECD.

Annex Table 4. Real public consumption expenditure

Percentage change from previous period

	Average 1975-85	1986	1987	1988	1989	1990	1991	1992	1993	1994	1995	1996	1997	1998	1999	2000	2001	2002	Projections	
																			2003	2004
Australia	3.7	4.2	2.0	2.2	3.6	3.7	3.1	0.5	0.3	3.1	4.0	2.9	2.6	3.4	2.9	5.8	1.5	4.3	2.5	3.5
Austria	2.3	1.8	0.1	1.1	1.7	2.3	3.2	3.5	3.7	3.0	1.3	1.2	-1.5	2.8	3.1	0.0	-0.5	1.3	0.5	0.7
Belgium	2.3	1.4	2.7	-0.8	1.1	-0.4	3.6	1.4	-0.1	1.6	1.3	2.2	0.3	1.1	3.5	2.4	2.1	1.5	1.5	1.8
Canada	2.3	1.8	1.3	4.6	2.8	3.5	2.9	1.0	0.0	-1.2	-0.6	-1.2	-1.0	3.2	1.9	2.3	3.3	2.0	3.7	3.2
Czech Republic	..	..	..	..	..	..	..	..	..	-2.4	-4.3	3.6	-4.4	-4.4	2.3	-1.0	5.3	5.7	1.8	1.4
Denmark	3.1	0.5	2.5	0.9	-0.8	-0.2	0.6	0.8	4.1	3.0	2.1	3.4	0.8	3.1	2.0	1.1	2.1	0.9	1.0	0.9
Finland	3.6	3.4	4.4	1.9	2.2	4.0	2.1	-2.4	-4.2	0.3	2.0	2.9	3.3	2.1	1.4	0.4	1.2	4.0	2.0	2.0
France	3.3	2.4	2.2	3.0	1.8	2.5	2.6	3.6	4.3	0.5	0.0	2.2	2.1	0.0	1.5	2.9	2.4	3.5	2.7	1.6
Germany	2.0	2.4	1.8	2.4	-1.1	3.1	1.9	5.0	0.1	2.4	1.5	1.8	0.3	1.9	1.0	1.2	0.8	1.5	0.8	0.4
Greece	3.6	-1.1	0.2	-5.5	5.4	0.6	-1.5	-3.0	2.6	-1.1	5.6	0.9	3.0	1.7	1.6	2.0	-0.9	6.2	0.0	0.2
Hungary	4.7	..	6.5	4.7	3.0	4.4	3.1	-0.7	2.3	-7.4	-5.7	-1.9	3.1	2.8	1.5	1.9	0.1	2.6	1.4	0.0
Iceland	2.8	7.3	-4.8	-5.0	-1.3	5.4	2.7	3.0	0.1	4.0	1.8	1.2	2.5	3.4	4.6	3.8	2.9	3.1	2.0	2.5
Ireland	3.0	2.6	4.8	4.0	0.2	2.5	1.7	0.6	-0.2	4.1	3.9	3.5	5.1	6.5	6.7	7.6	10.5	8.7	1.5	0.7
Italy	4.1	4.6	3.5	3.7	2.7	2.6	3.4	2.6	3.2	-0.9	-2.2	1.0	0.2	0.2	1.3	1.6	3.6	1.7	1.2	1.1
Japan	4.1	4.6	3.5	3.7	2.7	2.6	1.6	2.9	2.4	2.7	4.2	2.9	1.0	2.1	4.4	4.7	2.5	2.3	2.0	1.9
Korea	4.1	8.3	6.2	7.8	8.5	7.4	7.2	5.9	4.6	1.9	0.8	8.2	1.5	-0.4	1.3	0.1	1.3	2.9	2.0	2.0
Luxembourg	2.2	6.4	9.6	4.3	8.2	6.7	4.0	3.2	5.2	1.0	4.8	5.6	3.1	1.3	7.1	4.3	7.5	6.3	6.5	3.2
Mexico	5.6	1.4	-1.2	-0.5	2.2	3.3	5.4	1.9	2.4	2.9	-1.3	-0.7	2.9	2.3	4.7	2.0	-1.2	-1.3	2.8	3.0
Netherlands	2.6	3.6	2.6	1.8	1.9	2.2	3.0	2.9	1.6	1.5	1.5	-0.4	3.2	3.6	2.5	1.9	3.1	3.8	0.2	0.8
New Zealand	1.6	2.1	0.5	0.1	3.5	1.6	-0.6	1.1	1.3	0.8	4.8	2.1	7.6	-1.9	7.5	-1.9	3.5	4.6	2.9	2.5
Norway	4.0	1.9	4.6	-0.1	1.9	4.9	4.3	5.6	2.7	1.5	1.5	3.1	2.5	3.3	3.2	1.3	2.7	4.5	0.5	1.1
Poland	..	..	..	..	..	..	9.6	-0.9	-0.2	1.2	4.8	2.0	3.1	1.4	1.0	1.1	0.4	1.3	1.7	1.8
Portugal	5.7	7.2	3.8	8.6	8.3	6.3	6.0	3.5	2.7	4.3	1.0	3.4	2.2	4.1	5.6	4.0	3.4	3.2	-0.3	-0.3
Slovak Republic	..	..	..	..	..	..	..	..	..	-10.1	2.1	17.4	-4.5	11.5	-7.7	1.3	5.1	4.0	2.5	3.0
Spain	4.3	4.6	9.2	3.6	8.3	6.3	6.0	3.5	2.7	0.5	2.4	1.3	2.9	3.7	4.2	5.0	3.1	3.8	3.5	3.0
Sweden	2.4	1.8	1.2	1.1	3.0	2.5	3.4	0.2	-0.1	-0.8	-0.4	0.7	-0.9	3.4	1.7	-1.1	0.9	2.1	0.8	0.8
Switzerland	2.0	3.4	1.7	4.5	5.4	5.4	3.5	0.7	-0.1	2.0	-0.1	2.0	0.0	1.3	1.2	1.5	2.6	1.9	0.1	0.4
Turkey	5.3	9.2	9.4	-1.1	0.8	8.0	3.7	3.6	8.6	-5.5	6.8	8.6	4.1	7.8	6.5	7.1	-8.5	5.4	2.8	3.1
United Kingdom	0.9	1.6	-0.4	0.2	1.0	2.2	3.0	0.7	-0.7	1.0	1.7	1.2	0.1	1.5	3.1	2.1	2.5	3.8	2.1	2.8
United States	2.0	4.6	2.4	1.6	2.5	2.6	1.4	0.4	-0.3	0.2	0.0	0.5	1.8	1.4	2.9	2.8	3.7	4.4	5.3	2.0
Euro area	2.8	2.6	3.0	2.6	1.2	2.8	2.6	3.0	1.4	1.1	0.7	1.6	1.2	1.4	1.8	2.2	2.1	2.7	1.6	1.2
European Union	2.6	2.5	2.7	2.2	1.4	2.8	2.7	2.5	1.0	1.0	0.8	1.5	1.0	1.6	2.1	2.1	2.2	2.7	1.6	1.4
Total OECD	2.8	3.8	2.7	2.3	2.3	3.0	2.6	1.8	1.1	0.8	1.1	1.6	1.4	1.8	2.8	2.8	2.5	3.2	3.1	1.9

Note: The adoption of new national account systems, SNA93 or ESA95, has been proceeding at an uneven pace among OECD member countries, both with respect to variables and the time period covered. As a consequence there are breaks in many national series. Moreover, some countries are using chain-weighted price indices to calculate real GDP and expenditures components. See Table "National Account Reporting Systems and Base-years" at the beginning of the Statistical Annex and OECD Economic Outlook Sources and Methods (http://www.oecd.org/eco/sources-and-methods).

Source: OECD.

Annex Table 5. Real total gross fixed capital formation

Percentage change from previous period

	Average 1975-85	1986	1987	1988	1989	1990	1991	1992	1993	1994	1995	1996	1997	1998	1999	2000	2001	2002	Projections 2003	Projections 2004
Australia	4.7	-0.7	3.6	9.3	10.1	-7.6	-8.4	1.5	5.2	11.6	2.4	4.3	9.5	8.4	6.9	-0.4	-1.3	14.1	6.2	5.5
Austria	1.1	1.3	3.8	7.4	4.1	6.2	6.6	0.6	-0.9	4.6	1.3	2.2	2.0	3.9	2.1	5.9	-2.2	-4.8	0.8	2.9
Belgium	-0.4	3.4	5.1	15.6	12.2	7.8	-3.9	0.8	-1.7	-0.1	3.7	-0.5	8.5	3.2	4.5	3.2	0.5	-2.6	0.5	2.5
Canada	3.7	4.6	10.5	9.3	5.6	-3.9	-5.4	-2.7	-2.0	7.5	-2.1	4.4	15.2	2.4	7.8	6.5	1.7	2.5	3.4	5.2
Czech Republic	..	..	..	..	..	..	..	..	..	17.1	19.8	8.2	-2.9	0.7	-1.0	5.3	5.5	0.6	3.2	3.5
Denmark	1.2	17.1	-3.8	-6.6	-0.8	-2.1	-3.3	-2.0	-4.0	7.6	11.6	4.0	10.9	10.1	1.5	9.1	1.3	1.3	1.1	3.2
Finland	0.3	1.0	4.9	11.0	13.0	-4.6	-18.6	-16.7	-16.6	-2.7	10.6	7.5	13.1	8.2	1.8	4.0	3.8	-1.0	-1.3	2.6
France	0.6	4.6	5.7	9.0	7.6	3.3	-1.5	-1.8	-6.6	1.5	2.2	0.1	-0.2	7.3	8.3	8.3	2.6	-0.6	-1.4	2.3
Germany	1.1	2.9	1.8	4.6	6.7	7.7	5.2	4.5	-4.4	4.0	-0.6	-0.8	0.6	3.0	4.1	2.5	-5.3	-6.7	-0.5	1.8
Greece	0.1	0.1	-5.6	2.6	6.1	4.5	4.2	-3.5	-4.0	-3.1	4.1	8.4	6.8	10.6	6.2	8.0	5.9	6.7	8.6	6.8
Hungary	..	..	18.8	-0.2	-7.9	3.0	0.9	-11.1	-10.7	12.5	-4.3	6.7	9.2	13.3	5.9	7.7	3.1	5.9	2.6	2.1
Iceland	1.1	-1.6	-1.1	5.2	10.1	13.4	-7.0	0.0	-5.1	0.6	-1.1	25.7	10.0	33.4	-3.7	14.8	-6.3	-13.0	10.6	11.2
Ireland	2.8	-2.8	-1.1	2.7	14.5	12.4	-8.0	0.2	-5.6	11.8	15.3	16.8	18.1	14.8	14.0	7.0	1.0	-0.7	-0.2	2.1
Italy	1.0	2.3	4.2	6.7	4.2	4.0	1.0	-1.4	-10.9	0.1	6.0	3.6	2.1	4.0	5.0	7.1	2.6	0.5	1.1	3.5
Japan	2.9	5.0	9.0	12.1	8.6	8.1	2.3	-2.4	-2.8	-1.5	0.7	6.4	0.9	-3.9	-0.9	2.9	-1.2	-4.0	-1.3	-1.5
Korea	11.4	10.7	17.0	13.6	15.8	25.9	13.3	-0.7	6.3	10.7	11.9	7.3	-2.2	-21.2	3.7	11.4	-1.8	4.8	2.4	5.0
Luxembourg	-1.8	37.1	17.7	11.5	6.9	3.4	15.8	-15.1	20.6	0.0	-1.5	3.9	12.6	11.8	14.0	-6.3	5.9	-4.3	-3.1	3.4
Mexico	1.7	-11.8	-0.1	5.8	5.8	13.1	11.0	10.8	-2.5	8.4	-29.0	16.4	21.0	10.3	7.7	11.4	-5.8	-1.3	3.0	5.5
Netherlands	0.8	6.9	0.9	5.3	5.1	2.5	0.4	0.7	-3.2	2.1	3.9	6.3	6.6	4.2	7.8	3.5	-0.8	-3.1	-0.7	1.2
New Zealand	0.7	-1.8	-0.2	0.1	4.5	-0.8	-18.3	0.2	14.5	15.3	12.2	7.8	0.6	-5.2	4.4	7.4	-1.7	8.0	4.9	2.7
Norway	0.8	7.6	0.3	-1.8	-6.9	-10.8	-0.4	-1.1	6.5	5.3	3.9	10.3	15.5	13.1	-5.6	-3.6	-4.2	-3.3	2.1	0.6
Poland	..	..	..	..	..	..	..	..	..	9.2	16.6	19.7	21.7	14.2	6.8	2.7	-8.8	-7.2	3.5	7.0
Portugal	0.3	10.9	18.0	14.8	3.7	7.6	3.3	4.5	-5.5	2.7	6.6	5.7	13.9	11.5	6.4	4.4	0.1	-5.2	-2.4	4.2
Slovak Republic	..	..	..	..	..	..	..	..	..	-2.5	1.8	30.9	14.3	11.0	-18.5	1.2	9.6	-0.9	3.7	5.2
Spain	-0.9	10.5	12.2	13.6	12.0	6.5	1.7	-4.1	-8.9	1.9	7.7	2.1	5.0	10.0	8.7	5.7	3.2	1.4	2.6	4.1
Sweden	1.1	1.1	8.0	6.4	12.1	0.2	-8.6	-11.6	-15.0	6.6	9.9	4.5	-0.3	7.8	8.2	6.6	0.8	-2.5	0.2	4.4
Switzerland	1.9	5.4	4.0	8.1	5.3	3.8	-2.9	-6.6	-2.7	6.5	1.8	-2.4	1.5	4.5	2.7	5.8	-5.2	-6.5	-0.6	3.1
Turkey	-0.5	8.4	45.1	-1.0	2.2	15.9	0.4	6.4	26.4	-16.0	9.1	14.1	14.8	-3.9	-15.7	16.9	-31.5	-0.8	7.9	11.0
United Kingdom	1.5	2.1	9.0	14.9	6.0	-2.6	-8.2	-0.9	0.3	4.7	3.1	4.7	6.9	12.8	0.6	1.9	1.0	-3.2	1.9	6.7
United States	5.4	2.7	1.1	2.9	2.9	-0.2	-5.4	5.3	5.9	7.4	5.5	8.4	8.9	10.3	7.9	5.5	-2.6	-1.8	1.4	5.9
Euro area	0.7	4.0	4.3	7.6	7.1	5.0	1.0	0.0	-6.4	2.3	2.5	1.3	2.5	5.3	5.9	5.1	-0.2	-2.3	0.2	2.7
European Union	0.9	4.1	5.2	8.6	6.9	3.9	-0.4	-0.4	-5.6	2.6	3.5	2.3	3.4	6.7	5.1	4.9	0.1	-2.4	0.4	3.3
Total OECD	3.4	3.4	5.2	6.9	5.7	3.5	-1.5	1.7	0.3	4.4	3.2	6.2	6.3	5.7	4.9	5.3	-1.9	-1.7	1.1	3.9

Note: The adoption of new national account systems, SNA93 or ESA95, has been proceeding at an uneven pace among OECD member countries, both with respect to variables and the time period covered. As a consequence there are breaks in many national series. Moreover, some countries are using chain-weighted price indices to calculate real GDP and expenditures components. See Table "National Account Reporting Systems and Base-years" at the beginning of the Statistical Annex and *OECD Economic Outlook* Sources and Methods (*http://www.oecd.org/eco/sources-and-methods*).

Source: OECD.

Annex Table 6. **Real gross private non-residential fixed capital formation**
Percentage change from previous period

	Average 1975-85	1986	1987	1988	1989	1990	1991	1992	1993	1994	1995	1996	1997	1998	1999	2000	2001	2002	Projections 2003	2004
Australia	5.9	0.7	7.1	9.0	10.1	-7.6	-11.5	-1.9	2.2	12.1	8.0	10.5	8.1	7.4	6.6	-3.0	2.0	13.2	9.6	8.8
Austria	2.4	-0.6	8.5	9.4	6.3	13.2	6.1	-3.1	-4.4	3.7	-2.2	4.0	10.7	7.6	4.7	11.6	1.1	-5.6	0.6	3.5
Belgium	1.4	6.6	7.0	13.9	17.0	9.3	-3.3	-1.2	-4.7	-2.5	5.3	3.5	8.6	4.8	2.5	4.2	2.9	-3.6	1.0	2.9
Canada	5.4	2.4	10.0	14.7	5.5	-2.6	-3.3	-7.8	-1.4	9.4	4.8	4.4	22.6	5.3	7.8	8.2	-1.1	-3.9	4.2	8.4
Denmark	4.4	18.1	-4.8	-7.3	3.6	2.2	-1.4	-4.2	-8.3	7.6	13.9	2.7	13.7	13.5	1.9	9.4	4.1	2.0	0.8	3.5
Finland	0.4	5.8	5.7	10.2	15.9	-7.4	-23.3	-18.4	-17.8	-2.7	22.4	8.4	7.4	12.5	0.5	6.6	10.4	-2.5	-3.2	3.9
France	2.2	6.7	7.6	9.6	8.2	5.7	-1.1	-2.6	-8.0	0.7	3.3	0.0	0.9	10.2	9.1	9.2	3.0	-1.1	-2.0	2.8
Germany	1.5	0.2	1.9	5.6	7.1	9.0	6.0	0.7	-9.0	0.7	1.0	-0.8	2.2	4.9	5.2	6.2	-4.5	-7.3	-1.1	4.2
Greece	0.9	-10.5	0.6	2.8	15.3	6.6	5.2	0.7	1.1	0.9	2.9	14.7	5.4	12.0	8.5	9.7	7.8	7.4	9.8	7.9
Iceland	1.9	4.8	22.7	-11.4	-15.3	6.9	1.8	-18.0	-25.9	1.8	12.5	53.1	19.5	46.9	-5.8	14.9	-13.4	-20.5	18.7	15.5
Ireland	4.0	-4.4	6.4	19.4	9.5	18.9	-11.7	-2.5	-5.7	8.2	17.3	17.6	20.9	19.9	13.6	1.4	0.0	-4.8	-3.3	0.8
Italy	1.2	5.0	7.5	10.2	5.4	4.8	0.3	-1.3	-14.7	4.4	10.4	5.0	4.0	4.6	6.5	9.0	2.3	5.4	-1.0	3.9
Japan	5.5	5.1	6.2	15.3	14.9	10.4	4.1	-7.1	-11.2	-6.3	2.7	4.7	11.7	-2.0	-3.8	9.6	1.1	-3.6	1.3	1.1
Korea	13.2	12.9	20.4	12.8	15.7	16.7	13.4	0.1	5.3	15.1	14.1	7.3	-3.0	-29.2	11.4	18.0	-6.0	2.1	1.9	5.1
Mexico	..	-17.1	8.7	20.3	7.1	19.6	22.6	22.8	-5.6	-0.4	-38.9	45.8	34.0	18.3	8.8	10.0	-4.3	-3.7	2.8	5.7
Netherlands	2.2	12.1	0.3	3.4	8.0	4.7	1.9	-3.4	-5.2	-0.6	5.5	7.0	9.7	5.2	9.9	3.7	-3.0	-4.6	-2.9	1.0
New Zealand	4.4	-5.3	12.1	0.2	6.0	-5.1	-18.9	8.2	23.1	17.0	15.0	7.2	-6.5	-5.5	-1.5	17.5	2.0	5.7	5.4	3.8
Norway	0.9	6.6	-2.7	-1.2	-7.1	-9.8	3.3	-0.8	12.5	2.8	2.1	13.4	15.8	15.2	-8.6	-4.0	-7.8	-3.9	3.3	0.4
Spain	-1.2	17.3	19.6	14.0	12.1	3.9	3.7	-1.0	-13.5	3.5	12.4	3.6	6.4	9.1	9.5	7.6	3.7	-0.5	3.0	5.2
Sweden	1.9	3.1	8.7	5.3	14.2	-2.0	-15.0	-15.9	-12.3	18.3	21.3	8.0	4.3	9.2	8.5	9.5	-0.1	-6.3	-0.9	5.0
Switzerland	1.6	8.7	4.6	9.7	4.7	6.3	-2.6	-10.6	-5.9	2.0	4.9	2.3	4.3	9.0	1.3	5.3	-7.2	-9.0	-1.3	4.0
United Kingdom	3.2	1.1	10.4	16.1	12.6	0.1	-7.9	-3.5	-3.5	4.8	7.8	9.1	10.2	18.4	1.6	1.8	1.6	-8.0	0.5	6.4
United States	6.3	-2.7	-0.1	5.4	5.5	0.7	-4.9	3.4	8.4	8.9	9.8	10.0	12.2	12.5	8.1	7.8	-5.2	-5.7	1.7	9.5
Euro area	1.2	4.7	6.2	8.7	8.2	6.1	1.3	-1.3	-9.8	1.4	4.8	2.1	4.3	7.0	6.9	7.4	0.4	-2.2	-0.6	3.8
European Union	1.8	4.7	7.1	9.6	9.1	5.2	-0.3	-2.1	-8.8	2.7	6.4	3.7	5.2	8.9	6.1	6.7	0.7	-2.9	-0.4	4.2
Total OECD	4.6	1.4	4.7	9.4	8.5	4.4	-0.7	-0.2	-1.6	4.3	5.9	7.8	10.1	7.8	5.5	7.8	-1.9	-3.7	1.2	6.0

Note: The adoption of new national account systems, SNA93 or ESA95, has been proceeding at an uneven pace among OECD member countries, both with respect to variables and the time period covered. As a consequence, there are breaks in many national series. Moreover, some countries are using chain-weighted price indices to calculate real GDP and expenditures components. Some countries, United States, Canada and France use hedonic price indices to deflate current-price values of investment in certain information and communication technology products such as computers. See Table "National Account Reporting Systems and Base-years" at the beginning of the Statistical Annex. National account data do not always have a sectoral breakdown of investment expenditures, and for some countries data are estimated by the OECD. See also *OECD Economic Outlook* Sources and Methods, (*http://www.oecd.org/eco/sources-and-methods*).

Source: OECD.

Annex Table 7. **Real gross private residential fixed capital formation**

Percentage change from previous period

	Average 1975-85	1986	1987	1988	1989	1990	1991	1992	1993	1994	1995	1996	1997	1998	1999	2000	2001	2002	Projections 2003	Projections 2004
Australia	5.1	-7.7	-2.2	20.1	8.8	-10.8	-5.7	11.4	12.8	12.1	-7.6	-10.6	15.3	14.9	5.1	3.6	-10.2	25.1	-3.8	-3.0
Austria	0.9	1.8	1.3	9.2	-0.6	-8.2	9.4	10.7	4.3	7.7	13.1	2.4	-1.7	-2.5	-2.8	-5.0	-7.7	-1.4	1.1	1.3
Belgium	-4.4	-0.3	9.0	25.2	17.3	8.3	-9.0	4.9	1.8	5.5	4.3	-8.3	10.4	0.1	5.7	0.8	-2.0	-2.9	1.0	1.5
Canada	2.4	12.4	14.7	2.1	4.1	-10.5	-14.8	7.1	-3.4	4.1	-14.8	9.6	8.2	-3.5	5.4	3.5	4.7	16.0	0.8	-1.7
Denmark	-2.1	21.3	-3.2	-9.4	-8.4	-11.3	-10.1	0.1	6.3	8.9	8.5	5.8	7.1	4.2	-1.0	9.9	-14.2	1.6	2.2	2.5
Finland	-0.6	-7.8	0.9	15.8	17.4	-5.6	-16.6	-20.6	-14.3	-4.5	-2.7	4.6	24.0	6.5	6.8	3.4	-10.4	-1.4	3.4	2.2
France	-1.2	1.6	2.9	5.6	7.4	-1.7	-6.9	-3.7	-5.2	4.4	2.1	0.4	0.9	3.8	7.1	4.1	-0.9	0.2	-0.1	1.8
Germany	3.6	8.3	3.1	4.7	7.7	7.6	7.4	10.8	4.7	12.0	0.4	-0.2	0.4	0.3	1.6	-2.6	-7.1	-5.9	-0.1	-1.4
Greece	-1.9	20.9	-5.8	-0.6	-1.8	5.5	-0.3	-15.6	-10.5	-11.3	2.6	-1.2	6.6	8.8	3.9	-4.3	4.4	8.9	3.9	3.4
Iceland	-0.6	-13.9	14.2	14.9	2.8	-0.6	-3.7	-3.4	-5.2	4.1	-8.7	7.1	-9.3	1.3	0.3	15.2	17.8	5.2	-2.0	0.0
Ireland	2.5	8.1	6.2	0.3	13.2	-0.6	1.1	8.1	-11.7	23.6	14.9	18.4	16.1	5.8	11.3	15.5	-6.1	6.0	3.0	1.5
Italy	-0.4	-3.0	-2.1	2.2	3.0	3.7	3.3	1.3	-1.5	-2.3	-0.1	-1.4	-2.8	-0.6	1.9	5.3	1.7	0.9	2.2	2.6
Japan	-0.5	7.0	20.7	12.8	1.0	3.6	-5.4	-5.8	1.1	7.2	-4.7	11.8	-12.0	-14.3	0.2	0.7	-5.4	-4.8	-5.2	-3.9
Korea	6.2	17.0	9.3	22.3	19.4	60.1	10.8	-7.3	11.2	-1.7	8.3	1.5	-6.3	-7.9	-16.5	-10.0	11.5	14.5	1.1	3.7
Mexico	2.8	-1.6	4.4	-1.2	5.8	4.4	7.6	2.9	5.2	4.0	-7.9	2.5	4.5	3.4	2.9	5.2	-4.8	0.0	2.5	4.5
Netherlands	0.5	4.2	1.6	10.6	0.9	-3.3	-4.5	7.8	1.7	8.1	0.6	3.9	5.3	1.4	4.2	-0.4	-1.2	-2.0	2.5	4.0
New Zealand	-2.1	-3.1	-3.9	4.7	15.5	2.4	-15.5	3.8	17.1	13.1	3.3	5.9	6.8	-14.3	9.3	0.2	-9.7	20.4	8.2	-1.9
Norway	0.9	7.8	3.2	-6.9	-12.5	-17.8	-21.7	-9.2	-0.8	24.5	10.6	2.9	12.1	7.8	3.0	5.6	3.7	-3.9	-0.5	0.9
Spain	-2.6	2.1	6.3	11.4	3.3	6.4	-3.7	-4.0	-4.1	0.4	7.1	9.3	3.0	10.2	10.0	7.4	0.9	4.4	1.1	1.4
Sweden	-0.1	-2.2	8.8	8.4	4.8	7.2	-2.4	-11.6	-33.5	-34.1	-23.9	8.9	-11.5	-0.6	10.8	10.0	3.6	10.4	1.8	3.7
Switzerland	4.6	-1.6	2.7	4.9	5.8	-3.4	-7.7	-1.6	5.8	19.3	0.0	-10.2	-4.0	-0.6	0.8	2.5	-4.7	1.2	0.4	1.6
United Kingdom	1.6	10.2	9.8	19.0	-11.6	-17.5	-15.1	0.2	8.1	2.5	-3.0	6.9	5.1	-2.0	-2.8	0.8	-3.5	12.2	3.2	2.1
United States	4.1	12.0	0.2	-0.5	-4.1	-8.6	-12.8	16.3	7.3	9.7	-3.6	7.4	2.0	8.0	6.7	1.1	0.3	3.9	0.7	1.3
Euro area	0.2	2.9	2.1	6.3	5.9	2.9	0.0	2.8	0.0	6.3	1.8	0.8	1.5	2.1	3.9	1.3	-3.1	-1.5	0.8	1.0
European Union	0.6	4.4	3.5	8.2	2.9	-0.2	-2.4	1.9	-0.1	3.7	0.7	2.2	1.8	1.5	3.1	2.1	-2.6	1.3	1.3	1.3
Total OECD	2.6	7.7	5.2	5.6	0.6	-1.7	-6.8	6.2	3.5	6.7	-2.4	5.4	0.2	1.4	3.6	1.4	-1.6	2.6	0.0	0.5

Note: The adoption of new national account systems, SNA93 or ESA95, has been proceeding at an uneven pace among OECD member countries, both with respect to variables and the time period covered. As a consequence there are breaks in many national series. Moreover, some countries are using chain-weighted price indices to calculate real GDP and expenditures components. See Table "National Account Reporting Systems and Base-years" at the beginning of the Statistical Annex and *OECD Economic Outlook* Sources and Methods (*http://www.oecd.org/eco/sources-and-methods*).

Source: OECD.

Annex Table 8. Real total domestic demand
Percentage change from previous period

	Average 1975-85	1986	1987	1988	1989	1990	1991	1992	1993	1994	1995	1996	1997	1998	1999	2000	2001	2002	Projections 2003	2004
Australia	3.4	1.0	2.8	5.6	6.8	-0.7	-2.1	2.6	2.9	4.9	4.5	3.1	3.2	7.0	5.4	1.9	1.7	6.2	4.1	3.9
Austria	2.2	1.8	2.4	3.2	3.8	4.5	3.2	2.1	0.7	3.2	3.0	1.9	1.4	3.0	2.9	2.6	-0.2	-0.3	1.0	1.9
Belgium	1.6	2.6	3.4	4.6	4.1	3.1	1.7	1.7	-0.9	2.0	1.6	0.8	2.9	3.2	2.4	3.3	0.5	0.4	1.4	2.2
Canada	2.9	3.2	4.9	6.1	3.9	-0.5	-1.9	0.3	1.4	3.4	1.8	1.3	6.2	2.5	4.4	4.5	1.0	3.5	3.3	3.5
Czech Republic	:	:	:	:	:	:	:	:	:	6.3	8.4	7.3	-0.7	-2.4	0.3	4.0	5.1	3.4	3.3	3.6
Denmark	2.1	5.6	-1.7	-0.7	-0.1	-0.7	-0.1	0.9	-0.3	7.0	4.2	2.2	4.9	4.0	0.1	2.0	0.8	1.2	1.7	2.1
Finland	2.0	2.8	5.1	6.6	6.9	-1.5	-8.5	-6.1	-5.9	3.4	4.5	2.7	5.9	5.4	1.4	3.7	1.8	0.6	1.8	2.8
France	2.2	3.5	3.3	4.3	3.9	2.7	0.5	0.6	-1.6	1.9	1.7	0.7	0.6	4.1	3.6	4.3	1.6	1.1	1.1	2.9
Germany	1.8	3.7	2.4	3.7	3.2	4.7	4.4	2.8	-1.1	2.3	1.7	0.3	0.6	2.4	2.8	1.8	-0.8	-1.5	0.6	1.6
Greece	2.1	0.4	-2.7	5.9	5.3	2.2	3.5	-0.5	-1.0	1.1	3.5	3.3	3.5	4.6	2.8	3.9	3.1	3.9	3.7	3.5
Hungary	:	:	:	:	:	:	:	:	:	2.0	-2.8	0.6	3.9	7.6	4.0	5.1	2.1	5.3	4.0	3.1
Iceland	3.3	4.6	15.7	-0.7	-4.4	1.5	2.1	-4.5	-3.7	2.2	2.2	7.0	5.7	13.5	4.0	6.7	-3.4	-2.6	2.8	4.3
Ireland	2.7	1.2	-0.4	1.9	6.9	6.3	0.1	-0.3	1.1	5.6	7.3	7.9	9.9	9.7	8.3	8.5	4.4	2.5	2.2	2.7
Italy	2.9	3.1	4.3	4.1	3.1	2.7	2.1	0.9	-5.1	1.7	2.0	0.9	2.7	3.1	3.2	2.3	1.8	1.1	0.8	2.3
Japan	3.4	3.7	5.2	7.3	5.6	5.2	2.9	0.6	0.2	1.2	2.5	3.9	0.9	-1.5	0.2	2.4	1.1	-0.3	0.5	0.4
Korea	7.0	8.6	10.0	10.8	11.9	12.8	10.4	3.2	4.6	9.6	9.3	7.8	-0.8	-19.8	14.7	8.1	2.2	5.7	2.9	4.4
Luxembourg	1.8	9.1	8.2	7.7	6.2	4.7	8.5	-4.2	4.8	2.4	2.3	4.2	6.0	7.3	6.1	-0.3	6.3	1.0	0.7	2.5
Mexico	3.5	-4.9	1.1	3.9	5.6	7.0	5.7	6.0	1.1	5.6	-14.0	5.6	9.6	6.1	4.3	8.3	0.4	1.0	2.5	4.4
Netherlands	1.8	3.9	1.4	2.0	4.9	3.3	2.1	1.2	-1.7	2.0	3.5	2.8	3.9	4.8	4.3	2.8	1.4	-0.1	0.6	2.7
New Zealand	1.0	1.4	1.5	0.8	4.3	0.3	-6.0	2.0	4.9	6.9	5.4	4.6	2.6	-0.6	5.9	1.7	1.8	4.9	3.4	2.6
Norway	2.5	9.0	-1.8	-4.4	-2.0	1.0	0.1	2.1	3.2	4.3	4.8	4.0	6.6	5.7	0.3	2.4	0.4	2.1	1.9	1.7
Poland	:	:	:	:	:	:	:	:	:	4.2	7.5	9.0	10.4	6.4	4.9	2.8	-1.6	0.8	2.1	2.9
Portugal	2.1	6.0	8.8	9.9	4.9	5.3	6.1	3.4	-2.1	1.5	4.1	3.0	5.1	6.7	5.9	3.1	1.3	-0.4	-0.4	1.8
Slovak Republic	:	:	:	:	:	:	:	:	:	-4.5	10.3	17.9	3.8	6.9	-6.2	0.0	7.2	4.0	3.1	3.5
Spain	0.9	5.3	7.9	6.8	7.3	4.6	3.0	1.0	-3.3	1.5	3.1	1.9	3.5	5.7	5.6	4.4	2.7	2.2	2.6	3.4
Sweden	0.9	3.0	4.3	3.0	3.7	0.7	-1.6	-1.9	-4.6	3.1	2.3	0.9	1.2	4.3	3.5	4.1	0.0	0.6	1.5	2.4
Switzerland	1.8	4.0	2.0	3.0	4.2	3.9	-1.0	-2.4	-1.0	2.5	1.9	0.1	0.8	3.5	2.5	2.5	0.8	-1.3	0.4	1.8
Turkey	3.3	7.0	8.9	-1.3	1.5	14.6	-0.6	5.6	14.2	-12.5	11.4	7.6	9.0	0.6	-3.7	9.8	-18.5	9.2	3.4	3.0
United Kingdom	1.9	4.7	4.6	8.1	2.9	-0.3	-2.5	0.9	2.2	3.8	2.0	3.1	3.9	5.0	3.6	3.9	2.6	2.5	2.4	3.4
United States	3.7	3.6	3.1	3.2	2.9	1.4	-1.1	3.1	3.2	4.4	2.5	3.7	4.7	5.4	5.0	4.4	0.4	3.0	2.8	4.0
Euro area	2.1	3.4	3.4	4.3	4.0	3.5	2.3	1.3	-2.1	2.0	2.1	1.1	1.8	3.6	3.4	3.0	1.0	0.3	1.1	2.4
European Union	2.0	3.7	3.7	4.8	3.8	2.8	1.5	1.2	-1.6	2.4	2.2	1.4	2.3	3.9	3.5	3.2	1.2	0.7	1.3	2.5
Total OECD	3.1	3.6	3.8	4.6	4.0	3.0	0.8	2.1	1.1	3.1	2.4	3.2	3.4	3.1	3.8	3.9	0.6	1.9	2.0	2.9

Note: The adoption of new national account systems, SNA93 or ESA95, has been proceeding at an uneven pace among OECD member countries, both with respect to variables and the time period covered. As a consequence there are breaks in many national series. Moreover, some countries are using chain-weighted price indices to calculate real GDP and expenditures components. See Table "National Account Reporting Systems and Base-years" at the beginning of the Statistical Annex and *OECD Economic Outlook* Sources and Methods (*http://www.oecd.org/eco/sources-and-methods*).

Source: OECD.

Annex Table 9. Real exports of goods and services
Percentage change from previous period

	Average 1975-85	1986	1987	1988	1989	1990	1991	1992	1993	1994	1995	1996	1997	1998	1999	2000	2001	2002	Projections 2003	2004
Australia	4.9	4.3	12.2	3.5	2.9	8.5	13.1	5.4	8.0	9.0	5.0	10.6	11.5	-0.2	4.6	10.8	1.4	-0.1	3.4	8.4
Austria	6.1	-4.8	2.3	9.8	9.7	7.8	5.2	1.5	-1.4	5.6	3.0	5.2	12.4	8.1	8.5	13.4	7.4	2.6	3.0	6.4
Belgium	4.0	2.3	4.6	10.2	8.9	4.5	2.9	2.4	0.8	9.1	5.0	2.2	6.3	5.6	5.3	8.5	1.2	-1.0	2.6	6.6
Canada	6.5	4.3	2.9	8.9	1.0	4.7	1.8	7.2	10.8	12.7	8.5	5.6	8.3	9.1	10.0	8.0	-3.8	0.8	4.4	7.3
Czech Republic	..	..	..	..	..	..	..	..	..	0.2	16.7	8.2	9.2	10.0	6.1	17.0	11.9	2.8	6.3	9.8
Denmark	4.7	0.0	5.1	7.8	4.2	6.2	6.1	-0.9	-1.5	7.0	2.9	4.3	4.1	4.3	12.3	13.1	3.2	3.4	3.1	7.5
Finland	6.8	0.7	2.9	3.5	1.6	1.2	-7.3	10.3	16.7	13.1	8.6	5.7	13.7	9.2	6.5	19.3	-2.3	5.6	3.1	6.9
France	4.7	-0.8	2.7	8.5	10.6	4.9	5.5	5.1	-0.1	8.1	7.7	3.2	12.0	8.3	4.2	13.6	1.5	1.5	2.6	5.2
Germany	5.3	-1.3	0.7	5.5	10.3	13.2	12.9	-0.8	-5.5	7.6	5.7	5.1	11.2	7.0	5.6	13.7	5.0	2.6	3.2	6.0
Greece	5.6	16.8	5.9	-2.1	1.9	-3.5	4.1	10.0	-2.6	7.4	3.0	3.5	20.0	5.3	8.0	19.7	-1.6	-4.5	2.9	7.3
Hungary	..	..	..	..	..	0.0	-7.2	-2.0	7.0	13.7	13.4	8.4	26.4	16.7	13.1	21.8	9.1	5.9	4.6	8.0
Iceland	6.3	5.9	3.3	-3.6	2.9	8.7	5.7	13.9	9.7	9.9	-2.1	9.8	5.8	2.0	4.0	5.0	7.9	2.9	4.0	4.5
Ireland	8.8	2.9	13.7	9.0	10.3	7.5	-1.4	7.3	9.0	15.1	20.0	12.2	17.4	21.0	15.2	20.6	6.7	4.9	3.5	7.1
Italy	5.0	0.8	4.5	5.1	7.8	7.0	-1.4	7.3	9.0	9.8	12.6	0.6	6.4	3.4	0.1	11.7	1.1	-1.0	4.4	5.5
Japan	8.5	-5.5	-0.5	5.9	9.1	7.0	4.1	3.9	-0.1	3.5	4.1	6.5	11.3	-2.3	1.5	12.3	-6.1	8.1	7.7	9.4
Korea	13.0	27.0	22.7	12.2	-4.3	4.1	11.2	11.3	11.3	16.1	24.6	11.2	21.4	14.1	15.8	20.5	0.7	14.9	12.8	11.9
Luxembourg	4.2	2.8	3.3	11.1	12.6	5.6	9.2	2.7	4.8	7.7	3.4	5.6	13.6	14.3	12.0	19.1	1.2	-1.7	0.1	4.8
Mexico	10.8	4.5	9.5	5.8	5.7	5.3	5.1	5.0	8.1	17.8	30.2	18.2	10.7	12.1	12.4	16.4	-3.6	1.4	5.2	8.2
Netherlands	3.7	1.8	4.0	8.9	7.9	5.0	5.6	2.4	5.7	9.7	8.8	4.6	8.8	7.4	5.1	10.9	1.7	-1.4	1.4	7.0
New Zealand	5.7	-0.4	5.6	6.1	-1.4	4.9	10.8	3.7	4.6	10.0	3.8	3.7	3.9	1.6	8.2	6.8	2.0	7.6	4.6	6.4
Norway	5.4	2.2	1.1	6.4	11.0	8.6	6.1	4.7	3.2	8.4	4.9	10.2	7.7	0.6	2.8	4.0	4.1	-0.5	0.4	3.8
Poland	..	..	..	..	..	..	..	..	..	13.1	22.9	12.0	12.2	14.3	-2.6	23.2	3.1	5.7	8.5	13.6
Portugal	7.8	6.8	11.2	8.2	12.2	9.5	1.2	3.2	-3.3	8.4	8.8	7.1	7.1	9.1	2.9	8.0	1.9	2.0	3.2	7.7
Slovak Republic	..	..	..	..	..	..	..	..	..	12.2	4.8	-1.3	19.0	13.2	5.2	13.8	6.5	5.9	5.9	8.2
Spain	7.4	0.2	5.3	3.8	1.4	4.7	8.3	7.5	7.8	16.7	9.4	10.4	15.3	8.2	7.7	10.1	3.4	1.4	3.3	6.1
Sweden	4.6	3.4	4.3	2.8	3.2	1.8	-1.9	2.2	8.3	14.1	11.5	3.7	13.8	8.6	7.4	11.3	-0.8	0.4	2.2	7.5
Switzerland	4.7	0.2	2.0	5.7	5.3	2.6	-0.7	3.1	1.0	2.7	2.8	2.4	8.4	5.4	5.1	10.0	-0.1	0.4	3.0	4.9
Turkey	11.3	-5.1	26.4	18.4	-0.3	2.6	3.7	11.0	7.7	15.2	8.0	22.0	19.1	12.0	-7.0	19.2	7.4	11.0	8.7	12.1
United Kingdom	3.5	4.5	6.0	0.6	4.5	5.4	-0.1	4.3	4.4	9.2	9.0	8.2	8.3	3.0	5.3	10.1	0.9	-1.0	2.1	8.4
United States	4.0	7.4	11.2	16.1	11.8	8.7	6.5	6.2	3.3	8.9	10.3	8.2	12.3	2.1	3.4	9.7	-5.4	-1.6	4.0	9.0
Total OECD	5.9	3.2	7.0	9.8	8.5	7.4	5.5	5.2	3.1	9.0	9.6	7.3	11.6	4.2	4.3	11.8	-1.8	1.6	4.6	8.2

Note: The adoption of new national account systems, SNA93 or ESA95, has been proceeding at an uneven pace among OECD member countries, both with respect to variables and the time period covered. As a consequence there are breaks in many national series. Moreover, some countries are using chain-weighted price indices to calculate real GDP and expenditures components. See Table "National Account Reporting Systems and Base-years" at the beginning of the Statistical Annex and *OECD Economic Outlook* Sources and Methods (*http://www.oecd.org/eco/sources-and-methods*).
Source: OECD.

Annex Table 10. **Real imports of goods and services**

Percentage change from previous period

	Average 1975-85	1986	1987	1988	1989	1990	1991	1992	1993	1994	1995	1996	1997	1998	1999	2000	2001	2002	Projections 2003	Projections 2004
Australia	5.1	-3.3	2.7	17.1	20.6	-4.0	-2.4	7.1	4.2	14.3	7.9	8.3	10.5	6.0	9.2	7.1	-4.1	11.9	6.9	8.2
Austria	5.4	-6.0	4.8	9.3	8.0	6.9	5.8	1.4	-1.1	8.2	5.6	4.9	12.0	5.7	9.0	11.6	5.9	0.0	3.0	6.4
Belgium	3.2	3.8	6.8	10.5	10.1	4.8	2.9	3.1	0.6	7.3	4.1	2.2	5.0	7.4	4.3	8.3	0.8	-1.5	2.8	6.8
Canada	5.4	7.2	5.3	13.5	5.9	2.0	2.5	4.7	7.4	8.0	5.7	5.1	14.2	5.1	7.8	8.2	-5.8	0.8	6.1	8.0
Czech Republic	..	..	..	..	..	..	..	..	..	7.6	21.2	13.4	8.1	6.6	5.4	17.0	13.6	4.3	6.3	9.2
Denmark	3.0	6.8	-2.0	1.5	4.1	1.2	3.0	-0.4	-2.7	12.3	7.3	3.5	10.0	8.9	5.5	11.9	1.8	2.5	3.5	7.1
Finland	3.0	1.5	9.2	10.9	9.0	-0.8	-13.5	0.6	1.3	12.8	7.8	5.9	11.2	7.9	3.5	16.9	-0.2	1.7	3.5	6.3
France	4.5	6.4	7.5	8.5	8.4	5.5	2.4	1.6	-3.7	8.3	7.7	1.7	7.3	11.6	6.1	15.0	0.9	1.2	2.5	6.5
Germany	3.9	3.1	4.7	5.7	8.2	10.7	12.2	1.5	-5.5	7.4	5.6	3.1	8.3	9.1	8.5	10.5	1.0	-2.1	4.3	6.1
Greece	5.1	13.9	2.1	7.3	10.5	8.4	5.8	1.1	0.6	1.5	8.9	7.0	14.2	9.2	3.8	14.5	-3.4	-2.7	3.3	5.2
Hungary	..	..	..	..	..	..	..	..	..	8.8	-0.7	6.2	24.6	22.8	12.3	21.1	6.3	8.9	5.8	7.0
Iceland	3.9	0.9	23.3	-4.6	-10.3	1.0	4.1	-5.9	-7.7	4.2	4.0	16.7	8.5	23.5	4.2	8.0	-9.0	-2.4	6.0	6.5
Ireland	6.7	5.6	6.2	4.9	13.5	5.1	2.4	8.2	7.5	15.5	16.4	12.5	16.8	25.8	12.0	21.2	6.1	1.8	3.0	6.5
Italy	4.8	4.0	12.2	5.9	8.9	11.5	2.3	7.4	-10.9	8.1	9.7	-0.3	10.1	8.9	5.6	8.9	1.0	1.5	3.8	5.4
Japan	2.4	3.2	11.3	19.5	15.7	7.0	-1.1	-0.7	-1.4	7.8	12.8	13.2	1.2	-6.8	3.0	9.4	0.1	2.0	3.6	4.2
Korea	10.4	18.7	19.9	13.7	17.1	13.9	19.2	5.3	6.2	21.6	22.4	14.2	3.2	-22.1	28.8	20.0	-3.0	16.4	11.4	11.5
Luxembourg	3.6	1.7	7.3	10.5	9.1	5.0	9.1	-3.1	5.2	6.7	4.7	6.3	12.6	14.9	12.9	14.0	4.5	-2.2	0.4	5.0
Mexico	1.8	-7.6	5.1	36.7	18.0	19.7	15.2	19.6	1.9	21.3	-15.0	22.9	22.7	16.6	14.1	21.5	-1.5	1.6	4.8	9.3
Netherlands	3.3	3.5	4.2	6.9	8.2	3.6	5.1	1.4	0.7	9.4	10.6	4.4	9.5	8.5	5.8	10.6	1.9	-2.2	1.4	8.7
New Zealand	2.6	2.8	8.6	-0.9	13.5	3.6	-5.2	8.3	5.3	13.1	9.0	7.7	2.2	1.3	11.8	0.2	1.4	8.8	6.3	5.6
Norway	2.2	11.8	-6.5	-2.4	2.2	2.5	0.2	1.6	4.9	5.8	5.7	8.8	12.4	8.5	-1.8	2.7	0.9	1.7	2.3	3.2
Poland	..	..	..	..	..	..	..	..	..	11.3	24.2	28.0	21.4	18.5	1.0	15.6	-5.4	2.5	7.4	10.9
Portugal	3.0	16.9	23.1	18.0	5.9	14.5	7.2	10.7	-3.3	8.8	7.4	4.9	10.0	14.2	8.5	5.4	0.9	-0.4	0.8	5.4
Slovak Republic	..	..	..	..	..	..	..	..	..	-5.4	11.5	19.8	13.8	16.9	-6.3	10.2	11.7	5.3	5.2	7.1
Spain	2.3	17.2	24.8	16.1	17.7	9.6	10.3	6.8	-5.2	11.4	11.1	8.0	13.3	13.2	12.7	10.6	3.5	2.2	4.7	6.8
Sweden	2.4	3.8	7.6	4.5	7.7	0.7	-4.9	1.5	-2.2	12.2	7.2	3.0	12.5	11.3	4.9	11.5	-3.5	-2.7	2.0	7.0
Switzerland	6.1	7.9	5.9	5.5	4.8	3.0	-1.4	-3.7	-0.5	8.9	6.9	1.9	6.1	8.3	7.4	8.5	-0.3	-2.6	2.5	4.7
Turkey	6.8	-3.5	23.0	-4.5	6.9	33.0	-5.2	10.9	35.8	-21.9	29.6	20.5	22.4	2.3	-3.7	25.4	-24.8	15.7	12.9	13.9
United Kingdom	3.7	6.9	7.9	12.8	7.4	0.5	-4.5	6.8	3.3	5.7	5.4	9.6	9.7	9.6	8.7	11.7	2.3	1.5	2.9	9.6
United States	7.5	8.4	6.1	3.8	3.9	3.8	-0.5	6.6	9.1	12.0	8.2	8.6	13.7	11.8	10.9	13.2	-2.9	3.7	6.4	7.8
Total OECD	5.5	6.1	8.3	9.4	8.7	6.4	2.0	4.9	3.0	9.8	8.7	8.5	10.6	7.4	8.5	12.3	-1.2	2.7	5.1	7.2

Note: The adoption of new national account systems, SNA93 or ESA95, has been proceeding at an uneven pace among OECD member countries, both with respect to variables and the time period covered. As a consequence there are breaks in many national series. Moreover, some countries are using chain-weighted price indices to calculate real GDP and expenditures components. See Table "National Account Reporting Systems and Base-years" at the beginning of the Statistical Annex and *OECD Economic Outlook* Sources and Methods (*http://www.oecd.org/eco/sources-and-methods*).

Source: OECD.

Annex Table 11. **Output gaps**

Deviations of actual GDP from potential GDP as a per cent of potential GDP

	1985	1986	1987	1988	1989	1990	1991	1992	1993	1994	1995	1996	1997	1998	1999	2000	2001	2002	Projections 2003	2004
Australia	0.7	-1.3	-0.1	0.6	1.0	-1.2	-4.7	-4.8	-3.6	-1.7	-1.2	-0.5	-0.5	0.9	1.5	0.6	0.0	-0.3	-1.2	-1.4
Austria	-3.3	-3.1	-3.2	-1.8	0.0	1.9	2.3	1.6	-0.6	-0.4	-0.8	-0.8	-0.8	0.6	1.0	1.8	-0.2	-1.5	-2.5	-2.5
Belgium	-3.4	-3.3	-2.7	-0.2	1.1	1.7	0.9	-0.3	-3.1	-2.3	-2.0	-3.1	-1.3	-1.2	-0.1	1.3	-0.5	-1.9	-2.7	-2.4
Canada	0.3	0.2	1.7	3.8	3.6	1.2	-3.0	-4.1	-3.8	-1.4	-1.1	-2.2	-1.5	-1.0	0.9	1.9	-0.1	0.2	0.0	0.2
Denmark	2.1	3.8	2.3	1.3	0.0	-0.6	-1.1	-1.9	-3.4	-0.3	-0.1	0.2	0.7	0.7	0.9	1.2	0.2	-0.4	-0.8	-0.3
Finland	-1.1	-1.2	0.4	2.5	4.9	3.1	-4.5	-8.5	-10.8	-8.6	-6.7	-5.1	-2.1	-0.6	-0.4	2.4	0.1	-0.9	-1.3	-0.4
France	-4.0	-3.6	-2.9	-0.8	1.2	1.9	1.0	0.5	-2.1	-1.9	-1.9	-2.8	-3.1	-1.7	-0.7	1.2	0.8	-0.2	-1.2	-0.8
Germany	-2.2	-1.2	-1.3	0.4	1.0	3.4	2.2	1.6	-1.6	-1.1	-0.7	-1.4	-1.5	-1.1	-0.6	1.0	0.0	-1.3	-2.3	-2.0
Greece	-2.0	-2.0	-4.8	-1.5	1.1	-0.3	0.8	-0.5	-3.7	-3.5	-3.4	-3.5	-2.1	-2.9	-2.3	-1.1	0.1	0.8	0.9	1.1
Iceland	-2.9	0.4	5.5	2.0	0.1	-0.3	-2.9	-7.5	-7.7	-4.9	-5.8	-2.7	-0.6	1.4	2.1	4.0	3.9	0.6	0.0	0.7
Ireland	-1.5	-4.5	-3.4	-1.7	0.4	3.8	0.5	-1.7	-4.2	-4.5	-2.2	-1.7	0.8	0.6	3.6	6.8	5.8	5.7	3.2	2.1
Italy	-2.5	-2.0	-1.2	0.7	1.5	1.4	0.7	-0.5	-3.0	-2.2	-1.0	-1.5	-1.1	-1.0	-1.1	0.0	-0.1	-1.6	-2.2	-1.5
Japan	-1.1	-2.3	-2.0	0.4	1.6	3.4	3.2	1.4	-0.3	-0.8	-0.6	1.4	2.3	-0.1	-1.2	0.4	-0.6	-1.5	-1.8	-2.0
Netherlands	-1.0	-0.6	-1.4	-1.0	1.2	2.7	2.3	1.2	-0.2	-0.1	0.3	0.5	0.9	1.7	2.6	2.8	1.2	-1.0	-2.4	-2.4
New Zealand	2.9	2.7	1.7	-0.2	-0.5	-2.4	-5.4	-5.6	-2.5	0.6	1.2	1.5	0.3	-2.5	-1.0	0.5	0.5	1.2	0.8	0.3
Norway[a]	2.4	2.7	1.8	-1.3	-4.4	-4.4	-3.9	-3.4	-2.7	-1.7	-1.0	-0.1	1.5	2.6	2.5	2.3	1.4	0.9	-0.2	-0.3
Portugal	-9.7	-8.0	-4.7	-0.6	2.7	3.5	4.7	2.7	-2.0	-3.5	-1.8	-0.8	0.1	1.3	1.8	2.1	0.7	-1.1	-2.7	-2.5
Spain	-4.5	-4.8	-2.5	-0.2	1.2	1.9	1.6	-0.3	-3.8	-3.9	-4.0	-4.4	-3.3	-1.8	-0.5	0.4	0.0	-0.8	-1.5	-1.2
Sweden	1.3	2.3	3.7	4.4	4.6	3.3	0.2	-3.3	-6.1	-4.3	-2.6	-3.3	-2.8	-1.4	0.6	2.2	0.5	0.0	-0.6	0.0
Switzerland	1.9	1.4	0.0	0.9	3.1	4.5	1.1	-0.5	-1.7	-2.2	-2.1	-2.6	-1.7	-0.2	-0.8	0.1	-0.5	-1.3	-1.9	-1.4
United Kingdom	-2.6	-0.1	2.0	4.8	4.4	2.5	-1.8	-4.0	-4.2	-2.2	-1.6	-1.4	-0.4	0.1	-0.1	0.5	-0.2	-1.0	-1.4	-1.2
United States	-0.9	-0.7	-0.3	0.9	1.7	0.5	-2.5	-1.8	-1.8	-0.5	-0.6	0.0	0.9	1.8	2.4	2.2	-1.1	-1.5	-2.1	-1.2
Euro area	-2.8	-2.3	-1.8	0.1	1.5	2.4	1.4	0.5	-2.4	-2.0	-1.5	-2.0	-1.7	-1.0	-0.4	1.1	0.3	-0.9	-1.8	-1.5
European Union	-2.8	-1.9	-1.2	0.8	1.8	2.3	0.9	-0.3	-2.8	-2.1	-1.5	-2.0	-1.5	-0.8	-0.3	0.9	0.2	-0.9	-1.7	-1.4
Total OECD	-1.5	-1.4	-0.8	0.9	1.8	1.6	-0.4	-0.9	-2.1	-1.2	-1.0	-0.6	0.1	0.4	0.7	1.4	-0.4	-1.2	-1.8	-1.4

Note: Potential output for all countries except Portugal is calculated using the "production function method" described in Giorno et al, "Potential Output, Output Gaps, and Structural Budget Balances", *OECD Economic Studies*, No. 24, 1995/I. Using this methodology, two broad changes have been made to the calculation of potential output since the last *OECD Economic Outlook*. First, the "smoothing parameters" applied in the calculations have been standardised across the OECD countries. Second, as was previously the case for the major seven economies only, the calculations now incorporate trend working hours for other Member economies also, excepting Austria and Portugal where the data span is insufficient. Potential output for Portugal is calculated using a Hodrick-Prescott filter of actual output. See also *OECD Economic Outlook* Sources and Methods (http://www.oecd.org/eco/sources-and-methods).

a) Mainland Norway.

Source: OECD.

Annex Table 12. Compensation per employee in the business sector

Percentage change from previous period

	Average 1975-85	1986	1987	1988	1989	1990	1991	1992	1993	1994	1995	1996	1997	1998	1999	2000	2001	2002	Projections 2003	Projections 2004
Australia	8.9	6.7	5.5	6.5	7.7	8.3	2.4	3.8	3.4	0.9	3.1	6.4	3.3	2.6	2.4	3.6	4.0	2.9	4.5	3.9
Austria	7.0	5.7	4.1	4.2	4.5	5.2	6.0	5.5	4.3	3.7	4.0	1.0	2.9	1.7	1.5	2.7	2.0	2.0	2.2	2.4
Belgium	8.6	4.3	2.5	2.8	3.0	8.2	6.9	5.5	2.8	3.3	2.3	1.5	2.7	1.0	3.7	2.0	2.8	3.9	2.0	3.0
Canada	8.4	2.3	6.4	7.6	5.6	4.3	4.9	3.2	2.3	0.5	2.3	2.9	5.9	2.9	3.2	4.8	2.3	2.6	3.2	3.0
Czech Republic	..	..	..	..	..	..	..	..	..	16.4	17.3	17.4	7.9	4.8	5.0	7.3	7.9	6.4	7.0	7.0
Denmark	9.4	5.1	7.4	11.3	4.7	4.1	4.0	4.4	2.5	3.2	3.4	2.9	3.8	4.1	3.0	4.1	4.3	4.1	3.9	4.2
Finland	11.2	7.8	8.1	9.6	10.8	9.0	5.0	1.9	1.3	4.6	4.1	2.1	2.4	4.7	4.0	4.2	5.5	2.4	4.4	4.3
France	11.8	4.2	4.6	4.3	4.0	3.8	3.9	3.5	2.0	0.7	1.4	1.9	1.6	0.7	1.9	1.8	3.4	2.8	2.5	2.7
Germany	5.3	3.3	3.0	2.8	2.8	4.7	5.7	10.4	3.7	3.0	3.3	1.0	0.7	1.0	1.0	2.2	1.8	1.6	2.8	2.1
Greece	21.8	12.9	10.7	20.5	22.6	16.3	16.3	12.7	8.7	11.7	11.8	11.3	11.3	4.7	4.2	5.6	6.0	4.0	4.5	4.7
Hungary	..	..	..	..	..	..	..	..	..	..	23.6	21.5	18.7	12.4	1.8	16.7	14.8	12.2	8.1	7.3
Iceland	44.8	30.0	45.8	26.1	13.4	16.1	15.6	0.6	-4.1	3.8	5.3	8.1	5.7	8.5	8.7	10.7	7.9	8.2	4.9	5.0
Ireland	15.1	6.2	6.1	5.3	6.8	3.3	3.2	7.8	4.9	1.7	2.8	1.8	6.0	0.8	5.7	8.4	8.0	7.2	5.7	5.1
Italy	17.2	7.0	7.3	7.3	8.8	8.4	9.0	6.2	5.2	3.1	4.8	4.8	3.2	-0.8	2.3	2.8	1.8	2.5	3.3	3.1
Japan	6.0	2.5	2.0	3.0	3.8	3.7	4.4	0.7	0.5	1.3	1.1	0.2	1.5	-0.8	-1.1	0.4	-0.9	-1.7	-1.3	-0.8
Korea	18.1	10.5	10.2	17.5	10.0	16.3	19.1	11.1	10.8	11.2	15.0	11.2	3.4	2.0	1.9	4.0	5.4	10.5	6.9	7.0
Luxembourg	6.2	4.5	2.1	3.8	8.5	3.0	5.1	6.4	4.9	4.9	1.4	1.1	1.9	2.2	4.0	5.4	5.3	3.5	2.7	2.3
Mexico	..	..	..	..	27.0	27.7	29.9	24.1	15.2	11.4	17.7	22.9	21.0	18.0	13.5	11.5	9.3	5.5	5.0	4.7
Netherlands	5.5	2.7	1.5	1.3	0.9	3.3	4.5	4.3	3.1	2.8	1.4	1.7	2.1	3.6	2.4	4.7	5.0	4.8	4.0	2.9
New Zealand	12.1	18.2	11.1	9.3	6.6	0.9	0.2	2.9	3.0	2.1	-0.4	1.6	0.6	1.6	2.0	3.2	0.8	2.7	3.9	4.0
Norway	8.8	9.9	9.1	8.5	4.5	5.0	5.4	4.6	2.8	3.1	3.2	2.9	2.5	7.4	6.3	4.2	7.1	6.3	5.2	4.5
Poland	..	..	..	..	..	..	..	..	..	45.1	30.8	29.4	20.5	15.3	14.1	9.6	-1.2	3.4	3.2	3.8
Portugal	19.8	19.4	13.8	9.8	12.9	17.3	18.6	16.0	7.1	5.9	6.7	8.5	6.4	3.7	2.9	5.1	6.1	3.8	3.2	2.6
Spain	17.8	11.1	6.5	7.2	7.3	10.0	10.4	10.4	8.3	3.9	3.5	5.5	3.5	2.5	2.6	4.1	4.7	4.1	3.8	3.6
Sweden	10.6	8.3	7.6	8.1	12.3	9.7	6.2	3.2	8.5	7.3	2.3	6.4	4.4	3.6	0.7	6.9	5.2	4.1	4.2	4.3
Switzerland	4.9	4.2	3.3	3.6	4.6	5.2	6.5	4.6	2.0	2.4	2.8	0.7	3.9	1.0	1.7	3.2	3.1	2.3	1.7	1.3
Turkey	35.5	30.0	44.4	62.8	159.4	94.6	134.6	61.2	72.7	72.9	87.5	65.5	68.5	72.9	59.1	40.2	41.6	28.4	26.6	17.9
United Kingdom	11.7	8.4	4.7	6.6	9.0	10.0	8.7	4.9	4.3	4.6	3.3	3.2	4.2	5.7	4.2	5.2	5.1	3.9	4.4	4.0
United States	7.2	3.9	4.5	4.8	3.2	4.9	3.9	5.7	2.8	2.3	1.9	2.5	3.2	5.0	4.3	6.5	2.3	2.3	3.4	3.3
Euro area	11.0	6.0	5.1	4.6	4.8	6.9	6.6	8.0	5.5	3.1	3.7	1.8	1.7	0.8	1.2	2.3	2.5	2.4	2.8	2.6
European Union	11.5	6.3	5.1	5.6	6.2	7.1	7.2	7.0	4.3	3.3	3.3	3.0	2.7	1.9	2.3	3.3	3.4	3.0	3.3	3.0
Total OECD	9.4	5.3	5.3	6.3	8.1	8.0	8.6	6.9	4.8	4.7	5.1	4.8	4.8	4.6	4.0	5.1	3.3	2.9	3.3	3.1
Memorandum item OECD *less* high inflation countries [a]	9.0	4.8	4.6	5.3	4.8	5.9	5.6	5.4	3.2	2.8	2.8	2.7	2.9	2.8	2.6	4.2	2.4	2.3	2.8	2.8

Note: The business sector is in the OECD terminology defined as total economy less the public sector. Hence business sector employees are defined as total employees less public sector employees. See also *OECD Economic Outlook* Sources and Methods *(http://www.oecd.org/eco/sources-and-methods).*

a) High inflation countries are defined as countries which have had 10 per cent or more inflation in terms of the GDP deflator on average during the last 10 years based on historical data. Consequently, Hungary, Mexico, Poland and Turkey are excluded from the aggregate.

Source: OECD.

Annex Table 13. **Labour productivity in the business sector**

Percentage change from previous period

	Average 1975-85	1986	1987	1988	1989	1990	1991	1992	1993	1994	1995	1996	1997	1998	1999	2000	2001	2002	Projections 2003	2004
Australia	1.9	-2.6	3.2	0.9	-0.4	-0.3	1.5	3.6	4.1	1.5	-0.3	2.9	3.0	4.2	2.2	-0.1	1.8	1.6	1.4	2.2
Austria	2.7	2.0	1.9	3.3	3.5	3.6	2.2	2.4	1.2	3.2	2.0	3.0	1.9	3.1	1.6	3.1	-0.2	1.5	1.7	2.0
Belgium	2.9	1.5	2.0	3.4	2.3	2.2	1.3	1.6	-0.2	3.7	1.7	0.4	3.3	0.5	2.2	1.9	-1.0	1.2	1.6	1.8
Canada	2.8	-0.9	1.6	2.0	0.5	-0.4	-0.2	2.1	1.8	3.1	0.8	0.7	1.8	1.5	2.9	2.1	0.4	1.6	0.9	2.0
Czech Republic	..	..	..	..	..	..	..	..	..	1.3	5.6	4.4	-0.3	1.3	2.8	4.4	2.7	0.8	3.1	3.6
Denmark	2.3	0.1	0.7	-0.5	2.0	0.5	2.1	1.3	3.2	7.7	0.5	1.8	1.7	2.8	2.1	3.1	1.6	2.0	2.2	2.6
Finland	2.9	3.6	4.7	4.7	5.2	0.6	-0.4	5.5	6.6	6.6	2.6	3.1	3.6	3.1	0.7	3.6	-0.7	1.9	2.5	3.3
France	2.7	2.5	2.2	3.8	2.9	2.0	1.1	2.5	0.7	2.1	1.0	0.7	1.5	2.2	1.2	1.6	-0.5	0.5	1.5	2.1
Germany	2.0	0.6	0.2	2.6	2.3	2.8	2.4	4.3	0.2	2.7	1.5	1.1	1.6	0.8	0.8	1.0	0.0	0.8	1.4	1.8
Greece	1.1	0.2	-2.4	2.9	3.9	-1.5	6.4	-0.9	-2.7	0.1	1.3	3.1	4.8	-0.9	4.0	4.9	5.0	4.6	3.3	3.3
Hungary	..	..	..	3.4	2.3	1.7	-0.5	-3.6	1.0	4.0	-2.3	1.2	4.6	2.8	0.4	4.8	3.7	4.3	4.0	4.3
Iceland	2.4	3.6	3.2	6.5	6.9	4.4	2.5	3.3	1.3	2.7	-3.2	5.9	5.3	1.4	0.2	3.9	1.6	-0.4	1.7	2.1
Ireland	3.8	0.1	4.8	3.3	3.0	1.1	0.7	1.6	2.5	3.8	5.3	4.3	7.7	-1.6	5.0	5.4	3.2	5.2	2.8	3.1
Italy	2.4	1.9	2.9	3.3	3.0	1.1	0.7	1.6	2.5	3.8	1.7	0.8	1.7	0.7	0.9	1.5	0.2	-0.9	1.1	1.9
Japan	2.8	2.1	3.6	5.1	3.5	3.6	1.5	-0.1	0.1	1.0	1.7	3.0	0.9	-0.8	0.6	3.2	0.8	1.7	1.6	1.3
Korea	5.5	8.1	5.9	7.9	2.1	6.4	6.4	3.8	4.2	5.5	6.5	5.1	3.9	-1.5	10.2	5.6	1.7	4.0	4.0	4.4
Luxembourg	..	..	..	..	..	..	5.0	-0.9	2.7	1.4	-1.5	1.0	5.0	3.5	1.0	3.4	-4.9	-2.9	-0.6	0.9
Mexico	..	..	..	..	1.3	2.3	1.5	-0.3	-2.0	1.2	-6.5	0.9	0.5	1.4	3.1	5.5	0.1	-0.6	0.6	1.2
Netherlands	2.1	0.6	-0.5	1.4	3.3	1.8	1.1	0.5	0.9	3.2	1.7	0.4	0.5	1.5	1.8	1.6	-0.7	-0.5	1.3	2.0
New Zealand	0.7	2.0	0.1	3.4	4.2	-2.0	-0.9	-0.2	2.9	1.0	-1.6	0.2	1.6	0.4	2.8	2.5	0.2	1.7	2.2	2.1
Norway	2.1	-1.3	-0.4	-0.4	1.8	2.8	3.7	3.5	4.0	2.2	1.1	1.7	1.9	2.5	3.3	2.3	1.6	1.8	1.3	2.3
Poland	..	..	..	..	..	..	..	..	..	8.8	7.0	5.5	6.1	4.0	9.3	6.3	3.5	4.9	3.6	2.5
Portugal	1.1	4.6	4.2	5.5	4.8	0.0	1.5	0.6	-0.2	1.2	5.6	3.5	2.7	2.2	2.2	2.2	0.1	0.2	0.7	1.2
Spain	3.3	1.2	0.8	1.8	1.4	0.0	1.6	2.8	2.1	3.2	1.0	1.5	1.1	0.1	0.7	0.9	0.5	0.8	1.0	1.1
Sweden	1.5	2.4	2.7	1.4	1.4	0.1	0.5	3.5	6.1	5.9	2.3	2.4	4.3	2.2	2.6	0.8	-1.0	2.3	2.3	2.9
Switzerland	0.9	-0.9	-1.7	0.7	2.6	-1.9	-4.7	0.9	0.2	2.7	0.5	-0.2	2.6	0.9	0.3	2.3	-0.8	-0.2	1.2	1.5
United Kingdom	2.5	5.1	1.0	0.0	-1.0	0.2	1.5	2.5	2.8	3.5	1.3	1.1	1.0	1.8	1.0	2.2	1.5	1.1	2.1	2.4
United States	1.2	1.7	0.7	1.1	1.2	0.6	0.4	3.7	0.9	1.3	0.4	1.8	2.2	2.2	2.4	2.6	0.2	3.9	2.0	2.3
Euro area	2.5	1.7	1.6	3.0	2.9	1.8	..	2.8	1.1	3.0	1.8	1.0	1.7	0.9	0.7	1.4	-0.1	0.5	1.3	1.8
European Union	2.4	2.1	1.4	2.5	2.1	1.4	1.6	2.6	1.5	3.1	1.8	1.2	1.7	1.3	1.2	1.7	0.3	0.7	1.5	2.0
Total OECD	2.1	1.9	1.7	2.4	1.8	1.5	1.1	2.6	1.3	1.9	1.2	1.9	2.0	1.4	1.9	2.7	0.3	2.2	1.8	2.0
Memorandum item																				
OECD *less* high inflation countries [a]	2.1	1.9	1.6	2.4	1.9	1.4	1.1	2.6	1.2	2.1	1.3	1.8	1.9	1.3	1.9	2.4	0.4	2.2	1.8	2.1

Note: The adoption of new national account systems, SNA93 or ESA95, has been proceeding at an uneven pace among OECD member countries, both with respect to variables and the time period covered. As a consequence there are breaks in many national series. Moreover, some countries are using chain-weighted price indices to calculate real GDP and expenditures components. See Table "National Account Reporting Systems and Base-years" at the beginning of the Statistical Annex and OECD *Economic Outlook* Sources and Methods (*http://www.oecd.org/eco/sources-and-methods*).

a) High inflation countries are defined as countries which have had 10 per cent or more inflation in terms of the GDP deflator on average during the last 10 years based on historical data. Consequently, Hungary, Mexico, Poland and Turkey are excluded from the aggregate.

Source: OECD.

Annex Table 14. Unemployment rates: commonly used definitions

Per cent of labour force

	1999 Unemployment (thousands)	1986	1987	1988	1989	1990	1991	1992	1993	1994	1995	1996	1997	1998	1999	2000	2001	2002	Projections 2003	2004
Australia	661	7.9	7.8	6.9	5.9	6.7	9.1	10.4	10.7	9.4	8.3	8.2	8.3	7.8	7.0	6.3	6.8	6.3	6.1	5.8
Austria	226	4.0	4.3	4.1	3.8	4.1	4.5	4.7	5.4	5.3	5.3	5.6	5.7	5.7	5.3	4.7	4.8	5.3	5.9	5.9
Belgium	382	10.0	9.8	8.8	7.4	6.6	6.4	7.1	8.6	9.8	9.7	9.5	9.2	9.3	8.6	6.9	6.7	7.3	7.8	7.7
Canada	1 188	9.7	8.8	7.8	7.5	8.1	10.3	11.2	11.4	10.3	9.4	9.6	9.1	8.3	7.6	6.8	7.2	7.7	7.3	7.0
Czech Republic	454								4.3	4.4	4.1	3.9	4.8	6.5	8.8	8.9	8.2	7.3	7.2	7.2
Denmark	137	5.0	5.0	5.7	6.8	7.2	7.9	8.6	9.6	7.7	6.8	6.3	5.3	4.9	4.8	4.4	4.3	4.5	4.7	4.4
Finland	261	5.4	5.1	4.6	3.1	3.2	6.6	11.7	16.4	16.6	15.4	14.6	12.7	11.4	10.3	9.8	9.2	9.1	9.2	9.0
France	2 834	10.4	10.5	10.0	9.3	8.9	9.4	10.4	11.7	12.0	11.4	12.0	12.1	11.5	10.7	9.4	8.6	8.9	9.3	9.2
Germany	3 333	6.1	5.8	5.8	5.2	4.5	5.3	6.2	7.5	8.0	7.7	8.4	9.2	8.7	8.0	7.3	7.3	7.8	8.3	8.3
Greece	533	7.4	7.4	7.7	7.5	7.0	7.7	8.7	9.7	9.6	9.1	9.8	9.8	11.1	11.9	11.1	10.4	10.0	9.5	9.1
Hungary	285								12.1	11.0	10.4	10.1	8.9	7.9	7.1	6.5	5.8	5.9	6.0	6.4
Iceland	3	1.3	1.2	1.3	2.3	2.5	2.5	4.2	5.0	5.1	4.7	3.7	3.9	2.7	2.0	2.3	2.3	3.1	3.3	3.0
Ireland	95	17.0	16.7	16.2	14.9	12.8	14.4	15.1	15.7	14.7	12.2	11.7	10.4	7.6	5.6	4.3	3.9	4.2	5.0	5.2
Italy	2 669	9.9	10.2	10.5	10.2	9.1	8.6	8.8	10.2	11.2	11.7	11.7	11.8	11.9	11.5	10.7	9.6	9.1	9.2	8.9
Japan	3 171	2.8	2.8	2.5	2.3	2.1	2.1	2.2	2.5	2.9	3.2	3.4	3.4	4.1	4.7	4.7	5.0	5.4	5.7	5.7
Korea	1 353	3.8	3.1	2.5	2.6	2.4	2.3	2.4	2.8	2.4	2.0	2.0	2.6	6.8	6.3	4.1	3.7	3.0	3.2	3.0
Luxembourg	5	1.5	1.7	1.6	1.4	1.3	1.4	1.6	2.1	2.7	3.0	3.3	3.6	3.1	2.9	2.6	2.6	3.0	4.0	3.9
Mexico[a]	473		3.9	3.6	3.0	2.8	2.6	2.8	3.4	3.7	6.2	5.5	3.7	3.2	2.5	2.2	2.4	2.7	2.7	2.4
Netherlands	222	8.4	8.0	7.7	6.9	6.0	5.4	5.4	6.6	7.6	7.1	6.6	5.5	4.2	3.2	2.6	2.0	2.5	4.1	5.0
New Zealand	128	4.0	4.1	5.6	7.1	7.8	10.3	10.3	9.5	8.1	6.3	6.1	6.6	7.5	6.8	6.0	5.3	5.2	5.1	5.3
Norway	75	2.0	2.1	3.2	4.9	5.2	5.5	5.9	6.0	5.4	4.9	4.8	4.0	3.1	3.2	3.4	3.5	4.0	4.5	4.6
Poland	2 391								14.0	14.4	13.3	12.3	11.2	10.6	13.9	16.1	18.2	19.9	20.4	19.9
Portugal	226	8.7	7.3	5.9	5.2	4.9	4.3	4.1	5.5	6.9	7.2	7.3	6.7	5.0	4.4	4.0	4.1	5.1	6.4	6.3
Slovak Republic	417									13.7	13.1	11.3	11.9	12.6	16.4	18.8	19.3	18.6	17.7	16.8
Spain[b]	2 147	16.7	15.9	14.0	12.1	11.6	11.8	13.0	16.6	18.4	18.1	17.5	16.6	15.0	12.8	11.0	10.5	11.4	12.0	11.7
Sweden	241	2.5	2.1	1.7	1.5	1.7	3.0	5.3	8.2	8.0	7.7	8.0	8.0	6.5	5.6	4.7	4.0	4.0	4.5	4.3
Switzerland	99	0.8	0.8	0.7	0.6	0.5	1.1	2.5	4.5	4.7	4.2	4.7	5.2	3.9	2.7	2.0	1.9	2.8	3.7	3.4
Turkey[c]	1 774	7.7	8.1	8.2	8.4	7.8	7.9	8.1	8.5	8.2	7.3	6.4	6.6	6.7	7.5	6.6	8.5	10.6	10.5	10.6
United Kingdom	1 721	11.6	10.0	7.6	5.9	5.6	8.0	9.9	10.4	9.5	8.6	8.1	7.0	6.3	6.0	5.5	5.1	5.2	5.4	5.2
United States	5 882	7.0	6.2	5.5	5.3	5.6	6.8	7.5	6.9	6.1	5.6	5.4	4.9	4.5	4.2	4.0	4.8	5.8	6.0	5.8
Euro area	12 934	9.4	9.2	8.8	8.1	7.4	7.6	8.4	10.0	10.7	10.5	10.7	10.8	10.2	9.4	8.4	8.0	8.2	8.8	8.7
European Union	15 032	9.5	9.1	8.3	7.5	6.9	7.5	8.6	10.0	10.4	10.0	10.1	10.0	9.4	8.7	7.8	7.3	7.6	8.0	7.9
Total OECD	33 385	7.2	6.8	6.1	5.6	5.5	6.2	6.9	7.6	7.5	7.2	7.1	6.8	6.7	6.6	6.1	6.4	6.9	7.2	7.0

Note: Labour market data are subject to differences in definitions across countries and to many series breaks, though the latter are often of a minor nature. For information about definitions, sources, data coverage, break in series and rebasings, see *OECD Economic Outlook* Sources and Methods (*http://www.oecd.org/eco/sources-and-methods*).

a) Data based on the National Survey of Urban Employment; see *OECD Economic Outlook* Sources and Methods.

b) Spanish data on unemployment are revised since 1976 using the methodology to be applied by the LFS as from 2002. Revisions are OECD calculations based on information from INE in Spain

c) The figures incorporate important revisions to Turkish data; see *OECD Economic Outlook* Sources and Methods.

Source: OECD.

Annex Table 15. **Standardised unemployment rates**[a]

Per cent of civilian labour force

	1984	1985	1986	1987	1988	1989	1990	1991	1992	1993	1994	1995	1996	1997	1998	1999	2000	2001	2002
Australia	9.0	8.3	7.9	7.9	7.0	6.0	6.7	9.3	10.5	10.6	9.5	8.2	8.2	8.3	7.7	7.0	6.3	6.7	6.3
Austria	..	..	..	..	..	..	..	..	..	4.0	3.8	3.9	4.4	4.4	4.5	4.0	3.7	3.6	4.3
Belgium	10.8	10.1	10.0	..	8.8	7.4	6.6	6.4	7.1	8.6	9.8	9.7	9.5	9.2	9.3	8.6	6.9	6.7	7.3
Canada	11.3	10.7	9.6	8.8	7.8	7.5	8.1	10.3	11.2	11.4	10.4	9.4	9.6	9.1	8.3	7.6	6.8	7.2	7.7
Czech Republic	..	..	..	..	..	..	..	..	..	4.4	4.4	4.1	3.9	4.8	6.4	8.6	8.7	8.0	7.3
Denmark	7.9	6.6	5.0	5.0	5.7	6.8	7.2	7.9	8.6	9.6	7.7	6.8	6.3	5.3	4.9	4.8	4.4	4.3	4.5
Finland	5.9	6.0	6.7	4.9	4.2	3.1	3.2	6.6	11.6	16.4	16.8	15.2	14.5	12.6	11.4	10.2	9.8	9.1	9.1
France	9.4	9.8	9.9	10.1	9.6	9.1	8.6	9.1	10.0	11.3	11.8	11.4	11.9	11.8	11.4	10.7	9.3	8.5	8.7
Germany[b]	7.1	7.2	6.5	6.3	6.2	5.6	4.8	4.2	6.4	7.7	8.2	8.0	8.7	9.7	9.1	8.4	7.8	7.8	8.2
Hungary	..	..	..	..	..	..	..	..	9.9	12.1	11.0	10.4	9.6	9.0	8.4	6.9	6.3	5.6	5.6
Ireland	15.5	16.8	16.8	16.6	16.2	14.7	13.4	14.7	15.4	15.6	14.3	12.3	11.7	9.9	7.5	5.6	4.3	3.9	4.4
Italy	7.9	8.1	8.9	9.6	9.7	9.7	8.9	8.5	8.7	10.1	11.0	11.5	11.5	11.6	11.7	11.3	10.4	9.4	9.0
Japan	2.7	2.6	2.8	2.8	2.5	2.3	2.1	2.1	2.2	2.5	2.9	3.1	3.4	3.4	4.1	4.7	4.7	5.0	5.4
Luxembourg	3.0	2.9	2.5	2.5	2.0	1.8	1.6	1.6	2.1	2.6	3.2	2.9	2.9	2.7	2.7	2.4	2.3	2.1	2.8
Netherlands	8.9	7.9	7.8	7.7	7.2	6.6	5.9	5.5	5.3	6.2	6.8	6.6	6.0	4.9	3.8	3.2	2.8	2.4	2.8
New Zealand	5.7	4.2	4.0	4.1	5.6	7.1	7.8	10.3	10.3	9.5	8.1	6.3	6.1	6.6	7.5	6.8	6.0	5.3	5.2
Norway	3.2	2.6	2.0	2.1	3.2	5.4	5.7	6.0	6.5	6.5	5.9	5.4	4.8	4.0	3.2	3.3	3.4	3.6	3.9
Poland	..	..	..	..	..	..	..	..	..	14.0	14.4	13.3	12.3	10.9	10.2	13.4	16.4	18.5	19.9
Portugal	8.9	9.2	8.8	7.2	5.8	5.2	4.8	4.2	4.3	5.6	6.9	7.3	7.3	6.8	5.2	4.5	4.1	4.1	5.1
Slovak Republic	..	..	..	..	..	..	..	..	..	..	13.7	13.1	11.3	11.9	12.6	16.8	18.7	19.4	18.6
Spain	16.5	17.7	17.4	16.7	15.8	13.9	13.1	13.2	14.9	18.6	19.8	18.8	18.1	17.0	15.2	12.8	11.3	10.6	11.3
Sweden	3.3	2.9	2.7	2.2	1.8	1.5	1.7	3.1	5.6	9.1	9.4	8.8	9.6	9.9	8.2	6.7	5.6	4.9	4.9
Switzerland	..	..	..	..	..	..	..	1.8	2.8	3.8	3.7	3.3	3.7	4.1	3.4	2.9	2.6	2.5	..
United Kingdom	10.9	11.2	11.2	10.3	8.5	7.1	6.9	8.6	9.7	9.9	9.2	8.5	8.0	6.9	6.2	5.9	5.4	5.0	5.1
United States	7.5	7.2	7.0	6.2	5.5	5.3	5.6	6.8	7.5	6.9	6.1	5.6	5.4	4.9	4.5	4.2	4.0	4.7	5.8
Euro area	..	..	..	..	..	..	..	7.9	8.6	10.2	10.8	10.6	10.8	10.8	10.2	9.4	8.5	8.0	8.3
European Union	..	..	..	..	..	..	..	7.9	8.7	10.1	10.5	10.1	10.2	10.0	9.4	8.7	7.8	7.4	7.6
Total OECD	..	..	..	..	..	..	..	..	..	..	7.7	7.3	7.2	7.0	6.9	6.7	6.3	6.5	6.9

Note: In so far as possible, the data have been adjusted to ensure comparability over time and to conform to the guidelines of the International Labour Office. All series are benchmarked to labour-force-survey-based estimates. In countries with annual surveys, monthly estimates are obtained by interpolation/extrapolation and by incorporating trends in administrative data, where available. The annual figures are then calculated by averaging the monthly estimates (for both unemployed and the labour force). For countries with monthly or quarterly surveys, the annual estimates are obtained by averaging the monthly or quarterly estimates, respectively. For several countries, the adjustment procedure used is similar to that of the Bureau of Labor Statistics, U.S. Department of Labor. For EU countries, the procedures are similar to those used in deriving the Comparable Unemployment Rates (CURs) of the Statistical Office of the European Communities. Minor differences may appear mainly because of various methods of calculating and applying adjustment factors, and because EU estimates are based on the civilian labour force.

a) See technical notes in OECD *Quarterly Labour Force Statistics.*

b) Prior to 1993 data refers to Western Germany.

Source: OECD.

Annex Table 16. **Labour force, employment and unemployment**

Millions

	1986	1987	1988	1989	1990	1991	1992	1993	1994	1995	1996	1997	1998	1999	2000	2001	2002	Projections 2003	2004
Labour force																			
Major seven countries	296.1	299.7	303.7	307.8	312.0	322.7	325.0	326.2	328.6	330.3	333.1	337.2	339.7	342.6	347.0	348.9	350.4	352.3	354.6
Total of smaller countries[a]	97.1	112.8	115.0	117.4	119.4	121.8	122.9	149.4	154.3	156.3	158.7	160.4	162.5	164.8	165.5	167.4	169.4	171.1	173.0
European Union	151.6	152.9	154.6	155.7	157.2	166.5	166.4	166.0	166.5	167.1	168.2	169.5	171.4	173.3	175.1	176.7	178.0	178.8	179.8
Euro area	116.9	118.0	119.1	120.0	121.4	130.9	130.8	130.7	131.3	131.8	132.9	134.1	135.8	137.4	139.1	140.5	141.5	142.2	143.1
Total OECD[a]	393.2	412.4	418.6	425.2	431.4	444.5	447.9	475.6	482.9	486.5	491.8	497.6	502.2	507.4	512.4	516.3	519.8	523.4	527.7
Employment																			
Major seven countries	275.1	279.9	285.6	290.9	295.1	302.5	302.4	302.8	305.7	308.3	310.8	315.2	318.3	321.8	327.3	328.4	327.8	328.7	331.4
Total of smaller countries[a]	89.7	104.9	107.5	110.3	112.5	114.4	114.7	136.6	140.9	143.1	146.1	148.4	150.1	152.2	153.9	155.1	156.1	157.3	159.3
European Union	137.2	139.0	141.7	144.1	146.3	154.0	152.1	149.4	149.2	150.4	151.2	152.6	155.3	158.3	161.5	163.8	164.5	164.5	165.6
Euro area	105.9	107.1	108.6	110.3	112.4	121.0	119.8	117.6	117.3	118.1	118.6	119.6	122.0	124.5	127.4	129.3	129.9	129.8	130.7
Total OECD[a]	364.8	384.8	393.1	401.2	407.6	416.9	417.1	439.4	446.6	451.4	456.8	463.6	468.4	474.0	481.2	483.5	483.9	485.9	490.7
Unemployment																			
Major seven countries	21.0	19.8	18.1	16.9	16.9	20.2	22.6	23.4	22.9	22.0	22.3	22.0	21.4	20.8	19.6	20.5	22.6	23.6	23.3
Total of smaller countries[a]	7.4	7.8	7.4	7.0	6.9	7.4	8.2	12.7	13.4	13.1	12.6	12.1	12.4	12.6	11.6	12.3	13.2	13.8	13.7
European Union	14.4	13.9	12.9	11.6	10.9	12.5	14.2	16.6	17.2	16.7	17.1	16.9	16.1	15.0	13.6	12.9	13.5	14.4	14.3
Euro area	11.0	10.9	10.5	9.7	9.0	9.9	10.9	13.0	14.0	13.8	14.3	14.5	13.9	12.9	11.7	11.2	11.7	12.4	12.4
Total OECD[a]	28.4	27.6	25.5	24.0	23.7	27.6	30.8	36.2	36.3	35.1	34.9	34.0	33.8	33.4	31.2	32.8	35.8	37.5	37.0

a) The aggregate measures include Mexico as of 1987. There is a potential bias in the aggregates thereafter because of the limited coverage of the Mexican National Survey of Urban Employment
Source: OECD.

Annex Table 17. GDP deflators

Percentage change from previous period

	Average 1975-85	1986	1987	1988	1989	1990	1991	1992	1993	1994	1995	1996	1997	1998	1999	2000	2001	2002	Projections 2003	Projections 2004
Australia	9.2	6.5	7.9	8.6	7.1	4.9	2.3	1.3	1.2	0.9	1.5	2.3	1.7	0.3	0.8	4.3	3.0	2.7	1.8	2.6
Austria	4.9	2.9	2.2	1.2	2.9	3.3	3.8	3.6	2.9	2.7	2.5	1.3	0.9	0.5	0.7	1.4	1.6	1.3	1.7	1.1
Belgium	5.6	2.8	1.6	2.3	4.8	2.8	2.9	3.5	4.0	2.1	1.3	1.2	1.2	1.6	1.4	1.3	1.9	2.2	2.0	1.5
Canada	7.4	3.0	4.6	4.5	4.5	3.2	3.0	1.3	1.4	1.1	2.3	1.6	1.2	-0.4	1.7	3.9	1.0	1.2	3.5	2.1
Czech Republic	..	..	..	..	..	..	..	..	..	11.0	10.2	8.8	8.0	10.6	3.0	1.1	6.3	2.6	2.5	3.6
Denmark	8.2	4.6	4.7	3.4	5.2	3.7	2.8	2.9	1.4	1.7	1.8	2.5	2.2	1.0	1.8	3.1	2.0	1.1	2.4	2.6
Finland	9.1	4.3	4.2	8.1	6.1	5.4	1.8	0.9	2.3	2.0	4.1	-0.3	2.0	3.6	-0.3	2.9	3.6	1.3	1.5	1.3
France	9.7	5.1	2.9	3.2	3.2	2.9	3.0	2.0	2.4	1.8	1.7	1.4	1.3	0.9	0.5	0.5	1.5	1.7	1.5	1.6
Germany	3.6	3.3	1.8	1.5	2.3	3.2	3.5	5.0	3.7	2.5	2.0	1.0	0.7	1.1	0.5	-0.3	1.4	1.6	0.8	0.6
Greece	19.3	18.9	15.3	16.7	14.5	20.7	19.8	14.8	14.4	11.2	9.8	7.4	6.8	5.2	3.0	3.4	3.4	3.7	3.5	3.6
Hungary	..	..	..	..	..	..	..	..	..	19.5	25.6	21.2	18.5	12.6	8.4	9.7	9.0	8.8	7.1	4.3
Iceland	43.4	25.5	19.5	22.8	19.8	16.9	8.7	3.3	2.1	2.0	2.8	2.1	3.3	4.9	2.8	2.9	9.1	5.2	2.8	3.2
Ireland	12.7	6.5	2.2	3.2	5.5	-0.7	1.8	2.8	5.2	1.7	3.0	2.1	4.2	6.2	4.1	4.3	5.3	4.9	4.0	3.6
Italy	15.8	7.9	6.2	6.8	6.5	8.2	7.6	4.5	3.9	3.5	5.0	5.3	2.4	2.7	1.6	2.1	2.7	2.7	2.7	2.6
Japan	4.0	1.6	-0.1	0.7	2.0	2.4	2.9	1.6	0.5	0.1	-0.5	-0.8	0.3	-0.1	-1.5	-1.9	-1.6	-1.7	-2.2	-1.8
Korea	14.6	5.1	5.6	7.6	5.7	10.7	10.9	7.6	7.1	7.7	7.1	3.9	3.1	5.1	-2.0	-1.1	2.5	1.7	0.5	1.4
Luxembourg	6.5	-0.1	0.1	2.8	4.0	2.5	1.8	3.7	6.0	3.5	2.4	1.6	3.3	2.1	3.1	2.8	2.3	0.2	0.6	2.2
Mexico	39.0	73.4	140.7	101.2	26.5	28.1	23.3	14.4	9.5	8.5	37.9	30.7	17.7	15.4	15.2	12.2	6.4	4.6	4.1	3.6
Netherlands	4.6	0.1	-0.7	0.9	1.1	2.2	2.8	2.3	1.8	2.3	2.0	1.2	2.0	1.7	1.6	4.2	5.3	3.4	2.6	1.9
New Zealand	13.7	15.3	13.2	7.5	5.1	3.3	0.5	1.4	3.0	1.0	2.4	2.5	0.4	1.5	-0.1	2.4	4.8	0.3	1.1	2.5
Norway	8.2	-0.9	6.9	5.0	5.7	3.9	2.4	-0.6	2.3	-0.1	2.9	4.1	2.9	-0.7	6.6	15.9	1.9	-0.7	2.6	2.6
Poland	..	..	..	..	..	..	..	..	..	37.2	28.0	18.7	14.0	11.8	6.8	11.3	4.2	1.4	1.0	1.9
Portugal	21.4	20.5	10.1	11.2	10.5	13.1	10.1	11.4	7.4	7.3	3.4	3.0	3.8	3.8	3.1	3.2	4.8	4.6	3.6	2.3
Slovak Republic	..	..	..	..	..	..	..	..	..	13.7	9.9	4.4	6.7	5.2	6.4	6.4	5.4	4.0	7.4	5.2
Spain	14.7	10.9	5.9	5.9	6.9	7.3	6.9	6.7	4.5	3.9	4.9	3.5	2.3	2.4	2.7	3.5	4.2	4.4	3.0	2.4
Sweden	9.9	6.5	4.8	6.4	8.0	8.8	7.3	1.0	2.7	2.3	3.4	1.2	1.5	0.8	0.7	1.3	2.0	1.3	2.3	2.3
Switzerland	3.2	3.1	2.7	2.8	3.1	4.3	6.0	2.7	2.7	1.6	1.1	0.4	-0.2	0.0	0.7	1.2	1.4	0.4	0.8	0.4
Turkey	43.3	36.0	33.6	69.3	75.5	58.3	58.8	63.7	67.8	106.5	87.2	77.8	81.5	75.7	55.6	49.9	54.8	43.7	26.2	14.3
United Kingdom	10.8	3.1	5.5	6.1	7.5	7.5	6.6	4.0	2.6	1.4	2.6	3.3	2.9	2.9	2.5	2.2	2.3	3.2	1.8	2.3
United States	6.3	2.2	3.0	3.4	3.8	3.9	3.6	2.4	2.4	2.1	2.2	1.9	1.9	1.2	1.4	2.1	2.4	1.1	1.6	1.3
Euro area	8.9	5.5	3.5	3.8	4.2	4.9	4.8	4.3	3.6	2.8	2.9	2.1	1.6	1.7	1.1	1.3	2.4	2.4	1.9	1.7
European Union	9.9	5.5	4.1	4.5	5.0	5.6	5.3	4.3	3.5	2.7	3.0	2.5	1.9	1.9	1.4	1.5	2.4	2.5	1.9	1.8
Total OECD	9.3	6.3	7.9	7.8	6.0	6.1	5.8	4.4	3.9	4.6	5.2	4.3	3.7	3.2	2.4	2.7	2.9	2.1	1.7	1.4
Memorandum item																				
OECD *less* high inflation countries [a]	7.6	3.6	3.2	3.6	4.1	4.5	4.3	3.1	2.6	2.2	2.3	1.8	1.7	1.4	0.9	1.4	1.8	1.3	1.2	1.1

Note: The adoption of new national account systems, SNA93 or ESA95, has been proceeding at an uneven pace among OECD member countries, both with respect to variables and the time period covered. As a consequence there are breaks in many national series. Moreover, some countries are using chain-weighted price indices to calculate real GDP and expenditures components. See Table "National Account Reporting Systems and Base-years" at the beginning of the Statistical Annex and OECD *Economic Outlook* Sources and Methods (*http://www.oecd.org/eco/sources-and-methods*).

a) High inflation countries are defined as countries which have had 10 per cent or more inflation in terms of the GDP deflator on average during the last 10 years based on historical data. Consequently, Hungary, Mexico, Poland and Turkey are excluded from the aggregate.

Source: OECD.

Annex Table 18. Private consumption deflators
Percentage change from previous period

	Average 1975-85	1986	1987	1988	1989	1990	1991	1992	1993	1994	1995	1996	1997	1998	1999	2000	2001	2002	Projections 2003	2004
Australia	9.4	8.0	8.6	7.5	5.6	6.4	4.4	2.2	2.2	1.2	2.3	1.9	1.6	1.3	1.0	3.3	3.5	2.1	2.5	2.6
Austria	5.1	1.7	1.2	1.5	2.6	3.3	3.5	3.9	3.5	2.8	2.0	1.9	1.5	0.5	0.9	1.5	2.0	1.8	1.4	1.1
Belgium	6.2	0.4	1.6	1.1	3.8	2.8	2.8	1.8	2.5	2.3	1.5	2.2	1.7	1.1	1.2	2.3	2.5	1.9	1.7	1.2
Canada	7.9	4.3	3.9	3.9	4.4	4.2	5.0	1.7	2.3	1.1	1.3	1.6	1.6	1.2	1.7	2.1	1.9	1.9	2.8	2.1
Czech Republic	..	..	..	..	..	..	..	..	..	10.7	9.2	8.0	7.5	9.1	3.7	2.8	3.8	-0.1	2.0	2.3
Denmark	9.0	2.9	4.6	4.0	4.7	2.9	2.8	1.9	2.0	3.0	1.9	2.1	2.2	1.3	2.4	3.5	2.6	2.3	2.3	2.3
Finland	9.3	2.8	3.2	4.8	5.3	5.5	5.9	4.1	3.9	0.9	0.4	1.5	1.9	1.9	1.2	3.7	3.4	1.7	2.3	1.5
France	10.1	2.9	3.3	2.9	3.8	3.1	3.5	2.5	2.5	2.2	2.0	1.9	1.4	0.6	0.2	1.2	1.4	1.5	1.4	1.4
Germany	3.9	-0.5	0.5	1.3	2.8	2.6	3.8	4.4	3.9	2.6	1.9	1.7	2.0	1.1	0.4	1.5	1.9	1.4	0.8	0.4
Greece	18.1	22.4	17.3	15.1	13.5	19.8	19.7	15.7	14.1	11.0	9.0	8.2	5.6	4.5	2.2	3.2	3.1	3.5	3.3	3.4
Hungary	..	..	..	..	..	..	..	..	..	19.7	27.0	23.7	18.0	13.7	10.7	9.9	8.6	4.5	5.1	4.5
Iceland	44.4	20.1	15.9	25.4	23.3	16.7	8.9	3.5	3.6	1.4	1.9	2.4	-0.2	0.9	2.6	4.5	8.1	3.9	2.5	2.6
Ireland	13.1	4.6	2.4	3.8	4.1	2.1	2.7	3.0	2.2	2.7	2.8	2.6	2.6	3.8	3.1	4.0	4.2	4.8	4.2	3.2
Italy	15.4	6.4	5.2	5.9	6.7	6.4	7.0	5.5	5.5	4.9	6.0	4.4	2.2	2.1	2.1	2.9	2.7	3.0	2.4	1.9
Japan	4.7	0.7	0.4	0.6	2.1	2.6	2.7	1.6	1.0	0.5	-0.3	-0.1	1.0	-0.1	-0.7	-1.2	-1.5	-1.5	-1.6	-1.6
Korea	13.7	1.6	4.0	6.0	6.1	10.6	12.1	8.9	8.0	9.7	7.0	5.7	5.4	7.9	0.6	2.2	4.1	3.0	3.8	3.3
Luxembourg	6.9	0.3	0.9	2.3	3.2	3.6	3.4	4.2	4.0	2.6	2.2	1.7	1.5	1.2	1.4	2.6	2.8	2.2	2.2	1.4
Mexico	38.4	82.0	135.1	109.1	25.1	27.8	24.3	15.4	10.1	7.6	34.0	30.6	16.5	20.6	14.0	10.3	7.2	4.8	4.4	3.5
Netherlands	5.0	0.3	0.2	0.9	1.4	2.2	3.3	3.3	2.2	2.9	1.4	1.9	2.0	1.7	1.8	3.5	4.6	3.5	2.3	1.3
New Zealand	14.0	12.8	13.0	6.3	6.2	5.6	2.2	1.1	1.1	1.2	2.6	2.2	1.9	2.0	0.3	2.1	2.1	1.5	1.6	2.0
Norway	8.5	6.7	7.8	6.1	4.8	4.7	3.9	2.5	2.4	1.2	2.4	1.4	2.3	2.5	2.0	3.0	2.4	0.7	3.2	1.6
Poland	22.6	..	..	..	..	..	..	..	..	37.9	27.2	20.0	14.7	11.5	7.0	11.5	5.0	1.6	1.4	2.3
Portugal	..	13.8	9.9	11.5	12.8	11.6	11.8	9.2	6.9	5.6	4.3	3.7	2.9	2.8	2.1	2.8	4.2	3.6	3.1	2.2
Slovak Republic	15.0	9.3	5.5	4.8	6.7	6.6	6.4	6.6	5.3	4.9	4.8	3.5	2.6	2.2	2.4	3.2	3.3	3.6	2.9	2.4
Spain	..	..	..	..	..	..	..	..	..	14.1	9.2	4.9	6.2	5.8	8.7	10.5	5.6	2.4	7.1	6.1
Sweden	10.3	4.6	5.2	5.9	6.9	9.8	10.5	2.1	5.8	2.7	2.8	1.3	1.9	0.8	1.2	1.1	2.1	2.0	2.3	1.7
Switzerland	3.4	1.3	1.5	1.9	2.9	5.2	6.0	4.2	3.4	1.1	1.7	1.1	0.6	-0.2	0.3	1.1	1.2	0.8	0.7	0.3
Turkey	41.5	30.4	48.8	58.9	83.7	59.8	60.7	65.6	65.9	108.9	92.4	67.8	82.1	83.0	59.0	50.0	58.8	40.5	32.0	17.1
United Kingdom	10.4	4.0	4.7	5.2	6.3	7.5	7.9	4.7	3.2	1.9	3.1	3.1	2.3	2.7	1.6	0.7	0.9	0.8	0.9	1.0
United States	6.4	2.4	3.8	3.9	4.4	4.6	3.8	3.1	2.4	2.0	2.3	2.1	1.9	1.1	1.6	2.5	2.0	1.4	2.0	1.2
Euro area	9.2	3.4	3.1	3.4	4.6	4.5	5.1	4.6	4.2	3.3	3.0	2.5	2.0	1.5	1.1	2.1	2.4	2.2	1.7	1.4
European Union	9.9	3.8	3.6	3.9	5.0	5.1	5.7	4.5	4.0	3.2	3.1	2.7	2.1	1.7	1.2	1.9	2.2	2.0	1.6	1.4
Total OECD	9.4	5.8	8.2	7.7	6.3	6.3	6.2	4.9	4.2	4.9	5.2	4.4	4.0	3.5	2.6	3.0	2.8	2.0	2.0	1.3
Memorandum item																				
OECD *less* high inflation countries[a]	7.8	2.9	3.4	3.5	4.3	4.7	4.6	3.5	2.9	2.5	2.4	2.1	2.0	1.4	1.1	1.8	1.6	1.3	1.4	1.0

Note: The adoption of new national account systems, SNA93 or ESA95, has been proceeding at an uneven pace among OECD member countries, both with respect to variables and the time period covered. As a consequence there are breaks in many national series. Moreover, some countries are using chain-weighted price indices to calculate real GDP and expenditures components. See Table "National Account Reporting Systems and Base-years" at the beginning of the Statistical Annex and *OECD Economic Outlook* Sources and Methods (*http://www.oecd.org/eco/sources-and-methods*).

a) High inflation countries are defined as countries which have had 10 per cent or more inflation in terms of the GDP deflator on average during the last 10 years based on historical data. Consequently, Hungary, Mexico, Poland and Turkey are excluded from the aggregate.

Source: OECD.

Annex Table 19. **Consumer prices indices**
Percentage change from previous period

	Average 1975-85	1986	1987	1988	1989	1990	1991	1992	1993	1994	1995	1996	1997	1998	1999	2000	2001	2002	Projections 2003	Projections 2004
Australia	9.4	9.1	8.5	7.3	7.5	7.3	3.2	1.0	1.8	1.9	4.6	2.6	0.3	0.9	1.5	4.5	4.4	3.0	2.5	2.5
Austria	5.0	1.7	1.5	1.9	2.6	3.3	3.1	3.4	3.2	2.7	1.6	1.8	1.2	0.8	0.5	2.0	2.3	1.7	1.4	1.0
Belgium	6.7	1.3	1.6	1.2	3.1	3.4	3.9	2.2	2.5	2.4	1.3	1.8	1.5	0.9	1.1	2.7	2.4	1.6	1.4	1.2
Canada	8.1	4.2	4.3	4.0	5.0	4.8	5.6	1.5	1.9	0.2	2.2	1.6	1.6	1.0	1.7	2.7	2.5	2.2	3.7	2.1
Czech Republic	..	..	..	..	..	..	..	..	..	10.0	9.1	8.8	8.5	10.7	2.1	3.9	4.8	1.8	2.0	3.1
Denmark	9.2	3.7	4.0	4.5	4.8	2.6	2.4	2.1	1.3	2.0	2.1	2.1	2.2	1.8	2.5	2.9	2.4	2.4	2.4	2.3
Finland	9.4	2.9	4.1	5.1	6.6	6.1	4.6	3.2	3.3	1.6	0.4	1.1	1.2	1.4	1.3	3.0	2.7	2.0	1.4	1.2
France	10.1	2.5	3.3	2.7	3.5	3.6	3.4	2.5	2.2	1.7	1.8	2.1	1.3	0.7	0.6	1.8	1.8	1.9	1.6	1.4
Germany	3.9	-0.1	0.2	1.3	2.8	2.7	4.1	5.1	4.4	2.7	1.7	1.2	1.5	0.6	0.6	1.5	2.1	1.3	0.8	0.4
Greece	18.4	23.0	16.4	13.5	13.7	20.4	19.5	15.9	14.4	10.9	8.9	7.9	5.4	4.5	2.1	2.9	3.7	3.9	3.4	3.5
Hungary	..	..	..	..	..	..	..	..	..	18.9	28.3	23.5	18.3	14.2	10.0	9.8	9.2	5.3	5.2	4.6
Iceland[a]	..	22.1	18.3	25.7	20.8	15.5	6.8	4.0	4.1	1.6	1.7	2.3	1.8	1.7	3.2	5.1	6.4	5.2	2.5	2.6
Ireland	13.2	3.8	3.1	2.2	4.0	3.3	3.2	3.1	1.4	2.3	2.5	2.2	1.2	2.1	2.5	5.3	4.0	4.7	4.1	3.2
Italy	15.0	5.8	4.7	5.1	6.3	6.5	6.2	5.0	4.5	4.2	5.4	4.0	1.9	2.0	1.7	2.6	2.3	2.6	2.3	1.9
Japan	4.7	0.6	0.1	0.7	2.3	3.1	3.2	1.7	1.3	0.7	-0.1	0.1	1.7	0.7	-0.3	-0.7	-0.7	-0.9	-0.9	-1.0
Korea	12.0	2.3	3.5	7.1	5.7	8.5	9.3	6.2	4.8	6.3	4.5	4.9	4.4	7.5	0.8	2.3	4.1	2.8	3.8	3.3
Luxembourg	6.7	0.3	-0.1	1.4	3.4	3.3	3.1	3.2	3.6	2.2	1.9	1.2	1.4	1.0	1.0	3.8	2.4	2.1	2.3	1.2
Mexico	39.6	86.2	131.8	114.2	20.0	26.7	22.7	15.5	9.8	7.0	35.0	34.4	20.6	15.9	16.6	9.5	6.4	5.0	4.4	3.5
Netherlands	5.1	0.1	-0.7	0.7	1.1	2.5	3.2	2.8	1.6	2.1	1.4	1.4	1.9	1.8	2.0	2.3	5.1	3.9	2.4	1.5
New Zealand	13.4	13.2	15.7	6.4	5.7	6.1	2.6	1.0	1.3	1.7	3.8	2.3	1.2	1.3	-0.1	2.6	2.6	2.7	2.0	2.0
Norway	8.7	7.2	8.7	6.7	4.5	4.1	3.4	2.3	2.3	1.4	2.4	1.2	2.6	2.3	2.3	3.1	3.0	1.3	3.2	1.6
Poland	..	..	..	..	..	..	..	..	..	33.2	28.3	19.9	14.9	11.6	7.3	10.1	5.5	1.9	1.4	2.3
Portugal	23.3	11.8	9.4	9.7	12.6	13.4	11.4	8.9	5.9	5.0	4.0	2.9	1.9	2.2	2.2	2.8	4.4	3.7	3.2	2.2
Slovak Republic	..	..	..	..	..	..	..	..	..	13.4	9.8	5.8	6.1	6.7	10.6	12.0	7.3	3.1	8.7	7.4
Spain	15.4	8.8	5.2	4.8	6.8	6.7	5.9	5.9	4.9	4.6	4.6	3.6	1.9	1.8	2.2	3.5	2.8	3.6	2.9	2.4
Sweden	9.7	4.2	4.2	6.1	6.6	10.4	9.7	2.6	4.7	2.4	2.9	0.8	0.9	0.4	0.3	1.3	2.6	2.4	2.4	1.8
Switzerland	3.3	0.8	1.4	1.9	3.2	5.4	5.9	4.0	3.3	0.9	1.8	0.8	0.5	0.0	0.8	1.6	1.0	0.6	0.7	0.3
Turkey[b]	44.0	34.6	38.9	68.8	63.3	60.3	66.0	70.1	66.1	105.2	89.1	80.4	85.7	84.6	64.9	54.9	54.4	45.0	30.3	17.5
United Kingdom	10.6	3.6	3.7	4.6	5.9	8.1	6.8	4.7	3.0	2.4	2.8	2.9	2.8	2.7	2.3	2.1	2.1	2.2	3.1	2.8
United States[c]	7.2	1.9	3.6	4.1	4.8	5.4	4.2	3.0	3.0	2.6	2.8	2.9	2.3	1.5	2.2	3.4	2.8	1.6	2.4	1.7
Euro area	7.3	2.5	2.6	2.7	3.8	6.0	4.3	3.8	3.4	2.8	2.6	2.3	1.7	1.2	1.1	2.4	2.5	2.4	2.0	1.6

Note: Consumer price index. For the euro area countries and the euro area aggregate: Harmonised Index of Consumer Prices (HICP) and United Kingdom: retail price index excluding mortgage payments (RPIX).
a) Excluding rent, but including imputed rent.
b) Until 1981: Istanbul index (154 items); from 1982, Turkish index.
c) The methodology for calculating the Consumer Price Index has changed considerably over the past years, lowering measured inflation substantially.
Source: OECD.

Annex Table 20. **Oil and other primary commodity markets**

	1987	1988	1989	1990	1991	1992	1993	1994	1995	1996	1997	1998	1999	2000	2001	2002	Projections 2003	Projections 2004
Oil market conditions[a] (in million barrels per day)																		
Demand																		
OECD[b]	39.3	40.6	41.2	41.5	41.9	42.9	43.2	44.4	44.9	45.9	46.7	46.8	47.7	47.7	47.7	47.6	48.2	..
of which: North America	20.1	20.8	21.0	20.7	20.5	20.8	21.1	21.7	21.6	22.2	22.7	23.1	23.8	24.0	23.9	23.9	24.4	..
Europe[c]	13.2	13.4	13.5	13.6	14.0	14.2	14.2	14.3	14.6	14.9	15.0	15.3	15.2	15.1	15.3	15.1	15.1	..
Pacific	5.9	6.4	6.7	7.2	7.5	7.9	8.0	8.4	8.7	8.8	9.0	8.4	8.7	8.6	8.6	8.5	8.7	..
Non-OECD[d]	23.5	24.2	24.5	24.5	24.8	24.4	24.6	24.0	24.7	25.6	26.8	27.0	27.7	28.4	28.8	29.3	29.8	..
Total	62.8	64.8	65.8	66.0	66.7	67.2	67.8	68.4	69.6	71.5	73.5	73.8	75.4	76.2	76.5	76.9	78.0	..
Supply																		
OECD[b]	19.8	19.6	18.9	19.0	19.5	19.8	20.0	20.8	21.1	21.7	22.1	21.9	21.4	21.9	21.8	21.9	22.4	..
OPEC total	19.7	21.8	23.8	25.1	25.3	26.5	26.9	27.4	27.6	28.4	29.9	30.8	29.4	30.8	30.1	28.5	..	..
Former USSR	12.5	12.5	12.2	11.5	10.4	8.9	7.9	7.2	7.1	7.1	7.2	7.3	7.5	7.9	8.6	9.4	10.0	..
Other non-OECD[d]	10.4	10.8	11.2	11.4	11.6	12.1	12.6	13.4	14.5	15.1	15.4	15.8	16.0	16.2	16.3	..	..	..
Total	62.4	64.8	66.1	66.9	66.8	67.2	67.5	68.8	70.4	72.3	74.6	75.7	74.3	76.8	76.8	76.6	..	..
Trade																		
OECD net imports[b]	19.8	20.8	22.5	22.8	22.4	23.1	23.5	23.8	23.4	24.2	24.9	25.3	25.5	26.0	26.2	25.4	25.7	..
Former USSR net exports	3.6	3.6	3.5	3.1	2.2	2.0	2.0	2.7	2.8	3.1	3.4	3.6	3.9	4.3	4.9	5.6	6.2	..
Other non-OECD net exports[d]	16.2	17.2	19.0	19.7	20.2	21.1	21.4	21.1	20.6	21.1	21.5	21.7	21.6	21.7	21.3	19.7	19.5	..
Prices[e]																		
OECD crude oil import price (cif, $ per bl)	17.9	14.9	17.5	22.3	19.3	18.4	16.4	15.6	17.2	20.5	19.1	12.6	17.3	28.0	23.6	24.1	26.0	25.0
Prices of other primary commodities[e] ($ indices)																		
Food and tropical beverages	80	93	88	79	74	72	73	98	100	99	104	91	74	67	61	67	73	76
of which: Food	71	99	96	85	83	87	88	95	100	118	104	91	77	73	70	80	89	91
Tropical beverages	86	90	82	75	68	62	63	100	100	86	103	91	72	62	55	58	62	65
Agricultural raw materials	72	80	82	90	78	79	75	86	100	86	83	71	71	74	67	64	70	75
Minerals, ores and metals	78	112	107	99	88	85	74	85	100	90	91	78	74	84	77	75	82	85
Total	76	94	92	90	80	79	74	89	100	90	91	78	73	75	69	68	75	79
Memorandum item																		
Export prices of OECD manufactures (dollar index)	79	84	84	91	90	93	89	91	100	97	89	86	83	79	77	78	84	85

a) Based on data published in in various issues of the International Energy Agency, *Oil Market Report* and *Annual Statistical Supplement*, August 2002.
b) Excluding Czech Republic, Hungary, Korea, Mexico and Poland.
c) European Union countries and Iceland, Norway, Switzerland and Turkey.
d) Including Czech Republic, Hungary, Korea, Mexico and Poland.
e) Indices through 2002 are based on data compiled by the International Energy Agency for oil and by the Hamburg Institute for Economic Research for the prices of other primary commodities; OECD projections for 2003 and 2004.
Source: OECD.

Annex Table 21. **Employment rates, participation rates and labour force**

	Employment rates						Labour force participation rates						Labour force					
	Average 1981-83	Average 1991-93	2001	2002	2003	2004	Average 1981-83	Average 1991-93	2001	2002	2003	2004	Average 1981-90	Average 1991-00	2001	2002	2003	2004
	Per cent						Per cent						Percentage change					
Australia	64.8	66.3	70.4	70.8	70.9	71.0	70.1	73.7	75.6	75.5	75.5	75.4	2.4	1.4	1.5	1.5	1.5	1.5
Austria	76.1	73.9	73.8	73.3	72.8	72.8	78.2	77.7	77.5	77.5	77.4	77.4	0.4	0.3	0.8	0.2	0.2	0.2
Belgium	57.5	58.5	62.4	62.0	61.7	61.9	63.7	63.1	66.9	66.9	66.9	67.1	0.1	0.6	1.2	0.4	0.5	0.6
Canada	65.9	68.2	71.9	72.6	73.2	73.6	73.3	76.6	77.5	78.6	79.1	79.2	1.7	1.2	1.5	2.6	1.8	1.3
Czech Republic	..	69.2	65.6	66.3	66.3	66.3	..	72.3	71.5	71.6	71.5	71.4	..	0.1	0.0	0.2	0.0	0.0
Denmark	71.6	74.8	76.3	76.3	76.2	76.5	77.7	81.9	79.8	79.9	80.0	80.0	1.1	-0.1	0.1	0.2	0.2	0.2
Finland	72.1	65.3	68.0	68.0	67.9	68.1	76.1	73.8	74.8	74.8	74.8	74.9	0.5	0.2	0.7	0.1	0.1	0.3
France	62.2	59.8	63.7	63.7	63.4	63.5	67.6	66.9	69.7	69.9	69.9	70.0	0.5	0.7	0.7	0.7	0.4	0.5
Germany	64.8	68.5	70.2	69.9	69.4	69.4	68.0	73.1	75.8	75.8	75.6	75.7	1.3	0.3	0.4	-0.1	-0.4	0.1
Greece	58.0	55.3	57.2	57.0	57.2	57.6	61.6	60.6	63.8	63.3	63.2	63.3	0.9	1.3	-1.1	-0.6	0.0	0.4
Hungary	..	54.1	54.6				..	61.5	58.0				..	-0.2	-0.3	-0.1	-0.2	0.2
Iceland	83.3	81.6	85.5	84.0	83.4	83.9	84.5	84.9	87.5	86.7	86.3	86.5	1.6	1.5	1.7	0.6	0.8	1.2
Ireland	55.4	52.9	67.3	67.2	66.6	66.5	63.3	62.3	70.0	70.1	70.1	70.1	0.4	3.0	2.5	1.7	1.5	1.5
Italy	56.3	53.8	54.9	55.8	56.2	56.9	60.5	59.2	60.8	61.4	61.9	62.5	0.6	0.1	0.8	0.9	0.5	0.8
Japan	70.6	73.9	74.1	73.4	73.1	73.2	72.3	75.6	78.1	77.5	77.5	77.6	1.3	0.4	-0.2	-0.9	-0.3	-0.2
Korea	57.5	62.1	63.0	63.9	64.1	64.5	60.0	63.7	65.4	65.9	66.2	66.5	2.6	1.5	1.1	1.7	1.5	1.5
Luxembourg	60.0	60.7	63.9	64.4	64.0	64.3	60.8	61.8	65.6	66.3	66.6	66.9	0.8	1.4	2.5	2.0	1.3	1.3
Mexico	..	52.5	54.4	54.1	54.0	54.4	..	54.1	55.7	55.6	55.5	55.8	..	2.8	1.0	1.7	2.0	2.4
Netherlands	52.5	56.2	65.2	65.3	64.6	64.4	57.4	59.7	66.5	66.9	67.4	67.8	1.1	1.7	1.5	1.2	1.1	1.0
New Zealand	71.9	64.0	71.7	72.4			75.0	71.1	75.7	76.4			0.7	1.7	1.8	2.8	1.0	1.2
Norway	74.3	72.4	77.7	77.4	77.0	76.8	76.3	76.8	80.5	80.6	80.7	80.6	0.9	1.1	0.5	0.6	0.6	0.4
Poland	..	59.1	53.2	51.4	50.6	50.9	..	68.8	65.1	64.2	63.6	63.5	..	0.2	0.4	-0.9	-0.4	0.4
Portugal	62.9	69.8	72.6	72.5	71.9	72.4	68.4	73.2	75.7	76.3	76.8	77.3	1.1	0.7	1.7	1.3	1.1	0.9
Slovak Republic	..	..	56.6	56.6	57.0	57.4	..	..	70.1	69.6	69.3	69.0	..	0.9	1.7	-0.7	-0.5	-0.3
Spain	49.7	49.8	59.1	59.9	60.5	61.5	56.7	57.8	66.0	67.6	68.7	69.6	1.3	1.7	3.1	3.0	2.2	1.8
Sweden	78.7	75.6	73.7	73.3	72.6	72.5	81.1	79.9	76.8	76.4	76.0	75.7	0.6	-0.4	1.3	0.1	0.2	0.2
Switzerland	78.1	85.5	83.9	83.8	82.8	82.7	78.4	87.5	85.3	85.8	85.5	85.1	1.8	0.0	1.6	1.3	0.4	0.4
Turkey	62.4	53.5	45.8	44.5	43.9	43.3	67.1	58.3	50.1	49.8	49.1	48.5	1.8	0.4	1.1	1.9	1.0	1.3
United Kingdom	65.3	68.5	71.6	71.8	71.7	71.7	72.6	75.6	75.5	75.7	75.7	75.6	0.8	0.2	0.3	0.8	0.4	0.3
United States	65.1	71.0	72.3	..	..	..	71.5	76.5	76.0	..	..	..	1.6	1.4	0.8	0.8	1.1	1.2
Euro area	59.6	60.1	63.7	63.9	63.7	64.1	64.3	65.8	69.2	69.6	69.8	70.2	0.9	0.7	1.0	0.8	0.5	0.7
European Union	61.2	62.0	65.3	65.5	65.3	65.6	66.3	67.8	70.5	70.9	71.0	71.3	0.9	0.6	0.9	0.7	0.5	0.6
Total OECD	63.2	65.0	66.3	64.0	63.8	63.9	68.0	69.8	70.8	69.1	69.0	69.1	1.3	0.9	0.8	0.7	0.8	0.8

Note: Employment rates are calculated as the ratio of total employment to the population of working age. The working age population concept used here and in the labour force participation rate is defined as all persons of the age 15 to 64 years (16 to 65 years for Spain). This definition does not correspond to the commonly-used working age population concepts for the United States (16 years and above), Hungary and New Zealand (15 years and above). Hence for these countries no projections are available. For information about sources and definitions, see *OECD Economic Outlook* Sources and Methods (*http://www.oecd.org/eco/sources-and-methods*).
Source: OECD.

Annex Table 22. Potential GDP, employment and capital stock

Percentage change from previous period

	Potential GDP						Employment						Capital stock					
	Average 1981-90	Average 1991-00	2001	2002	2003	2004	Average 1981-90	Average 1991-00	2001	2002	2003	2004	Average 1981-90	Average 1991-00	2001	2002	2003	2004
Australia	3.5	3.3	3.5	3.8	4.1	4.0	2.3	1.8	1.1	2.0	1.7	1.8	4.6	4.1	3.5	4.0	5.1	5.4
Austria	2.2	2.4	2.7	2.3	2.1	2.1	0.2	0.3	0.7	-0.4	-0.4	0.3	3.9	4.1	4.6	3.7	3.4	3.2
Belgium	2.1	2.2	2.6	2.1	2.1	2.0	0.4	0.6	1.4	-0.2	-0.1	0.7	3.0	2.8	2.9	2.6	2.5	2.5
Canada	2.7	2.8	3.5	3.1	2.9	3.1	1.6	1.7	1.1	2.2	2.1	1.7	2.9	2.2	3.0	2.3	2.5	3.1
Czech Republic	..	..	..	..	..	..	..	-0.7	0.7	1.2	0.1	0.1	..	..	..	..	..	..
Denmark	1.9	2.2	2.4	2.2	2.1	2.1	1.1	0.3	0.2	0.1	0.0	0.5	3.1	2.8	3.3	3.0	2.5	2.2
Finland	2.8	2.2	2.9	2.7	2.6	2.5	0.7	-0.2	1.4	0.2	0.0	0.5	3.1	0.5	1.7	1.3	1.0	1.2
France	2.1	2.0	2.2	2.2	2.2	2.2	0.4	0.7	1.6	0.4	-0.1	0.7	3.5	2.9	3.1	2.8	2.4	2.5
Germany	2.1	1.7	1.6	1.4	1.4	1.4	1.1	0.1	0.4	-0.6	-1.0	0.0	3.0	2.3	2.0	1.4	1.1	1.1
Greece	1.1	2.5	2.9	3.2	3.5	3.7	0.6	0.9	-0.3	-0.1	0.6	0.9	..	..	..	..	..	..
Hungary	..	..	..	..	..	..	..	0.6	0.5	-0.2	-0.3	-0.2	..	..	..	..	..	..
Iceland	3.1	2.1	3.1	2.6	2.7	2.7	1.4	1.5	1.7	-0.2	0.5	1.5	3.0	2.4	4.2	1.8	3.1	4.1
Ireland	3.5	7.1	7.0	6.2	5.7	5.4	0.2	4.3	2.9	1.4	0.6	1.3	2.6	3.7	5.2	4.4	3.8	3.5
Italy	2.5	1.7	1.9	1.9	1.7	1.7	0.2	-0.2	2.0	1.5	0.5	1.2	3.0	2.9	3.5	3.6	3.4	3.4
Japan	3.9	1.6	1.4	1.3	1.3	1.3	1.3	0.1	-0.5	-1.3	-0.6	-0.2	6.1	4.0	3.5	3.0	2.9	2.7
Korea	..	..	..	..	..	..	2.9	1.3	1.4	2.4	1.3	1.7	..	..	..	..	..	..
Luxembourg	..	..	..	..	..	..	0.8	1.2	2.6	1.6	0.3	1.4	..	..	..	..	..	..
Mexico	..	..	..	..	..	..	2.0	2.8	0.8	1.4	2.0	2.7	..	..	..	..	..	..
Netherlands	1.9	2.9	2.8	2.6	2.1	1.9	1.1	2.0	2.1	0.7	-0.6	0.1	2.0	2.6	3.1	2.6	2.2	2.1
New Zealand	1.7	2.6	2.7	3.7	3.5	3.3	0.2	2.2	2.5	2.9	1.1	1.0	3.5	2.1	3.3	3.7	3.8	3.8
Norway	2.2	2.7	2.5	1.9	2.0	2.1	0.5	1.4	0.4	0.2	0.0	0.3	1.8	1.7	1.6	0.4	0.1	0.0
Poland	..	..	..	..	..	..	..	-0.2	-2.2	-3.0	-1.0	1.0	..	..	..	..	..	..
Portugal	2.9	2.9	3.0	2.3	2.0	2.0	1.5	0.7	1.6	0.3	-0.4	1.1	..	..	..	..	..	..
Slovak Republic	..	..	..	..	..	..	..	-0.4	1.0	0.2	0.6	0.8	..	..	..	..	..	..
Spain	2.3	2.8	3.1	2.8	2.8	2.8	1.2	1.8	3.7	2.0	1.4	2.1	3.5	3.9	4.1	3.5	3.3	3.2
Sweden	1.9	2.1	2.9	2.4	2.2	2.2	0.7	-0.6	2.0	0.1	-0.3	0.4	2.8	2.2	3.1	2.5	2.3	2.4
Switzerland	1.9	1.2	1.5	1.0	1.2	1.4	1.7	-0.1	1.7	0.6	-0.5	0.6	2.7	2.3	2.2	1.7	1.6	1.8
Turkey	..	..	..	..	..	..	1.7	0.6	-1.0	-0.4	1.1	1.2	..	..	..	..	..	..
United Kingdom	2.1	2.5	2.8	2.7	2.5	2.4	1.2	0.6	0.8	0.7	0.2	0.5	2.0	2.7	3.3	2.7	2.5	2.7
United States	2.9	3.1	3.5	2.9	3.0	3.1	1.9	1.7	0.0	-0.3	0.9	1.4	2.8	3.0	2.7	1.4	1.4	2.2
Euro area	2.2	2.1	2.2	2.1	2.0	2.0	0.7	0.6	1.5	0.4	-0.1	0.7	2.9	2.8	3.0	2.6	2.3	2.4
European Union	2.2	2.1	2.3	2.2	2.1	2.0	0.8	0.5	1.4	0.5	0.0	0.7	..	..	..	..	..	..
Total OECD	2.8	2.5	2.7	2.4	2.4	2.4	1.4	1.0	0.5	0.1	0.4	1.0	3.4	3.1	3.0	2.2	2.1	2.4

Note: Potential output is estimated using a Cobb-Douglas production function approach. For information about definitions, sources and data coverage, see *OECD Economic Outlook* Sources and Methods (*http://www.oecd.org/eco/sources-and-methods*).

Source: OECD.

Annex Table 23. **Structural unemployment, wage shares and unit labor costs**

	Structural unemployment rate						Wage shares in the business sector						Unit labour costs in the business sector					
	Per cent						*Per cent of business GDP*						*Percentage change*					
	Average 1981-83	Average 1991-93	2001	2002	2003	2004	Average 1981-83	Average 1991-93	2001	2002	2003	2004	Average 1981-90	Average 1991-00	2001	2002	2003	2004
Australia	5.9	7.0	6.2	5.8	5.6	5.5	46.4	44.7	45.9	45.3	46.0	45.8	6.9	0.9	2.1	1.3	3.0	1.7
Austria	2.5	5.0	4.9	4.9	5.0	5.0	58.1	54.8	53.0	52.7	52.2	52.1	2.1	0.6	2.1	0.5	0.5	0.4
Belgium	6.6	8.7	7.2	6.9	6.9	6.9	51.4	51.9	50.0	50.2	49.5	49.5	3.1	1.1	3.9	2.7	0.4	1.2
Canada	8.7	8.9	7.1	7.1	7.1	7.1	45.2	47.3	49.6	49.7	49.0	48.8	3.8	1.2	1.9	1.0	2.2	1.7
Czech Republic	..	..	..	..	..	..	..	45.1	46.0	47.4	47.6	47.3	..	6.6	5.0	5.6	3.8	3.2
Denmark	5.8	7.7	4.9	4.9	4.9	4.9	..	41.7	40.2	40.7	40.5	40.4	5.6	0.8	2.6	2.0	1.6	1.5
Finland	4.0	8.1	8.6	8.4	8.3	8.3	48.9	43.9	41.2	41.0	41.2	41.2	5.7	-0.8	6.3	0.4	1.8	0.9
France	5.7	10.0	9.3	9.2	9.1	9.0	52.3	45.0	42.6	42.5	42.3	42.1	3.8	0.3	3.1	1.9	1.0	0.6
Germany	4.3	6.6	7.3	7.3	7.3	7.3	53.6	52.3	52.7	52.4	52.9	53.1	1.7	1.3	1.7	0.8	1.3	0.3
Greece	5.0	8.5	9.8	9.7	9.6	9.4	55.1	46.2	43.3	41.2	40.4	39.7	..	..	..	..	..	..
Hungary	0.6	1.7	3.5	3.5	3.4	3.4	..	..	53.9	55.5	55.7	55.6	..	11.0	10.7	7.5	3.9	2.8
Iceland	13.0	14.1	6.4	5.9	5.7	5.5	48.4	52.6	42.0	40.8	40.5	40.0	31.8	3.5	6.2	8.6	3.2	2.8
Ireland	7.0	9.4	9.2	9.0	8.9	8.8	56.9	51.0	46.5	47.0	46.9	46.4	3.4	0.7	4.6	1.9	2.8	1.9
Italy	2.0	2.4	3.9	3.9	3.9	3.9	55.2	51.0	57.2	56.1	55.6	55.4	8.1	1.6	1.7	3.4	2.1	1.2
Japan	..	..	..	..	..	..	66.4	59.8	68.5	72.2	74.2	75.2	0.1	-0.6	-1.7	-3.3	-2.8	-2.1
Korea	..	..	..	..	..	..	..	..	47.8	50.2	51.0	50.6	4.6	2.8	3.7	6.3	2.8	2.4
Luxembourg	..	..	..	..	..	..	..	..	..	..	..	..	..	..	..	..	..	..
Mexico	..	..	..	..	..	..	..	..	..	..	..	..	24.8	16.7	9.2	6.2	4.4	3.4
Netherlands	5.7	6.8	4.0	3.7	3.6	3.5	46.9	46.8	46.7	47.0	47.1	46.8	0.6	1.5	5.7	5.4	2.6	0.9
New Zealand	2.2	7.5	5.4	5.4	5.4	5.4	48.2	44.7	41.9	41.9	42.2	42.0	7.1	0.8	0.7	1.1	1.6	1.9
Norway	2.2	5.1	3.6	3.6	3.6	3.6	40.5	37.0	32.8	34.2	34.3	34.0	6.7	1.6	5.5	4.4	3.8	2.1
Poland	..	..	..	..	..	..	..	51.3	43.0	42.0	41.5	41.4	..	12.5	-4.6	-1.5	-0.4	1.3
Portugal	6.1	4.6	3.8	3.8	3.8	3.8	..	..	49.0	48.7	48.3	48.2	14.4	4.5	6.0	3.6	2.5	1.4
Slovak Republic	..	..	..	..	..	..	..	..	34.5	35.1	35.2	35.8	..	5.7	5.3	3.8	7.1	7.0
Spain	8.8	13.4	11.5	11.3	11.0	10.7	54.1	49.6	48.5	47.8	47.6	47.5	7.7	3.4	4.2	3.2	2.8	2.4
Sweden	2.2	4.3	4.8	4.6	4.5	4.5	39.3	39.3	45.0	45.3	45.3	45.1	6.5	1.4	6.3	1.7	1.9	1.4
Switzerland	1.0	1.7	1.8	1.8	1.8	1.8	..	..	..	..	..	..	4.2	1.3	4.0	2.5	0.5	-0.1
Turkey	..	..	..	..	..	..	50.4	54.7	59.7	59.6	59.8	59.4	49.5	60.8	52.5	18.1	25.2	16.3
United Kingdom	5.3	7.6	5.5	5.3	5.2	5.1	50.4	49.7	50.9	49.6	49.5	49.4	5.4	2.4	3.5	2.8	2.2	1.6
United States	5.8	5.3	5.1	5.1	5.1	5.1	50.9	50.0	50.0	49.7	49.5	49.4	3.2	1.8	2.1	-1.5	1.4	1.0
Euro area	6.0	8.6	8.2	8.1	8.1	8.0	54.0	50.6	48.7	48.5	48.5	48.2	4.6	1.5	2.6	1.9	1.5	0.7
European Union	5.7	8.4	7.7	7.6	7.5	7.4	52.5	50.0	49.5	49.4	49.5	49.3	4.7	1.5	3.0	2.3	1.7	1.0
Total OECD	5.2	6.2	6.0	5.9	5.9	5.8	54.3	51.7	51.3	50.7	50.7	50.6	4.9	3.0	3.0	0.6	1.5	1.0

Note: The structural unemployment rate corresponds to NAIRU (Non Accelerating Inflation Rate of Unemployment). For more information about sources and definitions, see *OECD Economic Outlook* Sources and Methods *(http://www.oecd.org/eco/sources-and-methods)*.

Source: OECD.

Annex Table 24. **Household saving rates**

Per cent of disposable household income

	1985	1986	1987	1988	1989	1990	1991	1992	1993	1994	1995	1996	1997	1998	1999	2000	2001	2002	Projections 2003	2004
Australia	10.8	10.2	8.2	7.0	8.7	9.3	6.2	5.7	5.0	5.8	4.8	5.8	3.9	1.9	1.7	3.4	3.0	0.3	0.5	0.8
Austria	10.5	12.3	13.9	11.9	12.8	14.0	14.9	12.0	10.9	11.8	11.7	9.9	7.4	8.4	8.5	8.3	7.4	7.5	7.6	7.8
Belgium	15.9	18.5	16.9	17.0	15.3	18.0	17.9	19.0	19.4	19.3	18.8	17.0	15.7	14.5	14.1	13.4	13.0	13.7	13.8	14.1
Canada	15.8	13.4	11.9	12.3	13.0	13.0	13.3	13.0	11.9	9.5	9.2	7.0	4.9	4.9	4.1	4.8	4.6	4.4	3.8	4.5
Czech Republic	..	..	..	..	..	..	..	..	-1.1	-3.0	20.6	21.5	20.3	18.3	17.8	13.0	13.0	11.3	11.1	10.8
Denmark	..	..	..	7.4	8.4	11.2	10.8	9.7	8.3	4.2	6.9	5.6	3.6	5.0	1.4	4.8	6.0	6.2	6.0	6.1
Finland	3.4	2.1	3.8	-0.5	-0.3	2.2	7.2	9.5	6.9	1.8	5.2	0.9	2.5	0.7	1.8	-0.9	-0.9	-0.3	1.0	1.3
France	8.9	8.1	6.4	6.9	7.2	7.8	8.7	9.7	10.4	9.8	11.2	10.0	11.3	10.8	10.4	10.8	11.5	12.2	12.0	12.1
Germany	12.1	12.9	12.9	13.2	12.7	13.9	13.0	13.0	12.3	11.6	11.2	10.8	10.4	10.3	9.8	9.8	10.1	10.4	10.5	10.8
Italy	30.7	28.9	28.3	27.7	27.4	27.8	27.0	25.6	25.2	23.8	22.5	23.5	20.2	17.3	15.4	14.5	15.4	16.0	16.1	15.9
Japan	16.5	16.5	14.0	13.2	13.3	14.0	14.6	13.9	13.5	12.3	11.9	9.8	9.8	11.2	11.1	9.8	6.9	5.8	5.8	5.8
Korea	14.8	20.0	23.2	25.1	23.6	22.0	24.0	22.8	20.6	19.4	16.8	15.9	15.4	23.0	16.0	11.5	9.4	9.6	10.0	10.8
Netherlands	5.6	8.2	8.3	8.1	9.8	11.6	7.2	8.3	6.8	7.1	14.9	13.6	13.4	12.9	9.6	6.7	9.6	10.7	10.9	10.8
New Zealand	..	1.3	4.4	2.9	2.7	0.5	2.5	0.2	-0.6	-3.8	-3.6	-2.6	-4.6	-4.2	-5.3	-3.8	-1.7	-0.3	-2.5	-3.1
Norway	-3.3	-6.2	-6.2	-2.8	-0.4	0.8	2.9	5.0	6.1	5.2	4.6	2.2	2.8	5.8	5.5	4.5	3.7	7.0	5.5	5.9
Portugal	..	..	..	..	..	..	..	..	..	..	13.6	11.8	10.3	9.9	8.6	9.5	10.7	11.9	12.2	12.1
Spain	11.1	12.1	10.6	11.0	10.2	12.3	13.4	11.9	14.3	11.9	14.4	14.2	13.4	12.2	11.1	10.6	10.2	10.1	10.4	10.2
Sweden	3.2	1.9	-2.6	-4.5	-4.4	0.0	3.4	8.0	10.7	11.1	8.3	7.1	4.9	2.5	3.3	2.4	5.2	8.2	7.2	6.8
Switzerland	..	..	..	..	..	8.7	9.9	10.1	10.8	9.1	9.4	8.7	10.1	8.6	8.9	8.3	8.7	9.0	9.1	9.1
United Kingdom	9.8	8.2	6.4	4.9	6.6	8.0	10.0	11.4	10.8	9.3	10.0	9.1	9.5	6.0	5.3	4.3	5.5	5.2	5.5	5.8
United States	9.2	8.2	7.3	7.8	7.5	7.8	8.3	8.7	7.1	6.1	5.6	4.8	4.2	4.7	2.6	2.8	2.3	3.7	4.6	4.8

Note: The adoption of new national account systems, SNA93 or ESA95, has been proceeding at an uneven pace among OECD member countries, both with respect to variables and the time period covered. As a consequence, there are breaks in many national series. See Table "National Account Reporting Systems and Base-years" at the beginning of the Statistical Annex and *OECD Economic Outlook* Sources and Methods *(http://www.oecd.org/eco/sources-and-methods).* Countries differ in the way household disposable income is reported (in particular whether private pension benefits less pension contributions are included in disposable income or not), but the calculation of household saving is adjusted for this difference. Most countries are reporting household saving on a net basis (i.e. excluding consumption of fixed capital by households and unincorporated businesses). Five countries, Belgium, Denmark, Italy, Spain and the United Kingdom are reporting gross household saving. In most countries the households saving include saving by non-profit institutions (in some cases referred to as personal saving). Other countries (Czech Republic, Finland, France, Japan and New Zealand) report saving of households only.

Source: OECD.

Annex Table 25. Gross national saving
Per cent of nominal GDP

	1983	1984	1985	1986	1987	1988	1989	1990	1991	1992	1993	1994	1995	1996	1997	1998	1999	2000	2001
Australia	20.2	20.0	18.9	19.4	21.3	22.6	21.7	18.1	16.2	17.2	18.6	17.5	17.8	18.9	19.0	18.6	19.3	18.7	19.1
Austria	22.2	23.2	23.1	23.2	23.3	23.9	24.4	25.0	24.8	23.9	22.4	22.3	21.6	21.4	21.3	21.8	21.3	22.0	21.3
Belgium	16.4	17.8	17.9	19.0	19.8	22.5	23.6	23.9	23.1	23.5	24.6	25.9	25.8	24.6	25.7	25.7	26.0	25.9	24.8
Canada	20.0	20.8	20.2	18.8	20.0	20.8	20.1	17.6	14.9	13.6	14.2	16.5	18.6	19.1	19.9	19.4	21.3	24.2	22.7
Czech Republic	..	..	..	..	..	..	..	..	..	27.9	28.1	27.3	29.9	27.4	26.1	27.8	25.4	24.4	..
Denmark	15.5	17.1	17.4	18.3	18.6	19.2	19.5	20.7	20.0	20.3	19.2	19.1	20.4	20.4	21.2	20.8	21.5	22.8	23.5
Finland	25.7	27.0	25.8	25.2	25.0	27.8	27.9	25.8	16.5	13.0	14.1	18.4	22.3	21.5	24.7	26.0	25.8	27.7	27.9
France	18.6	18.3	18.1	19.4	19.6	20.8	21.6	21.5	20.9	20.5	19.0	19.2	19.5	19.2	20.4	21.4	22.3	22.1	21.4
Germany	..	..	..	..	..	..	..	..	23.3	23.1	21.9	21.9	21.8	21.3	21.4	21.5	20.8	20.8	19.8
Greece	21.9	23.0	22.6	22.4	18.9	21.3	19.0	19.1	20.7	20.0	18.5	19.4	18.0	17.4	17.9	17.8	18.1	18.6	18.6
Iceland	19.8	17.6	15.8	18.8	16.5	16.2	16.2	17.3	16.7	16.6	18.2	18.4	17.7	17.8	18.4	17.7	15.2	13.9	17.8
Ireland	14.3	14.1	13.5	13.4	14.5	14.7	15.0	18.0	17.7	15.6	17.7	18.0	20.8	22.3	24.2	25.7	24.6	25.0	23.4
Italy	23.1	23.1	22.6	22.4	21.9	21.8	21.0	20.7	19.6	18.3	19.2	19.7	21.6	21.9	21.6	21.2	20.7	20.0	20.0
Japan	30.3	31.2	32.0	32.2	32.8	33.6	33.6	33.6	34.4	33.6	32.1	30.3	29.4	29.7	29.9	29.0	27.8	27.7	26.4
Korea	28.8	30.6	30.6	34.6	38.4	40.7	37.6	37.6	37.4	36.5	36.2	35.6	35.4	33.7	33.3	33.7	32.6	32.2	29.8
Mexico	28.4	25.7	25.8	19.1	24.5	21.3	20.3	20.3	18.7	16.6	15.1	14.8	19.3	22.5	24.0	20.5	20.5	20.4	..
Netherlands	24.0	25.2	25.7	25.8	23.8	25.6	27.2	26.0	25.4	24.5	24.6	26.3	27.4	26.7	27.9	25.2	26.6	27.6	25.3
New Zealand	18.8	19.1	18.6	18.9	18.0	18.6	17.8	16.2	13.0	13.9	16.6	17.3	17.2	16.4	15.7	15.4	14.2	15.6	..
Norway	28.5	30.6	29.8	25.0	25.3	24.9	25.8	25.3	24.7	23.7	23.8	24.8	26.4	28.4	30.1	27.3	29.1	36.4	35.1
Poland	..	..	..	..	..	..	..	..	13.6	13.4	14.2	18.9	20.4	19.9	20.2	21.4	20.2	19.1	..
Portugal	8.2	7.5	8.7	10.6	11.9	11.6	12.4	11.1	8.6	8.0	5.0	4.1	4.7	3.8	3.7	4.3	3.1	1.5	1.0
Spain	19.5	21.2	21.9	22.9	22.6	23.5	22.9	22.9	22.3	20.5	20.5	20.0	22.3	22.0	22.5	22.4	22.4	22.4	22.7
Sweden	16.7	17.9	17.6	17.9	18.0	18.4	18.8	17.8	16.5	14.9	14.0	17.7	20.9	20.1	20.5	21.1	21.7	22.5	22.3
Switzerland	27.4	30.0	30.4	30.0	29.8	31.8	32.5	32.3	30.2	28.4	28.9	27.9	28.5	27.9	30.3	30.7	31.4	34.2	..
Turkey	15.5	16.3	20.7	23.9	24.3	28.9	26.4	21.5	17.7	18.5	18.7	18.9	20.1	22.6	21.6	20.6	13.7	15.2	12.6
United Kingdom	17.7	18.2	18.2	17.3	17.3	17.2	17.1	16.2	15.3	14.0	13.9	15.5	15.7	15.6	16.9	17.6	15.5	15.3	15.4
United States	16.3	18.5	17.2	15.4	15.9	17.2	16.7	15.9	16.1	15.1	15.0	15.8	16.4	16.7	17.6	18.3	17.9	18.0	16.1
European Union	19.6	20.1	20.0	20.3	20.1	20.8	20.8	20.5	20.4	19.6	19.1	19.7	20.4	20.2	20.7	20.9	20.5	20.5	20.0
Total OECD	20.6	21.8	21.4	20.7	21.3	22.2	21.9	21.2	21.0	20.1	19.7	20.0	20.7	20.8	21.4	21.5	21.0	21.1	19.8

Note: Based on SNA93 or ESA95 except for Switzerland and Turkey that report on SNA68 basis.
Source: OECD.

Annex Table 26. General government total outlays

Per cent of nominal GDP

	1985	1986	1987	1988	1989	1990	1991	1992	1993	1994	1995	1996	1997	1998	1999	2000	2001	2002	Projections	
																			2003	2004
Australia	40.0	40.0	38.7	36.0	35.2	36.0	37.3	39.2	39.4	38.7	38.8	38.3	37.2	36.7	36.1	36.0	37.0	36.0	36.0	35.7
Austria	54.7	55.7	56.0	55.2	53.6	53.1	54.2	54.9	57.9	57.4	57.3	56.8	54.1	54.1	54.0	52.3	52.1	51.9	52.3	51.8
Belgium	59.8	58.9	57.0	55.0	53.4	53.4	54.4	54.7	55.6	53.3	52.8	53.0	51.4	50.7	50.1	49.4	50.2	50.2	49.8	49.5
Canada	48.3	47.6	46.1	45.4	45.8	48.8	52.3	53.3	52.2	49.7	48.5	46.6	44.3	44.4	42.3	41.2	41.7	40.6	40.3	40.1
Czech Republic [a]	..	..	..	..	..	..	..	54.6	70.2	49.9	60.4	50.7	46.5	47.9	46.6	46.9	42.6	45.3	46.6	46.1
Denmark	57.3	53.7	55.4	57.2	57.3	57.0	57.8	59.0	61.7	61.6	60.3	59.8	58.0	57.6	56.3	54.8	55.3	55.3	55.0	54.2
Finland	47.0	48.0	48.5	47.1	45.2	48.8	57.9	63.2	64.4	62.9	59.4	59.5	56.3	52.8	52.1	48.9	49.0	49.2	50.0	49.9
France	53.3	52.7	51.9	51.4	50.4	50.7	51.5	53.0	55.3	54.9	55.2	55.5	55.0	53.8	53.6	52.7	53.0	54.0	54.6	54.1
Germany [b]	46.3	45.4	45.8	45.3	44.0	44.5	47.1	48.1	49.3	49.0	49.4	50.3	49.3	48.8	48.8	45.9	48.3	48.6	49.3	48.8
Greece	47.0	46.1	46.3	44.5	46.2	50.5	47.0	49.1	51.4	49.4	49.4	47.7	46.4	46.6	46.5	48.9	47.0	46.3	45.9	45.4
Hungary	..	..	..	..	..	..	56.7	60.3	59.8	63.4	56.9	53.9	54.9	56.7	51.8	49.1	50.9	52.2	49.0	48.7
Iceland	38.6	40.7	37.6	42.7	45.2	42.5	43.8	44.8	44.7	44.5	43.8	43.4	41.8	42.5	43.5	43.1	43.6	44.6	44.8	44.6
Ireland	54.0	53.9	51.4	48.7	42.5	43.2	44.8	45.2	45.1	44.3	41.5	39.6	37.1	35.0	34.7	31.9	33.5	34.4	34.6	34.5
Italy	50.9	51.4	50.8	51.5	52.9	54.3	55.5	56.7	57.7	54.6	53.4	53.2	51.1	49.9	48.9	46.9	48.5	47.7	47.1	46.7
Japan [c]	31.0	31.2	31.7	31.1	30.5	32.1	31.8	32.8	34.7	35.1	36.1	36.6	35.4	36.5	38.1	38.6	38.0	38.6	38.8	39.1
Korea	19.8	18.8	17.8	17.9	18.9	19.5	20.7	21.9	21.3	20.9	20.6	22.0	22.9	25.6	24.6	24.4	24.6	24.6	27.4	27.5
Luxembourg	..	..	..	..	..	43.3	44.5	45.5	45.8	44.5	45.5	45.5	43.3	42.1	41.7	39.6	40.2	46.1	49.7	50.0
Netherlands [d]	57.3	57.0	58.6	56.8	54.6	54.8	54.9	55.7	55.8	53.5	51.4	49.6	48.2	47.2	46.9	45.3	46.4	47.3	47.4	47.0
New Zealand	..	..	..	..	..	..	45.2	44.9	41.4	39.2	38.4	37.4	38.0	38.9	37.9	37.2	36.1	36.5	37.0	37.1
Norway	46.0	50.0	52.2	54.0	53.5	54.1	54.9	56.3	55.1	54.1	51.6	49.2	47.3	49.7	48.3	43.5	44.2	46.7	47.1	47.3
Poland	..	..	..	..	..	..	53.4	54.9	54.3	49.4	47.2	46.2	45.6	43.8	43.4	40.7	42.4	43.2	43.9	43.6
Portugal	40.8	41.3	40.0	38.5	38.8	42.1	45.1	46.2	47.8	46.0	45.0	45.8	44.8	44.1	45.3	45.2	46.3	46.1	46.1	45.4
Slovak Republic	..	..	..	..	..	..	..	..	..	58.2	57.0	61.2	63.0	60.1	56.7	58.8	53.1	50.6	48.2	46.5
Spain	43.1	42.6	41.1	40.9	42.3	43.4	44.9	45.9	49.4	47.3	45.0	43.7	42.2	41.7	40.9	40.2	39.9	39.8	39.9	39.8
Sweden	63.7	62.0	58.3	58.6	58.6	59.4	62.3	67.5	73.0	70.9	67.6	65.2	63.1	60.7	60.2	57.4	56.9	58.3	58.8	58.4
United Kingdom	45.9	44.8	43.6	41.1	40.5	42.2	44.0	45.7	45.7	45.0	44.6	43.0	41.1	39.8	39.1	37.0	40.4	40.9	41.7	42.2
United States [e]	36.5	37.0	36.7	35.8	35.6	36.5	37.2	38.0	37.5	36.5	36.4	35.9	34.8	34.0	33.7	33.6	34.9	35.6	36.1	35.8
Euro area	49.5	49.1	48.8	48.3	47.8	48.9	50.3	51.4	53.1	51.9	51.5	51.6	50.3	49.4	49.0	47.2	48.2	48.4	48.7	48.2
European Union	49.6	49.1	48.5	47.9	47.4	48.3	49.9	51.2	52.7	51.5	50.9	50.6	49.2	48.2	47.8	46.0	47.4	47.7	48.0	47.7
Total OECD	40.6	40.6	40.3	39.5	39.2	40.3	41.6	42.8	43.4	42.4	42.2	41.9	40.7	40.2	40.0	39.3	40.2	40.7	41.1	40.9

Note: Total outlays are defined as current outlays plus net capital outlays. Data refer to the general government sector, which is a consolidation of accounts for the central, state and local governments plus social security. One-off revenues from the sale of mobile telephone licenses are recorded as negative capital outlays for countries listed in the note to Table 28. See *OECD Economic Outlook* Sources and Methods (http://www.oecd.org/eco/sources-and-methods).

a) In 1993 and 1995 data reflect the large privatisation campaign which transferred some public enterprises to private ownership through vouchers distributed to the population. Data are based on ESA95 basis prior to 2001 and on the IMF methodology used for Government Finance Statistics from 2001 on.

b) The 1995 outlays are net of the debt taken on this year from the Inherited Debt funds.

c) The 1998 outlays would be 5.2 percentage points of GDP higher if account were taken of the assumption by the central government of the debt of the Japan Railway Settlement Corporation and the National Forest Special Account. The 2000 outlays include capital transfers to the Deposit Insurance Company.

c) The 1995 outlays would be 4.9 percentage points of GDP higher if capital transfers to a housing agency offering rentals to low income people were taken into account.

e) These data include outlays net of operating surpluses of public enterprises.

Source: OECD.

Annex Table 27. **General government total tax and non-tax receipts**

Per cent of nominal GDP

	1985	1986	1987	1988	1989	1990	1991	1992	1993	1994	1995	1996	1997	1998	1999	2000	2001	2002	Projections 2003	2004
Australia	34.9	35.8	36.5	35.7	34.8	34.2	33.5	33.2	33.9	34.1	35.0	36.1	36.7	37.3	37.2	36.3	36.3	35.9	36.2	36.2
Austria	52.1	51.9	51.6	51.7	50.5	50.6	51.2	52.9	53.7	52.4	52.0	52.8	52.1	51.7	51.7	50.8	52.3	51.3	51.0	50.7
Belgium	49.6	48.8	49.1	47.7	45.7	46.6	46.9	46.6	48.3	48.3	48.5	49.2	49.5	50.0	49.6	49.5	49.8	50.2	49.8	49.7
Canada	39.5	40.4	40.6	41.0	41.2	42.9	43.9	44.2	43.5	43.0	43.1	43.8	44.5	44.5	44.1	44.2	43.5	41.9	41.4	41.1
Czech Republic[a]	..	..	..	..	..	..	..	50.3	47.0	46.4	48.0	48.9	44.1	43.3	42.9	42.8	39.9	40.8	40.3	39.9
Denmark	55.8	57.0	57.9	58.7	57.6	56.0	55.4	56.8	58.9	59.1	58.0	58.8	58.3	58.7	59.5	57.3	58.1	57.1	56.7	56.1
Finland	50.2	51.5	49.7	51.9	51.7	53.9	56.6	57.4	56.9	57.0	55.5	56.5	55.1	54.3	54.1	55.9	54.2	54.0	53.1	52.8
France	50.3	49.5	49.9	48.9	48.6	48.6	49.1	48.8	49.3	49.4	49.7	51.4	52.0	51.2	51.8	51.3	51.4	50.9	51.0	50.9
Germany	45.1	44.3	44.1	43.3	44.1	42.5	44.1	45.5	46.2	46.6	46.1	46.9	46.6	46.6	47.3	47.0	45.5	45.0	45.6	45.5
Greece	35.4	36.5	36.7	33.1	32.0	34.7	35.6	36.5	37.8	39.5	39.3	40.3	42.4	44.1	44.7	47.0	45.6	45.1	44.9	44.7
Hungary	..	36.6	36.7	..	40.7	39.2	53.8	53.2	53.2	52.4	49.3	48.1	46.6	47.5	46.7	46.2	45.7	43.8	43.5	43.7
Iceland	36.9	36.6	36.7	40.6	40.8	40.4	40.9	41.9	40.1	39.7	40.8	41.7	41.8	43.0	45.9	45.6	44.1	44.9	44.8	44.7
Ireland	43.6	43.7	43.3	44.4	40.8	40.4	42.0	42.3	42.3	42.4	39.4	39.4	38.6	37.2	36.7	36.4	35.2	34.1	33.8	33.3
Italy	38.2	39.2	39.0	40.2	41.1	42.6	43.8	46.0	47.4	45.3	45.8	46.1	48.4	46.8	47.1	46.2	45.8	45.2	44.7	43.9
Japan[b]	30.4	30.6	32.0	32.2	32.3	34.1	33.7	33.6	32.2	31.4	31.4	31.6	31.6	31.0	30.9	31.1	31.9	31.4	31.1	31.3
Korea	20.9	20.4	20.4	21.5	22.4	23.0	22.5	23.3	23.7	24.0	24.8	25.8	26.5	27.5	27.7	30.5	30.0	30.5	30.9	31.4
Luxembourg	..	..	..	..	..	48.2	45.7	46.3	47.4	47.3	47.6	47.4	46.5	45.1	45.2	45.7	46.6	48.7	50.0	49.0
Netherlands	54.1	52.5	53.4	52.6	49.6	49.5	52.2	51.5	53.0	50.1	47.3	47.8	47.1	46.4	47.6	47.4	46.5	46.2	45.8	45.0
New Zealand	..	..	..	..	..	..	41.7	41.8	40.9	42.3	41.3	40.3	39.6	39.3	38.2	38.1	37.9	37.8	37.8	37.6
Norway	55.7	55.7	56.6	56.4	55.2	56.5	55.0	54.4	53.7	54.4	55.0	55.6	55.1	53.2	54.4	58.5	59.0	59.5	58.4	58.1
Poland	..	..	..	..	..	..	44.2	47.8	49.9	45.9	44.7	43.3	42.9	41.5	41.5	37.7	37.2	37.5	37.7	37.7
Portugal	31.7	33.4	32.8	34.8	35.7	35.5	37.5	41.5	39.7	38.3	39.6	41.0	41.2	41.0	42.4	42.3	42.1	43.5	43.0	42.7
Slovak Republic	..	..	..	..	..	..	..	..	..	54.8	54.5	53.4	57.5	55.4	50.3	48.1	45.8	43.4	42.1	41.4
Spain	36.1	36.6	38.0	37.8	39.6	39.6	40.3	42.3	42.5	40.8	38.4	38.8	39.0	39.1	39.7	39.6	39.8	39.8	39.6	39.6
Sweden	59.9	60.7	62.1	61.5	63.3	63.1	60.4	59.9	61.4	60.4	60.2	62.3	61.3	62.9	61.6	60.8	61.5	59.3	59.6	59.6
United Kingdom	43.0	42.3	41.8	41.6	41.3	40.7	40.9	39.3	37.7	38.2	38.9	38.6	38.9	40.1	40.3	40.9	41.1	39.6	39.8	40.0
United States[c]	31.4	31.7	32.4	32.2	32.4	32.1	32.2	32.2	32.5	32.9	33.3	33.7	33.9	34.3	34.4	35.1	34.4	32.2	31.6	31.6
Euro area	44.4	44.2	44.3	43.9	44.0	44.3	45.2	46.3	47.3	46.8	46.5	47.3	47.7	47.1	47.6	47.2	46.6	46.1	46.1	45.8
European Union	44.7	44.4	44.5	44.3	44.4	44.3	45.2	45.8	46.3	45.8	45.6	46.2	46.6	46.5	46.9	46.7	46.3	45.7	45.7	45.5
Total OECD	36.4	36.5	37.0	36.9	37.1	37.3	37.8	38.2	38.3	38.1	38.2	38.6	38.9	38.9	39.0	39.3	38.9	37.7	37.5	37.4

Note: Data refer to the general government sector, which is a consolidation of accounts for the central, state and local governments. Non-tax receipts include operating surpluses of public enterprises, property income, fees, charges, sales, fines, capital tranfers received by the general government, etc. See *OECD Economic Outlook* Sources and Methods (*http://www.oecd.org/eco/sources-and-methods*).
a) Data are based on ESA95 basis prior to 2001 and on the IMF methodology used for Government Finance Statistics from 2001 on.
b) Includes deferred tax payments on postal savings accounts in 2000, 2001 and 2002.
c) Excludes the operating surpluses of public enterprises.
Source: OECD.

Annex Table 28. General government financial balances

Surplus (+) or deficit (−) as a percentage of nominal GDP

	1985	1986	1987	1988	1989	1990	1991	1992	1993	1994	1995	1996	1997	1998	1999	2000	2001	2002	Projections 2003	2004
Australia	-5.1	-4.2	-2.2	-0.3	-0.3	-1.8	-3.8	-6.0	-5.5	-4.6	-3.7	-2.2	-0.5	0.6	1.1	0.3	-0.6	-0.1	0.2	0.5
Austria	-2.6	-3.8	-4.4	-3.5	-3.1	-2.4	-3.0	-2.0	-4.2	-5.0	-5.3	-4.0	-2.0	-2.4	-2.3	-1.5	0.2	-0.6	-1.3	-1.1
Belgium	-10.2	-10.1	-7.9	-7.3	-7.7	-6.8	-7.5	-8.1	-7.3	-5.0	-4.3	-3.8	-2.0	-0.7	-0.5	0.1	0.4	0.0	0.0	0.2
Canada	-8.9	-7.2	-5.4	-4.3	-4.6	-5.9	-8.4	-9.1	-8.7	-6.7	-5.3	-2.8	0.2	0.1	1.7	3.1	1.8	1.3	1.1	1.0
Czech Republic[a]	..	..	..	..	..	..	..	-4.4	-23.2	-3.4	-12.3	-1.9	-2.4	-4.7	-3.7	-4.0	-2.8	-4.5	-6.3	-6.2
Denmark	-1.4	3.3	2.5	1.5	0.3	-1.0	-2.4	-2.2	-2.9	-2.4	-2.3	-1.0	0.4	1.1	3.2	2.5	2.8	1.8	1.6	1.9
Finland	3.2	3.6	1.3	4.8	6.5	5.1	-1.4	-5.8	-7.5	-5.9	-3.9	-3.0	-1.3	1.5	2.0	6.9	5.1	4.7	3.1	2.9
France	-3.0	-3.2	-2.0	-2.5	-1.8	-2.1	-2.4	-4.2	-6.0	-5.5	-5.5	-4.1	-3.0	-2.7	-1.8	-1.4	-1.5	-3.2	-3.6	-3.3
Germany	-1.1	-1.1	-1.8	-2.0	0.1	-2.0	-2.9	-2.6	-3.1	-2.4	-3.3	-3.4	-2.7	-2.2	-1.5	1.1	-2.8	-3.6	-3.7	-3.3
Greece	-11.6	-9.6	-9.6	-11.4	-14.2	-15.9	-11.4	-12.6	-13.6	-9.9	-10.2	-7.4	-4.0	-2.5	-1.8	-1.9	-1.4	-1.2	-1.0	-0.7
Hungary	..	..	..	..	..	..	-3.0	-7.1	-6.6	-11.0	-7.6	-5.9	-8.3	-9.3	-5.2	-2.9	-5.2	-8.4	-5.6	-5.0
Iceland	-1.7	-4.1	-0.9	-2.0	-4.6	-3.3	-3.0	-2.9	-4.6	-4.8	-3.0	-1.6	0.0	0.5	2.4	2.5	0.5	0.2	0.0	0.1
Ireland	-10.3	-10.2	-8.2	-4.2	-1.7	-2.8	-2.9	-3.0	-2.7	-2.0	-2.1	-0.1	1.4	2.3	2.0	4.5	1.6	-0.3	-0.8	-1.2
Italy[b]	-12.7	-12.2	-11.8	-11.3	-11.7	-11.8	-11.7	-10.7	-10.3	-9.3	-7.6	-7.1	-2.7	-3.1	-1.8	-0.7	-2.7	-2.5	-2.4	-2.8
Japan[b]	-0.6	-0.7	0.3	1.1	1.8	2.0	1.8	0.8	-2.4	-3.7	-4.7	-5.0	-3.8	-5.5	-7.2	-7.4	-6.1	-7.1	-7.7	-7.8
Korea	1.2	1.6	2.7	3.6	3.5	3.5	1.8	1.4	2.5	3.1	4.2	3.8	3.6	1.9	3.1	6.2	5.3	6.0	3.4	3.9
Luxembourg	..	..	..	..	3.5	4.9	1.2	0.8	1.6	2.8	2.1	1.9	3.2	3.0	3.5	6.1	6.4	2.6	0.2	-1.0
Netherlands	-3.2	-4.5	-5.3	-4.2	-5.0	-5.3	-2.7	-4.2	-2.8	-3.5	-4.2	-1.8	-1.1	-0.8	0.7	2.2	0.1	-1.1	-1.6	-2.0
New Zealand	..	-6.4	-2.1	-4.6	-3.4	-4.6	-3.5	-3.1	-0.4	3.1	2.9	2.8	1.6	0.4	0.2	0.9	1.8	1.3	0.8	0.5
Norway	9.7	5.6	4.4	2.5	1.8	2.5	0.1	-1.9	-1.5	0.3	3.4	6.5	7.8	3.6	6.1	15.0	14.8	12.8	11.3	10.7
Poland	..	..	..	..	..	..	-6.5	-6.7	-2.8	-2.4	-2.5	-2.9	-2.8	-2.3	-2.0	-3.0	-5.1	-5.7	-6.2	-5.9
Portugal	-9.1	-7.9	-7.2	-3.8	-3.1	-6.6	-7.6	-4.8	-8.1	-7.7	-5.5	-4.8	-3.6	-3.2	-2.9	-2.9	-4.3	-2.7	-3.2	-2.7
Slovak Republic	..	..	..	..	..	..	..	..	..	-5.7	-2.5	-7.8	-5.5	-4.7	-6.4	-10.7	-7.3	-7.2	-6.2	-5.1
Spain	-7.0	-6.0	-3.1	-3.1	-2.6	-3.9	-4.6	-3.7	-6.9	-6.5	-6.6	-4.9	-3.2	-2.7	-1.1	-0.6	-0.1	-0.1	-0.4	-0.2
Sweden	-3.7	-1.3	3.8	2.9	4.7	3.7	-1.9	-7.6	-11.6	-10.5	-7.4	-2.9	-1.7	2.3	1.3	3.4	4.6	1.1	0.7	1.2
United Kingdom[c]	-2.9	-2.6	-1.8	0.5	0.8	-1.6	-3.1	-6.4	-7.9	-6.7	-5.8	-4.4	-2.2	0.2	1.1	3.9	0.8	-1.3	-1.9	-2.2
United States[c]	-5.1	-5.3	-4.3	-3.6	-3.2	-4.3	-5.0	-5.9	-5.0	-3.6	-3.1	-2.2	-0.9	0.3	0.7	1.4	-0.5	-3.4	-4.6	-4.2
Euro area	-5.0	-4.9	-4.6	-4.4	-4.2	-4.7	-5.1	-5.1	-5.8	-5.1	-5.0	-4.3	-2.6	-2.3	-1.3	0.1	-1.6	-2.3	-2.5	-2.4
European Union	-4.9	-4.6	-4.0	-3.6	-3.0	-4.1	-4.7	-5.4	-6.4	-5.7	-5.4	-4.3	-2.5	-1.7	-0.8	0.7	-1.1	-2.0	-2.3	-2.2
Total OECD	-4.2	-4.1	-3.3	-2.6	-2.1	-3.0	-3.8	-4.6	-5.2	-4.3	-4.1	-3.2	-1.8	-1.4	-1.0	0.0	-1.3	-2.9	-3.6	-3.5

Memorandum items

General government financial balances excluding social security

	1985	1986	1987	1988	1989	1990	1991	1992	1993	1994	1995	1996	1997	1998	1999	2000	2001	2002	Projections 2003	2004
United States	-5.3	-5.4	-4.8	-4.4	-4.2	-5.4	-5.9	-6.7	-5.7	-4.5	-3.9	-3.1	-2.0	-0.9	-0.7	-0.1	-2.1	-5.0	-6.1	-5.8
Japan[d]	-3.1	-3.5	-2.5	-2.0	-1.4	-1.4	-0.8	-1.7	-4.7	-5.7	-6.6	-6.8	-5.5	-6.8	-8.2	-7.9	-6.2	-7.2	-7.7	-7.8

Note: Financial balances include one-off revenues from the sale of the mobile telephone licenses where reported revenues are substantial: *i.e.* Australia (2000-2001), Austria (2000), Belgium (2001), Denmark (2001), France (2001-2002), Germany (2000), Greece (2001), Italy (2002), Netherlands (2000), New Zealand (2001), Portugal (2000), Spain (2000) and the United Kingdom (2000). Finally, being on a national account basis, the government financial balance may differ from the numbers reported to the European Commission under the Excessive Deficit Procedure for some EU countries and for some years. See *OECD Economic Outlook Sources and Methods (http://www.oecd.org/eco/sources-and-methods)*.
a) In 1993 and 1995 data reflect the large privatisation campaign which transferred some public enterprises to private ownership through vouchers distributed to the population. Data are based on ESA95 basis prior to 2001 and on the IMF methodology used for Government Finance Statistics from 2001 on.
b) Deferred tax payments on postal savings accounts are included in 2000, 2001 and 2002. The 2000 outlays include capital transfers to the Deposit Insurance Company.
c) The general government sector includes public enterprises.
d) From 1991 onwards data are based on SNA93 and thus exclude private pension funds.
Source: OECD.

Annex Table 29. **Cyclically-adjusted general government balances**

Surplus (+) or deficit (-) as a per cent of potential GDP

	1985	1986	1987	1988	1989	1990	1991	1992	1993	1994	1995	1996	1997	1998	1999	2000	2001	2002	Projections 2003	2004
Australia	-5.3	-3.8	-2.1	-0.5	-0.3	-0.9	-2.4	-4.5	-4.5	-4.1	-3.4	-2.0	-0.4	0.4	0.7	0.0	-0.8	-0.1	0.5	0.8
Austria	-1.6	-2.9	-3.4	-3.0	-3.1	-3.0	-3.6	-2.4	-4.0	-4.8	-5.0	-3.7	-1.8	-2.6	-2.6	-2.4	0.3	-0.1	-0.6	-0.4
Belgium	-7.8	-7.7	-6.1	-7.2	-8.4	-7.9	-8.0	-7.9	-5.2	-3.5	-3.0	-1.8	-1.1	0.0	-0.4	-0.7	0.5	1.2	1.6	1.7
Canada	-9.0	-7.3	-6.2	-6.0	-6.1	-6.4	-6.8	-7.0	-6.8	-6.0	-4.8	-1.8	0.8	0.5	1.4	2.4	1.8	1.3	1.1	0.9
Denmark	-3.1	0.4	0.7	0.4	0.3	-0.5	-1.6	-0.7	-0.1	-2.2	-2.2	-1.1	-0.2	0.6	2.5	1.6	2.4	2.1	2.2	2.2
Finland	3.8	4.3	1.0	3.3	3.6	3.1	1.9	0.8	1.0	1.0	1.1	0.8	0.2	1.9	2.3	5.5	5.1	5.3	3.9	3.2
France	-1.3	-1.7	-0.8	-2.2	-2.3	-2.9	-2.8	-4.4	-5.1	-4.7	-4.7	-2.9	-1.7	-1.9	-1.5	-1.9	-2.0	-3.1	-3.0	-2.9
Germany	-0.1	-0.6	-1.2	-2.2	-0.4	-3.5	-3.6	-3.4	-2.3	-1.8	-2.9	-2.7	-1.9	-1.7	-1.2	-1.9	-2.8	-3.0	-2.5	-2.2
Greece	-10.7	-8.8	-7.5	-10.7	-14.7	-15.7	-11.7	-12.4	-11.8	-8.3	-8.5	-5.9	-3.1	-1.2	-0.7	-1.4	-2.0	-1.6	-1.4	-1.2
Iceland	-0.7	-4.2	-2.8	-2.9	-4.6	-3.2	-1.8	0.3	-1.4	-2.8	-0.7	-0.5	0.2	-0.1	1.6	0.9	-1.1	0.0	0.0	-0.2
Ireland	-9.6	-8.0	-6.5	-3.5	-1.8	-4.3	-3.1	-2.3	-1.0	-0.1	-1.2	0.5	1.1	2.1	0.9	2.5	-0.2	-2.3	-1.8	-1.9
Italy	-11.5	-11.3	-11.2	-11.6	-12.5	-12.5	-12.1	-10.4	-8.7	-8.1	-7.1	-6.4	-2.2	-2.6	-1.2	-1.9	-2.6	-1.7	-1.4	-2.1
Japan [a]	-0.3	-0.2	0.8	1.0	1.4	1.3	1.4	0.5	-2.4	-3.5	-4.5	-5.4	-4.3	-5.5	-6.9	-7.5	-5.9	-6.7	-7.2	-7.2
Netherlands	-2.5	-4.0	-4.2	-3.4	-6.0	-7.5	-4.5	-5.2	-2.7	-3.4	-4.4	-2.1	-1.7	-1.9	-1.1	-0.3	-0.7	-0.5	0.0	-0.4
New Zealand	..	-8.1	-3.1	-4.5	-3.1	-3.1	-0.4	0.2	1.0	2.8	2.3	2.1	1.5	1.7	0.7	0.6	1.5	0.7	0.4	0.4
Norway [b]	4.5	5.9	5.2	5.6	5.4	4.0	-3.9	-6.0	-6.2	-4.9	-1.8	-1.7	-1.5	-3.0	-2.0	-0.9	-0.2	-0.6	-0.9	-1.0
Portugal	-3.8	-3.5	-3.9	-3.2	-3.1	-6.1	-9.4	-5.7	-7.3	-6.3	-4.8	-4.5	-3.6	-3.7	-3.5	-4.1	-4.6	-2.3	-2.1	-1.7
Spain	-5.2	-4.1	-2.1	-3.0	-3.1	-4.7	-5.2	-3.5	-5.2	-4.7	-4.9	-3.1	-1.8	-2.0	-0.9	-1.1	-0.1	0.2	0.2	0.3
Sweden	-4.6	-2.9	1.4	0.0	1.7	1.5	-2.0	-5.1	-6.7	-7.1	-5.4	-0.5	0.3	3.2	0.9	2.0	4.2	1.0	1.2	1.2
United Kingdom	-1.5	-2.5	-2.9	-1.9	-1.4	-2.8	-2.1	-4.1	-5.5	-5.5	-4.9	-3.7	-2.0	0.2	1.2	1.3	0.9	-0.8	-1.2	-1.5
United States	-4.8	-5.0	-4.2	-3.9	-3.7	-4.5	-4.3	-5.3	-4.4	-3.5	-2.9	-2.2	-1.2	-0.2	0.1	0.9	-0.2	-2.9	-4.0	-3.9
Euro area	-3.6	-3.8	-3.7	-4.5	-4.5	-5.9	-5.8	-5.3	-4.5	-4.1	-4.3	-3.3	-1.8	-1.8	-1.2	-1.5	-1.8	-1.9	-1.6	-1.6
European Union	-3.6	-3.8	-3.5	-4.0	-3.8	-5.2	-5.0	-5.1	-4.9	-4.6	-4.6	-3.4	-1.8	-1.4	-0.7	-1.0	-1.2	-1.6	-1.4	-1.5
Total OECD	-3.8	-3.8	-3.1	-3.1	-2.9	-3.8	-3.7	-4.4	-4.4	-4.0	-3.9	-3.1	-1.8	-1.4	-1.3	-1.1	-1.4	-2.8	-3.2	-3.2

Note: Cyclically-adjusted balances exclude one-off revenues from the sale of mobile telephone licenses for those countries listed in the note to Table 28. For details on the methodology used for estimating the cyclical component of government balances see *OECD Economic Outlook* Sources and Methods (*http://www.oecd.org/eco/sources-and-methods*).
a) Includes deferred tax payments on postal savings accounts in 2000, 2001 and 2002. The 2000 outlays include capital transfers to the Deposit Insurance Company.
b) As a percentage of mainland potential GDP. The financial balances shown exclude revenues from the petroleum activities.
Source: OECD.

Annex Table 30. General government primary balances

Surplus (+) or deficit (-) as a per cent of nominal GDP

	1985	1986	1987	1988	1989	1990	1991	1992	1993	1994	1995	1996	1997	1998	1999	2000	2001	2002	Projections 2003	2004
Australia	-1.2	0.1	1.9	3.5	3.5	1.7	-0.6	-2.3	-2.4	-0.4	0.4	1.3	2.3	2.9	3.3	2.4	1.3	1.7	2.0	2.3
Austria	0.3	-0.8	-1.2	-0.2	0.1	0.9	0.4	1.5	-0.6	-1.5	-1.6	-0.1	1.5	0.9	0.8	1.6	3.2	2.2	1.4	1.5
Belgium	0.0	0.6	2.2	2.6	3.2	4.4	3.3	2.7	3.3	4.2	4.5	4.7	5.7	6.5	6.2	6.6	6.6	5.7	5.2	5.1
Canada	-4.9	-3.1	-1.3	-0.1	0.1	-0.7	-3.2	-4.1	-3.7	-1.7	0.3	2.5	4.9	4.8	5.9	6.2	4.6	3.8	3.3	3.1
Denmark	4.8	8.4	7.5	5.8	4.3	2.8	1.6	1.0	0.6	0.9	0.9	1.9	3.3	3.6	5.6	4.4	4.3	3.2	2.8	2.8
Finland	2.3	2.5	0.4	3.9	5.3	3.4	-3.3	-7.8	-7.9	-4.8	-3.0	-1.5	0.6	3.3	3.6	8.0	5.8	4.8	3.2	2.9
France	-0.9	-1.0	0.2	-0.3	0.4	0.3	0.1	-1.4	-3.0	-2.4	-2.2	-0.6	0.2	0.5	1.2	1.5	1.4	-0.2	-0.4	-0.1
Germany	1.5	1.4	0.7	0.4	2.4	0.3	-0.6	0.1	-0.3	0.4	-0.1	-0.2	0.5	1.0	1.6	4.0	0.0	-0.8	-0.8	-0.2
Greece	-6.6	-4.2	-2.8	-4.0	-6.7	-5.9	-2.1	-1.1	-1.0	4.0	1.0	3.1	4.2	5.3	5.4	5.1	4.9	4.3	4.3	4.3
Iceland	-1.9	-3.9	-0.9	-1.3	-3.8	-2.1	-1.7	-1.8	-3.2	-3.4	-1.3	0.0	1.3	1.9	3.8	3.5	1.0	1.5	1.2	1.2
Ireland	-3.3	-3.4	-0.5	2.1	4.3	3.4	2.8	2.2	2.1	2.6	1.9	3.1	4.1	4.7	3.5	5.4	1.8	-0.1	-0.6	-1.1
Italy	-4.6	-3.9	-4.2	-3.3	-2.7	-1.8	-0.4	1.5	2.3	1.7	3.3	3.8	6.1	4.7	4.4	5.3	3.3	2.9	2.2	1.5
Japan	1.8	1.6	2.5	2.9	3.5	3.2	2.8	1.8	-1.3	-2.6	-3.5	-3.8	-2.6	-4.2	-5.8	-6.1	-4.7	-6.0	-6.3	-6.3
Korea	1.2	1.7	2.7	3.5	3.2	3.2	1.4	1.0	2.1	2.7	3.8	3.2	2.8	0.6	2.0	5.1	4.4	5.0	2.6	3.1
Luxembourg	..	..	..	..	..	2.7	-0.9	-1.1	0.0	1.5	1.0	1.0	2.4	2.1	2.8	5.2	5.5	1.9	-0.3	-1.5
Netherlands	1.0	-0.2	-0.7	0.3	-1.0	-1.3	1.6	0.2	1.6	0.9	0.6	2.9	3.3	3.4	4.5	5.4	2.8	1.5	0.7	0.3
New Zealand	..	-2.0	2.0	-1.2	0.5	-0.5	-0.7	-0.2	1.9	4.4	4.4	3.5	2.2	0.0	-0.2	1.1	1.8	1.5	0.9	0.7
Norway	8.5	3.9	2.7	0.1	-0.5	0.4	-3.6	-5.3	-4.3	-2.0	1.0	4.2	5.6	1.4	3.7	12.4	11.6	8.8	7.2	6.7
Portugal	-2.2	0.4	0.3	2.9	3.1	2.0	1.2	3.8	-0.3	-1.1	0.8	0.6	0.7	0.3	0.4	0.4	-1.1	0.4	-0.1	0.3
Slovak Republic	..	..	..	..	..	..	..	..	..	0.1	-0.2	-5.3	-3.3	-2.3	-3.0	-7.8	-3.9	-5.1	-3.0	-2.1
Spain	-4.7	-3.1	-0.6	-0.4	0.2	-0.8	-1.2	0.0	-2.3	-1.9	-1.8	0.0	1.2	1.3	2.2	2.4	2.7	2.6	2.2	2.2
Sweden	-0.8	0.9	5.5	3.9	5.3	3.9	-1.7	-7.2	-12.0	-9.7	-6.0	-1.3	0.2	3.6	2.7	4.2	5.3	1.9	1.5	1.8
United Kingdom	0.7	0.9	1.5	3.4	3.5	1.1	-0.8	-4.1	-5.5	-4.1	-2.8	-1.5	0.8	3.1	3.4	6.1	2.6	0.2	-0.4	-0.7
United States	-1.8	-2.0	-1.0	-0.3	0.2	-0.8	-1.3	-2.2	-1.4	-0.2	0.6	1.3	2.4	3.5	3.6	4.1	1.9	-1.4	-2.7	-2.4
Euro area	-1.1	-0.9	-0.6	-0.4	0.4	-0.1	-0.2	0.1	-0.5	-0.1	0.0	0.9	2.0	2.1	2.5	3.7	1.9	1.1	0.7	0.8
European Union	-0.9	-0.5	-0.1	0.3	1.0	0.2	-0.3	-0.7	-1.5	-0.9	-0.4	0.6	1.9	2.4	2.7	4.1	2.1	1.0	0.6	0.7
Total OECD	-0.9	-0.8	0.0	0.6	1.1	0.3	-0.3	-1.0	-1.4	-0.8	-0.3	0.4	1.6	1.8	1.8	2.6	1.2	-0.7	-1.5	-1.3

Note: The primary balance is the difference between the financial balance and net interest payments. For more details see footnotes of Annex Tables 28 and 32 and *OECD Economic Outlook* Sources and Methods (*http://www.oecd.org/eco/sources-and-methods*).
Source: OECD.

Annex Table 31. **Cyclically-adjusted general government primary balances**

Surplus (+) or deficit (−) as a per cent of potential GDP

	1985	1986	1987	1988	1989	1990	1991	1992	1993	1994	1995	1996	1997	1998	1999	2000	2001	2002	Projections 2003	2004
Australia	-1.4	0.4	2.0	3.3	3.6	2.6	0.5	-1.0	-1.4	0.0	0.7	1.4	2.4	2.7	3.0	2.0	1.1	1.8	2.3	2.6
Austria	1.2	0.0	-0.3	0.3	0.1	0.4	-0.2	1.1	-0.4	-1.4	-1.4	0.1	1.7	0.7	0.6	0.7	3.2	2.6	2.1	2.2
Belgium	2.1	2.6	3.8	2.6	2.6	3.5	2.9	2.8	5.1	5.5	5.7	6.4	6.4	7.2	6.2	5.8	6.7	6.8	6.7	6.4
Canada	-5.0	-3.2	-1.9	-1.5	-1.3	-1.1	-1.9	-2.2	-2.0	-1.1	0.7	3.3	5.4	5.2	5.6	5.6	4.7	3.8	3.3	3.0
Denmark	3.3	5.7	5.8	4.8	4.3	3.2	2.4	2.4	3.3	1.1	0.9	1.8	2.7	3.1	4.9	3.6	3.9	3.5	3.4	3.0
Finland	3.0	3.3	0.1	2.4	2.4	1.4	0.1	-1.0	0.7	2.0	1.9	2.2	2.1	3.6	3.9	6.6	5.8	5.4	4.0	3.2
France	0.7	0.4	1.3	0.0	0.0	-0.4	-0.3	-1.6	-2.1	-1.7	-1.5	0.5	1.4	1.2	1.5	1.0	1.0	-0.2	0.0	0.3
Germany	2.5	1.9	1.3	0.3	1.9	-1.2	-1.2	-0.6	0.5	1.0	0.2	0.5	1.3	1.6	1.9	1.1	0.1	-0.2	0.4	0.8
Greece	-5.8	-3.5	-1.0	-3.5	-7.1	-5.8	-2.3	-0.9	0.3	5.2	2.2	4.3	5.0	6.4	6.3	5.5	4.4	4.0	3.9	3.9
Iceland	-0.9	-4.1	-2.9	-2.1	-3.9	-1.9	-0.6	1.3	-0.1	-1.5	0.9	1.0	1.5	1.4	2.9	2.0	-0.6	1.2	1.2	0.9
Ireland	-2.7	-1.5	0.8	2.8	4.2	2.1	2.6	2.8	3.6	4.2	2.7	3.6	3.8	4.5	2.4	3.5	0.0	-2.1	-1.6	-1.7
Italy	-3.6	-3.2	-3.7	-3.5	-3.4	-2.4	-0.7	1.7	3.6	2.6	3.7	4.4	6.5	5.1	4.8	4.2	3.3	3.5	3.1	2.1
Japan[a]	1.8	1.8	2.7	2.6	3.0	2.6	2.5	1.6	-1.3	-2.4	-3.3	-4.1	-3.1	-4.2	-5.5	-6.2	-4.6	-5.6	-5.8	-5.8
Netherlands	1.7	0.3	0.3	1.1	-1.9	-3.3	-0.1	-0.7	1.8	1.0	0.4	2.6	2.8	2.3	2.9	3.0	2.0	2.2	2.3	1.9
New Zealand	..	-3.6	1.1	-1.1	0.8	0.9	2.3	2.9	3.2	4.1	3.8	2.8	2.1	1.3	0.3	0.9	1.5	0.9	0.6	0.5
Norway[b]	3.0	3.9	3.2	3.0	2.9	1.6	-8.1	-9.9	-9.4	-7.5	-4.5	-4.4	-4.2	-5.6	-4.9	-4.5	-4.5	-5.7	-6.0	-6.0
Portugal	3.4	4.2	3.3	3.4	3.0	2.0	-0.2	3.0	0.3	0.0	1.4	0.9	0.6	-0.1	-0.2	-0.7	-1.4	0.7	0.8	1.2
Spain	-3.0	-1.4	0.4	-0.3	-0.2	-1.6	-1.9	0.1	-0.7	-0.3	-0.2	1.7	2.4	2.0	2.4	1.9	2.7	2.9	2.7	2.7
Sweden	-1.7	-0.7	3.2	1.0	2.3	1.7	-1.8	-4.8	-7.0	-6.3	-4.0	1.0	2.2	4.6	2.3	2.8	5.0	1.9	1.9	1.8
United Kingdom	2.0	0.9	0.5	1.1	1.5	-0.2	0.1	-1.9	-3.2	-2.9	-2.0	-0.8	1.0	3.0	3.5	3.5	2.7	0.8	0.3	-0.1
United States	-1.6	-1.8	-0.9	-0.6	-0.2	-0.9	-0.6	-1.7	-0.9	0.0	0.7	1.3	2.1	3.0	3.0	3.6	2.1	-1.0	-2.1	-2.0
Euro area	0.2	0.1	0.2	-0.5	-0.2	-1.3	-0.9	-0.1	0.6	0.8	0.7	1.8	2.8	2.6	2.7	2.2	1.7	1.4	1.6	1.5
European Union	0.3	0.2	0.4	-0.1	0.2	-0.9	-0.5	-0.4	-0.1	0.1	0.3	1.4	2.6	2.7	2.9	2.4	2.0	1.5	1.5	1.3
Total OECD	-0.4	-0.4	0.2	0.2	0.5	-0.3	-0.2	-0.7	-0.7	-0.4	-0.1	0.6	1.6	1.8	1.7	1.6	1.1	-0.6	-1.0	-1.1

Note: The cyclically-adjusted primary balance is the difference between the cyclically adjusted balance and net interest payments. It excludes one-off revenues from the sale of mobile telephone licenses. See *OECD Economic Outlook* Sources and Methods (*http://www.oecd.org/eco/sources-and-methods*) for details on the methodology used for estimating the cyclical component of government balances. The 2000 outlays include capital transfers to the Deposit Insurance Company.
a) Includes deferred tax payments on postal savings accounts in 2000, 2001 and 2002.
b) As a percentage of mainland potential GDP. The financial balances shown exclude revenues from the petroleum activities.
Source: OECD.

Annex Table 32. General government net debt interest payments
Per cent of nominal GDP

	1985	1986	1987	1988	1989	1990	1991	1992	1993	1994	1995	1996	1997	1998	1999	2000	2001	2002	Projections 2003	2004
Australia	3.9	4.2	4.1	3.8	3.9	3.5	3.1	3.7	3.2	4.2	4.1	3.4	2.8	2.3	2.2	2.1	1.9	1.8	1.8	1.8
Austria	2.9	3.0	3.1	3.3	3.2	3.3	3.4	3.5	3.6	3.5	3.7	3.8	3.5	3.3	3.1	3.0	2.9	2.8	2.7	2.6
Belgium	10.3	10.7	10.1	9.9	10.9	11.3	10.8	10.8	10.6	9.2	8.9	8.5	7.7	7.3	6.6	6.5	6.2	5.7	5.2	4.9
Canada	4.0	4.1	4.2	4.3	4.7	5.2	5.1	5.1	5.0	5.0	5.6	5.3	4.7	4.7	4.2	3.1	2.8	2.5	2.2	2.2
Denmark	6.2	5.1	5.0	4.3	4.0	3.8	4.0	3.2	3.5	3.3	3.1	2.9	2.9	2.5	2.4	2.0	1.5	1.5	1.2	0.9
Finland	-0.9	-1.0	-0.9	-0.9	-1.2	-1.7	-1.9	-1.9	-0.3	1.1	0.9	1.5	1.9	1.7	1.6	1.1	0.7	0.0	0.1	0.1
France	2.1	2.2	2.2	2.1	2.2	2.4	2.6	2.7	3.0	3.1	3.3	3.4	3.3	3.2	3.0	2.9	2.9	3.0	3.1	3.2
Germany[a]	2.6	2.5	2.5	2.5	2.3	2.2	2.3	2.7	2.8	2.8	3.2	3.2	3.2	3.3	3.1	2.9	2.8	2.8	3.0	3.1
Greece	5.0	5.4	6.8	7.4	7.5	10.0	9.3	11.5	12.6	13.9	11.2	10.5	8.2	7.8	7.2	7.0	6.3	5.5	5.3	5.0
Iceland	-0.3	0.1	-0.1	0.7	0.8	1.3	1.2	1.0	1.4	1.4	1.7	1.6	1.3	1.4	1.3	1.0	0.6	1.2	1.2	1.1
Ireland	7.0	6.9	7.6	6.4	6.0	6.2	5.7	5.2	4.8	4.5	4.0	3.2	2.6	2.4	1.5	1.0	0.2	0.2	0.2	0.1
Italy	8.1	8.3	7.6	8.1	9.0	9.9	11.3	12.2	12.6	11.0	10.9	10.9	8.8	7.8	6.2	6.0	5.9	5.3	4.7	4.3
Japan[b]	2.4	2.2	2.1	1.8	1.7	1.2	1.0	1.0	1.1	1.1	1.2	1.2	1.2	1.3	1.4	1.4	1.4	1.2	1.4	1.5
Korea	0.1	0.1	0.1	0.0	-0.2	-0.4	-0.5	-0.5	-0.4	-0.4	-0.4	-0.6	-0.9	-1.3	-1.1	-1.1	-1.0	-0.9	-0.8	-0.9
Luxembourg	..	..	..	..	..	-2.2	-2.0	-1.9	-1.6	-1.3	-1.1	-0.9	-0.8	-0.9	-0.7	-0.9	-0.9	-0.7	-0.6	-0.5
Netherlands	4.2	4.3	4.6	4.5	4.0	4.0	4.3	4.5	4.5	4.4	4.7	4.7	4.4	4.2	3.8	3.2	2.6	2.7	2.3	2.3
New Zealand	..	4.4	4.1	3.4	3.9	4.1	2.9	2.9	2.3	1.3	1.4	0.7	0.6	-0.4	-0.4	0.3	0.0	0.2	0.2	0.2
Norway	-1.2	-1.7	-1.8	-2.4	-2.2	-2.1	-3.7	-3.4	-2.8	-2.2	-2.4	-2.3	-2.2	-2.2	-2.4	-2.6	-3.2	-4.0	-4.0	-4.0
Portugal	6.9	8.3	7.5	6.6	6.1	8.6	8.8	8.5	7.7	6.6	6.3	5.4	4.2	3.5	3.2	3.3	3.2	3.0	3.0	3.0
Slovak Republic	..	..	..	..	..	..	..	..	..	3.5	2.4	2.5	2.2	2.4	3.4	2.9	3.4	2.1	3.1	3.0
Spain	2.3	2.9	2.5	2.8	2.9	3.0	3.3	3.7	4.7	4.6	4.9	5.0	4.4	4.0	3.3	3.0	2.8	2.7	2.6	2.4
Sweden	2.9	2.2	1.7	1.0	0.6	0.2	0.2	0.4	-0.4	0.8	1.4	1.6	2.0	1.4	1.4	0.8	0.8	0.9	0.7	0.6
United Kingdom	3.5	3.4	3.3	2.9	2.7	2.6	2.3	2.2	2.4	2.6	2.9	2.9	3.0	2.9	2.3	2.1	1.8	1.5	1.5	1.5
United States	3.2	3.3	3.3	3.3	3.4	3.5	3.7	3.7	3.5	3.5	3.6	3.5	3.3	3.2	2.8	2.6	2.3	2.0	1.9	1.9
Euro area	3.9	4.0	3.9	4.0	4.2	4.5	4.8	5.2	5.3	5.0	5.0	5.2	4.7	4.4	3.8	3.6	3.5	3.3	3.2	3.2
European Union	4.0	4.1	4.0	3.9	4.0	4.2	4.4	4.7	5.0	4.8	4.9	4.9	4.4	4.1	3.6	3.4	3.2	3.0	2.9	2.9
Total OECD	3.3	3.4	3.3	3.2	3.3	3.4	3.5	3.6	3.6	3.5	3.7	3.6	3.3	3.1	2.8	2.6	2.4	2.1	2.1	2.1

Note: In the case of Ireland and New Zealand where net interest payments are not available, net property income paid is used as a proxy. For Denmark, net interest payments include dividends received. See *OECD Economic Outlook* Sources and Methods (*http://www.oecd.org/eco/sources-and-methods*).
a) Includes interest payments on the debt of the Inherited Debt Funds from 1995 onwards.
b) Includes interest payments on the debt of the Japan Railway settlement Corporation and the National Forest Special Account from 1998 onwards.
Source: OECD.

Annex Table 33. General government gross financial liabilities
Per cent of nominal GDP

	1985	1986	1987	1988	1989	1990	1991	1992	1993	1994	1995	1996	1997	1998	1999	2000	2001	2002	Projections 2003	2004
Australia	..	..	..	25.9	23.8	22.6	23.8	28.1	31.5	41.3	43.2	40.3	38.5	33.2	27.7	24.2	21.5	21.3	20.2	19.6
Austria	49.1	53.6	57.5	58.9	58.1	57.2	57.5	57.2	61.8	64.7	69.2	69.1	64.7	63.7	67.5	66.8	67.3	67.6	66.8	65.8
Belgium	118.1	123.3	127.8	127.9	124.6	129.1	130.9	132.8	138.1	135.8	133.9	130.5	124.8	119.5	114.8	109.6	108.5	105.4	102.4	98.6
Canada	66.9	71.0	71.5	71.1	72.3	75.1	82.8	90.9	96.2	97.2	99.9	99.2	97.5	94.3	92.5	83.3	83.2	80.4	77.3	74.8
Denmark	80.6	77.2	73.9	71.8	70.0	70.8	71.8	76.0	90.1	83.6	79.5	76.8	73.4	70.7	61.1	54.3	53.8	51.9	50.0	47.8
Finland	18.5	19.6	20.1	19.0	16.8	16.6	25.1	45.1	58.3	60.8	65.8	66.5	64.8	61.1	56.2	53.5	51.5	47.2	45.7	44.9
France	38.0	38.8	40.1	40.0	39.9	39.5	40.3	44.7	51.6	55.3	62.9	66.5	68.2	70.4	66.2	65.4	65.0	67.1	69.6	71.2
Germany[a]	40.8	40.7	41.8	42.3	40.9	41.5	38.8	41.8	47.4	47.9	57.1	60.3	61.8	63.2	61.2	60.5	60.2	62.4	64.9	66.5
Greece	47.1	47.7	53.0	62.7	65.7	79.6	82.2	87.8	110.1	107.9	108.7	111.3	108.2	105.8	105.1	106.2	107.0	104.9	102.4	98.7
Iceland	33.2	30.7	28.2	31.6	37.4	37.1	39.3	47.3	54.4	57.1	60.5	57.8	54.5	49.4	44.8	42.2	47.4	44.8	44.2	43.1
Ireland	..	..	..	..	..	94.2	95.6	92.5	96.5	90.9	82.9	74.1	65.0	54.9	49.3	39.3	36.7	33.7	31.8	31.4
Italy	89.1	93.8	98.3	100.6	103.7	112.8	116.8	126.3	128.2	134.8	133.9	136.0	133.3	133.5	128.0	124.3	121.7	121.2	120.1	118.3
Japan[b]	71.4	75.1	75.5	73.4	70.4	68.3	64.5	68.4	74.3	79.3	86.6	93.9	99.9	111.2	124.9	133.0	141.5	147.2	155.7	164.1
Korea	16.4	14.5	12.7	9.9	9.2	8.2	7.2	6.9	5.9	6.1	6.3	6.3	9.2	15.2	18.7	19.3	17.7	16.4	17.5	18.9
Luxembourg	..	..	..	..	..	4.4	3.8	4.7	5.7	5.4	5.6	6.2	6.1	6.3	6.0	5.6	5.6	5.8	5.5	6.2
Netherlands	69.1	71.0	73.5	76.4	76.2	77.0	76.9	77.8	79.0	76.3	77.2	75.2	69.9	66.8	63.1	55.8	52.8	52.7	52.2	52.7
New Zealand	32.3	..	..	32.8	32.7	..	..	..	70.6	63.9	57.2	51.7	49.5	50.0	47.4	44.9	42.6	41.0	39.7	38.4
Norway	..	40.6	33.6	..	..	29.2	27.5	32.2	40.5	36.9	34.4	30.7	27.5	26.2	26.8	30.0	26.2	23.5	20.8	20.0
Poland	..	..	..	..	..	..	..	..	..	..	..	..	48.7	44.5	44.4	39.4	40.3	45.0	49.8	53.2
Portugal	55.8	54.0	60.8	61.0	59.0	58.3	60.7	54.4	59.1	62.1	64.3	62.9	59.1	55.0	54.3	53.3	55.5	58.1	58.9	58.6
Slovak Republic	..	..	..	..	..	..	..	..	27.0	23.9	21.9	26.4	28.8	29.4	29.4	32.0	36.7	41.0	43.0	44.3
Spain	49.0	49.8	49.0	45.3	46.9	48.8	49.9	52.4	63.5	68.2	73.8	81.4	80.8	81.4	75.6	72.4	68.4	65.9	64.4	62.6
Sweden	69.2	68.6	61.1	54.8	49.8	45.7	55.1	73.9	78.9	83.4	82.1	84.6	82.7	81.1	71.5	64.2	63.2	59.7	59.2	58.3
United Kingdom	59.2	58.4	56.1	49.7	43.0	44.4	44.3	49.2	58.1	55.8	60.6	60.1	60.5	61.5	56.3	51.5	50.4	50.3	51.1	51.9
United States	59.0	62.6	64.1	64.7	65.0	66.6	71.4	74.0	75.6	74.8	74.2	73.5	70.8	67.6	64.5	58.8	58.9	61.0	63.8	65.7
Euro area	54.4	56.2	58.4	59.0	59.3	62.2	62.5	66.4	70.8	72.8	77.4	81.3	81.4	81.5	77.9	75.7	74.5	75.0	75.8	76.0
European Union	57.2	58.3	59.5	58.8	57.7	60.2	60.6	65.3	71.8	73.5	78.0	80.0	79.4	79.7	75.6	72.8	71.6	71.8	72.4	72.5
Total OECD	59.3	61.8	62.8	61.7	60.9	62.1	63.8	67.5	71.6	72.9	75.6	77.1	76.3	76.8	76.0	73.7	74.4	76.1	78.6	80.5

Note: Gross debt data are not always comparable across countries due to a different definition or treatment of debt components. Notably, they include the funded portion of government employee pension liabilities for some OECD countries, including Australia and the United States. The debt position of these countries is thus overstated relative to countries that have large unfunded liabilities for such pensions which according to ESA95/SNA93 are not counted in the debt figures, but rather as a memorandum item to the debt. General government financial liabilities presented here are defined according to ESA95/SNA93 for all countries with the exception of Austria, Belgium, Greece, Ireland, Luxembourg, Netherlands and Portugal where debt measures follow the definition of debt applied under the Maastricht Treaty. Maastricht debt for European Union countries is shown in Annex Table 58. For more details see *OECD Economic Outlook* Sources and Methods (http://www.oecd.org/eco/sources-and-methods).
a) Includes the debt of the Inherited Debt Fund from 1995 onwards.
b) Includes the debt of the Japan Railway Settlement Corporation and the National Forest Special Account from 1998 onwards.
Source: OECD.

Annex Table 34. General government net financial liabilities

Per cent of nominal GDP

	1985	1986	1987	1988	1989	1990	1991	1992	1993	1994	1995	1996	1997	1998	1999	2000	2001	2002	Projections 2003	Projections 2004
Australia	..	..	..	15.3	11.3	10.7	11.6	16.2	22.1	26.6	27.3	21.7	21.9	16.5	15.5	9.5	5.6	6.0	4.8	4.3
Austria	30.1	33.3	36.2	38.4	38.1	37.5	37.4	38.7	43.5	45.7	50.5	50.1	47.8	48.6	49.9	48.8	49.8	49.8	49.8	49.3
Belgium	108.2	113.5	117.7	118.1	115.1	116.8	118.1	119.3	123.9	123.1	123.2	120.6	115.9	110.4	105.6	100.7	98.1	95.8	93.2	89.9
Canada	35.3	39.7	39.3	38.2	41.0	43.4	50.1	59.6	64.0	66.7	68.0	66.6	64.3	60.8	55.5	46.6	43.6	40.4	36.9	34.0
Denmark	26.2	21.9	19.5	20.5	19.2	19.0	21.7	23.8	26.1	26.4	26.7	26.3	23.9	24.2	13.6	10.1	8.3	6.3	4.4	2.3
Finland	-27.0	-28.0	-27.8	-29.1	-33.2	-35.4	-34.1	-24.9	-16.1	-16.3	-12.5	-15.1	-15.5	-25.7	-62.0	-41.7	-42.0	-44.5	-46.0	-46.8
France	9.7	12.5	13.3	15.1	15.7	17.5	18.8	20.4	27.1	28.3	38.9	42.6	43.3	41.7	33.6	34.9	37.7	39.7	42.3	43.8
Germany[a]	19.9	20.1	21.1	22.0	20.5	21.0	20.2	24.4	27.9	29.1	39.6	42.4	43.4	46.0	44.8	41.9	44.3	47.2	50.3	52.4
Iceland	6.1	9.0	8.2	9.9	18.0	19.4	20.2	27.1	35.4	38.5	40.5	40.4	38.3	31.8	24.2	24.1	25.9	24.1	23.4	22.9
Italy	80.4	84.8	89.2	91.5	94.4	84.5	89.4	98.2	106.4	111.8	109.7	111.3	107.4	108.5	103.9	99.3	97.2	96.7	95.7	93.9
Japan[b]	69.7	67.1	55.7	47.1	38.6	24.8	12.7	14.5	17.9	20.5	24.8	30.5	35.3	46.2	52.8	58.6	63.7	71.7	80.2	88.6
Korea	-6.5	-8.2	-10.3	-13.7	-16.5	-17.2	-15.9	-15.3	-15.5	-15.2	-18.0	-19.4	-22.5	-24.5	-25.6	-28.4	-32.2	-35.8	-37.3	-38.6
Netherlands	40.9	44.0	27.3	31.1	34.6	35.6	36.2	39.7	40.7	42.3	53.2	53.7	55.3	53.7	50.2	44.5	41.4	41.0	41.3	41.8
New Zealand	..	..	..	..	..	..	..	..	48.0	42.0	35.5	31.1	28.7	26.5	24.0	21.4	20.0	19.5	18.0	16.6
Norway	-36.6	-41.1	-42.4	-42.6	-41.8	-41.6	-37.9	-35.6	-32.4	-31.0	-32.6	-36.5	-42.9	-46.9	-52.7	-60.1	-72.7	-85.2	-93.4	-99.9
Spain	26.1	29.3	29.9	30.6	30.7	31.8	33.2	35.4	42.3	43.3	49.2	53.3	52.4	51.9	46.0	42.9	41.5	39.0	37.5	35.7
Sweden	13.5	12.1	6.2	0.2	-5.8	-7.6	-4.9	4.5	10.3	20.4	25.2	25.7	23.1	19.9	9.4	1.4	-3.1	-4.1	-4.7	-5.6
United Kingdom	30.8	31.2	29.5	23.8	19.1	15.1	15.3	21.6	30.9	31.1	36.9	38.7	40.1	41.9	36.7	30.9	28.7	28.7	29.4	30.2
United States	41.9	45.4	47.4	48.5	48.7	49.9	53.6	57.0	58.9	59.5	58.9	58.4	56.1	52.3	47.9	43.0	42.1	44.2	47.1	48.9
Euro area	32.7	35.4	36.4	38.0	38.6	38.7	39.9	43.9	48.4	49.8	56.1	59.8	59.7	59.8	55.1	53.2	53.8	54.7	55.8	56.1
European Union	34.1	36.0	36.1	36.3	35.6	33.8	34.8	39.4	45.5	47.4	53.8	56.0	55.6	56.0	50.9	48.0	47.9	48.5	49.4	49.7
Total OECD	41.4	43.2	42.1	40.6	39.1	36.8	37.0	40.8	44.6	46.1	48.8	50.1	49.6	49.6	46.7	44.1	44.2	46.2	48.7	50.6

Note: Net debt measures are not always comparable across countries due to a different definition or treatment of debt (and asset) components. First, the treatment of government liabilities in respect of their employee pension plans may be different (see footnote to Annex Table 33). Second while general government financial liabilities presented here for most countries are defined by ESA95/SNA93, for some EU countries, i.e. Austria, Belgium, Greece, Ireland, Luxembourg, Netherlands and Portugal debt measures follow the definition of debt applied under the Maastricht Treaty. Third, a range of items included as general government assets differs across countries. For example, equity participation is excluded from government assets in some countries, whereas foreign exchange, gold and SDR holdings are considered as assets of the government in the United States and the United Kingdom. For details see *OECD Economic Outlook* Sources and Methods (*http://www.oecd.org/eco/sources-and-methods*).

a) Includes the debt of the Inherited Debt Fund from 1995 onwards.
b) Includes the debt of the Japan Railway Settlement Corporation and the National Forest Special Account from 1998 onwards.
Source: OECD.

Annex Table 35. **Short-term interest rates**

Per cent, per annum

	1985	1986	1987	1988	1989	1990	1991	1992	1993	1994	1995	1996	1997	1998	1999	2000	2001	2002	Projections 2003	2004
Australia	16.0	16.5	13.8	12.8	17.6	14.5	10.2	6.5	5.2	5.7	7.7	7.2	5.4	5.0	5.0	6.2	4.9	4.7	4.8	5.5
Austria	6.2	5.3	4.3	4.6	7.5	9.0	9.5	9.5	7.0	5.1	4.6	3.4	3.5	3.6	3.0	4.4	4.2	3.3	2.3	2.3
Belgium	9.5	8.1	7.1	6.7	8.8	9.6	9.4	9.4	8.2	5.7	4.8	3.2	3.4	3.6	3.0	4.4	4.2	3.3	2.3	2.3
Canada	8.6	8.1	7.8	9.5	12.1	12.7	8.8	6.6	5.0	5.5	7.1	4.4	3.5	5.0	4.9	5.8	4.0	2.6	3.6	4.6
Czech Republic	..	..	..	..	..	..	..	..	13.1	9.1	10.9	12.0	15.9	14.3	6.9	5.4	5.2	3.5	2.7	2.8
Denmark	10.3	9.1	10.1	8.5	9.6	10.9	9.7	11.0	10.4	6.1	6.1	3.9	3.7	4.1	3.3	4.9	4.6	3.5	2.5	2.5
Finland	13.5	12.7	10.0	10.0	12.6	14.0	13.1	13.3	7.8	5.4	5.8	3.6	3.2	3.6	3.0	4.4	4.2	3.3	2.3	2.3
France	9.9	7.7	8.3	7.9	9.4	10.3	9.6	10.3	8.6	5.8	6.6	3.9	3.5	3.6	3.0	4.4	4.2	3.3	2.3	2.3
Germany	5.4	4.6	4.0	4.3	7.1	8.5	9.2	9.5	7.3	5.4	4.5	3.3	3.3	3.5	3.0	4.4	4.2	3.3	2.3	2.3
Greece	18.4	18.5	19.0	19.2	19.0	23.0	23.3	21.7	21.3	19.3	15.5	12.8	10.4	11.6	8.9	6.1	4.2	3.3	2.3	2.3
Hungary	..	..	..	..	..	..	..	..	17.2	26.9	32.0	24.0	20.1	18.0	14.7	11.0	10.8	8.9	6.9	7.3
Iceland	..	..	..	31.0	27.9	14.8	14.6	10.5	8.8	4.9	7.0	7.0	7.1	7.4	8.6	11.2	11.0	8.0	6.0	8.0
Ireland	11.9	12.5	10.8	8.0	10.0	11.3	10.4	14.3	9.1	5.9	6.2	5.4	6.1	5.4	3.0	4.4	4.2	3.3	2.3	2.3
Italy	15.2	13.4	11.3	10.8	12.6	12.2	12.2	14.0	10.2	8.5	10.5	8.8	6.9	5.0	3.0	4.4	4.2	3.3	2.3	2.3
Japan	6.6	5.2	4.2	4.5	5.4	7.7	7.4	4.5	3.0	2.2	1.2	0.6	0.6	0.7	0.2	0.2	0.1	0.1	0.0	0.0
Korea	..	..	..	..	..	..	18.3	16.4	13.0	13.3	14.1	12.7	13.4	15.2	6.8	7.1	5.3	4.8	5.0	5.5
Luxembourg	9.5	8.1	7.1	6.7	8.8	9.6	9.4	9.4	8.2	5.7	4.8	3.2	3.4	3.6	3.0	4.4	4.2	3.3	2.3	2.3
Mexico	..	..	..	..	..	35.0	19.8	15.9	15.5	14.5	47.8	32.9	21.3	26.1	22.4	16.2	12.2	7.4	8.9	7.8
Netherlands	6.3	5.7	5.4	4.8	7.4	8.7	9.3	9.4	6.9	5.2	4.4	3.0	3.3	3.5	3.0	4.4	4.2	3.3	2.3	2.3
New Zealand	23.3	19.1	21.1	15.4	13.5	13.9	10.0	6.7	6.3	6.7	9.0	9.3	7.7	7.3	4.8	6.5	5.7	5.7	5.8	5.8
Norway	12.5	14.4	14.7	13.5	11.4	11.5	10.6	11.8	7.3	5.9	5.5	4.9	3.7	5.8	6.5	6.7	7.2	6.9	5.6	5.6
Poland	..	..	..	..	..	..	..	..	34.9	31.8	27.7	21.3	23.1	19.9	14.7	18.9	15.7	8.8	6.6	6.0
Portugal	22.4	15.6	13.9	13.0	14.9	16.9	17.7	16.1	12.5	11.1	9.8	7.4	5.7	4.3	3.0	4.4	4.2	3.3	2.3	2.3
Slovak Republic	..	..	..	..	..	..	..	..	11.7	8.0	9.4	11.5	20.2	18.1	14.8	8.2	7.5	7.5	7.5	6.5
Spain	12.2	11.7	15.8	11.7	15.0	15.2	13.2	13.3	11.7	8.0	9.4	7.5	5.4	4.2	3.0	4.4	4.2	3.3	2.3	2.3
Sweden	14.2	9.8	9.4	10.1	11.5	13.7	11.6	12.9	8.4	7.4	8.7	5.8	4.1	4.2	3.1	4.0	4.0	4.1	3.6	4.2
Switzerland	4.9	4.2	3.8	3.1	7.3	8.9	8.2	7.9	4.9	4.2	2.9	2.0	1.6	1.5	1.4	3.2	2.9	1.1	0.4	0.6
Turkey	..	..	..	..	..	51.9	109.6	97.8	90.3	150.6	136.3	143.6	119.2	115.7	96.6	37.0	70.2	64.2	37.1	17.6
United Kingdom	12.2	10.9	9.7	10.3	13.9	14.8	11.5	9.6	5.9	5.5	6.7	6.0	6.8	7.3	5.4	6.1	5.0	4.0	3.8	4.3
United States	8.3	6.8	7.1	7.9	9.3	8.2	5.9	3.8	3.2	4.7	6.0	5.4	5.7	5.5	5.4	6.5	3.7	1.8	1.4	3.0
Euro area	9.9	8.5	8.2	7.7	10.0	10.9	10.6	11.1	8.6	6.3	6.5	4.8	4.3	3.9	3.0	4.4	4.2	3.3	2.3	2.3

Note : Three-month money market rates where available, or rates on proximately similar financial instruments. See *OECD Economic Outlook* Sources and Methods (*http://www.oecd.org/eco/sources-and-methods*).
Source: OECD.

Annex Table 36. **Long-term interest rates**

Per cent, per annum

	1985	1986	1987	1988	1989	1990	1991	1992	1993	1994	1995	1996	1997	1998	1999	2000	2001	2002	Projections 2003	2004
Australia	14.0	13.4	13.2	12.1	13.4	13.2	10.7	9.2	7.3	9.0	9.2	8.2	6.9	5.5	6.1	6.3	5.6	5.8	5.8	6.3
Austria	7.8	7.3	6.9	6.7	7.1	8.7	8.5	8.1	6.7	7.0	7.1	6.3	5.7	4.7	4.7	5.6	5.1	5.0	4.3	4.4
Belgium	11.0	8.6	8.2	8.0	8.6	10.1	9.3	8.7	7.2	7.7	7.4	6.3	5.6	4.7	4.7	5.6	5.1	4.9	4.3	4.4
Canada	10.8	9.1	9.5	9.8	9.8	10.8	9.4	8.1	7.2	8.4	8.1	7.2	6.1	5.3	5.6	5.9	5.5	5.3	5.3	5.7
Denmark	11.6	10.1	11.3	9.9	9.7	10.6	9.3	9.0	7.3	7.8	8.3	7.2	6.3	5.0	4.9	5.7	5.1	5.1	4.4	4.5
Finland	10.7	8.9	7.9	10.3	12.1	13.2	11.9	12.1	8.8	9.0	8.8	7.1	6.0	4.8	4.7	5.5	5.0	5.0	4.4	4.5
France	11.9	9.1	9.5	9.1	8.8	9.9	9.0	8.6	6.8	7.2	7.5	6.3	5.6	4.6	4.6	5.4	4.9	4.9	4.3	4.4
Germany	7.2	6.3	6.4	6.6	7.1	8.7	8.5	7.9	6.5	6.9	6.9	6.2	5.7	4.6	4.5	5.3	4.8	4.8	4.2	4.3
Greece	..	..	..	..	..	..	..	..	..	..	..	..	9.8	8.5	6.3	6.1	5.3	5.0	4.4	4.4
Iceland	12.8	11.2	11.3	9.4	..	10.3	9.4	13.1	13.4	7.0	9.7	9.2	8.7	7.7	8.5	11.2	10.4	8.0	6.5	7.5
Ireland	13.7	11.5	10.6	10.9	12.8	13.5	13.3	9.3	7.6	8.0	8.2	7.2	6.3	4.7	4.8	5.5	5.0	5.0	4.8	5.3
Italy	13.7	11.5	10.6	10.9	12.8	13.5	13.3	13.3	11.2	10.5	12.2	9.4	6.9	4.9	4.7	5.6	5.2	5.0	4.6	4.5
Japan	6.5	5.1	5.0	4.8	5.1	7.0	6.3	5.3	4.3	4.4	3.4	3.1	2.4	1.5	1.7	1.7	1.3	1.3	0.9	1.1
Korea	13.9	11.9	12.4	13.0	14.2	15.1	16.5	15.1	12.1	12.3	12.4	10.9	11.8	12.8	8.7	8.5	6.7	6.5	5.6	6.7
Luxembourg	..	..	..	..	..	..	..	..	6.9	7.2	7.2	6.3	5.6	4.7	4.7	5.5	4.9	4.7	4.3	4.3
Mexico	..	..	..	..	..	34.8	19.7	16.1	15.5	13.8	39.8	34.4	22.5	24.8	24.1	16.9	13.8	8.5	9.8	8.8
Netherlands	7.3	6.3	6.4	6.4	7.2	8.9	8.7	8.1	6.4	6.9	6.9	6.2	5.6	4.6	4.6	5.4	4.9	4.9	4.3	4.4
New Zealand	17.7	16.4	15.7	13.1	12.8	12.4	10.1	8.4	6.9	7.6	7.8	7.9	7.2	6.3	6.4	6.9	6.4	6.5	5.8	6.2
Norway	12.6	13.3	13.3	12.9	10.8	10.7	10.0	9.6	6.9	7.4	7.4	6.8	5.9	5.4	5.5	6.3	6.2	6.1	5.7	5.7
Portugal	..	..	..	..	..	..	..	..	..	10.4	11.5	8.6	6.4	4.9	4.8	5.6	5.2	5.0	4.4	4.5
Slovak Republic	..	..	..	..	..	..	..	..	..	..	10.4	9.7	9.4	21.7	15.9	8.5	7.8	9.1	8.3	7.7
Spain	13.4	11.4	12.8	11.7	13.8	14.6	12.8	11.7	10.2	10.0	11.3	8.7	6.4	4.8	4.7	5.5	5.1	5.0	4.2	4.2
Sweden	13.2	10.5	11.7	11.4	11.2	13.2	10.7	10.0	8.5	9.5	10.2	8.0	6.6	5.0	5.0	5.4	5.1	5.3	4.6	4.8
Switzerland	4.7	4.2	4.0	4.0	5.2	6.4	6.2	6.4	4.6	5.0	4.5	4.0	3.4	3.0	3.0	3.9	3.4	3.2	2.3	2.4
Turkey	..	55.0	47.0	62.4	58.3	51.9	71.9	79.6	86.6	138.5	111.5	124.9	106.0	113.6	106.6	35.8	87.4	62.4	38.9	19.0
United Kingdom	11.0	10.1	9.6	9.7	10.2	11.8	10.1	9.1	7.5	8.2	8.2	7.8	7.1	5.5	5.1	5.3	4.9	4.9	4.5	5.1
United States	10.6	7.7	8.4	8.8	8.5	8.6	7.9	7.0	5.9	7.1	6.6	6.4	6.4	5.3	5.6	6.0	5.0	4.6	4.1	5.0
Euro area	..	..	..	..	..	11.1	10.5	10.0	8.3	8.2	8.6	7.1	6.0	4.8	4.7	5.4	5.0	4.9	4.3	4.4

Note: 10-year benchmark government bond yields where available or yield on proximately similar financial instruments (for Korea a 5-year bond is used). See also *OECD Economic Outlook* Sources and Methods (*http://www.oecd.org/eco/sources-and-methods*).
Source: OECD.

Annex Table 37. **Nominal exchange rates (*vis-à-vis* the US dollar)**

Average of daily rates

	Monetary unit	1992	1993	1994	1995	1996	1997	1998	1999	Estimates and assumptions[a]					
										1999	2000	2001	2002	2003	2004
Australia	Dollar	1.362	1.473	1.369	1.350	1.277	1.348	1.592	1.550	1.550	1.727	1.935	1.841	1.676	1.673
Austria	Schilling	10.99	11.63	11.42	10.08	10.58	12.20	12.38	12.91						
Belgium	Franc	32.15	34.55	33.46	29.50	30.98	35.76	36.30	37.86						
Canada	Dollar	1.209	1.290	1.366	1.372	1.364	1.385	1.483	1.486	1.486	1.485	1.548	1.570	1.479	1.470
Czech Republic	Koruny	..	29.15	28.79	26.54	27.15	31.70	32.28	34.59	34.59	38.64	38.02	32.73	29.61	29.660
Denmark	Krone	6.038	6.482	6.360	5.604	5.798	6.604	6.699	6.980	6.980	8.088	8.321	7.884	6.943	6.949
Finland	Markka	4.486	5.721	5.223	4.367	4.592	5.187	5.345	5.580						
France	Franc	5.294	5.662	5.552	4.991	5.116	5.837	5.899	6.157						
Germany	Deutschemark	1.562	1.653	1.623	1.433	1.505	1.734	1.759	1.836						
Greece	Drachma	190.5	229.1	242.2	231.6	240.7	272.9	295.3	305.7						
Hungary	Forint	..	91.9	105.1	125.7	152.6	186.6	214.3	237.1	237.1	282.3	286.5	257.4	230.2	231.2
Iceland	Krona	57.62	67.64	69.99	64.77	66.69	70.97	71.17	72.43	72.43	78.84	97.67	91.59	78.88	79.01
Ireland	Pound	0.588	0.683	0.670	0.624	0.625	0.660	0.703	0.739						
Italy	Lira	1232	1572	1613	1629	1543	1703	1736	1817						
Japan	Yen	126.7	111.2	102.2	94.1	108.8	121.0	130.9	113.9	113.9	107.8	121.5	125.3	119.8	120.1
Korea	Won	780.0	802.4	804.3	771.4	804.4	950.5	1400.5	1186.7	1 186.7	1 130.6	1 290.4	1 251.0	1 233.7	1 244.3
Luxembourg	Franc	32.15	34.55	33.46	29.50	30.98	35.76	36.30	37.86						
Mexico	Peso	3.095	3.115	3.389	6.421	7.601	7.924	9.153	9.553	9.553	9.453	9.344	9.660	10.756	10.733
Netherlands	Guilder	1.759	1.857	1.820	1.605	1.686	1.951	1.983	2.068						
New Zealand	Dollar	1.860	1.851	1.687	1.524	1.454	1.513	1.869	1.892	1.892	2.205	2.382	2.163	1.820	1.820
Norway	Krone	6.214	7.094	7.057	6.337	6.457	7.072	7.545	7.797	7.797	8.797	8.993	7.986	7.263	7.333
Poland	Zloty	..	1.814	2.273	2.425	2.695	3.277	3.492	3.964	3.964	4.346	4.097	4.082	4.013	4.050
Portugal	Escudo	134.8	160.7	166.0	149.9	154.2	175.2	180.1	188.2						
Slovak Republic	Koruna	..	30.77	32.04	29.74	30.65	33.62	35.23	41.36	41.36	46.23	48.35	45.30	39.12	39.170
Spain	Peseta	102.4	127.2	134.0	124.7	126.7	146.4	149.4	156.2						
Sweden	Krona	5.823	7.785	7.716	7.134	6.707	7.635	7.947	8.262	8.262	9.161	10.338	9.721	8.628	8.651
Switzerland	Franc	1.406	1.477	1.367	1.182	1.236	1.450	1.450	1.503	1.503	1.688	1.687	1.557	1.378	1.382
Turkey	Lira	6 861	10 964	29 778	45 738	81 281	151 595	260 473	418 984	418 984	624 325	1 228 269	1 512 342	1 837 745	2 151 252
United Kingdom	Pound	0.570	0.666	0.653	0.634	0.641	0.611	0.604	0.618	0.618	0.661	0.694	0.667	0.632	0.635
United States	Dollar	1.000	1.000	1.000	1.000	1.000	1.000	1.000	1.000	1.000	1.000	1.000	1.000	1.000	1.000
Euro area	Euro	..	..	..	..	..	..	..	0.939	0.939	1.085	1.117	1.061	0.935	0.936
	SDR	0.710	0.716	0.699	0.659	0.689	0.726	0.737	0.731	0.731	0.758	0.785	0.773	0.733	0.734

Note: No exchange rates are shown for individual euro area countries after 1999.
a) On the technical assumption that exchange rates remain at their levels of 26 March 2003, except for Turkey, where exchange rates vary according to official exchange rate policy.
Source: OECD.

Annex Table 38. **Effective exchange rates**
Indices 1995 = 100, average of daily rates

	1989	1990	1991	1992	1993	1994	1995	1996	1997	1998	1999	2000	2001	Estimates and assumptions[a] 2002	2003	2004
Australia	106.7	106.9	107.7	100.9	95.7	103.1	100.0	109.7	111.0	103.5	103.6	96.3	90.3	93.6	98.5	99.0
Austria	84.4	87.9	88.1	90.2	93.2	95.4	100.0	99.1	97.2	99.2	99.9	97.7	98.1	98.6	101.3	102.1
Belgium	79.7	85.2	86.1	88.7	90.7	94.7	100.0	98.4	94.5	96.8	96.3	92.5	93.6	95.2	98.8	99.1
Canada	109.7	113.2	116.5	110.7	105.6	100.8	100.0	101.9	102.2	97.4	97.1	98.0	95.1	93.6	98.6	99.3
Czech Republic	..	..	..	..	95.9	99.3	100.0	101.6	98.6	100.3	99.9	101.2	106.2	118.2	117.2	117.5
Denmark	80.0	86.5	86.0	88.7	92.9	95.1	100.0	99.1	96.8	99.3	98.7	94.8	96.4	97.6	101.0	101.4
Finland	96.1	99.9	97.0	85.2	76.7	87.0	100.0	97.6	95.4	98.2	101.1	96.6	98.6	100.3	104.4	104.8
France	80.5	86.4	85.9	89.6	93.3	96.1	100.0	100.4	97.7	100.0	99.3	95.7	96.6	98.0	101.7	102.2
Germany	73.2	79.4	80.1	84.0	88.6	93.0	100.0	98.6	95.2	98.7	98.6	94.3	95.5	97.1	101.8	102.6
Greece	142.4	133.8	120.8	113.7	106.0	101.2	100.0	98.4	96.6	93.9	94.6	88.4	89.1	90.7	93.9	94.3
Hungary	..	..	..	..	140.1	126.0	100.0	85.2	78.9	71.5	69.0	65.5	66.7	71.2	72.0	72.0
Iceland	121.9	110.4	110.9	110.5	104.0	99.6	100.0	99.5	101.7	104.5	106.3	107.4	91.0	93.2	99.3	99.6
Ireland	90.8	98.6	97.5	101.7	96.6	98.2	100.0	102.6	102.4	99.4	96.5	89.5	90.7	92.8	99.4	99.6
Italy	118.7	126.1	127.3	126.2	108.7	108.6	100.0	110.0	111.5	113.9	113.5	109.4	110.7	112.7	117.3	118.0
Japan	54.0	53.2	59.9	65.0	80.4	93.4	100.0	87.2	83.3	86.6	99.3	108.1	99.7	95.5	97.3	97.4
Korea	114.6	111.3	107.4	100.1	98.6	99.7	100.0	101.6	94.1	68.1	77.9	83.4	77.1	79.7	78.2	77.6
Luxembourg	86.8	91.0	91.6	93.5	94.1	96.8	100.0	98.9	96.7	97.7	97.5	94.9	95.4	96.5	99.1	99.2
Mexico	212.5	193.5	186.9	187.1	196.5	190.3	100.0	84.9	83.3	74.0	70.6	72.1	74.1	71.8	63.6	63.8
Netherlands	75.8	81.4	82.0	85.2	89.3	93.6	100.0	98.6	93.9	97.2	97.1	92.2	93.5	95.6	100.3	100.6
New Zealand	91.9	92.0	89.5	83.3	87.3	93.6	100.0	106.3	108.9	97.8	94.4	85.6	84.7	91.5	102.5	102.6
Norway	94.4	95.8	95.0	96.7	95.7	96.4	100.0	100.1	101.1	98.0	97.9	95.8	99.0	107.3	107.2	106.5
Poland	..	..	..		139.0	113.5	100.0	93.2	86.6	84.8	79.2	81.6	90.0	86.1	79.0	78.5
Portugal	91.8	93.3	95.8	101.3	97.8	96.9	100.0	99.6	98.3	98.2	97.7	95.4	96.3	97.2	99.6	99.9
Slovak Republic	..	..	..		97.9	96.7	100.0	100.9	105.6	106.6	100.6	102.3	99.8	100.1	104.4	104.6
Spain	109.7	117.0	118.4	117.1	104.6	99.7	100.0	101.0	96.9	98.1	97.3	94.3	95.4	96.8	99.7	100.1
Sweden	115.2	115.7	116.7	119.6	98.4	99.6	100.0	110.1	106.6	106.3	106.1	106.3	97.8	100.2	103.5	103.7
Switzerland	74.3	80.5	80.2	79.7	83.5	91.9	100.0	98.7	93.1	97.2	97.8	96.1	100.0	105.1	108.7	108.6
Turkey	2 008.1	1 546.9	1 023.7	610.9	427.8	173.5	100.0	58.6	34.9	21.1	14.1	10.3	5.8	4.3	3.2	2.8
United Kingdom	108.0	109.0	111.1	108.4	100.2	103.4	100.0	102.3	119.2	127.0	127.5	130.9	129.6	131.1	127.6	127.5
United States	79.2	83.3	85.4	87.1	92.6	98.0	100.0	105.6	113.1	124.8	124.4	127.5	134.3	134.8	131.3	131.6
Euro area	68.3	81.1	81.6	86.9	86.0	92.0	100.0	102.0	95.5	100.7	99.0	90.1	92.4	95.5	104.6	105.9

Note: For details on the method of calculation, see the section on exchange rates and competitiveness indicators in *OECD Economic Outlook* Sources and Methods (*http://www.oecd.org/eco/sources-and-methods*).
a) On the technical assumption that exchange rates remain at their levels of 26 March 2003, except for Turkey, where exchange rates vary according to official exchange rate policy.
Source: OECD.

Annex Table 39. **Export volumes**

Total goods, customs basis, percentage changes from previous year

	1985	1986	1987	1988	1989	1990	1991	1992	1993	1994	1995	1996	1997	1998	1999	2000	2001	2002	Projections	
																			2003	2004
Australia	9.0	3.1	8.1	0.1	4.8	7.2	16.2	6.3	6.2	6.3	3.0	12.3	8.0	0.1	4.9	9.7	1.4	0.6	3.7	8.9
Austria	9.5	1.2	2.0	7.6	15.0	10.7	7.1	3.7	-2.8	10.7	9.3	12.0	20.0	12.1	15.0	15.6	6.8	4.2	3.0	6.7
Belgium[a]	4.1	7.9	6.9	4.6	8.1	3.1	4.0	0.0	7.5	9.0	6.2	2.2	7.5	5.6	5.0	10.2	1.7	6.7	3.3	6.6
Canada	6.4	5.8	3.6	9.7	1.2	4.7	2.6	7.9	11.3	13.2	9.5	5.6	9.8	8.5	10.7	9.0	-4.3	0.6	4.1	7.4
Czech Republic	..	..	..	..	..	..	..	..	..	5.7	15.0	2.6	15.0	15.2	7.8	16.0	12.9	5.7	7.2	10.1
Denmark	4.6	1.4	2.4	7.6	7.4	6.5	7.1	5.3	0.1	7.5	6.0	3.4	6.3	1.5	6.7	10.8	2.2	6.1	3.8	7.9
Finland	1.0	0.6	1.4	3.2	-0.2	2.8	-8.7	9.0	18.6	13.9	7.0	6.0	12.0	9.0	4.1	9.1	-0.6	1.2	3.1	7.0
France[b]	2.5	0.1	4.2	9.7	10.1	5.1	5.2	4.8	-0.0	10.0	9.5	2.3	12.1	9.2	4.8	13.3	1.6	2.2	2.7	5.4
Germany	5.9	1.3	2.9	6.6	8.1	1.4	1.4	0.8	-6.3	9.0	6.7	7.1	10.7	5.7	6.3	12.8	4.7	4.4	4.4	6.0
Hungary	..	..	..	..	..	..	..	..	..	16.7	9.9	24.2	29.7	21.9	16.3	21.7	7.7	6.4	4.6	8.0
Iceland[c]	12.7	34.5	25.2	0.5	-2.1	3.8	-8.1	-0.9	4.9	12.2	-2.2	9.0	1.5	-2.5	7.3	-0.6	7.0	4.5	5.5	5.0
Ireland	5.3	2.8	18.2	8.7	9.2	7.7	6.7	11.4	15.4	11.6	20.8	9.9	14.9	24.5	16.3	18.9	5.1	6.4	2.7	7.2
Italy	7.4	1.8	2.5	5.6	8.6	3.3	0.2	3.7	8.8	11.9	13.2	1.2	3.8	2.6	1.8	10.2	0.3	1.6	4.4	5.7
Japan	5.0	-0.5	0.4	4.4	4.5	6.8	2.1	1.5	-2.4	1.4	4.2	1.2	11.6	-1.9	1.8	9.0	-10.9	9.6	8.2	9.6
Korea	10.7	24.5	23.2	19.4	-0.1	8.2	11.1	8.7	12.1	13.6	21.9	19.7	15.3	22.0	10.5	19.8	0.4	12.2	13.7	12.1
Luxembourg	-3.2	..	11.7	..	12.8	2.2	3.7	-0.5	-0.2	6.6	3.6	1.3	12.5	16.1	5.4	16.9	3.9	-3.2	0.8	6.2
Mexico	5.9	18.0	4.5	16.8	5.9	8.0	14.3	8.1	16.6	8.6	23.9	18.4	16.3	13.3	11.4	13.6	-2.7	-0.8	5.2	8.2
Netherlands	10.7	2.1	2.9	9.2	6.4	5.2	4.8	2.6	1.1	6.5	7.2	5.4	6.5	9.0	6.4	10.1	6.0	-2.2	3.4	7.2
New Zealand	3.5	-2.0	2.9	3.9	-2.7	5.7	10.4	2.6	4.2	10.1	2.9	4.8	5.9	-0.6	2.7	5.5	3.3	5.4	5.6	6.4
Norway	..	1.8	13.9	4.4	15.0	6.7	6.7	8.0	5.3	12.4	5.5	12.9	4.6	0.2	2.8	5.2	4.6	1.3	0.1	2.7
Poland	..	..	..	..	..	..	..	..	..	19.6	17.1	9.9	13.8	8.8	2.8	25.1	11.8	7.2	6.9	14.2
Portugal	10.6	7.8	11.7	9.3	20.5	12.7	0.6	7.5	-4.2	14.4	14.2	9.6	10.0	6.6	5.1	9.5	2.2	4.7	4.7	7.7
Slovak Republic	..	..	..	..	..	..	..	..	..	5.7	15.0	6.6	3.9	16.4	6.2	16.3	6.6	6.3	6.0	8.6
Spain	1.4	-3.4	7.5	6.0	4.8	11.9	11.3	4.9	11.7	21.2	9.7	12.0	14.1	6.9	6.4	12.2	2.0	1.4	2.3	6.2
Sweden	3.4	2.9	2.7	3.7	2.1	0.2	-2.2	1.0	9.8	16.9	10.8	6.1	10.7	8.5	6.1	11.4	-4.5	2.8	2.5	7.6
Switzerland	9.0	0.9	1.5	6.2	6.0	4.2	-1.0	3.8	0.4	4.8	3.8	2.5	7.6	3.5	3.6	7.0	1.2	3.1	3.3	5.3
Turkey	14.5	-20.8	21.9	8.8	-1.6	1.1	6.4	6.5	7.6	22.0	5.7	12.8	18.3	6.7	5.4	22.4	5.5	11.9	8.8	13.7
United Kingdom[b]	5.7	4.0	5.5	2.5	5.4	6.5	0.5	2.2	0.1	13.0	10.6	8.2	7.6	1.6	4.5	11.4	0.8	-1.8	0.5	9.0
United States[b]	3.6	5.1	11.4	18.8	12.6	8.3	7.1	6.8	3.0	9.7	11.9	8.7	14.5	2.1	3.8	11.3	-5.9	-3.6	3.6	9.9
Total OECD	5.2	2.6	4.9	7.9	7.3	5.2	3.7	3.8	2.0	9.3	9.3	6.5	11.0	5.7	5.7	12.0	-0.5	2.7	4.6	7.9

Note: Regional aggregates are calculated *inclusive* of intra-regional trade. Data are on a national account basis for the United States and France, otherwise from international trade statistics. See also *OECD Economic Outlook* Sources and Methods (*http://www.oecd.org/eco/sources-and-methods*).
a) Including Luxembourg until 1994.
b) Volume data use hedonic price deflators for certain components.
c) OECD estimates.
Source: OECD.

Annex Table 40. **Import volumes**

Total goods, customs basis, percentage changes from previous year

	1985	1986	1987	1988	1989	1990	1991	1992	1993	1994	1995	1996	1997	1998	1999	2000	2001	2002	Projections 2003	Projections 2004
Australia	7.9	-1.3	1.5	13.2	22.8	-7.3	-1.3	6.7	4.3	11.8	10.1	7.0	6.2	7.1	7.2	5.6	-4.7	13.6	8.6	8.6
Austria	5.4	5.2	5.3	7.7	10.6	11.0	3.3	2.8	-1.3	12.9	6.7	12.4	15.8	12.4	13.3	9.1	4.9	-0.6	2.6	6.3
Belgium[a]	3.8	10.6	8.3	4.9	6.8	5.2	4.1	1.0	1.2	7.8	4.9	4.3	4.6	8.1	3.3	10.3	0.2	5.4	3.4	7.0
Canada	10.4	9.1	5.4	13.5	5.2	0.6	3.1	7.6	8.7	10.6	7.5	6.0	17.1	6.2	8.8	9.5	-5.9	1.1	6.1	8.0
Czech Republic	..	..	..	..	..	..	..	..	..	18.8	26.7	10.9	8.8	11.4	2.4	14.1	13.8	4.8	6.4	9.4
Denmark	7.9	7.0	-1.7	0.0	2.4	4.5	4.7	4.7	-3.6	12.3	7.8	0.1	8.5	3.3	1.1	6.4	1.2	5.9	4.5	7.9
Finland	6.0	5.7	8.9	8.7	10.7	-4.0	-16.7	-2.1	-3.7	20.4	8.1	7.7	10.1	11.8	-0.5	4.4	-2.7	1.7	3.3	6.4
France[b]	5.7	6.6	8.8	11.1	9.6	5.4	2.8	0.9	-4.1	10.1	8.5	0.2	7.6	12.3	7.4	15.5	0.4	1.6	2.5	6.9
Germany	4.9	5.4	5.3	6.4	7.3	11.4	13.3	1.3	-9.8	7.9	6.9	5.5	6.1	11.0	6.6	9.9	2.4	-0.3	4.8	6.3
Hungary	..	..	..	..	..	..	..	..	..	14.9	-3.1	17.9	26.2	24.6	14.2	20.8	3.9	5.8	5.6	7.0
Iceland[c]	10.1	23.4	41.8	0.6	-12.3	3.3	3.0	-2.2	-12.2	6.5	6.8	15.9	5.0	24.4	3.4	3.2	-9.0	-2.9	7.0	7.4
Ireland	3.4	0.5	10.1	6.6	10.9	7.1	0.6	5.1	5.8	12.4	16.0	10.0	14.8	18.2	8.1	15.6	-0.0	4.4	2.2	6.0
Italy	8.8	4.6	10.2	7.0	8.3	4.5	4.6	3.2	-10.2	12.5	9.8	-3.1	8.9	8.5	7.9	8.3	-0.7	1.7	3.8	5.8
Japan	0.7	9.7	9.0	16.9	7.7	8.0	2.6	-1.0	2.7	12.5	14.9	7.7	1.9	-6.5	10.0	11.1	-1.9	1.6	4.7	4.3
Korea	5.6	1.6	17.8	19.8	15.8	15.1	23.1	3.2	4.7	23.5	24.4	16.1	2.2	-22.1	28.0	16.8	-3.3	13.7	12.3	12.3
Luxembourg	..	..	..	..	5.8	4.9	10.5	-2.9	2.5	4.9	2.9	-0.5	12.9	10.4	14.2	5.0	3.4	-1.9	0.1	4.9
Mexico	14.6	-6.9	8.9	41.1	18.8	17.4	19.7	23.2	3.8	18.5	-13.2	22.7	22.0	15.3	13.8	19.5	-4.1	0.3	4.7	9.3
Netherlands	7.2	3.7	4.7	8.0	6.8	4.7	4.3	1.3	-2.7	7.1	7.8	6.1	7.6	8.5	5.9	12.0	4.6	-2.7	1.2	9.3
New Zealand	-0.0	-1.4	10.4	-7.8	21.7	7.3	-9.6	10.7	4.3	16.3	6.5	3.4	3.6	2.4	13.4	-2.7	1.9	8.4	6.2	5.6
Norway	11.7	14.4	-2.0	-9.5	-5.7	10.3	2.6	3.3	0.7	16.1	8.1	10.4	7.9	10.5	4.3	6.4	1.3	2.5	2.8	2.9
Poland	..	..	..	..	..	..	..	..	..	15.3	20.8	28.2	22.2	15.1	4.2	10.8	3.1	9.9	7.4	11.0
Portugal	6.6	19.2	28.0	22.2	8.4	15.8	5.9	13.0	-9.5	12.2	9.4	5.1	12.8	15.0	9.8	5.6	2.3	-1.7	0.2	5.4
Slovak Republic	..	..	..	..	..	..	..	..	..	18.8	26.6	5.4	1.9	18.6	-5.5	13.1	12.4	4.8	5.5	7.1
Spain	8.4	21.6	26.3	19.2	16.8	9.9	11.5	6.8	-5.7	15.2	11.0	7.5	11.8	13.7	13.9	8.3	4.1	3.8	5.8	6.9
Sweden	9.2	3.7	8.9	5.4	7.1	0.2	-6.4	-0.8	2.5	14.9	9.0	2.4	10.5	10.3	2.9	12.7	-6.1	-3.3	1.4	7.7
Switzerland	5.5	8.2	5.7	4.7	5.8	2.3	-1.2	-4.3	-1.6	9.5	6.1	1.4	6.8	6.1	8.2	7.4	1.0	-0.8	2.6	4.8
Turkey	7.9	-5.0	14.1	-0.5	5.7	34.2	-2.0	10.6	37.2	-21.1	29.8	30.8	20.9	-2.2	-6.4	43.8	-25.6	16.4	13.3	14.6
United Kingdom	3.8	7.2	6.9	13.8	8.0	0.5	-5.2	6.2	0.4	6.3	6.0	10.1	9.4	9.6	7.6	11.8	2.9	1.4	2.2	9.6
United States[b]	6.3	10.3	4.8	4.1	4.2	3.0	-0.1	9.3	10.1	13.3	9.0	9.4	14.2	11.7	12.2	13.5	-3.3	3.9	6.6	7.7
Total OECD	5.9	7.3	7.1	8.6	7.7	5.6	3.7	4.1	0.3	11.0	9.0	7.3	9.7	8.2	9.0	12.0	-0.7	2.5	4.9	7.5

Note: Regional aggregates are calculated *inclusive* of intra-regional trade. Data are on a national account basis for the United States and France, otherwise from international trade statistics. See also *OECD Economic Outlook*
Sources and Methods (*http://www.oecd.org/eco/sources-and-methods*).
a) Including Luxembourg until 1994.
b) Volume data use hedonic price deflators for certain components.
c) OECD estimates.
Source: OECD.

Annex Table 41. **Export prices (average unit values)**

Total goods, percentage changes from previous year, national currency terms

	1985	1986	1987	1988	1989	1990	1991	1992	1993	1994	1995	1996	1997	1998	1999	2000	2001	2002	Projections 2003	2004
Australia	12.5	1.2	4.0	11.8	5.5	1.2	-9.1	2.1	1.3	-2.8	7.4	-4.1	1.8	4.9	-7.0	15.7	9.8	-2.9	-4.4	0.6
Austria	2.6	-4.3	-1.9	4.0	-2.6	-1.9	-4.1	-1.8	-1.4	-1.0	3.7	-6.1	-2.6	-3.3	-8.0	-1.5	-0.2	-2.3	0.3	1.6
Belgium[a]	1.7	-9.9	-6.1	4.7	7.9	-3.1	-1.9	-1.4	-1.6	1.2	1.8	2.7	5.3	-0.0	-0.6	8.7	2.2	0.1	-0.8	1.4
Canada	0.5	-2.4	1.4	-0.5	1.2	-1.2	-5.3	2.5	4.6	6.0	6.2	-0.0	-1.3	-0.6	1.4	6.3	1.8	-1.5	1.8	1.6
Czech Republic	:	:	:	:	:	:	:	:	:	4.7	7.2	1.0	5.5	3.6	-0.9	6.3	0.3	-6.8	-1.1	1.4
Denmark	3.4	-4.5	-1.0	-0.1	5.6	-1.5	-0.4	-1.7	-3.0	1.9	0.1	1.2	2.0	-0.8	0.4	6.7	2.5	-1.9	-0.9	2.6
Finland	2.8	-2.3	2.3	5.0	7.7	-1.2	0.5	6.1	4.8	1.3	7.0	-1.2	3.0	-0.6	-2.8	15.2	-2.5	-7.0	-4.2	0.3
France[b]	3.7	-4.5	-1.3	2.1	3.7	-1.9	-1.5	-2.3	-3.2	-0.6	0.4	1.7	2.1	-1.9	-1.8	1.6	0.4	-2.8	-1.0	1.9
Germany	3.9	-3.3	-2.7	0.9	4.5	-1.1	-0.6	0.7	0.0	1.0	1.7	0.2	1.6	0.1	-1.7	3.9	1.8	-2.6	-1.3	1.7
Hungary	:	:	:	:	:	:	:	:	:	18.0	31.2	18.9	15.1	13.1	3.5	9.9	2.1	-5.0	0.7	1.7
Iceland[c]	30.9	-1.0	-5.9	11.3	32.7	13.7	7.8	-3.1	2.7	6.0	5.8	-1.2	2.9	6.9	-1.2	3.7	22.7	0.2	0.8	1.8
Ireland	4.0	-5.7	-3.9	5.6	8.7	-8.7	-1.8	-0.6	3.7	3.1	0.6	-0.8	1.4	2.5	0.3	4.8	5.2	-5.4	-8.2	1.7
Italy	8.0	-4.7	1.2	5.0	6.3	2.1	2.9	0.8	11.3	3.7	9.2	0.8	0.5	0.9	-0.1	5.7	4.0	-2.3	-0.5	1.5
Japan	-0.7	-15.4	-6.0	-2.5	7.0	3.6	-0.3	-0.1	-4.6	-1.0	-1.8	6.9	1.9	0.7	-8.0	-0.7	5.5	-3.3	-1.1	0.8
Korea	-6.0	-8.4	10.5	8.5	-5.3	2.0	3.1	4.3	-1.5	2.8	2.4	-9.4	8.0	17.2	-17.0	-4.6	-0.8	-7.2	-3.0	-0.1
Luxembourg	:	:	:	:	15.7	5.2	-1.0	8.3	11.3	-10.9	2.7	-7.0	0.7	-7.1	16.1	-7.8	5.6	12.9	0.2	1.4
Mexico	60.7	35.6	152.0	53.3	18.4	22.2	-2.6	2.5	-3.0	17.9	100.0	20.3	3.1	8.7	8.2	6.5	-3.3	5.8	11.4	3.4
Netherlands	1.3	-17.1	-5.7	0.4	5.0	-1.2	-0.6	-2.9	-3.4	2.0	1.5	0.7	3.0	-2.8	-1.2	8.1	1.6	0.0	-2.0	2.1
New Zealand	9.3	-2.6	6.0	6.2	13.3	-1.4	-4.2	8.1	2.7	-4.1	-1.7	-3.5	-2.8	4.6	1.4	17.7	9.0	-10.3	-8.7	2.7
Norway	4.9	-24.8	-3.4	-0.1	12.3	4.1	-3.7	-8.4	0.6	-3.7	3.7	7.4	2.3	-11.3	12.8	44.6	-5.2	-7.7	1.6	2.8
Poland	:	:	:	:	:	:	:	:	:	29.0	20.8	8.0	12.7	6.5	7.9	1.1	-4.0	2.4	4.5	3.1
Portugal	15.7	3.3	8.4	10.4	5.8	2.9	0.2	-2.2	4.3	5.1	3.0	-1.1	0.4	-0.3	-0.7	4.8	-0.1	-4.3	-0.6	1.8
Slovak Republic	:	:	:	:	:	:	:	:	:	4.7	7.2	3.0	1.2	3.0	5.4	11.2	4.5	-0.8	-0.0	4.3
Spain	8.4	-4.1	2.7	5.4	4.6	-1.8	-0.9	1.1	5.1	4.2	6.3	1.0	3.5	-0.2	-0.8	6.1	2.4	0.3	-0.9	1.6
Sweden	3.8	-1.2	3.5	4.5	6.9	2.1	0.2	-3.0	8.4	3.9	5.4	-4.3	0.4	-2.5	-1.8	2.0	3.4	-1.5	-0.8	1.2
Switzerland	2.0	0.5	-1.0	2.2	5.7	1.3	2.4	1.2	0.2	-0.6	-1.8	-0.2	3.8	0.3	1.2	3.4	2.9	-3.2	-1.4	0.4
Turkey	35.9	25.7	45.6	59.5	50.4	35.8	58.2	66.9	55.4	163.7	72.1	69.7	77.8	64.1	50.4	24.3	105.0	25.8	34.1	25.7
United Kingdom	5.2	-10.6	3.8	0.4	8.3	4.0	0.6	1.2	9.7	0.4	3.7	1.1	-5.1	-5.7	-3.0	1.2	-0.2	-0.4	1.3	0.6
United States[b]	-5.0	-3.3	2.2	6.5	1.4	-1.0	-0.1	-1.5	-0.5	1.1	2.4	-2.6	-2.7	-3.1	-1.4	1.2	-0.7	-0.5	2.1	1.4
Total OECD	2.9	-5.9	1.7	3.8	5.0	0.8	-0.3	0.2	1.0	2.3	4.5	1.2	1.2	-0.1	-2.1	3.7	2.0	-1.8	-0.0	1.5

Note: Regional aggregates are calculated *inclusive* of intra-regional trade. Data are national accounts price deflators in the case of the United States and France.
a) Including Luxembourg until 1994.
b) Certain components are estimated on a hedonic basis.
c) OECD estimates.
Source: OECD.

Annex Table 42. **Import prices (average unit values)**
Total goods, percentage changes from previous year, national currency terms

	1985	1986	1987	1988	1989	1990	1991	1992	1993	1994	1995	1996	1997	1998	1999	2000	2001	2002	Projections 2003	2004
Australia	18.7	9.3	6.1	-2.4	-1.0	3.9	1.0	4.6	8.1	-2.4	3.6	-5.4	-0.1	8.4	-2.2	9.2	5.8	-4.7	-7.0	-0.7
Austria	3.8	-9.9	-4.1	1.8	3.0	-2.6	3.1	-2.5	-3.5	-1.2	-1.2	-5.2	-3.8	-5.3	-6.7	4.3	-1.0	-3.8	-2.1	1.3
Belgium[a]	-0.0	-16.2	-7.0	5.7	7.1	-1.8	-1.3	-3.2	-5.8	2.1	3.2	3.3	6.0	-1.6	1.1	9.7	4.0	0.9	-0.7	1.2
Canada	1.7	0.1	-1.8	-2.0	-0.3	0.7	-3.3	2.0	5.5	6.1	3.0	-2.5	-0.2	2.9	-0.9	1.5	2.5	0.4	-1.2	1.3
Czech Republic	..	..	..	..	..	..	..	..	..	-0.9	5.6	1.3	5.1	-2.3	2.0	11.9	-1.7	-8.8	-0.8	1.1
Denmark	2.4	-9.6	-4.1	1.8	7.1	-2.9	0.0	-2.9	-2.9	2.5	2.4	2.1	3.4	0.9	0.4	7.8	0.8	-1.5	-1.1	1.7
Finland	3.0	-9.8	-2.2	1.8	4.1	1.6	2.2	10.5	12.8	-3.1	-1.0	0.2	5.3	-3.9	2.6	18.3	0.6	-2.0	-4.1	0.5
France[b]	0.8	-14.9	-2.3	0.7	6.1	-2.1	-0.7	-3.8	-4.1	0.1	0.4	2.4	1.7	-3.1	-1.9	5.2	-0.4	-3.8	-1.7	1.7
Germany	2.5	-15.9	-6.1	0.9	7.4	-2.5	1.9	-2.4	-1.5	0.8	0.5	0.5	3.2	-3.2	-1.4	10.1	-0.2	-4.9	-1.5	1.5
Hungary	..	..	..	..	..	..	..	..	..	15.2	30.6	21.3	13.6	11.3	5.5	13.0	2.3	-5.4	1.4	1.9
Iceland[c]	30.9	-1.0	-5.9	11.3	32.7	9.6	2.9	-2.4	7.4	5.0	4.2	3.3	0.1	-0.9	-0.3	8.1	20.0	-0.5	4.6	1.8
Ireland	2.5	-8.5	-4.2	4.7	8.5	-5.2	2.4	-2.3	7.6	2.3	3.0	-1.2	0.5	2.1	3.1	8.5	2.2	-7.8	-10.7	0.1
Italy	7.4	-17.6	-1.5	4.0	7.7	-0.7	-0.8	-0.5	11.7	4.1	12.2	-1.3	1.4	-2.7	-0.9	14.2	2.0	-2.8	-0.7	1.6
Japan	-4.4	-36.5	-8.0	-5.4	11.9	10.9	-9.2	-6.9	-12.4	-7.7	-1.3	14.7	6.0	-5.4	-12.3	4.7	5.0	-2.4	2.0	1.8
Korea	-3.6	-0.2	10.1	3.3	-5.9	4.3	-1.8	3.3	0.7	-0.9	1.7	0.1	10.8	22.5	-15.3	9.5	3.7	-9.1	1.1	0.9
Luxembourg	..	..	..	..	6.1	-2.6	-3.5	4.7	8.5	3.1	-3.9	2.5	-1.5	-4.7	4.2	0.3	-0.4	6.8	1.0	0.6
Mexico	70.7	92.1	129.8	69.7	14.2	16.2	6.6	3.3	2.0	11.7	99.7	18.9	4.8	14.7	3.3	1.9	-0.6	3.9	12.6	2.9
Netherlands	0.9	-18.1	-3.0	-0.6	5.2	-1.7	-0.3	-2.7	-3.2	2.0	0.2	0.7	2.6	-2.7	0.8	7.6	-1.0	0.0	-2.1	1.7
New Zealand	10.5	-2.5	-4.3	-0.8	7.9	0.7	1.0	6.7	-0.6	-3.4	-0.1	-2.7	-0.9	3.8	2.3	16.5	1.2	-5.8	-5.6	2.5
Norway	6.5	0.0	2.8	2.9	6.0	0.9	-1.7	-2.1	1.0	0.7	0.9	-0.9	-1.0	1.4	-7.4	3.5	0.2	-7.6	2.4	3.4
Poland	..	..	..	..	..	..	..	..	..	28.3	18.6	11.1	13.3	2.1	7.2	5.2	-6.2	-0.7	5.7	3.5
Portugal	7.3	-8.6	6.1	7.1	7.8	3.3	0.2	-5.1	5.0	3.6	1.8	2.7	0.3	-2.1	-1.3	8.5	1.1	-1.4	-0.7	2.0
Slovak Republic	..	..	..	..	..	..	..	..	..	-0.9	5.6	5.5	2.6	-3.4	7.7	13.6	7.6	-0.8	-0.6	3.8
Spain	1.2	-20.1	-3.2	-2.1	2.1	-3.4	-2.7	-1.2	5.2	5.8	4.4	0.3	4.1	-2.9	0.0	12.9	-1.3	-2.4	-1.8	1.2
Sweden	2.4	-8.3	1.7	3.4	5.2	2.2	-0.6	-2.7	12.0	4.2	0.8	-3.8	0.9	-3.3	1.5	4.5	5.9	2.6	-2.0	0.7
Switzerland	4.4	-9.3	-3.6	4.8	8.1	-0.4	-0.1	2.2	-1.9	-4.9	-2.0	-0.1	5.0	-2.3	-1.9	5.6	0.1	-3.4	-0.4	0.9
Turkey	44.3	8.3	37.5	64.6	54.7	30.0	54.6	61.6	50.0	171.5	82.2	65.2	72.7	63.0	53.5	45.9	88.4	31.8	40.5	25.6
United Kingdom	3.9	-5.8	2.7	-0.5	5.9	3.0	-0.5	-0.3	7.8	3.6	6.7	-0.3	-7.1	-7.4	-3.3	0.4	-0.6	-2.5	2.4	0.6
United States[b]	-4.0	-2.2	6.9	4.8	2.8	1.8	-1.4	-0.4	-1.1	0.8	2.7	-2.4	-4.1	-6.0	0.1	4.8	-2.9	-1.7	3.6	1.1
Total OECD	2.0	-10.7	1.2	2.9	5.7	1.4	-0.7	-0.9	0.1	2.1	4.3	1.6	1.5	-1.9	-1.7	6.9	0.9	-2.2	0.8	1.5

Note: Regional aggregates are calculated *inclusive* of intra-regional trade. Data are national accounts price deflators in the case of the United States and France.
a) Including Luxembourg until 1994.
b) Certain components are estimated on a hedonic basis.
c) OECD estimates.
Source: OECD.

Annex Table 43. Competitive positions: relative unit labour costs

Indices, 1995 = 100

	1985	1986	1987	1988	1989	1990	1991	1992	1993	1994	1995	1996	1997	1998	1999	2000	2001	2002
Australia	224.0	180.8	164.6	161.5	163.9	149.9	133.2	115.8	101.4	102.9	100.0	103.5	104.5	93.1	91.4	86.8	81.7	85.8
Austria	94.2	109.2	115.6	109.8	103.9	104.2	102.1	103.6	105.8	98.9	100.0	102.0	91.9	82.0	79.1	72.1	70.5	70.2
Belgium	88.5	92.5	95.9	93.4	91.5	97.4	97.3	97.4	96.4	96.9	100.0	94.7	87.9	89.1	89.3	85.6	87.3	89.8
Canada	107.3	102.3	109.3	117.8	121.8	125.0	128.5	117.6	105.1	97.8	100.0	105.8	106.2	101.6	102.8	102.0	104.1	104.3
Czech Republic	..	..	..	..	..	..	..	..	90.2	98.1	100.0	107.1	104.9	115.2	116.6	115.8	119.1	125.3
Denmark	78.4	82.4	90.2	95.4	89.6	97.8	93.9	96.3	101.2	96.9	100.0	104.0	98.4	101.9	104.0	103.5	105.7	108.3
Finland	133.5	128.8	127.6	131.7	138.3	145.5	139.2	108.2	82.3	87.2	100.0	93.8	88.0	89.0	87.5	77.9	81.5	82.6
France	106.6	108.0	107.1	102.9	99.4	105.6	100.9	99.0	101.5	100.3	100.0	99.6	90.8	87.2	84.6	78.1	78.0	78.2
Germany	69.7	77.4	83.5	83.0	80.4	82.9	83.6	89.8	91.4	92.6	100.0	97.4	92.8	94.8	96.3	93.4	93.1	93.7
Greece	102.7	88.0	85.0	93.8	99.7	106.3	97.9	94.3	88.2	92.1	100.0	102.7	105.9	101.2	102.9	98.3	98.5	101.0
Hungary	..	..	..	..	..	..	..	..	122.7	122.2	100.0	92.5	92.6	85.5	85.5	78.2	86.2	97.8
Iceland	99.0	96.2	117.9	128.2	113.6	109.0	113.3	111.0	101.2	99.4	100.0	98.7	104.0	113.1	124.3	134.4	116.4	122.5
Ireland	152.8	163.6	151.0	138.6	127.6	133.0	126.8	123.0	113.0	109.0	100.0	99.1	91.7	85.3	81.5	74.3	72.1	75.4
Italy	135.4	133.9	133.5	130.9	130.7	130.0	133.2	131.3	120.0	114.1	100.0	111.8	114.1	120.3	121.1	113.6	115.3	119.2
Japan	49.4	65.6	69.5	71.8	65.2	60.9	66.6	73.5	89.1	98.5	100.0	84.7	80.1	87.7	98.6	101.7	97.5	89.1
Korea	82.6	65.2	68.4	84.0	99.4	96.7	98.4	90.7	87.3	89.8	100.0	107.0	93.4	64.8	67.5	70.9	67.4	75.1
Luxembourg	110.3	119.1	120.6	109.5	103.5	104.4	102.1	102.0	100.9	99.4	100.0	94.8	94.1	92.5	88.1	87.3	89.0	90.4
Mexico	134.5	103.5	105.0	109.1	120.9	123.0	137.4	153.0	164.7	160.6	100.0	101.8	111.8	118.3	113.8	122.7	132.4	133.7
Netherlands	98.9	106.7	112.5	108.9	101.2	102.6	99.6	102.6	101.6	97.6	100.0	96.7	93.8	97.9	97.1	93.7	95.1	99.8
New Zealand	77.6	79.9	89.8	99.9	92.8	93.0	92.0	82.4	85.4	93.3	100.0	111.1	116.5	107.7	108.0	97.2	95.4	104.2
Norway	93.4	94.1	95.4	100.6	98.9	97.7	95.7	93.6	90.6	94.4	100.0	101.0	107.0	109.0	116.1	119.3	124.9	139.4
Poland	..	..	..	..	..	..	..	..	90.2	96.3	100.0	102.7	102.4	108.0	101.0	100.4	104.7	93.8
Portugal	89.3	87.3	83.6	86.9	94.6	89.8	91.8	100.7	91.5	95.0	100.0	91.3	92.9	94.7	97.0	97.9	100.5	102.4
Slovak Republic	..	..	..	..	..	..	..	..	83.3	89.2	100.0	107.7	125.7	133.9	132.2	146.7	153.5	163.4
Spain	79.3	82.9	84.2	89.5	96.6	108.7	109.8	112.6	102.3	99.2	100.0	104.3	103.7	106.6	106.5	107.1	110.8	115.6
Sweden	127.7	128.8	129.8	134.7	141.3	145.7	148.3	145.5	103.9	97.2	100.0	113.1	108.7	105.9	101.2	98.2	90.0	91.7
Switzerland	69.4	76.6	81.9	83.4	78.9	84.9	85.3	83.6	82.7	91.3	100.0	96.5	92.8	96.1	96.4	96.2	101.2	106.5
Turkey	122.0	97.1	88.5	80.8	122.2	173.4	190.7	172.1	171.3	111.5	100.0	100.2	112.6	125.8	147.1	168.5	121.1	117.8
United Kingdom	111.9	105.7	109.0	116.3	112.5	116.5	120.1	111.2	98.2	100.6	100.0	103.2	125.3	138.0	143.1	145.2	143.7	146.5
United States	168.8	148.8	125.7	116.4	117.6	114.4	112.1	108.0	106.6	105.5	100.0	101.0	106.1	115.3	112.3	117.7	119.0	117.6
Euro area	83.7	94.5	101.8	97.3	92.3	101.1	98.8	103.1	99.3	96.8	100.0	100.5	90.5	92.3	91.1	82.1	83.7	87.6

Note: Competitiveness-weighted relative unit labour costs in the manufacturing sector in dollar terms. An increase in the index indicates a real effective appreciation and a corresponding deterioration of the competitive position. Competitiveness weights take into account the structure of competition in both export and import markets of the manufacturing sector of 42 countries. For details on the method of calculation see Durand. M., C. Madaschi and F. Terrible (1998), "Trends in OECD Countries' International Competitiveness: The Influence of Emerging Market Economies", *OECD Economics Department Working Papers*, No. 195. See also *OECD Economic Outlook Sources and Methods* (http://www.oecd.org/eco/sources-and-methods).

Source: OECD.

Annex Table 44. Competitive positions: relative export prices

Indices, 1995 = 100

	1985	1986	1987	1988	1989	1990	1991	1992	1993	1994	1995	1996	1997	1998	1999	2000	2001	2002
Australia	108.5	98.0	100.9	118.3	123.5	116.4	105.7	96.9	91.1	96.1	100.0	100.4	102.2	95.7	97.5	103.0	97.3	96.8
Austria	103.6	107.8	109.7	112.5	102.6	104.6	99.3	98.5	99.4	96.0	100.0	92.3	86.1	83.7	77.5	71.3	69.6	69.8
Belgium	89.8	93.5	93.1	92.8	95.2	97.3	95.0	95.9	94.0	95.9	100.0	100.2	100.1	102.6	102.3	104.0	105.0	108.4
Canada	100.0	97.3	99.2	102.8	105.6	103.1	100.4	96.3	95.3	95.6	100.0	101.3	102.3	100.1	100.9	102.5	100.4	99.1
Czech Republic	..	..	..	..	..	..	..	..	94.2	98.3	100.0	102.7	103.2	108.4	107.0	108.8	111.5	117.3
Denmark	89.4	96.1	98.6	95.5	93.2	98.7	97.2	98.8	98.7	100.0	100.0	99.6	97.9	101.0	102.7	99.2	100.0	102.3
Finland	88.4	88.6	91.2	94.6	99.3	99.3	98.0	90.1	79.5	85.1	100.0	95.3	94.6	96.8	94.5	100.5	98.4	94.9
France	105.1	108.6	109.0	107.4	104.0	106.8	102.5	103.0	100.3	99.8	100.0	101.7	99.5	99.3	97.6	91.9	90.6	90.0
Germany	80.6	89.8	93.0	90.5	89.1	92.9	91.5	94.9	96.4	96.6	100.0	97.8	93.4	95.3	94.2	91.2	91.2	91.0
Hungary	..	..	..	..	..	..	..	..	103.3	102.4	100.0	101.2	105.7	108.0	107.3	108.3	109.7	112.9
Iceland	148.5	122.1	108.0	101.8	102.6	99.6	79.9	75.0	72.8	91.4	100.0	85.7	99.3	86.4	91.3	111.9	107.6	112.9
Ireland	110.5	113.0	108.5	110.5	110.6	106.0	104.0	104.6	100.9	99.5	100.0	102.4	103.6	104.1	103.7	97.5	104.1	101.7
Italy	101.8	104.1	104.6	100.6	107.4	112.9	114.1	112.6	100.4	98.5	100.0	105.8	105.2	109.1	109.9	109.1	111.7	112.0
Japan	71.7	80.7	79.4	81.5	79.4	74.8	80.4	84.1	94.5	100.7	100.0	92.7	89.8	90.2	98.1	104.4	100.9	94.0
Korea	100.7	87.1	99.7	112.4	123.8	116.6	110.0	103.5	101.3	99.0	100.0	104.1	105.2	84.4	81.3	84.0	80.1	73.5
Luxembourg	71.8	73.9	73.9	74.0	81.0	89.2	88.6	97.6	108.2	96.9	100.0	91.1	87.8	82.2	96.1	84.0	87.1	100.5
Mexico	103.2	100.8	97.4	97.5	95.7	93.8	94.0	91.7	92.2	99.4	100.0	103.6	110.0	113.8	114.5	118.1	119.8	120.4
Netherlands	91.2	91.9	98.5	98.7	95.0	96.6	95.1	95.3	94.9	96.2	100.0	98.7	95.1	94.3	92.8	85.8	88.3	92.3
New Zealand	93.9	89.8	95.4	106.5	104.2	97.5	92.0	89.3	92.9	97.4	100.0	101.6	101.0	92.1	91.1	94.9	98.7	98.3
Norway	99.5	95.6	96.3	112.0	116.3	105.8	100.2	94.8	90.5	89.2	100.0	95.9	95.4	95.5	93.0	95.3	93.6	93.6
Poland	..	..	..	..	..	..	..	..	100.9	99.3	100.0	100.2	102.5	106.4	108.0	107.7	110.6	110.1
Portugal	108.7	106.9	104.9	104.9	100.4	101.7	103.6	105.5	100.5	99.6	100.0	98.6	95.0	94.5	94.5	93.9	92.0	88.8
Slovak Republic	..	..	..	..	..	..	..	..	102.7	99.7	100.0	101.9	104.2	106.7	103.6	111.8	114.8	118.9
Spain	104.0	106.7	106.9	113.3	111.4	111.5	112.9	112.4	106.1	100.1	100.0	100.8	101.0	101.6	100.5	100.3	105.8	113.2
Sweden	104.8	107.4	109.0	110.7	112.5	113.2	114.5	113.1	98.2	98.9	100.0	105.6	100.9	98.0	96.5	94.1	87.8	90.4
Switzerland	74.5	84.5	88.4	88.0	83.9	90.6	92.5	91.7	93.7	99.5	100.0	99.4	97.1	101.8	104.7	104.0	110.7	115.5
Turkey	142.2	112.7	119.9	108.8	106.4	104.9	104.7	102.3	101.0	98.6	100.0	97.2	99.2	96.7	95.9	85.1	94.2	89.9
United Kingdom	100.7	96.8	97.7	102.6	101.3	103.2	104.8	102.8	102.4	104.1	100.0	101.5	110.5	111.4	108.3	105.8	102.2	104.7
United States	151.3	134.1	123.5	119.3	119.5	114.9	114.5	111.3	112.6	108.7	100.0	98.9	101.4	105.2	105.5	106.7	109.9	110.4

Note: Competitiveness-weighted relative export prices in the manufacturing sector in dollar terms. Competitiveness weights take into account the structure of competition in both export and import markets of the manufacturing sector of 42 countries. An increase in the index indicates a real effective appreciation and a corresponding deterioration of the competitive position. For details on the method of calculation see Durand, M., C. Madaschi and F. Terrible (1998). "Trends in OECD Countries' International Competitiveness: The Influence of Emerging Market Economies", *OECD Economics Department Working Papers*, No. 195. See also *OECD Economic Outlook Sources and Methods (http://www.oecd.org/eco/sources-and-methods).*

Source: OECD.

Annex Table 45. Export performance for total goods
Total goods, percentage changes from previous year

	1985	1986	1987	1988	1989	1990	1991	1992	1993	1994	1995	1996	1997	1998	1999	2000	2001	2002	Projections 2003	2004
Australia	7.6	1.5	-1.9	-9.2	-1.5	2.3	9.0	0.5	1.8	-4.4	-6.0	6.2	1.8	-1.2	0.3	0.6	2.0	-3.0	-3.4	-0.3
Austria	5.0	-4.8	-3.9	0.5	6.8	4.0	0.4	2.5	-0.1	0.4	0.0	5.0	9.0	1.6	7.6	2.8	3.9	2.1	-1.9	-0.8
Belgium[a]	0.5	-1.1	0.0	-1.1	0.4	-2.7	-1.3	-2.5	10.7	0.1	-2.2	-3.0	-1.6	-3.4	-1.5	-1.5	-0.5	5.8	-0.5	-0.9
Canada	-0.7	-2.9	-1.3	2.5	-4.0	4.0	1.4	-0.9	1.4	0.6	1.0	-2.7	-3.1	-0.7	-0.3	-4.2	-0.7	-2.8	-2.4	-0.4
Czech Republic	..	..	..	..	..	..	..	..	..	-5.1	2.8	-4.9	4.9	2.6	3.3	5.5	8.6	2.9	1.9	2.3
Denmark	-0.0	-3.6	-2.8	2.2	1.3	2.1	2.4	2.4	1.4	-1.9	-0.8	-4.0	-1.5	-5.6	1.7	-0.7	2.2	3.8	-0.3	0.7
Finland	-2.6	-5.1	-4.0	-2.8	-6.2	-0.2	-12.1	7.6	20.1	8.4	-10.4	-3.4	0.6	1.8	-0.6	-3.6	-2.0	-1.4	-1.7	-1.4
France	1.7	-4.7	-1.5	0.8	1.0	-0.9	-1.5	1.0	2.1	-1.4	0.7	-3.8	1.4	0.2	-1.8	1.0	-0.6	0.8	-1.7	-2.1
Germany	1.5	-4.7	-3.6	-2.1	0.3	-2.7	-1.2	-2.5	-7.6	-1.8	-2.7	-0.4	-0.3	-2.5	-0.8	-0.2	3.6	1.7	-0.1	-2.3
Hungary	..	..	..	..	..	..	..	..	..	8.3	0.2	16.8	18.1	12.8	12.9	10.4	3.5	4.0	0.1	0.5
Iceland	9.4	26.8	18.4	0.8	-6.5	8.2	-0.1	-6.5	-1.6	-0.1	3.6	4.3	0.2	-6.8	3.2	-6.8	3.9	3.3	1.6	-1.3
Ireland	2.3	-0.9	6.4	-1.6	3.5	4.0	2.9	10.1	12.1	6.0	10.8	2.5	6.0	14.6	8.7	6.5	3.6	4.8	-1.1	-0.6
Italy	4.0	-5.2	-2.1	0.5	-1.8	-3.5	-4.4	0.0	12.5	2.4	-1.1	-2.5	-5.5	-6.3	-4.7	-2.6	-0.8	-0.6	-0.5	-2.2
Japan	-0.1	-6.3	-6.6	-5.9	-3.7	-0.5	-5.1	-7.0	-9.6	-10.7	-6.8	-7.4	-0.6	-1.9	-7.2	-6.7	-8.0	-4.0	0.2	-1.7
Korea	4.6	10.3	11.5	6.8	-12.8	2.6	6.1	1.3	0.7	2.6	7.6	-3.7	0.1	26.4	3.0	-0.4	-4.0	14.8	5.7	1.4
Luxembourg	..	..	..	..	-3.3	-9.8	-2.8	-13.9	-11.4	11.9	-5.0	2.8	1.6	16.3	-15.7	13.6	-0.1	-10.2	-3.2	-1.2
Mexico	..	1.2	5.0	9.4	3.2	7.5	10.2	-2.2	3.8	-3.9	16.6	8.3	0.4	-0.4	2.2	1.5	0.2	-2.1	-0.7	0.6
Netherlands	2.3	-2.1	-1.3	2.7	-0.3	-0.2	-0.5	-0.3	3.7	-2.2	0.3	-0.3	-1.1	0.8	1.3	-0.2	4.8	-4.1	-0.9	-0.1
New Zealand	9.8	-2.3	-4.9	-4.7	-11.3	5.3	6.5	-3.5	-1.1	1.0	-5.8	-1.3	-0.5	-2.3	-2.8	-1.3	2.4	0.8	-0.6	-1.2
Norway	0.2	-5.2	6.2	-0.8	9.1	2.9	3.3	3.6	5.3	4.4	-0.2	6.6	-2.0	-4.8	-0.7	-4.2	4.4	-0.2	-3.4	-4.3
Poland	..	..	..	..	..	..	..	..	..	8.1	7.2	3.8	4.4	0.1	-1.0	12.7	8.0	5.6	2.0	6.2
Portugal	6.2	0.9	2.9	-1.1	11.3	6.6	-4.4	3.9	0.2	4.4	6.3	4.3	0.8	-3.5	-3.4	-1.3	0.1	3.6	0.7	0.4
Slovak Republic	..	..	..	..	..	..	..	..	..	-7.1	-0.4	-3.1	-7.1	4.3	4.8	2.2	-1.3	2.4	-1.2	-0.0
Spain	-4.7	-8.1	0.5	-3.5	2.0	7.5	3.3	1.8	11.7	12.1	3.0	7.1	2.8	-1.4	0.9	0.1	-2.8	-2.5	-1.2	-1.0
Sweden	-1.8	-3.8	-2.3	-2.9	-4.3	-4.2	-5.1	-2.4	9.9	5.2	1.7	-1.4	0.8	0.3	-0.0	-0.2	-5.2	-0.1	-2.2	-0.3
Switzerland	6.0	-4.3	-4.9	-0.9	-2.3	-1.7	-7.3	0.3	2.6	-6.4	-4.8	-3.7	-3.8	-4.3	-2.9	-6.2	0.9	-0.1	-1.6	-2.7
Turkey	15.8	-22.9	18.7	3.8	-4.8	-2.3	3.0	5.9	11.6	11.9	-4.2	6.6	9.7	-0.1	2.3	9.9	1.1	8.9	3.4	5.5
United Kingdom	3.2	-1.1	1.0	-3.2	-1.2	1.0	-4.0	-1.9	1.1	2.6	1.3	2.3	-2.1	-6.3	-2.1	-0.6	0.8	-4.1	-3.9	1.2
United States	0.9	0.6	8.3	5.1	4.1	3.2	-0.3	-0.7	-2.2	-2.3	3.1	0.9	2.9	-0.7	-2.3	-1.0	-4.9	-6.1	-1.8	0.9
Total OECD	1.5	-3.3	-0.9	-0.6	-0.4	0.1	-1.4	-1.3	-0.2	-1.5	-0.3	-1.0	0.1	-0.6	-1.4	-1.1	-0.8	0.1	-0.8	-0.7
Memorandum items																				
China	..	..	..	..	..	..	6.1	7.5	7.5	15.4	0.1	13.2	18.9	5.5	-0.0	15.7	12.9	15.6	10.2	2.0
Dynamic Asia[b]	..	..	..	..	..	..	5.5	4.8	0.6	1.4	1.4	-4.6	1.0	-2.2	-1.4	-1.0	-7.6	0.6	1.6	3.7
Other Asia	..	..	..	..	..	..	4.4	4.6	4.6	-0.8	4.6	2.6	3.6	0.3	3.2	7.5	4.8	0.3	0.8	0.8
Latin America	..	..	..	..	..	..	-2.0	-4.1	3.3	-4.2	-7.1	0.5	-0.3	2.0	-0.4	0.7	2.7	2.8	0.4	-1.5
Africa and Middle-East	..	..	..	..	..	..	-0.7	-0.6	1.2	-5.1	-6.9	7.8	1.1	0.7	-1.3	-5.5	-0.7	0.9	1.6	-0.1
Central and Eastern Europe	..	..	..	..	..	..	-13.1	-13.3	-0.9	12.0	0.2	-4.1	-12.4	-2.8	5.1	-5.8	-0.2	0.3	-0.4	-0.7

Note: Regional aggregates are calculated *inclusive* of intra-regional trade. Export performance is the ratio between export volumes and export markets for total goods. The export volume concept employed is the sum of the exports of non-manufactured goods and manufactures. The calculation of export markets is based on a weighted average of import volumes in each exporting country's markets, with weights based on trade flows in 1995. The export markets for total goods facing each country is calculated as the weighted sum of the individual export markets for non-manufactured goods and manufactures, where the weights correspond to the commodity export structure of the exporting country in 1995.
a) Including Luxembourg until 1994.
b) Dynamic Asia includes Chinese Taipei; Hong Kong, China; Indonesia; Malaysia; Philippines; Singapore and Thailand.
Source: OECD.

Annex Table 46. **Shares in World exports and imports**
Percentage, values for total goods, customs basis

	1985	1986	1987	1988	1989	1990	1991	1992	1993	1994	1995	1996	1997	1998	1999	2000	2001	2002	Projections 2003	Projections 2004
A. Exports																				
Canada	4.9	4.5	4.2	4.3	4.2	3.9	3.8	3.7	4.0	4.0	3.9	3.9	4.0	4.2	4.5	4.6	4.5	4.2	4.2	4.2
France	5.4	6.1	6.2	6.1	6.0	6.4	6.2	6.4	5.7	5.6	5.7	5.5	5.3	5.8	5.5	4.9	5.0	5.0	5.1	5.0
Germany	10.2	12.4	12.8	12.2	11.9	12.3	11.8	11.9	10.5	10.3	10.6	10.3	9.6	10.3	9.9	8.9	9.6	9.9	10.2	10.0
Italy	4.2	4.8	4.9	4.7	4.7	5.0	4.9	4.8	4.6	4.5	4.6	4.8	4.3	4.5	4.2	3.8	4.0	4.0	4.1	4.0
Japan	9.7	10.6	9.9	9.9	9.5	8.8	9.4	9.5	10.1	9.7	9.0	8.0	7.8	7.3	7.6	7.7	6.7	6.6	6.5	6.5
United Kingdom	5.4	5.2	5.4	5.3	5.1	5.4	5.3	5.2	4.8	4.9	4.8	5.0	5.1	5.1	4.9	4.6	4.5	4.4	4.2	4.2
United States	11.5	10.6	10.3	11.3	11.9	11.3	11.8	11.7	11.9	11.6	11.1	11.2	11.9	12.1	11.9	11.9	11.6	10.6	9.9	10.1
Other OECD countries	19.6	20.5	21.5	21.8	21.4	22.2	22.0	22.0	22.4	22.6	23.6	23.7	23.1	24.3	24.3	23.5	24.3	24.9	24.9	24.8
Total OECD	70.9	74.8	75.1	75.7	74.7	75.4	75.3	75.2	73.9	73.3	73.3	72.3	71.4	73.5	72.9	69.9	70.2	69.5	69.2	68.7
Non-OECD Asia	9.4	9.3	10.2	10.8	11.3	11.3	12.6	13.6	14.9	15.7	15.8	16.1	17.1	16.1	16.5	17.8	17.4	18.3	18.9	19.8
Latin America	4.5	3.7	3.3	3.4	3.4	3.2	3.0	2.9	3.0	3.1	3.0	3.0	3.2	3.1	2.9	3.1	3.1	3.0	2.9	2.8
Other non-OECD countries	15.1	12.2	11.5	10.1	10.5	10.1	9.1	8.3	8.1	8.0	7.9	8.6	8.4	7.3	7.7	9.2	9.3	9.1	9.0	8.7
Total of non-OECD countries	29.1	25.2	24.9	24.3	25.3	24.6	24.7	24.8	26.1	26.7	26.7	27.7	28.6	26.5	27.1	30.1	29.8	30.5	30.8	31.3
B. Imports																				
Canada	3.8	3.7	3.4	3.6	3.6	3.3	3.2	3.2	3.4	3.3	3.1	3.0	3.4	3.5	3.6	3.6	3.4	3.3	3.2	3.2
France	5.7	6.1	6.4	6.3	6.3	6.8	6.5	6.3	5.5	5.4	5.5	5.2	4.8	5.3	5.1	4.8	4.8	4.7	4.8	4.7
Germany	8.4	9.2	9.4	9.0	9.0	10.0	10.9	10.8	9.1	8.9	9.0	8.7	8.0	8.6	8.3	7.7	7.9	7.6	7.9	7.7
Italy	4.4	4.4	4.7	4.6	4.7	4.9	4.8	4.6	3.7	3.7	3.8	3.6	3.5	3.7	3.6	3.4	3.5	3.5	3.6	3.5
Japan	6.1	5.5	5.5	6.0	6.2	6.3	6.1	5.6	5.8	5.8	5.9	6.0	5.7	4.7	5.0	5.4	5.1	4.8	4.7	4.5
United Kingdom	5.7	6.0	6.3	6.7	6.5	6.5	5.9	5.8	5.4	5.4	5.2	5.4	5.6	5.8	5.7	5.3	5.3	5.3	5.1	5.1
United States	18.3	18.0	17.3	16.4	16.3	15.0	14.4	14.7	16.1	16.2	15.2	15.4	16.3	17.4	18.8	19.7	19.2	18.9	18.4	18.2
Other OECD countries	20.5	21.8	23.0	23.3	23.5	24.5	24.3	24.0	23.7	24.0	24.5	24.7	24.0	24.7	24.8	24.0	24.1	24.7	25.0	24.9
Total OECD	72.9	74.7	76.1	75.9	76.2	77.2	76.1	75.1	72.8	72.6	72.1	72.0	71.2	73.6	75.0	73.9	73.3	72.7	72.8	72.0
Non-OECD Asia	9.3	8.8	9.2	10.5	10.9	10.9	12.1	13.3	15.4	15.9	16.3	16.5	16.7	14.3	14.6	16.1	15.7	16.6	17.1	18.1
Latin America	3.8	3.8	3.5	3.2	3.0	2.8	3.0	3.3	3.7	3.8	3.9	3.8	4.3	4.5	3.7	3.6	3.7	3.2	2.7	2.6
Other non-OECD countries	14.1	12.8	11.2	10.5	9.9	9.1	8.9	8.3	8.1	7.7	7.7	7.7	7.7	7.6	6.6	6.4	7.4	7.5	7.4	7.3
Total of non-OECD countries	27.1	25.3	23.9	24.1	23.8	22.8	23.9	24.9	27.2	27.4	27.9	28.0	28.8	26.4	25.0	26.1	26.7	27.3	27.2	28.0

Note: Regional aggregates are calculated *inclusive* of intra-regional trade.
Source: OECD.

Annex Table 47. **Trade balances**
$ billion

	1985	1986	1987	1988	1989	1990	1991	1992	1993	1994	1995	1996	1997	1998	1999	2000	2001	2002	Projections 2003	2004
Australia	-1.0	-1.9	0.5	-0.7	-3.4	0.4	3.5	1.6	-0.1	-3.3	-4.2	-0.6	1.8	-5.4	-9.7	-4.7	1.9	-5.3	-6.5	-5.7
Austria	-3.1	-4.0	-4.8	-4.8	-5.6	-7.0	-8.6	-7.7	-6.5	-7.9	-6.7	-7.3	-4.3	-3.7	-3.6	-2.7	-1.3	4.5	7.3	8.4
Belgium[a]	1.3	3.4	2.6	4.2	3.9	3.5	3.9	5.7	7.7	9.0	12.3	10.9	9.9	9.8	9.5	4.9	5.6	8.1	9.1	9.5
Canada	11.9	7.2	9.2	8.8	6.5	9.5	6.1	7.4	10.2	14.8	25.8	31.1	18.6	16.0	27.1	41.8	41.4	34.5	41.3	44.6
Czech Republic	..	..	..	..	..	..	..	..	-0.5	-1.4	-3.7	-5.7	-5.0	-2.6	-1.9	-3.1	-3.1	-2.3	-2.5	-2.3
Denmark	-0.7	-1.0	0.8	2.4	2.7	5.0	5.1	7.4	7.8	7.6	6.7	7.7	5.8	3.8	6.7	6.8	7.5	8.4	10.0	11.6
Finland	1.0	1.8	1.6	1.3	-0.1	0.9	2.4	4.0	6.4	7.7	12.4	11.3	11.6	12.5	12.2	13.7	12.7	13.4	14.9	16.1
France	-5.0	-1.4	-7.8	-7.6	-10.3	-13.3	-9.7	2.4	7.2	7.2	11.0	15.1	26.6	25.4	17.6	-3.2	3.2	10.9	12.8	9.0
Germany	28.3	54.6	67.6	76.3	74.9	68.4	19.5	28.2	41.2	50.9	65.1	70.6	71.3	77.8	70.9	58.4	90.7	123.3	139.8	149.5
Greece	-6.6	-5.9	-7.2	-8.0	-9.6	-13.2	-13.1	-15.0	-13.7	-14.7	-18.7	-20.1	-19.1	-17.1	-18.8	-20.5	-19.1	-21.5	-26.0	-27.4
Hungary	..	..	..	..	..	..	..	0.0	-3.3	-3.6	-1.5	-1.7	-1.3	-1.9	-2.2	-2.9	-2.2	-2.1	-3.0	-3.0
Iceland	-0.0	0.1	-0.1	-0.0	0.1	0.1	-0.0	0.0	0.2	0.3	0.2	0.0	0.0	-0.4	-0.3	-0.5	-0.1	0.1	0.1	0.0
Ireland	0.6	1.1	2.6	3.8	4.0	3.9	4.3	7.0	8.1	9.3	13.5	15.7	18.6	20.0	24.3	25.9	30.7	36.1	40.3	45.4
Italy	-5.4	4.8	0.1	-0.8	-2.7	-1.8	-2.5	-1.0	29.5	31.4	38.7	54.0	40.1	36.5	23.4	9.6	15.6	17.1	22.1	23.5
Japan	54.9	90.7	91.3	92.3	80.3	69.2	96.2	124.7	139.4	144.1	132.1	83.7	101.6	122.5	123.3	116.6	70.3	93.8	105.8	131.2
Korea	-0.0	4.3	7.5	11.3	4.4	-2.5	-6.8	-1.8	2.3	-2.9	-4.4	-15.0	-3.2	41.6	28.4	16.9	13.5	14.2	11.0	9.9
Luxembourg	..	..	..	..	..	..	..	..	..	..	-1.7	-1.9	-2.0	-2.3	-2.6	-2.4	-2.5	-2.1	-3.3	-3.3
Mexico	8.4	5.0	8.8	2.6	0.4	-0.9	-7.3	-15.9	-13.5	-18.5	7.1	6.5	0.6	-7.9	-5.6	-8.0	-9.9	-8.0	-9.4	-11.4
Netherlands	6.8	7.4	6.3	10.1	9.8	12.0	12.0	12.3	16.9	18.7	23.8	22.8	21.0	20.4	16.1	17.6	20.9	25.7	34.2	33.7
New Zealand	-0.0	0.1	0.6	2.2	1.0	0.9	2.1	1.6	1.7	1.4	0.8	0.5	0.9	0.9	-0.4	0.7	1.5	0.5	-0.1	0.0
Norway	3.0	-3.8	-2.6	-2.1	1.1	4.6	6.0	8.3	6.9	7.5	8.7	13.0	11.7	2.1	10.7	26.0	26.0	25.8	25.5	26.4
Poland	..	..	..	..	..	..	..	..	-2.5	-0.6	-1.6	-7.3	-9.8	-12.8	-15.1	-12.3	-7.7	-8.4	-10.5	-10.5
Portugal	-1.4	-1.6	-3.5	-5.3	-4.7	-6.6	-7.6	-9.3	-8.0	-8.2	-8.9	-9.2	-9.9	-12.2	-13.8	-14.0	-13.4	-12.4	-12.6	-12.8
Slovak Republic	..	..	..	..	..	..	..	..	-0.9	0.1	-0.2	-2.3	-2.1	-2.4	-1.1	-0.9	-2.1	-2.1	-2.4	-2.3
Spain	-4.7	-7.2	-13.7	-18.7	-25.4	-29.1	-30.4	-30.4	-15.1	-14.8	-18.4	-16.3	-13.5	-20.7	-30.4	-34.9	-31.6	-33.2	-42.8	-46.7
Sweden	2.4	5.1	4.5	4.8	4.0	3.4	6.3	6.2	7.2	9.4	16.9	18.8	19.0	17.1	16.8	14.9	13.0	15.1	18.3	20.2
Switzerland	-3.9	-4.3	-6.0	-6.3	-7.4	-7.1	-6.0	-0.9	1.6	1.5	0.8	0.9	-0.4	-1.6	-0.2	-2.5	-2.7	3.0	2.9	3.1
Turkey	-3.0	-3.1	-3.2	-1.8	-4.2	-9.6	-7.3	-8.2	-14.2	-4.2	-13.2	-10.6	-15.4	-14.2	-10.4	-22.4	-4.5	-8.6	-15.6	-19.8
United Kingdom	-4.2	-14.1	-19.4	-38.3	-40.6	-32.8	-18.2	-22.8	-19.6	-17.0	-19.0	-21.4	-20.2	-36.2	-44.3	-45.9	-48.2	-52.0	-65.9	-74.1
United States	-122.2	-145.1	-159.6	-127.0	-117.7	-111.0	-76.9	-96.9	-132.5	-165.8	-174.2	-191.0	-198.1	-246.7	-346.0	-452.4	-427.2	-484.4	-562.3	-593.6
Euro area	11.7	53.1	43.8	50.5	34.3	17.9	-29.8	-3.8	73.8	88.6	122.5	145.6	150.3	146.4	104.7	52.3	111.5	169.8	195.7	205.2
European Union	9.2	43.0	29.7	19.4	0.4	-6.5	-36.5	-13.0	69.2	88.6	127.1	150.7	154.9	131.2	83.8	28.1	83.7	141.3	158.0	162.8
Total OECD	-42.8	-7.8	-23.8	-1.3	-38.5	-52.8	-27.0	7.0	64.2	58.0	99.6	52.2	54.8	18.4	-119.6	-279.6	-221.2	-207.8	-267.5	-270.6

a) Including Luxembourg until 1994.
Source: OECD.

Annex Table 48. **Non-factor services, net**
$ billion

	1985	1986	1987	1988	1989	1990	1991	1992	1993	1994	1995	1996	1997	1998	1999	2000	2001	2002	Projections 2003	2004
Australia	-3.5	-2.9	-2.6	-2.4	-4.3	-3.6	-2.5	-2.6	-1.5	-1.3	-1.0	-0.0	-0.4	-1.1	-0.9	0.4	-0.4	-0.8	-1.5	-1.7
Austria	3.3	5.0	5.5	5.4	6.8	9.1	10.1	9.4	7.5	7.3	4.6	4.6	1.0	2.4	1.8	1.6	1.3	-0.7	-3.0	-3.5
Belgium[a]	0.1	0.4	1.0	0.6	-0.9	-0.1	-0.3	0.3	1.0	1.0	-0.1	0.2	1.3	0.8	1.4	2.1	1.8	1.0	1.1	1.7
Canada	-4.1	-4.1	-4.6	-5.4	-6.9	-9.1	-10.0	-10.1	-10.5	-8.5	-7.4	-6.7	-6.4	-4.3	-4.8	-5.0	-5.4	-5.1	-4.7	-5.4
Czech Republic	..	..	..	..	..	..	..	..	1.0	0.5	1.8	1.9	1.8	1.9	1.2	1.4	1.5	0.6	0.4	0.6
Denmark	0.7	0.3	0.5	0.8	0.7	1.8	2.8	2.3	1.6	0.5	0.7	1.3	0.1	-0.3	1.6	2.6	2.9	1.9	2.8	3.5
Finland	-0.5	-0.8	-1.3	-1.8	-2.3	-3.2	-3.6	-2.9	-2.2	-1.8	-2.2	-1.7	-1.6	-1.1	-1.4	-2.2	-2.3	-2.3	-2.8	-3.1
France	9.6	10.0	10.4	10.7	13.6	14.9	16.6	19.5	17.3	17.8	14.3	15.1	16.5	17.6	18.5	19.9	17.7	19.2	21.7	22.8
Germany	-4.5	-7.0	-10.7	-14.4	-13.7	-18.6	-22.6	-31.6	-33.8	-41.1	-47.0	-45.4	-42.5	-46.2	-53.0	-50.8	-52.0	-42.3	-47.0	-49.1
Greece	2.4	2.9	4.1	4.6	4.2	5.8	6.3	7.3	6.9	7.8	8.1	7.7	7.2	7.0	7.6	8.1	7.9	9.8	12.8	14.1
Hungary	..	..	..	..	..	..	..	..	0.2	0.2	1.4	1.9	1.8	1.2	0.9	1.1	1.5	0.6	0.7	1.0
Iceland	0.0	0.1	0.0	-0.0	0.0	0.0	-0.0	-0.0	0.0	0.0	0.0	0.0	0.0	-0.0	-0.1	-0.1	0.0	0.0	-0.0	-0.0
Ireland	-0.3	-0.6	-1.0	-1.4	-1.8	-1.7	-2.0	-3.1	-3.0	-4.1	-6.3	-7.7	-9.0	-10.1	-11.1	-12.9	-15.6	-13.5	-14.6	-16.0
Italy	3.4	3.4	3.5	1.6	2.5	3.6	3.3	0.6	3.2	5.2	6.4	7.2	7.9	4.9	1.2	0.9	0.3	-4.1	-2.6	-1.9
Japan	-9.6	-12.9	-20.4	-30.3	-36.7	-42.9	-41.9	-44.0	-43.0	-48.0	-57.3	-62.3	-54.1	-49.5	-54.1	-47.6	-43.8	-41.3	-41.5	-42.6
Korea	0.5	1.4	2.3	2.3	0.4	-0.6	-2.2	-2.9	-2.1	-1.8	-3.0	-6.2	-3.2	1.0	-0.7	-2.9	-3.8	-7.5	-9.4	-9.1
Luxembourg	..	..	..	..	..	..	..	..	..	..	3.2	3.5	4.0	4.3	5.4	6.8	6.4	7.7	9.8	10.4
Mexico	-0.6	-0.4	0.3	0.0	-0.5	-1.9	-1.8	-2.3	-2.1	-2.0	0.7	0.4	-0.7	-0.9	-1.8	-2.3	-3.6	-4.0	-4.6	-5.7
Netherlands	-1.2	-1.3	-1.5	-2.3	-1.4	-0.4	-0.8	-0.1	-0.1	0.2	1.1	2.0	3.2	2.5	2.5	-2.0	-2.5	-1.3	-0.9	-1.8
New Zealand	-0.3	-0.5	-0.5	-0.6	-0.8	-0.8	-0.8	-0.9	-0.6	-0.3	-0.2	-0.3	-0.7	-0.7	-0.2	-0.1	0.1	0.7	0.8	1.0
Norway	1.8	1.2	0.6	1.6	2.6	3.2	3.5	0.4	0.8	0.2	0.5	1.4	1.5	0.7	1.0	1.9	2.6	2.2	3.2	4.0
Poland	..	..	..	..	..	..	..	..	0.4	2.8	3.5	3.4	3.2	4.2	1.4	1.4	0.8	0.4	0.4	0.4
Portugal	0.6	0.8	1.0	0.7	0.9	1.0	0.8	0.6	1.3	1.2	1.5	1.4	1.5	1.9	1.9	1.9	2.5	3.0	3.9	4.5
Slovak Republic	..	..	..	..	..	..	..	..	0.3	0.8	0.7	0.2	0.1	0.2	0.2	0.4	0.5	0.5	0.7	0.7
Spain	8.1	11.8	13.4	13.9	12.7	11.9	12.1	12.4	11.7	14.9	18.6	20.4	20.0	21.9	23.0	22.3	24.3	24.8	27.3	28.7
Sweden	-0.6	-1.8	-1.7	-2.2	-3.0	-3.3	-2.6	-2.3	0.1	0.2	-0.4	-0.8	-1.4	-1.6	-1.4	-1.5	-0.6	-0.6	-1.4	-1.2
Switzerland	4.8	6.6	8.3	8.3	8.0	9.4	10.4	10.9	11.2	11.3	12.9	12.5	13.1	13.5	14.4	15.2	14.3	16.1	19.6	20.5
Turkey	1.5	1.6	2.1	3.7	3.9	4.9	5.2	5.8	6.7	7.0	9.6	6.6	10.9	13.5	7.4	11.3	9.1	7.9	9.3	10.2
United Kingdom	8.6	9.5	11.1	7.9	6.0	7.7	7.2	9.6	9.9	9.8	13.4	15.0	20.5	21.0	19.1	18.0	16.3	23.5	27.4	26.2
United States	0.3	6.5	7.9	12.4	24.6	30.2	45.8	60.4	63.7	69.2	77.8	89.2	90.4	79.8	83.8	73.7	68.9	48.8	47.8	49.1
Euro area	21.2	24.7	24.6	17.6	20.7	22.2	19.8	12.5	9.8	8.4	2.3	7.4	9.5	5.8	-2.3	-4.4	-10.0	1.5	5.6	6.6
European Union	30.0	32.7	34.6	24.1	24.3	28.3	27.2	22.1	21.4	18.9	16.0	22.9	28.7	24.9	17.0	14.7	8.6	26.3	34.5	35.2
Total OECD	20.8	29.2	28.0	13.7	14.7	17.1	33.0	36.9	45.8	49.0	56.1	64.9	85.8	84.3	64.7	63.6	50.9	45.4	55.7	58.1

Note: The classification of non-factor services and investment income is affected by the change in reporting system to the International Monetary Fund, *Fifth Balance of Payments Manual.*
a) Including Luxembourg until 1994.
Source: OECD.

Annex Table 49. **Investment income, net**
$ billion

	1985	1986	1987	1988	1989	1990	1991	1992	1993	1994	1995	1996	1997	1998	1999	2000	2001	2002	Projections 2003	2004
Australia	-4.5	-4.9	-5.8	-8.6	-10.4	-13.2	-12.2	-10.1	-8.1	-12.4	-14.0	-15.2	-13.8	-11.4	-11.6	-10.8	-10.2	-11.7	-11.9	-12.5
Austria	-0.2	-0.6	-0.8	-0.9	-0.9	-0.9	-1.4	-1.4	-1.5	-1.7	-2.4	-0.9	-1.5	-2.0	-2.9	-2.5	-3.0	-1.7	-2.2	-2.5
Belgium[a]	1.2	1.5	1.8	2.1	4.0	4.8	5.7	6.4	6.9	7.4	7.3	6.8	6.3	6.9	6.5	6.3	5.6	6.5	8.6	9.1
Canada	-12.8	-14.0	-17.1	-17.5	-20.5	-19.4	-17.4	-17.5	-20.8	-18.9	-22.7	-21.5	-20.9	-20.0	-21.6	-19.1	-17.8	-19.3	-21.1	-21.0
Czech Republic	..	..	..	..	..	..	..	..	-0.1	-0.0	-0.1	-0.7	-0.8	-1.1	-1.4	-1.4	-2.2	-3.0	-2.7	-3.1
Denmark	-2.6	-3.5	-4.1	-3.7	-3.8	-5.1	-5.1	-4.9	-3.8	-3.8	-3.8	-3.7	-3.4	-2.8	-2.5	-4.0	-3.0	-2.8	-3.6	-3.9
Finland	-1.0	-1.3	-1.6	-1.7	-2.7	-3.7	-4.7	-5.4	-4.9	-4.4	-4.4	-3.6	-2.4	-3.1	-2.0	-1.7	-1.1	-0.4	0.0	0.5
France	-2.3	-1.7	-1.7	-1.0	-0.3	-1.6	-3.3	-6.0	-6.6	-6.0	-8.4	-1.9	7.4	9.1	18.9	13.8	14.8	12.4	16.2	18.9
Germany	4.7	5.3	5.2	9.4	14.3	20.6	20.3	21.8	16.6	2.9	0.1	1.0	-1.4	-7.6	-9.6	-3.1	-11.3	-6.6	-1.5	-0.9
Greece	-1.3	-1.5	-1.7	-1.8	-1.9	-2.0	-2.0	-2.4	-1.7	-1.4	-1.8	-2.1	-1.7	-1.6	-0.7	-0.9	-1.8	-2.0	-2.2	-2.3
Hungary	..	..	..	..	..	..	..	..	-1.2	-1.4	0.1	0.0	-1.3	-1.8	-1.6	-1.4	-1.3	-1.6	-1.8	-1.8
Iceland	-0.1	-0.2	-0.2	-0.2	-0.2	-0.2	-0.2	-0.2	-0.1	-0.2	-0.2	-0.2	-0.2	-0.2	-0.2	-0.3	-0.3	-0.1	-0.2	-0.2
Ireland	-2.1	-2.6	-3.1	-3.9	-4.3	-5.0	-4.6	-5.6	-5.3	-5.4	-7.3	-8.2	-9.7	-10.6	-14.0	-13.7	-15.8	-23.7	-28.1	-28.4
Italy	-2.7	-4.2	-4.9	-5.5	-7.2	-14.6	-17.5	-22.0	-17.4	-16.9	-15.9	-15.4	-10.1	-10.9	-11.2	-12.0	-10.4	-14.9	-16.3	-17.1
Japan	6.8	9.3	16.3	20.6	22.9	22.7	26.0	35.7	40.7	40.4	44.1	53.4	58.1	54.7	57.8	60.3	69.1	66.1	73.1	80.6
Korea	-2.1	-2.3	-1.6	-1.3	-0.6	-0.1	-0.2	-0.4	-0.4	-0.5	-1.3	-1.8	-2.5	-5.6	-5.2	-2.4	-1.2	0.5	1.2	1.5
Luxembourg	..	..	..	..	..	..	..	..	..	..	1.6	1.3	0.5	0.2	-0.5	-1.3	-1.6	-2.3	-2.4	-2.6
Mexico	-9.0	-7.5	-6.8	-7.2	-8.3	-8.6	-8.6	-9.6	-11.4	-13.0	-13.3	-13.9	-12.8	-13.3	-12.9	-14.8	-13.8	-12.3	-12.0	-11.9
Netherlands	-0.2	-0.2	1.4	1.2	2.9	-0.6	0.4	-1.0	0.9	3.7	7.3	3.5	7.0	-2.7	3.6	-1.6	-3.5	-8.9	-10.6	-11.0
New Zealand	-1.3	-1.5	-2.0	-2.1	-1.9	-1.6	-2.5	-2.5	-2.9	-3.4	-4.0	-4.7	-4.9	-2.6	-3.1	-3.5	-3.1	-3.2	-4.0	-4.6
Norway	-1.2	-1.3	-1.4	-2.5	-2.8	-3.4	-4.0	-2.8	-2.8	-2.2	-1.9	-1.9	-1.7	-1.2	-1.9	-1.7	-0.9	0.4	0.6	2.1
Poland	..	..	..	..	..	..	0.2	0.6	-3.4	-2.6	-2.0	-1.1	-1.1	-1.2	-1.0	-1.5	-1.4	-1.8	-2.0	-2.4
Portugal	-1.1	-1.0	-0.8	-0.8	-0.6	-0.1	0.2	0.6	0.2	-0.6	-0.0	-1.0	-1.5	-1.6	-1.8	-2.5	-3.1	-3.3	-3.8	-4.0
Slovak Republic	..	..	..	..	..	..	..	..	-0.0	-0.1	-0.0	-0.0	-0.1	-0.2	-0.3	-0.4	-0.3	-0.5	-0.6	-0.7
Spain	-1.7	-1.8	-2.6	-3.3	-2.8	-3.5	-4.3	-5.8	-3.6	-7.8	-4.1	-6.1	-6.8	-7.5	-9.5	-8.3	-9.6	-10.8	-11.3	-11.9
Sweden	-2.0	-2.0	-1.6	-1.8	-2.3	-4.5	-6.4	-10.0	-8.8	-5.9	-5.5	-6.3	-4.9	-3.2	-2.0	-1.4	-1.4	-1.8	-2.4	-2.5
Switzerland	5.0	5.8	6.8	8.9	8.1	8.8	8.8	8.3	9.1	7.9	11.9	12.6	16.2	17.6	20.2	21.8	14.8	17.3	18.7	19.6
Turkey	-1.6	-1.9	-2.1	-2.5	-2.3	-2.5	-2.7	-2.6	-2.7	-3.3	-3.2	-2.9	-3.0	-3.0	-3.5	-4.0	-5.0	-4.5	-4.0	-3.4
United Kingdom	-0.0	4.2	1.4	1.3	-1.2	-5.1	-5.9	0.2	-0.3	5.1	3.3	1.8	6.4	20.8	4.2	14.2	23.6	29.0	31.2	30.2
United States	25.7	15.5	14.3	18.7	19.8	28.5	24.1	23.0	23.9	16.7	24.6	24.1	20.2	7.6	18.1	21.8	14.4	-11.9	-16.6	-27.6
Euro area	-6.8	-8.3	-8.7	-6.1	0.6	-6.7	-11.2	-20.8	-16.2	-30.1	-28.0	-26.8	-13.9	-31.4	-23.1	-27.4	-40.7	-55.7	-53.6	-52.0
European Union	-11.4	-9.6	-13.0	-10.2	-6.8	-21.4	-28.6	-35.4	-29.1	-34.7	-34.0	-34.9	-15.9	-16.5	-23.3	-18.5	-21.4	-31.3	-28.5	-28.3
Total OECD	-6.5	-12.5	-12.6	-4.0	-3.1	-10.5	-17.3	-14.1	-9.4	-27.7	-16.1	-8.9	15.6	13.0	8.5	24.3	19.3	-17.0	-11.8	-13.7

Note: The classification of non-factor services and investment income is affected by the change in reporting system to the International Monetary Fund, *Fifth Balance of Payments Manual*.
a) Including Luxembourg until 1994.
Source: OECD.

Annex Table 50. **Current account balances**
$ billion

	1985	1986	1987	1988	1989	1990	1991	1992	1993	1994	1995	1996	1997	1998	1999	2000	2001	2002	Projections	Projections
																			2003	2004
Australia	-7.8	-8.4	-6.7	-10.0	-16.3	-14.0	-9.2	-9.5	-8.1	-15.2	-17.4	-14.0	-10.7	-16.5	-20.6	-13.2	-7.1	-16.2	-18.2	-18.4
Austria	-0.1	0.3	-0.2	-0.3	0.3	1.2	-0.0	-0.7	-1.4	-3.3	-6.2	-5.4	-6.5	-5.2	-6.7	-5.0	-4.2	0.6	0.4	0.8
Belgium*a*	2.0	4.4	4.1	5.2	5.1	6.2	7.2	9.9	13.0	14.2	15.3	13.8	13.8	13.3	12.8	9.4	9.2	11.5	14.6	15.9
Canada	-5.7	-11.2	-13.5	-14.9	-21.8	-19.8	-22.4	-21.1	-21.7	-13.0	-4.4	3.4	-8.2	-7.7	1.3	18.6	19.5	11.0	16.4	19.1
Czech Republic	..	..	..	..	..	..	..	..	0.5	-0.8	-1.4	-4.1	-3.6	-1.4	-1.5	-2.7	-3.3	-3.7	-4.3	-4.4
Denmark	-2.7	-4.5	-3.0	-1.6	-1.7	0.6	1.2	3.2	3.9	2.3	1.2	2.7	0.7	-1.6	3.0	2.4	4.9	5.0	5.9	7.8
Finland	-0.8	-0.7	-1.7	-2.7	-5.8	-7.0	-6.8	-5.1	-1.1	1.1	5.4	5.1	6.8	7.3	7.7	9.2	8.6	10.0	10.5	11.7
France	-0.2	2.4	-4.5	-4.6	-4.6	-9.8	-5.7	4.8	9.6	7.4	11.0	20.8	37.8	39.3	41.3	17.2	21.2	29.4	39.2	38.3
Germany	18.3	40.2	45.8	52.7	57.1	48.6	-18.4	-14.5	-9.7	-24.3	-20.7	-7.9	-3.1	-6.2	-19.2	-20.5	3.5	50.3	66.6	74.6
Greece	-3.8	-2.1	-1.8	-1.5	-3.3	-4.7	-2.7	-3.6	-1.9	-1.4	-4.5	-6.4	-5.3	-3.7	-5.3	-7.7	-7.2	-8.7	-10.1	-10.1
Hungary	..	..	..	..	..	..	..	..	-3.5	-4.0	-2.5	-1.7	-0.7	-2.2	-2.4	-2.9	-1.7	-2.7	-3.6	-3.3
Iceland	-0.1	0.0	-0.2	-0.0	-0.1	-0.1	-0.3	-0.2	0.0	0.1	0.1	-0.1	-0.1	-0.6	-0.6	-0.9	-0.3	0.0	-0.0	-0.1
Ireland	-0.8	-0.9	-0.1	-0.0	-0.6	-0.4	0.3	0.5	1.8	1.5	1.7	2.0	1.9	0.7	0.4	0.1	-0.3	-0.3	-1.6	1.2
Italy	-4.2	2.2	-2.5	-7.0	-11.2	-16.8	-24.3	-30.2	7.9	12.5	25.0	39.1	33.7	23.0	8.1	-5.8	-0.3	-5.7	-0.8	0.5
Japan	50.7	85.4	84.1	79.2	63.3	44.1	68.3	112.6	131.9	130.4	111.1	65.8	96.8	119.0	114.8	119.5	87.7	113.6	128.7	160.5
Korea	-0.8	4.7	10.1	14.5	5.4	-2.0	-8.3	-3.9	1.0	-3.9	-8.5	-23.0	-8.2	40.4	24.5	12.2	8.2	6.1	1.8	1.3
Luxembourg	..	..	..	..	..	..	..	..	..	..	2.5	2.3	1.9	1.8	1.8	2.7	1.8	2.8	3.4	3.8
Mexico	0.8	-1.4	4.2	-2.4	-5.8	-7.5	-14.6	-24.4	-23.4	-29.7	-1.6	-2.5	-7.7	-16.1	-14.1	-18.2	-18.0	-14.0	-15.2	-18.3
Netherlands	4.4	4.3	4.2	7.1	9.4	8.1	7.5	6.8	13.2	17.3	25.8	21.5	25.1	13.0	15.7	7.8	8.1	9.1	15.0	13.0
New Zealand	-1.6	-1.8	-1.7	-0.4	-1.6	-1.4	-1.2	-1.7	-1.7	-2.1	-3.1	-3.9	-4.4	-2.1	-3.5	-2.7	-1.4	-1.8	-3.3	-3.5
Norway	3.0	-4.7	-4.4	-4.0	-0.1	3.1	4.3	4.4	3.6	3.8	5.2	11.0	10.0	0.0	8.4	24.8	25.9	26.3	26.8	29.9
Poland	..	..	..	..	..	..	..	..	-4.6	1.0	0.9	-3.3	-5.7	-6.9	-12.5	-10.0	-5.4	-6.7	-8.9	-9.3
Portugal*b*	0.4	1.2	0.4	-1.0	0.2	-0.2	-0.7	-0.3	0.3	-2.3	-0.2	-4.4	-6.1	-7.8	-9.8	-11.2	-10.5	-9.3	-8.7	-8.3
Slovak Republic	..	..	..	..	..	..	..	..	-0.6	0.8	0.5	-2.0	-2.0	-2.0	-1.0	-0.7	-1.8	-1.9	-2.1	-2.0
Spain	2.8	3.9	-0.2	-3.7	-10.9	-18.1	-19.9	-21.6	-5.7	-6.4	0.8	0.4	2.5	-3.0	-13.9	-19.5	-15.1	-16.8	-23.4	-26.3
Sweden	-1.0	0.0	-0.0	-0.6	-3.1	-6.3	-4.7	-7.5	-2.6	2.5	8.4	9.7	10.3	9.7	10.6	9.4	8.5	9.8	11.0	13.1
Switzerland	5.1	6.9	7.6	9.1	7.0	8.8	10.7	15.3	19.2	17.3	21.3	22.0	25.5	25.9	30.3	31.6	22.4	32.1	36.4	38.2
Turkey	-1.0	-1.5	-0.8	1.6	0.9	-2.6	0.3	-1.0	-6.4	2.6	-2.3	-2.4	-2.6	2.0	-1.4	-9.8	3.4	-1.8	-3.6	-5.0
United Kingdom	0.5	-3.5	-12.7	-35.4	-43.1	-39.1	-19.0	-22.9	-17.9	-10.3	-14.3	-13.5	-2.9	-8.0	-31.8	-28.7	-17.9	-13.1	-24.0	-36.6
United States	-118.2	-147.2	-160.7	-121.2	-99.5	-79.0	3.7	-48.5	-82.5	-118.2	-105.8	-117.8	-128.4	-203.8	-292.9	-410.3	-393.4	-503.4	-587.1	-629.5
Euro area	18.0	55.1	43.4	44.2	35.6	7.1	-63.4	-53.9	26.1	16.4	56.0	80.9	102.6	72.4	33.0	-23.2	14.7	72.8	105.2	115.2
European Union	14.8	47.1	27.7	6.7	-12.3	-37.6	-86.0	-81.2	9.4	10.9	51.4	79.8	110.7	72.6	14.9	-40.2	10.2	74.6	98.0	99.5
Total OECD	-60.9	-31.9	-54.2	-42.1	-80.9	-108.0	-54.6	-59.1	13.1	-20.1	46.2	8.9	60.7	0.5	-156.2	-304.7	-255.0	-288.5	-338.2	-345.3

Note: The balance-of-payments data in this table are based on the concepts and definition of the International Monetary Fund, *Fifth Balance of Payments Manual*.
a) Including Luxembourg until 1994.
b) Break between 1995 and 1996, reflecting change in methodology to the International Monetary Fund, *Fifth Balance of Payments Manual* (capital transfers from European Union are excluded from the current account as from 1996).
Source: OECD.

Annex Table 51. **Current account balances as a percentage of GDP**

	1985	1986	1987	1988	1989	1990	1991	1992	1993	1994	1995	1996	1997	1998	1999	2000	2001	2002	Projections 2003	2004
Australia	-4.7	-4.9	-3.3	-3.8	-5.6	-4.6	-3.0	-3.1	-2.7	-4.5	-4.8	-3.5	-2.7	-4.6	-5.3	-3.4	-2.0	-4.1	-3.9	-3.7
Austria	-0.1	0.3	-0.2	-0.2	0.2	0.7	0.0	-0.4	-0.8	-1.6	-2.6	-2.3	-3.2	-2.5	-3.2	-2.6	-2.2	0.3	0.2	0.3
Belgium[a]	2.4	3.8	2.8	3.3	3.2	3.1	3.6	4.4	6.0	6.0	5.5	5.1	5.6	5.3	5.1	4.1	4.0	4.7	5.0	5.3
Canada	-1.6	-3.0	-3.2	-3.0	-3.9	-3.4	-3.7	-3.6	-3.9	-2.3	-0.8	0.5	-1.3	-1.2	0.2	2.6	2.8	1.5	2.0	2.2
Czech Republic	..	..	..	..	..	..	..	..	1.3	-1.9	-2.6	-7.1	-6.7	-2.4	-2.8	-5.3	-5.7	-5.3	-5.3	-5.1
Denmark	-4.6	-5.3	-2.9	-1.4	-1.6	0.4	0.9	2.2	2.8	1.5	0.7	1.4	0.4	-0.9	1.7	1.5	3.1	2.9	2.9	3.6
Finland	-1.4	-0.9	-1.9	-2.5	-5.0	-5.1	-5.4	-4.7	-1.3	1.1	4.1	4.0	5.6	5.6	6.0	7.7	7.1	7.6	6.7	7.2
France	-0.1	0.3	-0.5	-0.5	-0.5	-0.8	-0.5	0.4	0.8	0.5	0.7	1.3	2.7	2.7	2.9	1.3	1.6	2.1	2.4	2.2
Germany	2.8	4.4	4.0	4.3	4.7	3.2	-1.0	-0.7	-0.5	-1.1	-0.8	-0.3	-0.1	-0.3	-0.9	-1.1	0.2	2.5	2.9	3.2
Greece	-9.2	-4.4	-3.1	-2.3	-4.9	-5.6	-2.9	-3.6	-2.1	-1.4	-3.8	-5.1	-4.4	-3.1	-4.2	-6.9	-6.2	-6.5	-6.2	-5.8
Hungary	..	..	..	..	..	..	-4.0	-2.4	-9.0	-9.5	0.9	0.5	-1.4	-4.7	-5.1	-6.3	-3.4	-4.0	-4.5	-3.8
Iceland	-3.8	0.5	-3.4	-3.7	-1.9	-2.1	0.7	1.0	0.7	2.0	0.8	-1.8	-1.7	-7.0	-7.0	-10.3	-4.3	0.3	-0.2	-0.9
Ireland	-3.7	-3.1	-0.2	-0.1	-1.5	-0.8	0.7	1.0	3.7	2.7	2.6	2.8	2.4	0.9	0.4	0.1	-0.3	-0.2	-1.1	0.8
Italy	-1.0	0.3	-0.3	-0.8	-1.3	-1.5	-2.1	-2.5	0.8	1.2	2.3	3.2	2.9	1.9	0.7	-0.5	-0.0	-0.5	-0.1	0.0
Japan	3.7	4.2	3.4	2.7	2.1	1.5	2.0	3.0	3.0	2.7	2.1	1.4	2.2	3.0	2.6	2.5	2.1	2.8	3.1	3.9
Korea	-0.8	4.4	7.5	8.0	2.4	-0.8	-2.8	-1.2	0.3	-1.0	-1.7	-4.4	-1.5	12.8	6.0	2.7	1.9	1.3	0.3	0.2
Luxembourg	..	..	..	..	..	..	..	..	..	..	13.9	12.8	11.0	9.4	8.9	14.0	9.3	13.6	14.4	15.6
Mexico	0.8	-0.8	2.8	-1.3	-2.7	-2.9	-4.7	-6.7	-5.8	-7.1	-0.5	-0.8	-1.9	-3.8	-2.9	-3.1	-2.9	-2.2	-2.5	-2.8
Netherlands	3.2	2.4	1.9	2.9	4.0	2.8	2.5	2.1	4.1	5.0	6.2	5.2	6.6	3.3	3.9	2.1	2.1	2.1	3.1	2.5
New Zealand	-7.2	-6.2	-4.9	-1.0	-3.8	-3.2	-2.8	-4.2	-4.0	-4.0	-5.2	-5.9	-6.5	-3.9	-6.2	-5.2	-2.8	-3.1	-4.6	-4.6
Norway	4.6	-6.0	-4.7	-4.0	-0.1	2.6	3.6	3.5	3.0	3.0	3.5	6.9	6.4	0.0	5.3	14.9	15.3	13.7	12.2	13.2
Poland	..	..	..	..	..	..	..	..	-5.2	1.0	0.7	-2.3	-4.0	-4.4	-8.1	-6.1	-2.9	-3.5	-4.5	-4.5
Portugal[b]	1.5	3.3	1.0	-2.0	0.3	-0.3	-0.8	-0.2	0.4	-2.4	-0.1	-3.9	-5.7	-6.9	-8.5	-10.5	-9.6	-7.6	-6.0	-5.5
Slovak Republic	..	..	..	..	..	..	..	..	-4.7	5.0	2.7	-9.6	-9.2	-9.0	-4.9	-3.8	-8.6	-8.1	-6.9	-6.1
Spain	1.6	1.6	-0.0	-1.0	-2.8	-3.5	-3.6	-3.6	-1.1	-1.3	0.1	0.1	0.4	-0.5	-2.3	-3.5	-2.6	-2.6	-3.0	-3.2
Sweden	-1.0	0.0	-0.0	-0.3	-1.5	-2.5	-1.8	-2.9	-1.3	1.1	3.4	3.6	4.2	3.9	4.2	3.9	3.9	4.1	3.9	4.4
Switzerland	5.2	5.0	4.4	4.9	3.9	3.8	4.6	6.3	8.1	6.6	6.9	7.4	9.9	9.9	11.7	13.2	9.1	11.9	11.9	12.2
Turkey	-1.5	-1.9	-0.9	2.0	0.9	-1.7	0.1	-0.6	-3.6	2.2	-1.5	-1.3	-1.3	1.1	-0.9	-4.9	2.4	-1.0	-1.9	-2.6
United Kingdom	0.1	-0.6	-1.8	-4.3	-5.1	-4.0	-1.8	-2.1	-1.9	-1.0	-1.3	-1.1	-0.2	-0.6	-2.2	-2.0	-1.3	-0.8	-1.4	-2.0
United States	-2.8	-3.3	-3.4	-2.4	-1.8	-1.4	0.1	-0.8	-1.2	-1.7	-1.4	-1.5	-1.5	-2.3	-3.2	-4.2	-3.9	-4.8	-5.4	-5.5
Euro area	0.8	1.8	1.1	1.0	0.8	0.1	-1.1	-0.8	0.5	0.3	0.8	1.1	1.6	1.1	0.5	-0.4	0.2	1.1	1.4	1.4
European Union	0.5	1.2	0.6	0.1	-0.2	-0.6	-1.2	-1.0	0.1	0.1	0.6	0.9	1.3	0.8	0.2	-0.5	0.1	0.9	1.0	1.0
Total OECD	-0.6	-0.3	-0.4	-0.3	-0.5	-0.6	-0.3	-0.3	0.1	-0.1	0.2	0.0	0.3	0.0	-0.6	-1.2	-1.0	-1.1	-1.2	-1.2

a) Including Luxembourg until 1994.
b) Break between 1995 and 1996, reflecting change in methodology to the International Monetary Fund, *Fifth Balance of Payments Manual* (capital transfers from European Union are excluded from the current account as from 1996).
Source: OECD.

Annex Table 52. Structure of current account balances of major world regions

$ billion

	1990	1991	1992	1993	1994	1995	1996	1997	1998	1999	2000	2001	2002	Projections 2003	Projections 2004
Trade balance															
OECD	-53	-27	7	64	58	100	52	55	18	-120	-280	-221	-208	-268	-271
Non-OECD *of which:*	68	52	29	-7	22	0	30	49	43	151	268	200	220	275	276
Non-OECD Asia *of which:*	7	9	3	-20	-12	-24	-21	23	91	100	90	85	97	115	119
China	9	9	5	-11	7	18	20	46	47	36	34	34	35	34	34
Dynamic Asia[a]	10	-9	8	1	-6	-23	-17	-3	65	81	76	71	82	102	105
Other Asia	-12	-9	-10	-10	-14	-19	-24	-20	-21	-17	-20	-19	-21	-22	-19
Latin America	31	19	10	2	2	-8	-6	-19	-33	-6	7	7	28	47	52
Africa and Middle-East	53	23	14	11	23	25	54	48	-11	33	118	73	65	77	74
Central and Eastern Europe	-23	1	2	-0	10	8	3	-3	-4	23	52	34	30	37	31
World[b]	15	25	36	57	80	100	83	103	61	31	-12	-21	12	8	6
Services and private transfers															
OECD	-11	0	3	18	-0	14	29	75	60	40	53	34	-10	3	0
Non-OECD *of which:*	-86	-102	-90	-84	-74	-101	-96	-106	-121	-105	-123	-113	-105	-105	-109
Non-OECD Asia *of which:*	-3	-0	-0	4	12	-7	3	4	-17	-10	-10	-5	-6	-6	-8
China	3	4	1	-1	0	-17	-13	-10	-15	-15	-14	-17	-17	-17	-18
Dynamic Asia[a]	-4	4	-1	4	0	9	9	4	-8	-4	-7	2	-0	5	6
Other Asia	-2	-0	0	1	5	4	6	10	6	9	11	2	6	6	5
Latin America	-27	-24	-21	-26	-26	-30	-33	-42	-44	-39	-39	-44	-34	-27	-25
Africa and Middle-East	-57	-73	-58	-56	-54	-54	-61	-58	-48	-48	-63	-55	-55	-63	-66
Central and Eastern Europe	1	-4	-10	-6	-5	-10	-5	-10	-12	-8	-11	-9	-9	-10	-10
World[b]	-96	-102	-87	-66	-74	-87	-67	-32	-61	-65	-70	-80	-115	-102	-109
Official transfers															
OECD	-45	-28	-69	-69	-78	-67	-72	-69	-78	-77	-78	-67	-70	-73	-75
Non-OECD *of which:*	4	-9	18	17	13	14	13	12	12	13	13	13	14	14	14
Non-OECD Asia *of which:*	2	2	2	2	2	3	2	3	2	3	3	3	2	2	2
China	0	0	0	0	-1	1	0	0	0	0	0	-0	-0	-0	-0
Dynamic Asia[a]	0	0	1	0	1	1	0	0	0	1	1	0	0	0	0
Other Asia	2	2	2	1	2	2	2	2	2	2	2	3	2	2	1
Latin America	2	2	2	1	1	2	2	1	2	2	2	1	2	2	2
Africa and Middle-East	-1	-20	10	10	8	7	7	6	6	6	6	7	7	7	7
Central and Eastern Europe	1	6	4	4	2	2	2	2	2	2	2	2	3	3	3
World[b]	-41	-37	-51	-52	-64	-54	-60	-56	-66	-64	-65	-54	-57	-60	-61
Current account balance															
OECD	-108	-55	-59	13	-20	46	9	61	1	-156	-305	-255	-289	-338	-345
Non-OECD *of which:*	-14	-59	-43	-74	-38	-87	-53	-45	-66	59	158	100	129	184	181
Non-OECD Asia *of which:*	6	11	6	-13	1	-29	-16	29	76	93	83	83	93	110	113
China	12	13	6	-12	7	2	7	37	31	21	21	17	19	18	15
Dynamic Asia[a]	6	6	7	6	1	-16	-7	1	58	77	69	73	88	108	111
Other Asia	-12	-7	-8	-8	-7	-14	-16	-9	-13	-6	-7	-8	-13	-15	-13
Latin America	6	-3	-9	-23	-22	-36	-37	-60	-76	-43	-29	-36	-5	22	29
Africa and Middle-East	-4	-70	-35	-35	-23	-22	-0	-4	-53	-9	62	25	17	21	15
Central and Eastern Europe	-21	3	-4	-3	6	-0	0	-11	-14	18	43	28	24	30	24
World[b]	-122	-113	-102	-61	-58	-41	-44	16	-66	-97	-147	-155	-159	-154	-164

Note: Historical data for the OECD area are aggregates of reported balance-of-payments data of each individual country. Because of various statistical problems as well as a large number of non-reporters among non-OECD countries, trade and current account balances estimated on the basis of these countries' own balance-of-payments records may differ from corresponding estimates shown in this table.
a) Dynamic Asia includes Chinese Taipei; Hong Kong, China; Indonesia; Malaysia; Philippines; Singapore and Thailand. There is a break in the current account, services and transfers series in 1997 for Dynamic Asia, as figures for Hong Kong, China are not included before these years but are afterward.
b) Reflects statistical errors and asymmetries. Given the very large gross flows of world balance-of-payments transactions, statistical errors and asymmetries easily give rise to world totals (balances) that are significantly different from zero.
Source: OECD.

Annex Table 53. **Semi-annual demand and output projections**

Percentage changes from previous period, seasonally adjusted at annual rates, volume

	2002	2003	2004	2002 I	2002 II	2003 I	2003 II	2004 I	2004 II
Private consumption									
Canada	2.9	2.8	2.9	3.7	3.0	2.7	2.8	3.0	2.9
France	1.8	1.6	2.2	1.3	2.2	1.5	1.3	2.5	2.6
Germany	-0.6	0.5	1.4	-1.7	0.9	0.4	0.5	1.5	2.0
Italy	0.4	1.0	2.4	-0.2	2.8	-0.2	1.8	2.6	2.8
Japan	1.4	0.6	0.7	2.0	2.1	0.1	0.4	0.7	0.8
United Kingdom	3.8	2.2	2.3	3.6	3.7	1.8	1.6	2.6	2.5
United States	3.1	2.3	3.6	3.5	3.0	1.5	3.0	3.9	3.6
Euro area	0.7	1.2	2.1	0.1	1.7	0.9	1.4	2.3	2.5
European Union	1.2	1.4	2.2	0.7	2.1	1.1	1.5	2.3	2.5
Total OECD	2.3	1.8	2.7	2.5	2.5	1.3	2.1	2.8	2.8
Public consumption									
Canada	2.0	3.7	3.2	1.2	3.2	4.0	3.6	3.1	3.1
France	3.5	2.7	1.6	3.8	3.1	3.0	1.7	1.6	1.6
Germany	1.5	0.8	0.4	2.7	0.6	0.8	0.8	0.3	0.3
Italy	1.7	1.2	1.1	2.2	-0.2	1.9	1.2	1.1	1.0
Japan	2.3	2.0	1.9	2.7	1.3	2.2	2.2	1.8	1.6
United Kingdom	3.8	2.1	2.8	4.9	0.4	2.7	2.7	2.8	2.8
United States	4.4	5.3	2.0	4.7	3.7	6.2	5.1	0.9	1.2
Euro area	2.7	1.6	1.2	3.4	1.7	1.6	1.2	1.2	1.2
European Union	2.7	1.6	1.4	3.5	1.4	1.7	1.4	1.4	1.4
Total OECD	3.2	3.1	1.9	3.5	2.7	3.4	3.0	1.5	1.5
Investment									
Canada	2.5	3.4	5.2	1.5	4.8	2.6	3.8	5.3	6.2
France	-0.6	-1.4	2.3	0.0	-2.1	-2.1	0.5	2.7	3.1
Germany	-6.7	-0.5	1.8	-8.6	-3.1	1.0	-0.8	2.3	3.4
Italy	0.5	1.1	3.5	-2.9	8.4	-2.9	2.4	3.8	4.2
Japan	-4.0	-1.3	-1.5	-4.7	2.3	-2.4	-2.4	-1.3	-0.7
United Kingdom	-3.2	1.9	6.7	-4.8	0.8	1.6	3.5	6.4	10.3
United States	-1.8	1.4	5.9	-0.5	0.5	0.8	3.5	6.8	6.4
Euro area	-2.3	0.2	2.7	-3.2	-0.2	-0.1	1.3	3.0	3.5
European Union	-2.4	0.4	3.3	-3.4	0.0	0.2	1.6	3.6	4.6
Total OECD	-1.7	1.1	3.9	-1.4	1.2	0.5	2.2	4.4	4.7
Total domestic demand									
Canada	3.5	3.3	3.5	4.6	5.0	2.5	3.2	3.5	3.6
France	1.1	1.1	2.9	1.7	0.6	1.2	1.6	3.4	3.4
Germany	-1.5	0.6	1.6	-1.9	0.6	0.7	0.4	1.8	2.4
Italy	1.1	0.8	2.3	1.6	0.9	0.4	1.5	2.5	2.8
Japan	-0.3	0.5	0.4	-0.4	3.2	-0.6	-0.2	0.5	0.7
United Kingdom	2.5	2.4	3.4	1.7	4.3	1.6	2.3	3.7	4.1
United States	3.0	2.8	4.0	4.2	3.3	2.1	3.8	4.2	3.8
Euro area	0.3	1.1	2.4	0.4	1.0	1.0	1.5	2.6	2.9
European Union	0.7	1.3	2.5	0.7	1.5	1.1	1.6	2.8	3.0
Total OECD	1.9	2.0	2.9	2.4	2.8	1.4	2.4	3.1	3.1
Export of goods and services									
Canada	0.8	4.4	7.3	2.8	3.1	4.1	6.2	7.8	7.2
France	1.5	2.6	5.2	3.8	4.6	1.2	3.5	5.7	6.0
Germany	2.6	3.2	6.0	1.5	7.5	1.5	2.4	6.7	8.0
Italy	-1.0	4.4	5.5	-3.0	12.0	0.3	5.8	5.5	5.3
Japan	8.1	7.7	9.4	17.0	11.5	5.4	8.8	9.9	9.0
United Kingdom	-1.0	2.1	8.4	3.4	-1.9	1.7	6.9	8.6	9.4
United States	-1.6	4.0	9.0	2.6	4.2	1.8	8.2	9.1	9.6
Total OECD [a]	1.6	4.6	8.2	4.8	6.2	2.6	7.0	8.5	8.7

Note: The adoption of new national account systems, SNA93 or ESA95, has been proceeding at an uneven pace among OECD member countries, both with respect to variables and the time period covered. As a consequence, there are breaks in many national series. Moreover, some countries are using chain-weighted price indices to calculate real GDP and expenditures components. See Table "National Account Reporting Systems and Base-years" at the beginning of the Statistical Annex and *OECD Economic Outlook* Sources and Methods (*http://www.oecd.org/eco/sources-and-methods*).

a) Includes intra-regional trade.

Source: OECD.

Annex Table 53. *(cont'd)* **Semi-annual demand and output projections**

Percentage changes from previous period, seasonally adjusted at annual rates, volume

	2002	2003	2004	2002		2003		2004	
				I	II	I	II	I	II
Import of goods and services									
Canada	0.8	6.1	8.0	2.1	7.7	4.6	7.6	8.3	7.8
France	1.2	2.5	6.5	4.6	2.3	1.7	4.3	7.0	7.7
Germany	-2.1	4.3	6.1	-5.5	8.1	3.0	3.3	6.7	7.8
Italy	1.5	3.8	5.4	2.1	11.0	-0.1	4.7	5.5	5.7
Japan	2.0	3.6	4.2	3.3	11.1	0.6	2.5	4.9	4.4
United Kingdom	1.5	2.9	9.6	4.6	1.9	1.5	6.6	10.1	11.4
United States	3.7	6.4	7.8	8.1	8.7	4.9	6.9	8.4	7.4
Total OECD[a]	2.7	5.1	7.2	5.0	8.3	3.3	5.7	7.7	7.6
GDP									
Canada	3.4	2.7	3.4	4.8	3.3	2.4	2.9	3.6	3.6
France	1.2	1.2	2.6	1.5	1.3	1.0	1.4	3.0	2.9
Germany	0.2	0.3	1.7	0.4	0.7	0.2	0.2	2.1	2.7
Italy	0.4	1.0	2.4	0.1	1.3	0.5	1.8	2.6	2.8
Japan	0.3	1.0	1.1	1.0	3.5	0.0	0.6	1.2	1.4
United Kingdom	1.8	2.1	2.6	1.3	3.1	1.7	2.1	2.8	2.9
United States	2.4	2.5	4.0	3.5	2.7	1.7	3.8	4.1	3.8
Euro area	0.9	1.0	2.4	1.1	1.1	0.9	1.4	2.6	2.9
European Union	1.0	1.2	2.4	1.2	1.4	1.0	1.5	2.6	2.8
Total OECD	1.8	1.9	3.0	2.5	2.4	1.4	2.4	3.2	3.2

Per cent of GDP

	2002	2003	2004	2002 I	2002 II	2003 I	2003 II	2004 I	2004 II
Current account balance									
Canada	1.5	2.0	2.2	1.7	1.3	2.0	2.0	2.1	2.2
France	2.1	2.4	2.2	1.9	2.2	2.4	2.4	2.4	2.1
Germany	2.5	2.9	3.2	1.9	3.1	2.9	2.9	3.1	3.3
Italy	-0.5	-0.1	0.0	-0.5	-0.5	-0.2	0.0	0.1	0.0
Japan	2.8	3.1	3.9	3.0	2.6	2.9	3.4	3.8	4.1
United Kingdom	-0.8	-1.4	-2.0	-0.9	-0.8	-1.3	-1.5	-1.8	-2.3
United States	-4.8	-5.4	-5.5	-4.6	-5.0	-5.4	-5.4	-5.5	-5.5
Euro area	1.1	1.4	1.4	0.9	1.3	1.3	1.4	1.4	1.4
European Union	0.9	1.0	1.0	0.7	1.0	1.0	1.0	1.0	0.9
Total OECD	-1.1	-1.2	-1.2	-1.0	-1.1	-1.2	-1.1	-1.1	-1.1

$ billions

	2002	2003	2004	2002 I	2002 II	2003 I	2003 II	2004 I	2004 II
Current account balance									
Canada	11.0	16	19	12.4	9.6	16	17	18	20
France	29.4	39	38	26.1	32.7	39	39	40	36
Germany	50.3	67	75	36.5	64.1	66	67	71	78
Italy	-5.7	-1	0	-5.4	-6.0	-2	1	1	0
Japan	113.6	129	160	117.4	109.7	119	138	154	167
United Kingdom	-13.1	-24	-37	-13.2	-12.9	-22	-26	-32	-41
United States	-503.4	-587	-629	-480.5	-526.4	-583	-591	-620	-639
Euro area	72.8	105	115	56.6	89.1	104	106	113	117
European Union	74.6	98	99	60.7	88.5	97	99	101	98
Total OECD	-288.5	-338	-345	-271.1	-305.9	-343	-333	-342	-348

Note: The adoption of new national account systems, SNA93 or ESA95, has been proceeding at an uneven pace among OECD member countries, both with respect to variables and the time period covered. As a consequence, there are breaks in many national series. Moreover, some countries are using chain-weighted price indices to calculate real GDP and expenditures components. See Table "National Account Reporting Systems and Base-years" at the beginning of the Statistical Annex and *OECD Economic Outlook* Sources and Methods (*http://www.oecd.org/eco/sources-and-methods*).

a) Includes intra-regional trade.

Source: OECD.

Annex Table 54. **Semi-annual price, cost and unemployment projections**

Percentage changes from previous period, seasonally adjusted at annual rates

	2002	2003	2004	2002		2003		2004	
				I	II	I	II	I	II
Private consumption deflator									
Canada	1.9	2.8	2.1	1.9	2.8	3.1	2.0	2.1	2.2
France	1.5	1.4	1.4	1.8	1.2	1.4	1.4	1.4	1.4
Germany	1.4	0.8	0.4	1.9	0.6	1.0	0.5	0.4	0.4
Italy	3.0	2.4	1.9	3.1	3.1	2.3	2.1	1.9	1.8
Japan	-1.5	-1.6	-1.6	-1.4	-1.5	-1.6	-1.6	-1.6	-1.6
United Kingdom	0.8	0.9	1.0	0.7	0.7	1.0	1.0	1.0	1.1
United States	1.4	2.0	1.2	1.4	2.0	2.6	0.8	1.3	1.3
Euro area	2.2	1.7	1.4	2.5	2.0	1.7	1.5	1.4	1.3
European Union	2.0	1.6	1.4	2.2	1.7	1.7	1.4	1.3	1.3
Total OECD	2.0	2.0	1.3	2.0	2.1	2.3	1.4	1.4	1.3
Total OECD *less* Turkey	1.4	1.5	1.1	1.5	1.5	1.8	1.0	1.1	1.1
GDP deflator									
Canada	1.2	3.5	2.1	2.4	3.6	4.0	2.1	2.1	2.1
France	1.7	1.5	1.6	1.8	1.4	1.5	1.6	1.6	1.5
Germany	1.6	0.8	0.6	2.1	0.8	0.8	0.8	0.5	0.6
Italy	2.7	2.7	2.6	2.6	2.7	2.7	2.6	2.6	2.5
Japan	-1.7	-2.2	-1.8	-1.7	-2.6	-2.1	-1.8	-1.8	-1.8
United Kingdom	3.2	1.8	2.3	4.3	2.3	1.5	2.0	2.3	2.5
United States	1.1	1.6	1.3	0.9	1.3	2.0	1.2	1.5	1.3
Euro area	2.4	1.9	1.7	2.5	2.1	1.9	1.8	1.6	1.6
European Union	2.5	1.9	1.8	2.8	2.1	1.9	1.9	1.8	1.8
Total OECD	2.1	1.7	1.4	2.0	1.7	1.9	1.5	1.4	1.3
Total OECD *less* Turkey	1.4	1.3	1.2	1.5	1.2	1.5	1.2	1.2	1.2
Unit labour cost (total economy)									
Canada	1.2	2.4	1.9	0.9	2.1	2.6	2.2	1.8	1.8
France	2.5	1.4	0.9	1.6	2.2	0.9	1.6	0.6	0.8
Germany	0.7	1.2	0.2	0.8	-0.1	1.6	1.6	-0.2	-0.3
Italy	3.9	2.9	2.4	5.1	0.8	4.1	2.5	2.4	2.3
Japan	-2.6	-2.3	-1.8	-4.2	-5.5	-0.8	-1.7	-1.8	-1.9
United Kingdom	3.0	2.4	1.9	3.4	2.5	2.1	2.3	1.7	1.7
United States	-0.7	1.3	1.2	-1.2	0.1	2.2	0.8	1.5	1.2
Euro area	2.4	1.8	1.1	2.3	1.6	1.9	1.8	0.9	0.9
European Union	2.6	2.0	1.4	2.6	1.8	2.1	1.9	1.2	1.2
Total OECD	1.3	1.7	1.3	0.7	0.8	2.2	1.5	1.3	1.2
Total OECD *less* Turkey	0.8	1.3	1.0	0.4	0.4	1.8	1.1	1.0	1.0
				Per cent of labour force					
Unemployment									
Canada	7.7	7.3	7.0	7.7	7.6	7.4	7.3	7.1	6.9
France	8.9	9.3	9.2	8.8	9.0	9.2	9.5	9.3	9.1
Germany	7.8	8.3	8.3	7.6	7.9	8.2	8.4	8.4	8.3
Italy	9.1	9.2	8.9	9.2	9.0	9.2	9.2	9.0	8.8
Japan	5.4	5.7	5.7	5.3	5.4	5.6	5.8	5.7	5.7
United Kingdom	5.2	5.4	5.2	5.1	5.2	5.4	5.3	5.3	5.2
United States	5.8	6.0	5.8	5.7	5.8	6.0	6.1	5.9	5.7
Euro area	8.2	8.8	8.7	8.1	8.3	8.7	8.8	8.8	8.6
European Union	7.6	8.0	7.9	7.5	7.7	8.0	8.1	8.0	7.9
Total OECD	6.9	7.2	7.0	6.8	7.0	7.1	7.2	7.1	6.9

Note: The adoption of new national account systems, SNA93 or ESA95, has been proceeding at an uneven pace among OECD member countries, both with respect to variables and the time period covered. As a consequence, there are breaks in many national series. Moreover, some countries are using chain-weighted price indices to calculate real GDP and expenditures components. See Table "National Account Reporting Systems and Base-years" at the beginning of the Statistical Annex and *OECD Economic Outlook* Sources and Methods *(http://www.oecd.org/eco/sources-and-methods)*.
Source: OECD.

Annex Table 55. **Contributions to changes in real GDP in OECD countries**

As a per cent of real GDP in the previous period, seasonally adjusted at annual rates

	2001	2002	2003	2004		2001	2002	2003	2004
Australia					**Germany**				
Final domestic demand	1.8	6.3	4.1	3.9	Final domestic demand	-0.2	-1.5	0.4	1.2
Stockbuilding	-0.1	-0.2	0.1	0.1	Stockbuilding	-0.6	0.1	0.2	0.3
Net exports	1.3	-2.6	-0.9	-0.2	Net exports	1.4	1.6	-0.2	0.2
GDP	2.8	3.5	3.2	3.8	GDP	0.6	0.2	0.3	1.7
Austria					**Greece**				
Final domestic demand	0.2	-0.3	1.0	1.8	Final domestic demand	3.3	4.1	3.9	3.8
Stockbuilding	-0.4	0.0	0.0	0.0	Stockbuilding	0.1	0.0	0.0	0.0
Net exports	0.8	1.4	0.1	0.2	Net exports	0.7	-0.2	-0.3	0.1
GDP	0.7	1.0	1.1	2.0	GDP	4.1	4.0	3.6	3.9
Belgium					**Hungary**				
Final domestic demand	1.1	0.1	0.9	1.9	Final domestic demand	3.3	7.0	3.9	2.7
Stockbuilding	-0.5	0.2	0.3	0.1	Stockbuilding	-1.2	-1.7	0.2	0.6
Net exports	0.3	0.3	0.0	0.3	Net exports	1.7	-2.0	-1.0	0.5
GDP	0.8	0.7	1.3	2.3	GDP	3.8	3.3	3.1	3.7
Canada					**Iceland**				
Final domestic demand	2.4	2.5	3.0	3.3	Final domestic demand	-2.9	-3.0	2.8	4.1
Stockbuilding	-1.3	0.8	0.2	0.1	Stockbuilding	-0.9	0.4	0.0	0.2
Net exports	0.6	0.0	-0.4	0.1	Net exports	6.8	2.0	-0.7	-0.8
GDP	1.5	3.4	2.7	3.4	GDP	3.1	-0.6	2.1	3.5
Czech Republic					**Ireland**				
Final domestic demand	4.8	3.4	3.7	3.9	Final domestic demand	4.2	2.3	1.6	2.1
Stockbuilding	0.7	0.3	0.0	0.0	Stockbuilding	-0.4	-0.2	0.2	0.1
Net exports	-2.3	-1.7	-0.7	-0.5	Net exports	1.6	3.6	1.1	1.8
GDP	3.1	2.0	3.0	3.5	GDP	6.0	6.0	3.2	4.2
Denmark					**Italy**				
Final domestic demand	1.0	1.5	1.4	2.0	Final domestic demand	1.8	0.7	1.1	2.4
Stockbuilding	-0.3	-0.4	0.2	0.0	Stockbuilding	0.0	0.4	-0.3	-0.1
Net exports	0.7	0.5	0.0	0.6	Net exports	0.1	-0.7	0.2	0.1
GDP	1.4	1.6	1.6	2.6	GDP	1.8	0.4	1.0	2.4
Finland					**Japan**				
Final domestic demand	1.8	1.7	1.3	2.0	Final domestic demand	1.0	0.1	0.4	0.3
Stockbuilding	-0.2	-1.2	0.3	0.5	Stockbuilding	0.0	-0.4	0.1	0.0
Net exports	-0.9	1.8	0.1	0.9	Net exports	-0.7	0.7	0.6	0.8
GDP	0.6	1.6	2.2	3.4	GDP	0.4	0.3	1.0	1.1
France					**Korea**				
Final domestic demand	2.6	1.7	1.2	2.1	Final domestic demand	2.0	5.0	2.4	3.6
Stockbuilding	-1.0	-0.6	-0.1	0.8	Stockbuilding	-0.1	-0.2	0.0	0.0
Net exports	0.2	0.1	0.1	-0.2	Net exports	1.4	2.0	2.7	2.4
GDP	1.8	1.2	1.2	2.6	GDP	3.1	6.3	5.2	6.0

Note: The adoption of new national account systems, SNA93 or ESA95, has been proceeding at an uneven pace among OECD member countries, both with respect to variables and the time period covered. As a consequence, there are breaks in many national series. Moreover, some countries are using chain-weighted price indices to calculate real GDP and expenditures components. See Table "National Account Reporting Systems and Base-years" at the beginning of the Statistical Annex and *OECD Economic Outlook* Sources and Methods *(http://www.oecd.org/eco/sources-and-methods)*. Totals may not add up due to rounding and/or statistical discrepancy.
Source: OECD.

Annex Table 55. *(cont'd)* **Contributions to changes in real GDP in OECD countries**

As a per cent of real GDP in the previous period

	2001	2002	2003	2004		2001	2002	2003	2004
Luxembourg					**Sweden**				
Final domestic demand	4.0	0.8	0.6	2.0	Final domestic demand	0.5	0.7	1.3	2.2
Stockbuilding	1.0	0.0	0.0	0.2	Stockbuilding	-0.4	-0.1	0.1	0.0
Net exports	-4.0	0.5	-0.4	0.5	Net exports	1.1	1.3	0.3	1.0
GDP	1.0	0.5	0.3	2.7	GDP	1.1	1.9	1.5	2.8
Mexico					**Switzerland**				
Final domestic demand	0.6	0.5	2.6	4.3	Final domestic demand	0.1	-0.8	0.4	1.8
Stockbuilding	-0.2	0.5	0.0	0.3	Stockbuilding	0.7	-0.5	0.0	0.0
Net exports	-0.7	-0.1	0.0	-0.7	Net exports	0.1	1.4	0.2	0.1
GDP	-0.3	0.9	2.5	3.9	GDP	0.9	0.1	0.6	1.9
Netherlands					**Turkey**				
Final domestic demand	1.1	0.7	0.5	1.6	Final domestic demand	-15.8	1.7	3.5	4.5
Stockbuilding	0.2	-0.7	0.1	0.9	Stockbuilding	-4.0	7.0	-0.3	-1.6
Net exports	0.0	0.4	0.1	-0.6	Net exports	12.4	-0.9	-1.1	-0.3
GDP	1.3	0.3	0.7	1.9	GDP	-7.5	7.8	2.5	2.6
New Zealand					**United Kingdom**				
Final domestic demand	1.6	4.6	3.5	2.5	Final domestic demand	3.4	2.8	2.3	3.3
Stockbuilding	0.2	0.2	-0.2	0.0	Stockbuilding	-0.6	-0.1	0.3	0.4
Net exports	0.2	-0.2	-0.5	0.3	Net exports	-0.6	-0.9	-0.5	-1.1
GDP	2.0	4.6	2.9	2.9	GDP	2.1	1.8	2.1	2.6
Norway					**United States**				
Final domestic demand	0.8	1.7	1.6	1.4	Final domestic demand	1.7	2.5	2.7	3.9
Stockbuilding	-0.5	0.0	0.0	0.0	Stockbuilding	-1.4	0.7	0.3	0.3
Net exports	1.6	-0.7	-0.5	0.8	Net exports	-0.2	-0.8	-0.6	-0.3
GDP	1.9	1.0	1.1	2.1	GDP	0.3	2.4	2.5	4.0
Poland									
Final domestic demand	-0.6	0.8	2.1	2.9					
Stockbuilding	-1.2	0.0	0.0	0.0					
Net exports	2.6	0.8	0.1	0.5					
GDP	1.0	1.3	2.3	3.5					
Portugal					**Euro area**				
Final domestic demand	1.4	-0.4	-0.3	2.0	Final domestic demand	1.4	0.4	1.1	2.0
Stockbuilding	0.0	0.0	-0.1	0.0	Stockbuilding	-0.4	-0.1	0.0	0.3
Net exports	0.2	0.9	0.8	0.4	Net exports	0.5	0.5	0.0	0.1
GDP	1.6	0.5	0.3	2.3	GDP	1.5	0.9	1.0	2.4
Slovak Republic					**European Union**				
Final domestic demand	5.8	3.3	3.2	3.6	Final domestic demand	1.7	0.8	1.3	2.2
Stockbuilding	1.4	0.8	0.0	0.0	Stockbuilding	-0.5	-0.1	0.0	0.3
Net exports	-4.0	0.3	0.4	0.7	Net exports	0.3	0.3	-0.1	-0.1
GDP	3.3	4.4	3.6	4.3	GDP	1.6	1.0	1.2	2.4
Spain					**Total OECD**				
Final domestic demand	2.8	2.1	2.7	3.5	Final domestic demand	1.3	1.6	1.9	2.8
Stockbuilding	0.0	0.1	0.0	0.0	Stockbuilding	-0.7	0.3	0.2	0.2
Net exports	-0.1	-0.3	-0.5	-0.4	Net exports	0.2	-0.1	-0.1	0.0
GDP	2.7	2.0	2.1	3.1	GDP	0.8	1.8	1.9	3.0

Note: The adoption of new national account systems, SNA93 or ESA95, has been proceeding at an uneven pace among OECD member countries, both with respect to variables and the time period covered. As a consequence, there are breaks in many national series. Moreover, some countries are using chain-weighted price indices to calculate real GDP and expenditures components. See Table "National Account Reporting Systems and Base-years" at the beginning of the Statistical Annex and *OECD Economic Outlook* Sources and Methods *(http://www.oecd.org/eco/sources-and-methods)*. Totals may not add up due to rounding and/or statistical discrepancy.
Source: OECD.

Annex Table 56. **Household wealth and indebtedness**[a]

	1990	1991	1992	1993	1994	1995	1996	1997	1998	1999	2000	2001
Canada												
Net wealth	416.5	427.5	441.6	455.1	475.3	480.8	494.8	509.6	511.2	514.3	506.9	503.2
Net financial wealth	177.5	186.2	195.2	201.5	212.0	222.2	233.2	245.1	245.4	246.5	242.7	236.5
Non-financial assets	239.0	241.3	246.4	253.6	263.4	258.6	261.6	264.6	265.8	267.8	264.2	266.7
Financial assets	270.4	279.5	291.4	300.4	314.4	325.0	339.3	353.8	355.9	358.3	353.5	348.2
of which: Equities	49.6	51.3	52.6	59.7	64.0	67.6	76.0	86.4	93.6	95.9	95.7	98.9
Liabilities	92.9	93.4	96.2	98.9	102.4	102.8	106.1	108.7	110.4	111.8	110.8	111.7
of which: Mortgages	59.2	61.4	64.7	66.4	68.6	68.8	70.9	71.5	71.7	71.4	69.8	70.0
France												
Net wealth	541.8	527.2	510.3	515.9	494.7	507.6	533.6	557.5	577.8	656.0	650.2	630.9
Net financial wealth	169.6	170.3	173.1	188.9	166.5	195.0	220.2	241.6	262.2	310.5	302.4	271.8
Non-financial assets	372.2	356.9	337.2	327.0	328.3	312.6	313.4	315.9	315.6	345.5	347.8	359.1
Financial assets	248.3	251.3	253.4	271.4	251.1	262.9	288.9	310.8	336.0	385.8	379.6	347.8
of which: Equities	114.1	118.6	115.5	126.2	94.9	89.6	104.5	117.1	137.6	177.6	174.2	144.3
Liabilities	78.7	80.9	80.3	82.6	84.6	67.9	68.7	69.2	73.8	75.3	77.2	76.0
of which: Long-term loans	53.4	53.4	53.0	54.7	53.7	51.6	52.2	52.6	52.9	55.0	55.4	55.3
Germany												
Net wealth	535.6	532.3	530.8	547.5	553.3	563.1	570.8	579.3	585.4	591.0	583.9	568.5
Net financial wealth	130.8	123.2	124.1	133.7	130.3	135.6	140.5	149.2	155.2	165.7	162.9	158.6
Non-financial assets	404.8	344.8	341.4	347.4	356.2	360.6	353.8	360.8	360.3	355.5	351.0	340.4
Financial assets	200.7	208.1	209.9	224.7	227.3	236.2	245.2	256.8	266.2	280.0	277.3	270.5
of which: Equities	11.6	30.4	30.8	37.8	40.7	42.4	46.8	55.2	53.0	75.0	75.0	67.0
Liabilities	70.0	84.9	85.7	91.0	97.0	100.6	104.8	107.6	111.0	114.2	114.4	112.0
of which: Mortgages	53.6	50.7	50.3	53.8	58.0	61.0	64.5	67.1	68.5	71.9	72.5	72.1
Italy												
Net wealth	636.9	653.9	723.8	762.4	708.2	699.3	699.6	693.3	713.2	736.7	748.3	714.2
Net financial wealth	196.3	202.4	207.0	229.2	224.1	224.0	231.3	239.7	266.4	293.9	294.6	251.7
Non-financial assets	440.5	451.5	516.7	533.2	484.2	475.3	468.3	453.6	446.9	442.8	453.7	462.5
Financial assets	225.4	232.2	237.7	261.0	256.0	254.6	263.3	268.0	296.7	327.7	329.8	287.0
of which: Equities	46.0	47.9	47.9	54.4	49.3	46.5	50.9	72.2	108.3	153.0	147.4	102.5
Liabilities	29.1	29.8	30.6	31.8	31.9	30.6	32.0	28.2	30.3	33.8	35.3	35.3
of which: Medium and long-term loans	13.7	14.3	14.4	14.9	15.2	18.6	19.1	19.3	21.2	24.3	25.7	26.0
Japan												
Net wealth	947.6	867.3	794.4	774.8	772.5	757.1	767.5	759.9	739.8	765.8	762.3	755.2
Net financial wealth	268.0	265.0	255.8	263.8	281.8	289.1	303.0	307.6	303.5	338.4	343.0	346.8
Non-financial assets	679.6	602.3	538.6	510.9	490.7	468.0	464.6	452.3	436.3	427.4	419.3	408.4
Financial assets	398.8	395.9	384.1	396.2	414.2	426.2	436.9	442.0	437.1	471.9	477.7	483.5
of which: Equities	57.3	52.8	37.1	38.3	47.0	45.9	41.1	36.8	26.5	48.7	42.8	31.6
Liabilities	130.8	130.9	128.3	132.4	132.4	137.1	133.9	134.4	133.6	133.5	134.7	136.7
of which: Mortgages	50.6	50.8	51.8	53.9	56.2	58.5	60.2	54.4	54.9	57.5	59.3	61.9
United Kingdom												
Net wealth	611.0	579.8	551.7	584.7	546.1	553.4	568.7	626.3	672.5	746.9	747.7	663.9
Net financial wealth	214.1	220.0	234.5	278.7	257.3	281.3	286.9	342.2	355.4	402.7	375.3	291.9
Non-financial assets	396.9	359.9	317.2	306.0	288.8	272.1	281.8	284.1	317.1	344.2	372.4	372.0
Financial assets	329.9	333.4	343.9	385.1	364.7	387.8	392.0	447.2	464.4	520.6	493.1	433.1
of which: Equities	61.2	58.9	61.2	73.5	70.2	71.7	70.2	96.2	92.1	120.6	110.9	78.8
Liabilities	115.8	113.5	109.4	106.4	107.5	106.5	105.1	105.0	109.1	111.8	115.6	118.7
of which: Mortgages	507.0	505.8	514.5	565.0	542.4	566.0	567.3	648.4	665.6	753.0	719.5	630.6
United States												
Net wealth	474.5	490.4	481.0	488.2	478.6	508.2	529.5	566.4	586.8	637.9	586.6	553.1
Net financial wealth	259.0	277.9	274.2	282.8	276.3	304.5	327.1	363.0	380.7	424.0	369.2	327.1
Non-financial assets	215.5	212.4	206.8	205.4	202.3	203.7	202.4	203.4	206.2	213.9	217.5	226.0
Financial assets	345.6	365.9	361.3	372.2	367.9	398.3	423.0	460.6	479.9	528.0	474.1	436.0
of which: Equities	52.1	69.7	75.2	85.1	79.0	97.7	112.2	137.6	149.5	184.6	147.3	121.4
Liabilities	86.6	87.9	87.1	89.5	91.6	93.7	95.9	97.6	99.3	103.9	104.9	108.8
of which: Mortgages	60.3	62.1	62.3	63.4	63.7	63.5	64.7	65.6	67.1	70.0	70.5	74.5

a) Assets and liabilities are amounts outstanding at the end of the period, in per cent of nominal disposable income. Vertical lines between columns indicate breaks in the series due to changes in the definitions or accounting systems. Figures after the most recent breaks in the series are based on the UN System of National Accounts 1993 (SNA 93) and, more specifically, for European Union countries, on the corresponding European System of Accounts 1995 (ESA 95).

Households include non-profit institutions serving households. Net wealth is defined as non-financial and financial assets minus liabilities; net financial wealth is financial assets minus liabilities. Non-financial assets include stock of durable goods and dwellings, at replacement cost and at market value, respectively. Financial assets comprise currency and deposits, securities other than shares, loans, shares and other equity, insurance technical reserves; and other accounts receivable/payable. Not included are assets with regard to social security pension insurance schemes. Equities comprise shares and other equity, including quoted, unquoted and mutual fund shares. See also *OECD Economic Outlook* Sources and Methods *(http://www.oecd.org/eco/sources-and-methods)*.

Sources: Canada: Statistics Canada, *National Balance Sheet Accounts.* France: INSEE, *Rapport sur les Comptes de la Nation* and *25 ans de Comptes de Patrimoine* (1969-1993); Banque de France, *Flow of Funds Accounts.* Germany: Deutsche Bundesbank, *Monthly Report* and *Financial accounts for Germany 1991 to 1999,* Special Statistical Publication, 2000. Italy: Banca d'Italia, *Supplements to the Statistical Bulletin* ; Ando, A., L.Guiso, I.Visco (eds.), *Saving and the Accumulation of Wealth,* Cambridge University Press, 1994; OECD, *Financial Accounts of OECD countries* . Japan: Economic Planning Agency, Government of Japan, *Annual Report on National Accounts.* United Kingdom: Office for National Statistics, *United Kingdom National Accounts,* and *Financial Statistics.* United States: Federal Reserve Statistical Release, *Flow of Funds Accounts* of the United States.

Annex Table 57. **Central government financial balances**

Surplus (+) or deficit (-) as a percentage of nominal GDP

	1993	1994	1995	1996	1997	1998	1999	2000	2001	2002	Projections 2003	Projections 2004
Canada	-5.5	-4.6	-3.9	-2.0	0.7	0.8	0.8	1.7	1.0	1.0	0.1	0.1
France	-4.9	-4.9	-4.2	-3.7	-2.8	-3.0	-2.5	-2.4	-2.3	-3.7	-3.4	-3.4
Germany	-1.9	-1.2	-1.4	-2.2	-1.6	-1.8	-1.6	1.3	-1.3	-1.6	-1.6	-1.4
Italy	-9.8	-9.2	-7.7	-6.9	-2.7	-2.5	-1.5	-1.1	-2.8	-2.5	-2.5	-2.9
Japan[a]	-3.5	-4.3	-4.3	-4.4	-3.9	-5.4	-7.7	-6.7	-6.2	-6.7	-6.8	-6.7
United Kingdom	-8.1	-6.7	-5.5	-4.6	-2.2	0.3	1.2	4.1	0.9	-1.3	-1.9	-2.1
United States	-4.4	-3.2	-2.6	-1.9	-0.6	0.5	1.1	2.0	0.6	-2.2	-3.5	-3.5
excluding social security	-5.1	-4.0	-3.4	-2.8	-1.7	-0.7	-0.3	0.5	-1.0	-3.7	-5.0	-5.0
Total of above countries	-4.7	-4.0	-3.5	-3.0	-1.7	-1.3	-1.2	-0.1	-1.3	-2.9	-3.6	-3.5

Note: Central government financial balances include one-off revenues from the sale of mobile telephone licenses.
a) Data are only available for fiscal years beginning April 1 of the year shown. The 1998 deficit would rise by 5.2 percentage points of GDP if account were taken of the assumption by the central government of the debt of the Japan Railway Settlement Corporation and the National Forest Special Account.
Source: OECD.

Annex Table 58. **Maastricht definition of general government gross public debt**

As a percentage of nominal GDP

	1993	1994	1995	1996	1997	1998	1999	2000	2001	2002	Projections 2003	Projections 2004
Austria	61.8	64.7	69.2	69.1	64.7	63.7	67.5	66.8	67.3	67.6	66.8	65.8
Belgium	138.1	135.8	133.9	130.5	124.8	119.5	114.8	109.6	108.5	105.4	102.4	98.6
Denmark	78.0	73.5	69.3	65.1	61.2	56.2	53.0	47.4	45.4	45.2	43.6	41.7
Finland	55.8	57.8	57.1	57.0	54.0	48.6	47.0	44.5	43.8	42.7	41.2	40.4
France	45.3	48.4	54.6	57.0	59.3	59.5	58.5	57.3	57.3	59.5	62.0	63.5
Germany	46.9	49.3	57.0	59.8	61.0	60.9	61.2	60.2	59.5	60.8	63.4	65.0
Greece	110.1	107.9	108.7	111.3	108.2	105.8	105.1	106.2	107.0	104.9	102.4	98.7
Ireland	96.5	90.9	82.9	74.1	65.0	54.9	49.3	39.3	36.7	33.5	31.6	31.2
Italy	118.1	123.8	123.2	122.1	120.2	116.3	114.9	110.6	109.5	106.7	106.1	105.0
Luxembourg	5.7	5.4	5.6	6.2	6.1	6.3	6.0	5.6	5.6	5.8	5.5	6.2
Netherlands	79.0	76.3	77.2	75.2	69.9	66.8	63.1	55.8	52.8	52.5	52.0	52.5
Portugal	59.1	62.1	64.3	62.9	59.1	55.0	54.3	53.3	55.5	58.1	58.9	58.6
Spain	58.4	61.1	63.9	68.1	66.6	64.6	63.1	60.5	56.9	54.0	53.0	51.8
Sweden	..	73.8	73.6	73.5	70.5	68.0	62.7	52.8	54.4	52.4	52.1	51.6
United Kingdom	45.4	48.5	51.8	52.3	50.8	47.7	45.1	42.1	38.9	38.4	39.7	41.0

Note: Debt figures are based on ESA95 definitions. For the period 1993-2002, they are provided by Eurostat, the Statistical Office of the European Communities, while GDP figures are provided by National Authorities. The 2003 to 2004 debt ratios are projected forward in line with the OECD projections for general government gross financial liabilities and GDP.
Source: OECD.

Annex Table 59. **Monetary and credit aggregates: recent trends**

Annualised percentage change, seasonally adjusted

		Annual change (to 4th quarter)					Latest twelve months	
		1998	1999	2000	2001	2002		
Canada	M2	0.6	3.8	7.2	5.7	6.0	5.6	(Mar. 2003)
	BL[a]	7.6	5.9	7.0	4.8	5.0	5.0	(Jan. 2003)
Japan	M2+CD	4.5	3.1	2.0	3.2	2.9	1.8	(Mar. 2003)
	BL[a]	-1.0	-0.6	2.5	-1.4	-3.1	-2.1	(Jan. 2003)
United Kingdom	M0	5.2	9.3	9.0	5.2	6.7	6.8	(Mar. 2003)
	M4	8.8	3.6	8.7	7.4	5.6	6.7	(Mar. 2003)
	BL[a]	8.1	9.1	14.1	10.0	8.8	8.3	(Mar. 2003)
United States	M2	8.5	6.3	6.0	10.2	6.9	7.2	(Mar. 2003)
	M3	10.8	7.6	9.2	12.7	6.4	6.4	(Mar. 2003)
	BL[a]	9.8	4.5	12.1	2.5	5.0	7.6	(Mar. 2003)
Euro area	M2	5.7	6.6	4.0	8.4	6.5	7.9	(Mar. 2003)
	M3	4.9	5.2	4.6	10.5	6.7	7.9	(Mar. 2003)
	BL[a]	6.4	6.6	5.9	7.2	3.8	4.3	(Feb. 2003)

a) Commercial bank lending.
Source: OECD.

Annex Table 60. **Export market growth and performance in manufactured goods**
Percentage changes from previous year

	Import volume				Export market growth				Export volume				Export performance[a]			
	2001	2002	2003	2004	2001	2002	2003	2004	2001	2002	2003	2004	2001	2002	2003	2004
Australia	-6.8	15.0	8.5	8.7	-2.5	7.0	8.6	11.7	5.5	5.0	4.1	11.3	8.2	-1.9	-4.2	-0.3
Austria	5.2	-0.7	2.5	6.3	2.9	2.0	5.1	7.6	6.5	4.2	3.0	6.8	3.5	2.2	-2.0	-0.8
Belgium	-0.3	6.5	3.2	7.5	2.0	0.7	3.9	8.0	2.0	7.2	3.1	6.8	-0.0	6.4	-0.8	-1.1
Canada	-7.0	1.4	6.2	8.3	-4.6	4.1	6.6	8.1	-6.0	-0.1	3.6	7.9	-1.5	-4.0	-2.7	-0.2
Czech Republic	15.9	5.1	6.3	9.7	4.7	2.5	5.1	7.8	14.6	6.0	7.3	10.3	9.5	3.4	2.0	2.4
Denmark	0.8	6.3	4.7	8.4	0.8	1.3	4.2	7.6	4.5	6.1	3.9	8.8	3.7	4.7	-0.3	1.1
Finland	-3.5	1.3	2.9	6.9	1.0	2.7	5.1	8.8	-0.6	1.3	3.2	7.5	-1.6	-1.3	-1.8	-1.2
France	0.1	1.6	2.7	7.5	1.3	1.8	4.6	8.0	1.8	1.9	2.7	5.6	0.5	0.1	-1.9	-2.3
Germany	3.7	-0.5	4.8	6.2	0.9	2.7	4.6	8.6	5.3	4.5	4.6	6.0	4.4	1.7	-0.1	-2.4
Hungary	4.2	5.9	5.8	7.1	4.0	2.2	5.0	7.9	8.0	7.6	5.3	8.1	3.8	5.3	0.4	0.2
Iceland	-12.6	-4.3	7.4	7.9	1.4	1.7	4.5	7.2	20.6	4.9	6.4	8.5	18.9	3.2	1.8	1.2
Ireland	-2.0	3.9	1.9	6.2	0.7	1.5	3.9	8.2	4.7	7.2	2.7	7.7	4.0	5.6	-1.1	-0.5
Italy	-0.2	1.3	4.3	6.2	1.1	2.4	4.9	8.3	0.3	1.8	4.7	5.8	-0.8	-0.6	-0.3	-2.3
Japan	-1.5	4.9	5.8	4.5	-3.0	5.5	8.0	11.6	-11.2	10.0	8.3	9.7	-8.4	4.3	0.3	-1.6
Korea	-2.9	20.4	13.4	12.6	-1.4	4.7	7.6	10.7	-5.4	23.2	13.9	12.2	-4.1	17.7	5.9	1.3
Luxembourg	10.5	-8.7	1.2	5.6	1.3	1.7	4.1	7.7	0.8	-10.5	0.5	6.8	-0.5	-12.0	-3.5	-0.9
Mexico	-3.7	1.1	4.4	9.4	-4.7	3.2	6.0	7.8	-3.4	0.5	5.1	8.5	1.4	-2.6	-0.9	0.6
Netherlands	5.0	-4.5	0.1	10.4	1.0	2.1	4.4	7.8	6.7	-4.5	3.6	8.0	5.7	-6.5	-0.7	0.2
New Zealand	1.7	8.5	6.5	5.2	-3.6	8.7	7.6	8.9	0.5	6.5	6.7	5.3	4.3	-2.1	-0.9	-3.3
Norway	0.5	3.8	2.9	2.7	-0.3	1.3	4.3	8.5	9.3	0.6	0.0	5.3	9.7	-0.7	-4.0	-3.0
Poland	3.5	11.3	7.1	11.2	3.5	1.4	4.8	7.8	12.1	8.4	6.9	14.9	8.3	6.8	1.9	6.6
Portugal	2.2	-2.2	-0.3	5.2	1.4	0.9	4.0	7.5	1.9	4.9	4.8	7.9	0.5	3.9	0.8	0.4
Slovak Republic	13.6	4.9	5.2	7.3	8.4	3.9	5.8	8.8	6.3	5.5	6.0	8.7	-1.9	1.5	0.2	-0.1
Spain	0.8	0.8	5.0	7.0	1.1	1.1	3.6	7.6	-2.4	-2.1	2.0	6.2	-3.4	-3.1	-1.6	-1.3
Sweden	-7.3	-4.4	1.3	8.0	0.6	2.9	4.8	8.1	-5.2	2.5	2.4	7.8	-5.8	-0.5	-2.3	-0.3
Switzerland	1.2	-1.1	2.8	4.9	0.5	2.2	5.1	8.3	1.7	2.1	3.3	5.3	1.1	-0.1	-1.7	-2.7
Turkey	-28.1	20.0	14.5	17.0	3.7	2.6	5.3	8.3	3.5	14.7	10.1	14.2	-0.2	11.7	4.5	5.5
United Kingdom	2.7	1.2	2.5	9.9	-0.0	2.4	4.7	8.1	1.6	-2.6	0.2	9.4	1.6	-4.8	-4.3	1.2
United States	-5.2	4.1	6.6	7.8	-2.3	2.6	5.6	9.4	-7.5	-4.8	3.9	10.6	-5.4	-7.2	-1.6	1.0
Total OECD	-1.2	2.8	5.0	7.8	-0.5	2.9	5.5	9.0	-1.2	3.0	4.7	8.2	-0.7	0.1	-0.8	-0.7
Memorandum items																
China	14.4	19.6	18.9	16.0	-3.3	4.6	7.2	10.8	9.3	21.0	18.8	13.0	13.0	15.7	10.8	2.0
Dynamic Asia[b]	-8.9	5.5	10.6	19.0	-1.3	6.1	8.7	11.5	-9.3	6.2	10.3	15.7	-8.1	0.1	1.5	3.8
Other Asia	17.3	2.7	5.5	6.7	-0.7	3.7	6.0	9.0	-0.2	3.3	6.6	9.3	0.5	-0.3	0.6	0.3
Latin America	1.5	-11.1	-5.1	4.5	-1.2	-0.7	3.1	7.7	3.0	2.5	4.4	5.8	4.2	3.3	1.2	-1.8
Africa and Middle-East	10.0	2.9	5.0	6.8	0.9	3.5	5.6	8.7	0.8	1.7	6.5	8.2	-0.2	-1.7	0.8	-0.4
Central and Eastern Europe	15.6	9.5	9.2	11.8	5.0	6.1	7.6	10.1	5.0	4.0	3.9	6.0	-0.0	-1.9	-3.4	-3.7

Note: Regional aggregates are calculated *inclusive* of intra-regional trade. The calculation of export markets is based on a weighted average of import volumes in each exporting country's market, with weights based on manufacturing trade flows in 1995.
a) Export performance is calculated as the percentage change in the ratio of export volumes to export markets.
b) Dynamic Asia includes Chinese Taipei; Hong Kong, China; Indonesia; Malaysia; Philippines; Singapore and Thailand.
Sources: OECD; Direction of trade data - United Nations Statistical Office; OECD, *International Trade by commodity Statistics.*

Annex Table 61. **Geographical structure of OECD trade**
Percentage of nominal GDP

Area or country	Source/destination		Source of imports						Destination of exports					
			1962	1972	1982	1992	2001	2002	1962	1972	1982	1992	2001	2002
OECD[a]	**OECD**		**6.17**	**8.20**	**10.66**	**11.22**	**13.47**	**13.03**	**5.89**	**8.08**	**10.31**	**11.01**	**13.59**	**13.22**
	of which:	European Union	3.53	4.93	6.15	6.62	7.10	7.08	3.48	4.85	6.37	6.73	7.31	7.21
		United States	1.25	1.27	1.65	1.66	2.19	1.95	0.88	1.38	1.67	1.84	3.01	2.85
		Other	1.40	2.00	2.86	2.94	4.17	4.00	1.53	1.85	2.27	2.43	3.26	3.16
	Non-OECD		**2.24**	**2.35**	**4.59**	**3.07**	**4.80**	**4.91**	**2.24**	**2.22**	**4.13**	**2.98**	**3.56**	**3.73**
	of which:	DAEs + China[b]	0.25	0.34	0.76	1.20	2.20	2.26	0.27	0.38	0.75	1.15	1.52	1.52
		OPEC	0.58	0.80	2.12	0.71	0.88	0.75	0.28	0.40	1.40	0.54	0.45	0.44
United States	**OECD**		**1.80**	**3.45**	**4.94**	**5.76**	**7.56**	**7.31**	**2.22**	**2.93**	**4.22**	**5.09**	**5.30**	**4.84**
	of which:	European Union	0.69	1.15	1.45	1.60	2.18	2.17	0.96	1.13	1.69	1.71	1.58	1.39
		Other	1.11	2.30	3.49	4.16	5.38	5.14	1.26	1.80	2.53	3.38	3.72	3.45
	Non-OECD		**0.99**	**1.03**	**2.55**	**2.67**	**3.76**	**3.83**	**1.46**	**1.08**	**2.29**	**2.00**	**1.95**	**1.80**
	of which:	DAEs + China[b]	0.14	0.30	0.72	1.45	2.07	2.20	0.12	0.18	0.54	0.83	0.91	0.88
		OPEC	0.24	0.21	0.90	0.49	0.59	0.51	0.17	0.21	0.67	0.33	0.20	0.18
Japan	**OECD**		**5.36**	**4.15**	**4.65**	**3.30**	**3.76**	**3.72**	**4.13**	**5.60**	**6.58**	**5.41**	**5.66**	**5.90**
	of which:	European Union	0.88	0.72	0.78	0.88	1.07	1.10	0.97	1.40	1.79	1.76	1.54	1.54
		United States	2.93	1.92	2.18	1.37	1.51	1.45	2.27	2.91	3.28	2.52	2.90	2.97
		Other	1.54	1.51	1.68	1.04	1.18	1.17	0.89	1.29	1.51	1.13	1.22	1.39
	Non-OECD		**3.78**	**3.57**	**7.25**	**2.82**	**4.60**	**4.72**	**3.85**	**3.82**	**5.94**	**3.51**	**3.99**	**4.53**
	of which:	DAEs + China[b]	1.08	0.75	1.43	1.22	2.60	2.75	1.24	1.50	2.08	2.33	2.97	3.46
		OPEC	1.09	1.48	4.38	1.02	1.35	1.32	0.51	0.60	1.95	0.49	0.38	0.42
European Union[c]	**OECD**		**12.48**	**13.62**	**18.13**	**17.88**	**22.47**	**21.27**	**11.52**	**13.67**	**17.25**	**17.12**	**23.98**	**23.22**
	of which:	European Union	8.50	10.34	13.34	13.62	16.10	15.49	8.21	10.31	13.46	13.60	17.56	16.93
		United States	1.97	1.45	2.06	1.53	2.32	1.97	1.17	1.38	1.56	1.31	2.68	2.60
		Other	2.02	1.83	2.74	2.73	4.05	3.81	2.13	1.98	2.22	2.21	3.73	3.69
	Non-OECD		**4.36**	**3.74**	**6.25**	**3.41**	**5.51**	**5.19**	**3.44**	**3.09**	**5.52**	**3.20**	**4.57**	**4.52**
	of which:	DAEs + China[b]	0.31	0.28	0.57	0.94	1.90	1.81	0.30	0.25	0.44	0.65	1.13	1.07
		OPEC	1.12	1.37	2.82	0.70	0.86	0.73	0.46	0.59	2.06	0.70	0.70	0.72

a) OECD includes Korea from 1988. Trade data for Greece in 2002 are partially OECD estimates.
b) DAEs are the Dynamic Asian Economies (Chinese Taipei; Hong Kong, China; Malaysia; Philippines; Singapore and Thailand).
c) Trade data for Greece in 2002 are partially OECD estimates.
Source: OECD.

OECD ECONOMICS DEPARTMENT

A wide range of news and information about recent Economics Department studies and publications on a variety of topics is now regularly available *via* INTERNET on the OECD website at the following address: ***www.oecd.org/eco***. This includes links to the *Economics Department Working Papers* series, which can be downloaded free of charge, as well as summaries of recent editions in the *OECD Economic Surveys* series and the *OECD Economic Outlook*.

OECD ECONOMIC OUTLOOK

OECD Economic Outlook Flashfile

A datafile containing a summary of the *Economic Outlook* forecasts is now available on INTERNET at the time of its preliminary publication (a month to six weeks before the final publication date) at the following address: ***www.oecd.org/eco/statistics***. This includes key macroeconomic variables for all OECD countries and regions in text file form, which can be input directly into most statistical and analytical software. The *Economic Outlook* Flashfile is available free of charge.

Statistics and projections on CD-ROM

The full set of historical time series data and projections underlying the *OECD Economic Outlook* is now available on CD-ROM at the same time as its publication. The *OECD Economic Outlook* CD-ROM contains approximately 4 000 macroeconomic time series for OECD countries and non-OECD zones, beginning in 1960 and extending to the end of the published forecast horizon.

The general subject and country coverage for both versions are as follows:

Subject coverage

- Gross domestic product and its components
- Government and households appropriation accounts
- Fiscal and monetary indicators
- Labour market and supply indicators
- Wages, prices and profitability
- International trade and payments
- Potential output and output gaps

Country coverage

- 30 OECD countries
- OECD area aggregations
- Non-OECD zones
- The euro area

Subscriptions, which also include the printed version of the *OECD Economic Outlook*, may be made at any time of the year. For special conditions (Academics, Government Agencies, etc.) and information on commercial redistribution rights, contact OECD Publications. For more information, register to the OECD newsletters at ***www.oecd.org/OECDdirect*** or visit the OECD bookshop at ***www.oecd.org/bookshop*** or send your order to:

OECD Publications
2, rue André-Pascal
75775 Paris Cedex 16
FRANCE

OECD ECONOMIC SURVEYS

For more in-depth, country-by-country analysis, read the *OECD Economic Surveys*. By providing rich information on economic and policy developments, this series constitutes a must for financial institutions, multinational enterprises, consulting firms, universities and libraries. Each issue contains OECD assessments of:

- Recent macroeconomic performance
- The short-term outlook
- Monetary policy
- The fiscal stance
- Structural reforms in various areas such as the labour market, the financial system, taxation, healthcare, environment, etc.
- Specific themes, among which: tax reform, ageing populations, sustainable development and public expenditure.

Surveys are available for the following countries:

Australia	Mexico
Austria	Netherlands
Belgium	New Zealand
Bulgaria	Norway
Canada	Poland
Czech Republic	Portugal
Denmark	Romania
Finland	Russian Federation
France	Slovak Republic
Germany	Slovenia
Greece	Spain
Hungary	Sweden
Iceland	Switzerland
Ireland	Turkey
Italy	United Kingdom
Japan	United States
Korea	

Available on subscription. You also create your own personalised collection by ordering just the books you need, for example, major seven OECD countries, European Union, Asia-Pacific, or central and eastern European countries, just a single country. For more information, register to the OECD newsletters at *www.oecd.org/OECDdirect* or visit the OECD bookshop at *www.oecd.org/bookshop* or send your order to:

OECD Publications
2, rue André-Pascal
75775 Paris Cedex 16
FRANCE

For customers in Germany and Austria
OECD Sales Office
August-Bebel-Allee 6, D-53175 Bonn
Tel.: (49-228) 959 1215
Fax: (49-228) 959 1218
E-mail: bonn.contact@oecd.org
Internet: *www.oecd.org/deutschland*

For customers in North America
OECD Washington Center
2001 L Street N.W., Suite 650
Washington DC, 20036-4922 USA
Tel.: 1 202 785 6323
Fax: 1 202 785 0350
E-mail: washington.contact@oecd.org
Internet: www.oecdwash.org

For customers in Japan and Asia
OECD Tokyo Centre
3rd Floor, Nippon Press Center Building
2-2-1, Uchisaiwaicho
Chiyoda-ku, Tokyo 100-0011
Tel.: 81 3 5532 0021
Fax: 81 3 5532 0035
E-mail: center@oecdtokyo.org
Internet: *www.oecdtokyo.org*

For customers in Central and South America
OECD Mexico Centre
Av. Presidente Mazaryk 526
Colonia: Polanco
C.P. 11560, Mexico D.F.
Tel.: 52 555 281 3810
Fax: 52 555 280 0480
E-mail: mexico.contact@oecd.org
Internet: *rtn.net.mx/ocde*

For customers in the rest of the world
OECD Paris Centre
2, rue André-Pascal
75775 Paris Cedex 16, France
Tel.: 33 1 45 24 94 16
Fax: 33 1 45 24 94 53
E-mail: sourceoecd@oecd.org
Internet: *www.sourceoecd.org*

Online ordering: *www.oecd.org/publications*
(secure payment with credit card)

OECD PUBLICATIONS, 2, rue André-Pascal, 75775 PARIS CEDEX 16
PRINTED IN FRANCE
(12 2003 73 1 P) ISBN 92-64-10057-1 – No. 52993 2003
ISSN 0474-5574